Inclusive Futures

This book offers a comprehensive analysis of the role of diversity, equity, and inclusion (DEI) in the technology sector from a global perspective. Comprising seven in-depth chapters, the book highlights inherent biases within technology and strategies for constructing inclusive products and services. It takes on a forward-looking outlook on the future of DEI in technology, visualizing a world in which technology functions as a unifying force for positive social transformation.

The authors examine DEI and their significance across different regions, to enhance readers' awareness and understanding. This increased understanding is crucial for professionals and policymakers to make informed decisions that foster an inclusive technological environment. The book equips the readers with knowledge to identify and address these biases in technology, including algorithms, datasets, and user interfaces, through an in-depth study of such biases. This is particularly valuable for technology developers, designers, and companies that aim to create fair and unbiased technology products and services. Through the global and local case studies and empirical research, readers learn valuable insights to developing inclusive technology products and services that cater to a diverse range of users. This book also addresses recruitment practices and cultural changes necessary within tech organizations to cultivate a diverse and inclusive workforce. The topic of how technology can bridge the digital divide and empower underrepresented communities is studied, providing new ideas for such initiatives in the future.

This book serves as a valuable resource for practitioners involved in the development of technology, hiring in the technology sector and leaders involved in policymaking of ethical and regulatory aspects of DEI in technology.

Inclusive Futures

Lessons from Emerging Contexts on Building Equitable Digital Systems

Edited by
Arif Perdana, Vijayakumar Bharathi S.,
Kanchan Patil, Grace Wangge,
Sabina Satriyani Puspita and Wei Kang

CRC Press
Taylor & Francis Group
Boca Raton London New York

CRC Press is an imprint of the
Taylor & Francis Group, an **informa** business

Designed cover image: Shutterstock

First edition published 2026
by CRC Press
2385 NW Executive Center Drive, Suite 320, Boca Raton FL 33431

and by CRC Press
4 Park Square, Milton Park, Abingdon, Oxon, OX14 4RN

CRC Press is an imprint of Taylor & Francis Group, LLC

ISBN: 9781032968858 (hbk)
ISBN: 9781032968841 (pbk)
ISBN: 9781003591078 (ebk)

DOI: 10.1201/9781003591078

Typeset in Palatino
by Newgen Publishing UK

Contents

Part III Designing Inclusive Digital Products and Ecosystems

Part IV Workforce Transformation and Digital Capability Building

Part V Technology and Marginalized Communities

Part VI Embedding DEIB in Digital Foundations

Preface: Digital Technology and the Quest for Structural Inclusion

The promise of digital technology is that it can equalise. That it can transcend geography, circumvent traditional gatekeepers, and offer scalable pathways to economic opportunity, education, and civic participation. Yet this promise remains only partially fulfilled. The acceleration of digital transformation across economies, industries, and public services has been marked by profound asymmetries: between those who design technology and those who use it, those who benefit and those who are further excluded, and those who belong and those rendered invisible.

This book is a response to those asymmetries. It does not begin with a celebration of innovation, but rather with a critical recognition that digital technology reproduces structural inequality unless intentionally designed otherwise. The integration of Diversity, Equity, Inclusion, and Belonging (DEIB) into technology development and governance is not an aspirational add-on; it is foundational to building systems that work for more than a narrow demographic of users.

The chapters assembled in this book provide a multi-layered, interdisciplinary exploration of DEIB in digital systems. They bring together scholars, practitioners, and case-based insights across domains, from artificial intelligence and financial inclusion to e-learning and urban safety. They do not merely critique existing systems but offer constructive frameworks for rethinking the architectures of inclusion across the design, deployment, and regulation of digital technologies.

Notably, many of the contributions in this volume originate from the Global South, contexts where innovation is often driven by necessity and scarcity rather than abundance. While the concept of DEIB is widely associated with Western corporate and academic discourse, its core concerns are neither alien nor imported in many low- and middle-income countries (LMICs). Traditions of communal life, social justice, and mutual obligation have long existed in these regions, albeit under different names and frameworks. In this sense, DEIB is not so much a Western export as it is a reframing of struggles that have always been present, against exclusion, marginalisation, and inequity. This book invites readers to reconsider the genealogy of inclusion and take seriously the insights, innovations, and institutional models emerging from the Global South as not peripheral but central to the future of inclusive technology.

Part I: Reframing the Discourse on DEIB

The opening part poses a difficult but necessary question: Is DEI going to die? Rather than defaulting to normative optimism, it dissects the evolving legitimacy crisis of diversity agendas, particularly in Western corporate environments. Drawing on organizational theory and empirical shifts in legal and cultural landscapes, this part argues that DEI must evolve from rhetorical affirmation to structural strategy. In contrast, the literature review that follows situates digital technology as a variable force, capable of reducing or exacerbating inequity depending on how it is governed. This sets the intellectual foundation of the volume. DEIB is not a static principle but a contested and dynamic field of action shaped by institutional, cultural, and technological constraints.

Part II: Addressing Embedded Bias in Digital Systems

The second part cluster confronts algorithmic bias directly. AI systems are not neutral. They encode and amplify historical inequalities embedded in data, social structures, and institutional practices. The chapter on Inclusive AI provides a grounded, ethical framework for understanding the mechanisms by which bias operates and how it may be mitigated, citing examples from hiring, law enforcement, healthcare, and finance. This is followed by an analysis of generative AI's failure to accurately or respectfully represent nonbinary individuals. Despite growing awareness, image generation systems remain overfitted to dominant cultural archetypes, producing outputs that erase gender complexity.

The chapter on AI art and gender extends this discussion into aesthetics and critique. Using metamodernism as a lens, it challenges both the assumptions of algorithmic objectivity and the binary logic of conventional gender classification in AI systems. Collectively, these works argue that bias in digital systems is not simply a matter of flawed data or poor engineering, but reflects deeper epistemic and cultural defaults that must be questioned at the design stage.

Part III: Designing Inclusive Digital Products and Ecosystems

The third part foregrounds the role of inclusive design in expanding access to core services such as finance, healthcare, urban mobility, and digital markets.

The chapter on financial inclusion in India and beyond explores how layered digital public infrastructure, comprising identity systems, payment protocols, and institutional interoperability, can bring millions into formal financial systems. Complementing this, the piece on algorithmic trading applies inclusive design to the financial services context, showing how human-centered AI and low-barrier interfaces can democratise complex digital tools.

Healthcare access, historically shaped by geography and institutional hierarchy, is interrogated in the chapter on eSanjeevani, India's national telemedicine platform. The analysis underscores how design decisions, such as doctor-to-doctor versus doctor-to-patient modalities, can serve different populations and shift care access across urban and rural lines. Meanwhile, Safetipin demonstrates how user-generated safety data, when systematized and geo-tagged, can shape municipal policy and urban design.

This section culminates with a benchmarking analysis of how corporate actors report and act on Sustainable Development Goals, revealing gaps between technological adoption and substantive impact. While digital systems proliferate, their ability to advance DEIB goals remains uneven, highlighting the need for more substantial alignment between design, regulation, and inclusive outcomes.

Part IV: Workforce Transformation and Digital Capability Building

Workforce diversity is not simply about hiring. It involves deep structural shifts in how organizations cultivate capability and redefine contribution. This part opens with an analysis of how inclusive leadership, cognitive bias training, and psychological safety practices are necessary complements to diversity recruitment. It explores how organizations like SAP and Basecamp have institutionalized DEIB through talent programs and cultural reorientation.

The chapter on Citizen Development introduces a compelling paradigm: enabling nontechnical employees to participate in digital innovation through low-code and no-code platforms. This is not just about productivity gains. It signals a redistribution of digital agency within the workplace. Similarly, the examination of cybersquatting law through a DEIB lens points to the vulnerabilities created when digital literacy and regulatory infrastructure do not keep pace with rapid innovation. Here, protection of digital identity becomes a key component of equity. Together, these chapters frame the digital workforce not as a monolith to be diversified, but as a fluid and contested space where inclusion must be actively negotiated across tools, practices, and legal frameworks.

Part V: Technology and Marginalized Communities

Where digital systems have the potential for greatest impact is often where they are least accessible. This section centers underrepresented and historically marginalized communities not as passive recipients of technology but as subjects of structural exclusion whose needs must shape system design. The chapter on COVID-19 and the Digital Divide presents sobering data on rural education access in Malaysia, where over 90% of students in some regions were unable to participate in online learning. Afghanistan's e-learning experience offers a contrasting yet equally constrained context. Here, digital learning has expanded through international partnerships, yet continues to struggle with infrastructural deficits, gender norms, and limited policy coherence.

The India-focused chapter, Bridging Divides, explores how digital tools can support both sustainability and community empowerment if deployed alongside infrastructure investments and inclusive governance. Financial inclusion is returned to through the case of bKash, which demonstrates how mobile money systems can reconfigure trust, access, and empowerment, especially for women. Kasikornbank adds nuance to this model by integrating AI-based credit scoring and social banking interfaces, providing a blueprint for inclusive banking in middle-income contexts. Finally, the chapter on blockchain governance unpacks how decentralized technologies may either reinforce or disrupt exclusionary legal systems. It emphasizes that technological innovation must be coupled with institutional reform if it is to advance equitable outcomes.

Part VI: Embedding DEIB in Digital Foundations

The final part is forward-looking. It asserts that DEIB must not be relegated to applications or user interfaces but embedded into the foundational layers of digital infrastructure. From cloud services to AI governance, from platform protocols to interoperability standards, every architectural decision is a political choice. These decisions determine who is visible, whose voice is encoded, and who benefits.

Rather than offering a universal prescription, the chapter presents multiple case studies, spanning platform labor, education, finance, and healthcare, that illustrate how inclusion is operationalized differently depending on regulatory environment, institutional readiness, and civic capacity. It argues for a shift from isolated pilot programs toward systemic transformation, in which DEIB is treated not as a checklist but as a principle that informs innovation cycles, compliance strategies, and social accountability. This is not a call for idealism. It is a call for alignment between policy and platform, between infrastructure and experience, and between metrics and meaning.

Concluding Remarks: From Rhetoric to Redesign

DEIB in digital technology is at a crossroads. On the one hand, the public discourse on inclusion has never been louder. On the other, rollback and resistance, especially in political and corporate contexts, threaten to reduce these principles to tokenism or legal risk management. The chapters in this book take a different route. They resist rhetorical inflation and instead provide granular analysis, grounded frameworks, and empirical insight into what inclusion demands in the digital age. They show that equitable systems are not simply the result of good intent, but of deliberate design choices, policy alignment, and participatory governance. Inclusion cannot be retrofitted. It must be foundational. This book is intended not just for scholars, but for practitioners, policymakers, technologists, and advocates. It is a guide for those building systems, shaping institutions, or setting norms. The contributors, diverse in expertise and geography, demonstrate that there is no single path to digital inclusion, but there are common principles: transparency, agency, accountability, and justice. The question is not whether DEIB belongs in digital technology. It is whether digital technology, without DEIB, can ever fulfill its potential as a force for shared progress.

About the Editors

Arif Perdana is an Associate Professor at Monash University and Director of the Action Lab Indonesia, specializing in digital strategy and data science. With over two decades of experience spanning academia and industry, he has worked with institutions such as the University of Queensland, Aarhus University, and the Singapore Institute of Technology. His research explores responsible AI, blockchain, machine learning, and digital transformation in finance, education, and healthcare. Arif has secured major funding from institutions including Bank Indonesia and the Singapore Government, published in leading journals, and trained over 700 professionals across 150 organizations in Singapore and Indonesia.

Vijayakumar Bharathi S. is a Professor at Symbiosis Centre for Information Technology, Symbiosis International (Deemed University). He holds post-graduate degrees in Commerce and Management and a PhD in Computer Science from Symbiosis International, specializing in ERP risk assessment for SMEs. A member of the SAP Academic Alliance Board for Asia Pacific and Japan, he is a global SAP trainer for S4 HANA, ECC6.0, and ByD across multiple countries. His expertise includes intelligent ERP, SAP Analytics Cloud, design thinking, and blockchain applications. He collaborates with SAP headquarters in Germany and contributes to global pilot projects for SAP curriculum development.

Kanchan Patil is Deputy Director and Professor at Symbiosis Centre for Information Technology. She holds a Doctorate in Management and a Master's in Marketing Management from the University of Pune, with a background in Electronics and Telecommunications Engineering. With over 21 years of experience in academia, research, and administration, her teaching spans Industry 4.0, digital transformation, IoT, and marketing. An approved PhD guide, she has secured research grants, published in Scopus and Web of Science journals, and presented at IIMs and IIT Delhi. She also leads faculty and management development programs and is a recipient of multiple education leadership awards.

Grace Wangge is an Associate Professor in Public Health at Monash University, Indonesia, where she leads the Master of Public Health program. A medical doctor and epidemiologist, she earned her MD from Universitas Indonesia and PhD in Pharmacoepidemiology from Utrecht University, followed by a postdoctoral fellowship at Harvard Medical School/Brigham and Women's Hospital. Since returning to Indonesia in 2014, her research has focused on public health policy, community medicine, nutrition, and pharmacovigilance. She has advised national health initiatives, including the G20 Health Working Group, and continues to explore digital health governance and health science communication in the Indonesian context.

Sabina Satriyani Puspita is an Assistant Professor and Interim Course Coordinator for the Public Policy and Management program at Monash University, Indonesia, where she also serves as Deputy Director of the Monash Herb Feith Indonesian Engagement Centre. She joined Monash in 2022 as a Research Fellow at the Institute for Advanced Research. Sabina's research examines democratisation, political institutions, social movements, gender politics, and sustainable communities, with a focus on Southeast and Northeast Asia. She earned her PhD in comparative politics and international relations from Northwestern University, USA, and previously worked as a policy analyst at Indonesia's Ministry of Education.

Wei Kang is a Senior Lecturer in Accounting and Finance at Anglia Ruskin University's Faculty of Business and Law, where she also directs the postgraduate accounting and finance program. Her expertise spans finance, sustainable development, and fintech innovations, with a particular focus on their role in advancing environmental and social impact. Wei actively bridges academia and industry, collaborating on initiatives to influence sustainability policies and practices. Her research interests include organisational behaviour, international business, and gender in entrepreneurship. She holds advanced degrees in finance and is committed to preparing graduates for evolving challenges in global finance and sustainability.

Contributors

Smita Barik is an Assistant Professor at the Institute of Technology & Science, Mohan Nagar, Ghaziabad. She specializes in human resources, organizational behavior, and analytics with extensive teaching and research experience.

Siddiqullah Barikzai is Associate Professor of Information Systems at Kabul Education University, specializing in technology integration in education. He holds a master's in computer education from the University of Massachusetts and is pursuing a PhD in e-learning at Symbiosis International University, Pune.

Vijayakumar Bharathi S. is Professor at the Symbiosis Centre for Information Technology. He earned a PhD in computer science focusing on ERP risk assessment. His research interests include design thinking, technology adoption, immersive technologies, and blockchain.

Sumant Devasthali is Senior Adjunct Faculty at Narsee Monjee Institute of Management Studies (NMIMS) School of Business Management. He is an MBA-finance professional and former Accenture director with expertise in IT strategy, outsourcing, and global industrial solutions.

Parul Gupta is an Assistant Professor in the area of General Management at the Institute of Technology & Science, Mohan Nagar, Ghaziabad.

Ika Karlina Idris is an Associate Professor at Monash University Indonesia and Co-Director of the Monash Data and Democracy Research Hub. Her work bridges government communication, digital policy, and public service, with consultancy experience for key Indonesian agencies and international training in digital public relations.

Nuurrianti Jalli is an Assistant Professor of Professional Practice at the School of Media and Strategic Communications, Oklahoma State University. She has previously served as faculty at institutions across the United States, Malaysia, and Indonesia.

Shaji Joseph is Professor of Management at Symbiosis International University, specializing in organizational behavior, human resources, governance, ethics, community development, and micro, small, and medium enterprises.

Apoorva Joshi is a Junior Research Fellow at Symbiosis International University, focusing on algorithmic trading, fintech, and behavioral finance.

Pearpilai Jutasompakorn is an associate professor in the Accountancy program at Singapore Institute of Technology. She earned her PhD in Finance from Monash University and has research interests in credit risk management, banking, financial stability, regulation, and FinTech.

Wei Kang is Senior Lecturer in Accounting and Finance at Anglia Ruskin University. She specializes in sustainable finance, fintech innovations, and their role in driving social and environmental impact, bridging academia and industry.

Ridoan Karim is a lecturer in business law at Monash University Malaysia. His research focuses on science, technology and law, privacy and data protection law, energy justice, and Asian comparative law.

Rajwinder Kaur is an assistant professor at Symbiosis Institute of Business Management, Noida, specializing in Human Resource Management and Organizational Behavior with expertise in HR analytics, talent management, and leadership.

Sirin Kumar is a PhD scholar at Symbiosis Centre of Information Technology, Pune, and General Manager at RBI Mumbai, India.

Ujwal Prabhakar Nandekar is an assistant professor at Symbiosis Law School, Pune, specializing in Intellectual Property Law.

Tanuj Negi is an assistant professor at FLAME University, Pune. He teaches courses related to Human Resource Management, with research interests in transformative learning, HRM, and emerging technologies.

Neha Parashar is Director at Symbiosis School of Banking and Finance, Pune. She is an award-winning academic leader in finance, banking, and management education.

Kanchan Patil is Deputy Director and Professor at Symbiosis Centre for Information Technology. She is a doctorate in management with expertise in Industry 4.0, digital transformation, IoT, and marketing. She is an approved PhD guide, recipient of national research grants, and awardee of the Education Leadership Award, with extensive experience in academics, research, and corporate training.

Arif Perdana is an associate professor at Monash University and Director of the Action Lab Indonesia, specializing in digital strategy and data science.

Eka Permanasari is an associate professor in urban design, architecture, and Southeast Asian studies. She is an internationally recognized scholar with over two decades of experience in community-based development and urban planning.

Sabina Satriyani Puspita is an assistant professor, Interim Course Coordinator for the Public Policy and Management program, and Deputy Director of the Monash Herb Feith Indonesian Engagement Centre at Monash University, Indonesia. A Northwestern-trained political scientist, her research focuses on democratisation, gender politics, and sustainable communities in Southeast and Northeast Asia.

Jay Rosenbaum is a Melbourne AI artist and researcher working with 3D modelling, artificial intelligence, and extended reality technologies.

Janhavi A. Sakalkar is a student at Symbiosis Law School, Pune, focusing on advanced legal studies and research.

Mitali Sengupta is an associate professor at the Department of Management, Eastern Institute for Integrated Learning in Management (EIILM), Kolkata.

Manisha Sharma is Professor and Area Chair at NMIMS, specializing in data analytics, operations, and supply chain management, with extensive teaching, research, and editorial experience.

Shruti Shree is an LL.M. candidate in Innovation, Technology, and Intellectual Property Law at Symbiosis Law School, Pune. She holds a BBA LL.B. from Bharati Vidyapeeth and focuses on emerging legal issues in technology and IP.

Ananthanarayanan Venkateswaran is Founder & CEO of Techdivine Creative Services. He is a digital ROI strategist, visiting faculty, executive coach, corporate trainer, and speaker with global client experience across 14 countries. He is currently pursuing a PhD at Symbiosis International University.

Nala Edwin Widjaja is an expert in social statistics, holding degrees in Communication and Development Studies from Ohio University and Economics from Paramadina. A former journalist at Detik.com, his research explores media narratives, fertility trends, and socio-political issues in Indonesia and Southeast Asia.

Part I

Reframing the Discourse on DEIB

1

DEI - Is it going to DIE?

Parul Gupta and Smita Barik

1.1 Introduction

The concept of diversity, equity, and inclusion in the workplace, while a subject of conversation for many years, has gained significant momentum in recent times. DEI aims to provide an inclusive atmosphere in which every individual, irrespective of their race, ethnicity, gender, age, sexual orientation, disability, or any other attribute, is treated with fairness, dignity, and afforded equal opportunities for personal and professional advancement (Thomas et al., 2014). Racial inequality was there in the society as well as in workplace from very beginning, but just waiting for the solution or being patient towards the inequality will not fix the issue. Instead of believing that the inequality will be neutralized on its own over time, organizations must come together to bring real change to the society and the workplace by changing their rules structures and way of operation backed by research or evidences and by supporting DEIs. Beyond being an important attribute among employees, promoting an inclusive work culture generally results in increased outcomes for teams and organizations, establishing as greater innovation, enhancing feelings of belonging, and more robust social interactions within the workplace (Gill et al., 2018; Hicks-Clarke & Iles, 2000; Nishii, 2013; Shore et al., 2018).

Historically, the concepts of Diversity, Equity, and Inclusion (DEI) have transitioned from a focus on affirmative action and equal employment opportunity requirements to more holistic approaches that tackle systemic inequalities and encourage an inclusive culture (Thomas & Ely, 1996). This evolution towards acknowledging the inherent worth of diversity and cultivating an inclusive atmosphere signifies a deeper comprehension of the role diversity plays in enhancing organizational resilience and adaptability (Roberson, 2006). The emergence of social movements championing racial, gender, and various other forms of equity has emphasized the significance of Diversity, Equity, and Inclusion (DEI) within organizations. These movements have brought to light ongoing inequalities and the necessity for

DOI: 10.1201/9781003591078-2

systemic reform, encouraging organizations to reassess and enhance their DEI initiatives (Dobbin & Kalev, 2016; Manjare, 2024). As society today is under substantial transformation induced by dynamic technology, demographic shifts, globalization, workforce fluidity, and uncertainties like geopolitical turbulence, the challenge is to decipher how DEI must evolve to cater to the changing paradigms and also whether it truly holds futuristic relevance for organizations.

This book chapter therefore attempts to delve deeper into the idea and examine two research questions:

RQ1: What are the complex and multifaceted dimensions of Diversity, Equity, and Inclusion (DEI) in organizational settings?

RQ2: What are the future prospect and direction that DEI practices may take depending upon the current trends?

1.2 Evolution of DEI

The conceptualization of DEI has witnessed evolution in last few decades. It has been frequently misinterpreted as only catering to certain groups, such as the LGBTQIA+ community. In reality, DEI includes race, ethnicity, gender, socioeconomic status, handicap, religion, and age, among other factors. It aims to break down the historical and systematic barriers that limit the fair access to the opportunities and resources for all the individuals irrespective of their background, gender, race, and identity so that everyone in an organizational setting can have equal right fostering equalities and inclusivity in a workplace (Beavers, 2018a; Olzmann, 2020).

Diversity: To understand diversity formally, it means all the ways in which people differ from one another. It respects and welcomes all the visible differences such as gender, race, culture, ethnicity, nationality, skills and ability, languages, spiritual orientation, and one's sexual orientation. It may also include the dimensions which are invisible such as thought process, personality, psychometric profiles, experiences, leadership style, philosophical views, and tenure. In the context of a particular identity, diversity refers to the differences among individuals focusing on race, gender, or sexual orientation (Cox & Blake, 1991). Also it includes both apparent and concealed aspects of a person's identity and life experiences (Beavers, 2018b; Olzmann, 2020).

Equity: Equity and equality seem to have a thin line difference yet they are way apart in terms of their definition. Traditionally, equality is understood as equal access to individuals despite if their inequalities and differences, but equity acknowledges that all people don't start with the same opportunities hence we should make adjustments to fix this imbalance (Friedman & Cole, 2025). Equity ensures fair treatment, access, and fair opportunities for everyone while finding and removing the obstacles that has brought unequal participation for specific groups. This means making sure that everyone should be treated fairly, has equal chance to grow, and can participate fully in reaching the organizational goals by removing all the obstacles coming in between. In order to achieve equity in the society, it is the need to find out the root causes such disparities that some groups are facing to support them for getting better results (Friedman & Cole, 2025; Young, 2008).

***Inclusion*:** The word inclusion is understood building spaces where all employees are valued, supported, respected, and being accepted. By going beyond simple tolerance, it actively encourages everyone to take part fully and feel like they belong (Bush, 2025; Shore et al., 2018). In organizational context, it means creating a work environment which promotes and integrates diversity and can make everyone feel welcomed, respected, and valued, thereby facilitating full participation. Furthermore, studies say that by giving such inclusive environment where people feel welcomed and respected, they can share their unique ideas and talents (Cox, 1994). Interestingly, inclusion is typically viewed as a positive approach. It refers to using good practices to improve diversity and equality in organizations, especially in human resource management (HRM) practices (Li et al., 2024). Although, inclusion is understood as creating more comfort for maximum of the people of organization, it may also bring discomfort to some not comfortable with the inclusivity approach. Researchers (Sherbin & Rashid, 2017) have aptly established inclusion as a source of positive work-related outcomes such as work satisfaction and commitment.

The interplay between diversity, equity, and inclusion (DEI) forms the foundation of effective DEI initiatives, which have evolved through historical movements, policy changes, and organizational shifts. Many historical movements have shaped the DEI journey. The understanding of human diversity was introduced in a new concept in United States as during Civil Rights movements 1960, all military, education, local communicates, and businesses promoted DEI. Antidiscriminatory laws and philosophy of social justice acted as stimuli for encouraging different sectors to do things rightly although it faces challenges initially. Later on, gender, sexual preference, age, ethnicity, religion, disability, and gender identity were added to inclusion in training programs with passage of time. Diversity education programs were encouraged during 1980s to ensure compliance. But still its importance was not properly understood by the society. Figure 1.1 represents a brief on the important milestones of the journey.

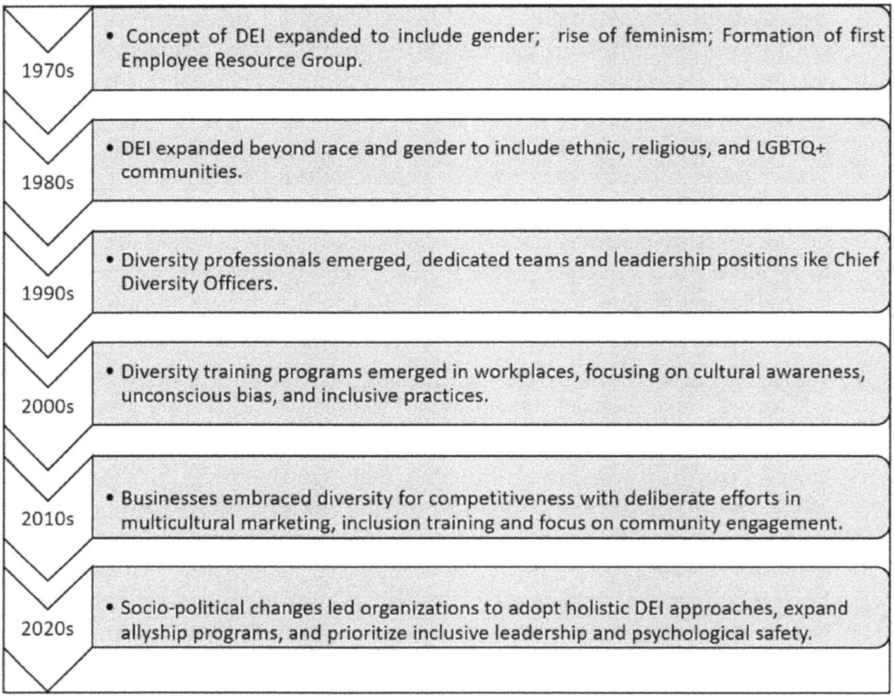

FIGURE 1.1
DEI milestones of evolution over years [*Source*: Kratz, J. (2024, December 29)].

1.3 Theoretical Perspectives

Although researches claim that commitment to DEI can increase a company's financial success through stronger leadership, diverse innovation and an enhanced brand image, deeper connections with consumers and workers, and higher sales, which can attract investment (Li et al., 2024) but theories related to DEI do not completely claim for a positive relationship with group performance. This section presents the contradictory theoretical perspectives with reference to DEI.

1.3.1 Resource-Based Theory of Diversity Management

This theory focuses on how embracing diversity affects an organization's resources (Barney & Clark, 2007). Physical capital, financial capital, human capital, and corporate capital are four crucial resources for every organization. These resources are used very carefully by the organizations so that they lead to growth and success. From a business perspective, organizations that prioritize diversity often gain a competitive edge over those that remain homogenous. Research has shown that racial diversity, when implemented for a growth or innovation strategy, can significantly increase financial performance (Richard, 2000). Furthermore, companies with strong diversity management practices leads to lower employee turnover. When companies link diversity efforts with a focus on innovation, they see better productivity and stronger market results. Simply put, organizations that promote diversity benefit from higher profits and a more motivated, creative team. Those who fail to implement these diversity policies risk missing these benefits. This theory advocates the positive impact of DEI on performance, which many of the other theories like Cognitive-Diversity Theory and Institutional Theory of Diversity Management (Bairoh, 2008) also concur.

1.3.2 The Similarity-Attraction Paradigm

The Cognitive Diversity Hypothesis (Miller et al., 1998) meticulously highlights the positive impact of diversity on organizational performance, while the Similarity-Attraction Paradigm explains why diversity can sometimes create challenges (Byrne, 1997). Research suggests that employees in diverse teams may feel less connected to their coworkers, leading to higher absenteeism and turnover rates. Some studies even indicate that workplace diversity can contribute to conflicts and dissatisfaction (Tsui et al., 1992). The Similarity-Attraction Theory helps explain this by suggesting that people naturally gravitate toward those who share similar attitudes and beliefs. While shared values and perspectives play a key role in forming connections, other factors like race, age, gender, and socioeconomic background can also shape interpersonal dynamics. One study found that organizations promoting diversity in their hiring materials appeal more to racial minorities and women compared to White candidates (Lambert, 2015). Another study revealed that targeted diversity messaging for sexual minorities led to a decline in attraction among heterosexual job seekers. Similarly, international job candidates are more drawn to organizations that highlight global diversity in their workforce (Lambert et al., 2019).

According to this theory, organizations need to strike the right balance when creating inclusive policies and hiring strategies. This view is backed by other theories that question the need for DEI practices in organizations. These are Social Cognitive Theory, Social Identity theory, Schema Theory, and Justification Suppression Model.

1.4 DEI and Business Organizations

DEI has proven to have far-reaching societal impact on organizations. For long, DEI has enhanced workplace culture, innovation, and market reach while ensuring legal compliance and reducing business risks. It is believed that companies with strong DEI initiatives outperform competitors and foster a more inclusive, successful environment. To build a fair and inclusive society, we must first acknowledge that the world is naturally unequal and diversity is a fundamental part of it. Therefore, organizations should reject the idea that racial equality will happen on its own over time. Instead, DEI should be seen as a deliberate process of structural change, driven by evidence-based policies that transform how organizations operate from within. Research indicates that embracing and highlighting diversity fosters creativity, better ideas, and higher engagement, as compared to suppressing differences for group harmony (Rock & Grant, 2016).

Additionally, diverse teams exhibit improved problem-solving ability compared to more homogeneous teams. Further research also claims that Brands are increasingly using DEI to reflect their identity and align with consumer values (Ferraro et al., 2023). When elimination of DEI was studied across various sectors, it was found that it may hinder talent retention, stifles innovation, and increases legal and financial risks, leaving companies at a competitive disadvantage in workplaces (Rock & Grant, 2016). Health care sector worsens disparities, reduces cultural competency, and weakens crisis response, endangering vulnerable populations (Betancourt et al., 2005). Eliminating DEI in education reduces access, weakens critical thinking, and harms institutional reputation and funding (Engle & Tinto, 2008; Gurin et al., 2002). These long-held views accompanied with Government directives have prompted businesses to focus on DEI practices and how organizations have adopted DEI practices. It also examines the catalytic changes prompting for the abandonment of the same. This section therefore attempts to answer the research questions RQ1 and RQ2.

1.4.1 Embracing DEI

Ideologically organizations are expected to consciously avoid discrimination based on any criteria from all its practices. They are also expected to design and implement DEI practices in all their processes. The heightened focus on DEI has made it morally and socially imperative for organizations to prioritize DEI in their operations. Organizations are working to become more diverse, inclusive, and equitable. The real challenge, however, is to pursue this not just because it's trendy but because it genuinely reflects and supports society's desire for unity and fairness. Interestingly, many organizations which are publicly committing to the DEI goals are clueless about the implications and efforts which must be made for success in the direction (Kraus et al., 2022).

Nevertheless, globally, many organizations have made conscious efforts to embrace, design, and implement DEI practices. Some of the key practices as adopted by the industry front-runners of DEI are as follows:

- **Sensitization trainings for DEI**: These aim to educate the employees and eliminate the conscious/unconscious bias, which lead to discriminatory practices. The methodologies include workshops, seminars, discussions etc, which focus on building an inclusive environment.
- **Transformation of hiring practices**: This implies implementing equitable recruitment practice. Consequently, job descriptions and advertising are designed with a focus on equity. The aim is to actively recruit from categories which are underrepresented in the organization.
- **Affinity groups**: These groups are formed around specific identities based on gender, race, sexual orientation etc and aim to provide support and build a sense of belongingness among the employees who feel marginalized in the workplace.
- **Commitment of leadership**: This implies that the leadership is committed to accomplishment of DEI goals. Additionally, it entails that the leadership will ensure availability of assistance and all forms of resources to the team working for successful implementation of DEI.
- **Cultural affinity:** Organizations now have a higher acknowledgement of the diverse cultural composition of their workforce. Offering flexible leaves; celebrating festivals from various cultures; transforming written and verbal communications to make the language more inclusive and encouraging feedback and transparency are some of the key initiatives which organizations take for cultural assimilation of diversity.
- **Monitoring:** Continuous follow-up and monitoring of the DEI initiatives coupled with realistic deadlines is a must for organizations engaged with DEI. It also implies that various stages for completing the tasks are pre-defined keeping in mind the endeavor's complexity and scalability. Celebration of the completion of milestone stages is also a common practice to keep the commitment strong and momentum going.

Table 1.1 shows the visual representation of key practices of DEI adopted by various industries.

This is not an exhaustive list of the industry practices. Organizations have extended and innovated the practices for better fit with the organization. A look at the global players who have pioneered various initiatives and are recognized as leaders in DEI implementation shall further explain how corporate has embraced the DEI implementation.

- **Gender Parity**: Empowerment of female employees, running mentorship programs, and creating leadership opportunities are amongst the most common practices by companies to implement DEI and ensure gender-based inclusion. Organizations like Tata Consultancy Services (TCS), Infosys, Hindustan Unilever Limited (HUL), Wipro, Mahindra, and Accenture are some of the global giants taking such initiatives. HUL

TABLE 1.1

Key DEI practices adopted by industries

Practice	Description
Sensitization trainings	Educates employees to eliminate conscious/unconscious biases through workshops, seminars, and discussions that foster an inclusive work environment
Transformation of hiring	Focuses on equitable recruitment by designing inclusive job descriptions and actively sourcing candidates from underrepresented groups
Affinity groups	Employee-led groups based on shared identities (e.g., gender, race, sexual orientation) that offer support and a sense of belonging for marginalized employees
Leadership commitment	Involves leadership actively supporting DEI goals, providing resources, and setting a clear tone from the top for organizational culture and accountability
Cultural affinity practices	Embraces diverse cultural backgrounds through inclusive language, flexible leave policies, multicultural celebrations, and transparent feedback mechanisms
Monitoring and accountability	Involves setting clear goals, defining milestones, tracking progress, and celebrating achievements to maintain momentum and ensure successful DEI implementation

Source: Authors' compilation.

also consciously gives opportunity to women who wish to start their career after a break. This involves offering training and support to help individuals return to full-time work, along with mentorship programs, leadership development, and networking opportunities.

- **Diverse workforce**: Organizations like Salesforce, Infosys, Wipro, Mahindra, Accenture, Cisco, Proctor, and Gamble are actively taking initiatives for inclusion of underrepresented groups (women, multiracial, differently-abled, and LGBTQIA+ employees). Substantial investments are being channeled into nurturing a diverse workforce. These include provisions like transforming hiring practices that are designed to be inclusive and to address systemic barriers for underrepresented communities. This ensures that discrimination is quelled and all levels of the organizational hierarchy are represented by diverse workforce. This provision is further supported by the organizations through dedicatedly designed recruitment drives and specifically tailored training programs that upskill individuals from these groups and ensure that their inclusion does not end with hiring rather. It continues till complete integration in to the organization is successfully achieved.
- **Value added initiatives**: Many organizations like Intel, Apple Inc, and Google offer child care leaves to its LGBTQIA+, single, and nonbiological parents. They also undertake projects and work as partner with non-profit organizations for generating funds and support for marginalized sections of the society. These companies actively collaborate and strive to create better opportunities for underrepresented communities.

Additionally, companies like Estée Lauder, and Tata Consultancy Services run Employee Resource Groups (ERGs) with thousands of participants to offer support to the underrepresented groups of the organization and for women, families, veterans among others. In a unique initiative, Hindustan Unilever Limited runs a Supplier Diversity Program where it ensures that its supplier base if diverse and actively engages the minority – owned businesses for instance the businesses owned by women or by marginalized communities.

- **Technology for DEI**: Organizations are also harnessing the power of technology for adoption and implementation of DEI initiatives. Companies like Salesforce, Cisco, and Infosys are using data to identify gaps, study trends and recognize opportunities and barriers for improving diversity, equity, and inclusion. For instance, study of real-time data on representation, attrition, and promotions by race and gender may enable an organization to adopt a well-structured approach to DEI initiatives and to forge new frontiers of inclusion. Digital tools are being leveraged to ensure equity in recruitment processes. The use of artificial intelligence-driven platforms that aid in attracting diverse talent also ensures reduced biases in hiring. Additionally, the use of augmented reality and virtual reality technologies to train employees on DEI enables organizations to creating an immersive experience and simultaneously addresses the problem of unconscious biases. The use of assistive technologies, such as screen readers and automated mobility tools, helps specially abled workforce with the resources they need for their unhindered functioning.

Table 1.2 shows a visual representation of DEI implementation by global leaders.

TABLE 1.2

DEI implementation by global leaders

Category	Key Practices	Organizations Involved
Gender parity and empowerment	Mentorship programs Leadership opportunities Return-to-work support	TCS, Infosys, HUL, Wipro, Mahindra, Accenture
Diverse workforce inclusion	Inclusive hiring practices Training for underrepresented groups Systemic barrier reduction	Salesforce, Infosys, Wipro, Mahindra, Accenture, Cisco, Procter & Gamble
Value-added initiatives	Childcare leave for LGBTQIA+, single, non-biological parents Support via ERGs Supplier diversity programs	Intel, Apple, Google, Estée Lauder, TCS, HUL
Technology for DEI	Data-driven gap analysis AI-based hiring AR/VR for DEI training Assistive tech for accessibility	Salesforce, Cisco, Infosys

Source: Author Self Compilation.

1.4.2 Abandoning DEI

The global wave of adopting diversity, equity, and inclusion as a corporate norm seems to be receding as the voices opposing the DEI practices grow stronger. In the later part of year 2024 and early 2025, numerous organizations have announced substantial changes in their policies related to DEI. These changes are being done across the various functions of the organization. A reduction or complete stop on the spending for DEI related projects is one of the most common ways of abandoning the DEI practices. As businesses focus on cutting costs and maximizing profits, DEI efforts often lose priority. Some organizations feel these initiatives don't lead to meaningful changes in workplace culture, viewing them as less impactful than goals like innovation, efficiency, and productivity. As a result, DEI is sometimes seen as nonessential and receives less attention or funding. This short-term mindset can hinder long-term growth by ignoring the role of DEI in fostering innovation and strengthening organizational resilience. Thus, as a result, these organizations tend to scale back the programs focusing on DEI.

Recent turn of socio-political events in the US has triggered retractions by organizations on their DEI commitment. In the year 2024, out of top Fortune 50 companies, only 10 have publicly released their DEI reports. Figure 1.2 depicts a review of S& P 500 companies report found that DEI has fallen sharply over the years.

As concerns over legal exposures grow stronger, the organizations have become more cautious towards the reporting of their diversity, equity, and inclusion-related initiatives in public domain (Purpose Brand, 2025). Simultaneously, organizations are also revisiting their DEI efforts and reassessing how much attention, dedication, and resources they want to

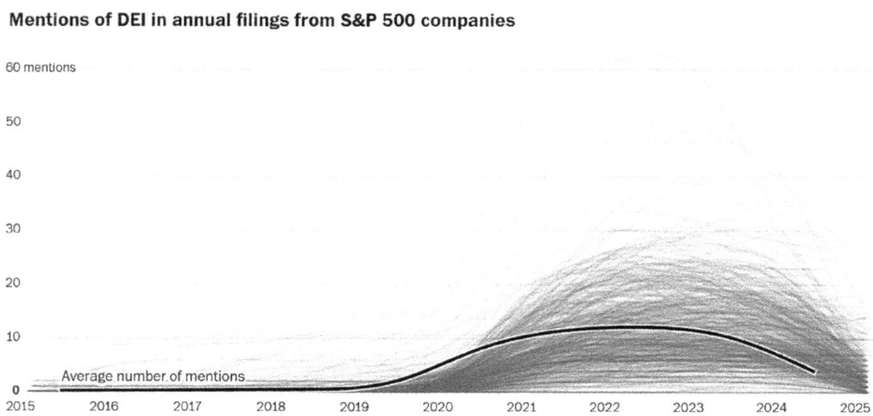

FIGURE 1.2

A review of S&P 500 companies' report to find diversity, equity and inclusion.

Source: **(Lau & Telford, 2025).** ***"DEI" vanishing from corporate filings, mirroring broader retreat. The Washington Post. www.washingtonpost.com/business/interactive/2025/dei-companies-sec-filings/***

commit to the same. This has led to DEI plans being restructured, reworded, or being completely retracted. Some of the major changes as announced by Giant corporations like Ford, Lowe's, Harley Davidson, Walmart, Boeing, PepsiCo, Goldman Sachs, Salesforce, Meta, and Amazon are as follows:

- Ceased participation in surveys related to diversity, equity, and inclusion in the company.
- Evolution and restructuring of Employee Resource Groups so that their focus shifts to nurturing networks, strengthening mentorship, enhanced community service, and promoting personal and professional development.
- Dismantle of teams/departments and positions which were dedicated to run the diversity, equity, and inclusion efforts of the organization.
- Ceased allocation of funds to the programs run under DEI initiatives.
- Change in use of language and vocabulary in official communications both internally and externally.
- Removal of targets related to diversity hiring; change in recruitment practices to build a workforce based on merit rather than on the grounds of diversity.
- Put a stop to employee training for 'equity and inclusion'.

As these steps gain momentum and are implemented by industry leaders, others are highly likely to follow the trend. This is expected to result in a set back to the Global DEI initiatives. However, many companies engaged and committed to the DEI efforts may continue to do so due to multiple reasons. For instance, organizations operating in India carry a DEI accountability framework due to Government mandate and similar other related provisions like Maternity benefits, Prevention of Sexual Harassment (POSH) Act among others. Consequently, they view continuing their DEI efforts as an opportunity to be an attractive workplace for individuals with diverse talent. At the same time, such companies can also enjoy strengthened reputation among its various stakeholders like employees, suppliers, and customers, who believe that an ideal workplace must have human resources from diverse backgrounds enabling employees to engage, interact, and develop connect among themselves; a less diverse organization will not be able to facilitate the same (Basu, 2025).

1.5 Conclusion

The ongoing debate around DEI practices has brought forward the challenges associated with the same. The larger agreement on ensuring social equity and inclusion remains unquestioned. However, the challenge is to have a consensus on the components of diversity, equity, and inclusion and to adopt their universally acceptable definition. Yet another prominent challenge is to outline the right methods of achieving DEI without losing its larger purpose that aims to establish equitable practices which mitigate biases of all kinds. As many organizations abandon or change their DEI commitments, the extent to which others follow the suit still remains to be seen. Many Indian and non-U.S.-based companies continue to uphold their DEI commitments without interruption, while a significant number have opted to modify their approaches to better align with evolving business needs and local contexts (Sharan, 2025). This may reflect the cultural mindset of a nation in which the organizations are based where a diverse talent pool and other stakeholders necessitate organizations' DEI commitment to continue. As of now, conclusive verdicts are a challenge. Whatever be the future of DEI initiatives on organizational fronts, it must be ensured that the society consciously eliminates biases, promises, and delivers equity to all its members for generations to come.

1.6 Implications

DEI can be welcomed in the organizations in a hope to bring diversity of talent pool so that more creative solutions with improved decision making can be possible. Studies also support that a diversified team brings increased financial performance of an organization (Lorenzo et al., 2018). From societal point of view, DEI as reducing discrimination will help the society to become inclusive and bring harmony. Effective implementation of Diversity, Equity, and Inclusion (DEI) initiatives can help cultivate a workplace culture where individuals are judged fairly and free from bias. By ensuring that no single group is discriminated against and that all employees are valued based on their skills and contributions, organizations can promote a sense of equity and belonging. This inclusive environment enhances employee morale, encourages open collaboration, and fosters psychological safety. As a result, employees are more likely to feel committed to the organization, leading to increased engagement, lower turnover, and a stronger, more cohesive workforce.

1.7 Future Directions of Research

As DEI has been considered under scrutiny and facing backlash, the future research must focus on quantifying its impact which means measuring the performance, turnover, employee satisfaction, and employee engagement in DEI over non-DEI environment. Future research also must focus on the ways or methods to make DEI sustainable. The future research can also focus on how DEI brings advantage to long term value and growth of organization. Also, more of quantitative researches can be done to better analyze the impact of DEI on organizations.

References

Bairoh, S. (2008). *Current debates on classifying diversity management: Review and a proposal.* https://helda.helsinki.fi/bitstream/10227/267/2/534-978-951-555-978-4.pdf

Barney, J. B., & Clark, D. N. (2007). *Resource-based theory: Creating and sustaining competitive advantage.* OUP Oxford.

Basu, S. (2025, February 11). Some US MNCs may slow DEI efforts, but Indian companies not to let up momentum. *The Economic Times.* https://economictimes.indiatimes.com/jobs/hr-policies-trends/some-us-mncs-may-slow-dei-efforts-but-indian-companies-not-to-let-up-momentum/articleshow/118124415.cms?from=mdr

Beavers, D. (2018a). Diversity, equity and inclusion framework. *The Greenlining Institute.* https://greenlining.org/wp-content/uploads/2018/03/DEI-Framework-Appointment.pdf

Beavers, D. (2018b). *Diversity, equity and inclusion framework.* The Greenlining Institute.

Betancourt, J. R., Green, A. R., Carrillo, J. E., & Park, E. R. (2005). Cultural competence and health care disparities: Key perspectives and trends. *Health Affairs, 24*(2), 499–505.

Bush, L. (2025). DEI definitions, theories, and concepts. In *Diversity, Equity, and Inclusion in Strategic Communications* (pp. 3–17). Routledge.

Byrne, D. (1997). An overview (and underview) of research and theory within the attraction paradigm. *Journal of Social and Personal Relationships, 14*(3), 417–431. https://doi.org/10.1177/0265407597143008

Cox, T. (1994). *Cultural diversity in organizations: Theory, research and practice.* Berrett-Koehler Publishers.

Cox, T. H., & Blake, S. (1991). Managing cultural diversity: Implications for organizational competitiveness. *Academy of Management Perspectives, 5*(3), 45–56. https://doi.org/10.5465/ame.1991.4274465

Dobbin, F., & Kalev, A. (2016). Why diversity programs fail. *Harvard Business Review, 94*(7), 14.

Engle, J., & Tinto, V. (2008). Moving beyond access: College success for low-income, first-generation students. In *Pell Institute for the Study of Opportunity in Higher Education.*

Ferraro, C., Hemsley, A., & Sands, S. (2023). Embracing diversity, equity, and inclusion (DEI): Considerations and opportunities for brand managers. *Business Horizons, 66*(4), 463–479. https://doi.org/10.1016/j.bushor.2022.09.005

Friedman, Z., & Cole, M. (2025). A diversity, equity, and inclusion (DEI) group experience. In *Group Dynamics in Occupational Therapy* (pp. 385–423). Routledge.

Gill, G. K., McNally, M. J., & Berman, V. (2018). Effective diversity, equity, and inclusion practices. *Healthcare Management Forum, 31*(5), 196–199. https://doi.org/10.1177/0840470418773785

Gurin, P., Dey, E., Hurtado, S., & Gurin, G. (2002). Diversity and higher education: Theory and impact on educational outcomes. *Harvard Educational Review, 72*(3), 330–367.

Hicks-Clarke, D., & Iles, P. (2000). Climate for diversity and its effects on career and organisational attitudes and perceptions. *Personnel Review, 29*(3), 324–345.

Kraus, M. W., Torrez, B., & Hollie, L. (2022). How narratives of racial progress create barriers to diversity, equity, and inclusion in organizations. *Current Opinion in Psychology, 43*, 108–113. https://doi.org/10.1016/j.copsyc.2021.06.022

Lambert, J. R. (2015). The impact of gay-friendly recruitment statements and due process employment on a firm's attractiveness as an employer. *Equality, Diversity and Inclusion: An International Journal, 34*(6), 510–526.

Lambert, J. R., Basuil, D. A., Bell, M. P., & Marquardt, D. J. (2019). Coming to America: Work visas, international diversity, and organizational attractiveness among highly skilled Asian immigrants. *International Journal of Human Resource Management, 30*(15), 2293–2319.

Lau, E., & Telford, T. (2025, April 30). *'DEI' vanishing from corporate filings, mirroring business world's retreat*. The Washington Post. www.washingtonpost.com/business/interactive/2025/dei-companies-sec-filings/

Li, F., Lo, C. K. Y., Tang, C. S., & Zhou, P. (2024). Will diversity, equity, and inclusion commitment improve manufacturing firms. In *Market performance? A signaling theory perspective on DEI announcements. Production and Operations Management*. https://doi.org/10.1177/10591478241265479

Lorenzo, R., Voigt, N., Tsusaka, M., Krentz, M., & Abouzahr, K. (2018, January 23). *How Diverse Leadership Teams Boost Innovation*. BCG. www.bcg.com/publications/2018/how-diverse-leadership-teams-boost-innovation

Manjare, S. O. (2024). From theory to practice: Implementing DEI in organizational policy. In Diversity, Equity and Inclusion (1st ed., pp. 1–26). Bluerose Publishers.

Miller, C. C., Burke, L. M., & Glick, W. H. (1998). Cognitive diversity among upper-echelon executives: Implications for strategic decision processes. *Strategic Management Journal, 19*, 39–58.

Nishii, L. H. (2013). The benefits of climate for inclusion for gender-diverse groups. *Academy of Management Journal, 56*(6), 1754–1774.

Olzmann, J. A. (2020). Diversity through equity and inclusion: The responsibility belongs to all of us. *Molecular Biology of the Cell, 31*(25), 2757–2760. https://doi.org/10.1091/mbc.e20-09-0575

Purpose Brand. (2025, January 13). Fortune 500 Companies Retool Diversity Marketing in DEI Reports. *Fortune 500 Companies Retool Diversity Marketing in DEI Reports*. https://purposebrand.com/blog/fortune-500-dei-reports-2024/

Richard, O. C. (2000). Racial diversity, business strategy, and firm performance: A resource-based view. *Academy of Management Journal, 43*(2), 164–177.

Roberson, Q. M. (2006). Disentangling the meanings of diversity and inclusion in organizations. *Group & Organization Management, 31*(2), 212–236. https://doi.org/10.1177/1059601104273064

Rock, D., & Grant, H. (2016). Why diverse teams are smarter. *Harvard Business Review, 4*(4), 2–5.

Sharan, G. (2025, February 27). *While US companies step back from DEI, India is moving ahead*. People Matters. www.peoplematters.in/article/diversity/while-us-companies-step-back-from-dei-india-is-moving-ahead-44543

Sherbin, L., & Rashid, R. (2017). Diversity doesn't stick without inclusion. *Harvard Business Review, 1*, 1–5.

Shore, L. M., Randel, A. E., Chung, B. G., Dean, M. A., Ehrhart, K. H., & Singh, G. (2018). Inclusion and diversity in work groups: A review and model for future research. *Journal of Management, 44*(1), 118–146.

Thomas, D. A., & Ely, R. J. (1996). Making differences matter. *Harvard Business Review, 74*(5), 79–90.

Thomas, K. M., Plaut, V. C., & Tran, N. M. (2014). *Diversity ideologies in organizations*. Routledge New York.

Tsui, A. S., Egan, T. D., & O'Reilly III, C. A. (1992). Being different: Relational demography and organizational attachment. *Administrative Science Quarterly, 37*(4), 549–579. https://doi.org/10.2307/2393472

Young, I. M. (2008). Justice and the politics of difference. In *The New Social Theory Reader* (2nd ed.). Routledge.

2

A Literature Review on the Role of Digital Technologies in Addressing Social and Economic Inequities

Mitali Sengupta

2.1 Introduction

Equitable distribution of resources is not only something that one strives for, but is also the need of the hour. Recognizing that various groups may need varying degrees of support to achieve fairness, equity makes ensuring that people and communities have access to the opportunities and resources they need to prosper (Bopaiah, 2021). Cycles of poverty and marginalization are sustained by social and economic injustices, which originates from structural obstacles including discrimination, income inequality, and unequal access to healthcare and education. Investigating methods for advancing more inclusive and just institutions is crucial since these disparities have wide-ranging effects on social mobility, economic stability, and general societal well-being.

The social and economic inequities depict the presence of significant gaps in terms of allocation and distribution of vital resources, wealth, access, income, and opportunities across individuals or communities that are cohabit in different geographical locations. Aspects of economic inequity are best observed through various indicators of mismatched income distribution, wealth-related gaps and access to various economic services. Social inequity includes differential access to health, education, infrastructural services, and participation in the process of decision-making (Bahn et al., 2020). Gender, education, technology, race/ethnicity, occupation, sexual orientation, earnings, and population structure are some of the factors that are highlighted in the literature on social equality (Peltzman, 2009; Healey and Stepnick, 2019). Nonetheless, a number of scholars have generally stated that the most important component of social equality is economic disparity. Peltzman (2009) demonstrates that disparities in life expectancy, or mortality inequality, highlight the importance of lifetime inequality in the relationship

DOI: 10.1201/9781003591078-3

between wealth and longevity. The nature of social equality and the social relationships that underlie it are examined by Helliwell et al. (2023). The impact of gender on social equality in England is examined by Netto et al. (2020), who find that gender patterns have a significant role in equality. Skare and Porada (2022) distinguish between results favoring chance as a tool of human advancement and equality of chance. Feldblum (2005) explores the relationship between equality and sexual orientation, emphasizing related limitations. Djerf-Pierre (2018) discusses social equality, gender inequality, and disparities in living conditions, primarily based on the corresponding income level. Equality of opportunity is significantly impacted by the Rawlsian style (Rawls, 2005) relationship between race and education (Voigt, 2017). Destabilizing economic and social equity can negatively impact community cohesiveness and social and economic growth (Corbera et al., 2020). Additionally, such inequities can give rise to problems associated with poverty, socioeconomic status, unemployment, and quality of life to name a few. It is, therefore, very important to address facets of social and economic inequity for inclusive and sustainable development of mankind. The importance of technology lies in addressing and curbing issues of inequity.

Recent studies emphasize how important technology is to promoting social equality and better thriving conditions. Various researchers like Johnson et al. (2022) and Acemoglu and Restrepo (2019) have highlighted that while the different technological advancements and implementations have been identified to be one of the leading reasons to significantly enhance inequity among people on one side. It also offers potential solutions to curb the same. An instance for the same can be looked at from the perspective of creation of varied work domains using technology primarily to employ people across all socioeconomic strata and elevate their position. At the same time, people who lack access to technology are excluded from the facets of technological upliftment happening to provide equitable distribution of resources. Given the fact that the main transformative process utilized by the society to allocate the different social and economic resources pertaining to work, unequal access to technology and correspondingly, the work or jobs could further accentuate inequity amongst people. Thus, advancements in technology may act as a stabilizing influence for inequalities created by society. The advancement of assistive technology has the potential to enhance the quality of life for individuals with special needs (Klochikhin, 2012). Through the Pareto resource allocation, such a policy's significant macroeconomic benefits lead to increased income and employment, cost savings, and growth.

Rapid structural and qualitative changes brought about by the quick adoption of cutting-edge technology, such as digital technologies; define the current stage of socioeconomic system development. The processes of economic and social digitalization promote deeper interactions between all participants of an environment that transcend national boundaries, formulating the conditions for GDP growth, boost worker productivity, and introduce and disseminate innovations in all areas of life (Grybauskas et al., 2022).

Rapid technology advancements that have a multiplier impact necessitate the development of qualitatively novel, flexible models, and methodologies for the management of economic processes at all scales.

Strategies for the economic development of the state, regions, and particular sectors are useless if they do not include the impact of significant digitalization trends being followed in the society on the evolution of economic and social processes. The introduction and broad use of technologies for processing and storing vast amounts of data (cloud computing, big data), the Internet of Things, end-to-end information technologies, cyber security technologies, robotization and complete automation of the majority of processes and industries, and other areas of development of cutting-edge technologies that alter the role of humans in the economic system form the foundation of the digital economy (Kaur et al., 2020).

In recent years, both developed and developing economies have seen a rapid increase in the influence of technology in business and society. As a result, digital technologies are now being studied and used in many other domains, from social communication, education, and healthcare to government policy, business, and finance. In the context of the so-called "digital divide" between wealthy and developing nations, numerous writers have explored the relationship between emerging technologies and society. Increased cost and accessibility of technology has been crucial to socioeconomic progress across social classes, regions, and countries, and it has often been hypothesized that nation characteristics attenuate the productivity effects of technology (Pick and Azari, 2008). Socioeconomic development is significantly influenced by healthcare and education.

The rapid changes and significant developments in the field of digital technologies have a direct impact on different dimensions of our life, especially in the social and economic attributes. Though advances in electronic and communication technologies have created newer avenues for growth and development, but at the same time it has also triggered different challenges related to economic and social equity. The subsequent section shall highlight the impact of digital transformation towards digital divide.

2.1.1 Digital Transformation and Digital Divide

Digital transformation has led to significant revolutions in terms of how individuals and businesses operate. All essential activities and transactions including healthcare, education, and other regular services have been shifted to online platforms as a result of this transformation. The availability of dependable internet connectivity, gadgets, and technical infrastructure that let people interact with the digital world is referred to as digital access (Haleem et al., 2022). The capacity to communicate, study, and work efficiently using digital tools, software, and online platforms is referred to as digital skills. To navigate the current digital landscape and effectively participate in society, one must possess digital literacy, which is based on digital access and abilities.

By increasing the digital divide, this change has worsened social and economic inequality even if it has increased efficiency and connectivity. People with access to digital technologies and the necessary skills can access financial services, online education, and better job opportunities, while people without these resources are becoming isolated. This inequality disproportionately affects low-income communities, rural areas, and developing countries, limiting their ability to participate in the modern economy (Ho and Tseng, 2006). Since the repercussions of this divide extend beyond economic inequality and impact social mobility, healthcare access, and overall quality of life, addressing digital inclusion as part of broader equality initiatives is crucial.

One of the most significant ways that digital technology impacts social and economic inequality is through the digital divide, or unequal distribution of access to and usage of this technology. According to a research done by International Telecommunication Union (ITU) in Canton (2021), approximately 51.2% of people globally have an internet connection, with significant disparities between rich and developing countries. In many low-income and marginalized communities, access to digital technology and issues in adopting the same bear numerous challenges, including cost, infrastructure, and a lack of digital literacy (Kandachar and Halme, 2017). This lack of access to digital technology and absence or limited digital skills add upon already-existing social and economic inequality, as digital technologies are now essential for a variety of engagement, employment, and education.

The economic and social inequity continues to be a cause of global concern and without proper dissemination of digital technology, the gap surrounding disparity in education, health, and employment shall increase manifolds. Individuals having access to technology shall make good use of the same compared to the ones that struggle for technological access. The role of digital transformation in education, healthcare services, and employment needs to be explored to properly utilize the potential of technology from creating barriers to removing them.

2.1.2 Digital Transformation in Education

In addition to changing how we obtain and exchange information, digital technologies have opened up new avenues for education and skill improvement. However, not everyone has equal access to these opportunities. According to research, students of color and those with lower incomes are less likely to have access to digital devices and the internet at home, which may hinder their capacity to finish homework, take part in online courses, and take part in digital literacy initiatives (Oliveira and De Souza, 2022). Since students without access to digital technologies are less likely to be ready for the demands of a labor market driven by technology, this lack of access can lead to educational success inequalities (Mukul and Büyüközkan, 2023).

2.1.3 Digital Transformation in Healthcare Services

The healthcare industry has undergone a substantial transition due to digitalization, which has improved patient care, accessibility, and efficiency through telemedicine, electronic health records, and AI-driven diagnostics. However, the digital divide has also grown as a result of this quick change, disproportionately impacting people who lack digital knowledge, dependable internet access, or the money to purchase essential technologies (Kraus et al. (2021)). People in low-income and rural areas have difficulty accessing digital health resources, online appointment scheduling, and telehealth services, which restricts their capacity to get timely and high-quality care. Addressing digital inclusion in healthcare is crucial to ensuring equitable access for everyone, as this barrier not only exacerbates already-existing health disparities but also perpetuates larger social and economic imbalances.

2.1.4 Digital Transformation in Employment

Significant changes in employment have also been brought about by digital technology, which have opened up new career paths in industries like software development, digital marketing, and e-commerce. Nevertheless, not everyone has access to these opportunities, and some groups face major obstacles to finding work in these industries. For instance, STEM fields—which are essential for many careers involving digital technology—are underrepresented in women and people of color (Eisenhart and Allen, 2020). Furthermore, many low-skilled jobs have been automated by digital technologies, which have resulted in job displacement and wage stagnation for individuals who lack the education and skills necessary to adjust to these changes (Lloyd and Payne, 2023).

Technology can serve as an enabler to reduce social and economic inequity or be the cause. However, the exact role of technology toward social or economic inequity or equitable distribution is quite complex and also contested. While technology helps in enhancing productivity and drives economic growth, but limited access to technology might dampen the efforts and cause disparity. Similarly, while technology can create growth and learning opportunities for the remotest locations, but digital divide can lead to improper distribution of technological advancements and implementations.

2.1.5 Social Inequity and Technology

Despite the fact that multiple studies have highlighted how income distribution, which is significantly biased toward a small number of individuals, undercuts the general public's economic potential, the literature's investigation of the relationship between income inequality and technical innovation is somewhat limited (Mhlongo and Dlamini, 2022). On the one hand, some research ignores the possible consequences of technological innovation on income inequality in favor of concentrating on how it affects economic growth. However, despite being a well-researched and significant topic, the impact of technological innovation in wealth redistribution frequently lacks either empirical backing or theoretical depth.

There are several facets to the connection between inequality and technology. Technology has boosted economic growth, increased productivity, made knowledge and sharing of information and easier access to essential services. It has, nevertheless, also contributed to inequality. As a meta-infrastructure, information and communications technologies (ICT) transform all other infrastructures into intelligent systems that hasten socioeconomic development. More significantly, artificial intelligence (AI), or machines that can think and act like humans, has emerged as the next technological frontier of sustainable development as the Third Industrial Revolution turns into the Fourth Industrial Revolution with the Internet of Things (IoT) at its center (Mhlanga, 2021). As AI goes mainstream, its disruptive implications are likely to be seen at an unprecedented speed and scale, which underlines the need for governments and stakeholders to discuss and determine their common destiny.

2.1.6 Economic Inequity and Technology

Global economic structures have changed as a result of the quick development of technology, but social and economic disparities have also gotten worse, especially in the areas of employment, healthcare, and income distribution (Lloyd and Payne, 2023). Traditional low-skilled employment has been replaced by automation, artificial intelligence, and digitalization in the labor market. Workers in emerging nations are disproportionately affected since they do not have access to chances for reskilling and upskilling.

Employment inequities are made worse by the digital divide, as individuals who are proficient in technology are able to land higher-paying, tech-driven jobs, while others experience job displacement and unstable finances. Similar to this, telemedicine, electronic health records, and AI-driven diagnostics have all enhanced service delivery in the healthcare industry as a result of digital transformation; nevertheless, marginalized populations that lack dependable internet connectivity or digital literacy are still generally unable to take advantage of these advancements (Lloyd and Payne, 2023). By restricting access to urgent medical interventions, preventive care, and vital health information, this restriction exacerbates already-existing health inequities. Additionally, since the digital economy benefits those who have the resources and know-how to use technology, income inequality has increased, further stratifying economic prospects and widening the wealth disparity. These changes in technology highlight the urgent need for laws and programs that support digital inclusion, provide fair access to new developments, and stop socioeconomic marginalization from getting worse.

Implementation of technology on one side has been crucial to enhance job productivity, average wages, quality of life, and income potential; however, automation and utilization of technology without access or knowhow can be detrimental to the growth of communities as individuals struggle to utilize technology ending up losing jobs and impacting their social quality of life. It is therefore essential to explore how technological upgradations and its implementation can positively impact the social and economic attributes of individuals and communities. This review systematically highlights two important areas of equity research linked to digital transformation and technology adoption. At first it focuses on identifying the role of digital technology in widening or lessening social and economic inequities. Subsequently, it seeks to identify different interventions and policy frameworks which pave the way forward as to how digital technology can be utilized for developing social and economic equity utilizing technology with specific reference to education, employment, and securing healthcare services.

2.2 Methodology

As per the classical Preferred Reporting Items for Systematic Reviews and Meta-Analysis (PRISMA) criteria have been implemented as per PRISMA guidelines (2020) that helps to systematically report literature reviews and critically synthesize and analyze the information highlighted (Sahoo et al., 2024; Mishra and Mishra, 2023; Page et al., 2021). The current research has been undertaken to explore how technology promotes economic and social equity. The criteria of PRISMA utilize a comprehensive methodology to find, evaluate, filter, and complete research literature in a very systematic manner. This approach has been widely used in areas like social and economic equity, digital inclusion, and technology-driven societal change among others.

The following actions have been implemented for the search strategy:

1) Determining the original body of literature
2) Implementing a strict screening procedure
3) Evaluating the suitability of particular studies
4) Finalizing the corpus for examination

The search technique, inclusion and exclusion criteria, and data extraction procedure are thoroughly explained in the parts that follow.

2.3 Search Strategy

We used a systematic search approach in Scopus, a well-known and reputable research database, to guarantee a thorough coverage of the literature on the relationship between technology and economic and social equity.

Search Terms and Query Formulation

The main search terms used were "digital transformation AND economic equity," "digital transformation AND social equity," "technology AND economic AND equity," and "technology AND social AND equity," "digital divide AND social AND economic and equity," and similar term combinations. These terms were chosen to include studies that specifically focus on technology, digital divide, digital transformation and highlight the role of technology in widening or narrowing the social and economic equity, thereby addressing systemic biases in technological applications. The search was conducted in January 2025, with no restriction on publication date to ensure the inclusion of both historical and contemporary research. We formulated search queries using a combination of keywords and Boolean operators to ensure coverage of pertinent literature.

2.4 Eligibility Criteria

Specific inclusion and exclusion criteria have been established to refine the corpus of studies (see Figure 2.1).

Inclusion Criteria

The study considered journal research articles and excluded conference papers, posters, and editorial commentary. Research that specifically addresses the connection between technology and social or economic equity have been considered. Peer-reviewed articles from conferences and publications with indexes, along with theoretical articles, empirical research, and systematic reviews that add to the ongoing discussion around the role of technology in social and economic equity are included in the study protocol.

Exclusion Criteria

Papers that just discuss technological developments without taking social or economic equity into account or do not provide any linkage on technological transformations in social and economic equity, opinion pieces, gray literature, and nonpeer-reviewed articles have been excluded. Studies that are not written in English or where full texts are not available have also not been considered.

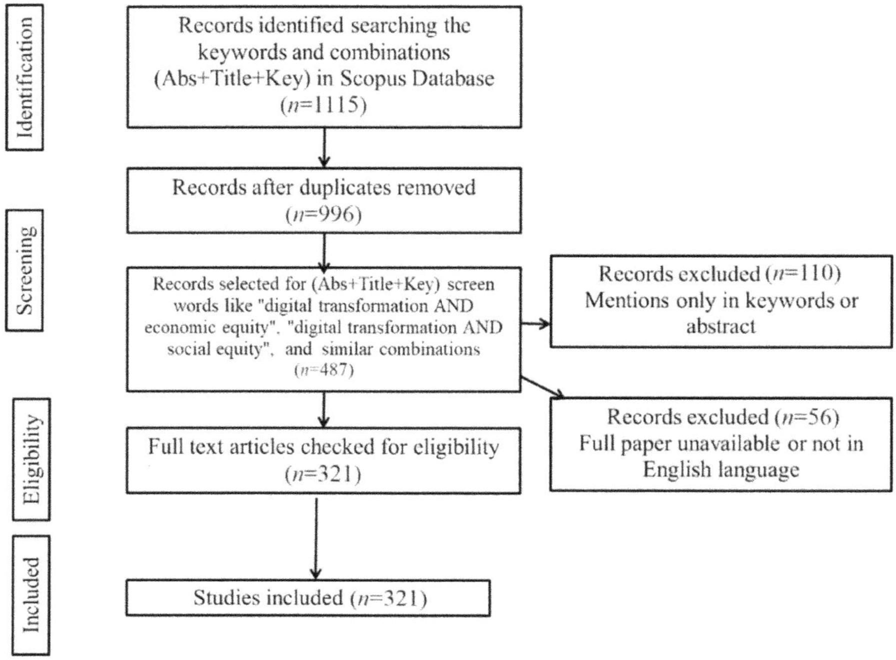

FIGURE 2.1
The PRISMA flow to select research articles.

2.5 Screening Protocol

The screening protocol has been a two-step process

Title and Abstract Screening
The initial search returned all entries matching the provided search terms.

Using predetermined inclusion and exclusion criteria, titles, abstracts, and keywords (Title+Abs+Key) were examined to exclude articles that weren't relevant.

2.6 Full-Text Review

To make sure they were in line with the goals of the study, articles that made it past the first round were subjected to full-text review. Thematic relevance, methodological rigor, and contribution to technology and equity discourses were used to classify the studies.

2.7 Data Extraction and Synthesis

After the corpus was finalized, a structured coding methodology was used to extract the data. Important characteristics taken from every investigation are as follows:

Research questions and study objectives

- The analytical techniques and methodology employed.
- Important conclusions about how technology contributes to social and economic justice; issues and
- suggestions for fair technological advancement

2.8 Results

In order to incorporate findings from several studies and provide an exhaustive overview of themes, trends, and research gaps in the field, a narrative synthesis was used.

2.8.1 The Role of Digital Technology in Social and Economic Inequities

This combination of words approximately yielded about 1115 search results. The examination of citation data from several datasets in Scopus database shows that the relationship between digital technology and equity is becoming more and more of an academic concern. With 3,936 citations, the most cited work highlights its significance in this discussion (Ghisellini et al., 2016). The need for more research in this area is shown by the median citation count, which indicates that although some works have gained traction, others are still neglected.

Digital Divide

Different researchers have highlighted the findings related to technology acceptance, transformation, and adoption and their individual roles in equity amongst individuals. This section identifies and highlights research articles of digital divide and their role in establishing (in) equity. This combination of words with equity application approximately yielded about 92 search results in Scopus database.

Researchers working in the field of technology and social and economic equity emphasize the advantages and disadvantages of digital innovations that have happened from time to time within the society. In these studies, the digital divide—the difference between people or communities with and without access to digital technologies—recurs frequently. According to Benjelloun (2023), technology can improve learning chances within individuals, but it also highlights how differences in internet access and digital skills might pose significant restrictions to these advantages. Similarly, the study conducted by Holmes (2003) explore the role of interactive media and whether it could possibly help marginalized people develop their digital literacy and engagement. A policy-driven approach is used by Afzal et al. (2023), which examine the role played by international organizations that might help alleviate these disparities, especially in the field of education. It can therefore be said that, these studies show that although technology can democratize access to knowledge and education, structural obstacles like financial limitations and poor infrastructure still prevent its fair distribution.

The influence of technology in social and economic change is another important aspect that the study examines. Researchers like Alfaraz and Tully (2025) and Cortinois, and Birn (2021) have identified the different applications of digital technologies in creating digital divide. It specifically refers to whether digital technologies impact activism, government, and societal institutions. While the latter questions whether digital innovations have actually promoted inclusivity or have instead concentrated power among elite groups controlling mass media, the former contends that technology can empower marginalized communities by offering platforms for social movements and political participation. Additionally, Cortinois, and Birn (2021) examines how the various political systems and technology interact and the role of digital tools to uphold preexisting power structures.

Zhao et al. (2024), described various means as to how the digital economy might help solve energy and environmental issues, demonstrates how economic ramifications are also a major area of interest with technological interventions. Furthermore, Sengupta and Sengupta (2022) in their research article evaluated the ways in which digital innovations support sustainable urban development while highlighting inconsistencies between economic inclusion and technological advancement. Although these studies recognize the revolutionary potential of digital innovations, they also warn that, in the absence of deliberate policy frameworks and equitable implementation, technology may unintentionally exacerbate rather than lessen social and economic inequality (see Table 2.1).

Economic Equity and technology

This combination of words with equity application approximately yielded about 94 search results in Scopus database. The recent developments in the field of digital technology have been found to open up newer arenas to lessen economic inequity. The various digital platforms have been able to create successful job opportunities as well as entrepreneurial ventures. It is now possible for individuals to earn additional income or start their own ventures via ecommerce platforms and gig economy without any limitations

TABLE 2.1

Selected important literature on digital divide and equity

Author	Year	Title	Aim/Purpose of the study
Afzal, A., Khan, S., Daud, S., Ahmad, Z., & Butt, A. .	2023	Addressing the digital divide: Access and use of technology in education	Examines technology and its influence in widening social inequity if policies are not implemented effectively
Benjelloun W.	2023	Bridging the digital divide in higher education: north African challenges and initiatives. In *Higher Education in the Arab World: E-Learning and Distance Education*	Examines how technology can enhance education but also deepen inequities due to access issues
Holmes N.	2003	The digital divide, the UN, and the computing profession	Analyzes the role of international organizations in addressing digital inequalities
Alfaraz, C., & Tully, C	2025	Mobilizing social transformation with technology. The shaping of social processes since the development of industrial society and beyond: innovation input and social processes	Discusses how technology can be leveraged for activism and social change
Cortinois, A. A., & Birn, A. E.	(2021).	What's technology got to do with it? Power, politics, and health equity beyond technological triumphalism	Examines how technology intersects with political structures and reinforces power dynamics
Zhao, C., Dong, K., Liu, Z., & Ma, X.	2024	Is digital economy an answer to energy trilemma eradication? The case of China. *Journal of Environmental Management*	Explores the role of the digital economy in addressing environmental and economic challenges
Sengupta, U., & Sengupta, U.	2022	SDG-11 and smart cities: Contradictions and overlaps between social and environmental justice research agendas	Assesses the contribution of digital innovation to sustainable urban development and economic inclusivity

regarding geographical locations. Issues of unemployment can be addressed to a large extent through utilising digital technologies in this manner to promote economic equity (Fisher et al., 2020). Additionally, various aspects of digital technology can be successfully utilised to enhance the transparency of transactions and increase responsibility and accountability. It will further strengthen judicious utilisation of resources and ease monitoring systems to check resource allocation, utilisation and performance across all sectors and all strata of people. Armitage and Nellums (2020) are of the opinion that it will help to alleviate poverty effectively and reduce inequality of income to a large extent.

Research papers on economic equity and digital transformation, including topics like education, entrepreneurship, and socioeconomic inequities, are included in the dataset. Numerous studies demonstrate how digital technology is changing economic systems and impacting the distribution of income. Mhlanga (2023) for instance, studied the linkage between digital technologies and equity and showed that digital technologies both increase learning accessibility and distance institutions with digital infrastructure from those without having it. Analyzing the differing impacts of digitalization on economies, a very recent study by Baffour Gyau et al. (2025) demonstrates that although some countries see economic growth, others face growing income disparities. These results imply that although digital transformation offers chances for economic expansion, but the true potential and advantages are not equally shared, thereby favoring nations that have technological advantage in implementation.

While some studies contend that automation and digital platforms perpetuate structural inequality, others contend that they open up new economic opportunities (Studley, 2021). Millions of people have found work thanks to the growth of platform economies and gig work, yet many digital workers face unstable circumstances with little social protection and little job security (Graham et al., 2017). On the other hand, new types of microfinance and entrepreneurship have been made possible by technological developments in some industries, such as fin-tech, which have democratized financial access for underserved groups (Mamtaz, 2024).

Other studies examine the effects of digital technologies on economic and social fairness at the individual and corporate levels and its overall impact on entrepreneurship. Pérez-Barea (2025) examined the different ways that entrepreneurs can adopt to scale social impact projects using digital platforms, although there are still obstacles like funding and market access. Researchers examine how digital adoption can boost corporate competitiveness while simultaneously posing challenges for smaller, less resource-rich companies as opined by Thanh et al. (2025). According to this research, policies and investments in digital infrastructure are essential to prevent technology breakthroughs from already-existing disparities, even though they can promote economic inclusion. Overall, the findings show that technology is a significant driver in changing economic environments, but proactive steps are required to ensure that all socioeconomic groups have possibility of access to and benefits from it in a fair environment (see Table 2.2).

Though the optimal utilization of digital technology still is under progress, more efforts of comprehensive nature are required to ensure equitable access. This is more relevant in the context of digital literacy across various strata of the society and development of technology infrastructure across various locations and sectors. It is important to establish a synergy between private and public sector infrastructure upliftment coupled with tech literacy for the greater mass. Only with a strong, but staggered collaborative approach, the potential of digital technology towards positive transformation of the

TABLE 2.2

Selected important literature on economic equity and technology

Author	Year	Title	Aim/Purpose of the study
Mhlanga, D.	2023	Digital transformation education, opportunities, and challenges of the application of ChatGPT to emerging economies	Explores how digital tools enhance learning accessibility but also widen the gap between institutions
Baffour Gyau, E., Li, Y., & Appiah, M	2025	Global digital transformation: discovering the impact of digitalization on income inequality in OECD countries, the moderating role of globalization	Examines how digitalization affects economic growth and income disparity across nations
Pérez-Barea, J. J.	2025	The Evolution of Social Entrepreneurship: Broadening the Framework for the Digital and Sustainable Era	Analyzes how digital platforms help scale social entrepreneurship but also present market access challenges
Thanh, T. C., Nguyen, P. M., Nguyen-Nhu-Y, H., Hanh, N. T. H., Son, T. L., & Hang, H. M.	2025	Factors Affecting the Commitment to Digital Transformation Toward Achieving Sustainable Development Goals: Evidence from Vietnamese Small and Medium-Sized Enterprises	Studies how digital adoption enhances business competitiveness while creating barriers for smaller firms

economic dimensions of the society can be harnessed, otherwise the economic disparities shall always remain a fundamental issue at hand (Bapuji et al., 2020).

Social Equity and technology

This combination of words with equity application approximately yielded about 135 search results in Scopus database. The inclusion of digital technology toward promoting social equity is an important landmark to promote social equity. The utilisations of digital platforms like Google pay, Phone-pe, and other digital wallets have been instrumental in enhancing the access to financial services for individuals beyond their geographical boundaries. Such facilities in mobile banking services are being commonly used by people to save or transfer money for various purposes. This definitely helps to promote financial equity and inclusion within the formal system (Czymara et al., 2021). In the field of education, digital technologies have been used to access online content, self-paced courses, and other video lectures to enhance one's knowledge about a particular subject. Knowledge exchange is no longer limited to classrooms and one can pursue degrees even while they are working or involved in other activities, thanks to digital technology, thereby bringing in equity in education and dissemination of knowledge (Bywaters et al., 2020).

The important problem of unequal internet access and its effects on marginalized people is brought to light in the research articles on technology and social disparity. Government and organizational initiatives to close the digital gap have been examined by Johansson (2025) where they have highlighted the significance of digital literacy initiatives and infrastructure investment. In particular, gender discrepancies in digital access have been studied in details by Marín-Raventós & Calderón-Campos (2016), which highlights the ways in which cultural and economic variables impact women's engagement in the digital economy. Similarly, another study by Lim et al. (2018) explores the ways in which mobile technology might enhance social mobility and education, especially in underprivileged areas. Together, these studies highlight how socioeconomic inequality is still reinforced by differences among people to access, digital transformation benefits enhancing discriminations in the field of affordability, and digital skills, even if digital transformation has the potential to promote inclusivity.

Other research focuses on how various demographic groups are impacted by technological improvements, especially vulnerable groups like older folks and those from low-income backgrounds. The study by Golomski et al (2022) examines the relationship between social isolation and digital exclusion among seniors, emphasizing the necessity of specific measures to improve their digital engagement. While digital platforms can promote economic inclusion, they frequently favor those with prior technological access and skills, as per Räsänen et al. (2021), that consider digital transformation both in terms of opportunities and challenges for low-income groups. These studies highlight the need for comprehensive approaches, such as inclusive technology design, educational programs, and public regulations to achieve social equality in the digital age and guarantee that all society groups may profit from technological breakthroughs.

In healthcare, telemedicine and online consultations make way for accessing healthcare services even from remote locations. Additionally, several other digital health-based buddy apps help individuals to take up preventive measures for nonemergency health situations from the comfort of their own homes. Esping-Andersen (2024) have highlighted that it is especially important for elderly, differently able people or individuals staying in remote locations to get in time healthcare access and support from the comfort of their homes, without going to the healthcare facility (see Table 2.3).

2.8.2 Healthcare and Education Disparities

Research shows that online education and digital healthcare services can increase access, but they also point out issues with affordability and digital literacy (West, 2015). While some benefited from the COVID-19 pandemic's acceleration of telemedicine and virtual learning, others who lacked dependable

TABLE 2.3

Selected important literature on social equity and technology

Author	Year	Title	Aim/Purpose of the study
Johansson, M.	2025	Bridging the Digital Divide: Strategies for Inclusive Digital Transformation	Analyzes government and organizational efforts to bridge the digital divide through policy interventions
Marín-Raventós, G., & Calderón-Campos, M.	2016	Typifying mechanisms for gender digital equity in Latin America. In *ICT for Promoting Human Development and Protecting the Environment*	Explores gender disparities in digital access and participation, focusing on cultural and economic influences
Lim, C. P., Tinio, V. L., Smith, M., & Bhowmik, M. K.	2018	Achieving equity, quality, and efficiency in education. *Routledge International Handbook of Schools and Schooling in Asia*, 369	Investigates how mobile technology can support education and improve social mobility in underserved communities
Golomski, C., Corvini, M., Kim, B., Wilcox, J., & Valcourt, S.	2022	Aspects of ICT connectivity among older adults living in rural subsidized housing: reassessing the digital divide	Examines how digital exclusion among seniors impacts social isolation and suggests strategies for engagement
Räsänen, P., Koivula, A., & Keipi, T.	2021	Online information seeking patterns and social inequality in a digital economy	Studies how digital transformation can both create opportunities and reinforce barriers for low-income groups

internet or digital literacy skills saw their digital divide worsen (Aissaoui, 2022). In tackling disparities, the study emphasizes the potential and risks of technology-driven healthcare and education. Finding solutions and policy suggestions that help advance digital equity in healthcare, work, and education is the main goal of the second study topic. The following strategies are identified by the evaluated literature:

Education

To guarantee equal learning opportunities, policies that support digital literacy, reasonably priced internet access, and investments in digital infrastructure in underprivileged areas are essential (Jaeger et al., 2012; Bailey and Nyabola, 2021). The educational digital divide has shrunk in nations that have made investments in school technology initiatives and nationwide internet connectivity (Asadullah and Bhattacharjee, 2022; Bandhopadhyay et al., 2021). Disparities still exist, nevertheless, when it comes to culturally inclusive digital material and teacher preparation.

Employment

Research shows that in order to prepare people for the digital economy, reskilling and upskilling programs are necessary, as are labor laws that guarantee equitable compensation and protections for gig workers (Rushambwa, 2024). Strategic measures like government-sponsored retraining programs have demonstrated promise in reducing workforce displacement, even while automation poses a danger to some job categories (Silalahi & Walsh, 2023).

Healthcare

According to research, telemedicine, AI-powered diagnostics, and mobile health apps can increase access to healthcare; nevertheless, data privacy and ethical issues need to be addressed (Harini, 2024). Mobile health apps have been especially successful in providing rural communities with access to essential healthcare services in low-resource environments. Nonetheless, data privacy issues and legislative obstacles continue to exist (McGraw and Mandi, 2021).

2.9 Discussion

2.9.1 Digital Technology's Dual Role in Equity

The findings suggest that social and economic justice is shaped differently by digital technology. On the one hand, it makes it easier to connect, engage economically, and obtain services. It may, however, reinforce systemic disadvantages if it is not used inclusively. For instance, research has shown that AI-driven hiring practices and automation may lead to biased hiring decisions that disproportionately affect marginalized individuals (Bose, 2025; Drage and McKareth, 2022).

Digital tools can bridge gaps, but there are still systemic obstacles to overcome. Research indicates that biased algorithmic conclusions resulting from underrepresentation in AI training datasets can lead to discriminatory employment and lending practices (Kothandapani, 2025). Strict regulatory policy framework inplementations and continuous algorithmic audits are required to fix these issues and ensure equity (Krause, 2024; Murikah et al., 2024).

2.9.2 Effective Interventions and Policy Strategies

The development of AI has significantly altered several facets of international business. It has simplified many activities and produced amazing results that were previously impossible for humans to accomplish. However, its impact also prompts worries about possible constitutional and human rights abuses.

Therefore, a system as part of checks and balances must be put in place to control the influence of AI, especially when it comes to protecting job possibilities from possible disruptions (Gaikwad, 2024).

Subjective opinions and philosophical stances are frequently used in discussions on AI ethics and human rights. For researchers, coming to an agreement on how to balance the development of AI with the defense of human rights can be a difficult task. An interdisciplinary approach is required for integrating technical understanding of AI with perspectives on human rights, ethics, and law. It could be challenging to reach comprehensive conclusions or workable solutions due to the complexity of integrating several domains. Targeted policy actions are necessary to address disparities. Government action is crucial to ensuring universal broadband access, enacting fair labor laws for digital workers, and embracing AI ethics frameworks to reduce bias in automated decision-making, according to a number of studies (Dhir and Verma, 2024).

2.9.3 Expanding Digital Infrastructure

Traditional forms of communication, business, education, how we live and work, and even government are being disrupted by digital technology. It is accelerating and expanding communications and information access, lowering the price of technology, increasing efficiency and productivity, accelerating innovation, propelling economic growth, enabling financial inclusion, creating resilient and creative solutions, and promoting openness in government and citizen–government communication (Ingram, 2021). Public–private collaborations to increase broadband availability and provide reasonably priced connectivity. In order to support community-led internet initiatives and subsidize internet access in underserved areas, governments must intervene proactively (Junod and Scally, 2025).

Workforce Development

Achieving sustainable and high-quality economic development requires increasing total factor productivity (TFP). The work now in publication mostly concentrates on how old infrastructure affects TFP, but it frequently overlooks the contribution of new digital infrastructure to TFP, doesn't evaluate impact mechanisms, and doesn't examine if effects vary (Tang and Zhao, 2023). Programs for lifetime learning and training in digital skills to get workers ready for changing employment markets are helpful (Li, 2024). Research identifies effective methods where governments and digital companies work together to develop skill-building initiatives for underserved areas (Mukul et al., 2024).

Regulating AI and Digital Platforms

After decades of research and experimenting to find an organizational structure that would work with the affordances of digital technology, the platform became a dominating model. The platform model engages in a type of privatized governance by leveraging digital technology's unparalleled ability to influence lives by emulating social infrastructure (Törnberg, 2023). Rules to guarantee accountability, openness, and equity in algorithmic judgment are needed. Comprehensive AI ethical frameworks that uphold equity in automated decision-making processes are demanded by an expanding corpus of research (Saheb and Saheb, 2024).

Healthcare Equity through Digital Tools

In order to support the efforts of industry leaders and developers, health systems operations, and academics, a framework for digital health equality outlining important DDoHs is required as digital health becomes more and more important. Product managers, software architects, computer scientists, and user experience designers are among the professionals who build digital health solutions. Leaders and developers involved in the digital revolution of health must comprehend the ways in which digital factors affect health inequalities (Richardson et al., 2022). Making sure AI diagnoses, digital health records, and mobile health solutions adhere to moral principles and are available to everyone, especially in underprivileged areas (Kanagarajah, 2024).

2.10 Conclusion and Scope for Further Research

Using the PRISMA methodology, this study conducted a systematic evaluation of the literature on the relationship between technology and social and economic fairness. The results show that although digital technology can help decrease economic and social equity disparities, its effects are contingent on implementation tactics and policy choices. Even while efforts to promote digital inclusiveness have advanced significantly, structural disparities in representation, affordability, and access still exist. Although it is clear that technology can help close gaps in healthcare, work, and education, interventions must be built with fairness and inclusivity at their center.

Future studies should examine the following topics to further this field: The long-term impacts of policies promoting digital inclusion on economic mobility. The moral and legal ramifications of AI-powered healthcare and employment decision-making are imperative to lessen digital divide. The efficiency of continuous government initiatives to bridge digital divides. The effect of digital literacy initiatives on enhancing access to necessary services and workforce preparedness is needed. In order to establish inclusive digital ecosystems that promote social and economic fairness, policymakers, researchers, and industry players must collaborate. Digital technology has the potential to revolutionize equitable development by removing structural obstacles and guaranteeing equitable access. In order to guarantee that digital breakthroughs are used as a tool for inclusion rather than exclusion, more research and advocacy are required, as evidenced by the expanding body of literature.

References

Acemoglu, D., & Restrepo, P. (2019). Automation and new tasks: How technology displaces and reinstates labor. *Journal of Economic Perspectives, 33*(2), 3–30.

Afzal, A., Khan, S., Daud, S., Ahmad, Z., & Butt, A. (2023). Addressing the digital divide: Access and use of technology in education. *Journal of Social Sciences Review, 3*(2), 883–895.

Aissaoui, N. (2022). The digital divide: A literature review and some directions for future research in light of COVID-19. *Global Knowledge, Memory and Communication, 71*(8/9), 686–708.

Alfaraz, C., & Tully, C. (2025). Mobilizing social transformation with technology: The shaping of social processes since the development of industrial society and beyond—innovation input and social processes. *Innovation: The European Journal of Social Science Research, 38*(2), 589–605. https://doi.org/10.1080/13511610.2024.2346813

Armitage, R., & Nellums, L. B. (2020). COVID-19 and the consequences of isolating the elderly. *The Lancet Public Health, 5*(5), e256. https://doi.org/10.1016/S2468-2667(20)30061-X

Asadullah, M. N., & Bhattacharjee, A. (2022). Digital divide or digital provide? Technology, time use, and learning loss during COVID-19. *The Journal of Development Studies, 58*(10), 1934–1957.

Baffour Gyau, E., Li, Y., & Appiah, M. (2025). Global digital transformation: Discovering the impact of digitalization on income inequality in OECD countries, the moderating role of globalization. *Economic Change and Restructuring, 58*(1), 6.

Bahn, K., Cohen, J., & van der Meulen Rodgers, Y. (2020). A feminist perspective on COVID-19 and the value of care work globally. *Gender, Work & Organization, 27*(5), 695–699.

Bailey, L. E., & Nyabola, N. (2021). Digital equity as an enabling platform for equality and inclusion. *Pathfinders for Peaceful, Just, and Inclusive Societies/NYU Center on International Cooperation, June 2021.* https://cic.nyu.edu/wp-content/uploads/1662/65/cic_pathfinders_digital_equity_as_an_enabling_platform_june_2021.pdf

Bandhopadhyay, S., Bardhan, A., Dey, P., & Bhattacharyya, S. (2021). *Bridging the Education Divide Using Social Technologies*. Springer.

Benjelloun, W. (2023). Bridging the digital divide in higher education: North African challenges and initiatives. In *Higher Education in the Arab World: E-Learning and Distance Education* (pp. 169–189). Springer Nature Switzerland.

Bopaiah, M. (2021). *Equity: How to Design Organizations Where Everyone Thrives*. Berrett-Koehler Publishers.

Bapuji, H., Patel, C., Ertug, G., & Allen, D. G. (2020). Corona crisis and inequality: Why management research needs a societal turn. *Journal of Management, 46*(7), 1205–1222.
Bose, M. (2025). Bias in AI: A societal threat: A look beyond the tech. In *Open AI and Computational Intelligence for Society 5.0* (pp. 197–224). IGI Global Scientific Publishing.
Bywaters, P., Scourfield, J., Jones, C., Sparks, T., Elliott, M., Hooper, J., ... & Daniel, B. (2020). Child welfare inequalities in the four nations of the UK. *Journal of Social Work, 20*(2), 193–215.
Canton, H. (2021). International telecommunication union—ITU. In *The Europa Directory of International Organizations 2021* (pp. 355–358). Routledge.
Corbera, E., Anguelovski, I., Honey-Rosés, J., & Ruiz-Mallén, I. (2020). Academia in the time of COVID-19: Towards an ethics of care. *Planning Theory & Practice, 21*(2), 191–199.
Cortinois, A. A., & Birn, A. E. (2021). What's technology got to do with it? Power, politics, and health equity beyond technological triumphalism. *Global Policy, 12*, 75–79.
Czymara, C. S., Langenkamp, A., & Cano, T. (2021). Cause for concerns: Gender inequality in experiencing the COVID-19 lockdown in Germany. *European Societies, 23*(S1), S68-S81.
Dhir, M., & Verma, S. (2024). *AI for good: India and beyond: Detailed analysis of AI & laws, policies, ethical frameworks and judgements*. Notion Press.
Djerf-Pierre, M. (2018). The difference engine: Gender equality, journalism and the good society. In *Current Perspectives in Feminist Media Studies* (pp. 38–46). Routledge.
Drage, E., & Mackereth, K. (2022). Does AI debias recruitment? Race, gender, and AI's "eradication of difference". *Philosophy & Technology, 35*(4), 89.
Eisenhart, M., & Allen, C. D. (2020). Addressing underrepresentation of young women of color in engineering and computing through the lens of sociocultural theory. *Cultural Studies of Science Education, 15*(3), 793–824.
Esping-Andersen, G. (2024). Citizenship and socialism: De-commodification and solidarity in the welfare state. In *Stagnation and renewal in social policy* (pp. 78–101). Routledge.
Feldblum, C. R. (2005). Gay is good: The moral case for marriage equality and more. *Yale JL & Feminism, 17*, 139.
Fisher, J., Languilaire, J. C., Lawthom, R., Nieuwenhuis, R., Petts, R. J., Runswick-Cole, K., & Yerkes, M. A. (2020). Community, work, and family in times of COVID-19. *Community, Work & Family, 23*(3), 247–252.
Gaikwad, B. (2024). The Intersection of AI with constitutional and human rights with focus on employment impact. *International Journal of Legal Science and Innovation, 6*(6), 108–142.
Ghisellini, P., Cialani, C., & Ulgiati, S. (2016). A review on circular economy: The expected transition to a balanced interplay of environmental and economic systems. *Journal of Cleaner production, 114*, 11–32.
Golomski, C., Corvini, M., Kim, B., Wilcox, J., & Valcourt, S. (2022). Aspects of ICT connectivity among older adults living in rural subsidized housing: Reassessing the digital divide. *Journal of Enabling Technologies, 16*(1), 17–27.
Graham, M., Hjorth, I., & Lehdonvirta, V. (2017). Digital labour and development: Impacts of global digital labour platforms and the gig economy on

worker livelihoods. *Transfer: European Review of Labour and Research, 23*(2), 135–162.
Grybauskas, A., Stefanini, A., & Ghobakhloo, M. (2022). Social sustainability in the age of digitalization: A systematic literature review on the social implications of industry 4.0. *Technology in Society, 70*, 101997.
Haleem, A., Javaid, M., Qadri, M. A., & Suman, R. (2022). Understanding the role of digital technologies in education: A review. *Sustainable Operations and Computers, 3*, 275–285.
Harini, M. (2024). Telemedicine and health care accessibility: AI-powered remote diagnostics. *Bulletin of Nexus: Journal of Multidisciplinary International Research Studies, 1*(1), 1–5.
Healey, J. F., & Stepnick, A. (2019). *Diversity and society: Race, ethnicity, and gender*. Sage Publications.
Helliwell, J. F., Huang, H., Norton, M., Goff, L., & Wang, S. (2023). World happiness, trust and social connections in times of crisis. *World happiness report, 2023.*
Holmes, N. (2003). The digital divide, the UN, and the computing profession. *Computer, 36*(12), 142–144.
Ho, C. C., & Tseng, S. F. (2006). From digital divide to digital inequality: The global perspective. *International Journal of Internet and Enterprise Management, 4*(3), 215–227.
Ingram, G. (2021). Bridging the global digital divide: A platform to advance digital development in low-and middle-income countries. Available at: www.brookings.edu/wp-content/uploads/2021/05/bridging-the-digital-divide_final.pdf
Jaeger, P. T., Bertot, J. C., Thompson, K. M., Katz, S. M., & DeCoster, E. J. (2012). The intersection of public policy and public access: Digital divides, digital literacy, digital inclusion, and public libraries. *Public Library Quarterly, 31*(1), 1–20.
Johnson, B. A., Coggburn, J. D., & Llorens, J. J. (2022). Artificial intelligence and public human resource management: Questions for research and practice. *Public Personnel Management, 51*(4), 538–562.
Johansson, M. (2025). Bridging the digital divide: Strategies for inclusive digital transformation. *Available at SSRN 5078871.*
Junod, A. N., & Scally, C. P. (2025). Expanding digital opportunity in rural communities. Available at: www.urban.org/sites/default/files/additional-materials/Expanding_Digital_Opportunity_in_Rural_Communities_.pdf
Kanagarajah, A. (2024). AI-driven innovation in healthcare product development: Challenges and ethical implications (Master's thesis, School of Engineering Science, Tuotantotalous). https://urn.fi/URN:NBN:fi-fe20241216102846
Kandachar, P., & Halme, M. (Eds.). (2017). *Sustainability Challenges and Solutions at the Base of the Pyramid: Business, Technology and the Poor*. Routledge.
Kaur, M. J., Riaz, S., & Mushtaq, A. (2020). Cyber-physical cloud computing systems and internet of everything. In Peng, SL., Pal, S., Huang, L. (eds) *Principles of Internet of Things (IoT) Ecosystem: Insight Paradigm. Intelligent Systems Reference Library*, vol 174. Springer. https://doi.org/10.1007/978-3-030-33596-0_8
Klochikhin, E. A. (2012). Linking development and innovation: What does technological change bring to the society?. *The European Journal of Development Research, 24*(1), 41–55.
Kothandapani, H. P. (2025). Social implications of algorithmic decision-making in housing finance: Examining the broader social impacts of deploying machine

learning in lending decisions, including potential disparities and community effects. *Journal of Knowledge Learning and Science Technology*, *4*(1), 78–97.

Kraus, S., Schiavone, F., Pluzhnikova, A., & Invernizzi, A. C. (2021). Digital transformation in healthcare: Analyzing the current state of research. *Journal of Business Research, 123,* 557–567. https://doi.org/10.1016/j.jbusres.2020.10.030

Krause, D. (2024). Addressing the challenges of auditing and testing for AI bias: A comparative analysis of regulatory frameworks. *SSRN*: https://ssrn.com/abstract=5050631

Kurtuluş, S. A., & Çakiroğlu, O. Ç. (2020). Digital transformation in healthcare services. *Advances in Health Sciences Research*, 523.

Li, L. (2024). Reskilling and upskilling the future-ready workforce for industry 4.0 and beyond. *Information Systems Frontiers*, *26*(5), 1697–1712.

Lloyd, C., & Payne, J. (2023). Digital skills in context: Working with robots in lower-skilled jobs. *Economic and Industrial Democracy*, *44*(4), 1084–1104.

Lim, C. P., Tinio, V. L., Smith, M., & Bhowmik, M. K. (2018). Achieving equity, quality, and efficiency in education. *Routledge International Handbook of Schools and Schooling in Asia*, 369.

Mamtaz, S. (2024). *Leveraging FinTech to Enhance Access to Finance for Small Enterprises in Bangladesh* (Doctoral dissertation, © University of Dhaka).

Marín-Raventós, G., & Calderón-Campos, M. (2016). Typifying mechanisms for gender digital equity in Latin America. In *ICT for Promoting Human Development and Protecting the Environment: 6th IFIP World Information Technology Forum, WITFOR 2016, San José, Costa Rica, September 12-14, 2016, Proceedings 6* (pp. 159–170). Springer International Publishing.

McGraw, D., & Mandl, K. D. (2021). Privacy protections to encourage use of health-relevant digital data in a learning health system. *NPJ Digital Medicine*, *4*(1), 2.

Mhlanga, D. (2021). Artificial intelligence in the industry 4.0, and its impact on poverty, innovation, infrastructure development, and the sustainable development goals: Lessons from emerging economies?. *Sustainability*, *13*(11), 5788.

Mhlanga, D. (2023). Digital transformation education, opportunities, and challenges of the application of ChatGPT to emerging economies. *Education Research International*, *2023*(1), 7605075.

Mhlongo, S., & Dlamini, R. (2022). Digital inequities and societal context: Digital transformation as a conduit to achieve social and epistemic justice: Digital transformation as a conduit to achieve social and epistemic justice. In *Innovation practices for digital transformation in the global South: IFIP WG 13.8, 9.4, invited selection* (pp. 1–15). Springer International Publishing.

Mishra, V., & Mishra, M. P. (2023). PRISMA for review of management literature–method, merits, and limitations–an academic review. In *Advancing methodologies of conducting literature review in management domain*, pp. 125–136.

Mukul, E., & Büyüközkan, G. (2023). Digital transformation in education: A systematic review of education 4.0. *Technological forecasting and social change*, *194*, 122664.

Mukul, B., Taneja, S., Özen, E., & Bansal, N. (2024). Challenges and opportunities for skill development in developing economies. In *Contemporary Challenges in Social Science Management: Skills Gaps and Shortages in the Labour Market*, pp. 1–22.

Mukul, Taneja, S., Özen, E., & Bansal, N. (2024). Challenges and opportunities for skill development in developing economies. In *Contemporary Issues in Business and Globalization* (Vol. 112, pp. 1–xx). Emerald Publishing. https://doi.org/10.1108/S1569-37592024000112B001

Murikah, W., Nthenge, J. K., & Musyoka, F. M. (2024). Bias and ethics of AI systems applied in auditing-A systematic review. *Scientific African, 25,* e02281. https://doi.org/10.1016/j.sciaf.2024.e02281

Netto, G., Noon, M., Hudson, M., Kamenou-Aigbekaen, N., & Sosenko, F. (2020). Intersectionality, identity work and migrant progression from low-paid work: A critical realist approach. *Gender, Work & Organization, 27*(6), 1020–1039.

Oliveira, K. K. D. S., & De Souza, R. A. (2022). Digital transformation towards education 4.0. *Informatics in Education, 21*(2), 283–309.

Page, M. J., McKenzie, J. E., Bossuyt, P. M., Boutron, I., Hoffmann, T. C., Mulrow, C. D., Shamseer, L., Tetzlaff, J. M., Akl, E. A., Brennan, S. E., Chou, R., Glanville, J., Grimshaw, J. M., Hróbjartsson, A., Lalu, M. M., Li, T., Loder, E. W., Mayo-Wilson, E., McDonald, S., … Moher, D. (2021). The PRISMA 2020 statement: An updated guideline for reporting systematic reviews. *BMJ, 372,* n71. https://doi.org/10.1136/bmj.n71

Peltzman, S. (2009). Mortality inequality. *Journal of Economic Perspectives, 23*(4), 175–190.

Pérez-Barea, J. J. (2025). The evolution of social entrepreneurship: Broadening the framework for the digital and sustainable era. *Administrative Sciences, 15*(2), 55.

Pick, J. B., & Azari, R. (2008). Global digital divide: Influence of socioeconomic, governmental, and accessibility factors on information technology. *Information Technology for Development, 14*(2), 91–115.

Räsänen, P., Koivula, A., & Keipi, T. (2021). Online information seeking patterns and social inequality in a digital economy. *The International Review of Retail, Distribution and Consumer Research, 31*(2), 211–228.

Rawls, J. (2005). *A Theory of Justice: Original Edition*. Harvard University Press. https://doi.org/10.2307/j.ctvjf9z6v

Richardson, S., Lawrence, K., Schoenthaler, A. M., & Mann, D. (2022). A framework for digital health equity. *NPJ Digital Medicine, 5*(1), 119.

Rushambwa, T. (2024). Rethinking social policy in the era of digital transformation: Social policy and reinvigorated social contracts, a qualitative analysis. *SSRN*. https://doi.org/10.2139/ssrn.4974999

Saheb, T., & Saheb, T. (2024). Mapping ethical artificial intelligence policy landscape: A mixed method analysis. *Science and engineering ethics, 30*(2), 9.

Sahoo, P., Saraf, P. K., & Uchil, R. (2024). Identification of critical success factors for leveraging Industry 4.0 technology and research agenda: A systematic literature review using PRISMA protocol. *Asia-Pacific Journal of Business Administration, 16*(3), 457–481.

Sengupta, U., & Sengupta, U. (2022). SDG-11 and smart cities: Contradictions and overlaps between social and environmental justice research agendas. *Frontiers in Sociology, 7,* 995603.

Silalahi, M. S., & Walsh, S. (2023). Analyzing government policies in addressing unemployment and em-powering workers: Implications for economic stability and social welfare. *Law and Economics, 17*(2), 92–110.

Skare, M., & Porada-Rochoń, M. (2022). Technology and social equality in the United States. *Technological Forecasting and Social Change, 183,* 121947.

Studley, M. (2021). Onshoring through automation; Perpetuating inequality? *Frontiers in Robotics and AI, 8,* 634297.

Tang, J., & Zhao, X. (2023). Does the new digital infrastructure improve total factor productivity?. *Bulletin of Economic Research, 75*(4), 895–916.

Thanh, T. C., Nguyen, P. M., Nguyen-Nhu-Y, H., Hanh, N. T. H., Son, T. L., & Hang, H. M. (2025). Factors affecting the commitment to digital transformation toward achieving sustainable development goals: Evidence from Vietnamese small and medium-sized enterprises. *Journal of Lifestyle and SDGs Review*, *5*(2), e04387–e04387.

Törnberg, P. (2023). How platforms govern: Social regulation in digital capitalism. *Big Data & Society*, *10*(1), 20539517231153808.

Voigt, K. (2017). Distributive equality, relational equality and preferences about higher education. *Theory and Research in Education*, *15*(2), 109–128.

West, D. M. (2015). Digital divide: Improving Internet access in the developing world through affordable services and diverse content. *Center for Technology Innovation at Brookings*, *1*, 30.

Zhao, C., Dong, K., Liu, Z., & Ma, X. (2024). Is digital economy an answer to energy trilemma eradication? The case of China. *Journal of Environmental Management*, *349*, 119369.

Part II

Addressing Embedded Bias in Digital Systems

3

Inclusive AI: Mitigating Algorithmic Discrimination for a Fairer Society

Arif Perdana and Ridoan Karim

3.1 Introduction

In 2018, Amazon scrapped an AI-driven recruiting tool after it systematically disadvantaged female applicants. Trained on a decade of resumes, primarily from male candidates, the system penalised applicants who attended women's colleges or mentioned "women" in their resumes. This case exemplifies how AI, often seen as objective, can reinforce and amplify historical biases. It poses significant challenges to social equity.

AI and machine learning (ML) systems increasingly mediate decisions that affect access to employment, financial services, healthcare, and legal protection (Arowosegbe, 2023; Chen et al., 2024; Liebrenz et al., 2024; Xiong & Kim, 2025). Although perceived as neutral, empirical research shows they frequently reproduce and amplify historical biases (Mehrabi et al., 2021). Bias in AI refers to systematic distortions in automated decision making that result in unfair outcomes and disproportionately disadvantaging historically marginalised groups without justifiable causes (Pot et al., 2021; Van Giffen et al., 2022; Wei et al., 2025). As AI becomes more embedded in high-stakes decision-making, concerns have been raised over its implications for fairness, accountability, and social equity (Dignum, 2019; Floridi, 2021; Theodorou & Dignum, 2020).

Bias in AI systems manifests across critical domains, reinforcing systemic disparities. In employment, AI-driven hiring tools have perpetuated historical discrimination, disproportionately disadvantaging women and minority candidates (Drage & Mackereth, 2022). In law enforcement, predictive policing algorithms have intensified over-policing in certain communities, exacerbating structural inequities in criminal justice (Hung & Yen, 2023). Healthcare algorithms exhibit diagnostic biases, particularly in underrepresented populations, leading to disparities in treatment and medical outcomes (Hussain et al., 2025; Seyyed-Kalantari et al., 2021). Similarly, financial AI models in credit scoring and lending systematically disadvantage minority applicants,

DOI: 10.1201/9781003591078-5

even when economic risk factors are accounted for (Das et al., 2023; Mathen & Paul, 2025). These examples illustrate that AI bias is not a mere technical flaw but a pervasive issue shaping economic opportunities, legal rights, and access to essential services (Alvarez et al., 2024; Nitzberg & Zysman, 2022).

Despite the growing recognition of these challenges, a fundamental question emerges: How can we develop a comprehensive understanding of algorithmic bias that bridges conceptual foundations, theoretical frameworks, and practical interventions to effectively promote fairness in AI-driven decision-making? This research question underlies a critical gap in the existing literature, where technical solutions, ethical frameworks, and policy responses are often addressed in isolation, limiting their collective effectiveness in addressing systemic bias.

To address these biases, fairness-aware machine learning techniques, such as pre-processing data, modifying model architectures, and adjusting decision thresholds, have been introduced (Li et al., 2023; Pagano et al., 2023; Wan et al., 2023). However, these approaches often require trade-offs between competing fairness metrics—such as demographic and predictive parity—which cannot always be reconciled (Buijsman, 2024). The challenge is not merely technical but deeply normative, demanding careful deliberation on fairness in different contexts (Floridi, 2021; Floridi et al., 2021; Heyder et al., 2023). Effective bias mitigation requires an integrated framework that aligns conceptual understanding, ethical principles, and practical interventions in a continuous cycle. Moreover, algorithmic fairness is inseparable from broader concerns of diversity, equity, inclusion, and belonging (DEIB), as AI-driven decision-making can reinforce systemic inequalities if these factors remain unaddressed (Akbarighatar et al., 2023; Arowosegbe, 2023; Liebrenz et al., 2024).

Recognizing these risks, regulatory frameworks are evolving to enhance AI oversight. The European Union's proposed AI Act categorises high-risk applications and mandates transparency and bias audits (Laux et al., 2024). In the United States, agencies are issuing guidelines to prevent discriminatory AI outcomes in hiring and lending, while scholars continue to push for legal protections against algorithmic discrimination (Bains, 2024). At the industry level, technology firms have introduced AI ethics boards and bias mitigation initiatives, though their effectiveness remains contested. Despite these efforts, algorithmic bias persists, underscoring the need for a holistic approach that integrates technical, legal, and ethical considerations.

Against this backdrop, this chapter aims to: (1) synthesise the conceptual foundations that explain how bias emerges in AI systems across data, algorithmic, and human dimensions; (2) critically examine the theoretical frameworks that guide normative evaluations of fairness and their inherent trade-offs; (3) analyse the empirical manifestations of bias across key application domains including hiring, healthcare, finance, and law enforcement; (4) evaluate the effectiveness of current mitigation strategies and identify their limitations; and (5) assess global policy responses and corporate governance efforts in addressing algorithmic bias.

Our chapter's contribution lies in its synthesis of three distinct but interrelated perspectives: (1) the conceptual foundations that explain how bias emerges in AI systems, (2) the theoretical frameworks that guide normative evaluations of fairness, and (3) the practical strategies for bias mitigation across diverse application domains. By bridging these perspectives, we offer a theoretically grounded and practically applicable framework for addressing algorithmic bias.

The chapter is organised as follows. Section 3.2 explores the conceptual foundations of bias. It distinguishes between data, algorithmic, and human biases that contribute to unfair outcomes. Section 3.3 reviews the theoretical frameworks, including ethical perspectives and formal fairness definitions. It highlights the inherent trade-offs in bias mitigation. Section 3.4 analyses the empirical manifestations of bias across hiring, healthcare, finance, and law enforcement. Section 3.5 evaluates mitigation strategies, and Section 3.6 discusses global policy responses and corporate governance efforts. Finally, Section 3.7 concludes our chapter.

3.2 Conceptual Foundations of Bias in Digital Technologies

Bias in AI emerges when automated decision-making systems produce systematically unfavorable outcomes for certain groups without justifiable distinctions between them. At its core, bias reflects embedded disparities within the data, algorithms, and human decision-making processes that shape AI systems (Hooker, 2021; Mehrabi et al., 2021; Pagano et al., 2023). Data bias stems from unrepresentative, historically skewed, or imbalanced datasets, leading models to reinforce societal prejudices. Algorithmic bias results from design choices, such as optimisation criteria, that inadvertently privilege specific attributes. Even ostensibly neutral AI systems can inherit human biases through developer assumptions, deployment contexts, or interpretation of outputs. AI thus functions as both a mirror and amplifier of existing social structures, capable of perpetuating inequities if left unchecked. While bias is not unique to AI, its systematisation within digital tools necessitates critical scrutiny of how it encodes, perpetuates, or challenges historical disadvantages. As explored in Section 3.3, these foundational sources of bias intersect with ethical frameworks such as utilitarianism, deontology, and virtue ethics, offering distinct perspectives on AI fairness.

3.2.1 Data Bias

Data bias is a fundamental source of AI prejudice. When models train on datasets lacking diversity or reflecting historical biases, they replicate and amplify these disparities. For example, facial recognition systems consistently misidentify darker-skinned individuals due to training data imbalances (Buolamwini & Gebru, 2018). Similarly, hiring algorithms trained on past employment patterns may perpetuate gender and racial biases (Xiong & Kim, 2025). Underrepresentation in datasets further compounds bias, medical AI trained primarily on male patients may misdiagnose female patients (Cirillo et al., 2020). These systemic disparities challenge statistical fairness metrics like demographic parity and equalised odds, necessitating value judgments about which fairness criteria should be prioritised (Arowosegbe, 2023; Hussain et al., 2025; Ntoutsi et al., 2020).

3.2.2 Algorithmic Bias

Algorithmic bias emerges from model design, feature selection, and optimisation choices (Hooker, 2021; Kordzadeh & Ghasemaghaei, 2022). Predictive policing models trained on biased crime data disproportionately target minority communities (Hung & Yen, 2023), while credit scoring algorithms can disadvantage certain groups by relying on correlated demographic factors (Mathen & Paul, 2025). Optimisation trade-offs further entrench bias, a hiring algorithm maximizing productivity may favour candidates from elite universities, excluding qualified individuals from marginalised backgrounds. These biases underscore the tension between fairness definitions explored in Section 3.3: deontological ethics emphasise equal treatment, whereas utilitarianism prioritises overall utility despite potential disparities. Effective mitigation requires context-sensitive ethical evaluations of algorithmic design.

3.2.3 Human Bias

Even with unbiased data and algorithms, human biases infiltrate AI through decisions made during design, deployment, and interpretation (Militello et al., 2025; Nguyen, 2024; Van Giffen et al., 2022). Subjective choices in data labeling or feature engineering introduce bias, while human interactions with AI outputs reinforce prejudices (Van Giffen et al., 2022). Additionally, the way AI outputs are interpreted and acted upon by humans can reinforce existing prejudices (Varsha, 2023). For example, Obermeyer et al. (2019) identified systemic bias in a U.S. healthcare algorithm that underestimated Black patients' needs by using healthcare costs as a proxy for health requirements. This case inadvertently reinforced historical disparities in access to care. Law enforcement's disproportionate use of facial recognition in minority neighbourhoods further exemplifies bias in deployment (Lee & Chin-Rothmann, 2022). These examples illustrate the complex relationship between human decision-making and algorithmic outcomes. The sociotechnical lens and intersectionality theory discussed in Section 3.3 are critical for understanding human bias, highlighting how AI systems function within broader social structures influenced by historical discrimination and intersecting inequalities. Virtue ethics further reinforces this perspective, emphasizing the need to foster ethical awareness and accountability among AI developers and users to mitigate bias effectively.

3.3 Theoretical Frameworks of Fairness and Bias

Addressing bias in AI systems is not just a technical issue but a fundamentally theoretical and ethical challenge (Kordzadeh & Ghasemaghaei, 2022; Nishant et al., 2024; Ntoutsi et al., 2020). Over the past decade, researchers have developed formal fairness frameworks to better understand and mitigate bias in algorithms (Alvarez et al., 2024; Das et al., 2023; Dignum, 2019; Floridi, 2021; Floridi et al., 2021; Wan et al., 2023). These frameworks reveal that fairness is, however, multifaceted and often involves trade-offs and value judgments. To fully grasp the complexities of AI fairness, it is essential to synthesise insights from broad ethical frameworks, such as utilitarianism, deontology, and virtue ethics, using formal fairness definitions, sociotechnical contexts, and intersectionality theory (Akbarighatar et al., 2023; Heyder et al., 2023; Theodorou & Dignum, 2020). This integrated approach highlights the interplay between abstract principles and real-world applications, underscoring the need for holistic understanding of bias in AI.

3.3.1 Utilitarianism

At the foundation of any discussion on fairness, there are broad ethical frameworks with long-informed debates about justice and equality (Etzioni & Etzioni, 2017; Yampolskiy, 2018). Utilitarianism, with its emphasis on maximizing overall happiness or utility, offers one lens through which to evaluate AI systems (Cvik, 2022; Nida-Rümelin & Weidenfeld, 2022). A utilitarian approach may prioritise algorithms that produce the greatest good for the greatest number of people, even if this results in unequal outcomes for certain groups. For instance, a predictive policing algorithm designed to minimise overall crime rates might disproportionately target specific communities, raising ethical concerns about sacrificing minority rights for aggregate benefits. While utilitarianism provides a pragmatic framework for decision-making, its potential to overlook individual rights and perpetuate systemic inequalities has drawn significant criticism (Eggleston & Miller, 2014; Etzioni & Etzioni, 2017; Nida-Rümelin & Weidenfeld, 2022).

3.3.2 Deontology

In contrast, deontological ethics, rooted in Immanuel Kant's philosophy, emphasise duty and adherence to moral principles, such as treating individuals as ends in themselves rather than means to an end (Kim & Schönecker,

2022; Ulgen, 2017). In the context of AI fairness, a deontological approach prioritises algorithms that respect individual rights and ensure equal treatment, regardless of the consequences. For example, a hiring algorithm might be designed to avoid discriminatory practices, even if this reduces overall efficiency (Hofeditz et al., 2022). This principled stance aligns with the notion that fairness is a moral imperative. However, it can struggle to address the complex, context-specific trade-offs that often arise in AI applications. The rigidity of deontological ethics may also limit their applicability to dynamic and multifaceted domains. Figure 3.1 presents the connection between the conceptual foundations of bias and the relevant theoretical frameworks.

3.3.3 Virtue Ethics

Drawing from Aristotle, virtue ethics shifts the focus from abstract rules or outcomes to the cultivation of moral character and virtues, such as fairness,

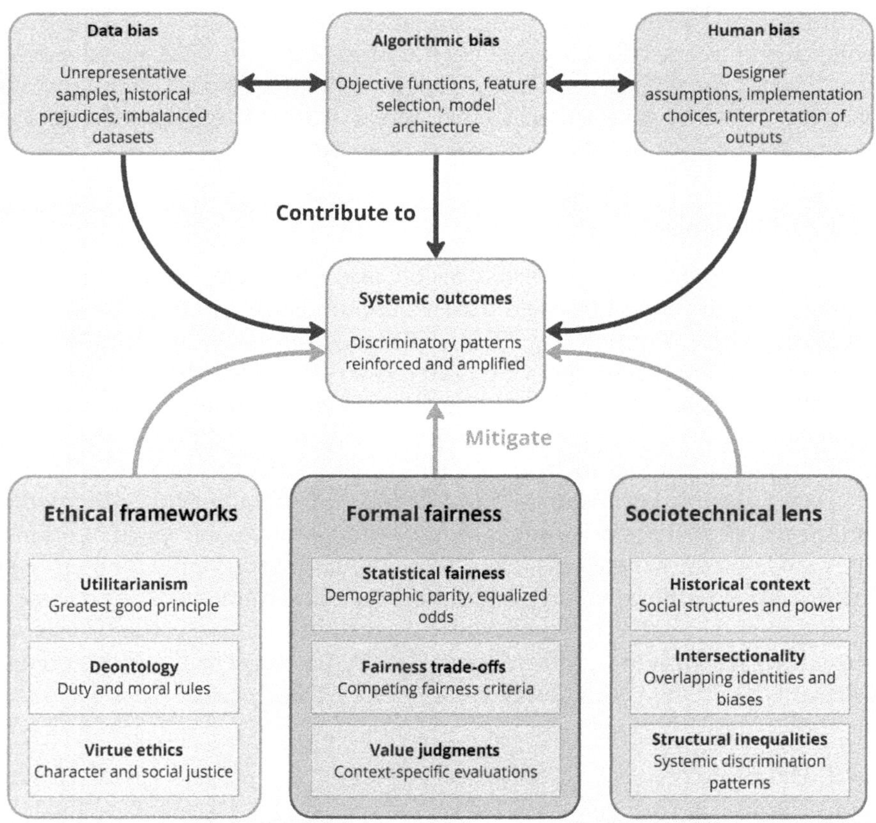

FIGURE 3.1
Conceptual foundation of bias and theoretical frameworks for mitigations.

compassion, and integrity (Farina et al., 2024). This approach emphasises the ethical responsibilities of developers and organisations in designing systems that reflect these virtues (Neubert & Montañez, 2020). Neubert and Montañez, for instance, suggest that a virtue ethics perspective might encourage transparency, accountability, and commitment to social justice in developing and deploying AI systems. While this framework fosters a culture of ethical responsibility, its subjective nature and lack of clear decision-making guidelines can pose practical challenges. Nevertheless, virtue ethics provide a valuable complement to utilitarianism and deontology by highlighting the importance of moral character and intentionality in addressing bias (Hagendorff, 2022).

3.3.4 Formal Fairness and Sociotechnical Lens

Building on these broad ethical frameworks, researchers have developed formal fairness definitions to address AI challenges, recognizing that fairness is a collection of sometimes incompatible concepts (Bell et al., 2023). For example, equalised odds aim to equalise error rates across demographic groups, while demographic parity requires equal positive prediction rates, and predictive parity ensures parity in predictive value. These definitions often conflict, making it impossible to satisfy all criteria simultaneously. Kleinberg et al. (2017) demonstrated inherent trade-offs in risk assessment, showing that optimizing for one fairness metric can preclude another. This highlights the necessity of value judgments in determining which fairness criteria to prioritise in different contexts.

Context plays a crucial role in operationalizing fairness. In hiring, demographic parity may ensure equal opportunities for underrepresented groups, whereas, in criminal justice, equalised odds may prevent unfair targeting. These decisions must balance abstract principles with real-world applications, requiring an understanding of the broader sociotechnical environment. Critical theorists argue that algorithmic bias cannot be fully understood or mitigated in isolation; it must be examined within historical and structural contexts (Akbarighatar et al., 2023; Krijger, 2022; Selbst et al., 2019; Theodorou & Dignum, 2020). Selbst et al. (2019) emphasised that fairness extends beyond technical solutions to include awareness of discrimination, power imbalances, and systemic inequalities. For instance, a credit scoring algorithm may reflect past discriminatory practices, necessitating both technical corrections and an understanding of historical economic disparities (Kordzadeh & Ghasemaghaei, 2022; Nishant et al., 2024; Ntoutsi et al., 2020).

Intersectionality further deepens the analysis by highlighting how multiple forms of oppression intersect (Atewologun, 2018; Crenshaw, 2022). In AI fairness, this means acknowledging how algorithms may disproportionately disadvantage individuals with multiple marginalised identities, such as women of color (Diniz et al., 2024; Mangal & Pardos, 2024). For instance,

TABLE 3.1

Summary of theoretical frameworks of fairness and bias

Framework	Key Idea	Example Application	Limitations
Ethical framework			
Utilitarianism	Maximise overall benefit, even if some groups are disadvantaged	Crime prediction favors majority but harms minorities	May sacrifice minority rights for aggregate benefits
Deontology	Follow moral rules; fairness is a principle, not just an outcome	Hiring AI ensures equality, even if efficiency drops	Rigid application may not consider real-world trade-offs
Virtue ethics	Focus on ethical character and responsible AI development	Encourages fairness, transparency, and social justice	Lacks clear decision-making guidelines; subjective
Nonethical framework			
Formal fairness	Different fairness definitions exist and often conflict	Fair loan approvals may trade off different fairness goals	Requires value judgments; fairness criteria often incompatible
Sociotechnical context	Bias is shaped by history, power, and social structures	Credit scoring AI may reflect past discrimination	Fairness needs broader social analysis, not just technical fixes
Intersectionality	Multiple disadvantages can overlap and amplify bias	Facial recognition struggles with marginalised identities	Fails if demographic categories are considered in isolation

facial recognition systems often perform poorly for women of color, reflecting the compounded effects of racial and gender biases in training (Leslie, 2020; Yucer et al., 2025). This perspective challenges simplistic fairness approaches and calls for nuanced analyses that consider the complex interplay of identities and systemic biases. Table 1 provides an overview of the ethical and nonethical frameworks for fairness and bias.

AI fairness and bias are complex, spanning statistical, ethical, and sociotechnical dimensions (Saheb & Saheb, 2024). While broad ethical frameworks like utilitarianism, deontology, and virtue ethics provide a foundation, AI introduces additional complexities. Formal fairness frameworks highlight multiple, sometimes incompatible, fairness definitions, necessitating value judgments and context-specific solutions. Critical theorists and intersectionality theory emphasise the importance of considering historical discrimination, power imbalances, and intersecting oppressions in understanding algorithmic bias. Addressing bias in AI requires a holistic, interdisciplinary approach integrating philosophy, social science, and computer science to create truly fair and just systems.

3.4 Manifestations of Bias in AI and Machine Learning

Empirical studies have consistently demonstrated that biases in AI and machine learning (ML) models often originate from preexisting societal biases (Mehrabi et al., 2021; Mikołajczyk-Bareła & Grochowski, 2023). Research on word-embedding models trained on large text corpora, for example, has shown that these models internalise gender and racial stereotypes embedded in language (Buolamwini & Gebru, 2018; Charlesworth et al., 2023; Dusi et al., 2024). Gender bias in Transformer models, for instance, appears in word embeddings (e.g., "nurse" → female, "engineer" → male), machine translation (e.g., "she is a doctor" → "he is a doctor"), and sentiment analysis (e.g., female-associated phrases rated angrier) (Nemani et al., 2024). Buolamwini and Gebru (2018), for example, found that commercial face recognition systems exhibited significantly lower accuracy for individuals with darker skin tones, particularly women, than for lighter-skinned males. Some systems produced error rates for dark-skinned women that were substantially higher than those for white men, highlighting the impact of nondiverse training data and evaluation methodologies on algorithmic performance. These findings illustrate a broader issue: AI models do not function as neutral entities, but rather replicate and reinforce historical patterns of bias when trained on data that reflect such inequities. Search and recommendation algorithms frequently "reflect and reproduce inequities" in society (Noble, 2018). Without deliberate intervention, AI systems risk perpetuating and legitimizing social biases under the guise of technological objectivity.

3.4.1 Bias in Hiring Algorithms

AI-driven hiring tools risk perpetuating bias, as seen in Amazon's experimental recruiting algorithm, which systematically discriminated against female applicants due to training on historically male-dominated hiring data (Fritts & Cabrera, 2021; Martin, 2022). Broader concerns extend to AI-based résumé screening and video interview analytics, which have been found to reinforce racial, gender, and disability biases, particularly penalizing nontraditional career paths and disabilities affecting motor skills and cognition (Tilmes, 2022). Researchers emphasise that without proactive auditing, transparency, and inclusive design, AI hiring systems may function as "black boxes" that legitimise structural inequalities rather than mitigating them (Hofeditz et al., 2022; Martin, 2022; Xiong & Kim, 2025).

3.4.2 Bias in Healthcare Algorithms

Algorithmic bias in healthcare presents significant risks, particularly when determining access to critical medical resources. Obermeyer et al. (2019) examined a widely used commercial algorithm allocating care to high-risk patients and found it systematically underestimated the health risks of Black patients. The model used healthcare spending as a proxy for health needs, overlooking structural disparities in healthcare access. As a result, more than half of the Black patients requiring high-risk care were overlooked. Adjusting for bias would have increased the proportion of Black patients receiving additional support from 17.7% to 46.5%.

Algorithmic healthcare bias arises from nonrepresentative training data, reinforcing racial disparities (Hussain et al., 2025; Loftus et al., 2022). Biases include race-based misdiagnoses, missing data for vulnerable populations, and confounding biases associating socioeconomic status with poor health outcomes. Diagnostic tools and clinical decision systems frequently underperform for minority populations, exacerbating health inequities. Policymakers have called for rigorous evaluation and fairness constraints, such as equalised odds, to mitigate algorithmic discrimination in healthcare (Abràmoff et al., 2023).

3.4.3 Bias in Finance and Credit Algorithms

The financial services sector has increasingly relied on algorithmic decision-making for credit scoring, loan approval, fraud detection, and related functions; however, evidence of bias in these systems continues to emerge. Despite legal frameworks being designed to ensure fair lending practices, algorithmic discrimination can manifest in subtle yet impactful ways. Bartlett et al. (2021) noted that algorithmic mortgage lending systematically imposes higher interest rates on minority borrowers, even after controlling for credit risk. Latinx and Black borrowers paid 4.7–7.7 basis points more in interest, even when controlling for credit risk. Fintech lending models inadvertently penalised minority applicants through proxy variables such as zip codes and income levels.

Algorithmic bias extends to credit scoring, insurance pricing, and property appraisals, disproportionately disadvantaging minority applicants (Garcia et al., 2024) Algorithmic credit scoring systems, for example, have been shown to disproportionately disadvantage minority applicants in underserved areas, often resulting in lower approval rates or less favorable loan terms. Such disparities stem from statistical discrimination within the training data, where patterns reflecting past lending biases are learned and reproduced by predictive models (Garcia et al., 2024).

Similar concerns have emerged in insurance pricing and automated property appraisals, where algorithms have systematically undervalued homes in minority communities or assigned higher risk scores to minority applicants (Kuppan et al., 2024). Researchers have noted that while algorithmic fairness interventions primarily address direct forms of discrimination, structural biases such as disparities in financial history and data availability remain less examined. These underlying systemic barriers pose a significant challenge as they shape the inputs used in financial decision-making models, potentially entrenching inequities rather than mitigating them (Garcia et al., 2024).

These findings underscore a fundamental tension: while algorithmic decision-making is often framed as more objective and consistent than human judgment, it can systematically reproduce financial disparities if trained using data that reflect past discrimination. Regulatory bodies have begun to address these issues. The U.S. Consumer Financial Protection Bureau, for example, emphasised that lenders employing opaque machine learning models remain liable under the Equal Credit Opportunity Act if their algorithms result in disparate impacts[1,2]. As algorithmic decision-making becomes more integrated into financial services, continuous auditing and the application of fairness constraints are crucial to prevent digital red-lining disguised as technological neutrality.

3.4.4 Bias in Law Enforcement and Criminal Justice Algorithms

Algorithmic bias in criminal justice has drawn significant scrutiny, particularly regarding risk assessment scores and predictive policing systems (Dressel & Farid, 2018; Hung & Yen, 2023). ProPublica's 2016 investigation of the COMPAS algorithm, a widely used tool for predicting recidivism, revealed substantial racial disparities (Dressel & Farid, 2018). Black defendants who did not reoffend were nearly twice as likely as their white counterparts to be misclassified as high risk, while white defendants who later reoffended were more frequently classified as low-risk (Grant, 2023). The case underscores the challenge of defining fairness in criminal justice algorithms, as competing fairness criteria yield conflicting outcomes.

Predictive policing algorithms also reinforces systemic bias. Trained on historical crime data, these tools justify increased policing in minority neighborhoods, creating self-reinforcing cycles of over-surveillance (McDaniel & Pease, 2021). Empirical studies indicate such tools institutionalise racial profiling under the guise of data-driven policing (Fountain, 2022). Additionally, errors in facial recognition technology have led to wrongful arrests, disproportionately affecting non-white individuals (Leslie, 2020). Legal scholars argue these biases may violate constitutional protections, prompting some jurisdictions to restrict predictive policing until fairness can be validated (Yang & Dobbie, 2020). Greater transparency and accountability are needed to mitigate algorithmic biases in law enforcement.

3.4.5 Bias in Social Media and Online Platforms

Algorithmic bias in digital platforms influences societal structures, shaping public discourse and reinforcing systemic inequities (Rodilosso, 2024). Search engine algorithms replicate and amplify racial and gender biases rather than functioning as neutral classifiers. Noble (2018) demonstrated that Google Search results reflect societal prejudices, as seen in early 2010s searches for "Black girls," which yielded disproportionately derogatory content, whereas similar searches for "white girls" produced neutral or positive results. Noble argues that such patterns privilege whiteness by reinforcing dominant narratives and marginalizing minority identities. Targeted advertising algorithms also exhibit bias (Ali et al., 2019). Cecere et al. (2024) examined gender disparities in STEM-related ads targeting teenagers on Facebook. Their experiments found that gender-oriented messaging mitigates bias but reduces overall ad visibility, while ad text length affects algorithmic evaluation and ad reach. These findings highlight the persistent nature of bias in digital advertising and the trade-offs in bias-mitigation strategies.

Beyond search and advertising, social media recommendation systems contribute to ideological polarisation through "filter bubbles" (Kitchens et al., 2020; Rodilosso, 2024). Rodilosso (2024) contends that AI-driven personalisation fosters epistemic isolation and political extremism, while Kitchens et al. (2020) provide evidence of platform-dependent effects, with Facebook fostering polarisation and Reddit moderating slant. Synthesizing these perspectives, filter bubbles not only constrain exposure but actively entrench ideologies, necessitating interventions beyond algorithmic transparency.

Overall, algorithmic bias shapes digital ecosystems, reinforces structural inequities, and impacts democratic processes. Without targeted interventions, these biases risk amplifying misinformation, deepening social divisions, and perpetuating disparities along racial, gender, and ideological lines.

3.5 Bias Mitigation Strategies in AI Systems

Algorithmic bias extends beyond technical errors, reflecting systemic and historical inequalities embedded in training data, model design, and decision-making processes. Addressing this issue requires a holistic approach that integrates fairness-aware machine learning, intersectional trade-offs, and strategies for mitigating bias in emerging AI technologies, such as generative and multimodal AI (Hort et al., 2024).

3.5.1 Fairness-Aware Machine Learning Techniques

Efforts to mitigate bias in AI systems have led to the development of fairness-aware machine learning techniques that intervene at different stages of the AI pipeline: before training, during model development, and after deployment (Hort et al., 2024). A key strategy is addressing bias at the data level, as historical datasets often encode societal prejudices. Pre-processing techniques, such as reweighting datasets, help achieve more equitable representation (Shahrezaei et al., 2023). For instance, oversampling images of darker-skinned individuals in facial recognition software improves accuracy and reduces disparities.

In-processing methods modify algorithms during training to incorporate fairness constraints. Adversarial debiasing, where a secondary network detects and corrects bias, has been applied in hiring algorithms to reduce gender and racial disparities (Wan et al., 2023). Similarly, fairness-aware regularisation techniques penalise demographic disparities in models like credit-scoring systems by removing proxy variables such as postal codes, which correlate with race.

Even with fairer data and training methods, bias can persist in AI outputs. Post-processing techniques adjust decision thresholds to refine results before reaching end users (Petersen et al., 2021). For example, in medical AI, modifying risk assessment thresholds ensures equitable treatment across racial groups. However, fairness trade-offs arise when competing principles, such as equal opportunity versus individual fairness, conflict, making AI fairness a nuanced and context-dependent challenge rather than a universal solution.

3.5.2 Intersectionality and the Trade-offs in Bias Correction

Fairness in AI is not a singular concept, and different definitions, such as demographic parity and equalised odds, can lead to conflicting objectives (Hort et al., 2024; Mehrabi et al., 2021; Mikołajczyk-Bareła & Grochowski, 2023; Ntoutsi et al., 2020). Intersectionality further complicates bias mitigation, as AI interventions that focus solely on race or gender may overlook the compounded effects on marginalised subgroups (Crenshaw, 2022). For instance, black women experience both racial and gender disparities, which broad fairness measures may fail to address.

Bias trade-offs are evident in criminal justice algorithms like COMPAS, where adjustments to equalise false-positive rates across racial groups inadvertently created disparities in false-negative rates, raising ethical questions about acceptable bias (Dressel & Farid, 2018; Grant, 2023). Similarly, AI-driven credit scoring systems face challenges when implementing fairness constraints, as demographic parity can unintentionally increase default rates, affecting lending practices (Baesens et al., 2003; Chen et al., 2024; Mathen & Paul, 2025). These dilemmas emphasise the importance of involving diverse stakeholders in defining fairness in AI systems.

3.5.3 Emerging Challenges in Bias Mitigation: Generative AI and Multimodal Systems

Generative AI and multimodal systems introduce new complexities in bias detection and mitigation (Balasubramaniam et al., 2024). Unlike traditional predictive models, generative AI produces open-ended content that can unpredictably reflect societal biases, even after rigorous filtering (Zhou et al., 2024). Studies reveal that AI-generated content (AIGC) systematically underrepresents females and Black individuals, reinforcing stereotypes (Fang et al., 2024). Although ChatGPT demonstrates lower bias and can refuse biased prompts, it remains vulnerable to adversarial manipulation.

Multimodal AI, which integrates text, images, and speech, compounds these issues. Hiring algorithms that analyse video interviews, for example, may introduce bias through facial recognition errors, speech misinterpretation, and culturally insensitive body language analysis (Tilmes, 2022). Similarly, deepfake technology, initially developed for entertainment, has been found to reinforce racial biases by overrepresenting white individuals in authoritative roles while assigning minorities to subordinate positions (Agarwal & Ratha, 2024; Hussain et al., 2025; Obermeyer et al., 2019; Yucer et al., 2025). The risk extends beyond representation, as biased deepfake content can be weaponised for misinformation and propaganda. These concerns underscore the need for stronger safeguards against biased AI content generation. Figure 3.2 presents bias mitigation strategy in AI systems.

3.5.4 Future Research Directions in Bias Mitigation

The evolving landscape of AI bias mitigation underscores several critical areas for further research. Dynamic fairness approaches are necessary to adapt to shifting societal norms, as static definitions risk obsolescence over time. While most efforts focus on supervised learning, unsupervised and self-supervised models present largely unexplored challenges. Federated learning offers a promising strategy to mitigate bias while preserving data privacy by enabling models to learn from decentralised datasets. Additionally, interdisciplinary approaches integrating social sciences, legal studies, and ethics are essential for developing comprehensive bias assessment frameworks considering AI's broader sociotechnical context. Cross-cultural fairness is another key concern, as bias is context-dependent, requiring culturally informed approaches that balance local norms with universal principles of equity and nondiscrimination.

A major challenge in addressing bias in generative AI is its inherent opacity. Unlike interpretable models such as decision trees, deep learning functions as a black box, making identifying bias sources difficult. Explainable AI (XAI) techniques aim to improve transparency, but no single method can fully eliminate bias (Adadi & Berrada, 2018). Instead, continuous auditing, human oversight, and policy interventions are necessary to ensure that generative AI aligns with ethical standards. These challenges highlight that bias mitigation is a technical issue and an ongoing sociotechnical process requiring continuous adaptation as AI and societal contexts evolve.

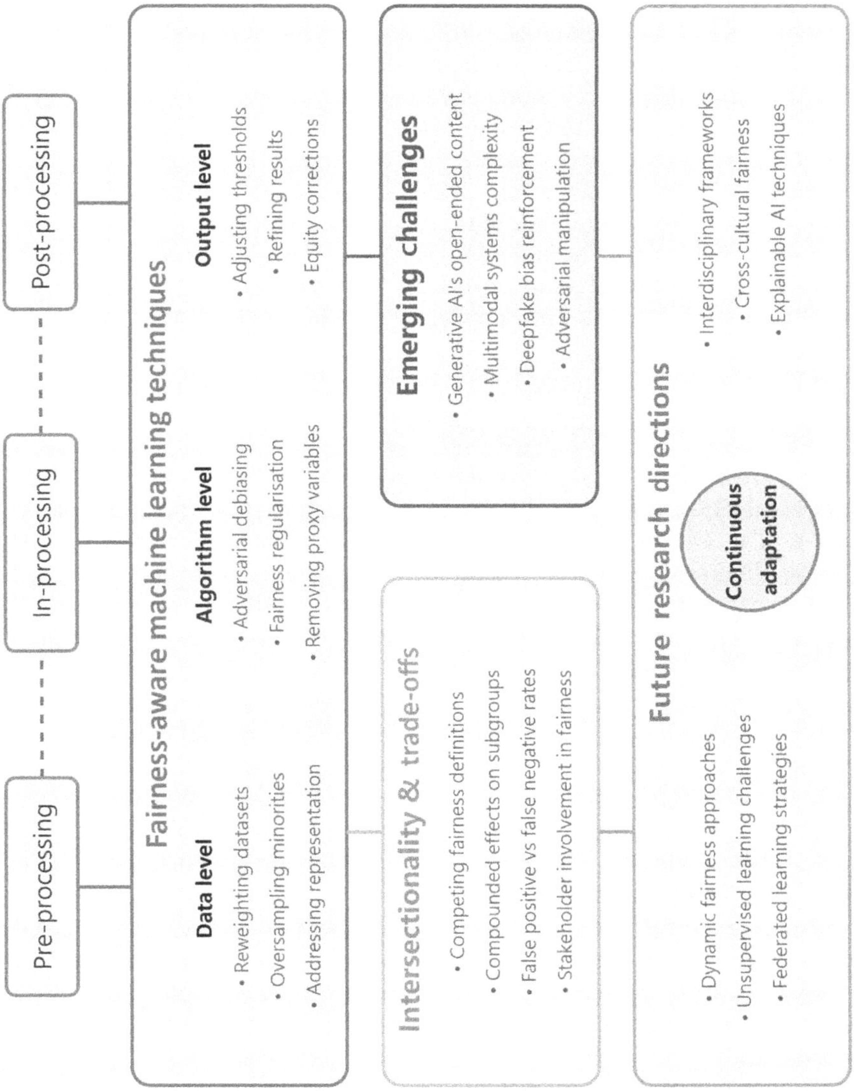

FIGURE 3.2
The strategy for mitigating bias in AI systems.

3.6 Global Impact and Policy Implications

The increasing reliance on AI in decision making has raised concerns about algorithmic bias, prompting responses from researchers, policymakers, and industry leaders. A distinct research domain now focuses on fairness, accountability, and transparency (FAT) in machine learning, developing methodologies to identify and mitigate bias (Zhdanov et al., 2022). Key interventions include preprocessing techniques to rebalance training data, in-processing adjustments to integrate fairness constraints, and postprocessing modifications to minimise discriminatory outcomes (Petersen et al., 2021; Shahrezaei et al., 2023; Wan et al., 2023). Transparency initiatives such as "datasheets for datasets" and "model cards" have also emerged to document model intent, performance across demographic groups, and bias evaluations (Gebru et al., 2021; Mitchell et al., 2019). However, bias in AI is not merely a technical issue but a governance challenge that requires broader structural interventions.

3.6.1 Regulatory Governance Approaches

Regulatory responses to algorithmic biases have evolved along distinct philosophical lines, reflecting different underlying values and governance traditions. The European Union's Ethics Guidelines for Trustworthy AI emphasise diversity, non-discrimination, and fairness, with the proposed EU AI Act mandating risk assessments for AI applications in hiring, credit scoring, and policing[3]. This rights-based approach prioritises individual protections and preventative oversight.

In the United States, the National Institute of Standards and Technology (NIST) has advanced socio-technical approaches to AI fairness, cautioning that current efforts focus too narrowly on data and algorithms while neglecting systemic biases.[4] (Schwartz et al., 2022) categorised bias as systemic, statistical, or human, advocating for organisational accountability across the AI life cycle. Meanwhile, the White House's Blueprint for an AI Bill of Rights enshrines freedom from algorithmic discrimination as a core principle[5]. The U.S. approach generally favors innovation-friendly frameworks with targeted interventions for high-risk applications. These initiatives signal a policy shift toward greater regulatory oversight, reflected in emerging laws such as New York City's bias audit requirement for AI hiring tools (Kestenbaum, 2023) and the EU's General Data Protection Regulation (GDPR)[6], which grants individuals the right to challenge automated decisions.

In state-directed governance systems, AI oversight is integrated into broader social control mechanisms. China's social credit system (SCS) exemplifies state-driven AI governance by assessing individual and business "trustworthiness" to determine access to loans, travel, and employment. Critics argue that the system disproportionately disadvantages low-income groups that lack the resources to maintain high scores, reinforcing social inequities (Heeks, 2022). However, Kostka (2019) found that China's SCSs enjoy surprisingly high public approval, particularly among wealthier, better-educated, and urban citizens as well as older individuals. While privacy concerns might be expected, these groups perceive SCSs as mechanisms for improving societal trust and regulatory enforcement rather than as surveillance tools.

3.6.2 Accessibility and Inclusion Challenges

The implementation of AI systems raises distinct equity concerns in contexts with limited digital infrastructure or diverse socioeconomic conditions. In India, the Aadhaar biometric identity system has expanded access to government services and financial transactions but has also introduced exclusionary risks. Authentication failures, particularly affecting rural populations and manual laborers, have resulted in denied access to essential services, such as food rations and healthcare, highlighting the intersection of algorithmic fairness and digital accessibility (Rao & Nair, 2019).

Developing economies increasingly deploy AI in financial services, employment matching, and public administration; however, the absence of strong regulatory safeguards heightens the risk of discriminatory outcomes. In Latin America and Africa, fintech firms leverage alternative data, such as mobile phone usage, social media activity, and psychological traits, for credit scoring (Bernards, 2019; Klinger et al., 2013; Óskarsdóttir et al., 2020; Shema, 2019). While this expands access, studies suggest that these models can reinforce socioeconomic disparities, penalizing individuals with a limited digital footprint. Policymakers must balance the gains in AI efficiency with protection against algorithmic discrimination. Figure 3.3 provides an overview of AI's global impact and policy implications.

3.6.3 Industry Self-Regulation and Economic Incentives

Corporate responses to AI fairness concerns include the establishment of internal ethics boards, with companies such as Google and Microsoft outlining principles that emphasise transparency and bias mitigation[7,8]. These governance structures typically involve fair audits, bias detection tools, and proactive model adjustments. Beyond ethics commitments, forward-thinking companies increasingly recognise fair AI as a competitive advantage. Market incentives for bias mitigation include reputation management, litigation avoidance, expanded customer bases, regulatory preparedness, and investor pressure for ESG compliance. These economic motivations may prove more sustainable drivers for corporate action than purely ethical considerations. However, the effectiveness of self-regulation remains debated as corporate commitments often lack enforceability and may be constrained by business priorities. Industry-wide frameworks have been developed to address these limitations. IEEE's ethically aligned design guidelines advocate

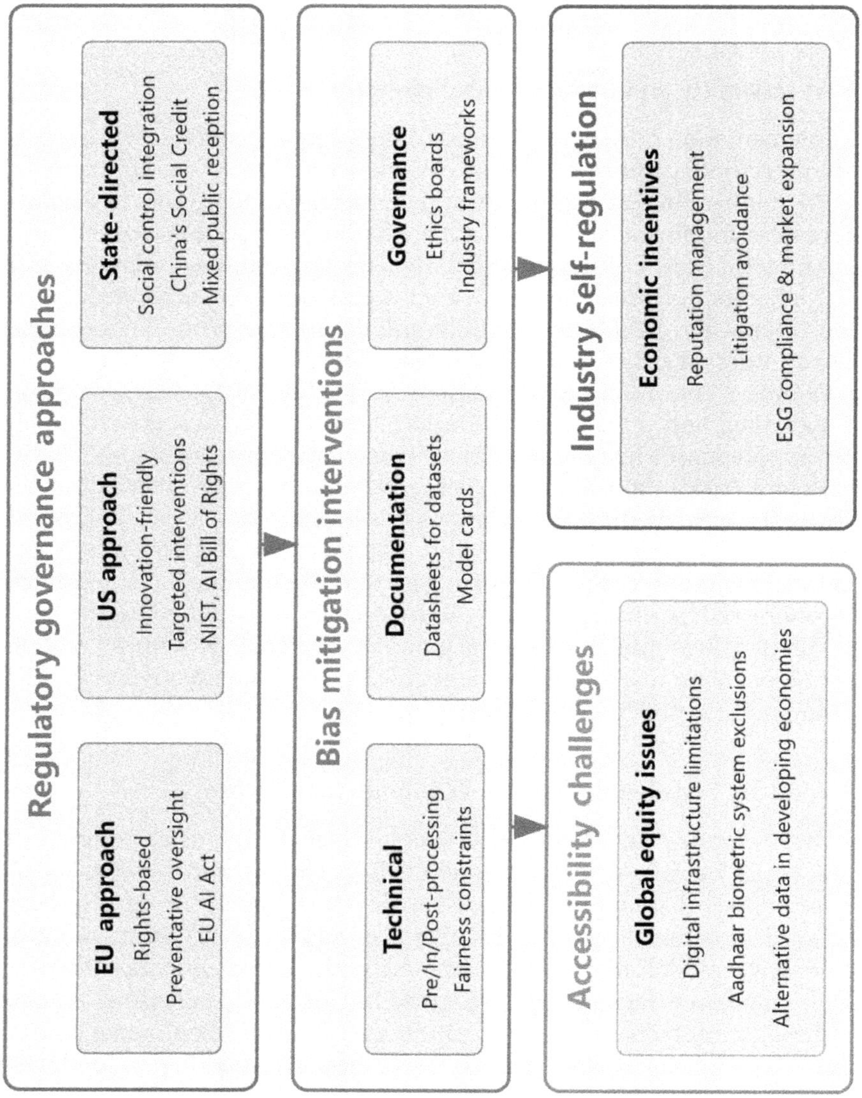

FIGURE 3.3
AI's worldwide influence and its policy implications.

human-centric AI principles[9], while ISO AI risk assessment standards provide structured methodologies for fairness evaluations[10]. Despite these initiatives, compliance remains voluntary in many jurisdictions, resulting in an uneven adoption across industries.

Efforts to mitigate algorithmic bias have increasingly focused on integrating fairness principles throughout the AI life cycle. Organizations employ fairness-aware machine-learning techniques, conduct bias impact assessments, and develop XAI methods to enhance transparency. In finance, credit-scoring firms experiment with fairness constraints to reduce bias in lending decisions (Kisten & Khosa, 2024). These initiatives highlight the growing role of industry in shaping AI fairness standards, even in the absence of stringent regulatory mandates.

3.7 Conclusion

Algorithmic fairness extends beyond a technical challenge to a broader socio-technical issue that reflects and reinforces systemic inequalities. As AI and ML systems shape critical life decisions, addressing biases in data, model design, and decision-making processes becomes essential. While fairness-aware machine learning techniques help detect and mitigate bias, their application often involves trade-offs between competing fairness metrics. Ethical frameworks such as utilitarianism, deontology, and virtue ethics offer theoretical insights, but achieving fairness requires context-specific solutions grounded in legal, social, and economic realities.

Global perspectives highlight the varied expressions of algorithmic fairness and the diverse policy responses across regions. The U.S. and EU have introduced regulatory measures for high-risk AI applications, while China, India, and developing economies confront fairness challenges in state-controlled AI, biometric authentication, and alternative credit scoring. Corporate AI ethics initiatives, such as IEEE's ethically aligned design and ISO risk assessments, seek to embed fairness in AI development, yet self-regulation remains insufficient without enforceable oversight. All in all, algorithmic bias is a structural issue embedded in data collection, interpretation, and application across various domains, necessitating an interdisciplinary approach that combines technical solutions—such as fairness-aware training, bias metrics, and rigorous testing—with legal protections, ethical oversight, and regulatory frameworks to ensure accountability, align bias mitigation research with global policy coordination, and uphold equity and human rights in automated decision-making.

Notes

1 CFPB warns lenders that using opaque algorithms does not exempt them from explaining credit denials under ECOA. www.consumerfinance.gov/about-us/newsroom/cfpb-acts-to-protect-the-public-from-black-box-credit-models-using-complex-algorithms/
2 Clarifies that lenders must give accurate, specific reasons for denials even when AI or complex models are used. www.consumerfinance.gov/about-us/newsroom/cfpb-issues-guidance-on-credit-denials-by-lenders-using-artificial-intelligence/
3 European Commission framework: trustworthy AI must be lawful, ethical, and robust, with principles of transparency, fairness, accountability, and human oversight. https://digital-strategy.ec.europa.eu/en/library/ethics-guidelines-trustworthy-ai
4 U.S. NIST launches ARIA (Advancing Responsible Innovation in AI) to develop sociotechnical testing and evaluation frameworks for AI systems. www.nist.gov/news-events/news/2024/05/nist-launches-aria-new-program-advance-sociotechnical-testing-and
5 U.S. framework outlining five principles to protect the public in the AI era: safe systems, algorithmic discrimination protections, data privacy, notice/explanation, and human alternatives. www.aasa.org/resources/blog/white-house-releases-blueprint-for-an-ai-bill-of-rights?
6 Official General Data Protection Regulation site; provides legal text and interpretations of EU's cornerstone data protection framework. https://gdpr-info.eu/
7 Google's commitment to develop AI responsibly, focusing on social benefit, safety, privacy, accountability, and avoiding bias or misuse. https://ai.google/responsibility/principles/
8 Microsoft's responsible AI approach built around fairness, reliability, safety, privacy, inclusiveness, transparency, and accountability. www.microsoft.com/en-us/ai/principles-and-approach
9 IEEE guidelines promoting human-centric AI aligned with ethics and values, offering recommendations for developers, policymakers, and organizations. https://standards.ieee.org/wp-content/uploads/import/documents/other/ead_v2.pdf
10 International standard defining AI terms and concepts to ensure clarity and consistency across stakeholders. www.iso.org/standard/77304.html

References

Abràmoff, M. D., Tarver, M. E., Loyo-Berrios, N., Trujillo, S., Char, D., Obermeyer, Z., Eydelman, M. B., Foundational Principles of Ophthalmic Imaging and Algorithmic Interpretation Working Group of the Collaborative Community for Ophthalmic Imaging Foundation, Washington, D.C., & Maisel, W. H. (2023).

Considerations for addressing bias in artificial intelligence for health equity. *Npj Digital Medicine*, *6*(1), 170. https://doi.org/10.1038/s41746-023-00913-9

Adadi, A., & Berrada, M. (2018). Peeking inside the black-box: A survey on explainable artificial intelligence (XAI). *IEEE Access*, *6*, 52138–52160. https://doi.org/10.1109/ACCESS.2018.2870052

Agarwal, A., & Ratha, N. (2024). Deepfake: Classifiers, fairness, and demographically robust algorithm. In *2024 IEEE 18th International Conference on Automatic Face and Gesture Recognition (FG)*, 1–9. https://doi.org/10.1109/FG59268.2024.10581915

Akbarighatar, P., Pappas, I., & Vassilakopoulou, P. (2023). A sociotechnical perspective for responsible AI maturity models: Findings from a mixed-method literature review. *International Journal of Information Management Data Insights*, *3*(2), 100193. https://doi.org/10.1016/j.jjimei.2023.100193

Ali, M., Sapiezynski, P., Bogen, M., Korolova, A., Mislove, A., & Rieke, A. (2019). Discrimination through optimization: How facebook's Ad delivery can lead to biased outcomes. *Proceedings of the ACM on Human-Computer Interaction*, *3*(CSCW), 1–30. https://doi.org/10.1145/3359301

Alvarez, J. M., Colmenarejo, A. B., Elobaid, A., Fabbrizzi, S., Fahimi, M., Ferrara, A., Ghodsi, S., Mougan, C., Papageorgiou, I., Reyero, P., Russo, M., Scott, K. M., State, L., Zhao, X., & Ruggieri, S. (2024). Policy advice and best practices on bias and fairness in AI. *Ethics and Information Technology*, *26*(2), 31. https://doi.org/10.1007/s10676-024-09746-w

Arowosegbe, J. O. (2023). Data bias, intelligent systems and criminal justice outcomes. *International Journal of Law and Information Technology*, *31*(1), 22–45. https://doi.org/10.1093/ijlit/eaad017

Atewologun, D. (2018). Intersectionality theory and practice. In D. Atewologun, *Oxford Research Encyclopedia of Business and Management*. Oxford University Press. https://doi.org/10.1093/acrefore/9780190224851.013.48

Baesens, B., Van Gestel, T., Viaene, S., Stepanova, M., Suykens, J., & Vanthienen, J. (2003). Benchmarking state-of-the-art classification algorithms for credit scoring. *Journal of the Operational Research Society*, *54*(6), 627–635. https://doi.org/10.1057/palgrave.jors.2601545

Bains, C. (2024). *The legal doctrine that will be key to preventing AI discrimination*. www.brookings.edu/articles/the-legal-doctrine-that-will-be-key-to-preventing-ai-discrimination/

Balasubramaniam, S., Chirchi, V., Kadry, S., Agoramoorthy, M., Gururama, P. S., K., S. K., & T. A., S. (2024). The road ahead: Emerging trends, unresolved issues, and concluding remarks in generative AI—A comprehensive review. *International Journal of Intelligent Systems*, *2024*(1), 4013195. https://doi.org/10.1155/2024/4013195

Bartlett, R., Morse, A., Wallace, N., & Stanton, R. (2021). Algorithmic discrimination and input accountability under the civil rights acts. *Berkeley Technology Law Journal*, *36*(2), 675–736. https://doi.org/10.15779/Z381N7XN5B

Bell, A., Bynum, L., Drushchak, N., Zakharchenko, T., Rosenblatt, L., & Stoyanovich, J. (2023). The possibility of fairness: Revisiting the impossibility theorem in practice. In *2023 ACM Conference on Fairness, Accountability, and Transparency*, pp.400–422. https://doi.org/10.1145/3593013.3594007

Bernards, N. (2019). The poverty of fintech? Psychometrics, credit infrastructures, and the limits of financialization. *Review of International Political Economy*, *26*(5), 815–838. https://doi.org/10.1080/09692290.2019.1597753

Buijsman, S. (2024). Navigating fairness measures and trade-offs. *AI and Ethics*, *4*(4), 1323–1334. https://doi.org/10.1007/s43681-023-00318-0
Buolamwini, J., & Gebru, T. (2018). Gender shades: Intersectional accuracy disparities in commercial gender classification. In *Proceedings of the 1st Conference on Fairness, Accountability and Transparency*.
Cecere, G., Jean, C., Le Guel, F., & Manant, M. (2024). Artificial intelligence and algorithmic bias? Field tests on social network with teens. *Technological Forecasting and Social Change, 201*, 123204. https://doi.org/10.1016/j.techfore.2023.123204
Charlesworth, T. E. S., Sanjeev, N., Hatzenbuehler, M. L., & Banaji, M. R. (2023). Identifying and predicting stereotype change in large language corpora: 72 groups, 115 years (1900–2015), and four text sources. *Journal of Personality and Social Psychology*, *125*(5), 969–990. https://doi.org/10.1037/pspa0000354
Chen, Y., Calabrese, R., & Martin-Barragan, B. (2024). Interpretable machine learning for imbalanced credit scoring datasets. *European Journal of Operational Research*, *312*(1), 357–372. https://doi.org/10.1016/j.ejor.2023.06.036
Cirillo, D., Catuara-Solarz, S., Morey, C., Guney, E., Subirats, L., Mellino, S., Gigante, A., Valencia, A., Rementeria, M. J., Chadha, A. S., & Mavridis, N. (2020). Sex and gender differences and biases in artificial intelligence for biomedicine and healthcare. *Npj Digital Medicine*, *3*(1), 81. https://doi.org/10.1038/s41746-020-0288-5
Crenshaw, K. (2022). *On Intersectionality: Essential Writings*. The New Press.
Cvik, Š. (2022). Categorization and challenges of utilitarianisms in the context of artificial intelligence. *AI & SOCIETY*, *37*(1), 291–297. https://doi.org/10.1007/s00146-021-01169-1
Das, S., Stanton, R., & Wallace, N. (2023). Algorithmic fairness. *Annual Review of Financial Economics*, *15*(1), 565–593. https://doi.org/10.1146/annurev-financial-110921-125930
Dignum, V. (2019). *Responsible Artificial Intelligence*. Springer International Publishing. https://doi.org/10.1007/978-3-030-30371-6
Diniz, E. H., Sanches, B. H., Pozzebon, M., & Luvizan, S. (2024). Do black fintechs matter? The long and winding road to develop inclusive algorithms for social justice. *MIS Quarterly*, *48*(4), 1721–1744. https://doi.org/10.25300/MISQ/2024/18288
Drage, E., & Mackereth, K. (2022). Does AI debias recruitment? Race, gender, and AI's "Eradication of Difference." *Philosophy & Technology*, *35*(4), 89. https://doi.org/10.1007/s13347-022-00543-1
Dressel, J., & Farid, H. (2018). The accuracy, fairness, and limits of predicting recidivism. *Science Advances*, *4*(1), eaao5580. https://doi.org/10.1126/sciadv.aao5580
Dusi, M., Arici, N., Emilio Gerevini, A., Putelli, L., & Serina, I. (2024). Discrimination bias detection through categorical association in pre-trained language models. *IEEE Access*, *12*, 162651–162667. https://doi.org/10.1109/ACCESS.2024.3482010
Eggleston, B., & Miller, D. E. (2014). *The Cambridge Companion to Utilitarianism*. Cambridge University Press.
Etzioni, A., & Etzioni, O. (2017). Incorporating ethics into artificial intelligence. *The Journal of Ethics*, *21*(4), 403–418. https://doi.org/10.1007/s10892-017-9252-2
Fang, X., Che, S., Mao, M., Zhang, H., Zhao, M., & Zhao, X. (2024). Bias of AI-generated content: An examination of news produced by large language models. *Scientific Reports*, *14*(1), 5224. https://doi.org/10.1038/s41598-024-55686-2

Farina, M., Zhdanov, P., Karimov, A., & Lavazza, A. (2024). AI and society: A virtue ethics approach. *AI & Society*, *39*(3), 1127–1140. https://doi.org/10.1007/s00146-022-01545-5

Floridi, L. (Ed.). (2021). *Ethics, Governance, and Policies in Artificial Intelligence* (Vol. 144). Springer International Publishing. https://doi.org/10.1007/978-3-030-81907-1

Floridi, L., Cowls, J., Beltrametti, M., Chatila, R., Chazerand, P., Dignum, V., Luetge, C., Madelin, R., Pagallo, U., Rossi, F., Schafer, B., Valcke, P., & Vayena, E. (2021). *An Ethical Framework for a Good AI Society: Opportunities, Risks, Principles, and Recommendations* (pp. 19–39). https://doi.org/10.1007/978-3-030-81907-1_3

Fountain, J. E. (2022). The moon, the ghetto and artificial intelligence: Reducing systemic racism in computational algorithms. *Government Information Quarterly*, *39*(2), 101645. https://doi.org/10.1016/j.giq.2021.101645

Fritts, M., & Cabrera, F. (2021). AI recruitment algorithms and the dehumanization problem. *Ethics and Information Technology*, *23*(4), 791–801. https://doi.org/10.1007/s10676-021-09615-w

Garcia, A. C. B., Garcia, M. G. P., & Rigobon, R. (2024). Algorithmic discrimination in the credit domain: What do we know about it? *AI & Society*, *39*(4), 2059–2098. https://doi.org/10.1007/s00146-023-01676-3

Gebru, T., Morgenstern, J., Vecchione, B., Vaughan, J. W., Wallach, H., III, H. D., & Crawford, K. (2021). Datasheets for datasets. *Communications of the ACM*, *64*(12), 86–92. https://doi.org/10.1145/3458723

Grant, D. G. (2023). Equalized odds is a requirement of algorithmic fairness. *Synthese*, *201*(3), 101. https://doi.org/10.1007/s11229-023-04054-0

Hagendorff, T. (2022). A virtue-based framework to support putting AI ethics into practice. *Philosophy & Technology*, *35*(3), 55. https://doi.org/10.1007/s13347-022-00553-z

Heeks, R. (2022). Digital inequality beyond the digital divide: Conceptualizing adverse digital incorporation in the global South. *Information Technology for Development*, *28*(4), 688–704. https://doi.org/10.1080/02681102.2022.2068492

Heyder, T., Passlack, N., & Posegga, O. (2023). Ethical management of human-AI interaction: Theory development review. *The Journal of Strategic Information Systems*, *32*(3), 101772. https://doi.org/10.1016/j.jsis.2023.101772

Hofeditz, L., Clausen, S., Rieß, A., Mirbabaie, M., & Stieglitz, S. (2022). Applying XAI to an AI-based system for candidate management to mitigate bias and discrimination in hiring. *Electronic Markets*, *32*(4), 2207–2233. https://doi.org/10.1007/s12525-022-00600-9

Hooker, S. (2021). Moving beyond "algorithmic bias is a data problem." *Patterns*, *2*(4), 100241. https://doi.org/10.1016/j.patter.2021.100241

Hort, M., Chen, Z., Zhang, J. M., Harman, M., & Sarro, F. (2024). Bias mitigation for machine learning classifiers: A comprehensive survey. *ACM Journal on Responsible Computing*, *1*(2), 1–52. https://doi.org/10.1145/3631326

Hung, T.-W., & Yen, C.-P. (2023). Predictive policing and algorithmic fairness. *Synthese*, *201*(6), 206. https://doi.org/10.1007/s11229-023-04189-0

Hussain, S. A., Bresnahan, M., & Zhuang, J. (2025). The bias algorithm: How AI in healthcare exacerbates ethnic and racial disparities – A scoping review. *Ethnicity & Health*, *30*(2), 197–214. https://doi.org/10.1080/13557858.2024.2422848

Kestenbaum, J. (2023, July 5). NYC's new AI bias law broadly impacts hiring and requires audits. *Bloomberg*. https://news.bloomberglaw.com/us-law-week/nycs-new-ai-bias-law-broadly-impacts-hiring-and-requires-audits

Kim, H., & Schönecker, D. (Eds.). (2022). *Kant and Artificial Intelligence*. De Gruyter. https://doi.org/10.1515/9783110706611

Kisten, M., & Khosa, M. (2024). Enhancing fairness in credit assessment: Mitigation strategies and implementation. *IEEE Access, 12*, 177277–177284. https://doi.org/10.1109/ACCESS.2024.3505836

Kitchens, B., Johnson, S. L., & Gray, P. (2020). Understanding echo chambers and filter bubbles: The impact of social media on diversification and partisan shifts in news consumption. *MIS Quarterly*, *44*(4), 1619–1649. https://doi.org/10.25300/MISQ/2020/16371

Kleinberg, J., Lakkaraju, H., Leskovec, J., Ludwig, J., & Mullainathan, S. (2017). Human decisions and machine predictions. *The Quarterly Journal of Economics, 33*(1), 237–293. https://doi.org/10.1093/qje/qjx032

Klinger, B., Khwaja, A. I., & LaMonte, J. (2013). *Improving Credit Risk Analysis with Psychometrics in Peru* (Technical Note: No. IDB-TN-587; Inter-American Development Bank: Capital Markets and Financial Institutions Division (CMF), Institutions for Development (IFD)).

Kordzadeh, N., & Ghasemaghaei, M. (2022). Algorithmic bias: Review, synthesis, and future research directions. *European Journal of Information Systems, 31*(3), 388–409. https://doi.org/10.1080/0960085X.2021.1927212

Kostka, G. (2019). China's social credit systems and public opinion: Explaining high levels of approval. *New Media & Society, 21*(7), 1565–1593. https://doi.org/10.1177/1461444819826402

Krijger, J. (2022). Enter the metrics: Critical theory and organizational operationalization of AI ethics. *AI & Society, 37*(4), 1427–1437. https://doi.org/10.1007/s00146-021-01256-3

Kuppan, K., Bhaskar Acharya, D., & B, D. (2024). Foundational AI in insurance and real estate: A survey of applications, challenges, and future directions. *IEEE Access, 12*, 181282–181302. https://doi.org/10.1109/ACCESS.2024.3509918

Laux, J., Wachter, S., & Mittelstadt, B. (2024). Trustworthy artificial intelligence and the European Union AI act: On the conflation of trustworthiness and acceptability of risk. *Regulation & Governance, 18*(1), 3–32. https://doi.org/10.1111/rego.12512

Lee, N. T., & Chin-Rothmann, C. (2022). *Police surveillance and facial recognition: Why data privacy is imperative for communities of color*. www.brookings.edu/articles/police-surveillance-and-facial-recognition-why-data-privacy-is-an-imperative-for-communities-of-color/

Leslie, D. (2020). *Understanding bias in facial recognition technologies* (arXiv:2010.07023).

Li, Y., Chen, H., Xu, S., Ge, Y., Tan, J., Liu, S., & Zhang, Y. (2023). Fairness in recommendation: Foundations, methods, and applications. *ACM Transactions on Intelligent Systems and Technology, 14*(5), 1–48. https://doi.org/10.1145/3610302

Liebrenz, M., Bhugra, D., Alibudbud, R., Ventriglio, A., & Smith, A. (2024). AI in health care and the fragile pursuit of equity and social justice. *The Lancet, 404*(10455), 843. https://doi.org/10.1016/S0140-6736(24)01604-0

Loftus, T. J., Shickel, B., Ozrazgat-Baslanti, T., Ren, Y., Glicksberg, B. S., Cao, J., Singh, K., Chan, L., Nadkarni, G. N., & Bihorac, A. (2022). Artificial intelligence-enabled

decision support in nephrology. *Nature Reviews Nephrology, 18*(7), 452–465. https://doi.org/10.1038/s41581-022-00562-3
Mangal, M., & Pardos, Z. A. (2024). Implementing equitable and intersectionality-aware ML in education: A practical guide. *British Journal of Educational Technology, 55*(5), 2003–2038. https://doi.org/10.1111/bjet.13484
Martin, K. (2022). *Ethics of Data and Analytics: Concepts and Cases* (1st ed.). Auerbach Publications. https://doi.org/10.1201/9781003278290
Mathen, M. P., & Paul, A. (2025). Toward an evolving framework for responsible AI for credit scoring in the banking industry. *Journal of Information, Communication and Ethics in Society, 23*(1), 148–163. https://doi.org/10.1108/JICES-08-2024-0122
McDaniel, J. L. M., & Pease, K. G. (Eds.). (2021). *Predictive Policing and Artificial Intelligence* (1st ed.). Routledge. https://doi.org/10.4324/9780429265365
Mehrabi, N., Morstatter, F., Saxena, N., Lerman, K., & Galstyan, A. (2021). A survey on bias and fairness in machine learning. *ACM Computing Surveys, 54*(6), 1–35. https://doi.org/10.1145/3457607
Mikołajczyk-Bareła, A., & Grochowski, M. (2023). *A survey on bias in machine learning research* (Version 1). arXiv. https://doi.org/10.48550/ARXIV.2308.11254
Militello, L. G., Diiulio, J., Wilson, D. L., Nguyen, K. A., Harle, C. A., Gellad, W., & Lo-Ciganic, W.-H. (2025). Using human factors methods to mitigate bias in artificial intelligence-based clinical decision support. *Journal of the American Medical Informatics Association, 32*(2), 398–403. https://doi.org/10.1093/jamia/ocae291
Mitchell, M., Wu, S., Zaldivar, A., Barnes, P., Vasserman, L., Hutchinson, B., Spitzer, E., Raji, I. D., & Gebru, T. (2019). Model cards for model reporting. In *Proceedings of the Conference on Fairness, Accountability, and Transparency*, pp. 220–229. https://doi.org/10.1145/3287560.3287596
Nemani, P., Joel, Y. D., Vijay, P., & Liza, F. F. (2024). Gender bias in transformers: A comprehensive review of detection and mitigation strategies. *Natural Language Processing Journal, 6*, 100047. https://doi.org/10.1016/j.nlp.2023.100047
Neubert, M. J., & Montañez, G. D. (2020). Virtue as a framework for the design and use of artificial intelligence. *Business Horizons, 63*(2), 195–204. https://doi.org/10.1016/j.bushor.2019.11.001
Nguyen, J. K. (2024). Human bias in AI models? Anchoring effects and mitigation strategies in large language models. *Journal of Behavioral and Experimental Finance, 43*, 100971. https://doi.org/10.1016/j.jbef.2024.100971
Nida-Rümelin, J., & Weidenfeld, N. (2022). Digital optimization, utilitarianism, and AI. In J. Nida-Rümelin & N. Weidenfeld, *Digital Humanism* (pp. 31–34). Springer International Publishing. https://doi.org/10.1007/978-3-031-12482-2_6
Nishant, R., Schneckenberg, D., & Ravishankar, M. (2024). The formal rationality of artificial intelligence-based algorithms and the problem of bias. *Journal of Information Technology, 39*(1), 19–40. https://doi.org/10.1177/02683962231176842
Nitzberg, M., & Zysman, J. (2022). Algorithms, data, and platforms: The diverse challenges of governing AI. *Journal of European Public Policy, 29*(11), 1753–1778. https://doi.org/10.1080/13501763.2022.2096668
Noble, S. U. (2018). *Algorithms of Oppression: How Search Engines Reinforce Racism*. New York University Press.

Ntoutsi, E., Fafalios, P., Gadiraju, U., Iosifidis, V., Nejdl, W., Vidal, M., Ruggieri, S., Turini, F., Papadopoulos, S., Krasanakis, E., Kompatsiaris, I., Kinder-Kurlanda, K., Wagner, C., Karimi, F., Fernandez, M., Alani, H., Berendt, B., Kruegel, T., Heinze, C., … Staab, S. (2020). Bias in data-driven artificial intelligence systems—An introductory survey. *WIREs Data Mining and Knowledge Discovery, 10*(3), e1356. https://doi.org/10.1002/widm.1356

Obermeyer, Z., Powers, B., Vogeli, C., & Mullainathan, S. (2019). Dissecting racial bias in an algorithm used to manage the health of populations. *Science, 366*(6464), 447–453. https://doi.org/10.1126/science.aax2342

Óskarsdóttir, M., Bravo, C., Sarraute, C., Baesens, B., & Vanthienen, J. (2020). *Credit scoring for good: Enhancing financial inclusion with smartphone-based microlending* (Version 1). arXiv. https://doi.org/10.48550/ARXIV.2001.10994

Pagano, T. P., Loureiro, R. B., Lisboa, F. V. N., Peixoto, R. M., Guimarães, G. A. S., Cruz, G. O. R., Araujo, M. M., Santos, L. L., Cruz, M. A. S., Oliveira, E. L. S., Winkler, I., & Nascimento, E. G. S. (2023). Bias and unfairness in machine learning models: A systematic review on datasets, tools, fairness metrics, and identification and mitigation methods. *Big Data and Cognitive Computing, 7*(1), 15. https://doi.org/10.3390/bdcc7010015

Petersen, F., Mukherjee, D., Sun, Y., & Yurochkin, M. (2021). Post-processing for individual fairness. *Advances in Neural Information Processing Systems, 34*, 25944–25955. https://proceedings.neurips.cc/paper_files/paper/2021/file/d9fea4ca7e4a74c318ec27c1deb0796c-Paper.pdf

Pot, M., Kieusseyan, N., & Prainsack, B. (2021). Not all biases are bad: Equitable and inequitable biases in machine learning and radiology. *Insights into Imaging, 12*(1), 13. https://doi.org/10.1186/s13244-020-00955-7

Rao, U., & Nair, V. (2019). Aadhaar: Governing with biometrics. *South Asia: Journal of South Asian Studies, 42*(3), 469–481. https://doi.org/10.1080/00856401.2019.1595343

Rodilosso, E. (2024). Filter bubbles and the unfeeling: How AI for social media can foster extremism and polarization. *Philosophy & Technology, 37*(2), 71. https://doi.org/10.1007/s13347-024-00758-4

Saheb, T., & Saheb, T. (2024). Mapping ethical artificial intelligence policy landscape: A mixed method analysis. *Science and Engineering Ethics, 30*(2), 9. https://doi.org/10.1007/s11948-024-00472-6

Schwartz, R., Vassilev, A., Greene, K., Perine, L., Burt, A., & Hall, P. (2022). *Towards a standard for identifying and managing bias in artificial intelligence* (NIST SP 1270; p. NIST SP 1270). National Institute of Standards and Technology (U.S.). https://doi.org/10.6028/NIST.SP.1270

Selbst, A. D., Boyd, D., Friedler, S. A., Venkatasubramanian, S., & Vertesi, J. (2019). Fairness and abstraction in sociotechnical systems. In *Proceedings of the Conference on Fairness, Accountability, and Transparency*, 59–68. https://doi.org/10.1145/3287560.3287598

Seyyed-Kalantari, L., Zhang, H., McDermott, M. B. A., Chen, I. Y., & Ghassemi, M. (2021). Underdiagnosis bias of artificial intelligence algorithms applied to chest radiographs in under-served patient populations. *Nature Medicine, 27*(12), 2176–2182. https://doi.org/10.1038/s41591-021-01595-0

Shahrezaei, M. H., Loughran, R., & Daid, K. M. (2023). Pre-processing techniques to mitigate against algorithmic bias. In *2023 31st Irish Conference on Artificial*

Intelligence and Cognitive Science (AICS), 1–4. https://doi.org/10.1109/AICS60730.2023.10470759

Shema, A. (2019). Effective credit scoring using limited mobile phone data. In *Proceedings of the Tenth International Conference on Information and Communication Technologies and Development*, 1–11. https://doi.org/10.1145/3287098.3287116

Theodorou, A., & Dignum, V. (2020). Towards ethical and socio-legal governance in AI. *Nature Machine Intelligence*, *2*(1), 10–12. https://doi.org/10.1038/s42256-019-0136-y

Tilmes, N. (2022). Disability, fairness, and algorithmic bias in AI recruitment. *Ethics and Information Technology*, *24*(2), 21. https://doi.org/10.1007/s10676-022-09633-2

Ulgen, O. (2017). Kantian ethics in the age of artificial intelligence and robotics. *Questions of International Law*, *43*.

Van Giffen, B., Herhausen, D., & Fahse, T. (2022). Overcoming the pitfalls and perils of algorithms: A classification of machine learning biases and mitigation methods. *Journal of Business Research*, *144*, 93–106. https://doi.org/10.1016/j.jbusres.2022.01.076

Varsha, P. S. (2023). How can we manage biases in artificial intelligence systems – A systematic literature review. *International Journal of Information Management Data Insights*, *3*(1), 100165. https://doi.org/10.1016/j.jjimei.2023.100165

Wan, M., Zha, D., Liu, N., & Zou, N. (2023). In-processing modeling techniques for machine learning fairness: A survey. *ACM Transactions on Knowledge Discovery from Data*, *17*(3), 1–27. https://doi.org/10.1145/3551390

Wei, X., Kumar, N., & Zhang, H. (2025). Addressing bias in generative AI: Challenges and research opportunities in information management. *Information & Management*, *62*(2), 104103. https://doi.org/10.1016/j.im.2025.104103

Xiong, Y., & Kim, J. K. (2025). Who wants to be hired by AI? How message frames and AI transparency impact individuals' attitudes and behaviors toward companies using AI in hiring. *Computers in Human Behavior: Artificial Humans*, *3*, 100120. https://doi.org/10.1016/j.chbah.2025.100120

Yampolskiy, R. V. (Ed.). (2018). *Artificial Intelligence Safety and Security* (1st ed.). Chapman and Hall/CRC. https://doi.org/10.1201/9781351251389

Yang, C., & Dobbie, W. (2020). Equal protection under algorithms: A new statistical and legal framework. *Michigan Law Review*, *119.2*, 291. https://doi.org/10.36644/mlr.119.2.equal

Yucer, S., Tektas, F., Al Moubayed, N., & Breckon, T. (2025). Racial bias within face recognition: A survey. *ACM Computing Surveys*, *57*(4), 1–39. https://doi.org/10.1145/3705295

Zhdanov, D., Bhattacharjee, S., & Bragin, M. A. (2022). Incorporating FAT and privacy aware AI modeling approaches into business decision making frameworks. *Decision Support Systems*, *155*, 113715. https://doi.org/10.1016/j.dss.2021.113715

Zhou, M., Abhishek, V., Derdenger, T., Kim, J., & Srinivasan, K. (2024). *Bias in generative AI* (Version 1). arXiv preprint arXiv:2403.02726. https://doi.org/10.48550/arXiv.2403.02726

4

Augmenting Humanity Through Strategic Artificial Intelligence Applications in DEIB

Arif Perdana and Sabina Satriyani Puspita

4.1 Introduction

Despite decades of organisational efforts to address persistent disparities in workforce representation, advancement opportunities, and workplace inclusion, progress toward truly equitable workplaces remains gradual and uneven (Rothwell et al., 2022; Singh & Ramdeo, 2023). Organisations continue to struggle with unconscious biases that permeate decision-making processes, systemic barriers that disadvantage underrepresented groups, and workplace cultures that discourage authentic participation from diverse employees (King, 2024; Meyer & Baogui, 2025; Williams, 2023). This limited progress persists despite substantial investments in diversity training, unconscious bias education, and formal policies designed to enhance equity (Carter-Veale et al., 2025; Ellul & Friggieri, 2025; Jerab, 2025). As these traditional interventions demonstrate inconsistent efficacy, forward-thinking organisations increasingly turn to artificial intelligence (AI) as a potentially transformative tool to accelerate diversity, equity, inclusion, and belonging (DEIB) initiatives (Gao et al., 2024; McClung & Linton, 2024; Wilder & Stratchan, 2025).

The application of AI to organisational DEIB challenges emerges at the intersection of two significant developments. First, organisations face mounting pressure from stakeholders, including employees, consumers, and investors, who increasingly view workplace equity not merely as a moral imperative but also as a strategic business necessity linked to innovation, market responsiveness, and talent acquisition (Gholidoust, 2024; Jay, 2025). Second, rapid advances in AI capabilities, particularly in natural language processing, pattern recognition, and predictive analytics, offer unprecedented opportunities to identify, measure, and address subtle forms of bias that often escape human detection (Gao et al., 2024; Sanyi et al., 2025). This technological evolution comes precisely as organisations recognise the limitations of human

DOI: 10.1201/9781003591078-6

judgment in consistently applying fair evaluation criteria across diverse candidates and employees.

The theoretical rationale for integrating AI into DEIB initiatives stems from organisational justice frameworks that distinguish between distributive, procedural, and interactional forms of fairness (Chauhan et al., 2025; Greenberg, 1987; Harriott, 2025). AI systems promise to enhance procedural justice by applying consistent evaluation standards across candidates and employees. This can potentially mitigate inconsistencies in human decision-making processes (Kleinberg et al., 2020). Similarly, the computer science community has developed increasingly sophisticated algorithmic fairness frameworks that formalise various definitions of fairness, from group fairness, ensuring similar outcomes across protected categories to individual fairness, treating similar individuals similarly regardless of protected characteristics (Barocas et al., 2023; Voria et al., 2025). These frameworks provide mathematical rigor that allows organizations to precisely define and measure fairness in previously impossible ways.

The application of AI to DEIB initiatives, however, creates profound tensions and paradoxes that demand thoughtful navigation. First, AI systems fundamentally learn from historical data, risking the perpetuation or amplification of existing patterns of exclusion rather than their disruption (Buolamwini & Gebru, 2018; Cirillo et al., 2020; Xiong & Kim, 2025). When algorithms are trained on data reflecting historical biases such as male-dominated leadership or racially homogeneous talent pools, they risk encoding these biases into seemingly objective recommendations. This phenomenon creates a troubling possibility: the systems designed to enhance fairness may legitimise discrimination by clothing it in technological objectivity (Martin, 2022).

Second, many sophisticated AI algorithms operate as "black boxes" with decision-making logic that remains opaque even to their developers (Hofeditz et al., 2022; Martin, 2022; Xiong & Kim, 2025). The lack of transparency and DEI principles and practices in the ethical guidelines for AI systems create significant challenges for accountability and trust, particularly in DEIB contexts, where the explanation and justification of decisions are essential for building organisational legitimacy (Adadi & Berrada, 2018; Cachat-Rosset and Klarsfeld, 2023). When employees face rejection by an AI screening tool or receive negative performance evaluations from algorithmic systems without clear explanations, the perceived fairness of these systems deteriorates, regardless of their technical sophistication (Jabagi et al., 2025).

Third, DEIB challenges typically emerge from complex structural and deeply nuanced social dynamics that algorithmic systems may struggle to adequately capture or address adequately (D'Ignazio & Klein, 2020; Hilton, 2025). Organisations may view AI as a technical panacea for fundamental human problems that require contextual understanding and qualitative judgment (Gao et al., 2024; Jabagi et al., 2025; Kleinberg et al., 2020). Technological solutionism potentially reduces complex and dynamic social phenomena to oversimplified metrics that fail to address the root causes of inequity. As the critical race theory and intersectionality frameworks remind us, discrimination operates through systemic patterns embedded in institutional structures that require human intervention to be dismantled effectively (Conyers & Fields, 2025; Crenshaw, 1995; Guo & Lei, 2025).

Finally, even with sophisticated bias mitigation techniques, ensuring fairness across all demographic groups simultaneously is mathematically impossible owing to the inherent trade-offs between different fairness criteria (Barocas et al., 2023; Kleinberg et al., 2020; Voria et al., 2025). Improving fairness along one dimension (such as equalizing false-positive rates between groups) may degrade performance along other dimensions (such as overall accuracy or outcomes for different groups). These trade-offs require normative judgments about which conception of fairness to prioritise in specific organisational contexts and decisions that cannot be outsourced to algorithms alone (Hort et al., 2024; Voria et al., 2025).

Despite these significant challenges, preliminary evidence suggests that thoughtfully implemented AI applications can significantly enhance workplace equity (Abdelhalim et al., 2024; Marabelli et al., 2023; Rahimi et al., 2024). Organisations implementing AI writing platforms to optimise recruiting communications have documented increases in applications from women candidates while simultaneously reducing time-to-hire (Xiong & Kim, 2025). Similarly, AI analytics examining performance data along multiple dimensions have helped organisations identify and address disparities when certain groups consistently receive evaluations inconsistent with their objective performance indicators (Tambe et al., 2019). These early successes point toward AI's potential to function as a powerful tool for illumination and accountability, rather than as a substitute for the difficult organisational change processes required for truly inclusive workplaces.

The critical question is not whether to implement AI in DEIB initiatives but how to design and deploy these systems in ways that enhance rather than undermine equity objectives. This challenge demands integrated frameworks that reconcile technical approaches to fairness with socially constructed notions of justice and frameworks that position AI as an augmentation rather than a replacement for human empathy and expertise in navigating complex DEIB challenges. This leads to our central research question: *How can organisations develop and implement sociotechnically integrated AI systems that effectively advance DEIB objectives while mitigating the risks of bias perpetuation, procedural opacity, and reductionist approaches to complex social phenomena?*

By addressing this question, we aim to advance both the theoretical understanding and practical guidance at the intersection of AI and DEIB. We propose a comprehensive framework integrating justice theories, sociotechnical system perspectives, critical approaches, and psychological frameworks to navigate the promise and paradox of AI in DEIB initiatives. This framework acknowledges that meaningful progress requires technical sophistication paired with critical awareness and participatory approaches, recognizing that AI represents not merely a technical tool but also a sociotechnical intervention within complex organisational systems (Orlikowski, 2007). In doing so, we contribute to the emerging literature on algorithmic fairness, organisational justice, and ethical implementation of AI in high-stakes contexts where both technical performance and social impact must be optimised simultaneously.

The remainder of this paper is organised as follows. Section 4.2 examines the theoretical and conceptual foundations of AI in the DEIB, integrating justice frameworks, sociotechnical perspectives, and psychological approaches. Section 4.3 explores the strategic applications of AI across the employee life cycle. Section 4.4 analyses the critical challenges and risks associated with AI-enabled DEIB. Section 4.5 presents the proposed sociotechnical framework for responsible implementation. Section 4.6 provides practical implementation guidance for organisational case studies. Section 4.7 outlines future research directions, and Section 4.8 concludes the paper.

4.2 Theoretical and Conceptual Foundations

Organizations are increasingly turning to AI to address persistent DEIB challenges and develop strategic DEIB initiatives (Marabelli et al., 2023). This approach emerges from a convergence of organisational justice theories and computational fairness frameworks, which together suggest that AI can enhance procedural justice by applying consistent evaluation criteria where human judgment has historically faltered (Jiang et al., 2023; Lee et al., 2019a). The theoretical underpinnings of this movement merit deeper examination, as they reveal both promising avenues and paradoxes that demand thoughtful navigation.

4.2.1 Justice and Fairness Paradigms

The foundational rationale for AI in DEIB initiatives lies in the recognition that human decision-making processes remain susceptible to unconscious biases, despite decades of awareness and training. Organisational justice theory distinguishes between distributive, procedural, and interactional forms of fairness, each offering a lens through which to understand how AI might transform workplace equity (Greenberg, 1987). Procedural justice is affected when different evaluators apply inconsistent standards across candidates or employees. Provided candidates' or employees' level of accountability in disclosing their personal information or circumstance, AI systems promise consistency in the application of criteria, potentially enhancing the fairness of processes that determine how opportunities and resources are distributed throughout organisations.

This promise gains further theoretical support from the bias suppression literature, which suggests that, while blinding decision-makers to sensitive attributes can initially enhance objectivity, its long-term effectiveness depends on sustained accountability (Solomon et al., 2022). Solomon et al. argue that bias suppression is not inherently self-reinforcing and can be undermined when accountability fluctuates, particularly when decision makers initially operate under high accountability but later face reduced oversight. In such cases, counterfactual thinking and regret may lead to decision reversals, ultimately reintroducing bias into the process. The AI-enabled blind screening of résumés exemplifies this approach by removing demographic information to ensure that evaluators focus solely on merit-based factors. However, this approach assumes that merit can be objectively defined and measured, an assumption challenged by critical theoretical perspectives that highlights how seemingly neutral criteria often reflect and perpetuate existing power hierarchies.

The computer science community has responded to these challenges by developing increasingly sophisticated algorithmic fairness frameworks (Barocas et al., 2023; Voria et al., 2025). These formalise various definitions of fairness, from group fairness ensuring similar outcomes across protected categories to individual fairness treating similar individuals similarly, regardless of protected characteristics (Voria et al., 2025). The mathematical rigor these frameworks bring to DEIB efforts allows organizations to precisely define and measure fairness in ways previously impossible (Caton & Haas, 2024). Technical approaches to operationalise these definitions include preprocessing techniques that modify training data to remove historical biases, in-processing techniques incorporating fairness constraints directly into algorithms, and post-processing techniques that adjust model outputs to ensure fair results (Hort et al., 2024; Petersen et al., 2021; Shahrezaei et al., 2023).

However, the proliferation of formal fairness definitions reveals an uncomfortable truth: different fairness metrics often cannot be satisfied simultaneously. This impossibility results from computer science literature mirroring longstanding tensions in philosophical approaches to justice. Organisations must make explicit value judgments about which forms of fairness matter most in particular contexts and decisions that cannot be outsourced to algorithms alone (Hort et al., 2024; Mehrabi et al., 2021; Mikołajczyk-Bareła & Grochowski, 2023; Ntoutsi et al., 2020). Here, we observe the crucial intersection of sociotechnical systems theory with AI in DEIB applications (Dolata et al., 2022).

4.2.2 Sociotechnical Systems and Critical Perspectives

Sociotechnical systems theory reminds us that technology operates within complex social contexts (Orlikowski, 2007). For AI in DEIB, this means that technical solutions alone cannot solve deeply embedded social problems (Dolata et al., 2022). The naive application of AI to diversity challenges risks technological solutionism, in which the belief is that adding technology can solve social problems without addressing underlying power structures and organisational cultures. AI systems must be designed with an awareness of organisational power dynamics, historical patterns of exclusion, and ways in which technology can inadvertently reinforce existing hierarchies. The interaction between AI tools and human users ultimately determines the DEIB outcomes, not the sophistication of algorithms.

This insight connects to institutional theory's explanation of how organisations adopt similar practices due to external pressures, regulations, and normative expectations. The current wave of AI adoption in DEIB reflects technological opportunities and changes in stakeholder expectations regarding diversity and inclusion. Organisations increasingly measure their practices against industry benchmarks, comply with evolving regulations, and seek to maintain legitimacy with stakeholders who value diversity. AI tools facilitate these comparisons and compliance efforts, providing metrics and monitoring capabilities that help organisations demonstrate commitment to DEIB goals. However, without critical awareness, such efforts may become ceremonial rather than substantive, focusing on measurement rather than on meaningful change.

Critical perspectives, including the critical race theory and intersectionality frameworks, provide essential theoretical counterweights to overly optimistic views of AI in the DEIB (Crenshaw, 1995). These approaches examine how systemic forms of discrimination become embedded in institutional structures and data (Banaji et al., 2021; Favaretto et al., 2019). When AI systems are trained on historical data reflecting past discrimination, they risk perpetuating or amplifying these patterns unless specifically designed to counteract them. Intersectionality recognizes that individuals may face multiple, compounding forms of discrimination based on overlapping identities, in which complexities that simplistic algorithmic approaches may fail to address (Crenshaw, 2022). These critical frameworks challenge us to question whether technological interventions address root causes or merely treat the exclusion symptoms.

The limitations of purely technical approaches have led to an increasing emphasis on the participatory design and democratic governance of AI systems (Ahrweiler et al., 2025; Lee et al., 2019b). These emerging theoretical frameworks highlight the importance of involving diverse stakeholders in defining, designing, and implementing fairness metrics. When employees from underrepresented groups participate in determining how AI will evaluate candidates or monitor inclusion, the resulting systems are more likely to reflect diverse perspectives rather than merely reinforce dominant viewpoints. Some scholars propose that AI systems should not merely avoid perpetuating disadvantages, but should actively work to redress historical injustices through algorithmic affirmative action, a proposition that raises both legal and ethical questions demanding careful consideration (Bent, 2020; Hummerick, 2020; Salib, 2022).

4.2.3 Psychological and Ethical Frameworks: Fostering Belonging and Ethical Guidance

Beyond justice frameworks and critical perspectives, psychological theories offer crucial insights into AI in the DEIB (Brown, 2000; Crenshaw, 1995; Hogg, 2016; Morrow & Brown, 1994; Pettigrew & Tropp, 2008). Social identity theory explains how individuals categorize themselves and others into social groups, often leading to in-group favouritism and out-group discrimination (Abbink & Harris, 2019; Balliet et al., 2014). AI can potentially identify these patterns in historical decisions and help create balanced representations of teams and leadership. Fostering the inclusion climate is essential; however, psychological safety is also essential. Without it, employees may remain silent, thereby increasing their burnout. Empowering voice through impact perception strengthens workplace engagement (Sherf et al., 2021). We argue that AI tools analysing employee feedback, communication patterns, and language use can identify exclusionary practices and provide guidance for more inclusive behaviours, potentially transforming organizational climate.

Contact theory suggests that under appropriate conditions, interpersonal contact between majority and minority group members reduces prejudice (Pettigrew et al., 2011; Pettigrew & Tropp, 2008). AI can support this by facilitating diverse team formation based on complementary skills rather than homophily, and identifying potential mentoring relationships across demographic boundaries. Similarly, emerging work on neurodiversity emphasizes the organisational benefits of cognitive differences. AI can support neurodivergent individuals through personalised accommodation, identify complementary cognitive styles when forming teams, and make communication more accessible across cognitive differences. These applications demonstrate how AI may enhance inclusion beyond the conventional demographic diversity. Figure 4.1 presents the theoretical and conceptual foundations of AI in DEIB.

Ethical frameworks provide essential normative guidance for AI in DEIB initiatives (Akbarighatar et al., 2023; Heyder et al., 2023; Theodorou & Dignum, 2020). The ethics of care emphasise response to others' needs and relational interdependence, suggesting that AI in DEIB should prioritise the well-being of all organisational members, recognise unique individual circumstances, and support diverse communities (Villegas-Galaviz & Martin, 2024). International human rights standards establish expectations for organizations regarding non-discrimination and workplace rights, while regional frameworks such as the EU's Ethics Guidelines for Trustworthy AI set standards for responsible development. Explainability requirements

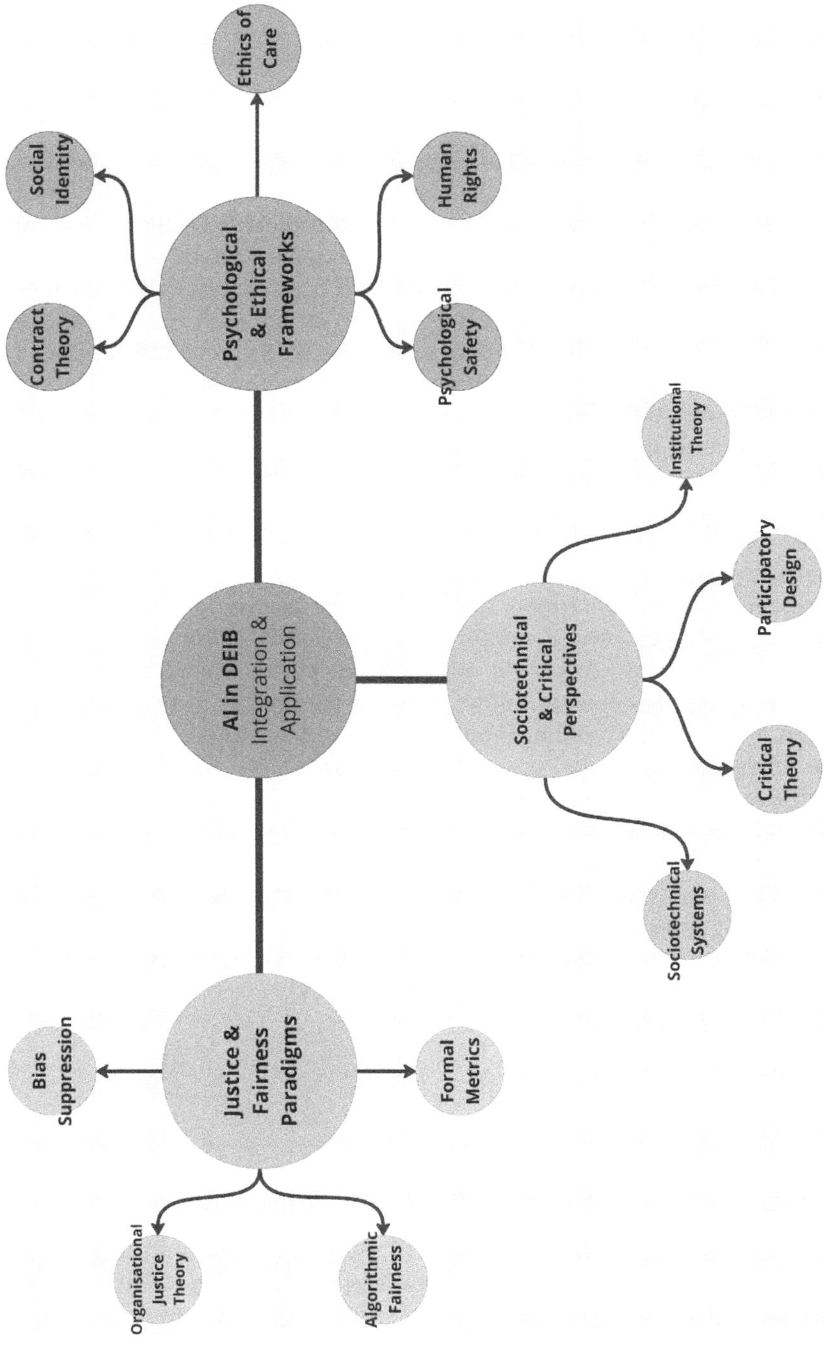

FIGURE 4.1
Theoretical and conceptual foundation of AI in DEIB.

ensure that algorithmic decisions remain transparent and accountable, which is crucial for building trust among employees affected by AI-influenced decisions (Adadi & Berrada, 2018).

4.2.4 Integration and Implications

The integration of these theoretical perspectives, namely justice frameworks, sociotechnical and critical perspectives, and psychological and ethical approaches, reveals both the promise and paradox of AI in DEIB. The promise lies in AI's potential to enforce consistent standards, detect subtle patterns of exclusion, facilitate diverse connections, and provide ongoing monitoring that is impossible through human effort alone (Aminizadeh et al., 2024; Nasir et al., 2024; Truby, 2020). The paradox emerges in the recognition that the systems designed to overcome human bias may themselves reproduce discrimination if not guided by diverse perspectives, contextual understanding, critical awareness, and ethical principles.

This paradox reflects a more profound tension in organisational approaches to DEIB. Technical solutions appeal because they promise to bypass the messiness and discomfort of confronting deep-seated biases and power differentials (Mehrabi et al., 2021; Voria et al., 2025). They rely on mathematical calculations to address discrimination, assuming that algorithmic interventions suffice without genuinely understanding the social contexts, organisational cultures, or power structures at play. However, meaningful progress requires this confrontation, with AI serving as a tool for illumination and accountability rather than a substitute for complex organisational change processes.

Organisations that successfully navigate these theoretical tensions will develop AI approaches to DEIB that enhance rather than replace human judgment, reflect on rather than obscure diverse perspectives, and advance substantive rather than merely symbolic inclusion. The journey requires ongoing dialogue between technical and social disciplines, between theory and practice, and between diverse stakeholders whose experiences must inform both the development and evaluation of AI systems in the service of truly inclusive workplaces.

4.3 Strategic Applications Across the Employee Lifecycle

AI technologies fundamentally transform how organisations approach DEIB initiatives. This transformation spans the entire employee lifecycle and offers promising avenues for addressing the persistent challenges in creating truly inclusive workplaces. This section examines how AI applications reshape DEIB practices across key organisational domains, synthesises emerging evidence of their effectiveness, and proposes a framework for their strategic implementation.

4.3.1 Mitigating Bias in Recruitment and Selection

The recruitment and selection process represents a critical juncture in which organisations can either perpetuate or disrupt patterns of exclusion (Dattner et al., 2019). AI systems are increasingly deployed to reduce implicit biases and broaden candidate pools. Natural language processing algorithms now analyse job descriptions to identify gender-coded or exclusionary language, while AI-driven resume screening tools standardise candidate evaluations based on skills rather than demographic characteristics. Organizations implementing these technologies have reported measurable improvements in diversity outcomes (Dattner et al., 2019; Van Den Broek et al., 2021). For instance, after integrating AI-powered writing platforms to optimise recruitment communications, several large enterprises have observed an increase in applications from diverse candidate pools, including more women, while also enhancing efficiency and reducing time-to-hire by streamlining job advertisement and screening processes (Chen, 2023). The mechanism appears straightforward: by focusing attention on capabilities rather than identity markers, these tools help organisations access previously overlooked talent pools.

Blind hiring practices facilitated by AI systems that automatically redact identifying information from applications further enhance equity in recruitment. Evidence suggests that such interventions significantly increase the likelihood that candidates from underrepresented groups receive fair evaluation based on qualifications alone (Chen, 2023; Jabagi et al., 2025; Van Den Broek et al., 2021; Xiong & Kim, 2025). Importantly, the most successful implementations maintain human oversight of AI recommendations while using carefully curated bias-neutral training data.

4.3.2 Enhancing Equity in Performance Evaluation and Advancement

Traditional performance management processes often rely on cognitive biases that disadvantage certain groups. AI analytics have the potential to address these limitations by introducing greater objectivity and standardisation. Advanced systems now analyse performance data along multiple dimensions, flagging potential disparities when certain groups consistently receive evaluations that are inconsistent with their objective performance indicators. Text analytics tools examine narrative evaluations to identify differential language patterns; for example, when male employees are described in terms of achievement. Simultaneously, women employees are evaluated based on their interpersonal attributes (Nyathani, 2023).

The most sophisticated applications can be extended beyond detection to prescriptions. AI systems that analyse historical promotion patterns can identify when employees from specific backgrounds systematically wait longer for advancement, despite equivalent qualifications. By standardizing evaluation frameworks and applying consistent rubrics across managers, these tools reduce idiosyncratic biases in assessments. The emerging evidence suggests that organisations leveraging such technologies as "fairness watchdogs" are better positioned to ensure high-potential individuals from all backgrounds receive equitable recognition and advancement opportunities (Achara & Chhabra, 2025).

4.3.3 Fostering Inclusive Communication and Culture

The daily fabric of organisational culture is woven through numerous interactions. AI tools now monitor and improve the inclusivity of workplace communication at scale (Inuwa-Dutse, 2023; Régis, 2024). Real-time language analysis systems process text in emails, chats, and documents to identify potentially biased or exclusionary terminology, offering immediate alternatives that promote a more inclusive discourse. Sentiment analysis algorithms, when applied to aggregated employee communication or survey responses, reveal patterns that might otherwise remain invisible, such as certain groups consistently expressing feelings of marginalisation or teams developing toxicity in their communication norms. This "listening at scale" provides organisations with unprecedented insight into the lived experiences of inclusion, enabling more targeted interventions.

AI-powered chatbots further support inclusive cultures by serving as always available resources. These systems answer questions about diversity policies, facilitate anonymous reporting of concerns, and provide personalised guidance on inclusive practices. By embedding DEI principles into everyday workflows, such tools reinforce organisational values while lowering barriers to information and support, particularly for employees who may hesitate to approach human representatives. The key to effectiveness lies in designing systems with robust DEI safeguards, including careful control of training inputs and continuous oversight of outputs.

4.3.4 Advancing Accessibility and Accommodation

True inclusion encompasses providing equitable access to employees with disabilities or different linguistic backgrounds (Shore et al., 2018). AI has dramatically improved accessibility technologies, with speech-to-text and text-to-speech applications enabling real-time captioning of meetings and enhanced screen readers for visually impaired employees (Reddy et al., 2023). These tools fundamentally alter who can fully participate in workplace activities, aligning with the equity dimension of the DEI by providing tailored resources that address diverse needs. Language translation represents another domain in which AI enhances inclusion (Nataraj et al., 2024). Real-time translation services powered by advanced machine learning models enable seamless collaboration across linguistic boundaries. This technology ensures that employees are not marginalised because of language differences, and that everyone can contribute to their preferred tongue. This is particularly valuable in global organisations, where language barriers might otherwise impede equal participation. Personalisation algorithms further advance accessibility by adapting digital interfaces to individual needs, for instance, by simplifying layouts for neurodivergent users or implementing colour-blind friendly design elements (Wald, 2021). These applications directly advance equity by aligning technology with diverse cognitive and physical characteristics and reducing barriers to full participation.

4.3.5 Enabling Data-Driven DEI Strategy

Aside from direct interventions, AI provides powerful analytical capabilities that transform how organisations approach the DEI strategy. Machine learning models analyse workforce data to identify hidden patterns of inequality, such as detecting pay gaps correlated with gender or race after controlling for role and experience, spotting departments lagging in representation, and highlighting disproportionate attrition among specific demographics (Chandana et al., 2024; Eichenseer et al., 2025; Pandya et al., 2022; Talpur et al., 2024). Predictive analytics enables scenario planning for DEI initiatives, forecasting the likely impact of proposed policies, such as diverse interview panels or targeted mentorship programs. This capability shifts the DEI strategy from intuition-driven to evidence-based, allowing organisations to allocate resources to interventions with the highest probability of meaningful impact. AI dashboards for DEI serve as accountability mechanisms, regularly monitor progress against goals, and provide early warnings when metrics begin to diverge from their targets. By making patterns of inequality visible and tracking intervention effectiveness in real time, these tools help organisations maintain focus on DEI objectives amidst competing priorities.

4.3.6 Organisational Case Studies: Successes and Cautions

The theoretical possibilities of AI for DEIB take concrete form in organisational implementations, with both successes and instructive failures offering valuable practical insights. Amazon's attempt to develop an AI recruitment tool in the mid-2010s is a cautionary tale (Fritts & Cabrera, 2021; Martin, 2022). The system, trained on historical resume data, inadvertently learned to penalise indicators of women applicants, such as participation in women's organisations. This algorithmic bias mirrored the male dominance in Amazon's historical hiring patterns. Despite efforts to correct the model, Amazon ultimately disbanded its project when it could not guarantee bias-free recommendations. This case illustrates how historical bias in the training data translates into algorithmic discrimination and underscores the necessity of rigorous bias auditing before deployment.

By contrast, Unilever's implementation of AI in entry-level recruitment demonstrates the positive potential of these technologies (Agnihotri & Bhattacharya, 2024). Facing global applicant volumes, Unilever deployed a combination of AI-driven gamified assessments and video interview analysis to standardise candidate screenings. By deliberately using a balanced training dataset and focusing on behavioural indicators rather than traditional resume credentials, Unilever achieved a 16% increase in the diversity of candidates, advancing to final interviews (Psico-smart, 2024). This success stemmed from fundamental process redesign, replacing inherently biased resume screening with skills-based assessment rather than merely adding AI to existing practices.

T-Mobile's experience with AI-powered language analysis offers another success story (Kondra et al., 2025). By implementing Textio, an AI-powered solution that optimises recruiting language for inclusivity, T-Mobile enhances its job postings and recruits emails to engage a more diverse candidate pool. This strategic implementation resulted in a 17% increase in applications from women, accelerated the hiring process by filling positions an average of five days faster, and improved the HR team's understanding of the DEI issues. This case demonstrates how AI tools can effectively support inclusive recruitment messaging, representing a practical application that delivers measurable results while reinforcing an organisation's commitment to diversity, equity, and inclusion (Kondra et al., 2025).

Implementing AI fairness audits in technology companies such as Microsoft and IBM represents an emerging best practice (Bellamy et al., 2018; Weerts et al., 2023). These organisations have established dedicated audit teams to continuously evaluate AI systems for bias before and after deployment. One approach for addressing bias in machine learning models is continuous monitoring and iterative refinement. IBM's development of the AI Fairness 360 toolkit exemplifies this commitment by providing a framework for detecting, understanding, and mitigating bias in machine-learning models (Bellamy et al., 2018). For instance, in real-world applications, biases can emerge because of cultural or contextual differences in data. A hypothetical scenario might involve an algorithm scoring employees in a particular region lower on collaboration metrics because of an overlooked culturally specific collaboration pattern. Such disparities highlight the need for ongoing vigilance rather than one-time validation, reinforcing the principle that fairness must be actively maintained throughout a model's lifecycle. Microsoft's Fairlearn aligns with IBM's emphasis on continuous monitoring and iterative refinement to address AI bias. It treats fairness as a sociotechnical challenge, offering disaggregated evaluation and mitigation techniques across preprocessing, in-training, and post-processing stages. By identifying the allocation and quality-of-service harms, Fairlearn reinforces that fairness must be actively managed throughout the lifecycle of a model. This supports

IBM's stance that bias mitigation requires ongoing vigilance, especially when addressing contextual and cultural disparities (Weerts et al., 2023).

4.4 Challenges and Risks of AI in DEIB

While AI offers transformative potential for advancing DEIB initiatives in organisations, it simultaneously introduces substantial challenges and ethical risks that require careful consideration. Without vigilant management, AI systems risk reinforcing existing biases or generating novel forms of discrimination that undermine their objectives they aim to support.

4.4.1 Perpetuation of Historical Inequities Through Training Data

AI systems fundamentally learn from historical data, inherit and potentially amplify the biases embedded within these datasets (Mehrabi et al., 2021). When deployed in an organisational context, these systems risk reproducing past patterns of discrimination rather than disrupting them (Pot et al., 2021; Van Giffen et al., 2022; Wei et al., 2025). For instance, when an AI hiring tool analyses past hiring decisions dominated by homogeneous groups, it may inadvertently learn to prefer candidates that resemble the dominant demographic, systematically disadvantaging others (Fritts & Cabrera, 2021; Martin, 2022).

This phenomenon manifests when algorithmic systems identify correlations between protected characteristics and positive outcomes, and then operationalise these correlations in ways that perpetuate exclusionary practices. Organisations have discovered this problem when implementing recruitment tools that systematically downgrade candidates from underrepresented groups because historical hiring data reflect biased selection patterns (Hofeditz et al., 2022; Van Den Broek et al., 2021, 2021; Xiong & Kim, 2025). Such cases demonstrate that AI systems merely reflect fairness, or lack thereof, in their training data. When historical organisational data contain embedded societal biases, AI systems risk replicating these patterns and potentially amplifying them through feedback loops, which further entrench disadvantages.

4.4.2 Opacity in Decision-Making Processes

Many sophisticated AI algorithms, particularly complex neural networks and deep learning models, operate as "black boxes" with decision-making logic that remains opaque even to their developers (Hofeditz et al., 2022; Martin, 2022; Xiong & Kim, 2025). This lack of transparency creates significant challenges for accountability and trust, especially in DEI contexts, where explanation and justification of decisions are paramount for building organisational legitimacy.

When employees face rejection by an AI screening tool or receive negative performance evaluations from algorithmic systems, stakeholders require transparency to verify the fairness of these determinations (Jabagi et al., 2025). Without explainability mechanisms, biases may persist undetected within the algorithmic systems. The development of Explainable AI (XAI) techniques represents an important advancement in addressing this challenge by making AI decisions more interpretable and contestable (Adadi & Berrada, 2018). Without such measures, the rationale underlying algorithmic determinations remains obscured, undermining the organisational capacity to identify bias or implement corrective measures.

This opacity also raises significant legal and compliance concerns, as emerging regulatory frameworks increasingly assert individuals' right to meaningful explanations for algorithmic decisions that affect their employment or advancement opportunities. Organisations deploying opaque systems risk not only ethical breaches but also potential legal liability as regulatory scrutiny intensifies.

4.4.3 Reductionist Approaches to Complex Social Phenomena

DEIB challenges typically emerge from the complex structural and deeply nuanced social dynamics that algorithmic systems may struggle to adequately capture or address. Organisations face the significant risk of viewing AI as a technical panacea for fundamental human problems that require contextual understanding and qualitative judgment. Subtle contextual factors, such as cultural differences, power dynamics, or individual experiences of inclusion, often make it difficult for AI systems to quantify or incorporate into their analyses. Excessive reliance on algorithmic solutions may lead organisations to neglect essential human judgment and qualitative input in DEIB initiatives. For example, a purely algorithm-driven approach might emphasise easily measurable diversity metrics while overlooking more nuanced aspects of inclusion such as psychological safety or belonging. Such reductionist approaches risk creating a false sense of progress by focusing exclusively on quantifiable outcomes, rather than addressing the root causes of inequity.

AI should function as an augmentation rather than a replacement for human empathy and expertise in navigating complex DEIB challenges (Raisch & Krakowski, 2021). When organisations delegate DEIB responsibilities primarily to algorithmic systems, subtle forms of exclusion and bias may persist undetected simply because these systems lack the sensitivity to identify them. Therefore, algorithmic recommendations must be situated within the comprehensive DEIB strategies that acknowledge the limitations of computational approaches to social problems.

4.4.4 Surveillance Tensions and Privacy Implications

Certain AI applications designed to promote inclusion, such as tools monitoring communication for biased language or analysing behavioural data for exclusionary patterns, introduce significant privacy concerns that may undermine trust and psychological safety. Employees frequently report discomfort when subjected to algorithmic surveillance of their communications or interactions, even when the stated purpose aligns with the creation of more inclusive environments (Kosta, 2022; Murphy, 2017; Newlands, 2021).

This tension creates a delicate balance between leveraging AI to foster respectful organisational cultures and respecting individual privacy and autonomy (Schlund & Zitek, 2024). To mitigate these risks, organisations must implement robust data governance frameworks and maintain transparent communication with employees regarding surveillance practices. Furthermore, collecting sensitive demographic data necessary for bias detection requires careful handling to comply with privacy regulations and to prevent potential misuse. Finding an appropriate equilibrium between analytics capabilities and privacy protection represents an ongoing challenge for organisations seeking to promote inclusion through technological means while respecting individual rights and maintaining trusting relationships with employees.

4.4.5 Competing Fairness Criteria and Value Trade-offs

Even with sophisticated bias mitigation techniques, ensuring fairness across all demographic groups simultaneously is mathematically impossible owing to the inherent trade-offs between different fairness criteria. Recall that improving equity in one dimension, such as equalizing error rates between demographic groups, may come at the expense of other important considerations, including overall system precision and the creation of new inequalities across different population segments. (Hort et al., 2024; Voria et al., 2025). These trade-offs require normative judgments about which conception of fairness is prioritised in specific organisational contexts.

These decisions have significant ethical implications and should ideally involve diverse stakeholders rather than remain exclusively within the purview of technical teams. When these deliberations exclude affected communities, the resulting algorithmic conception of fairness may diverge substantially from what impacted employees or the broader society would consider only. Moreover, certain subtle forms of bias, such as linguistic biases or proxy variables for protected attributes, are exceptionally difficult to eliminate entirely from algorithmic systems (Warner & Sloan, 2021). These challenges create persistent risks that AI systems initially deemed fair may produce inequitable outcomes in practice, necessitating continuous monitoring, evaluation, and refinement, rather than one-time validation processes.

4.4.6 Ambiguous Accountability Structures

The integration of AI into human resource functions complicates the traditional accountability frameworks. When algorithmic systems produce discriminatory outcomes, responsibility may be diffused across multiple parties such as technology vendors, algorithm developers, and organisations deploying these tools, creating accountability gaps that leave bias unaddressed. Organisations implementing AI for DEI purposes must establish clear governance policies and oversight committees specifically tasked with regularly reviewing algorithmic decisions and their impact on workforce equity. Forward-thinking organisations should establish dedicated algorithmic audit teams with diverse expertise, including ethicists, legal advisors, and representatives from affected groups, to systematically examine the effects of AI systems on employment outcomes. From a legal perspective, regulatory bodies have increasingly clarified that organisations cannot evade liability for discriminatory outcomes by attributing decisions to algorithmic systems. This evolving regulatory landscape creates an urgency for organisations to rigorously validate AI systems for fairness prior to deployment and maintain ongoing oversight throughout their operational lifecycle.

The challenges of leveraging AI for DEIB initiatives extend across the technical, ethical, and organisational dimensions. Implementing algorithmic systems without adequate safeguards risks introducing or amplifying discrimination, undermining transparency, reducing complex social phenomena to oversimplified metrics, eroding privacy, enforcing contested notions of fairness, and creating accountability vacuums. Organisations must approach AI implementation with appropriate humility, recognizing both its significant potential and equally significant limitations in addressing deeply rooted social inequities. Understanding these multifaceted challenges constitutes an essential prerequisite for developing robust frameworks that harness AI capabilities in the service of authentic organisational inclusion.

4.5 A Proposed Sociotechnical Framework for AI-Enabled DEIB

Organisations are increasingly deploying AI to address the persistent challenges in DEIB. This integration emerges from a convergence of organisational justice theories and computational fairness frameworks, suggesting that AI can enhance procedural justice by applying consistent evaluation criteria in which human judgment has historically been faltered. While promising, these applications create tension between technical approaches to fairness and socially constructed notions of justice.

This article presents an integrated framework for responsible AI-DEIB implementation that reconciles theoretical tensions while providing practical guidance for organisations.

4.5.1 Theoretical Foundations and Framework Integration

Our framework builds upon the intersection of justice theories, sociotechnical system perspectives, critical approaches, and psychological frameworks. It acknowledges the paradox that systems designed to overcome human bias may reproduce discrimination, if not guided by diverse perspectives, critical awareness, and ethical principles. The framework presents a cyclical, iterative approach with four interconnected domains: (1) value-driven design and data, (2) sociotechnical implementation, (3) governance and critical safeguards, and (4) evaluative feedback. Throughout the cycle, the framework emphasises participatory approaches and continuous learning, aligned with organisational justice principles.

4.5.2 Framework Components

4.5.2.1 Value-Driven Design and Data

The foundation of AI-DEIB integration begins with the explicit articulation of organisational values and justice priorities. Rather than treating AI implementation as a primary technical exercise, this stage demands that organisations make value judgments about which forms of fairness matter most in their context in which decisions cannot be outsourced to algorithms. Based on organisational justice theory's distinctions between distributive, procedural, and interactional forms of fairness, organisations must determine their priorities when these forms of justice become tense (Chauhan et al., 2025; Greenberg, 1987; S. A. M. Harriott, 2025).

This value-clarification process should involve diverse stakeholders, particularly those from underrepresented groups, in participatory design. When employees who experience exclusion contribute to defining fairness metrics and system requirements, the resulting AI applications are more likely to reflect diverse perspectives rather than to reinforce dominant viewpoints. This participatory approach combines technological solutionism by ensuring that technical developments remain anchored in substantive, rather than ceremonial, inclusion efforts.

Following value clarification, organisations must assemble training data with awareness of how historical patterns may embed bias (Drage & Mackereth, 2022; Mehrabi et al., 2021). Pre-processing techniques should be employed to audit and modify training data and remove or counterbalance historical biases (Shahrezaei et al., 2023). For example, if historical promotion data show gender disparities, organisations might apply pre-processing algorithms that statistically adjust for these patterns before using the data to train promotion-recommendation systems. Alternatively, they might enhance data collection to ensure adequate representation of underrepresented groups, even when they are historically underrepresented in the organisation.

The framework acknowledges the tensions between individual and group fairness, recognizing the impossibility theorem that different fairness metrics often cannot be simultaneously satisfied. Rather than treating this as a purely technical challenge, organisations should explicitly link fairness definitions to stated DEIB values and document these choices for transparency. This documentation becomes essential for ongoing evaluation and potential adjustment, as values and technical capabilities evolve.

4.5.2.2 Sociotechnical Implementation

The sociotechnical implementation domain recognises that technology operates within complex social contexts and that technical solutions alone cannot solve deeply embedded social problems (Orlikowski, 2007). The framework integrates AI applications within organisational processes, emphasizing technical fairness measures and organisational change management.

Technical implementation involves selecting and applying appropriate algorithmic fairness approaches (Voria et al., 2025). These range from in-processing techniques that incorporate fairness constraints directly into algorithms to post-processing techniques that adjust the model outputs to ensure fair results (Petersen et al., 2021). Organisations may deploy blind screening of résumés using natural language processing to strip away demographic information, implement balanced representation requirements in candidate recommendation systems, or build communication analysis tools that identify exclusionary language patterns.

However, the framework emphasises that these technical implementations must be paired with organisational interventions addressing the underlying power structures (Koutsikouri et al., 2024; Raisch & Krakowski, 2021). Following sociotechnical systems theory, the framework positions AI tools as enablers within broader change initiatives rather than standalone solutions. These organisational interventions include leadership development around inclusive practices, creating psychological safety in teams, and redesigning workflows to accommodate diverse working styles, all of which are informed by insights from AI systems.

The implementation must also consider the social dynamics of technology adoption. Based on institutional theory, organisations should be mindful of internal acceptance and external legitimacy concerns. Internally, this means engaging employees at all levels in co-creating implementation plans, building transparent communication about AI use, and providing adequate and regular training. Externally, it involves benchmarking against industry standards, while developing distinctive approaches that reflect the organisation's specific context and values.

4.5.2.3 Governance and Critical Safeguards

The governance domain establishes controls to ensure that AI systems advance, rather than undermine, DEIB objectives. Drawing on critical perspectives such as critical race theory and intersectionality frameworks, this domain builds safeguards against perpetuating systemic forms of discrimination (Crenshaw, 1995). It establishes oversight mechanisms that maintain human accountability for algorithmic decision making while ensuring conformity with ethical principles and legal requirements. A multilevel governance approach begins with technical safeguards built directly into the AI systems. These include XAI methods that make algorithmic reasoning transparent, fairness constraints that maintain demographic parity or equal opportunity across protected groups, and intersectional approaches that address compounding forms of disadvantages (Angelov et al., 2021). Rather than treating individuals as members of a single demographic category, algorithms should consider how multiple identities interact to create unique experiences of inclusion or exclusion.

Beyond technical safeguards, organisational governance includes human oversight at key decision points. This "human-in-the-loop" approach ensures that algorithmic recommendations receive appropriate contextual evaluation, particularly for high-stakes decisions like hiring, promotion, or performance assessment (Wu et al., 2022). Governance bodies should include diverse representations, with specific attention paid to involving individuals with both technical expertise and lived experience of exclusion. These bodies should have the clear authority to question algorithmic recommendations and override them when necessary. Figure 4.2 illustrates the proposed framework.

Transparency forms another critical safeguard, with organisations establishing clear policies about when and how AI informs DEIB decisions. Employees should understand what data are collected, how they are used, and what influence they have on decisions that affect them. This transparency builds trust while creating accountability for both algorithmic and human decision-makers. It also enables external stakeholders to evaluate an organisation's DEIB commitments against actual practices, aligning with institutional theory's emphasis on organisational legitimacy. The framework additionally emphasises ethical guardrails, drawing on care ethics, human rights standards, and domain-specific ethical principles. These include respecting individual dignity and autonomy, ensuring accessibility across cognitive differences, and prioritizing well-being within diverse communities. By embedding these principles in governance structures, organisations ensure that the efficiency and scale benefits from AI do not come at the expense of human-centered values.

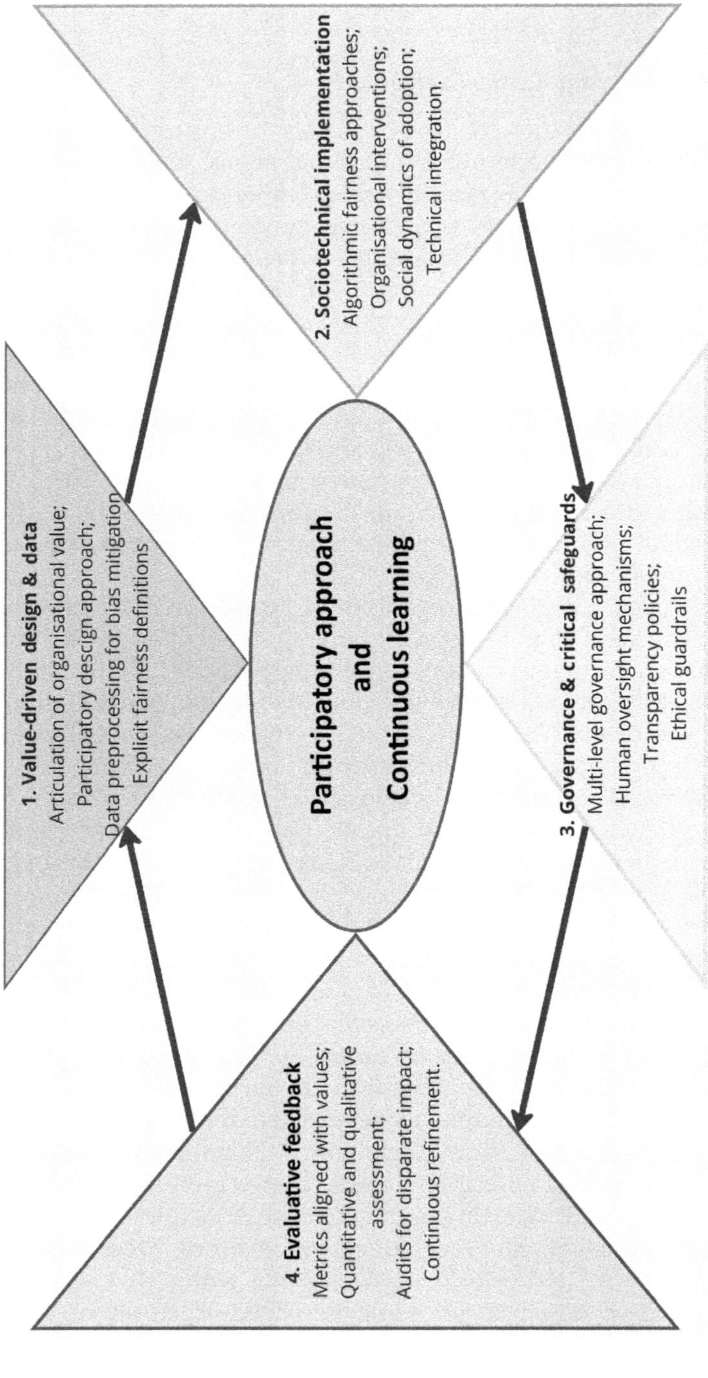

FIGURE 4.2
Framework for AI-DEIB integration.

4.5.2.4 Evaluative Feedback

The final domain of the framework establishes continuous evaluation and learning processes that complete the cycle by informing ongoing refinement. This domain measures both the intended outcomes and unintended consequences of AI-DEIB integration, creating accountability for results while generating insights for improvement. The evaluation begins by defining clear metrics that align with organisational values. These typically include representation metrics across organisational levels, equity indicators, such as pay gaps or promotion rates, and inclusion measures from employee surveys or communication patterns. AI systems can assist in generating these metrics by analysing patterns that might escape human attention. However, the framework emphasises complementing quantitative metrics with a qualitative assessment of lived experiences, particularly from underrepresented groups.

Feedback mechanisms should detect improvements and potential harm. Regular audits should examine whether algorithmic systems produce disparate impacts across demographic groups, while listening sessions can surface exclusionary experiences that metrics may miss. Organisations should implement formal mechanisms for employees to question or challenge algorithmic recommendations, creating bidirectional accountability. Following the diversity climate theory, one way of measuring an organisation's DEIB impact is through analysing three dimensions: intentionality, programming and praxis (Cachat-Rosset et al., 2021; Cachat-Rosset and Klarsfeld, 2023). These dimensions not only assess the employees' views about the organisation's commitment to and values of DEIB through its policies and programs, but also the managers' attitude and behaviour towards diverse employees, the realization equity and fostering of employees' sense of belonging in the organisation. The cycle is completed as evaluation insights inform refinement across other domains. For instance, unexpected disparities might trigger the reexamination of training data or fairness definitions, while positive outcomes in one business unit might lead to expanded implementation in others. This adaptive approach recognises that organisational contexts and AI capabilities evolve continuously, requiring ongoing recalibration rather than one-time solutions.

4.6 Practical Implementation Guidance

The integrated framework presented in Section 4.5 navigates the promise and paradox of AI in DEIB initiatives. It acknowledges that meaningful progress requires technical sophistication, paired with critical awareness and participatory approaches. Organisations can leverage AI's pattern-recognition capabilities and scale while avoiding technological solutionism by systematically addressing value alignment, sociotechnical implementation, governance safeguards, and continuous evaluation. This approach positions AI as a tool for illumination and accountability, rather than as a substitute for the problematic organisational change processes required for genuinely inclusive workplaces.

Organisations that successfully implement this framework will develop AI approaches to DEIB that enhance rather than replace human judgment, reflect on rather than obscure diverse perspectives, and advance substantive rather than merely symbolic inclusion. The journey requires ongoing dialogue between technical and social disciplines, theory and practice, and diverse stakeholders whose experiences must inform both the development and evaluation of AI systems in the service of organisational justice. This section offers practical implementation guidance using the Amazon, T-Mobile, Unilever, Microsoft, and IBM case studies. The guidance provides ideas on how the framework can be implemented.

4.6.1 Strategic Implementation Pathways

The journey toward effective AI-enabled DEIB requires a thoughtful progression from low-to high-stakes applications. Drawing lessons from successes and failures in the field, organisations benefit from a phased implementation strategy that builds capabilities while minimizing potential harm. The contrast between Amazon's failed recruiting tool and its successful implementations at T-Mobile and Unilever illuminates this pathway (Kondra et al., 2025; Psico-smart, 2024). While Amazon attempted to transform high-stakes hiring decisions with AI trained on historically biased data, leading to discriminatory outcomes and project abandonment, more successful organisations began with targeted, lower-risk applications before scaling to more consequential domains.

Organisations should begin with low-risk, high-value applications that deliver immediate benefits while building institutional capacity for more complex implementations. T-Mobile's experience with Textio exemplifies this approach, by analysing and improving language in job descriptions, they achieved a 17% increase in women applicants without disrupting core decision processes (Kondra et al., 2025; Psico-smart, 2024). Language analysis tools provide an ideal entry point, enabling organisations to identify exclusionary patterns in communications, enhance inclusive messaging across channels, and monitor whether diverse voices receive equitable attention in meetings and decision forums. These applications build essential governance capabilities while generating tangible improvements in the inclusion signals.

As organisations gain confidence and capacity, they can progress to more ambitious process redesign applications that address the structural barriers to inclusion. Unilever's approach represents this second phase, rather than attempting to debase traditional resume screening (Amazon's unsuccessful approach), they fundamentally reimagined assessment through gamified evaluations that directly measure capabilities. This approach allows organisations to replace proxy-based evaluations with direct skills measurement, implement blind evaluation mechanisms that mask potentially triggering demographic characteristics, and develop alternative pathways for candidates with non-traditional backgrounds but transferable skills. Although they require more substantial change management, these interventions address root causes rather than the symptoms of exclusion. Figure 4.3 presents an overview of the implementation phase.

Only after establishing robust governance mechanisms should organisations implement AI in high-stakes domains such as hiring, promotion, or performance evaluation. As Amazon's experience demonstrates, the reputational and practical risks of premature implementation are substantial. Organisations advancing to this phase must implement comprehensive bias testing before deployment, establish clear human-AI collaboration protocols that maintain human responsibility for final decisions, and create documented override mechanisms for cases where human judgment detects potential inequities that algorithms miss. These safeguards ensure that even as organisations leverage AI's efficiency in consequential decisions, they maintain ethical guardrails to prevent harm.

4.6.2 Implementation Structures and Processes

Successful AI-DEIB integration requires organisational structures that transcend traditional functional silos while creating robust accountability mechanisms. The mature implementations in Microsoft and IBM demonstrate how intentional governance structures enable responsible AI use in people's processes.

Cross-functional collaboration forms the foundation for effective implementation. Rather than treating AI-DEIB as either a technical initiative or a diversity program, organisations should create integrated teams that bring together diverse expertise. These teams should include technology specialists who understand algorithmic fairness approaches, organisational development professionals who can integrate AI within broader cultural initiatives, legal experts familiar with evolving regulations, DEIB practitioners with domain knowledge of inclusion challenges, and business leaders who ensure practical alignment with operational realities. Microsoft's Aether Committee exemplifies this approach, bringing together varied perspectives to evaluate AI applications for potential bias before deployment[1].

Formal governance structures create essential guardrails for AI-DEIB integration. Following IBM's and Microsoft's lead, organisations should establish AI ethics committees with diverse memberships and apparent authority to review applications that affect people's decisions[2]. These committees should oversee algorithmic impact assessments that evaluate potential disparate impacts before deployment and document mitigation

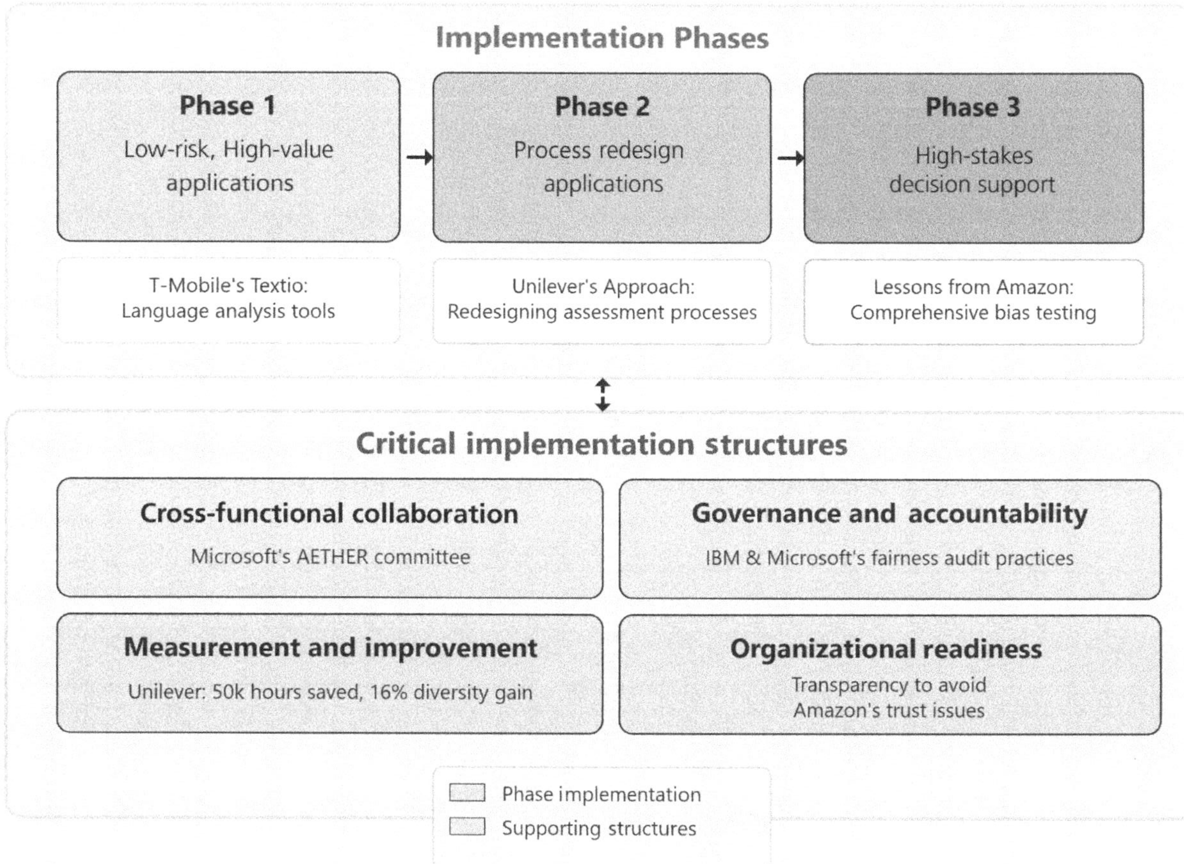

FIGURE 4.3
Implementation phases and critical implementation structures for AI-DEIB.

strategies for the identified risks. Regular fairness audits provide ongoing evaluations of AI system outputs, with protocols for addressing discovered issues, as demonstrated by IBM's detection and correction of biased performance evaluations. Transparent reporting to both leadership and affected employees maintains accountability, while building trust in AI applications. These mechanisms acknowledge that achieving fairness is not a one-time achievement, but a continuous process of detection and improvement.

Measurement and continuous improvement processes transform the AI-DEIB implementation from a static initiative to an adaptive learning system. Organisations should define multidimensional success metrics that capture both operational improvements, such as Unilever's 50,000 hours of recruiter time saved, and substantive inclusion outcomes, such as a 16% increase in candidate diversity (Psico-smart, 2024). Establishing baseline measurements before implementation enables meaningful comparison of progress, while regular disparate impact analysis across demographic groups identifies potential inequities that require correction. Feedback channels for affected individuals create bidirectional accountability, allowing employees to question or challenge the algorithmic assessments that affect them. Formal learning processes allow implementation teams to analyse successes and failures, and refine approaches based on emerging insights. This commitment to measurement and learning prevents the framework from becoming a one-time implementation, instead creating a cycle of continuous improvement that adapts to evolving organisational contexts and capabilities.

4.6.3 Building Organisational Readiness

Beyond technical and structural elements, successful AI-DEIB integration requires cultural preparedness throughout the organisation. Without attentive development of organisational readiness, even technically superior solutions may falter because of resistance, misuse, or misunderstanding. Educational initiatives build essential AI literacy among stakeholders, creating realistic expectations about what AI can or cannot accomplish in DEIB efforts. By demystifying AI capabilities while acknowledging limitations, organisations reduce techno-optimism, which leads to overreliance and techno-skepticism, which blocks the adoption of beneficial applications. These educational programs should target different stakeholder groups with appropriate depth, providing executives with strategic understanding, managers with practical application knowledge, and employees with awareness of how AI influences their experiences.

Transparency in AI use builds trust and prevents the "black box" problem that undermines Amazon's recruiting tool (Fritts & Cabrera, 2021; Martin, 2022). Organisations should communicate with employees when and how

AI influences decisions, explaining the rationale for algorithm use, the nature of data being analysed, and the relationship between algorithmic recommendations and human judgment. This transparency reduces suspicion while increasing engagement with AI-enabled processes.

Participatory design approaches ensure that AI applications address actual, rather than presumed, inclusion barriers. By involving diverse employees in defining fairness criteria and system requirements, organisations capture varied perspectives on inclusion challenges while building ownership of solutions. These workshops may include exercises mapping current exclusion points in processes, collaborative development of fairness definitions for specific contexts, and joint design of AI application user experiences. The resulting systems are more likely to reflect diverse needs rather than reinforce dominant perspectives.

Change management support enables managers to effectively incorporate AI insights into their leadership practices, while maintaining appropriate human judgment. As front-line implementers of many AI-DEIB applications, managers require training to interpret algorithmic outputs, recognise potential limitations or biases, and integrate insights into contextual understanding. Support resources may include interpretation guides for AI-generated recommendations, decision frameworks balancing algorithmic and human judgment, and coaching through complex cases in which equity considerations create tension with algorithmic outputs.

Together, these readiness activities establish the foundation for successful technical implementation, while building an organisational buy-in essential for sustained impact. They acknowledge that AI-DEIB integration represents not merely a technical change but also a sociotechnical transformation requiring aligned capabilities across human and technological dimensions.

4.7 Future Directions in AI for DEIB

Despite promising advancements at the intersection of AI and DEIB, significant research gaps remain. This section outlines the critical future directions that could substantively advance both scholarship and practice in this emerging field.

4.7.1 From Short-Term Solutions to Longitudinal Understanding

The predominance of short-term case studies and simulations underscores the need for longitudinal research to examine the sustained impacts of AI-driven DEIB interventions. Questions persist about whether initial diversity gains translate into improved retention and advancement over time, or whether benefits plateau without corresponding cultural transformation. Rigorous temporal analysis would illuminate whether AI truly catalyses lasting organisational change or merely produces ephemeral improvements in demographic representation. This is not to say that we assume AI can do the transformative work by itself. Parallel to building such longitudinal research, organisations ought to start financing initiatives or programs that enables such AI-facilitated cultural transformation. We can imagine those programs can be in the form of promoting AIS literacy among underrepresented population within and beyond universities to diversify the talent pool of AI creators. Alternatively, it can be in the form of running executive classes for AI creators and management professionals on practising DEIB values and interventions. AI can then shape organisations' increasing interests in DEIB interventions are no longer because of market pressure or utilitarian motives, but more because of wanting to make a real social impact.

4.7.2 Expanding Beyond Recruitment

Although recruitment represents a logical entry point for AI in DEIB work, other dimensions of inclusion remain underexplored. AI applications for enhancing recruiters or manager's attitude and perspectives toward employees with historically disadvantaged identities, improving fair and equal pay structure, boosting team dynamics, mitigating microaggressions, and fostering day-to-day inclusion warrant further investigation. Natural language processing offers preliminary insights, but integrating audio analysis and computer vision can detect nonverbal exclusionary behaviours in workplace interactions. Although such integration can be a breakthrough in advancing workplace equity, deeper and more careful research of its innovation is warranted for fears of the captured audio-visuals evolving into a database or tool for profiling people and, in turn, perpetuating further gender or racial biases (West et al., 2019; Ruberg and Ruelos, 2020). Similarly, personalised AI-driven learning experiences tailored to diverse cultural backgrounds represent fertile grounds for development. These "softer" dimensions of inclusion may yield the most profound organisational transformations.

4.7.3 Frameworks, Guidelines, and Interdisciplinary Collaboration

The field urgently requires comprehensive frameworks that integrate ethical AI principles with organisational DEIB objectives. "DEIB by Design" guidelines in which analogous to privacy by design approaches, would provide structured methodologies for embedding equity considerations throughout the AI development cycle. Such frameworks should emerge from interdisciplinary collaborations spanning computer science, organisational psychology, the humanities and social sciences, legal studies, and user-centered design. The technical challenges of algorithmic fairness must be addressed alongside the questions of user perception, legal compliance, and AI literacy among practitioners.

4.7.4 Policy Evolution and Global Context

The evolution of regulatory landscapes will significantly shape this domain. Given the sophistication of AI in improving workplace equity and the technology's reliance on historical data for generating results, policymakers should view it as an window of opportunity to support the innovation and, at the same time, to further regulate the enforcement of privacy laws that effectively protect citizens' personal information stored digitally. In this way, policymakers can not only restore the public's trust in disclosing relevant digital personal information for better job opportunity but also encourage organisations to comply with DEIB objectives.

Furthermore, research should examine how emergent policies influence organisational behaviour and DEIB outcomes. Do biased audit requirements effectively mitigate algorithmic discrimination, or do they inadvertently discourage AI adoption due to liability concerns? Additionally, comparative studies across diverse cultural contexts would illuminate how conceptions of fairness and inclusion vary globally, enabling more nuanced approaches to AI implementation in different legal and cultural environments. This is especially important.

4.7.5 Diversity in Development and Emerging Technologies

The composition of AI development teams represents another understudied variable. Systematic research examining whether diverse creators produce measurably less biased systems would provide valuable insights, potentially strengthening the case of representation within the AI industry itself. By diverse AI creators we mean not only of diverse demographic attributes but also disciplinary expertise (West et al., 2019). Addressing the social implications of AI development necessitates experts beyond the computer science community. Experts in the gender, indigenous or critical race studies fields, for instance, can contribute in efforts to detect historical data that are assumed to be universal but have, in fact, erased minorities' lived experiences (Losh and Wernimont, 2019; Perez, 2019). Additionally, integrating AI with emerging technologies such as virtual and augmented reality offers novel opportunities for experiential learning and perspective-taking in DEI contexts. Similarly, AI-powered organisational network analysis can reveal exclusionary patterns within communication structures, providing appropriate privacy safeguards.

4.8 Conclusion

Integrating AI into organisational DEIB initiatives represents a significant opportunity and substantial risk. Our sociotechnical framework addresses this tension by emphasizing participatory design, critical awareness, and continuous evaluation, rather than viewing AI as a technical panacea for fundamental human challenges. Successful implementation requires organisations to make explicit value judgments about fairness priorities, embed technical solutions within broader cultural transformations, establish robust governance mechanisms with diverse oversight, and maintain continuous learning processes. The proposed implementation pathways recommend starting with low-risk applications, such as communication analysis before progressing to process redesign and eventually high-stakes decision domains, incrementally building organisational capacity and safeguards.

Future research must address significant gaps, mainly longitudinal studies examining sustained impacts beyond initial diversity gains, applications beyond recruitment that enhance day-to-day inclusion, and comprehensive frameworks integrating ethical AI principles with organisational DEIB objectives. Cross-cultural research exploring how conceptions of fairness vary globally would enable more nuanced implementation approaches across different contexts. Simultaneously, studies on development team diversity might strengthen the case for representation within the AI industry. Ultimately, AI should function as a tool for illumination and accountability, rather than as a substitute for complex organisational change processes. By thoughtfully navigating these sociotechnical challenges, organisations can leverage AI to enhance procedural justice while building genuinely inclusive workplaces that reflect diverse perspectives and advance substantive rather than symbolic inclusion.

Notes

1 Review of literature (~60 studies) by Microsoft's AETHER group (AI, Ethics, and Effects in Engineering and Research) about how users can over-rely on AI (accepting incorrect outputs), its consequences, and strategies to mitigate that risk. www.microsoft.com/en-us/research/wp-content/uploads/2022/07/aether-datadoc-082522.pdf

2 Describes IBM's organizational approach to ethical AI governance, including its AI Ethics Board, use of watsonx.governance tools, risk-management, bias monitoring, model metadata tracking, and ensuring compliance and transparency throughout AI lifecycle. www.ibm.com/think/insights/a-look-into-ibms-ai-ethics-governance-framework

References

Abbink, K., & Harris, D. (2019). In-group favouritism and out-group discrimination in naturally occurring groups. *PLOS ONE, 14*(9), e0221616. https://doi.org/10.1371/journal.pone.0221616

Abdelhalim, E., Anazodo, K. S., Gali, N., & Robson, K. (2024). A framework of diversity, equity, and inclusion safeguards for chatbots. *Business Horizons, 67*(5), 487–498. https://doi.org/10.1016/j.bushor.2024.03.003

Achara, A., & Chhabra, A. (2025). Watching the AI watchdogs: A fairness and robustness analysis of AI safety moderation classifiers (Version 1). arXiv. https://doi.org/10.48550/ARXIV.2501.13302

Adadi, A., & Berrada, M. (2018). Peeking inside the black-box: A survey on explainable artificial intelligence (XAI). *IEEE Access, 6*, 52138–52160. https://doi.org/10.1109/ACCESS.2018.2870052

Agnihotri, A., & Bhattacharya, S. (2024). *Artificial Intelligence for Hiring and Induction: The Unilever Experience*. SAGE Publications: SAGE Business Cases Originals. https://doi.org/10.4135/9781071921470

Ahrweiler, P., Späth, E., Siqueiros García, J. M., Capellas, B. L., & Wurster, D. (2025). Inclusive technology co-design for participatory AI. In P. Ahrweiler (Ed.), *Participatory Artificial Intelligence in Public Social Services* (pp. 35–62). Springer Nature Switzerland. https://doi.org/10.1007/978-3-031-71678-2_2

Akbarighatar, P., Pappas, I., & Vassilakopoulou, P. (2023). A sociotechnical perspective for responsible AI maturity models: Findings from a mixed-method literature review. *International Journal of Information Management Data Insights, 3*(2), 100193. https://doi.org/10.1016/j.jjimei.2023.100193

Aminizadeh, S., Heidari, A., Dehghan, M., Toumaj, S., Rezaei, M., Jafari Navimipour, N., Stroppa, F., & Unal, M. (2024). Opportunities and challenges of artificial intelligence and distributed systems to improve the quality of healthcare service. *Artificial Intelligence in Medicine, 149*, 102779. https://doi.org/10.1016/j.artmed.2024.102779

Angelov, P. P., Soares, E. A., Jiang, R., Arnold, N. I., & Atkinson, P. M. (2021). Explainable artificial intelligence: An analytical review. *WIREs Data Mining and Knowledge Discovery, 11*(5), e1424. https://doi.org/10.1002/widm.1424

Balliet, D., Wu, J., & De Dreu, C. K. W. (2014). Ingroup favoritism in cooperation: A meta-analysis. *Psychological Bulletin, 140*(6), 1556–1581. https://doi.org/10.1037/a0037737

Banaji, M. R., Fiske, S. T., & Massey, D. S. (2021). Systemic racism: Individuals and interactions, institutions and society. *Cognitive Research: Principles and Implications, 6*(1), 82. https://doi.org/10.1186/s41235-021-00349-3

Barocas, S., Hardt, M., & Narayanan, A. (2023). *Fairness and Machine Learning: Limitations and Opportunities*. The MIT Press.

Bellamy, R. K. E., Dey, K., Hind, M., Hoffman, S. C., Houde, S., Kannan, K., Lohia, P., Martino, J., Mehta, S., Mojsilovic, A., Nagar, S., Ramamurthy, K. N., Richards, J., Saha, D., Sattigeri, P., Singh, M., Varshney, K. R., & Zhang, Y. (2018). *AI Fairness 360: An extensible toolkit for detecting, understanding, and mitigating unwanted algorithmic bias*. In *arXiv [cs.AI]*. 1–20 https://doi.org/10.48550/ARXIV.1810.01943

Bent, J. R. (2020). Is algorithmic affirmative action legal? *The Georgetown Law Journal, 108*, 803–853.

Brown, R. (2000). Social identity theory: Past achievements, current problems and future challenges. *European Journal of Social Psychology, 30*(6), 745–778. https://doi.org/10.1002/1099-0992(200011/12)30:6%3C745::AID-EJSP24%3E3.0.CO;2-O

Buolamwini, J., & Gebru, T. (2018). Gender shades: Intersectional accuracy disparities in commercial gender classification. In *Proceedings of the 1st Conference on Fairness, Accountability and Transparency*.

Cachat-rosset, G., K. A. Carillo, and A. Klarsfeld. 2021. Exploring the impact of diversity climate on individual work role performance: A novel approach. *European Management Review*, 19 (2):248–62. doi:10.1111/emre.12483

Cachat-Rosset, G., & Klarsfeld, A. (2023). Diversity, equity, and inclusion in artificial intelligence: An evaluation of guidelines. *Applied Artificial Intelligence, 37*(1), 1–28. https://doi.org/10.1080/08839514.2023.2176618

Cappelli, P., Tambe, P., & Yakubovich, V. (2018). Artificial intelligence in human resources management: Challenges and a path forward. *SSRN Electronic Journal*. https://doi.org/10.2139/ssrn.3263878

Carter-Veale, W. Y., Cresiski, R. H., Sharp, G., Lankford, J. D., & Ugarte, F. (2025). Cultivating change: An evaluation of departmental readiness for faculty diversification. *Frontiers in Education, 10*, 1553580. https://doi.org/10.3389/feduc.2025.1553580

Caton, S., & Haas, C. (2024). Fairness in machine learning: A survey. *ACM Computing Surveys, 56*(7), 1–38. https://doi.org/10.1145/3616865

Chandana, C., Sarkar, A., Deshmukh, K., Kulkarni, P., Bikash Acharjee, P., & Lourens, M. (2024). Analysing employee management using machine learning techniques and solutions in human resource management. In *2024 4th International Conference on Innovative Practices in Technology and Management (ICIPTM)*, 1–6. https://doi.org/10.1109/ICIPTM59628.2024.10563736

Chauhan, V., Shaik, A. S., & Gupta, M. (2025). Consumer response to diversity and inclusion initiatives in hospitality: Role of brand integrity and materialism. *Journal of Hospitality Marketing & Management, 34*(4), 1–18. https://doi.org/10.1080/19368623.2025.2449857

Chen, Z. (2023). Collaboration among recruiters and artificial intelligence: Removing human prejudices in employment. *Cognition, Technology & Work, 25*(1), 135–149. https://doi.org/10.1007/s10111-022-00716-0

Cirillo, D., Catuara-Solarz, S., Morey, C., Guney, E., Subirats, L., Mellino, S., Gigante, A., Valencia, A., Rementeria, M. J., Chadha, A. S., & Mavridis, N. (2020). Sex and gender differences and biases in artificial intelligence for biomedicine and healthcare. *Npj Digital Medicine, 3*(1), 81. https://doi.org/10.1038/s41746-020-0288-5

Conyers, A., & Fields, C. W. (2025). Paralyzing DEI: A critical analysis of anti-CRT legislation. *Administrative Theory & Praxis*, 1–19. https://doi.org/10.1080/10841806.2025.2449783

Crenshaw, K. (Ed.). (1995). *Critical race theory: The key writings that formed the movement*. New Press.

Crenshaw, K. (2022). *On Intersectionality: Essential Writings*. The New Press.

Dattner, B., Chamorro-Premuzic, T., Buchband, R., & Schettler. (2019). The legal and ethical implications of using AI in hiring. *Harvard Business Review*. https://hbr.org/2019/04/the-legal-and-ethical-implications-of-using-ai-in-hiring

D'Ignazio, C., & Klein, L. F. (2020). *Data feminism*. The MIT Press.

Dolata, M., Feuerriegel, S., & Schwabe, G. (2022). A sociotechnical view of algorithmic fairness. *Information Systems Journal, 32*(4), 754–818. https://doi.org/10.1111/isj.12370

Drage, E., & Mackereth, K. (2022). Does AI debias recruitment? Race, gender, and AI's "Eradication of Difference." *Philosophy & Technology*, *35*(4), 89. https://doi.org/10.1007/s13347-022-00543-1

Eichenseer, P., Hans, L., & Winkler, H. (2025). A data-driven machine learning model for forecasting delivery positions in logistics for workforce planning. *Supply Chain Analytics*, *9*, 100099. https://doi.org/10.1016/j.sca.2024.100099

Ellul, D. B., & Friggieri, J. (2025). A thriving future through diversity, equity, and inclusion for resilient and innovative communities. In *Poverty—Associated Risks and Alleviation [Working Title]*. IntechOpen. https://doi.org/10.5772/intechopen.1008368

Favaretto, M., De Clercq, E., & Elger, B. S. (2019). Big Data and discrimination: Perils, promises and solutions. A systematic review. *Journal of Big Data*, *6*(1), 12. https://doi.org/10.1186/s40537-019-0177-4

Fritts, M., & Cabrera, F. (2021). AI recruitment algorithms and the dehumanization problem. *Ethics and Information Technology*, *23*(4), 791–801. https://doi.org/10.1007/s10676-021-09615-w

Gao, G. Y., Lyu, J., & Cheung, C. M. K. (2024). AI recruiting and workplace diversity, equity, and inclusion: A literature analysis. *Pacific-Asia Conference on Information Systems*. pp 1–17. https://aisel.aisnet.org/pacis2024/track08_digtech_fow/track08_digtech_fow/4

Gholidoust, A. (2024). Unleashing creativity: The interplay of innovation and diversity. In H. Taherdoost (Ed.), *Advances in Business Strategy and Competitive Advantage* (pp. 47–76). IGI Global. https://doi.org/10.4018/979-8-3693-3759-2.ch003

Greenberg, J. (1987). A taxonomy of organizational justice theories. *The Academy of Management Review*, *12*(1), 9. https://doi.org/10.2307/257990

Guo, S., & Lei, L. (2025). Combating racism with critical race theory: Theorizing social movement learning from anti-racism movements in Canada. *Educational Philosophy and Theory*, 1–14. https://doi.org/10.1080/00131857.2025.2451338

Harriott, S. A. M. (2025). Breaking the silence: Creating brave spaces for true diversity, equity, inclusion, and belonging in the modern workplace. In S. A. M. Harriott (Ed.), *Advances in Human Resources Management and Organizational Development* (pp. 1–40). IGI Global. https://doi.org/10.4018/979-8-3693-3876-6.ch001

Heyder, T., Passlack, N., & Posegga, O. (2023). Ethical management of human-AI interaction: Theory development review. *The Journal of Strategic Information Systems*, *32*(3), 101772. https://doi.org/10.1016/j.jsis.2023.101772

Hilton, M. (2025). Building inclusive culture: Leveraging soft skills to enhance DEIB in organizational settings. In S. A. Harriott (Ed.), *Advances in Human Resources Management and Organizational Development* (pp. 249–274). IGI Global. https://doi.org/10.4018/979-8-3693-3876-6.ch010

Hofeditz, L., Clausen, S., Rieß, A., Mirbabaie, M., & Stieglitz, S. (2022). Applying XAI to an AI-based system for candidate management to mitigate bias and discrimination in hiring. *Electronic Markets*, *32*(4), 2207–2233. https://doi.org/10.1007/s12525-022-00600-9

Hogg, M. A. (2016). Social identity theory. In S. McKeown, R. Haji, & N. Ferguson (Eds.), *Understanding Peace and Conflict Through Social Identity Theory* (pp. 3–17). Springer International Publishing. https://doi.org/10.1007/978-3-319-29869-6_1

Hort, M., Chen, Z., Zhang, J. M., Harman, M., & Sarro, F. (2024). Bias mitigation for machine learning classifiers: A comprehensive survey. *ACM Journal on Responsible Computing, 1*(2), 1–52. https://doi.org/10.1145/3631326

Hummerick, J. D. (2020). Reprogramming fairness: Affirmative action in algorithmic criminal sentencing. *HRLR Online*. https://hrlr.law.columbia.edu/files/2020/04/8-Humerick_FINAL.pdf

Inuwa-Dutse, I. (2023). FATE in AI: Towards algorithmic inclusivity and accessibility. *Equity and Access in Algorithms, Mechanisms, and Optimization*, 1–14. https://doi.org/10.1145/3617694.3623233

Jabagi, N., Croteau, A.-M., Audebrand, L. K., & Marsan, J. (2025). Do algorithms play fair? Analysing the perceived fairness of HR-decisions made by algorithms and their impacts on gig-workers. *The International Journal of Human Resource Management, 36*(2), 235–274. https://doi.org/10.1080/09585192.2024.2441448

Jay, A. D. (2025). Ethical leadership and diversity, equity, inclusion, and belonging: A synergistic approach to inclusive excellence. In S. A. Harriott (Ed.), *Advances in Human Resources Management and Organizational Development* (pp. 275–304). IGI Global. https://doi.org/10.4018/979-8-3693-3876-6.ch011

Jerab, D. (2025). Diversity and inclusion in leadership positions. *SSRN Electronic Journal*. https://doi.org/10.2139/ssrn.5086945

Jiang, L., Qin, X., Yam, K. C., Dong, X., Liao, W., & Chen, C. (2023). Who should be first? How and when AI-human order influences procedural justice in a multi-stage decision-making process. *PLOS ONE, 18*(7), e0284840. https://doi.org/10.1371/journal.pone.0284840

King, M. (2024). *A Qualitative Phenomenological Study: The Experiences of Blacks in Executive Leadership at Predominantly White Institutions*. Marymount University.

Kleinberg, J., Ludwig, J., Mullainathan, S., & Sunstein, C. R. (2020). Algorithms as discrimination detectors. *Proceedings of the National Academy of Sciences, 117*(48), 30096–30100. https://doi.org/10.1073/pnas.1912790117

Kondra, S., Medapati, S., Koripalli, M., Chandra Nandula, S. R. S., & Zink, J. (2025). AI and Diversity, Equity, and Inclusion (DEI): Examining the potential for AI to mitigate bias and promote inclusive communication. *Journal of Artificial Intelligence and Machine Learning, 3*(1). https://doi.org/10.55124/jaim.v3i1.249

Kosta, E. (2022). Algorithmic state surveillance: Challenging the notion of agency in human rights. *Regulation & Governance, 16*(1), 212–224. https://doi.org/10.1111/rego.12331

Koutsikouri, D., Hylving, L., Bornemark, J., & Lindberg, S. (2024). Human judgment in the age of automated decision-making systems. In I. Constantiou, M. P. Joshi, & M. Stelmaszak (Eds.), *Research Handbook on Artificial Intelligence and Decision Making in Organizations* (pp. 144–159). Edward Elgar Publishing. https://doi.org/10.4337/9781803926216.00017

Lee, M. K., Jain, A., Cha, H. J., Ojha, S., & Kusbit, D. (2019a). Procedural justice in algorithmic fairness: Leveraging transparency and outcome control for fair algorithmic mediation. *Proceedings of the ACM on Human-Computer Interaction, 3*(CSCW), 1–26. https://doi.org/10.1145/3359284

Lee, M. K., Kusbit, D., Kahng, A., Kim, J. T., Yuan, X., Chan, A., See, D., Noothigattu, R., Lee, S., Psomas, A., & Procaccia, A. D. (2019b). WeBuildAI: Participatory framework for algorithmic governance. *Proceedings of the ACM on Human-Computer Interaction, 3*(CSCW), 1–35. https://doi.org/10.1145/3359283

Losh, E., & Wernimont, J. (Eds.). (2019). *Bodies of information: Intersectional feminism and the digital humanities*. University of Minnesota Press.

Marabelli, M., Zaza, S., Masiero, S., Li, J. (Lydia), & Chudoba, K. (2023). Diversity, equity and inclusion in the AIS: Challenges and opportunities of remote conferences. *Information Systems Journal, 33*(6), 1370–1395. https://doi.org/10.1111/isj.12458

Martin, K. (2022). *Ethics of Data and Analytics: Concepts and Cases* (1st ed.). Auerbach Publications. https://doi.org/10.1201/9781003278290

McClung, K. T., & Linton, D. M. (2024). *An Introduction to Inclusive Healthcare Design* (1st ed.). Routledge. https://doi.org/10.4324/9781003414902

Mehrabi, N., Morstatter, F., Saxena, N., Lerman, K., & Galstyan, A. (2021). A survey on bias and fairness in machine learning. *ACM Computing Surveys, 54*(6), 1–35. https://doi.org/10.1145/3457607

Meyer, C., & Baogui, D. (2025). Examining the gender gap in STI policy: Addressing factors contributing to women's underrepresentation. *Sage Open, 15*(1), 21582440251320769. https://doi.org/10.1177/21582440251320769

Mikołajczyk-Bareła, A., & Grochowski, M. (2023). *A survey on bias in machine learning research* (Version 1). arXiv. https://doi.org/10.48550/ARXIV.2308.11254

Morrow, R., & Brown, D. (1994). *Critical Theory and Methodology*. SAGE Publications, Inc. https://doi.org/10.4135/9781452243696

Murphy, M. H. (2017). Algorithmic surveillance: The collection conundrum. *International Review of Law, Computers & Technology, 31*(2), 225–242. https://doi.org/10.1080/13600869.2017.1298497

Nasir, S., Khan, R. A., & Bai, S. (2024). Ethical framework for harnessing the power of AI in healthcare and beyond. *IEEE Access, 12*, 31014–31035. https://doi.org/10.1109/ACCESS.2024.3369912

Nataraj, V., Liao, W.-H., Chang, Y.-S., Chiang, C.-Y., Lin, C.-Y., Lin, Y.-A., & Day, M.-Y. (2024). Generative AI in multimodal cross-lingual dialogue system for inclusive communication support. In *2024 IEEE International Conference on Information Reuse and Integration for Data Science (IRI)*, 204–209. https://doi.org/10.1109/IRI62200.2024.00051

Newlands, G. (2021). Algorithmic surveillance in the gig economy: The organization of work through Lefebvrian conceived space. *Organization Studies, 42*(5), 719–737. https://doi.org/10.1177/0170840620937900

Ntoutsi, E., Fafalios, P., Gadiraju, U., Iosifidis, V., Nejdl, W., Vidal, M., Ruggieri, S., Turini, F., Papadopoulos, S., Krasanakis, E., Kompatsiaris, I., Kinder-Kurlanda, K., Wagner, C., Karimi, F., Fernandez, M., Alani, H., Berendt, B., Kruegel, T., Heinze, C., … Staab, S. (2020). Bias in data-driven artificial intelligence systems—An introductory survey. *WIREs Data Mining and Knowledge Discovery, 10*(3), e1356. https://doi.org/10.1002/widm.1356

Nyathani, R. (2023). AI in performance management: Redefining performance appraisals in the digital age. *Journal of Artificial Intelligence & Cloud Computing, 2*(4), 1–5.

Orlikowski, W. J. (2007). Sociomaterial practices: Exploring technology at work. *Organization Studies, 28*(9), 1435–1448. https://doi.org/10.1177/0170840607081138

Pandya, F. H., Jain, S., & Atchyutuni, N. (Eds.). (2022). *Building Resilient Organizations: Predicaments & Prospects*. Routledge. https://doi.org/10.4324/9781003313663

Perez, C. C. (2019). *Invisible Women: The Sunday Times Number One Bestseller Exposing the Gender Bias Women Face Every Day*. Random House.

Petersen, F., Mukherjee, D., Sun, Y., & Yurochkin, M. (2021). *Post-processing for Individual Fairness* (Version 1). arXiv. https://doi.org/10.48550/ARXIV.2110.13796

Pettigrew, T. F., & Tropp, L. R. (2008). How does intergroup contact reduce prejudice? Meta-analytic tests of three mediators. *European Journal of Social Psychology, 38*(6), 922–934. https://doi.org/10.1002/ejsp.504

Pettigrew, T. F., Tropp, L. R., Wagner, U., & Christ, O. (2011). Recent advances in intergroup contact theory. *International Journal of Intercultural Relations, 35*(3), 271–280. https://doi.org/10.1016/j.ijintrel.2011.03.001

Pot, M., Kieusseyan, N., & Prainsack, B. (2021). Not all biases are bad: Equitable and inequitable biases in machine learning and radiology. *Insights into Imaging, 12*(1), 13. https://doi.org/10.1186/s13244-020-00955-7

Psico-smart. (2024). *The Impact of Psychometric Testing on Diverse Candidate Selection in Hiring Processes*. Psico-smart Editorial Team. https://psico-smart.com/en/blogs/blog-the-impact-of-psychometric-testing-on-diverse-candidate-selection-in-hiring-processes-162910

Rahimi, S. A., Shrivastava, R., Brown-Johnson, A., Caidor, P., Davies, C., Idrissi Janati, A., Kengne Talla, P., Madathil, S., Willie, B. M., & Emami, E. (2024). EDAI framework for integrating equity, diversity, and inclusion throughout the lifecycle of AI to improve health and oral health care: Qualitative study. *Journal of Medical Internet Research, 26*, e63356. https://doi.org/10.2196/63356

Raisch, S., & Krakowski, S. (2021). Artificial intelligence and management: The automation–augmentation paradox. *Academy of Management Review, 46*(1), 192–210. https://doi.org/10.5465/amr.2018.0072

Reddy, V. M., Vaishnavi, T., & Kumar, K. P. (2023). Speech-to-text and text-to-speech recognition using deep learning. In *2023 2nd International Conference on Edge Computing and Applications (ICECAA)*, 657–666. https://doi.org/10.1109/ICECAA58104.2023.10212222

Régis, C. (Ed.). (2024). *Human-centered AI: A multidisciplinary perspective for policymakers, auditors, and users* (First edition). Chapman & Hall: CRC Press.

Rothwell, W. J., Ealy, P. L., Campbell, J., & EBSCOhost (Eds.). (2022). *Rethinking organizational diversity, equity, and inclusion: A step-by-step guide for facilitating effective change*. Routledge.

Ruberg, B., & Ruelos, S. (2020). Data for queer lives: How LGBTQ gender and sexuality identities challenge norms of demographics. *Big Data & Society, 7*(1), 2053951720933286.

Salib, P. N. (2022). Big data affirmative action. *Northwestern University Law Review, 117*(3). https://scholarlycommons.law.northwestern.edu/nulr/vol117/iss3/4/

Sanyi, A., Byiringiro, S., Dabiri, S., Jacobson, M., Boyd, A., Ogunniyi, M. O., Morris, A. A., Kohn, R., Dickert, N. W., Lane-Fall, M. B., Lewis, E. F., Halpern, S. D., & Fanaroff, A. C. (2025). Measuring representativeness in clinical trials. *Circulation, 151*(5), 318–330. https://doi.org/10.1161/CIRCULATIONAHA.124.070299

Schlund, R., & Zitek, E. M. (2024). Algorithmic versus human surveillance leads to lower perceptions of autonomy and increased resistance. *Communications Psychology, 2*(1), 53. https://doi.org/10.1038/s44271-024-00102-8

Shahrezaei, M. H., Loughran, R., & Daid, K. M. (2023). Pre-processing techniques to mitigate against algorithmic bias. In *2023 31st Irish Conference on Artificial Intelligence and Cognitive Science (AICS)*, 1–4. https://doi.org/10.1109/AICS60730.2023.10470759

Sherf, E. N., Parke, M. R., & Isaakyan, S. (2021). Distinguishing voice and silence at work: Unique relationships with perceived impact, psychological safety, and burnout. *Academy of Management Journal*, *64*(1), 114–148. https://doi.org/10.5465/amj.2018.1428

Shore, L. M., Cleveland, J. N., & Sanchez, D. (2018). Inclusive workplaces: A review and model. *Human Resource Management Review*, *28*(2), 176–189. https://doi.org/10.1016/j.hrmr.2017.07.003

Singh, R., & Ramdeo, S. (2023). From diversity to inclusion in the workplace. In R. Singh & S. Ramdeo, *Contemporary Perspectives in Human Resource Management and Organizational Behavior* (pp. 79–98). Springer International Publishing. https://doi.org/10.1007/978-3-031-30225-1_5

Solomon, B. C., Hall, M. E. K., & Muir (Zapata), C. P. (2022). When and why bias suppression is difficult to sustain: The asymmetric effect of intermittent accountability. *Academy of Management Journal*, *65*(5), 1450–1476. https://doi.org/10.5465/amj.2020.0441

Talpur, N., Gakeer Alier, N. C., Matsom, H., Afifi Abdullah, M. H., & Khatoon, S. (2024). Predicting employee performance using machine learning to enhance workforce efficiency. In *2024 8th International Conference on Computing, Communication, Control and Automation (ICCUBEA)*, 1–4. https://doi.org/10.1109/ICCUBEA61740.2024.10774749

Tambe, P., Cappelli, P., & Yakubovich, V. (2019). Artificial intelligence in human resources management: Challenges and a path forward. *California management review*, *61*(4), 15–42. https://doi.org/10.1177/0008125619867910

Theodorou, A., & Dignum, V. (2020). Towards ethical and socio-legal governance in AI. *Nature Machine Intelligence*, *2*(1), 10–12. https://doi.org/10.1038/s42256-019-0136-y

Truby, J. (2020). Governing artificial intelligence to benefit the UN sustainable development goals. *Sustainable Development*, *28*(4), 946–959. https://doi.org/10.1002/sd.2048

Van Den Broek, E., Sergeeva, A., Universiteit Amsterdam, Huysman Vrije, M., & Universiteit Amsterdam. (2021). When the machine meets the expert: An ethnography of developing AI for hiring. *MIS Quarterly*, *45*(3), 1557–1580. https://doi.org/10.25300/MISQ/2021/16559

Van Giffen, B., Herhausen, D., & Fahse, T. (2022). Overcoming the pitfalls and perils of algorithms: A classification of machine learning biases and mitigation methods. *Journal of Business Research*, *144*, 93–106. https://doi.org/10.1016/j.jbusres.2022.01.076

Villegas-Galaviz, C., & Martin, K. (2024). Moral distance, AI, and the ethics of care. *AI & SOCIETY*, *39*(4), 1695–1706. https://doi.org/10.1007/s00146-023-01642-z

Voria, G., Sellitto, G., Ferrara, C., Abate, F., De Lucia, A., Ferrucci, F., Catolino, G., & Palomba, F. (2025). Fairness-aware practices from developers' perspective: A survey. *Information and Software Technology*, *182*, 107710. https://doi.org/10.1016/j.infsof.2025.107710

Wald, M. (2021). AI data-driven personalisation and disability inclusion. *Frontiers in Artificial Intelligence*, *3*, 571955. https://doi.org/10.3389/frai.2020.571955

Warner, R., & Sloan, R. H. (2021). Making artificial intelligence transparent: Fairness and the problem of proxy variables. *Criminal Justice Ethics*, *40*(1), 23–39. https://doi.org/10.1080/0731129X.2021.1893932

Weerts, H., Dudik, M., Edgar, R., Jalali, A., Lutz, R., & Madaio, M. (2023). Fairlearn: Assessing and improving fairness of AI systems. *Journal of Machine Learning Research*, *24*, 1–8.

Wei, X., Kumar, N., & Zhang, H. (2025). Addressing bias in generative AI: Challenges and research opportunities in information management. *Information & Management*, *62*(2), 104103. https://doi.org/10.1016/j.im.2025.104103

West, S.M., Whittaker, M. and Crawford, K. (2019). Discriminating systems: Gender, race and power in AI. AI Now Institute. Retrieved from https://ainowinstitute.org/publications/discriminating-systems-gender-race-and-power-in-ai-2

Wilder, T. L., & Stratchan, N. E. (2025). Artificial intelligence-enhanced interview success: Leveraging eye-tracking and cognitive measures to support self-regulation in college students with attention-deficit/hyperactivity disorder. *Education Sciences*, *15*(2), 165. https://doi.org/10.3390/educsci15020165

Williams, T. M. (2023). *Underrepresentation of African American Women in Senior Leadership: A Qualitative Study*. California Baptist University.

Wu, X., Xiao, L., Sun, Y., Zhang, J., Ma, T., & He, L. (2022). A survey of human-in-the-loop for machine learning. *Future Generation Computer Systems*, *135*, 364–381. https://doi.org/10.1016/j.future.2022.05.014

Xiong, Y., & Kim, J. K. (2025). Who wants to be hired by AI? How message frames and AI transparency impact individuals' attitudes and behaviors toward companies using AI in hiring. *Computers in Human Behavior: Artificial Humans*, *3*, 100120. https://doi.org/10.1016/j.chbah.2025.100120

5

Generative AI and Nonbinary Representation: Identifying Bias in Generative AI Systems

Jay Rosenbaum

5.1 Introduction

Picture a nonbinary person. What do they look like? What is their age? Their race? How do they dress? Generative AI systems tend to lack of nuance in their generations (Drushchak, 2024). The systems tend to smooth out outliers and create images along standard deviations, overfitting (Hawkins, 2004) to the most common entries into the dataset. This leads to problems with diversity and inclusion as the generated images of people are generally Eurocentric, conventionally attractive, young, slender, able, and cisgender-appearing. It can be challenging to generate images of people outside of those limited views without actively specifying. Even when specifically requesting different diverse image sets, the people shown still cling to those modalities of bias. The bias of image generation systems has been noted with regards to careers, race, and binary gender representation, and these issues remain ongoing in these systems (Zhou et al., 2024). This research, however, is concerned specifically with nonbinary representation. As the political climate changes and transgender people are coming under attack, it feels salient and timely to examine the images generated representing nonbinary people and what they mean for representation.

Initially, prompt-driven image generation systems were completely devoid of nonbinary representation as illustrated later in this document. With later models, it is now possible to generate images of nonbinary people, however, they still fit a stereotype. This research seeks to answer the question: *What are the stereotypes and biases associated with non-binary people in generative AI systems?* And *What are the implications for the stereotypical images generated?* This research will explore different generative AI models using the same prompt set in each image generation system and establish a comprehensive exploration of AI representations of nonbinary people to date, examining

 DOI: 10.1201/9781003591078-7

the stereotypes and biases that emerge. By examining these representations, the research will identify and analyze the stereotypes present in generative images of nonbinary people, examining the potential harms they can perpetuate.

This research was developed through an exploration of existing image generation systems. It seeks to examine how larger out-of-the-box systems have bias built in and further perpetuate that bias. The focus is specifically on the attribute of nonbinary gender to examine the expression of bias. The value of this research is in exploring the work of larger corporate systems, to see the results generated without fine control. This provided an opportunity to view the inherent biases of these datasets and learn how these systems work and how they affect each other.

5.1.1 Literature Review

Existing literature on the subject of gender representation in AI is limited and often binary. AI classification of gender dates back to SexNet (Golomb et al., 1991) and has encompassed facial classification, gait (Azhar et al., 2022), language (Verhoeven et al., 2016), and body shape (Q. Wu & Guo, 2014). These systems are almost always binary by nature. The Gender Shades project (Buolamwini, 2018) discusses how facial classification systems are often biased, particularly towards women of colour. The authors note that this research was necessarily binary as the systems analysed only allowed for binary classification. The ways AI systems perceive gender has been explored in depth by Rosenbaum (2022) resulting in several artistic explorations of nonbinary gender and AI generation and interpretation and by Scheuerman et al. (2019) exploring facial recognition and classification systems. Wu et al. (2024) explored the biases inherent in Stable Diffusion (2024); however, they note that their exploration is focused on binary genders. This analysis revealed how neutral prompts defaulted to masculine presentations, and that when the gender is changed, woman may be placed in less authoritative positions. This observation is critical to understanding the AI hierarchies that are assumed by generative AI systems. Parks (2025) explores how transgender and neurodivergent people are represented in generative AI and briefly explores the representation of individuals at this intersection in text to image generators, revealing that these systems perpetuate stereotypes that can further harm marginalized communities. AI agents and perceived gender crossed with the prisoner's dilemma are explored in depth in the paper *AI's assigned gender affects human-AI cooperation* (Bazazi et al., 2024) revealing tendencies to mistrust or exploit their partner based on their gender, whether or not the partner is a human or an AI agent. Ranjan, Gupta, and Singh explore the gender biases in OpenAI's o1 mini model by analyzing the stereotypes and gendered patterns present in generated personas (Ranjan et al., 2025). Ghosh and Caliskan (2023) discuss the stereotypical presentation of people in stable diffusion and prove the tendency to default to whiteness and also the tendency to over sexualize some women of color. Their paper specifically also analyses the lack of nonbinary representation and echoes the depersonalization shown in this research.

5.2 Methods

This research examines the biases present in large-scale image generation systems, with a specific focus on nonbinary gender identities. The study employs a comparative approach, generating and analysing images from pretrained generative AI systems and evaluating their outputs using independent AI-based classifiers. Images were generated using the specified prompts with no additional tailoring.

5.2.1 Systems used

- AttnGAN (Xu et al., 2018)
- Clip+VQGAN (Miranda, 2021)
- Midjourney V1 – V6 (Holz, 2022)
- Stable Diffusion 1.4 (Mostaque, 2022)
- Stable Diffusion XL (Podell et al., 2023)
- Flux.1 [Schnell] (Blattmann et al., 2024)

5.2.2 Prompt Methods

To assess how gender bias manifests in its outputs, a selection of prompts was used. For each prompt, the first image generated was accepted, and the visual elements within these outputs were analyzed using contrastive language-image pretraining (Ibarrola et al., 2022) through Clip Interrogator 2 (pharmapsychotic, 2025) and Imagga (Image Recognition API, Computer Vision AI – Imagga, 2023). These prompts were tested:

- "A man"
- "A woman"
- "A non-binary person"

5.2.3 Qualitative Analysis of Generated Images

The generated images were assessed for recurring patterns that indicated systemic bias. The key variables examined included:

- Presence or absence of a discernible human figure
- Apparent skin tone of the generative figures using the Fitzpatrick Skin Scale (Fitzpatrick, 1997)
- Apparent age of generative figures

5.2.4 Secondary Classification Using Clip Interrogator and Imagga

To investigate how secondary AI systems interpret the generated images, selected outputs were submitted to Clip Interrogator, a classification tool that uses Clip (Radford et al., 2021), a system that underpins many generative AI systems by creating captions based on the image submitted. Imagga is an image tagging tool that supports key words. With the Imagga results, the top six words were chosen.

5.2.5 Ethical Considerations

This study acknowledges the ethical implications of AI bias in gender representation. The research does not seek to define gender but to highlight the limitations and gaps in existing generative AI models. The results of Clip Interrogator may include some offensive terminology which has been left in for full accountability. The findings contribute to broader discussions on AI fairness and representation; however, it is acknowledged that this is a small snapshot and further research is needed.

5.3 Results

The generated images, prompts, apparent age, apparent skin tone, Clip Interrogator captions, Imagga tags, and generative system used have been broken down into a table for comparative purposes (see Table 5.1). The language of the Clip Interrogator system has not been altered from the AI response and may contain spelling mistakes and inappropriate content. Viewer discretion is advised as some responses may be potentially offensive.

This section will be broken down into the table of results and graphs showing the diversity breakdowns of each and a short summary of the findings. Nonparametric tests were used throughout due to ordinal and non-normally distributed data. Kruskal–Wallis H tests assessed group-level differences, followed by Bonferroni-corrected Mann–Whitney U tests for pairwise comparisons.

5.3.1 Table of Images

TABLE 5.1

Images with apparent age, Fitzpatrick scale, imagga tags, clip interrogator caption, prompt, and system

Image	Apparent Age	Apparent Fitzpatrick Skin Scale	Clip Interrogator	Imagga tags	System
Prompt: "A Man"					
	N/a	N/a	A man flying through the air while riding a skateboard, a picture, inspired by Anna Füssli, abstract illusionism, damaged webcam image, reflected in giant mirror, hands hidden, covered in transparent cloth	Suit, business, man, businessman, office, male	AttnGAN
	40	2	A man flying through the air while riding a skateboard, a picture, inspired by Anna Füssli, abstract illusionism, damaged webcam image, reflected in giant mirror, hands hidden, covered in transparent cloth	Suit, business, man, businessman, office, male	Clip+ VQGAN
	24	4	A shirtless man standing in front of a painting, by Aurél Bernáth, instagram, visual art, jeffrey wright, wearing black shorts, in a oil painting style, metzinger	Swimming trunks, swimsuit, garment, clothing, man, muscular	Stable Diffusion 1.4

	62	2	A black and white painting of a man with a mustache, a character portrait, inspired by Henry Woods, digital art, eugene de blaas, clint eastwood, portrait of a Victorian-era duke, digital painting	Bowtie, necktie, garment, man, male, portrait	SDXL
	50	2	A close up of a man with a beard, a photorealistic painting, inspired by Alexander Scott, marton csokas, blonde british man, gif, Tomas Kinkade	Person, smile, people, adult, portrait, smiling	Flux Schnell
	N/a	2	A painting of a man with a beard and no shirt, a digital painting, inspired by Henry Macbeth-Raeburn, figurative art, christopher shy, hastur, jesse mccree, jacket over bare torso	Cave, geological formation, stone, religion, old, dark	Midjourney V1

(Continued)

TABLE 5.1 (Continued)

Images with apparent age, Fitzpatrick scale, imagga tags, clip interrogator caption, prompt, and system

Image	Apparent Age	Apparent Fitzpatrick Skin Scale	Clip Interrogator	Imagga tags	System
	N/a	N/a	A painting of a man standing in the middle of a field, digital art, by Artur Tarnowski, beksinski and dan mumford, portrait of hide the pain harold, clothed in ancient suit, style of simon stalenhag	Suit, person, man, lighting, male, jacket	Midjourney V2
	N/a	N/a	A painting of a man standing in front of a window, digital art, inspired by Beksinski, paranoid android, wojtek fus, symmetrical long head, slenderman	Cloak, covering, people, person, attractive, dress	Midjourney V3
	34	2	A close up of a man wearing a hat, a character portrait, inspired by Sam Spratt, digital art, portrait of rugged male ranger, concept art of single boy, a beautiful artwork illustration, anthro portrait	Beard, man, male, portrait, handsome, guy	Midjourney V4

	78	2	A black and white photo of a man wearing a hat, by Etienne Delessert, pexels contest winner, photorealism, portrait of a old, looking happy, stockholm city portrait, years old	Grandfather, man, senior, male, portrait, person	Midjourney V5
	20	3	A painting of a man wearing a hat, a photorealistic painting, inspired by Sam Spratt, Artstation contest winner, portrait of a rugged young man, nick alm, oil on canvas 8 k, rob rey and kentarõ miura style	Person, portrait, attractive, pretty, hat, face	Midjourney V6
Prompt: "A Woman"					
	N/a	N/a	A reflection of a person laying on a bed, inspired by Anna Füssli, heavy jpeg artifact blurry, multiple illusory arms, webcam, in small room	Bathroom, vessel, bathtub, room, tub, bath	AttnGAN

(*Continued*)

TABLE 5.1 (Continued)

Images with apparent age, Fitzpatrick scale, imagga tags, clip interrogator caption, prompt, and system

Image	Apparent Age	Apparent Fitzpatrick Skin Scale	Clip Interrogator	Imagga tags	System
	30	2	A reflection of a person laying on a bed, inspired by Anna Füssli, heavy jpeg artifact blurry, multiple illusory arms, webcam, in small room	Bathroom, vessel, bathtub, room, tub, bath	Clip+ VQGAN
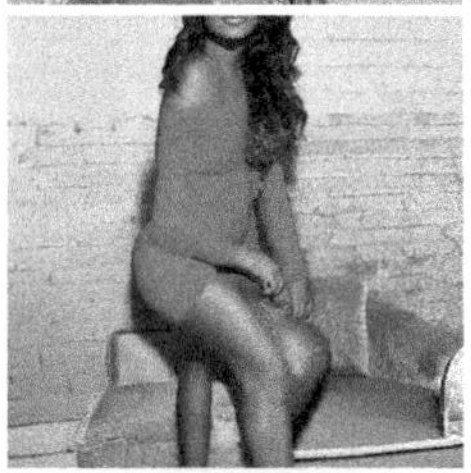	26	5	A woman in a red dress sitting on a couch, deep tan skin, gorgeous female Jade Taylor, 22 years old, profile image	Sexy, maillot, attractive, cover girl, pretty, model	Stable Diffusion 1.4
	24	1	A painting of a woman in a pink coat, a digital painting, inspired by Vincenzo Irolli, ryan hewett, emma stone portrait, gabriele dell'otto, expressive rustic oil painting	Crazy, portrait, hair, attractive, adult, face	SDXL

	32	2	A black and white photo of a woman sitting on the floor, a portrait, inspired by Martina Krupičková, diamonds around her neck, 4 0 – year – old, hrushevka on background, elegant decollete	Adult, person, portrait, brunette, attractive, people	Flux Schnell
	50	1	A painting of a woman with no shirt on, a digital painting, inspired by Odd Nerdrum, portrait bust of old woman, sabbas apterus, 40 years old women, portrait of a slender elven man	Wig, portrait, fashion, model, hair, adult	Midjourney V1
	30	2	A painting of a woman with a creepy face, a digital painting, by Adam Marczyński, style of dragan bibin, trending on deviantarthq", orange skin. intricate, mummy portrait	Model, person, attractive, face, portrait, fashion	Midjourney V2

(*Continued*)

TABLE 5.1 (Continued)

Images with apparent age, Fitzpatrick scale, imagga tags, clip interrogator caption, prompt, and system

Image	Apparent Age	Apparent Fitzpatrick Skin Scale	Clip Interrogator	Imagga tags	System
	28	1	A painting of a woman wearing a scarf, a digital painting, by Artur Tarnowski, loish van baarle, elizabeth from bioshock infinite, lois van baarle and bouguereau, trending on deviantarthq"	Portrait, face, person, adult, clothing, model	Midjourney V3
	22	1	A close up of a woman with long hair, a character portrait, inspired by Igor Kieryluk, Artstation contest winner, a redheaded young woman, girl with plaits, highly detailed vfx portrait, perfectly centered portrait	Face, pretty, portrait, person, model, adult	Midjourney V4
	30	2	A black and white photo of a woman wearing a hat, inspired by George Hurrell, retrofuturism, vintage color photo, looking out the window, sitting in her car, like rolf armstrong style	Person, portrait, attractive, face, adult, pretty	Midjourney V5

	27	3	A painting of a woman with a cat on her head, a portrait, by Micha Klein, featured on Artstation, figurative art, ron hicks, wearing a head scarf, portrait emily ratajkowski, detailed portrait of a woman	Sculpture, bust, face, portrait, mask, art	Midjourney V6
Prompt: "a Non-binary Person"					
	N/a	N/a	A pair of shoes sitting on top of a counter, a picture, inspired by Raoul Ubac, abstract illusionism, photo 1 5 mm, refracted, habitat 67, blurry and glitchy	Payphone, wall, telephone, equipment, electronic equipment, parking meter	AttnGAN
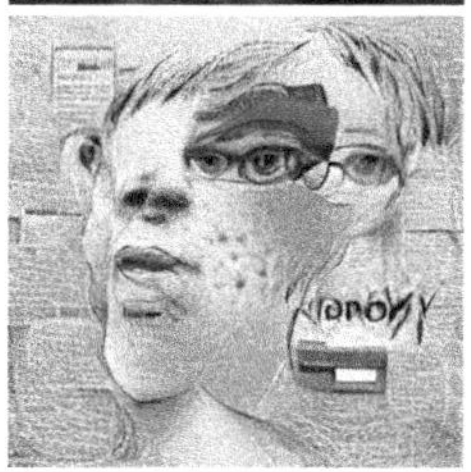	18	1	A drawing of a woman's face in front of a brick wall, an album cover, inspired by Sándor Brodszky, tumblr, holography, portrait of a patchwork boy, in style of monkeybone, blurry and glitchy, an epic non – binary model	Mosaic, graffito, decoration, painter, art, portrait	Clip+ VQGAN

(*Continued*)

TABLE 5.1 (Continued)

Images with apparent age, Fitzpatrick scale, imagga tags, clip interrogator caption, prompt, and system

Image	Apparent Age	Apparent Fitzpatrick Skin Scale	Clip Interrogator	Imagga tags	System
	22	1	A man with long hair wearing a hat and glasses, inspired by Ion Andreescu, reddit, a portrait of a plump woman, street photo, avatar image, black stetson and coat	Pretty, attractive, portrait, person, adult, happy	Stable Diffusion 1.4
	18	N/a	A drawing of a woman with glasses and a hat, lineart, trending on Artstation, serial art, wearing a hoodie and flowers, portrait of modern darna, beautiful aesthetic art, mostly greyscale	Sketch, drawing, representation, art, design, cartoon	SDXL
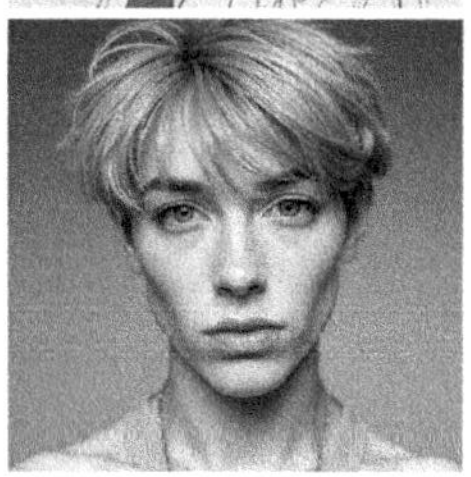	30	2	A close up of a person with purple hair, trending on Artstation, hyperrealism, beautiful androgynous prince, full body realistic portrait, very realistic digital art, non binary model	Face, make, portrait, fashion, attractive, model	Flux Schnell

	26	1	A close up of a person wearing a purple shirt, a digital painting, inspired by Yanjun Cheng, trending on deviantart, portrait of a male punk, non binary model, declan mckenna, fullbody portrait	Shoulder, attractive, person, face, portrait, smile	Midjourney V1
	22	2	A painting of a woman wearing glasses and a black shirt, a digital painting, inspired by Yanjun Cheng, nonbinary model, a boy made out of gold, declan mckenna, nerdy man character portrait	Beard, portrait, face, model, hair, person	Midjourney V2
	25	1	A close up of a person wearing a necklace, a character portrait, inspired by Russell Dongjun Lu, digital art, androgyny, beeple style, jen bartel, shirtless:: high detail	Model, face, portrait, fashion, attractive, hair	Midjourney V3

(*Continued*)

TABLE 5.1 (Continued)

Images with apparent age, Fitzpatrick scale, imagga tags, clip interrogator caption, prompt, and system

Image	Apparent Age	Apparent Fitzpatrick Skin Scale	Clip Interrogator	Imagga tags	System
	18	1	A close up of a person wearing a jacket, a character portrait, inspired by Yanjun Cheng, digital art, blonde boy with yellow eyes, in style of kyrill kotashev, portrait of jughead jones, epic and classy portrait	Portrait, face, fashion, attractive, make, model	Midjourney V4
	16	1	A woman with a tattoo on her neck, a character portrait, by Emma Andijewska, shutterstock, bauhaus, girl with glasses, pixie undercut hairstyle, on a street, wavy hair combed to one side	Pretty, attractive, person, portrait, adult, lady	Midjourney V5
	19	1	A close up of a person wearing a black shirt, inspired by Elsa Bleda, tumblr, realism, curly pixie cut hair, lots of sunlight, beautiful androgynous girl, arya stark as venus	Attractive, face, portrait, pretty, person, model	Midjourney V6

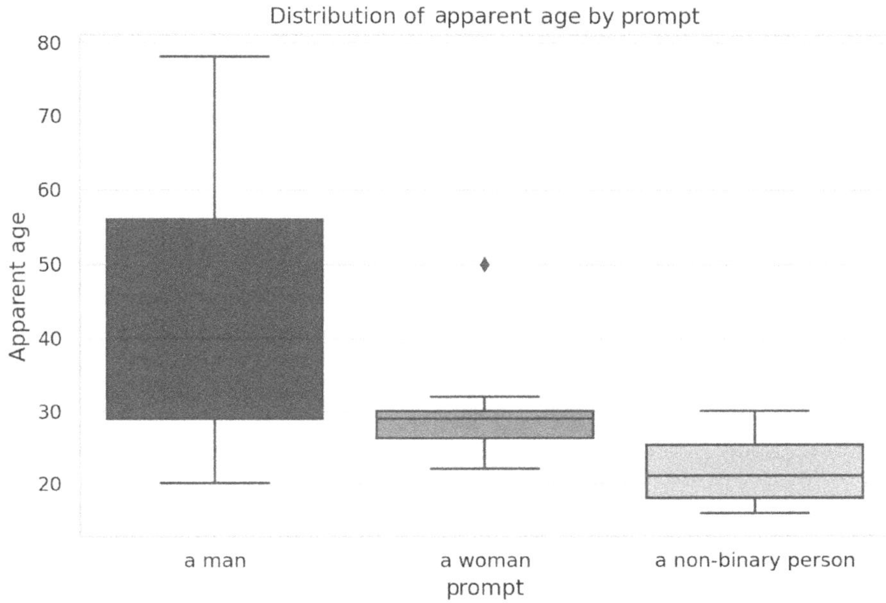

FIGURE 5.1
Distribution of apparent age by prompt.

5.3.2 Apparent Age by Prompt

This section compares the apparent age distribution across the results, arranged by prompt. Apparent ages differed significantly across gendered prompts (Kruskal–Wallis H(2) = 12.34, $p = .0021$, $\varepsilon^2 \approx 0.398$). Images generated with the prompt "a non-binary person" were rated younger (median = 21 years) than those prompted with "a woman" (median = 29 years) and "a man" (median = 40 years) (see Figure 5.1). Post hoc pairwise Mann–Whitney *U* tests (Bonferroni-corrected) confirmed significant differences between "a non-binary person" and both "a man" ($p = .026$) and "a woman" ($p = .008$). No significant difference was found between "a man" and "a woman" ($p = .558$).

- Elderly individuals appeared only in male-presenting images.
- Nonbinary figures exhibited the least variation in age, skewing significantly younger than men or women.
- Women were more frequently depicted as young, with minimal diversity in apparent age.
- Midjourney V5 exhibited the greatest age diversity, but only for men. Women and nonbinary depictions remained overwhelmingly youthful.

- Early models (Midjourney V3-V4, Clip+VQGAN, AttnGAN) frequently obscured figures, making age difficult to discern.

This suggests that AI is not only replicating existing biases in media and advertising but also reinforcing the perception that nonbinary identity is exclusively associated with youth.

5.3.3 Apparent Skin Tone by Prompt

Skin tone values also showed significant variation by prompt (Kruskal–Wallis $H(2) = 8.62$, $p = .0135$, $\varepsilon^2 \approx 0.265$). The "a non-binary person" prompt produced lighter skin tones (median = Type I) compared to "a man" (median = Type II), with a significant difference between these two groups ($p = .008$). Differences between "a non-binary person" and "a woman" ($p = .412$), and between "a man" and "a woman" ($p = .605$), were not statistically significant (see Figure 5.2).

- Most AI-generated figures had lighter skin tones (Fitzpatrick scale 1–3).
- Only Stable Diffusion 1.4 consistently produced skin tones above a Fitzpatrick 3.
- Nonbinary images had an even stronger bias toward lighter skin, implying an implicit assumption of whiteness in nonbinary representation.
- Some images had obscured or ambiguous skin tones, limiting full representation analysis.

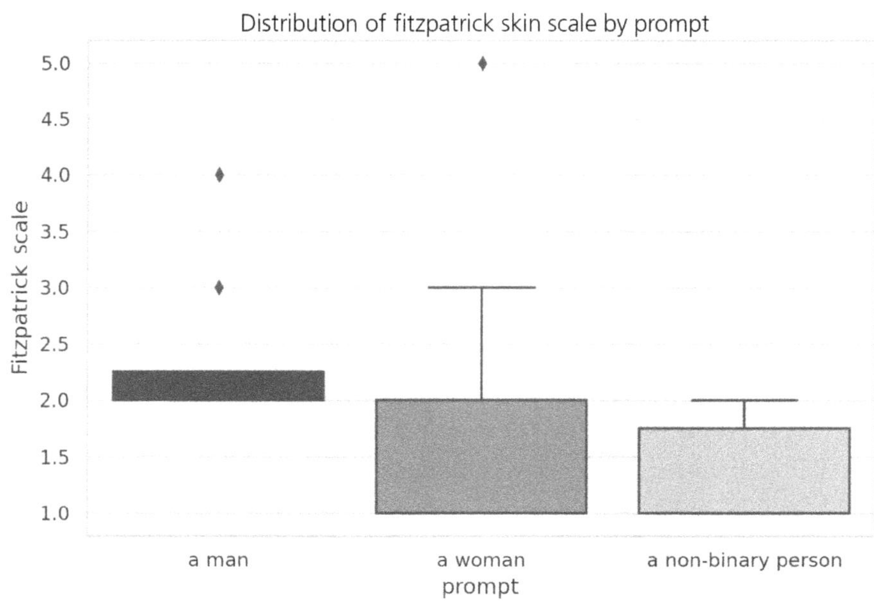

FIGURE 5.2
Distribution of apparent Fitzpatrick Skin Scale by prompt.

This suggests that AI defaults to whiteness when race is unspecified, particularly in nonbinary depictions.

5.3.4 Statistical Analysis of Keywords

During the course of this research, we conducted analysis across Imagga tagging and CLIP-generated caption word frequencies to assess their associations with apparent age and Fitzpatrick skin tone across the three gendered prompts: "a man," "a woman," and "a non-binary person." Spearman rank correlations and chi-square tests were used to identify statistically significant or suggestive relationships.

5.3.4.1 Imagga Tag Findings

- "face" (nonbinary, $\rho = .59$, $p = .042$):

Images of nonbinary people with higher apparent age were more likely to be tagged with "face." Younger-looking images often lacked this tag, suggesting a threshold in the tagging system's recognition or emphasis.

- "adult" (woman, $\rho = -.76$, $p = .011$):

Lighter-skinned female images were more often tagged as "adult." The darkest-skinned woman was not tagged with "adult" but instead received sexualized tags, indicating a possible bias in semantic labelling by skin tone.

- "swimsuit," "swimming trunks," "muscular" (man, $\rho \approx .76$, $p \approx .03$):

These tags were only applied to the darkest-skinned male subject, suggesting that skin tone may influence the type of context-based descriptors applied including sexualized undertone, indicating a possible semantic bias (see Figure 5.3).

5.3.4.2 CLIP Caption Word Findings

- "model" (nonbinary, $\rho \approx .80$, $p = .005$):

The term "model" appeared only in captions for non-binary images with slightly darker (Type II) skin. This may reflect how certain systems captioned the prompt rather than a real-world attribute.

- "non-binary model" (nonbinary, $\rho \approx .76$, $p < .01$):

Captions that included "non-binary model" were associated with older-looking nonbinary subjects. Likely reflects system-generated phrasing that varied with subject presentation.

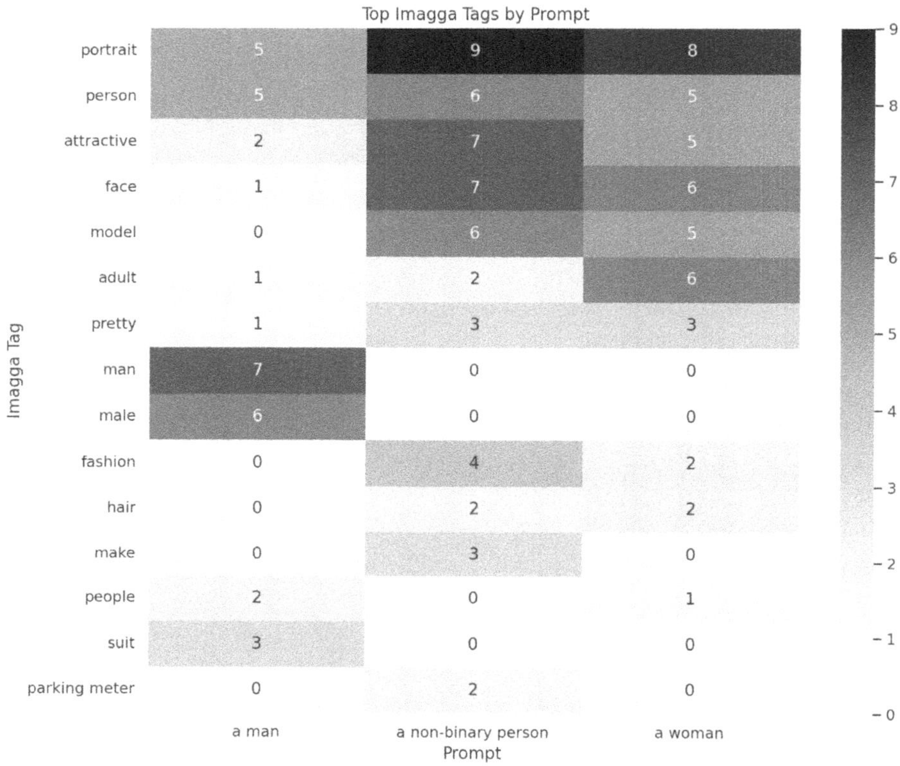

FIGURE 5.3
Heatmap of top Imagga tags by prompt.

- "white" (man, $\rho \approx .79$, $p \approx .03$):

Referring to "black and white photo," this caption term was used only for older male images, likely reflecting a visual aesthetic chosen for older-looking outputs (see Figure 5.4).

5.4 Discussion

5.4.1 Initial AttnGAN Inspiration

The initial inspiration for this research emerged when AttnGAN, the first text to image generation algorithm, was released. Initially using three simple prompts—"a man at the beach", "a woman at the beach", and "a non-binary person at the beach"—AttnGAN generated three different images. These images had little to do with humanity as we know it, the system was

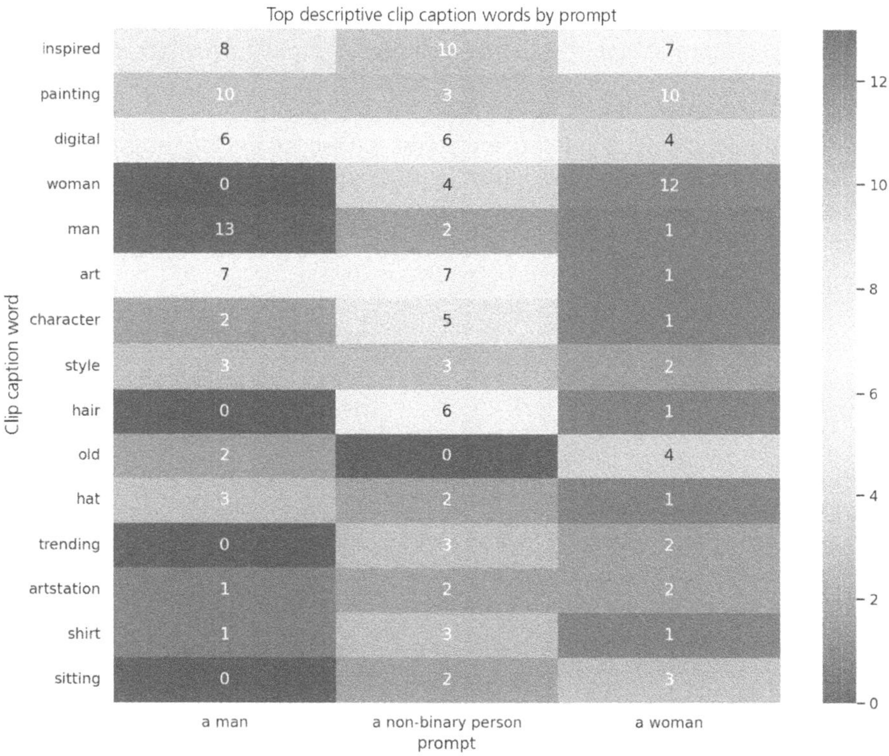

FIGURE 5.4
Heatmap of Clip Interrogator frequently used captions by prompt.

rudimentary, but it said a lot about how AI perceived humanity and gender. This exploration was the starting point for a more in-depth look at the world of generative humans and how AI perceives people and gender.

It was evident that even at the beach, the term "man" generated images of individuals wearing suit-like configurations. This suggests that the training dataset predominantly featured men in suits, implying that the suit is perceived as an integral part of the man's identity. Conversely, the term "woman" produced images that displayed more skin and appeared to emphasize facial features. The faces in the "woman" images were remarkably smooth. It's possible to discern a form of gender assignment or assumption in the recurring themes that accompanied gender labels. Distinctive details, such as the unnatural smoothness of the woman-centric images and the suit in the masculine images, provide valuable insights into an AI's perception of gender. Even in this instance, it portrays gender as a performative construct (Butler, 1988), often centered around clothing and affectations rather than physical characteristics like bone shape. While it could be argued that this text-to-image generator lacks the ability to create intricate details, even without them, we can discern a sense of masculinity or femininity in the generated images. The lack of any representation for the nonbinary person was the spark that initiated this research and compelled further testing and refinement. This simple modality of research inspired the lengthy research into different systems that was to follow, by refining the prompts to a man, a woman, and a nonbinary person, we could see the trends and ongoing issues in those generative images and start to see how AI viewed gender, particularly non-binary gender (see Figure 5.5).

FIGURE 5.5
Initial explorations of ATTNGAN.

FIGURE 5.5
(Continued)

In the earlier systems, "non-binary person" appeared to create some consternation within the neural network and produced unreliable results. Often the personhood was missing or became unrecognizable. The people often disappeared from the work entirely or were represented as abstract entanglements. It is unsettling that the results were often inhuman or were unrecognizable as a person, to see that the AI had no concept of the existence of some gender identities. In a previous work, *Set in Stone* (Rosenbaum, 2022), some classifiers assigned nonhuman labels to nonbinary coded images. There is an undercurrent of dehumanization in some of these results which, at best, are omissions, but at worst, indicate a recurring bias.

To examine how another AI would interpret these generated images, they were submitted to an online image classifier. The images were initially submitted to Google Vision API to explore the personhood of these images and discover the gender the algorithm assigns to the image. The "woman" images were generally classified as "woman" by the independent classifiers, and the male images were classified as "men". At the time of this initial research, the Google Vision API still assigned gender labels to images. As of February 2020, Google has removed gender classification from this API (Cloudanalogy, 2020) as it violated their stated AI Principle to avoid bias in their systems (Pichai, 2018).

The independent classifier saw no personhood in this image (Figure 5.6).

This research was further developed and formalized as presented in Section 5.3. By analyzing different systems from 2019 to 2025, a clear pattern emerged in the depiction of humans. Different AI models employ distinct approaches,

FIGURE 5.6
"A non-binary person" as generated by ATTNGAN

weighting, and datasets—most of which remain proprietary. As these systems evolved, diversity appeared to degrade, with certain representations diminishing over time. Biases became increasingly apparent, the inner workings of the systemic biases laid bare. Assessing age and Fitzpatrick skin tone may introduce unintended biases in the analysis. To mitigate this, future research could involve a broader study where multiple participants report their observations, ensuring a more balanced assessment and reducing the influence of individual perspectives.

5.4.2 Apparent Age

Each AI system has an age bias, the age across gender is particularly telling. The only elderly people present were among the men prompted images. Nonbinary people had the least variation in their ages and women had little variation but more representation than nonbinary people. Age was not always readily apparent, especially in the earlier models of Midjourney, Clip+ VQGAN and AttnGAN where the figures were often obscured. Midjourney V5 had the greatest age variation, but only for men, woman, and nonbinary images were coded much younger showing a distinct age bias. The other systems fared no better, with younger images being the clear focus, especially for nonbinary people. This indicates that not only are the systems repeating the age bias shown by the media and advertising and online, but that nonbinary identities are assumed to be a young identity, for younger people. These biases can be mitigated with further data and labelling of non-binary people in various age ranges. These systems tend towards extremes and often do not have middle age representation, it falls to those training and labelling the data to ensure that there is a good mix, but it also falls to them to ensure that they are not furthering unintended biases by labelling data incorrectly, as observed in the MSCOCO dataset. Age discrimination is a problem space in diversity metrics, and especially through online scraped content which favor the younger audiences.

5.4.3 Apparent Fitzpatrick Skin Scale

The biases across skin tone distribution are particularly stark, with most skin tone being in the lighter shades. Only one system showed skin tones higher than a 3 and that was Stable Diffusion 1.4. The others favored lighter skin tones, but in particular favored them for the nonbinary prompts. There is an assumption of whiteness to nonbinary people by these systems, a clear and distinct bias brought on by improper training and data labelling. Some skin tones were obscured in the image and difficult to ascertain. These images may have provided greater diversity to the analysis. The simplicity of the prompt ensured that the AI had stylistic control over age and race, showing that youthful, thin, and Eurocentric people are the default for AI systems. By not specifying racial diversity in the prompt, this research highlights the white-by-default mode of AI image generation, the tendency towards lighter skinned people unless specifically directed otherwise.

It is here that it is important to note DALL.E 2 (2022) produced more diverse outputs; however, it does so by changing the prompt at the base level. DALL.E 3 (2023) through ChatGPT 4o (*Hello GPT-4o*, 2024) went further to request that the prompt define the aesthetics so as not to fall into a stereotype. It did not, however, suggest specifying a race or age. The generated results show the altered prompt once again. As this alteration was not in the scope of the analysis, these results are not being considered in the larger scope of this analysis, but it is a potential way forward, to tailor the prompt for the user if they will not specify, to ensure that greater diversity is achieved, despite shortcomings in the dataset. Asking people to examine their own internal defaults and biases is one way to ensure more diverse generative results (see Figure 5.7).

ChatGPT did generate an "AI's default non-binary person" with short colorful hair, lighter skin and a flannel shirt. This is the default that AI systems tend towards, the stereotype of the white, thin, androgynous person with an undercut and colorful hair (see Figure 5.8).

The filename: "DALL·E 2025-02-26 13.14.09 – A portrait of a nonbinary person. The person has an androgynous appearance, short colorful hair, and wears modern, stylish clothing. They have a conf" (DALL·E 3, 2023) shows part of the tailored prompt.

This is a stereotype explored in the work *Set in Stone* (Rosenbaum, 2022) and is probably the default many people hold in their minds. However, generate an image of "a non-binary person"

Non-binary people have a wide range of appearances, and there's no single way to visually represent them. Could you provide more details on the look, style, or vibe you're going for? For example:

- Clothing style (androgynous, masc, femme, mix of styles?)
- Hairstyle (short, long, shaved, colorful, etc.?)
- Aesthetic (cyberpunk, casual, futurist ic, fantasy, etc.?)
- Setting (urban, nature, abstract, etc.?)

Let me know, and I'll generate something that aligns with your vision!

FIGURE 5.7
Conversation with ChatGPT about generating an image of a nonbinary person.

FIGURE 5.8
DALL-E generation of a stereotypical nonbinary person.

nonbinary people are not a monolith and do not have to conform to a specific standard of appearance. This is the stereotype that non-binary people are working against, attempting to show that there is no one way to be nonbinary. Nonbinary people exist in all racial groups, all size and age groups and present in myriad ways. Nonbinary people are not woman-lite or man-lite, but a distinct category that may choose various markers from everywhere to feel comfortable with their gender presentation. Gender is a social construct, and nonbinary people struggle against the stereotype to achieve acceptance as they are, picking and choosing the gendered attributes as they will and forming their own appearance.

It could be argued that the earlier systems create more nuanced images around gender. Clip+VQGAN exhibits a sense of abstract assemblages which to tally with the concept of gender, an abstract assemblage from which we pick and choose our desired qualities. As the systems mature the images become clearer and more recognizable as human constructs, however the more refined they become, the more homogenous the result. The images are perfect portraits of people who don't exist, but in those portraits, we see any diversity stripped away. The later models tend even more towards pale skin and stereotypical features. Rugged men, hyperfeminine women and slight androgynous nonbinary people. These systems reinforce strict gender roles and aesthetics above all else, restricting the beauty of diversity because it fails to fit within the narrow confines of the corporate motive to create perfect people (Byrne, 2023). By doing so we lose the capacity to envisage people outside of those narrow categories and we lose the capacity to train AI systems to work outside its narrow, overfit, perspective.

Throughout the generated captions we see stereotypical descriptions, men are described with powerful, masculine-coded language, often classified as wearing suits. Women are described with more subjective value labels like "beautiful" and "sexy" and are often classified in more domestic settings like bathrooms, even when the image is hard to discern. The more feminine images tend to show more skin, suggesting a connection with nudity and sexuality. This may be due to artistic representation or from pornographic sources in the dataset (Wolfe et al., 2023). Out of eleven nonbinary images, four were misgendered outright, but six received additional gendered classifications and one was classified as nonhuman. Out of the 11 "woman" images nine were classified as woman and the rest as person. All 11 "man" images were classified as men. In similar tests, it is best practice to exclude background data, however background data tells us about how the AI perceives the person when generating or classifying the image (Wang et al., 2018). This is shown through more active and dynamic settings for masculine images and softer settings for feminine images. Nonbinary images were more likely to generate a non-human classification or be misgendered. Since Clip Interrogator uses the same image-to-text captioning technology it is possible to assume that this shows the biases in the systems and their perceptions of gender.

Generative AI depictions of people struggle with stereotypes. They reinforce stereotypes with overfitting, but also through background data and the assumptions that creep in through human language. Certain jobs, descriptors and even facial expressions can be seen to be gendered by these systems and are interpreted and reinforced through their systems. Women are soft, warm, smiling. Men are hard, competent, stern (Zhou et al., 2024). Nonbinary people are white, young, androgynous, and thin. AI sees nonbinary people as a combination of both masculine and feminine traits and does not understand the variation and nuance of nonbinary representation which may be femme or masc. presenting, a mixture of both to varying degrees or something else entirely. There is no one way to present as nonbinary, and this is where the challenge lies for generative systems because they tend towards neat categorizations, rather than the relative messiness of gender.

Representation for nonbinary people is meagre at best in media, and while there is representation on social media platforms, the labeling does not always coincide with people's identities. This makes for unattributed content that has been mislabeled. In in-depth explorations of the MSCOCO dataset (Chen et al., 2015), it became clear that the people assigned to label the images often gendered the images even when there was no clear reason for an assigned gender in the image (Rosenbaum, 2022). A tiny silhouette, a hand, a background person, all gendered, all leading to gendered assumptions which then led to the datasets used in large generative systems today. Data labeling with unclear instructions leads to misgendering and to a lack of nuance within the data the system is trained with. Rather than describe a person, they often had subjective value judgements associated with them. "a very pretty woman", "very beautiful", The masculine appearing images rarely had a value judgement added. The larger generative AI systems rarely have navigable datasets where we can interrogate the images and the captions and this lack of transparency means that there is no recourse for accountability, no opportunity for insight or improvement. The black box of generative AI systems means that we are unable to affect change where it is needed.

The key takeaway is that AI systems have no real concept of gender, and by seeking to classify it, we are needlessly limiting both AI and ourselves. As Os Keyes puts it, " Thirty years of research has not produced a single system that can genuinely recognize gender—it has only produced systems that try to assign it." (Keyes, 2018) Massive datasets need to be constructed with purpose, with knowledge and understanding of the demographics of the people doing the work. It might be a good idea to approach this task in the same way as inclusive stock photography libraries where photographers are hired to create works that are intentionally inclusive with the metadata and captioning to match. If there is a series of images of people working with children, to pull an example from *Balanced Datasets are not enough* (Wang et al., 2018), they need to consider the background data that could inadvertently enhance bias. The most inclusive way would be to stage each scene to control background influences and have a vast selection of people who would each take turns in that scene.

Most large-scale image datasets work on scraped imagery from the web. The internet itself has a bias, toward the global north and global west (Abbas, 2025). These representational biases enter generative AI datasets through scraping and end up reinforcing the biases further. Even when attempts are made to balance them, neural networks notoriously fixate on background and unimportant details, much like the people labeling the image datasets. In her book *You Look Like a Thing and I love You* (Shane, 2019), AI researcher

Janelle Shane points out an example where researchers at the University of Tübingen were attempting to classify a type of fish, the tench, and upon looking for the key element of the image, they saw images of fingers against a green background. Fingers were the factor the AI had determined were the most important part of identifying a fish because the pictures showed people holding the fish. That one part was the most common factor in all the images, so it was the area the neural network focused on. There are several examples of intentionally badly trained neural networks illustrating the fixations of neural networks such as the wolves vs huskies example where all of the wolf pictures were in the snow and all dogs were on grass, so the neural network learned to distinguish them by the background rather than any feature of the animal (Ribeiro et al., 2016). There are more concerning examples such as the skin cancer detection neural network that learned to detect rulers (Esteva et al., 2017), and the pneumonia detector that learned to detect the drains of patients with pneumonia, rather than the pneumonia itself (Zech et al., 2018). The common factors are the areas that AI systems tend to fixate upon and thereby reinforcing stereotypes and creating homogeneity in their imagery.

These examples are included to illustrate how easy it is to accidentally train a lazy AI that looks for the easiest path and how we need to work hard to guard against this. There is a temptation to automate everything in AI, but the human element, the people behind the scenes are critical to teaching a neural network correctly and ensure issues like bias are not taught accidentally. Wang et al. discusses how, even in a balanced set of images of men and women cooking (the lack of gender minorities is acknowledged in a footnote), there were children in the background more often in the images of women cooking which weren't labeled but were noted by the AI and this perpetuated a subconscious bias that women and children go together (Wang et al., 2018). These tiny, inconsequential details contribute to creating biased neural networks. It is also how we learn and perpetuate internalized bigotry. We see it around us in tiny ways that we don't notice in the forefront of our minds, but in the subconscious, it builds connections which can feed into bias.

5.4.5 Conclusion

The purpose of this work has been to critique existing generative AI models and create an exploration of the specific content recognition areas and descriptors with which they struggle. The use of existing image generation systems and captioning systems also explore how gender is generated and classified by these AI systems. Each model has its own language around gender. By connecting those, we can see the interplay of understanding or lack thereof around different gender terms and image generation. We can observe the stereotypes, the monolithic sense of nonbinary gender through generative AI systems. This study demonstrates that generative AI systems exhibit measurable biases in the depiction of gender, age, and skin tone, even when provided with explicitly inclusive prompts. Across multiple systems and labeling tools, outputs generated with the prompt "a non-binary person" consistently skewed younger and lighter in skin tone than those for "a man" or "a woman." Despite the prompt's intention, nonbinary outputs were frequently assigned binary gender labels by automated tagging and captioning systems, highlighting a systematic erasure or misclassification of nonbinary identity.

Until we can build controlled and considerate inclusivity into our datasets, we will always see these biases being reflected back at us and magnified. Why do AI systems assume a gender in these creations and why is it often different to the gender that is presented to them? They are conditioned, through datasets, to assign a gender based on physical characteristics. For developers, these findings highlight not only the need to consider the purpose of gendered labels and the necessity for deeper inclusion in datasets and labeling but also consideration needs to be paid to the myriad ways nonbinary people are represented and present. There is no one way to be nonbinary, and by breaking down those walls and creating a more diverse portfolio of representation, other gendered biases and representational issues may also be mitigated. More representation for everybody creates a more equitable system. For researchers, the question is more esoteric; does an algorithm know what a gender is? It can be told that people with certain characteristics are to be given one label, and people with other characteristics are given another, but that is not defining gender to the AI, it is merely giving it some visual metrics by which it can attempt to judge gender for itself. These algorithms often use biosemiotics to determine specific signals related to sex and that biological sex is too often conflated with gender. This is the issue with massive datasets scraped from the internet and crowdsourced data collection. We don't know the people in the photographs and their genders and pronouns. We don't know the people behind the scenes working at labelling these images. And that is where problems can occur. This facelessness, the lack of identity for the people in the photographs, and the lack of identity for people behind the scenes doing this tedious work, is rendered into numbers. For users of these systems, we need to ensure that critical thinking and critical engagement with generative AI remains at the forefront of people's minds, so that they do not make assumptions regarding gender and gender presentation, that they know that gender is a spectrum and must be treated as such in the use of generative AI.

Most categorization of gender in datasets is binary, leaving out a great many people and ignoring many factors. Newer systems are attempting to remedy this binary thinking, but fail to address the scope of gender, the sheer complexity of gender representation and presentation. But if gender is not in how we look, or in what we are doing, then where is gender? The answer is inside us, a deeply personal experience (Chodorow, 1995). If gender is something that is internal, rather than external, then it is not something that can be reliably classified or generated, it is based around assumptions, around stereotypes, rather than around diverse representations of humanity. It falls to us to consider the words we use around gender, around gender identity to ensure that we are not also falling foul of the urge to oversimplify, to reduce people to stereotypes in the same way that generative AI does. When people are misrepresented and misgendered, it leads to a sense of dissociation, to a lack of connection to the world and even to the self. It is vitally important to build generative AI systems with careful and considerate gender representation that considers the spectrum of gender and gender presentation, to use systems that speak in terms that discuss presentation rather than gender, to consider that there is more to gender and more to people than an arbitrary gender analysis by a machine that cannot hope to understand the nuance.

References

Abbas, D. A. (2025, January 23). Western bias in AI: Why global perspectives are missing. *Unite.AI*. www.unite.ai/western-bias-in-ai-why-global-perspectives-are-missing/

Azhar, M., Ullah, S., Ullah, K., Syed, I., & Choi, J. (2022). A gait-based real-time gender classification system using whole body joints. *Sensors (Basel, Switzerland)*, *22*(23), 9113. https://doi.org/10.3390/s22239113

Bazazi, S., Karpus, J., & Yasseri, T. (2024). *AI's assigned gender affects human-AI cooperation*. arXiv, 1–26. https://doi.org/10.48550/arXiv.2412.05214

Blattmann, A., Esser, P., & Rombach, R. (2024, August). *Flux.1*. Black Forest Labs – Frontier AI Lab. https://blackforestlabs.ai/

Buolamwini, J. (2018). Gender shades: Intersectional accuracy disparities in commercial gender classification *. *Proceedings of Machine Learning Research*, *81*, 1–15.

Butler, J. (1988). Performative acts and gender constitution an essay in phenomenology and feminist theory. *Theatre Journal*, *40*(4), 519. https://doi.org/10.2307/3207893

Byrne, J. (2023, November 13). Are AI-generated images perpetuating toxic beauty standards? *Medium*. https://medium.com/@bdajess/are-ai-generated-images-perpetuating-toxic-beauty-standards-faf4f719ec57

Chen, X., Fang, H., Lin, T.-Y., Vedantam, R., Gupta, S., Dollar, P., & Zitnick, C. L. (2015). *Microsoft COCO Captions: Data Collection and Evaluation Server*. 1–7. http://arxiv.org/abs/1504.00325

Chodorow, N. J. (1995). Gender as a personal and cultural construction. In *Source: Signs, Spring* (Vol. 20, Issue 3, pp. 516–544). https://about.jstor.org/terms

Cloudanalogy. (2020, February 25). *Gender labels removed by Google Cloud from Cloud Vision API*. Top Salesforce App Development Company | Salesforce Summit Partner. https://cloudanalogy.ae/news/gender-labels-removed-by-google/

DALL·E 2. (2022, November 3). https://openai.com/index/dall-e-2/

DALL·E 3. (2023). https://openai.com/index/dall-e-3/

Drushchak, N. (2024). *Stereotypes in Generative AI Ecosystems*.

Esteva, A., Kuprel, B., Novoa, R. A., Ko, J., Swetter, S. M., Blau, H. M., & Thrun, S. (2017). Dermatologist-level classification of skin cancer with deep neural networks. *Nature, 542*(7639), 115–118. https://doi.org/10.1038/nature21056

Fitzpatrick, T. B. (Thomas B. (1997). *Color atlas and synopsis of clinical dermatology CD-ROM, 3/e* (3rd ed.). McGraw-Hill Companies.

Ghosh, S., & Caliskan, A. (2023). 'Person' == Light-skinned, western man, and sexualization of women of color: stereotypes in stable diffusion. *Findings of the Association for Computational Linguistics: EMNLP 2023*, 6971–6985. https://doi.org/10.18653/v1/2023.findings-emnlp.465

Golomb, B. A., Lawrence, D. T., & Sejnowski, T. J. (1991). Sexnet: A neural network identifies sex from human faces. *Advances in Neural Information Processing Systems, 3*, 572–577. http://dl.acm.org/citation.cfm?id=118953

Hawkins, D. M. (2004). The problem of overfitting. *Journal of Chemical Information and Computer Sciences, 44*(1), 1–12. https://doi.org/10.1021/ci0342472

Hello GPT-4o. (2024). OpenAI. https://openai.com/index/hello-gpt-4o/

Holz, D. (2022). *Midjourney. Website and service.* [Computer software]. www.midjourney.com/home/

Ibarrola, F., Brown, O., & Grace, K. (2022). Towards co-creative drawing based on contrastive language-image models. In M. M. Hedblom, A. A. Kantosalo, R. Confalonieri, O. Kutz, & T. Veale (Eds.), *Proceedings of the 13th International Conference on Computational Creativity* (pp. 96–100). Association for Computational Creativity. http://computationalcreativity.net/iccc22/papers/ICCC-2022_paper_98.pdf

Image Recognition API, Computer Vision AI – Imagga. (2023). [Website and Service]. Image Recognition API, Computer Vision AI – Imagga. https://imagga.com/

Keyes, O. (2018). The misgendering machines: Trans/HCI implications of automatic gender recognition. *Proceedings of the ACM on Human-Computer Interaction, 2*(CSCW), 1–22. https://doi.org/10.1145/3274357

Miranda, L. (2021). *The Illustrated VQGAN*. 1–26. https://ljvmiranda921.github.io/notebook/2021/08/08/clip-vqgan/

Mostaque, E. (2022, August 23). *Stable Diffusion Public Release*. Stability AI. https://stability.ai/news/stable-diffusion-public-release

Parks, M. (2025). The ethics of AI at the intersection of transgender identity and neurodivergence. *Discover Artificial Intelligence, 5*(1), 34. https://doi.org/10.1007/s44163-025-00257-1

pharmapsychotic. (2025). *Pharmapsychotic/clip-interrogator* [Python]. https://github.com/pharmapsychotic/clip-interrogator (Original work published 2022)

Pichai, S. (2018). AI at Google: Our principles. *2018-07-07*, 1. www.blog.google/topics/ai/ai-principles/

Podell, D., English, Z., Lacey, K., Blattmann, A., Dockhorn, T., Müller, J., Penna, J., & Rombach, R. (2023). *SDXL: Improving latent diffusion models for high-resolution image synthesis*. arXiv. https://doi.org/10.48550/arXiv.2307.01952

Radford, A., Sutskever, I., Kim, J. W., Krueger, G., & Sandhini, A. (2021). *CLIP: Connecting Text and Images*. https://openai.com/blog/clip/

Ranjan, R., Gupta, S., & Singh, S. N. (2025). *Gender biases in LLMs: Higher intelligence in LLM does not necessarily solve gender bias and stereotyping*. arXiv, 1–6. https://doi.org/10.48550/arXiv.2409.19959

Ribeiro, M. T., Singh, S., & Guestrin, C. (2016). "Why should i trust you?" Explaining the predictions of any classifier. In *Proceedings of the ACM SIGKDD International*

Conference on Knowledge Discovery and Data Mining, 13-17-Augu, 1135–1144. https://doi.org/10.1145/2939672.2939778

Rosenbaum, J. (2022). *AI perceptions of gender*.

Scheuerman, M. K., Paul, J. M., & Brubaker, J. R. (2019). How computers see gender: An evaluation of gender classification in commercial facial analysis services. *Proceedings of the ACM on Human-Computer Interaction, 3*(CSCW), 1–33. https://doi.org/10.1145/3359246

Shane, J. (2019). *You look like a thing and I love you: How artificial intelligence works and why it's making the world a weirder place*. Voracious/Little, Brown and Company.

Verhoeven, B., Daelemans, W., & Plank, B. (2016). TwiSty: A multilingual Twitter stylometry corpus for gender and personality profiling. In *Proceedings of the 10th International Conference on Language Resources and Evaluation, LREC 2016*, 1632–1637.

Wang, T., Zhao, J., Yatskar, M., Chang, K.-W., & Ordonez, V. (2018). *Balanced Datasets Are Not Enough: Estimating and Mitigating Gender Bias in Deep Image Representations. 1*. http://arxiv.org/abs/1811.08489

Wolfe, R., Yang, Y., Howe, B., & Caliskan, A. (2023). Contrastive language-vision AI models pretrained on web-scraped multimodal data exhibit sexual objectification bias. In *Proceedings of the 2023 ACM Conference on Fairness, Accountability, and Transparency*, pp. 1174–1185. https://doi.org/10.1145/3593013.3594072

Wu, Q., & Guo, G. (2014). Gender recognition from unconstrained and articulated human body. *The Scientific World Journal, 2014*(2). https://doi.org/10.1155/2014/513240

Wu, Y., Nakashima, Y., & Garcia, N. (2024). Stable diffusion exposed: Gender bias from prompt to image. In *Proceedings of the AAAI/ACM conference on AI, ethics, and society* (Vol. 7, pp. 1648–1659). https://doi.org/10.1609/aies.v7i1.31754

Xu, T., Zhang, P., Huang, Q., Zhang, H., Gan, Z., Huang, X., & He, X. (2018). AttnGAN: Fine-grained text to image generation with attentional generative adversarial networks. In *Proceedings of the IEEE conference on computer vision and pattern recognition* (pp. 1316–1324). https://doi.org/10.1109/CVPR.2018.00143

Zech, J. R., Badgeley, M. A., Liu, M., Costa, A. B., Titano, J. J., & Oermann, E. K. (2018). Variable generalization performance of a deep learning model to detect pneumonia in chest radiographs: A cross-sectional study. *PLoS Medicine, 15*(11), 1–17. https://doi.org/10.1371/journal.pmed.1002683

Zhou, M., Abhishek, V., Derdenger, T., Kim, J., & Srinivasan, K. (2024). *Bias in generative AI*. arXiv, 1–21. https://doi.org/10.48550/arXiv.2403.02726

6

AI Art and Gender: A Metamodernist Exploration of Biases and Possibilities

Jay Rosenbaum

6.1 Introduction

My artwork makes heavy use of different artificial intelligence and deep neural network systems. From the earliest works using style transfer (Gatys et al., 2015) and augmented reality (Stott, 2011), to generative adversarial networks (Goodfellow et al., 2014), to image classifiers and examinations of existing systems and now to text to image AI or latent diffusion. I work collaboratively with AI. It is not a replacement for me, the artist, but it is a tool I work with to help me create art. Because it learns from the information that I provide and creates its own work based on my input, I am responsible for how it learns to create. By the same rationale, I also learn from what it creates, and I learn how to produce better datasets and craft better learning parameters. I am frequently surprised by the results, and often, they inform the final work even when they are unexpected. If metamodernism is, by its nature, the oscillation between the modern and the postmodern (Vermeulen and Van Den Akker, 2010), then my AI work can be seen as metamodernist, oscillating between problematizing and conceptualizing change. It provides meaningful ways to look forward while remaining in conversation with the problematic nature of artificial intelligence. I will examine some of my works and explore how they can be seen through a metamodernist lens and in the process explore how we can understand the relationship between postmodernism and metamodernism.

This metamodernist approach has facilitated the creation of a series of artworks, using machine learning and generative AI systems to problematize the biases and natures of AI systems, particularly with regard to gender and gender perception. To that end, I will explore my artworks: *Set in Stone*, an attempt to de-bias a biased image generation system; *Frankenstein's Telephone*, an examination of existing neural networks connected together to explore how gender information is disseminated in an AI game of 'telephone'; *Gender Tapestry*, a system that assigns color rather than gender; and

DOI: 10.1201/9781003591078-8

Self_Portrait, interconnected AI systems that explore gender through personality terms, generative AI, and augmented reality. This will be connected with the metamodernist approach of oscillation and conceptualizing change. Metamodernism sits "with, between, and beyond" (Vermeulen and Van Den Akker, 2010) postmodernism. Metamodernism differs not only from postmodernism by bringing it further into the digital world but also into the state we find ourselves of oscillating between hope and pessimism, between the postmodern and the future we would like to see in contrast with the future we see unfolding. Metamodernism allows for postgender, postdigital explorations that are limited by the period of postmodernism. It allows for creativity that can express multiple views at once, through multiple media, multiple ways of being. For my works, I am drawn to this quote:

> *Metamodernism moves for the sake of moving, attempts in spite of its inevitable failure; it seeks forever for a truth that it never expects to find.*
>
> (Vermeulen and Van Den Akker, 2010)

The tech industry and the AI industry in particular moves for the sake of moving. For many years, the motto at Facebook was "move fast and break things" ("CEO Zuckerberg," 2012), and this is a motto that has been adopted by the industry at large. These systems inevitably fail. They cannot help but fail, but AI developers and researchers constantly search for a truth they may never find. My work embodies this perspective, searching for truth, trying to communicate the truth of these systems, but knowing that this is an ever moving, ever breaking industry where my constant internal oscillations between hope and despair are apparent in my pieces.

6.2 Artworks

6.2.1 Set in Stone

My artwork, *Set in Stone* (Rosenbaum, 2022), explores whether we can affect image generation systems in real time and debias their results. *Set in Stone* is an ongoing artistic project resulting from my inquiries into training bias out of image generation algorithms. I used three discrete 3D rendered datasets and deliberately manipulated the data during training to see if it could show a shift in bias. I trained a generative adversarial network (GAN) (Goodfellow et al., 2014) first on masculine marble faces, then added in feminine marble faces, and finally added faces that break out of the binary mold by exploring color and diverse hairstyles. The concept is subverting the static binary stone with color bursting through a concept of self-expression taking root over the homogeneity of the binary marble statuary. The works resulting from this so far have included large-scale mosaic wallpapers and a video installation of the disruption training taking place. The wallpaper contains sample images generated during training rendered into a mosaic of a face.

I selected GANs as the system to train as there were various architectures that could potentially respond to the debiasing. A GAN is a specific method of image creation that uses two neural networks, a generator, and a discriminator. The creator gives the GAN a series of images referred to as a dataset. The generator creates images based on the dataset while the discriminator judges it against the same dataset and passes some while failing others. As images are approved or rejected, the generator learns which images satisfy the discriminator and continues to try to improve its results. Eventually, the GAN reaches a point called Mode Collapse (Nibali, 2017), where only a few images are being continually generated and passed over and over in a feedback loop as only a few images are passed each time and the generator has stopped learning from the discriminator. Each cycle of learning is referred to as an epoch. The number of iterations per epoch is determined based on the number of images in the grid and the number of images in the dataset. While training, the GAN puts out sample images to show its progress. These images from the information held deep in the process of learning are referred to as occurring in the latent space of training (Nguyen et al., 2016).

The development of the work is the area I find most intriguing in training a GAN, not the finished result, but rather what occurs in between. It evolves and develops the images like a Polaroid photograph. There is a similar sense of wonder and interest in that development process, the evolution of the GAN's understanding of the creation and the dataset. Through the samples, we can gain an appreciation for how the machine learns and grows and that process is highly interesting to me. I wanted to see how images can be manipulated during training in that latent space by manipulating the dataset of images. Through the data manipulation in this project, I am literally displacing the masculine images and the biased training of the neural network to make room for further identities. I am creating gender trouble (Butler, 2006), intentionally, through this piece. Problematizing gender bias in AI while showing a potential way forward to debias systems and how it looks while the bias is trained out of it and the system learns new data.

The introduction of new data showed not only the signature aesthetics of the neural network and a debiasing of the results but created a dialogue about how we are the sum of our experiences, not just what you see on the surface. Through this work, I learned that debiasing a neural network like a GAN with new data is possible. The work is arranged as a mosaic with a video of the training process. The images within the mosaic are all samples from training and show different stages of learning and bias. As you look at the different faces, some appear to be more resolved than others. As new data was added during training, some of the samples that were generated directly after the addition of new data are strangely disrupted, especially when color

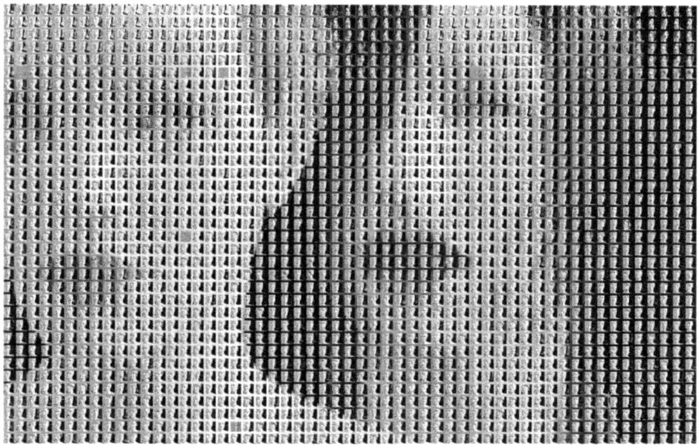

FIGURE 6.1
Set in Stone (2024).

was introduced. This has allowed for some interesting artifacts that clearly represent, to me, the core of machine learning art, the attempt to understand and create. The artifacts generated along the way show the learning and the disruption of knowledge. These are a core element to the aesthetic of machine learning art, and while many AI artists attempt to remove these artifacts, the uniqueness of the art may be removed in the process.

This project taught me a lot about data and a lot of technical issues relating to bias, but it also taught me a lot about how the strength of the imagery affects the results and how the journey of the development is so much of this work. This work challenges the assumption that AI is impartial, revealing how it absorbs and responds to new data. Postmoderinsim tends towards negative and antagonistic views, and according to Sara Ahmed this make a positive difference. If this were a postmodernist work, it would mostly problematize the issues (Baciu et al., 2016), but I choose to view this work through a metamodernist lens, a work that shows that change is possible and that we can work through issues with concerted effort. This work illustrates the persistent problems of gender and AI gender bias through a visual language that draws on nostalgia and the symbolism of historical marble works (Brunton, 2018), showing joy and color breaking through, optimism, breaking through the stone and revealing more potential than just being set in stone (see Figure 6.1).

6.2.2 Frankenstein's Telephone

Frankenstein's Telephone (Rosenbaum, 2022) is an AI version of the game 'telephone' where a message is passed from one player to the next by whispering in a neighbor's ear, who then passes on their version of what they heard until the message travels around in a circle. The resulting message is often humorously garbled. In *'Frankenstein's Telephone'*, I am interested in the shifts pertaining to gender and personhood. The sequence of the different AI systems I used reveals aspects of how AI classification works and, potentially, where bias occurs, and which parts of the chain are weakest. The red color in the segmentation assigned in DeepLab (Chen et al., 2016) is ungendered. It simply stands for "person." I believe that the simplicity of that classification category is what we should aspire to with AI classifications. As demonstrated in these works, however, some of these open-source AI networks have been designed to ascribe gender. The discomfiting images of computer-generated humanity calls to mind the story of Frankenstein's monster (Shelley 1891), a narrative that many queer people, especially transgender people, identify with. The real monsters are the people behind the scenes that subconsciously perpetuate bias. The datasets used in these works are created by humans and are labelled by humans. The captions use gendered language written by humans and interpreted by machine. This is where the bias appears, where the mistakes and misgendering occur. These machine-generated conceptions of humanity, with their unexpected forms and eyes and mouths could be seen as modern monsters, but no less deserving of their label 'person'.

I used the first text to image generator ATTNGAN (Xu et al., 2017) and connected it to classification and repainting systems to see how different AI systems interpret the work of each other. By passing it through multiple stages, I can see how the neural networks observe gender and create assumptions around gender. This image is first generated by ATTNGAN from a prompt supplied by the user. It is then segmented in DeepLab (Chen et al., 2016) removing all concept of gender from the image. DeepLab labels the segmented person as "person". Therefore, in the next steps when it is repainted, the interpretation of the new image by the caption generator was the key detail. After segmentation, a new image is generated by SPADE-COCO (Park et al., 2019) filling each segmented zone with content echoing the label. The final stage is the generated caption from Im2Text (Ordonez et al., 2011).

This is an ongoing issue with massive datasets scraped from the internet and crowdsourced data collection. This facelessness, the lack of agency for the people in the photographs, and the lack of identity for people behind the scenes doing this tedious work, is rendered into numbers. I observed some clear gendering of the people in the MSCOCO (Lin et al., 2014) dataset images and captions. As I read more about how mass workers are used to caption dataset images, and the instructions they are given and the conditions they work under, I gained an understanding of the reasons behind the gendering of these barely human appearing images. Background data plays a large part in the gender of the person (Wang et al., 2019), as does the action they are supposedly doing. The biases of the workers and the level of detail in the instructions and oversight also play a role, often perpetuating bias. This work problematizes the large corporate datasets that we are becoming increasingly reliant upon and the use of underpaid mass worker groups (Aguinis et al., 2021) but presents the results in a humorous game of linked AI systems that highlight the absurdity of our reliance on such systems. This oscillation speaks to the core of metamodernism. With a shift away from AI fanaticism and toward irony (Vermeulen & Van Den Akker, 2010), absurdism has been used to draw attention to the problems (see Figure 6.2).

6.2.3 Gender Tapestry

We often say gender is a spectrum without considering that it is more than a linear construct. *Gender Tapestry* (Rosenbaum, 2022) is a gender classification artwork where instead of a gender, the user receives a custom mixed color, the results of a custom, multilabel image classifier.

I began this project to explore not only the history of facial recognition and gender classification but also color perception. Like different computer monitors, most humans experience color in different ways. Some differences are huge while some are very small, but we all see color uniquely (Emery and Webster, 2019). The theory that I explored through this work was to consider that gender perception and experience is much the same as color perception, that everyone has a slightly different experience of gender because it is informed by our life experiences and culture and our own personal perception of our gender.

I wanted to create something that equated color with gender, so that instead of receiving a gender classification, people would receive their own unique color mix. *Gender Tapestry* (Rosenbaum, 2022) is a work that explores gender as a 3D color space. The result was an evolving mosaic using the color results of the users and a GAN trained on their faces. The mosaic gained in complexity as more people interacted with the system and received their custom gender colors. I particularly enjoy working with multiple AI systems in a complex network of multimodal interaction. Throughout my research, I have explored gender classification and its fallibility and lack of inclusiveness. I may have started *Gender Tapestry* with the aim of creating a better way to look at gender classification, but in the process, I think I have explored a better, metamodernist, way to look at gender. *Gender Tapestry* is a community work. It works best the more people interact with it and help it learn and grow. It problematizes gender classifiers but educates through the medium of classification and color. Color and gender have long been associated together, but to take it beyond the binary, into a full spectrum of color possibilities is to make gender as a social construct more tangible. The classifier was trained using pronouns and largely artificial faces in a multilabel system (Fürnkranz et al., 2008) that acknowledges that people use multiple sets of pronouns. Pronouns are a key element to the understanding of gender, understanding through semantic relationships (Lauscher et al., 2022), and understanding through exploration and discovery of our own identities (Pullen Sansfaçon et al., 2020). A pronoun is a personal label, a way of announcing our identity

FIGURE 6.2
Frankenstein's telephone chain images and captions.

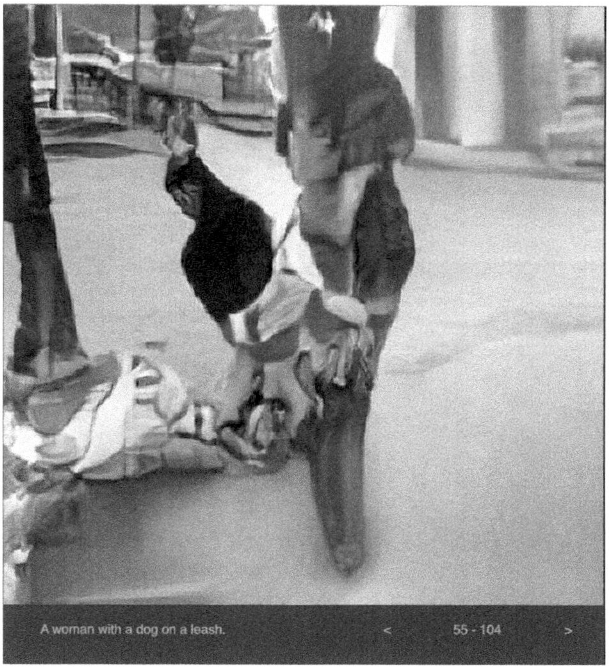

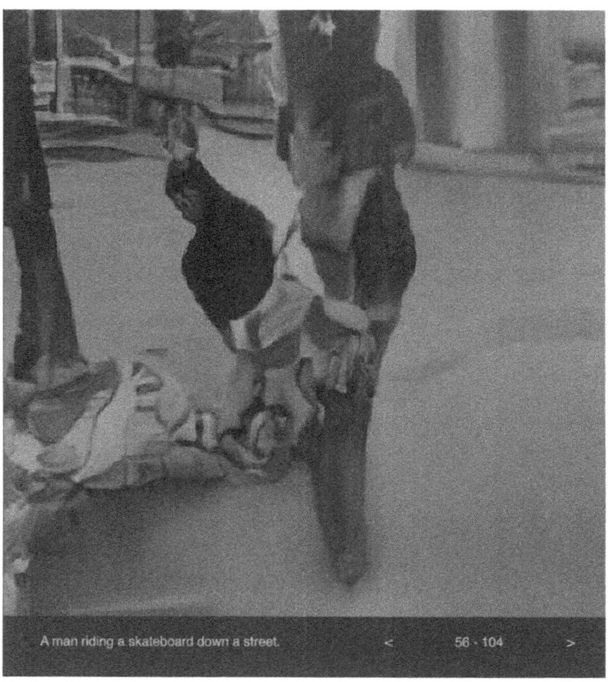

FIGURE 6.2
(Continued)

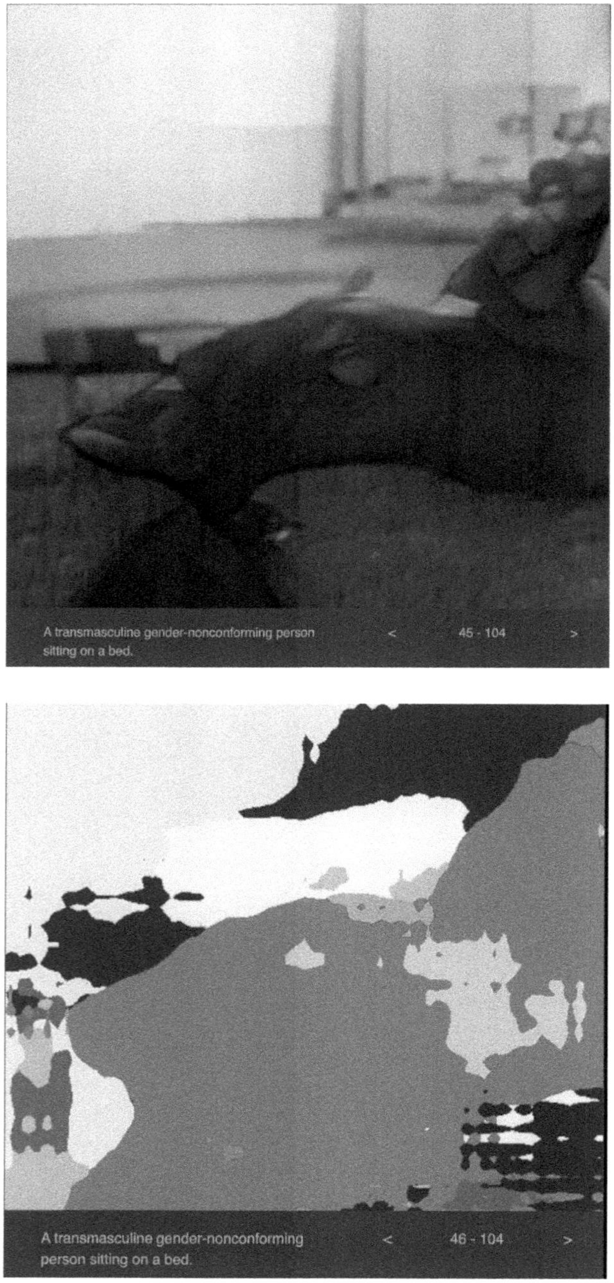

FIGURE 6.2
(Continued)

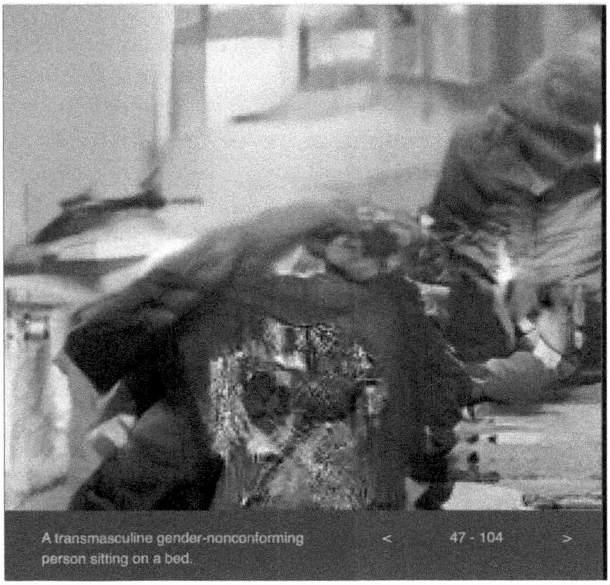

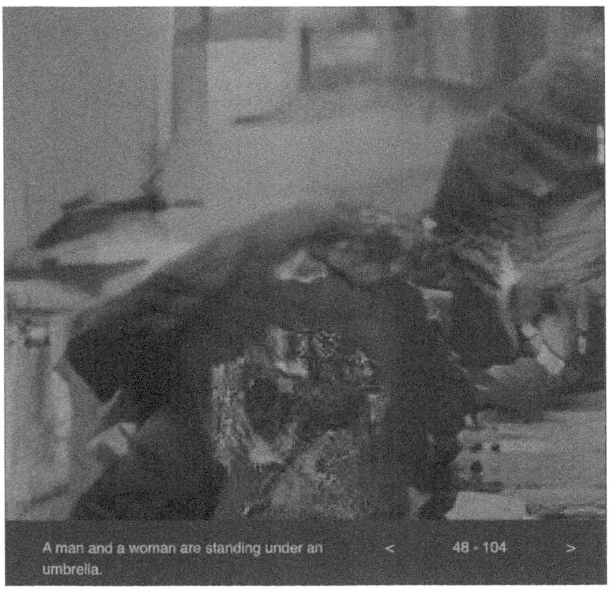

FIGURE 6.2
(Continued)

to the world. It is also a way to learn about and understand gender and explore our relationship with the nature of gender and what it means to us on a personal level. Further to this, rather than sanitizing the images that went into the classifier, as is typical in most gender classifiers (Golomb et al., 1991), I queered the results by leaning in to the performativity of gender (Butler, 1988). Therefore, while each image will always receive the same color, different ways of expressing yourself and your gender will receive different results. This work explores a wholesome different way to perceive gender, beyond the confines of a binary, to an optimistic future of acceptance (see, Figure 6.3). An opportunity to believe in gender as more than a biology, more than a binary, and to believe that we can get past limited AI perceptions of gender. This belief, this sense of hope and optimism characterizes metamodernism over postmodernism (Koford, 2022).

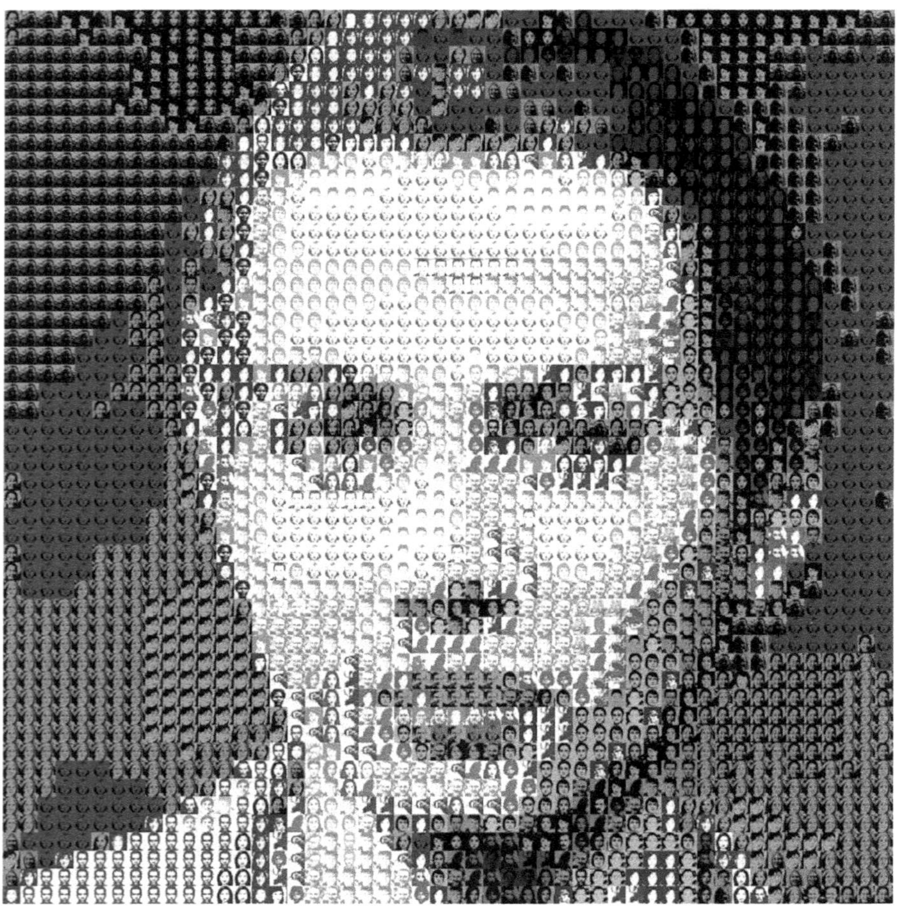

FIGURE 6.3
Gender Tapestry examples and finalized mosaic.

6.2.4 Self_Portrait

Continuing my explorations of gender and AI, *Self_Portrait* explores gender through different connected AI systems that examines how certain words, like personality terms, such as domineering, nurturing, or strong, can have gendered connotations. *Self_Portrait* uses a multilabel classifier (Fürnkranz et al., 2008) trained on certain word groups and assigns those to the user. It then passes a prompt using those assigned words to stable diffusion (Rombach et al., 2022) using ControlNets (Zhang et al., 2023) to mimic the viewer's position. The AI draws its impression of what a person with those personality terms looks like. However, a truly metamodernist work would not simply accept what an AI classifies a person as, so there is a second stage to the work where the user can choose to accept the assigned terms or change them to better suit themselves. A new portrait is generated and then transplanted onto the viewers face using augmented reality.

All of this must use AI. There is no way that users will get original works every time without using a system like stable diffusion. The AI is intrinsically tied to this artwork, just as gender is, because it is an examination of the assumptions AI makes about us. Different AI systems make snap judgements of us every day, from our browsing habits on Facebook to our style of writing on twitter (Verhoeven et al., 2016). Every action becomes a part of profiling users individually on each of these sites (Flekova and Gurevych, 2013). As it is algorithmically determined, our profile may not always be what we choose. Because of profiling and the biases that get reinforced, more insidious systems may end up causing issues, like job searching and applications (Keinert-Kisin, 2016), the justice system (Richardson et al., 2019) and financial systems (Johnson et al., 2019). *Self_Portrait* cannot show the breadth of AI access and overreach, but it can show how we take the labels different AI systems assign us for granted. I consulted for the classifier with ChatGPT (OpenAI, 2021) to produce a list of words associated with genders and generated batches of faces using those terms in stable diffusion to help fill in the dataset. Because this work is about what AI perceives with specific words, by using systems like stable diffusion and ChatGPT, we can directly show how generative AI systems process inputs to see their assumptions and biases writ large. Large language models in particular are increasingly referential with knowledge of AI bias and difficulty trained into the systems. This makes generative AI uniquely suitable for interrogating itself and AI. This is a particularly metamodernist approach, oscillating between pure research and academic understanding, and interrogations with machines which neither have intelligence, nor understanding but distill information in a forever moving and changing cycle of training and development. Working with these systems tie into the metamodernist approach of hope and despair, an attempt at finding reason and truth within a system that, by its nature, cannot have reason or know objective truth. Increasingly, I use AI in multiple stages of development, from ideation and planning to dataset and programming support. This isn't because I believe AI is faultless, but rather because I believe that interrogating AI with AI is the best way to understand the limitations of AI. AI magnifies biases, so what better way to hold a mirror up to those issues and biases than with AI?

Self_Portrait is about labels, and about accepting, or not, the labels that are given us by external forces. I think that, in the past labels were something that happened to us, that people hung on us. They ostracized us for our labels. Now labels are something we claim for ourselves. They help us find communities and connection. They can still be sources for ostracization, but now they are most often chosen and accepted, embraced. This work is about not just accepting the labels thrust upon us by an unknowing and uncaring machine but choosing our labels for ourselves. I enjoyed watching people use the system and laugh as their labels came up and then take great care choosing their own. That care and interest in what these words mean for us is what this work is truly about. Rather than the acceptance of a bleak post-modernist society where we accept the assignations of AI systems, this is a metamodernist look at how we can work with AI to accept ourselves. This work was created in concert with Melanie Huang for a site-specific work for the Science Gallery Melbourne. The collaboration that built this work from a small concept to a cohesive artwork experienced by 20,000 people is part of the spirit of Metamodernism, working together, using open source technology, creating a large communal mood board together and working towards a metanarrative (Stoev, 2022) that informed the final work (see Figure 6.4).

FIGURE 6.4
Self_Portrait in action, photos by Alan Weedon and the Science Gallery Melbourne.

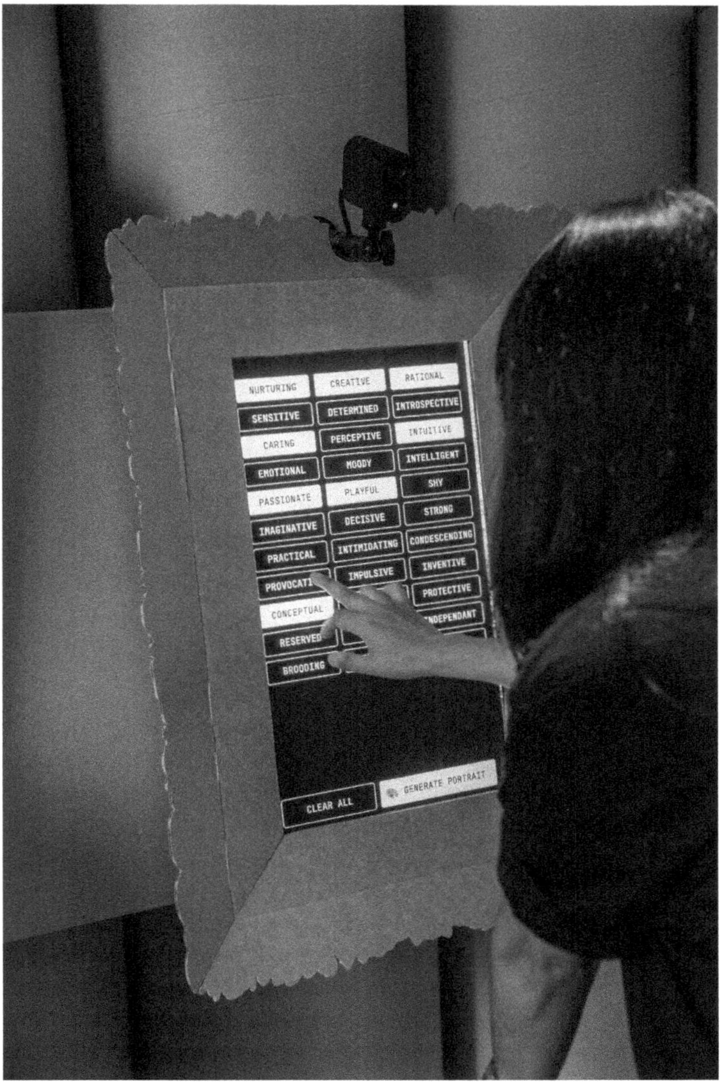

FIGURE 6.4
(Continued)

6.2.5 Discussion

In exploring the intersections of AI, gender, and perception, my work embodies the spirit of metamodernism. Metamodernism calls for an oscillation between opposing concepts, acknowledging the limitations and biases of AI systems while still using them to shed light on societal issues. Just as metamodernism seeks to transcend the binary nature of modernism and postmodernism, I aim to challenge the binary categorization of gender

FIGURE 6.4
(Continued)

within AI systems. My work oscillates between castigating AI for its biases and shortcomings and using AI to highlight and explore those shortcomings in a way that allows viewers to engage with the subject. Balancing that oscillation to ensure that neither the critique nor the engagement is lost is a key part of my artistic approach, just as I must balance the scientific and the artistic.

Metamodernism encourages a reevaluation of grand narratives and a departure from cynicism towards a more sincere and optimistic perspective. In my work, I strive to challenge the existing gender classification systems and question why AI needs to know a person's gender in the first place. By redirecting the focus towards pronouns, a more inclusive and respectful approach is possible. My aim with my work is not only to highlight the possibilities of AI but also why we must approach it with caution. Exploring the biases while showcasing an optimistic view towards creating work that engages with the problems of AI as it works with AI systems itself. My work *Set in Stone* highlights an optimistic view of AI bias through the artistic debiasing of a biased neural network, showcasing a metamodernist optimism beyond the postmodernist problematization. Through my works *Frankenstein's Telephone* and *Self_Portrait*, I explore the biases inherent in existing AI systems using irony to highlight the issues and challenges, promoting interactive engagement with these serious problems in a lighthearted way. *Gender Tapestry* provides an optimistic way to explore gender classification and further our understanding of gender. Allowing engagement between people and AI to create a collaborative dialogue that fosters understanding of the limitations of gender categorization, and a joyous use of color and community engagement.

My multidisciplinary use of AI systems and collaboration with other artists and experts reflect the metamodernist idea of embracing complexity and hybridity. Through the integration of various AI techniques, such as style transfer, GANs, and latent diffusion, I create multimodal interactive experiences that engage participants in a dialogue about the assumptions and biases embedded in AI.

By exploring the potential of AI and questioning its limitations, my work embodies the metamodernist spirit of critical engagement, sincere exploration, and a constant reevaluation of existing systems. I believe that through this lens, we can strive for a more nuanced and inclusive understanding of gender and challenge the assumptions made by AI systems.

Gender remains a critical issue in AI systems, from the categorization and gendering of people to the biases and the continued perception of gender as a binary rather than as a spectrum. Most gender classification systems work on a binary and don't allow for the myriad differences of humanity and are therefore incorrect much of the time, but, through my research I have largely ended up with the question, why? Why do these systems need to know people's genders at all? Why is so much time and energy taken up with trying to classify something that could be deduced with a simple question? Instead of trying to use AI to determine your gender, all that really needs to be asked is 'what are your pronouns'?

References

Aguinis, H., Villamor, I., & Ramani, R.S. 2021. MTurk research: Review and recommendations. J. Manag., 47, 823–837. https://doi.org/10.1177/0149206320969787

Baciu, C., Opre, D., Riley, S. 2016. A new way of thinking in the era of virtual reality and artificial intelligence. *Educatia 21*(14), 43–48. https://doi.org/10.13140/RG.2.1.3986.6483

Brunton, J. 2018. Whose (Meta)modernism?: Metamodernism, race, and the politics of failure. J. Mod. Lit., 41, 60. https://doi.org/10.2979/jmodelite.41.3.05

Butler, J. 2006. Gender Trouble: Feminism and the Subversion of Identity. Taylor & Francis Group, Florence, UK.

Butler, J. 1988. Performative acts and gender constitution an essay in phenomenology and feminist theory. Theatre J., 40, 519. https://doi.org/10.2307/3207893

CEO Zuckerberg: Facebook's 5 core values – CBS News [WWW Document]. 2012. www.cbsnews.com/news/ceo-zuckerberg-facebooks-5-core-values/ (Accessed 5 July 2025).

Chen, L.-C., Papandreou, G., Kokkinos, I., Murphy, K., Yuille, A.L. 2016. DeepLab: Semantic image segmentation with deep convolutional nets, atrous convolution, and fully connected CRFs. *arXiv*. https://doi.org/10.48550/arXiv.1606.00915

Emery, K.J., Webster, M.A. 2019. Individual differences and their implications for color perception. Curr. Opin. Behav. Sci., 30, 28–33. https://doi.org/10.1016/j.cobeha.2019.05.002

Flekova, L., Gurevych, I. 2013. Can we hide in the web? Large scale simultaneous age and gender author profiling in social media. In P. Forner, R. Navigli, D. Tufis, & N. Ferro (Eds.), *Working notes for CLEF 2013 conference* (pp. 411–423). CEUR-WS. http://ceur-ws.org/Vol-1179/

Fürnkranz, J., Hüllermeier, Eyke, Loza Mencía, Eneldo, Brinker, Klaus, Fawcett Fürnkranz, T.J., Loza Mencía, E, Hüllermeier, E, Brinker, K. 2008. Multilabel classification via calibrated label ranking. Mach. Learn., 73, 133–153. https://doi.org/10.1007/s10994-008-5064-8

Gatys, L.A., Ecker, A.S., Bethge, M. 2015. A neural algorithm of artistic style. *arXiv*. https://doi.org/10.48550/arXiv.1508.06576

Golomb, B.A., Lawrence, D.T., Sejnowski, T.J. 1991. Sexnet: A neural network identifies sex from human faces. Adv. Neural Inf. Process. Syst., 3, 572–577.

Goodfellow, I.J., Pouget-Abadie, J., Mirza, M., Xu, B., Warde-Farley, D., Ozair, S., Courville, A., Bengio, Y. 2014. Generative adversarial networks. *arXiv*. https://doi.org/10.48550/arXiv.1406.2661

Johnson, K., Pasquale, F., Chapman, J. 2019. Artificial intelligence, machine learning, and bias in finance: Toward responsible innovation. *Fordham Law Rev*. 88. Acticle 5.

Keinert-Kisin, C. 2016. Corporate social responsibility and discrimination: gender bias in personnel selection. Springer International Publishing, Cham.

Koford, K.L. 2022. A hug for humanity: Metamodernism and masculinity on television in Ted Lasso (Master's thesis, Brigham Young University). BYU ScholarsArchive. https://scholarsarchive.byu.edu/etd/9753

Lauscher, A., Crowley, A., Hovy, D. 2022. Welcome to the modern world of pronouns: Identity-inclusive natural language processing beyond gender. In N. Calzolari, C.-R. Huang, H. Kim, J. Pustejovsky, L. Wanner, K.-S. Choi, P.-M. Ryu, H.-H. Chen, L. Donatelli, H. Ji, S. Kurohashi, P. Paggio, N. Xue, S. Kim, Y. Hahm, Z. He, T. K. Lee, E. Santus, F. Bond, & S.-H. Na (Eds.), *Proceedings of the 29th International Conference on Computational Linguistics (COLING 2022)* (pp. 1221–1232). International Committee on Computational Linguistics. https://aclanthology.org/2022.coling-1.105/

Lin, T.-Y., Maire, M., Belongie, S., Bourdev, L., Girshick, R., Hays, J., Perona, P., Ramanan, D., Zitnick, C.L., Dollár, P. 2014. Microsoft COCO: Common objects in context. ArXiv E-Prints. https://doi.org/10.48550/arXiv.1405.0312

Nguyen, A., Clune, J., Bengio, Y., Dosovitskiy, A., Yosinski, J. 2016. Plug & play generative networks: Conditional iterative generation of images in latent space, Proceedings – 30th IEEE Conference on Computer Vision and Pattern Recognition, CVPR 2017. Institute of Electrical and Electronics Engineers Inc. https://doi.org/10.1109/CVPR.2017.374

Nibali, A. 2017. Mode collapse in GANs. AidenNibali.org. https://aiden.nibali.org/blog/2017-01-18-mode-collapse-gans/

Ordonez, V., Kulkarni, G., Berg, T.L. 2011. Im2Text: Describing images using 1 million captioned photographs. In Adv. Neural Inf. Process. Syst. 24 25th Annu. Conf. Neural Inf. Process. Syst. 2011 NIPS 2011 1–9.

Park, T., Liu, M.-Y., Wang, T.-C., Zhu, J.-Y. 2019. Semantic image synthesis with spatially-adaptive normalization. arXiv:1903.07291. https://doi.org/10.48550/arXiv.1903.07291

Pullen Sansfaçon, A., Medico, D., Suerich-Gulick, F., Temple Newhook, J. 2020. "I knew that I wasn't cis, I knew that, but I didn't know exactly": Gender identity development, expression and affirmation in youth who access gender affirming medical care. Int. J. Transgender Health, 21, 307–320. https://doi.org/10.1080/26895269.2020.1756551

Richardson, R., Schultz, J.M., Crawford, K. 2019. Dirty data, bad predictions: How civil rights violations impact police data, predictive policing systems, and justice. N. Y. Univ. Law Rev. 94.

Rombach, R., Blattmann, A., Lorenz, D., Esser, P., Ommer, B. 2022. High-resolution image synthesis with latent diffusion models. In *Proceedings of the IEEE/CVF Conference on Computer Vision and Pattern Recognition (CVPR 2022)* (pp. 10684–10695). IEEE. https://doi.org/10.1109/CVPR52688.2022.01042

Rosenbaum, J. 2022. *AI perceptions of gender* (Doctoral dissertation, RMIT University). RMIT University Research Repository.

Shelley, M. W. (1891). Frankenstein: Or, The Modern Prometheus. London: George Routledge & Sons.

Stoev, D. 2022. Metamodernism or metamodernity. Arts, 11, 91. https://doi.org/10.3390/arts11050091

Stott, P. 2011. Transcendental imaging and augmented reality. Technoetic Arts J. Specul. Res., 9, 49–64. https://doi.org/10.1386/tear.9.1.49_1

Verhoeven, B., Daelemans, W., Plank, B. 2016. TwiSty: A multilingual Twitter stylometry corpus for gender and personality profiling. In Proc. 10th Int. Conf. Lang. Resour. Eval. LREC 2016 1632–1637.

Vermeulen, T., Van Den Akker, R. 2010. Notes on metamodernism. J. Aesthet. Cult., 2, 5677. https://doi.org/10.3402/jac.v2i0.5677

Wang, T., Zhao, J., Yatskar, M., Chang, K.-W., Ordonez, V. 2019. Balanced datasets are not enough: estimating and mitigating gender bias in deep image representations. *arXiv*. https://doi.org/10.48550/arXiv.1811.08489

Xu, T., Zhang, P., Huang, Q., Zhang, H., Gan, Z., Huang, X., He, X. 2017. AttnGAN: Fine-grained text to image generation with attentional generative adversarial networks. arXiv. https://doi.org/10.48550/arXiv.1711.10485

Part III

Designing Inclusive Digital Products and Ecosystems

7

Building Inclusive Technology Products and Services: Insights from Financial Inclusion Efforts in India and Beyond[1]

Sirin Kumar and Vijayakumar Bharathi S.

7.1 Introduction

> ***"True economics, stands for social justice, it promotes the good of all equally including the weakest, and is indispensable for decent life."*** –
> Excerpts from the book "My Religion" by Mahatma Gandhi

The role of financial inclusion is well recognized for achieving economic growth and poverty reduction. Therefore, policymakers and major participants in the financial system need to act to achieve maximum financial inclusion. The issue is more important for emerging countries than for developed countries due to differences in the extent of exclusion, the state of respective economies, and societal norms. The increasing digitalization of the economy, technology adoption by traditional financial players, and the role of fintech have opened new avenues and tools for the delivery of financial services by enhancing reach and lowering costs. It would be useful to evaluate policy measures and models of successful countries to draw learnings and suitably adapt as per the conditions of any other. It is also important to understand the new challenges of a digital economy and adopt high-level principles and a structured approach while framing policies for financial inclusion to achieve maximum benefit.

While the topic of financial inclusion globally and in India has been covered extensively, the studies have addressed fragmented aspects of the subject, such as researching factors that influence financial inclusion or providing historical context or discussion on some policy measures in a limited manner. Most literature tends to focus on or discuss the policy aspects based on literature review in a limited manner. Falaiye et al. (2024), based on a literature review, provide historical contexts, trends, and challenges in the

DOI: 10.1201/9781003591078-10

use of key technologies for financial inclusion in select emerging markets. Oanh (2024) investigated the relationship between digital financial inclusion, technological advancement, environmental conditions, and economic growth. Pandya and Budhedeo (2025) examine macroeconomic and socio-economic factors influencing financial inclusion in India. Srinivasan et al. (2024) analyze banking sector reforms in India and their impact on financial inclusivity and performance. Solanki & Chhikara (2024) focus on the impact of the Pradhan Mantri Micro Units Development and Refinance Agency (MUDRA) Yojana on Financial inclusion in India. Mishra et al. (2024) undertake a systematic literature review of relevant articles on financial inclusion. Maity & Majumder (2025) create a financial inclusion index and rate countries on financial inclusion. Given the importance of the financial inclusion topic, there is an urgent need to provide information on replicable policies and models which are based on successful examples.

This chapter provides comprehensive coverage of the evolution of financial inclusion in India, spanning the cooperative movement in the 1950s to the latest initiatives on digital financial services with the idea of drawing learnings for implementation in other countries or dealing with new world challenges in the digital world. With analysis of secondary data and charts, it demonstrates the success of the ongoing efforts in India. It provides a multistakeholder model with the involvement of the Government, regulators, banks, nonbanks, business correspondents, and all stakeholders. It incorporates the new national level indices such as the Financial Inclusion Index and Digital Payments Index. It delves into the role of fintech and the latest technologies and provides examples of successful efforts by major countries across the world. More importantly, the chapter goes beyond India to provide valuable insights on cross-country analysis of successful products of other countries. It examines the unresolved challenges and provides future direction and approach that should be considered while formulating a strategy for financial inclusion in any country. Therefore, the chapter not only bridges the academic gap but also offers a replicable framework that can be adopted by other countries while implementing equitable financial systems in the current digital environment. The notes on numerals and abbreviations used in this chapter are provided in Appendices I and II, respectively.

7.1.1 Defining Financial Inclusion and Its Significance

Financial inclusion refers to providing individuals and businesses with access to useful and affordable financial products and services[2]. It includes the provision of basic facilities such as bank accounts, credit, payments, and insurance products. This helps in improving financial savings and facilitates credit for business or other needs, thereby improving livelihoods, providing economic resilience, and reducing poverty. Financial inclusion is important for economic development as it facilitates income generation, smooths consumption patterns, and enables investments[3]. It is integral to achieving global SDGs and helps in promoting inclusive growth and reducing economic disparities[4].

7.1.2 India's Journey Toward Financial Inclusion

The significant progress of India in achieving financial inclusion can be validated by observing the position of India vis-a-vis other countries on some parameters of financial inclusion and the progress in indices introduced by the RBI. Brief discussion and trends on these aspects are as follows.

According to the 79th round of survey by the National Sample Survey Office (NSSO) of India published in October 2024, 94.6% of India's population aged 18 and above owned financial accounts. An important parameter to measure the position of financial inclusion in a country is the percentage of citizens beyond a certain age group who hold financial accounts for undertaking financial transactions. Figure 7.1 provides a relative position of India compared to other key jurisdictions on this parameter. It is observed that India is very close to developed countries' financial inclusion status and much beyond the world average of 76%. It may be noted that for India, the data from 2024 have been provided based on a national survey, whereas for other countries, it is based on a 2021 survey, which is the latest available World Bank Findex survey. The data capture the rapid strides by India in achieving financial inclusion in recent years. However, it also needs to be recognized that comprehensive financial inclusion involves the availability of various financial products and services and active participation in the financial system.

The **Financial Inclusion Index** (FI-Index), introduced by the RBI in March 2021[5], measures financial inclusion across three dimensions: Access (availability of financial services), Usage (adoption of financial products), and Quality (financial literacy and consumer protection). Scored between 0 and 100, the index is computed annually without a base year. The FI Index improved from 43.4 in March 2017 to 64.2 in March 2024, reflecting progress driven by initiatives like Pradhan Mantri Jan Dhan Yojana (PMJDY) and UPI expansion. By identifying gaps and guiding policies, the FI Index supports India's efforts to enhance financial inclusion and promote equitable access to financial services nationwide. The annual progress is provided in Figure 7.2.

The **Payments Index** of India, introduced by the RBI in 2018, tracks the adoption and growth of digital payment systems nationwide. It evaluates parameters like transaction volume, value, and reach. The index has shown remarkable growth due to innovations like the UPI, Bharat Bill Payment System (BBPS), and RuPay cards. The index rose from 100 (base year 2018) to 445.5 in 2024, reflecting a 249% growth. This surge underscores India's progress towards a cashless economy and its commitment to enhancing financial inclusion through digital payments (Lenka et al., 2022). Figure 7.3 shows the annual progress.

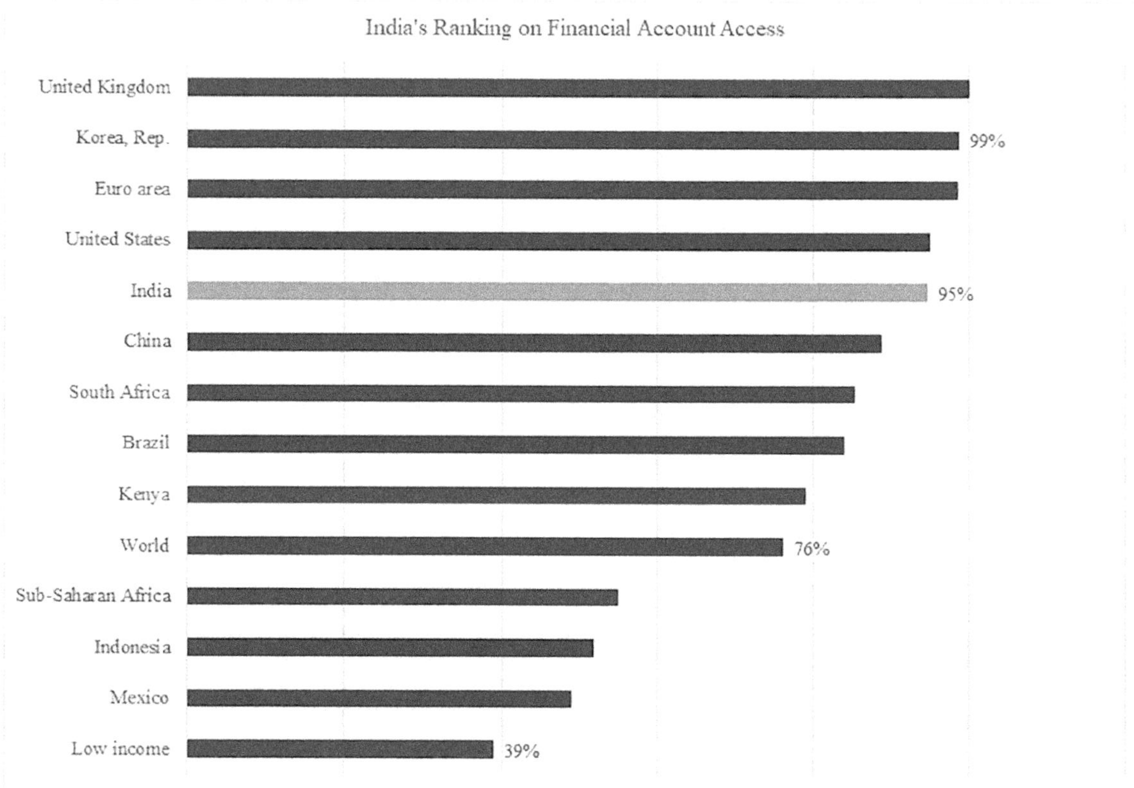

FIGURE 7.1
India's ranking on financial account access.

Source:

- ***World Bank Findex database of 2021 for all countries (except India) on financial account access (age 15+)***
- ***For India the latest data from the 79th round of the NSS of India published in Oct 2024 on financial account access (age 18+).***

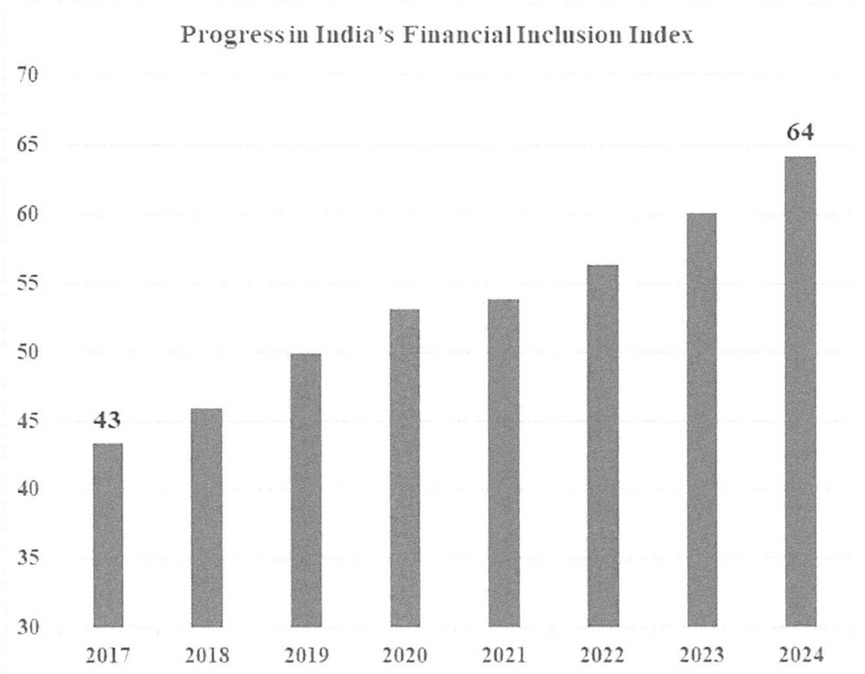

FIGURE 7.2
Progress in India's financial inclusion index.
Source: **RBI Annual Report 2023-24 and RBI press release dated July 9, 2024. www.rbi.org.in/Scripts/BS_PressReleaseDisplay.aspx?prid=58259**

The above figures highlight the remarkable progress in Indian Financial Inclusion efforts in the recent period. While India's achievements are commendable, learning from global financial inclusion initiatives (discussed in Chapter 5) offers valuable insights for India as well. In the next section the evolution of policies and actions which have led to this achievement are discussed in a sequential manner.

7.2 Financial Inclusion Landscape in India

7.2.1 Evolution of Policy Frameworks

India's financial inclusion journey is a testament to decades of policy reform, institutional innovation, and strategic planning aimed at reducing socioeconomic disparities and enhancing access to financial services (Figure 7.4).

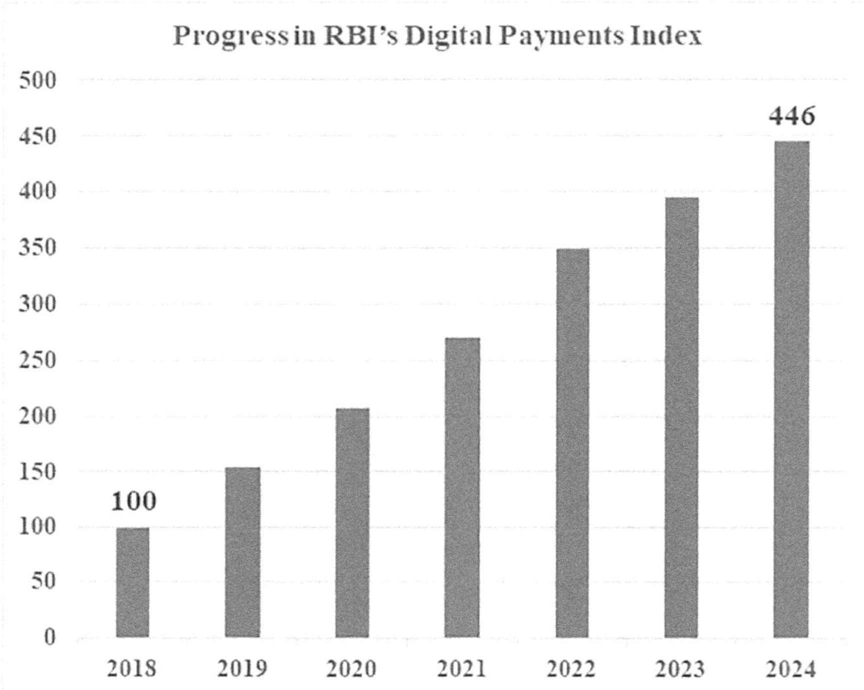

FIGURE 7.3
Progress in RBI's Digital Payments Index.
Source: **RBI press release dated Jan 29, 2025**
www.rbi.org.in/Scripts/BS_PressReleaseDisplay.aspx?prid=59632

1900–1950: The Cooperative Movement and Institutional Foundations

The evolution of financial inclusion in India can be traced to the cooperative movement, which started in the early 1900s. It sought to alleviate rural poverty and reduce dependence on exploitative moneylenders by introducing formal credit systems tailored to rural households. Inspired by European models, cooperatives initially succeeded but faced challenges such as political interference and operational inefficiencies, limiting their long-term impact (Sethy et al, 2018). Thereafter, during the period 1930–1950, the Agricultural Credit Department was established by the RBI to formalize credit access for the agriculture sector. These initiatives provided the institutional framework and policies to improve rural financial inclusion.

1950–1990: Nationalization and Expansion

The nationalization of banks in 1969 was a major milestone, which significantly expanded banking networks in rural and semi-urban areas. Policies such as the Lead Bank Scheme and priority sector lending helped in providing credit access for agriculture, small-scale industries, and marginalized

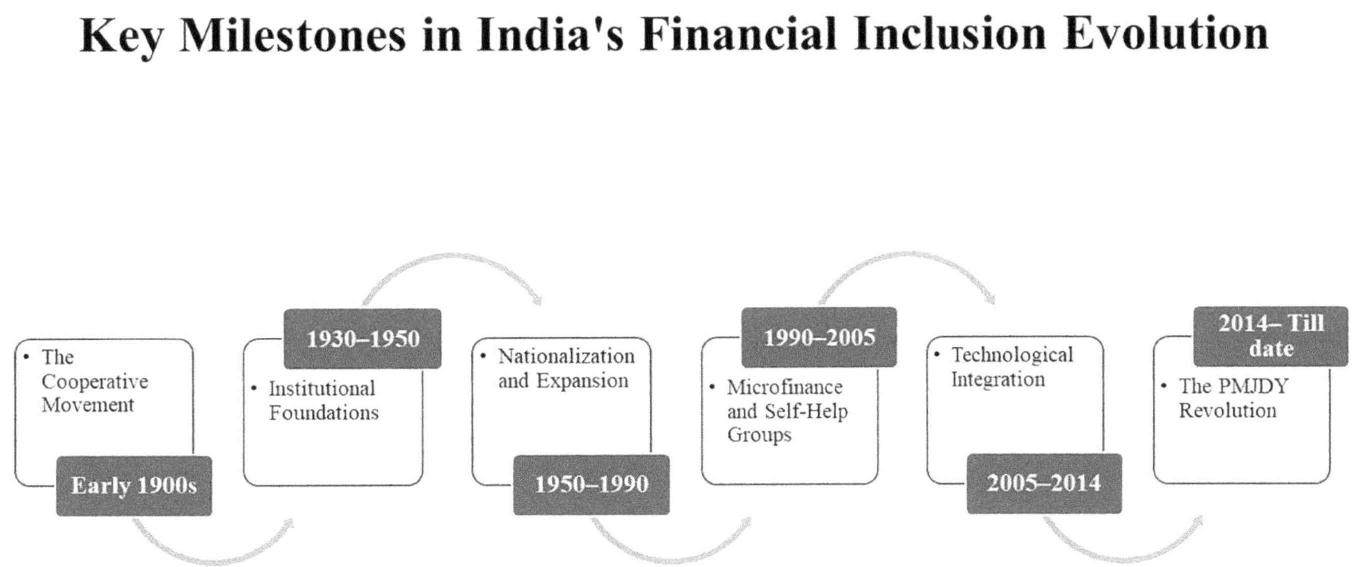

FIGURE 7.4
Key milestones in India's financial inclusion evolution.
Source: **Author depiction of the timeline.**

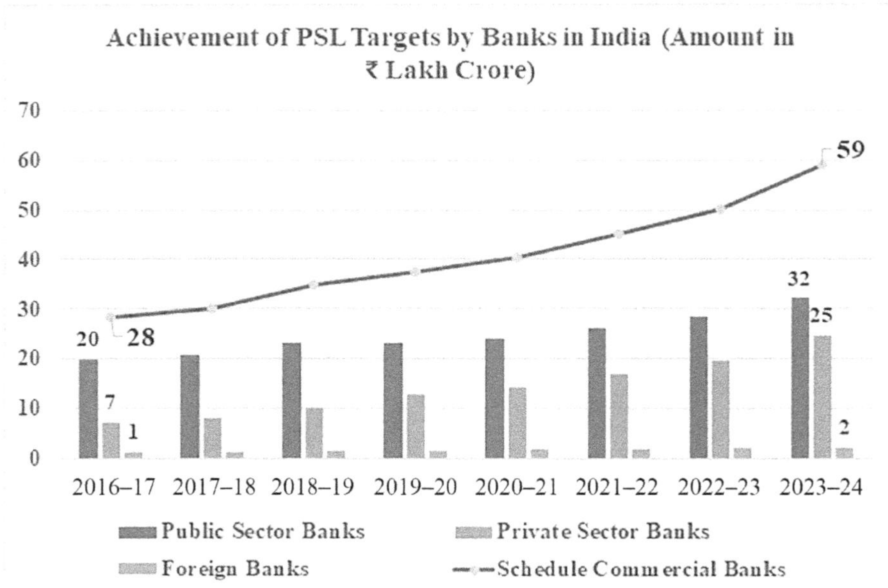

FIGURE 7.5
Achievement of PSL targets by banks (Amount in ₹ lakh crore*).

*Equal to INR 1 trillion
Source: **RBI Annual Reports 2016–17 to 2023–24.**

sections of society. The establishment of the National Bank for Agriculture and Rural Development (NABARD) in 1982 and the enactment of the Regional Rural Banks Act in 1975 further bolstered rural financial systems. The trend in the amount of loans disbursed by banks for achieving the Priority Sector Lending (PSL) targets is in Figure 7.5. The growth in the achievement of PSL targets by the scheduled commercial banks from 2016–17 to 2023–24 from Rs.28 Lakh crore to Rs.59 Lakh crore, respectively, is indicative of the success of the policy in ensuring the flow of funds to potentially excluded segments. The segment-wise analysis of the growth reveals the increasing role of private sector banks over time from Rs.7 lakh crore to Rs.25 lakh crore, which is a much higher annual growth compared to the public sector. This may be the case because of additional private banks getting licenses and also on account of comparatively much higher growth. However, the role of foreign banks is comparatively limited in providing funding to the priority sectors.

1990–2005: Microfinance and SHGs

The emergence of microfinance in the 1990s revolutionized financial inclusion as it provided small-ticket financial services, thereby bringing the unbanked segments to the formal financial fold. Further, the role of Self-Help Groups (SHG) and Joint Liability Groups (JLGs) enabled women, especially in rural

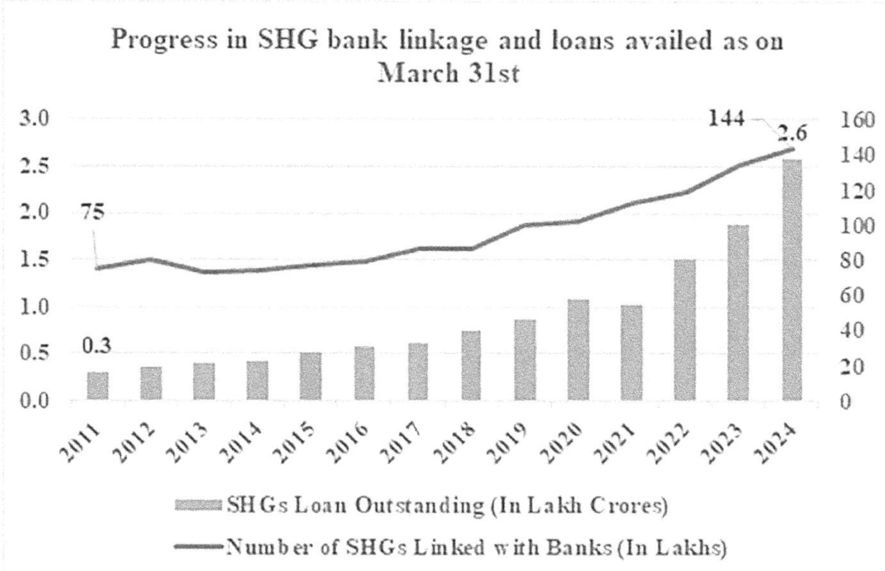

FIGURE 7.6

Progress in SHG-Bank linkage in India.

***Source*: NABARD Status of Microfinance in India reports from 2012 to 2024.**

areas, to form groups for collective savings and credit access (Figure 7.6). These models addressed the challenges of limited banking infrastructure by fostering group-based financial practices (Dar et al., 2021). Figure 7.6 shows the huge growth of SHGs linked with banks and availing credit facilities from banks. The number of SHGs went up from 75 lakhs in 2011 to 144 lakhs in 2024. With a similar trend, the loan outstanding with SHGs went up from 0.3 lakh crore in 2011 to 2.6 lakh crore in 2024. This is indicative of the inclusion of rural women and credit support from the formal financial system, which has led to their active employment and well-being.

2005–2014: Technological Integration

This period marked a significant policy shift with the introduction of no-frills accounts, simplified Know Your Customer (KYC) norms, and the Business Correspondent (BC) Model. Aadhaar's launch in 2009 provided a unique digital identity, streamlining account opening and enabling direct benefit transfers (DBTs). These measures expanded banking services to remote areas. The progress of India's no-frills accounts or the Basic Savings Bank Deposit (BSBD) accounts is given in Figure 7.7 which shows that the number of BSBD accounts held by individuals has gone up from 7 crores in 2010 to about 71 crores in 2024. This shows the tremendous progress in making affordable financial accounts available to the excluded segments and providing a window for availing the formal financial services.

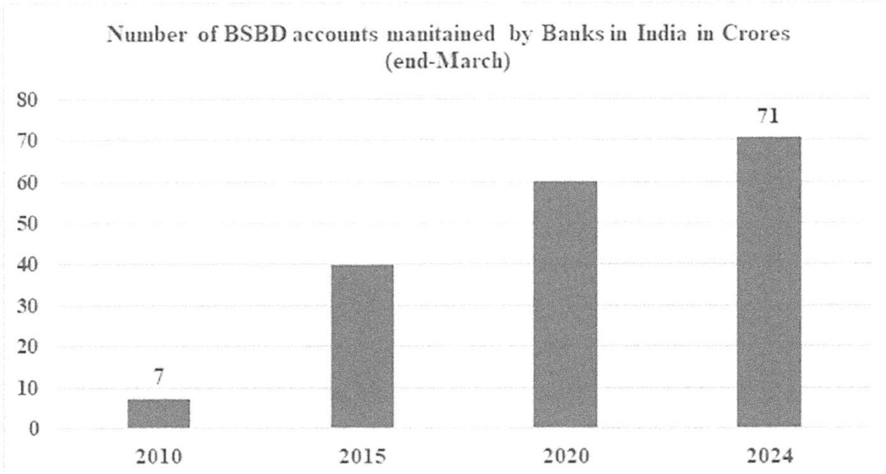

FIGURE 7.7
No. of BSBD accounts in Lakh (end-March)*
*INR 1 Lakh = INR 0.1 million
Source: **RBI Trend and Progress 2022–23 and 2023–24.**

2014 onwards: The Emergence of Digital Public Infrastructure
Since 2014, India has undergone a transformative shift in financial inclusion with the advancement of Digital Public Infrastructure (DPI) which has enabled the provision of digital financial services. These advancements have strengthened financial inclusion, bridged urban-rural divides, and integrated crores of people into the formal economy. Digital financial services have been pivotal in bridging financial gaps and leveraging technology to enhance accessibility, affordability, and security. Transaction volumes of digital payments have surged from 2,071 crores in FY 2017–18 to 18,592 crore in FY 2023–24, at a CAGR of 44%. The following section delves into various initiatives which have made this possible in detail.

7.2.2 JAM Trinity and Digital Infrastructure: Overcoming Barriers to Financial Inclusion

The Jan Dhan, Aadhaar, and Mobile (JAM) ecosystem exemplifies the transformative potential of digital technologies in financial inclusion. Further, payment systems, UPI, Aadhaar-enabled Payment Systems (AePS), and the emergence of fintechs are instrumental in building an inclusive digital financial ecosystem.

The **Jan Dhan** accounts opened under the Pradhan Mantri Jan Dhan Yojana (PMJDY) initiative enabled almost universal access to bank accounts. The PMJDY, launched in 2014, expanded banking access, bringing crores of people into the formal financial system. By January 2025, PMJDY had opened

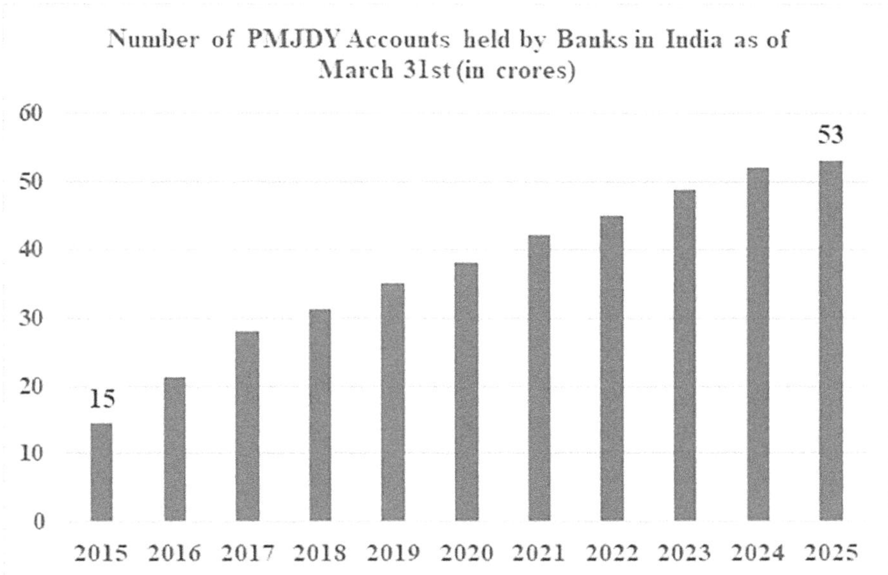

FIGURE 7.8
Number of PMJDY accounts as of March 31st (in crores).
*INR 1 Crore = INR 10 million
Source: **PIB www.pib.gov.in/PressReleasePage.aspx?PRID=2049231**

over 54 crore bank accounts with deposits exceeding ₹2.37 lakh crore[6]. Out of the above, around 67% of accounts were linked to rural and semi-urban branches. This initiative facilitated Direct Benefit Transfers (DBTs), ensuring timely and transparent government subsidy disbursement. Figure 7.8 shows the growth in the number of PMJDY accounts from about 15 crores in 2015 to 53 crores in 2025, which enabled the inclusion of hereby financially excluded individuals.

Aadhaar's biometric authentication has simplified account opening, while mobile penetration has facilitated access to banking and financial services. Aadhaar has also streamlined Direct Benefit Transfers (DBTs), reducing leakage in welfare delivery (Sethy et al., 2019). Figure 7.9 shows the increase in the number of Aadhaar generated, eKYCs, and authentications done through Aadhaar. The cumulative number of Aadhaar generated has gone up to 141 crores in 2025. The eKYC and other authentications done using Aadhaar have gone up to 2198 and 12760 crores, respectively, in 2025. This figure provides a sense of the increased coverage of Aadhaar and its usage for online financial and authentication services.

Mobile Connectivity: With nearly 116 crore mobile internet users[7], affordable devices and connectivity have expanded banking access to remote areas. Figure 7.10 illustrates key trends based on data from the Government[8]. Internet

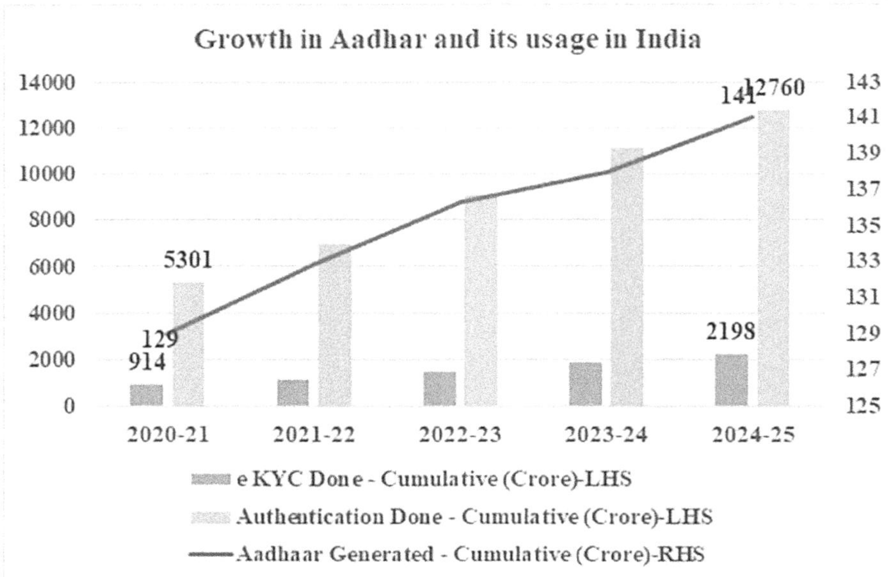

FIGURE 7.9
Growth in Aadhaar and its usage.
Source: **Meity Dashboard https://meity.dashboard.nic.in/DashboardF.aspx**

subscribers grew from 25 crores as of the end of March 2014 to 97 crores as of the end of June 2024, reflecting rapid digital adoption. Average data consumption surged from 61.66 MB in March 2014 to 21.30 GB per user in June 2024, indicating greater internet reliance and highlighting advancements in network infrastructure.

Payment Systems and UPI

India's fast payment systems, including UPI and Immediate Payment Service (IMPS), have set global benchmarks for speed, affordability, and scalability. The launch of UPI in 2016 revolutionized digital transactions, enhancing accessibility and cost efficiency. UPI transaction volume surged from 92 crores in FY 2017–18 to 13,116 crore in FY 2023–24 (CAGR 129%), while transaction value grew from ₹1 lakh crore to ₹200 lakhs crores (CAGR 138%)[9] over the same period, reinforcing its role in India's digital economy (Figure 7.11).

The Aadhaar Payment Services

The rise of Aadhaar-enabled payment services has enhanced authentication, enabling seamless biometric-based banking transactions, even in remote areas. It facilitates cash withdrawals, deposits, balance inquiries, and fund transfers through Aadhaar-linked accounts, eliminating the need for cards or PINs and expanding financial access for the unbanked. The

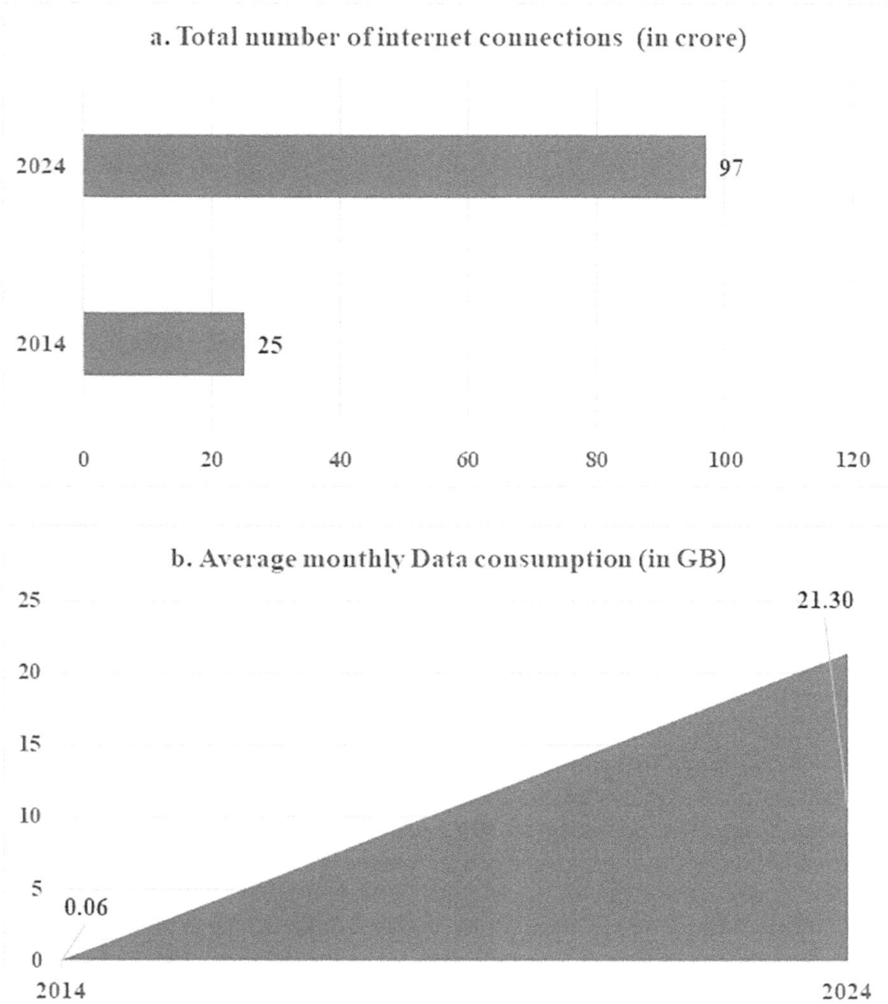

FIGURE 7.10
Progress in internet and data availability.
Source: **Govt of India www.pib.gov.in/PressReleaseIframePage.aspx?PRID=2098487**

trend shown in Figure 7.12 reveals that after the initial offtake, there has been a decline in its usage due to a decrease in the BCs that enable the use of these services and as a part of normalization in the post-Covid period. However, this aspect needs to be examined further. On the other hand, the use of Aadhaar payment systems, which are used for the disbursement of government welfare schemes, has seen a continuous rise, as can be observed in Figure 7.12.

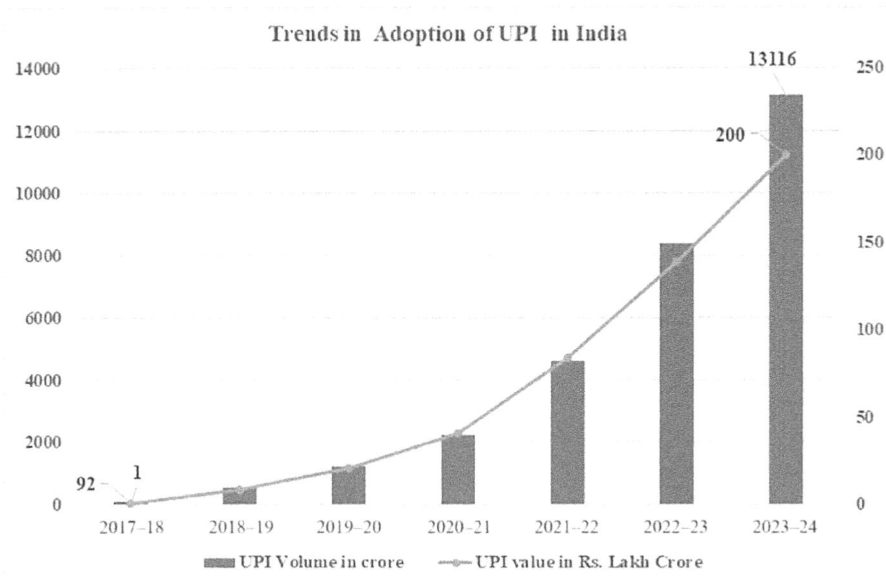

FIGURE 7.11
Trends in the adoption of UPI.

Source: **RBI Annual Reports 2013-14 to 2023-24 (Table on Payment System Indicators – Annual) and https://pib.gov.in/PressReleaseIframePage.aspx?PRID=2057013**

Digital Acceptance Infrastructure: Expanding Reach and Usability

Digital acceptance infrastructure is key to enabling seamless transactions and reducing cash dependency through Point of Sale (PoS) terminals, Micro-ATMs, QR payments, and online gateways. As shown in Figure 7.13, PoS terminals grew from about 44 lakh in March 2020 to 89 lakh in March 2024, while Micro-ATMs rose from about 4 lakh to 18 lakh during the same period, reflecting increased digital adoption in semi-urban and rural areas.

Initiatives like the Payment Infrastructure Development Fund (PIDF) and zero Merchant Discount Rate (MDR) policies on UPI and RuPay have helped in this expansion. Private sector contributions, including inventory management and micro-automated teller machine (ATM) services, have further strengthened last-mile access. To sustain growth, continued investment in offline payment solutions, contactless technology, and cybersecurity will be essential for a more inclusive digital financial ecosystem.

Microfinance and Digital Lending

Microfinance institutions and digital lenders have played a key role in providing financial services to low-income and unbanked groups. They offer microloans to small businesses, helping to generate income and improve livelihoods. These entities have leveraged technology to address credit

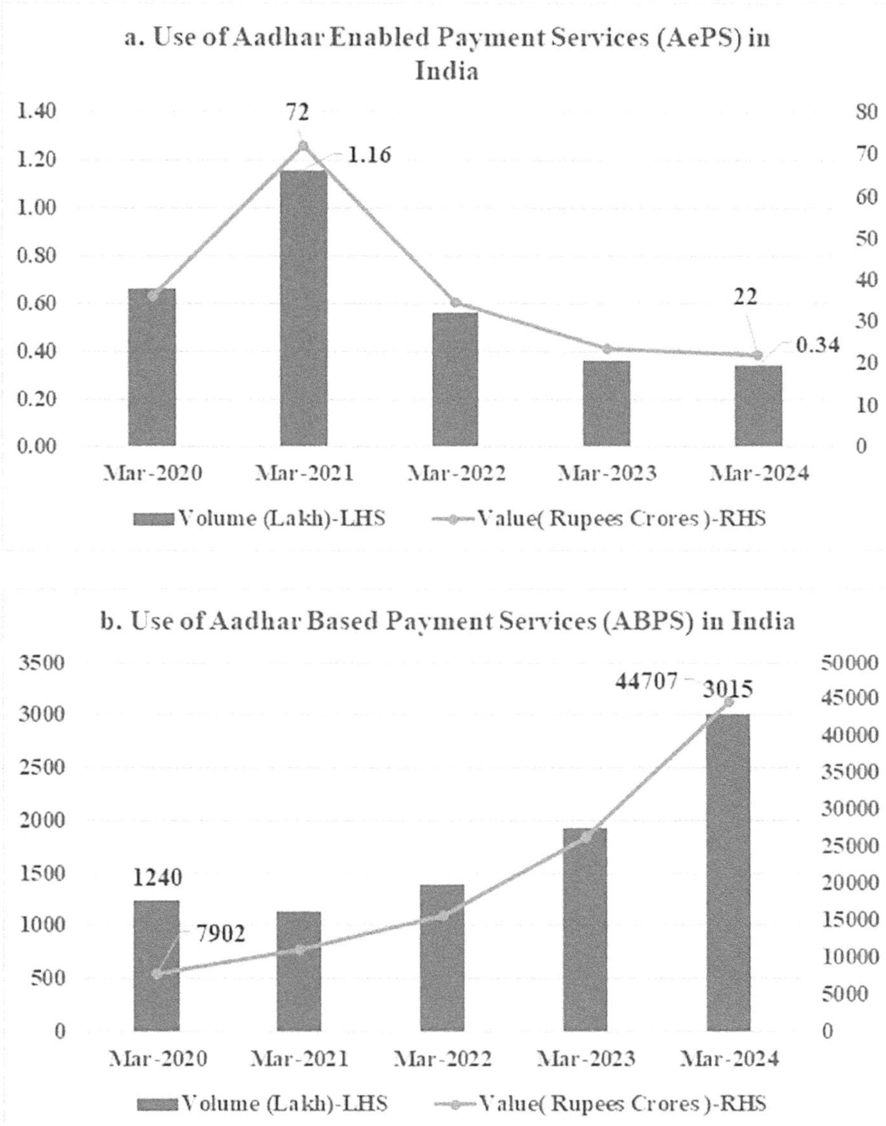

FIGURE 7.12
Usage of Aadhaar-based payments (AePS and ABPS).
Source: **RBI DBIE Payment systems indicators (Publications – Monthly Bulletin).**

constraints for underserved populations. They use various data sources to assess creditworthiness to provide credit access without collateral requirements, enabling broader access to credit, empowering borrowers, and fostering financial growth for the marginalized segments. The examples of

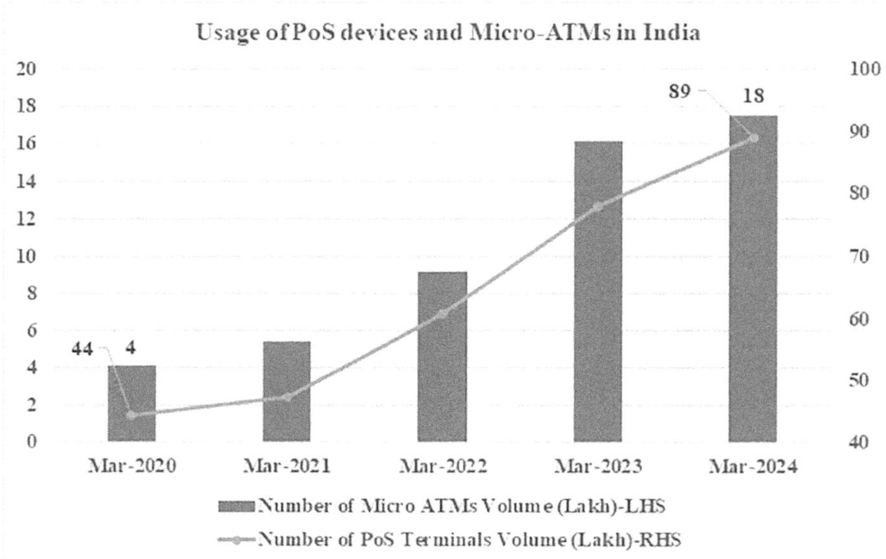

FIGURE 7.13
Usage of PoS and micro-ATM.
Source: **RBI DBIE Payment systems indicators (Publications – RBI Monthly Bulletin).**

data used for credit decisions are transaction histories, mobile usage, social media activity, utility payments, etc. Using business innovations such as product co-creation, strategic partnerships, and collaborations among banks, microlenders, and FinTech, they have enhanced the industry's overall value proposition.

Priority Sector Lending Certificates

Priority sector lending certificates (PSLCs) were introduced in 2016 by the RBI to facilitate compliance with priority sector lending (PSL) targets in an innovative way using technology. This instrument enables banks that are not in a position to provide the required credit to the priority sector as per extant norms to buy PSLCs from surplus banks at a market-determined premium, thereby helping the whole ecosystem. There are four categories of PSLCs, viz., PSLC-General, PSLC-Agriculture, PSLC-Small & Marginal Farmers, and PSLC-Micro Enterprises. These categories are aligned with the sub targets under the priority sector guidelines as these sub targets must be exclusively met by the banks. The total trading volume of PSLCs during 2023–24 stood at about Rs. 8,93,000 crores[10].

Trade Receivables Discounting System

The Trade Receivables Discounting System (TReDS), launched in 2017, enhances SME financing by enabling receivable discounting via platforms like RXIL,

M1xchange, and Invoicemart. By FY24, it processed over ₹3.5 lakh crore in transactions, benefiting more than 75,000 Micro, Small, and Medium Enterprises (MSMEs). TReDS fosters liquidity, timely payments, and economic growth.

The Unified Lending Interface (ULI) and the new JAM Trinity
The ULI, being piloted by the Reserve Bank Innovation Hub under the guidance of RBI, leverages consent-based data sharing and advanced analytics to streamline credit access for underserved segments like MSMEs, farmers, and women entrepreneurs. By enabling real-time tailored credit solutions, ULI enhances equitable access to formal financial systems. The new JAM Trinity integrates other applications, such as the UPI, e-KYC, and ULI, into the original JAM Trinity. This enhanced framework simplifies digital onboarding, enables real-time payments, and expands credit access, driving the next wave of financial inclusion and fostering inclusive economic growth in India.

7.3 Stakeholder Collaboration and Fintech Innovations in Financial Inclusion

7.3.1 Regulatory Ecosystem

Role of Government
The Government has a very important role in ensuring financial inclusion in the country. The Government of India (GoI) has taken several steps to enhance the reach of financial services to every nook and corner of the country and to all sections of society. Some major efforts by the GoI in this direction include enhancing the role of the public sector in financial services by the nationalization of banks and insurance companies, creation of specialized entities, direct benefit transfers, creation of specialized funds, interest subvention, facilitating mobile and internet connectivity through policies and several schemes of the government targeting focussed sectors, etc.

The Government nationalized the Life Insurance companies in 1956, general insurance companies in 1972, and banks in 1969 and 1980 to better serve the needs of the development of the economy in conformity with national policy and objectives. Specialized institutions such as Regional Rural Banks, NABARD, Small Industries Development Bank of India (SIDBI), etc, were created to focus on providing financial services to rural segments and Micro, Small, and Medium Enterprises (MSMEs). The Government also took steps to revitalize the cooperative banking system. Based on the Rangarajan Committee on Financial Inclusion recommendations in the year 2006, the Financial Inclusion Fund, and the Financial Inclusion Technology Fund were created to meet the costs for technology adoption and promotional initiatives by the stakeholders. Later, the Rural Infrastructure Development Fund was also created, where contributions could come in from banks with a shortfall in achieving priority sector targets. The GoI has administered various schemes. The prominent of them in the recent period are the Pradhan Mantri Jan Dhan Yojana, Atal Pension Yojana, Pradhan Mantri Jeevan Jyoti Bima Yojana, Pradhan Mantri Suraksha Bima Yojana, Stand-Up India Scheme, and Pradhan Mantri Mudra Yojana, etc. The Government through funding and policy support has facilitated the successful creation and use of various components of DPI including Aadhaar, Mobile, Internet, UPI, and near-universal accounts which has significantly enhanced the reach of financial services

The Financial Stability and Development Council (FSDC) is the apex-level body with several mandates, including financial stability, financial inclusion, and financial literacy. The FSDC is chaired by the Union Finance Minister, and heads of financial sector regulators and other concerned entities are its members that have financial inclusion and financial literacy as one of its important mandates. The Technical Group on Financial Inclusion and Financial Literacy (TGFIL) under the FSDC is responsible for formulating policies, monitoring progress, and ensuring coordination among regulators to enhance financial inclusion and literacy in India.

Role of the RBI

The role of RBI as a regulator of banks, NBFCs, and other financial institutions places it in a unique position to further the financial inclusion objective in the country through regulatory and monitoring measures. The developmental role is an important function of RBI in terms of which it performs a wide range of promotional functions for supporting national objectives. In coordination with the Government of India, the RBI has taken several important measures to achieve financial inclusion. The RBI has issued the guidelines on the Lead Bank Scheme, Priority Sector Lending, Business Correspondent model, frameworks for licensing of specialized banks, NBFCs including microfinance institutions, peer-to-peer lending platforms and Account Aggregators, financial literacy initiatives and customer service guidelines, etc.

RBI, in its role as a regulator and supervisor of payments systems, has ensured continuous innovation, the latest one being the fast payment system, the UPI being administered by the NPCI under the policy and guidance of RBI. Digital KYC norms and initiatives such as Aadhaar enabled payment services to have been facilitated with RBI policy actions.

The RBI has made several efforts to enable and encourage responsible innovation in the financial sector through initiatives such as Regulatory Sandbox and HaRBInger. It supports several initiatives to enable digital adoption for paperless, secure, and affordable financial services, driving inclusive lending and digital credit accessibility. The Digital Banking Units (DBUs) framework of RBI is helping banks to improve last-mile accessibility through assisted and self-service digital solutions. TReDS facilitates access to credit for MSMEs.

A National Strategy for Financial Inclusion (NSFI) is a vision document, introduced in the year 2019 by RBI in coordination with other stakeholders. NSFI aims to provide access to affordable formal financial services across India. It focuses on increasing and using digital infrastructure, financial literacy, and inclusive banking to accelerate financial inclusion in the country. It uses a multistakeholder approach for achieving effective financial inclusion with the involvement of financial sector regulators, government, developmental financial institutions and various agencies.

7.3.2 Role of Stakeholders

Banks: Cornerstones of Financial Inclusion

Banks have a central role in India's financial inclusion journey. Initiatives like the PMJDY have enabled individuals to access formal banking services, offering features like zero-balance accounts and RuPay cards. Rural outreach has been bolstered through branch expansion (Figure 7.15) and the deployment of Bank Mitras. Additionally, priority sector lending mandates ensure critical sectors, such as agriculture and small enterprises, receive adequate credit. Banks are collaborating with fintechs and partnering in innovations such as UPI and mobile banking to provide niche solutions for achieving inclusion objectives in a cost-effective manner. The regional rural banks, cooperative banks, and specialized banking institutions such as payment banks, small finance banks are providing savings, payments, and credit solutions tailored to rural populations, thereby furthering financial inclusion. Figure 7.14 shows that the number of functioning offices of commercial banks has gone up from 71873 in 2006 to 173556 in 2024. The number of commercial bank branches per 1,000 km^2 has gone up from 23 in 2004 to 52 in 2023. This shows the increased availability and reach of bank branches in the country.

Nonbanks: Extending the Reach

Nonbanking financial companies (NBFCs) have evolved in recent decades as important players complementing banks in providing financial services in the economy. Their size and role have gone up significantly and they constitute an important segment of our financial system. Under the current regulatory framework, NBFCs are classified on the basis based on activities and business models. NBFC Investment and credit companies have a wide variety of companies that provide credit and other financial services. However, select categories of NBFCs, such as microfinance institutions and NBFC factors, have emerged as important players furthering financial inclusion by catering to low-income groups, MSMEs, and underserved sections. Additionally, leveraging on their outreach and risk-sharing capabilities, NBFCs engage in colending partnerships with banks, to provide credit access for MSMEs and priority sectors.

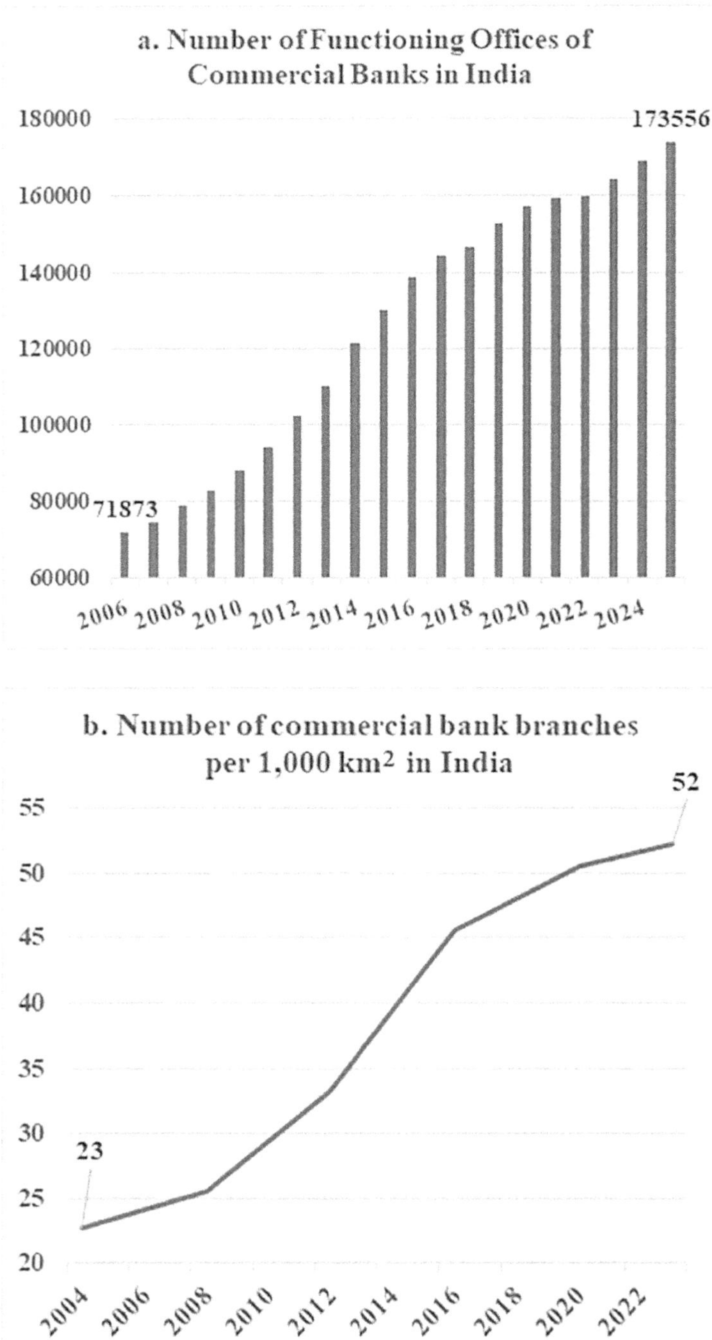

FIGURE 7.14

Commercial bank branches – number and spread in India.

Source: **1. RBI DBIE (Home > Publication > Time-Series Publications > Bank Branch Statistics > Quarterly > Functioning Offices>Bank Group-wise**
2. IMF Financial Access Survey

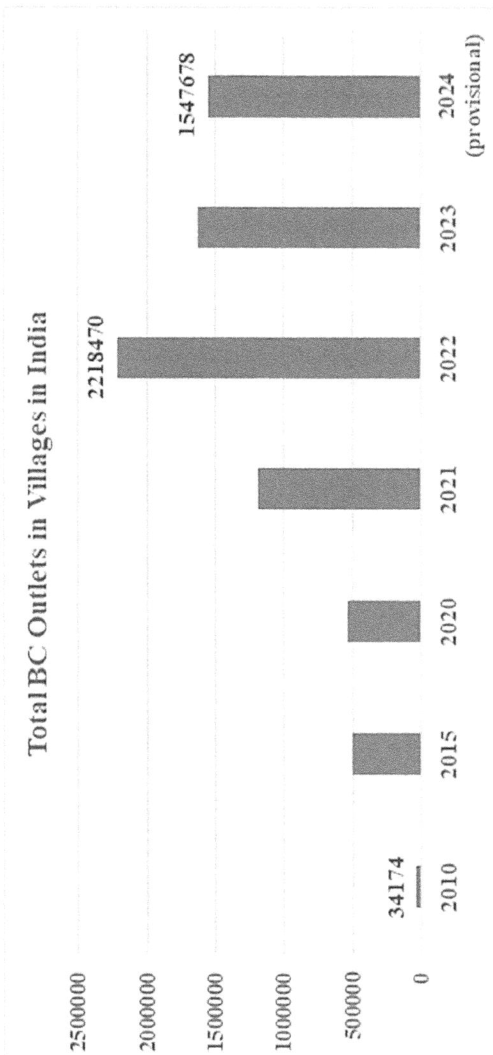

FIGURE 7.15
Total banking correspondent outlets in villages in India.
Source: **RBI Report on Trend and Progress 2022–23 and 2023–24.**

Business Correspondents: Strengthening Last-Mile Financial Access

The Business Correspondent model (BC) was introduced by the RBI in 2006 to enable banks to appoint BCs as agents to provide basic financial services to remote and underserved areas. The BCs, as an extended arm of the banks, are expected to carry out regular banking activities[11]. This includes identification of borrowers, preliminary processing of loan applications, creating awareness about financial products, processing and submission of applications to banks, supporting Self Help Groups, credit monitoring, recovery, small value deposits, sale of third-party financial products, and distribution of coins and banknotes. Over time, BCs have evolved significantly, and they now operate under different models. Individual BCs consist of local shopkeepers or retired bank employees delivering basic banking services via Kirana stores connected to banks such as SBI. Corporate BCs are large firms managing networks of individual BCs, like FINO payments bank. On the other hand, technology-driven BCs use digital platforms to facilitate smooth transactions, for example PayNearby. The growth in the BC network over time from 34174 in 2010 to 1.55 crore in 2024 (Figure 7.15) exemplifies the successful role being played by them for financial inclusion efforts. However, there has been a decline in the number of BCs in the last few years due to some issues concerning business models and normalization in their services post the heightened use during the Covid period. The importance of BCs in providing physical touchpoints across the country is important as the banking outlets by commercial banks can expand in a limited manner only as seen by its growth from 33378 to 53893, which is much less compared to the percentage (Figure 7.16) growth of BCs.

However, the BCs are facing challenges in fulfilling their mandate due to factors such as low remuneration, inadequate rural infrastructure, and high attrition rates (Jaiswal et al., 2019). Some reforms have been introduced, such as registration of BCs by the Indian Banks' Association, certification programs, and mandatory training. However, more needs to be done to scale the BC model, including higher capacity building, sufficient remuneration, and technological support for handheld devices and mobile-based solutions.

Insurance and Pension: Social Safety Nets

Insurance schemes mitigate risks and provide financial security. Programs like Pradhan Mantri Suraksha Bima Yojana (PMSBY) and Pradhan Mantri Jeevan Jyoti Bima Yojana (PMJJBY) offer affordable coverage to low-income families. Innovations like microinsurance cater to rural populations, and digital platforms streamline processes, ensuring accessibility and efficiency.

Pension schemes like Atal Pension Yojana (APY) and the National Pension System (NPS) provide long-term economic stability. With over 7 crore APY subscribers[12], pension systems cater to the unorganized sector, ensuring retirement security. Digital platforms enable seamless pension management, enhancing accessibility for participants.

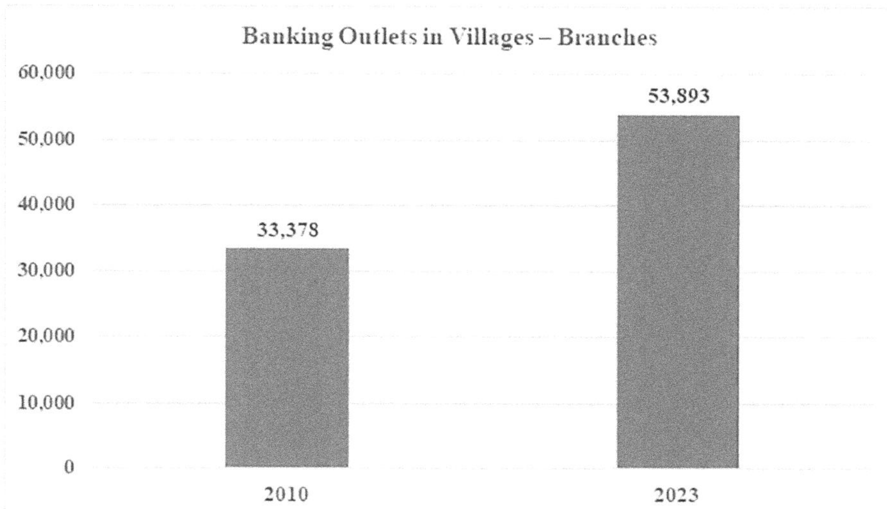

FIGURE 7.16
Progress in branch outlets.
Source: **RBI Annual Report 2023-24 (Table IV.4: Financial Inclusion Plan: A Progress Report)**

Emergence and Role of Fintechs

The advent of FinTech has significantly transformed the traditional financial services landscape, making financial service delivery faster, more efficient, cost-effective, and accessible. Fintech firms are driving financial inclusion through digital solutions, enhancing efficiency, and affordability (Adelaja et al., 2024). Innovations such as embedded finance, which integrates financial services into e-commerce and agritech, ensure seamless access to credit and payments. Similarly, neobanks cater to underserved populations, including MSMEs, by providing banking, payment, and compliance solutions. These models help overcome traditional barriers, fostering broader financial inclusion (Hegde & Bhowmik, 2024). By eliminating physical infrastructure and leveraging technology, fintech has lowered service costs.

India's FinTech ecosystem is driving innovation and scalability for global competitiveness. It is the third largest globally and comprises about 10,244 entities[13]. It is expected to generate around $190 billion in revenue by 2030, accounting for approximately 13% of the global FinTech industry's total revenue[14]. These projections underscore the increasing significance of the Indian Fintech sector. Third-party apps like PhonePe and Google Pay simplify payments, while data-driven credit assessments enable cash-flow-based lending for individuals without formal credit histories. Account Aggregators facilitate financial data consolidation and enhance decision-making. The peer-to-peer lending model provides platforms for connecting borrowers and lenders directly, providing an alternative model. Table 7.1 lists the key

TABLE 7.1

Select fintech success stories in India

No.	Fintech Company	Year found	Key Focus	Impact
1	Grameen Financial Services[a]	1999	Microloans for rural entrepreneurs	Uses alternative data analytics to extend microloans without traditional collateral, enhancing credit access for excluded populations
2	PolicyBazaar[b]	2008	Insurance comparison and distribution	Simplifies insurance selection with a digital platform, increasing insurance penetration in urban and semi-urban areas
3	Zerodha[c]	2010	Stock trading and investments	Democratized equity trading with low-cost platforms, empowering retail investors and increasing stock market participation
4	NeoGrowth[d]	2013	Small business lending	Offers working capital loans to MSMEs by leveraging POS transactional data, supporting growth and formal economic integration
5	Razorpay[e]	2014	Payment gateways and business finance	Enables businesses to accept online payments and offers credit solutions, promoting digital adoption for small enterprises
6	PhonePe[f]	2015	Digital payments	Integrated with UPI in 2016, enabling real-time bank-to-bank transfers. By 2024, had over 400 million users, contributing to financial inclusion
7	PayNearby[g]	2016	Financial services for rural areas	Partners with micro-entrepreneurs to deploy micro-ATMs and provide banking services, ensuring connectivity for unbanked communities
8	Dvara SmartGold[h]	2018	Microsavings and gold investment	Targets rural women, offering small-scale savings and investments via mobile platforms, fostering financial literacy and resilience

[a] A case study showing how CreditAccess Grameen used Temenos' technology to scale microfinance operations and improve outreach. www.temenos.com/community/success-stories/creditaccess-grameen-success-story/?utm_medium=organic-search&utm_page_title=CreditAccess+Grameen+-+Success+Story+-+Temenos&utm_page_url=https%3A%2F%2Fwww.temenos.com%2Fcommunity%2Fsuccess-stories%2Fcreditaccess-grameen-success-story%2F&utm_source=google

[b] A narrative on Yashish Dahiya's entrepreneurial journey in founding Policybazaar and its role in India's fintech / insurtech space. www.sovrenn.com/knowledge/yashish-dahiya-the-journey-of-building-policy-bazaar

[c] A LinkedIn article recounting how Nithin and Nikhil Kamath grew Zerodha into one of India's major discount brokerage platforms. https://thekarostartup.com/zerodha-success-story-business-model/

[d] An article profiling NeoGrowth, a fintech startup in India focused on providing unsecured business loans via digital processes. https://yourstory.com/2018/03/neogrowth-unsecured-loans

[e] A success story on Razorpay, highlighting its evolution as a payments gateway and its impact in India's digital payments ecosystem. www.marketfeed.com/read/en/the-success-story-of-razorpay

[f] A case study tracing the growth of PhonePe in India's mobile payments landscape, covering strategy, challenges, and scale. www.linkedin.com/pulse/rise-fintech-payments-case-study-phonepe-theinvestorco-lxcnc/

[g] A press release announcing that PayNearby received an award for fintech innovation in financial inclusion, recognizing its role in bridging the inclusion gap. https://paynearby.in/media/paynearby-wins-best-fintech-innovation-in-financial-inclusion-award/

[h] News that Dvara SmartGold was selected for the Inclusive Fintech 50 award in 2020, acknowledging its innovative model for financial inclusion. https://timesofindia.indiatimes.com/dvara-smartgold-selected-for-the-inclusive-fintech-50-award-for-2020/amp_articleshow/78785012.cms

focus and impact of selected fintech entities on financial inclusion and digital transformation efforts to provide a flavor of successful and innovative models being adopted by fintech in India.

It may be observed that fintech entities have the potential to drive financial inclusion by focusing on niche segments, providing innovative solutions, promoting digital adoption, and supporting underserved segments of society.

Having covered in detail the various initiatives and trends of the Government, RBI, banks, non-banks, and fintech, it would also be useful to review the actual impact on the targeted segments and the same is covered briefly in the following sections.

7.4 Social and Economic Impact of Financial Inclusion

Financial inclusion has played an important role in reducing poverty and fostering economic empowerment for underserved populations. It helps households to manage financial risks and shocks more effectively, thereby helping in poverty alleviation (Omar et al, 2020). Initiatives like PMJDY have enabled the integration of citizens without basic financial services to get integrated into the formal financial system. It helps in promoting savings and reducing dependence on informal credit sources. The widespread availability and adoption of digital payment systems such as UPI and Bharat BillPay help in providing access to financial services across the country. Further, Government insurance schemes like PMJJBY and PMSBY offer affordable insurance coverage and provide a crucial safety net for vulnerable families. As per the latest data as of November 2024, about ₹17,211 crore and ₹2,931 crore, respectively, have been disbursed so far.[15]

Another important factor in poverty reduction efforts is enabling access to affordable credit. Priority sector lending (PSL) guidelines of RBI ensure that banks allocate a mandated portion of their lending to underserved sectors such as agriculture, micro-enterprises, and weaker sections. The PSL guidelines have been revised to make it comprehensive and include sustainable finance as a priority sector. During 2023–24, the total lending under the priority sector targets of banks amounted to Rs. 59 lakh crores, which is 45.1% of the adjusted net bank credit (ANBC) of the banks[16].

Pradhan Mantri Mudra Yojana (PMMY) was launched by the government in 2015 to provide collateral-free microcredit to MSMEs. PMMY loans empower micro-entrepreneurs, enabling them to establish sustainable livelihoods. Figure 7.17 illustrates the growth in Mudra accounts and loans sanctioned under the scheme and is indicative of the funds flow to MSMEs which often face difficulties in obtaining credit from banks at reasonable costs. This steady increase highlights the rising demand for microcredit, particularly among small businesses, women entrepreneurs, and first-time

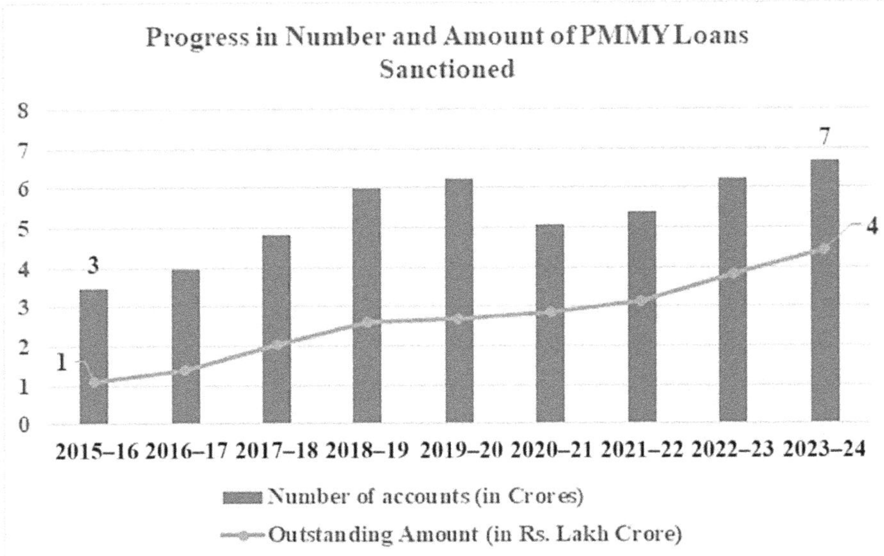

FIGURE 7.17
Progress in no. and amount of PMMY loans sanctioned.
Source: **Mudra website (PMMY Reports).**

borrowers. As of 31 March 2024, about 4 crore accounts and Rs.7 Lakh crore loans are outstanding under the scheme.

Similarly, the Kisan Credit Card (KCC) scheme has seen a steady adoption and growth in its use in India. KCC is a single window facility for providing working capital and investment credit to farmers for cultivation, animal husbandry, and fisheries. As of 31 March 2024, the KCC scheme has an outstanding loan of ₹5.75 lakh crore to the farmers, and there are 2.98 crore operative KCC accounts in the country, bolstering rural economies by supporting farming activities and related ventures (Figure 7.18).

Role in Women's Empowerment and Rural Development

Financial inclusion is a big catalyst for women's empowerment by providing them with the tools to gain financial independence. Programs like PMJDY, where 55.7% of account holders are women, promote gender equality and improve household decision-making. Access to microloans through initiatives like PMMY enables women entrepreneurs to contribute to their family's income and the local economy. About 21% of PMMY loans have been extended to new entrepreneurs, 69% to women, and 51% to SC/ST/OBC borrowers, promoting inclusive economic growth. Fintech entities, such as Dvara SmartGold, allow rural women to save amounts starting with ₹10 daily for gold investments, thereby providing tailored solutions for the financial empowerment of women.

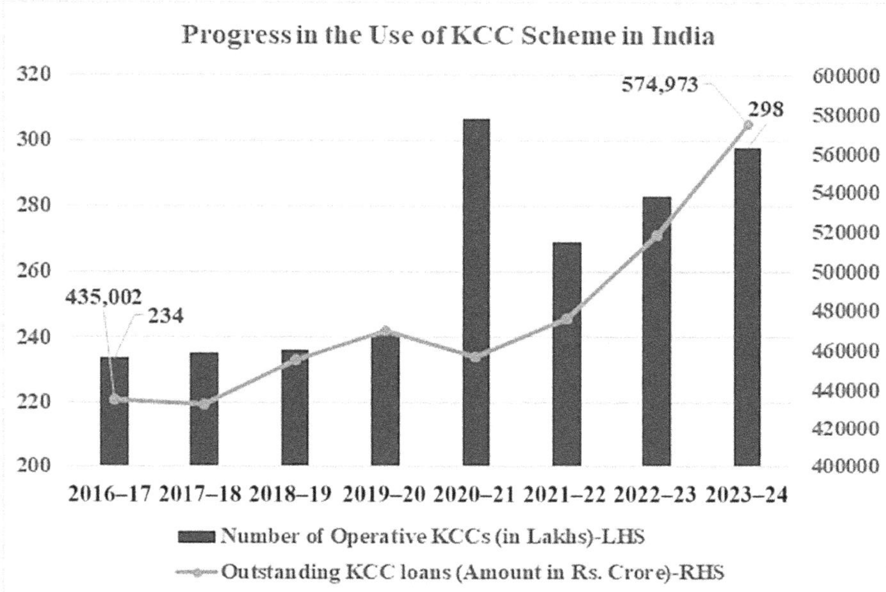

FIGURE 7.18
Progress in the KCC scheme.
***Source*: RBI Annual Report 2023-254 (Table IV.2: Kisan Credit Card Scheme).**

Digital Literacy Challenges and Efforts to Bridge the Knowledge Gap

Despite making significant progress, challenges remain in bridging gaps for digital and financial literacy. Limited knowledge and awareness of digital tools prevent individuals from fully utilizing financial services. For instance, many rural users struggle to navigate mobile banking applications. Addressing these challenges requires a multipronged approach. The National Strategy for Financial Education (NSFE) 2020–2025[17] is an important step by financial sector regulators to integrate financial literacy into school curricula and expand literacy programs. Financial literacy is being promoted through Centres for Financial Literacy (CFLs), established by NGOs with support from RBI, NABARD, and banks. With 2,421 CFLs operating nationwide, these centers enhance grassroots financial awareness. In Karnataka, 79 CFLs and 177 Financial Literacy Centres (FLCs) are actively educating communities on financial products[18].

After covering comprehensively, the Indian efforts at financial inclusion and evaluating the results, it is worthwhile to compare the differences in the approaches for financial inclusion and review the successful efforts in other parts of the country to draw replicable practices.

7.5 Comparing Outcomes and Identifying Replicable Practices

7.5.1 Comparison of the Role of Governments and Regulators for Financial Inclusion Across Key Jurisdictions

The role played by the government, regulators, and financial intermediaries differ from country to country. In developed economies such as the US, UK, Japan, and Europe, the public sector plays mostly as a facilitator as financial inclusion is market-driven. These economies rely on the private sector for innovation, financial technology, and inclusion efforts. The role of regulators is largely limited to customer protection, financial stability, regulatory oversight, and financial literacy. In contrast, in emerging market economies, the public sector plays a more direct and proactive role in pursuing financial inclusion, and there is a centralized push through targeted policies and schemes of the Government. The developmental role is included in the mandate of central banks and commercial banks in the public sector in some emerging market economies. However, within emerging market economies also, the approach and mandate vary from country to country. While Brazil and Indonesia rely on mobile money platforms and partnerships with telecom companies to drive inclusion, in India the Government and the RBI play a direct and proactive role in advancing financial inclusion through policies, digital public infrastructure, and various government schemes, as detailed throughout the chapter. The success of the role of the public sector in promoting innovation and financial inclusion provides a good roadmap for other emerging economies as it provides synergies to the much-required push for the collective effort of the financial system in the absence of deep pockets and priorities of individual players of requisite size.

7.5.2 Replicable Successful Financial Inclusion Initiatives for Key Jurisdictions

Financial inclusion has become a cornerstone for economic growth and poverty alleviation globally. By integrating underserved populations into the formal financial ecosystem, countries have developed innovative strategies through technology, policy frameworks, and public–private partnerships. Some examples of outstanding financial inclusion efforts and their relevance for other nations, including India, are given in Table 7.2.

These initiatives provide valuable insights for addressing specific challenges in diverse contexts. For countries like India, leveraging these models while accounting for local conditions offers a pathway to enhance financial inclusion.

TABLE 7.2

Learnings from successful products of select countries for financial inclusion

Country	Key Initiative	Details	Impact	Relevance to Other Nations
Kenya	M-Pesa and Mobile Money Transformation (Shaikh et al, 2023).	A mobile-based platform for sending, receiving, and storing money, as well as paying bills and accessing credit/insurance	Empowered 90% of Kenyan households by 2023; transformed rural economies and reduced poverty	M-Pesa's integration of financial services like savings and microloans with an agent-based cash-in/cash-out model can complement the existing systems in other countries
Bangladesh	Grameen Bank and Microfinance Innovations (Ghimire, Thapa & Zheng, 2025).	Small, collateral-free loans to rural women for economic independence	Served over 9 million borrowers by 2024, 97% of whom are women; advanced gender equality and sustainable development	Demonstrates the potential of microfinance for poverty alleviation and gender empowerment
Brazil	Pix and Real-Time Payments (Aurazo & Gasmi, 2024).	Instant, 24/7 digital money transfers with no fees for individuals	Registered over 140 million users by 2022; critical for delivering COVID-19 social welfare payments	Highlights the importance of inclusive, real-time payment systems for underserved populations
China	Digital Ecosystems for Financial Inclusion (Lee, Lou & Wang, 2023).	Integrated payments, microloans, and insurance through platforms like Alipay and WeChat Pay	Served over 1 billion users; bridged financial gaps in rural and urban areas alike	Illustrates the role of scalable, technology-driven solutions for financial inclusion
Mexico	Financial Literacy and Direct Transfers through Prospera (Beltran & Delgado, 2023).	Combines financial education with direct cash transfers, partnering with community banks and cooperatives	Reduced dependence on informal credit and advanced financial literacy	Demonstrates how integrating education with cash transfers fosters economic resilience
Rwanda	SACCOs and Mobile Money Integration (Mhlanga & Dzingirai, 2023).	Savings and Credit Cooperatives combined with mobile money platforms	Enhanced financial access and economic resilience in rural areas	Provides a model for combining financial literacy with digital platforms for inclusion

(Continued)

TABLE 7.2 (Continued)

Learnings from successful products of select countries for financial inclusion

Country	Key Initiative	Details	Impact	Relevance to Other Nations
South Africa	Mzansi Accounts and Social Grants (Mahalika et al, 2023)	Low-cost banking solutions and distribution of social grants through bank accounts	Expanded financial access to low-income populations; supported inclusive economic growth	Highlights fintech's role in addressing financial inclusion among underserved populations
Philippines	GCash and Financial Inclusion in Remote Areas (Rey & Rey, 2024).	Mobile wallet integrated with PhilSys digital ID system	Simplified account opening and extended access to microloans and insurance in rural communities	Demonstrates the impact of combining digital wallets with national ID systems for inclusion
Ghana	Mobile Money and Financial Inclusion Strategy (Osabutey & Jackson, 2024).	Platforms like MTN Mobile Money for savings, credit, and payments	Emphasized digital payments and financial literacy as critical components of inclusion	Provides an example of leveraging digital platforms for financial services in areas without traditional banking infrastructure
Indonesia	Digital Payment Ecosystems and Agent Banking (Jameaba, 2024).	Platforms like GoPay and OVO provide digital payments, while agent banking extends services to rural areas	A large section of the population uses digital payments, with agent banking improving access in remote areas	Highlights the role of combining digital wallets and agent networks to improve financial inclusion in geographically diverse nations

7.6 Challenges and Future Directions for Financial Inclusion

Financial inclusion, a critical enabler of equitable economic growth, faces various global challenges, ranging from infrastructural and regulatory barriers to technological and social inequalities. Addressing these challenges requires a nuanced approach to ensure financial services are accessible, affordable, and effectively utilized. Key challenges to financial inclusion in India and the measures taken to address them are outlined below.

7.6.1 Challenges and Future Directions

Bridging the Digital and Economic Divide in Financial Inclusion
India's financial inclusion efforts are hindered by digital and economic disparities, particularly in rural and remote areas. Uneven internet access, limited smartphone affordability, and low digital literacy contribute to a digital divide, with rural teledensity at 59.19% compared to 133.72% in urban areas (March 2024)[19]. Initiatives like BharatNet[20] aim to improve connectivity and bridge this gap.

Economic and geographic barriers continue to limit financial access, as high operational costs discourage traditional financial institutions from reaching underserved regions. The BC model and the JAM Trinity have played a key role in expanding financial access, while priority sector lending guidelines and RBI incentives have supported rural banking growth, particularly in the Northeastern regions. Strengthening last-mile digital infrastructure and enhancing inclusive banking models remain crucial for achieving sustainable financial inclusion.

Regulatory and Policy Challenges
Inconsistent regulatory frameworks hinder financial innovation and scalability. The RBI has implemented several initiatives to foster a conducive environment for innovation. Regulatory sandboxes provide controlled environments for testing innovative financial products safely, enabling the development of inclusive solutions. The RBI has recently recognized the Fintech Association for Consumer Empowerment (FACE) as a Self-Regulatory Organization (SRO) in the fintech sector[21]. The SRO is responsible for promoting industry standards and accountability. Hackathons like "HaRBInger"[22] encourage participants to come out with innovative solutions. The establishment of a Fintech Repository provides an avenue for collaboration among stakeholders and information to RBI for informed policymaking in the sector.

Financial and Digital Literacy
Financial and digital literacy are very important for financial inclusion and for creating awareness about fraud and trust in the financial system. Low

literacy and limited awareness of financial products prevent effective usage of financial services. For example, only 30% of adults in developing countries have adequate financial literacy[23]. In India, the National Strategy for Financial Education (NSFE) plays a pivotal role in addressing this gap by promoting financial literacy through structured programs aimed at different demographic groups. The establishment of Centres for Financial Literacy (CFLs) at the block level helps in financial education at the grassroots level by leveraging upon the use of local languages and engagement of all stakeholders to ensure inclusivity.

Cybersecurity and Fraud Concerns

With the proliferation of digital financial services, cybersecurity threats and fraud have become significant concerns. The progress in tech advancements comes with rising cyber frauds in India, with 1.1 million cases reported in just 1 year in 2023[24]. Common threats include phishing attacks, unauthorized access, and misuse of customer data. Vulnerabilities in the digital ecosystem can erode trust in financial services, deterring adoption among first-time users.

Cybersecurity remains a top priority, with the RBI implementing frameworks to mitigate risks such as data breaches and cyber fraud. The Digital Payment Security Controls Guidelines[25] mandate robust cybersecurity measures for regulated entities, including multifactor authentication and regular audits. Reserve Bank Innovation Hub (RBIH) is developing MuleHunter ™, an artificial intelligence (AI) driven system designed to identify and curb mule accounts used in financial fraud.

Customer Protection

Public awareness campaigns and regulatory vigilance are pivotal in building a secure digital financial ecosystem that fosters trust and confidence among users. (Afzal et al, 2024). The RBI has undertaken several awareness initiatives, including the RBI Kehta Hai campaign, to educate consumers about digital fraud, secure banking practices, and the importance of vigilance in online financial transactions. Additionally, the Reserve Bank-Integrated Ombudsman Scheme[26] simplifies grievance redressal by integrating existing frameworks into a single platform. The RBI's Limited Liability Guidelines protect customers from undue financial loss due to unauthorized electronic transactions by defining liability limits for banks and users, thereby enhancing trust and confidence in the financial system.

Data Privacy

The lack of robust data protection frameworks, especially in developing countries, undermines consumer trust. The Digital Personal Data Protection (DPDP) Act 2023 has been introduced by the government and rules are being framed to establish a comprehensive legal framework for the collection, processing, storage, and protection of personal data, ensuring data privacy, security, and accountability in the digital ecosystem. The Act lays down important principles such as data minimization, purpose limitation, and user consent. It safeguards personal data and encourages underserved populations to adopt formal financial services. These measures mitigate risks of data breaches and misuse and is particularly important for vulnerable and first-time users. (Gupta & George, 2025).

Emerging Technologies: AI, Blockchain, and Their Potential Role in Inclusivity

Emerging technologies, such as mobile banking, digital wallets, and blockchain technologies, have an important role in fostering financial inclusion in emerging markets. These innovations have played an important role in breaking down traditional barriers and enabling individuals to access affordable financial services (Falaiye et al, 2024). Mobile wallets and fintech solutions have made banking accessible to remote populations. Agent-based services are leading to cost-effective last-mile delivery in rural areas and helping to expand financial inclusion to underserved regions (Kandpal et al, 2019).

The decentralized design of Blockchain reduces trust and cost barriers It streamlines loan disbursement, cross-border payments, and remittances. It enables secure identity verification and facilitates tokenized assets. It also promotes micro-investments and broader financial participation (Mhlanga, 2023; Harvey et al, 2023). Authorities are exploring the potential of blockchain to modernize international payment infrastructure, enhancing financial accessibility.

AI has the potential to transform financial inclusion. It enhances digital access by improving risk assessment, fraud detection, and chatbot-based support. Through these improvements it helps marginalized groups such as women, youth, and small businesses to overcome barriers to banking (Mhlanga, 2020). However, the use of Artificial Intelligence (AI) and Machine Learning (ML) in financial services can introduce biases that perpetuate existing inequalities. Algorithms trained on historical data can discriminate by denying credit or charging higher interest rates. For example, a lack of diverse datasets can result in discriminatory credit scoring models. These models can also overlook applicants from underserved regions or those without formal credit histories. To mitigate biases and ensure fairness in decision-making using these tools, there is a need for transparent AI/ML practices, ethical guidelines, and algorithm audits (Nwaimo et al., 2024). In India, the RBI is looking to develop a framework for responsible and ethical enablement of artificial intelligence (FREE-AI) in the Indian financial sector.

7.6.2 Policy Recommendations for Financial Inclusion

G20's 2016 "High-Level Principles for Digital Financial Inclusion"[27] and 2023 "Policy Recommendations for Advancing Financial Inclusion and Productivity Gains Through Digital Public Infrastructure"[28] provide very important principles for developing policies on financial inclusion by any country.

Further, a multifaceted approach is required for enhancing financial inclusion. This includes improving digital infrastructure, technology, collaboration, and targeted interventions. Some important policy recommendations based on discussions and learnings from this chapter for countries to consider while framing financial inclusion framework and policies are given below.

By implementing the policy recommendations mentioned in Table 7.3, any country can strengthen and secure its financial ecosystem and ensure sustained inclusion. A holistic approach focusing on the integration of emerging technologies and the implementation of inclusive policies with strong institutional support can establish a globally replicable model for equitable economic growth.

7.7 Conclusion

This chapter has provided key insights into the proactive role of the public sector in India in implementing successful policies, schemes, and models for financial inclusion. Using secondary data, the progress and success of these initiatives have been evaluated. It provides clues and guidance to other countries to emulate some of these policies to achieve similar objectives. The chapter has also provided focus areas and approaches of select fintech entities in India. It goes on to provide successful financial inclusion products of other countries and how they could be adopted. The challenges of digital financial services have been discussed, along with suggestions on how they can be addressed. It also provides some high-level principles and key aspects to be considered while considering financial inclusion framework and policies of any countries.

Financial inclusion is the cumulative efforts of the stakeholders in the financial system towards ensuring the provision of basic financial services, including savings, credit, and other financial products to everyone. This helps in the formalization of the economy, improves monetary policy transmission, and enables overall development in the financial sector. The importance of financial inclusion is recognized by the Government and regulatory authorities, and they have taken several steps to further this objective. The digitization of finance, the use of emerging technologies, and the proliferation of fintech entities have provided huge momentum to financial inclusion efforts. These developments have enabled the cost-effective provision of financial services with a wider reach and customized solutions.

TABLE 7.3

Policy recommendations for further financial inclusion

Policy Area	Recommendations
Expanding infrastructure	Continue development of digital infrastructure in rural and remote locations by ensuring reliable internet connections and offline payment solutions. Initiatives like the Payment Infrastructure Development Funds enhance digital penetration
Leveraging inclusive technology	Promote multilingual voice-enabled financial services and Internet of Things (IoT)-based tools to cater to diverse user needs, such as for the elderly, students, and differently abled individuals. These innovations can make financial services more accessible and intuitive
Enhancing authentication systems	Implement secure and user-friendly authentication methods such as biometric and multifactor authentication to build trust in digital financial systems and reduce fraud risks
Targeted interventions for vulnerable groups	Develop financial products and literacy programs tailored for students, rural women, and elderly populations. Simplified digital payment platforms and local-language interfaces enhance inclusivity
Fostering collaboration	Strengthen partnerships between government, fintech, and private institutions to spur innovation while maintaining regulatory oversight. Such collaboration fosters inclusive financial products and services
Strengthening cybersecurity	Implement strict security protocols, including two-factor authentication, end-to-end encryption, and tokenization. The Digital Personal Data Protection Act of 2023 needs to be adhered to enhance privacy. More public awareness campaigns are required to educate users on safe digital practices
Investing in advanced technologies	Leverage AI and ML for real-time fraud detection and cyber threat mitigation. Implement blockchain for transparency and quantum-resistant cryptography to counter emerging risks
Building cyber resilience	Establish robust incident response frameworks including the Computer Emergency Response Teams and the Cybersecurity Incident Response Teams. There is a need to implement systems for resilience against cyberattacks. Facilitate the sharing of threat intelligence among various stakeholders to counter cyber threats
Education and community outreach	Integrate financial literacy into school curricula and other education programs for developing foundational knowledge. Community-based initiatives, with the help of SHGs and local leaders, can create further awareness at ground level
Innovative digital tools	Use of gamified mobile applications, interactive videos, and vernacular-language content to make financial education engaging and accessible. These tools can empower individuals to make informed financial decisions

In India, efforts towards financial inclusion can be traced from the cooperative movement which started in the 1900s. The prominent initiatives include the nationalization of banks, establishment of specialized banks and institutions (such as Regional Rural Banks, NABARD, National Payments Corporation of India (NPCI), microfinance institutions, payment banks, and small finance banks, etc.), priority sector lending targets for banks, and use of models such as banking correspondents and self-help groups. The notable developments in the past decade are the creation of Digital Public Infrastructure, the JAM trinity, UPI, AePS, initiatives in the payments sector, the role of the fintech sector, and the use of emerging technologies. More recently, the vision documents such as NSFI are complementing the efforts of financial inclusion and financial literacy in a structured way. The development of indices such as FI Index and Payment Index are helping to monitor the important elements of financial inclusion.

The successful implementation of financial inclusion requires the active participation of all stakeholders, including the Government, regulators, banks, NBFCs, specialized banks, banking correspondents, insurance, pension, and fintech entities. Some examples of successful Indian fintech entities, along with key focus and impact, have been furnished in the chapter. They employ innovative business models and with the use of technology. They can focus on various target groups and provide financial services in an innovative way.

The financial inclusion efforts have ensured that credit is allocated to underserved sectors such as agriculture, microenterprises, and weaker sections, which help in creating business and furthers poverty alleviation and inclusive economic growth. This has driven economic activities and digitization in rural areas and small towns. It is observed that government schemes and initiatives are enabling the provision of microcredit, particularly among small businesses, women entrepreneurs, and first-time borrowers.

Globally several outstanding efforts are ongoing to enhance financial inclusion. The prominent examples are M-Pesa of Kenya, Grameen Bank of Bangladesh, Pix of Brazil, Prospera of Mexico, Mzansi Accounts of South Africa, GCash of the Philippines, and Digital Payment Ecosystems of China and Indonesia. The impact of these use cases and their relevance for other nations have been discussed in the chapter.

While the new ecosystem and emerging technologies are helping the financial system, there are some challenges as well. The major ones are regulatory and policy challenges, cybersecurity and fraud concerns, customer protection, data privacy, and risks from emerging technologies such as biases and model risk. To deal with these challenges, some recommendations have been enumerated in the chapter. It includes the need for continued development of digital infrastructure, use of inclusive technologies, targeted plans for vulnerable groups, building cyber resilience, ensuring customer protection, and using innovative digital tools.

Financial inclusion has come a long way, but it is still some distance to travel, which is possible by leveraging the use of technology and coordination among all stakeholders, including the public sector and private sector, domestic and global. There is a need for effective collaboration at the global level and continuous learning from the efforts of other countries.

Notes

1 The views expressed in this article are those of the authors and do not represent the views of the organizations they represent.
2 Financial inclusion is a key enabler to reducing poverty and boosting prosperity. www.worldbank.org/en/topic/financialinclusion/overview#1
3 Financial Development and Financial Inclusion (FDFI) www.imf.org/en/Capacity-Development/Training/ICDTC/Courses/FDFI.
4 Inclusive Finance www.un.org/esa/ffd/topics/inclusive-local-finance/inclusive-finance.html#:~:text=Financial%20inclusion%20is%20universal%20access,small%20and%20medium%2Dsized%20enterprises.
5 Reserve Bank of India introduces the Financial Inclusion Index https://rbi.org.in/scripts/FS_PressRelease.aspx?prid=52068&fn=2754.
6 JAM(Jan Dhan, Aadhar, Mobile)TRINITY and digital revolution: A Decade of Financial Inclusion, Transparency and Corruption Free India. https://pib.gov.in/PressReleasePage.aspx?PRID=2086611#:~:text=Inclusive%20Healthcare%20Paradigm-,There%20are%20more%20than%2054%20crore%20Jan%20Dhan%20Yojana%20accounts,15%20times%20since%20its%20inception.
7 Telecom Regulatory Authority of India. www.trai.gov.in/sites/default/files/2025-05/PR_No.35of2025_0.pdf
8 Digital Infrastructure in India. www.pib.gov.in/PressReleaseIframePage.aspx?PRID=2098487
9 DFS drives expansion of digital payments in India and abroad. https://pib.gov.in/PressReleaseIframePage.aspx?PRID=2057013
10 RBI Annual Report 2023–24
11 RBI Master Circular on Branch Authorisation dated July 1, 2014
12 Gross enrolments under Atal Pension Yojana (APY) cross 7 crore mark, with over 56 lakh enrolments in current Financial Year 2024-25. https://pib.gov.in/PressReleasePage.aspx?PRID=2063311#:~:text=by%20PIB%20Delhi-,The%20total%20gross%20enrolments%20under%20the%20Atal%20Pension%20Yojana%20(APY,the%20Banks%20and%20SLBCs/UTLBCs
13 Union Finance Minister Smt. Nirmala Sitharaman interacts with start-up and fintech ecosystem stakeholders. https://pib.gov.in/PressReleasePage.aspx?PRID=2009261
14 State of the Fintech Union 2024. https://web-assets.bcg.com/11/05/8c4b6ccf476fbcf0a173ae7d65d8/state-of-the-fintech-union-2024.pdf
15 Ministry of Finance Year Ender 2024: Department of Financial Services. https://pib.gov.in/PressReleasePage.aspx?PRID=2088182#:~:text=In%20digital%20payments%2C%20the%20DFS,enabler%20of%20India's%20digital%20economy
16 RBI Annual Report 2023–2024
17 National Strategy for Financial Education. https://ncfe.org.in/nsfe/#
18 A speech by an RBI official highlighting India's progress in financial inclusion and the need to deepen usage and service-quality across underserved regions. https://rbi.org.in/Scripts/BS_SpeechesView.aspx?Id=1467
19 This press release reports on mobile connectivity under the Digital India / Universal Connectivity initiatives. https://pib.gov.in/PressReleaseIframePage.aspx?PRID=2040566

20 This press release reports on mobile connectivity under the Digital India / Universal Connectivity initiatives. https://pib.gov.in/PressReleaseIframePage.aspx?PRID=2040566
21 This press release reports on mobile connectivity under the Digital India / Universal Connectivity initiatives. https://rbi.org.in/scripts/FS_PressRelease.aspx?prid=58586&fn=2765
22 Reserve Bank of India's Third Global Hackathon. https://fintech.rbi.org.in/FT_HaRBInger_2024
23 A report by the OECD outlining global trends, strategies, and best practices to improve financial education and literacy across countries. www.oecd.org/finance/financial-education/advancing-financial-literacy-2021.pdf
24 Government and Meta join forces for "Scam se Bacho" Campaign to tackle rising online scams. https://pib.gov.in/PressReleasePage.aspx?PRID=2065959
25 Reserve Bank of India detailing regulations or guidelines. www.rbi.org.in/scripts/NotificationUser.aspx?Id=12032&Mode=0
26 An FAQ that explains RB-IOS (RBI's Ombudsman Scheme) and clarifies which kinds of grievances are covered under this scheme. www.rbi.org.in/commonman/English/scripts/FAQs.aspx?Id=3407#:~:text=RB%2DIOS%2C%202021%20has%20simplified,are%20covered%20under%20RB%2DIOS.
27 The G20's High-Level Principles for Digital Financial Inclusion, setting international guidelines for policy, regulation, innovation, and inclusion goals. https://g7g20-documents.org/fileadmin/G7G20_documents/2016/G20/China/Leaders/2%20Leaders%27%20Annex/G20%20High-Level%20Principles%20for%20Digital%20Financial%20Inclusion_05092016.pdf
28 A World Bank document (project or report) relevant to digital financial inclusion or infrastructure investment. https://documents1.worldbank.org/curated/en/099092023121016458/pdf/P178703046f82d07c0bbc60b5e474ea7841.pdf

References

Adelaja, A. O., Umeorah, S. C., Abikoye, B. E., & Nezianya, M. C. (2024). Advancing financial inclusion through fintech: Solutions for unbanked and underbanked populations. World Journal of Advanced Research and Reviews, 23(01), 427–438.

Afzal, M., Meraj, M., Kaur, M., & Shamim Ansari, M. (2024). How does cybersecurity awareness help in achieving digital financial inclusion in rural India under escalating cyber fraud scenario? Journal of Cyber Security Technology, 1–39.

Aurazo, J., & Gasmi, F. (2024). Digital payment systems in emerging economies: Lessons from Kenya, India, Brazil, and Peru. Information Economics and Policy, 69, 101113.

Beltran, L. D., & Delgado, M. C. (2023). Estimating the economic and social impact of conditional cash transfers from the Prospera Program in Mexico. Evaluation and Program Planning, 100, 102321.

Dar, A. B., & Ahmed, F. (2021). Financial inclusion determinants and impediments in India: Insights from the Global Financial Inclusion Index. Journal of Economic Policy Research, 4(1), 56–73.
Falaiye, T., Elufioye, O. A., Awonuga, K. F., Ibeh, C. V., Olatoye, F. O., & Mhlongo, N. Z. (2024). Financial inclusion through technology: A review of trends in emerging markets. International Journal of Management & Entrepreneurship Research, 6(2), 368–379.
Ghimire, S., Thapa, B. S., & Zheng, R. (2025). Microfinance for change: How financial innovation enables structural transformation. Financial Innovation, 11(1), 60.
Gupta, N., & George, A. (2025). Digital Personal Data Protection Act, 2023: Charting the future of India's data regulation. In Data Governance and the Digital Economy in Asia (pp. 34–53). Routledge.
Harvey, C. R., Ramachandran, A., & Santoro, M. (2023). Blockchain technology and financial inclusion. Financial Review, 58(1), 23–48. https://doi.org/10.1111/fire.12345
Hegde, A., & Bhowmik, B. (2024, April). Big data insights: Pioneering changes in FinTech. In 2024 IEEE 9th International Conference for Convergence in Technology (I2CT) (pp. 1–6). IEEE.
Jaiswal, P. P., & Dhar, S. N. (2019). Business correspondent agents for promoting financial inclusion: A study of glitches and gaps in appointment and operations. International Journal of Research and Analytical Reviews, 6(2), 566–576.
Jameaba, M. S. (2024). Digitalization, emerging technologies, and financial stability: Challenges and opportunities for the Indonesian banking sector and beyond. Emerging Technologies and Financial Stability: Challenges and Opportunities for the Indonesian Banking Sector and Beyond (April 26, 2024).
Kandpal, V., & Mehrotra, R. (2019). Financial inclusion: The role of fintech and digital financial services in India. Indian Journal of Economics and Business, 18(1), 85–93.
Lee, C. C., Lou, R., & Wang, F. (2023). Digital financial inclusion and poverty alleviation: Evidence from the sustainable development of China. Economic Analysis and Policy, 77, 418–434.
Lenka, S. K. (2022). Relationship between financial inclusion and financial development in India. International Journal of Financial Studies, 11(1), 112–135.
Maity, S., & Majumder, A. (2025). A comparative study on the financial inclusion status of G20 countries. Journal of Decision Analytics and Intelligent Computing, 5(1), 14–24.
Mahalika, R., Matsebula, V., & Yu, D. (2023). Investigating the relationship between financial inclusion and poverty in South Africa. Development Southern Africa, 40(1), 109–132.
Mhlanga, D. (2020). Industry 4.0 in finance: The impact of artificial intelligence (AI) on digital financial inclusion. International Journal of Financial Studies, 8(3), 45.
Mhlanga, D., & Dzingirai, M. (2023). Post-independence development and financial inclusion in Africa: Case studies and the way forward to support further financial inclusion. In Economic Inclusion in Post-Independence Africa: An Inclusive

Approach to Economic Development (pp. 149–166). Cham: Springer Nature Switzerland.
Mishra, D., Kandpal, V., Agarwal, N., & Srivastava, B. (2024). Financial inclusion and its ripple effects on socio-economic development: A comprehensive review. Journal of Risk and Financial Management, 17(3), 105.
Nwaimo, C. S., Adegbola, A. E., & Adegbola, M. D. (2024). Predictive analytics for financial inclusion: Using machine learning to improve credit access for underbanked populations. Computer Science & IT Research Journal, 5(6), 1358–1373.
Oanh, T. T. K. (2024). Digital financial inclusion in the context of financial development: Environmental destruction or the driving force for technological advancement. Borsa Istanbul Review, 24(2), 292–303.
Omar, M. A., & Inaba, K. (2020). Does financial inclusion reduce poverty and income inequality in developing countries? A panel data analysis. Economic Structures, 9(1), 37. https://doi.org/10.1186/s40008-020-00214-4
Osabutey, E. L., & Jackson, T. (2024). Mobile money and financial inclusion in Africa: Emerging themes, challenges and policy implications. Technological Forecasting and Social Change, 202, 123339.
Pandya, N. P., & Budhedeo, S. H. (2025). Mapping financial inclusion through financial innovations in India: A study of the past decade. International Journal of Banking, Risk & Insurance, 13(1).
Rey, W. P., & Rey, K. W. J. D. (2024, February). The role of mobile wallets in promoting cashless transactions: A case study of the Philippines. In International Conference on E-Business and Applications (pp. 155–170). Singapore: Springer Nature Singapore.
Sethy, B. K., & Mishra, S. K. (2018). The evolution of financial inclusion in India: Past, present, and future. Indian Journal of Economic Development, 14(2), 123–140.
Sethy, S. K. (2019). Financial technology and its role in financial inclusion: A study on India. In Financial Inclusion and Rural Development: A Road Map for Inclusive Growth (pp. 143–159).
Shaikh, A. A., Glavee-Geo, R., Karjaluoto, H., & Hinson, R. E. (2023). Mobile money as a driver of digital financial inclusion. Technological Forecasting and Social Change, 186, 122158.
Solanki, P., & Chhikara, K. S. (2024). Constraints to the promotion of financial inclusion in India: An empirical study of implementing agencies under Pradhan Mantri MUDRA Yojana. International Journal of Social Economics, 51(8), 1076–1092.
Srinivasan, K., Ramesh, K., Gunasekaran, K., & Sivasubramanian, K. (2024). Reforms in Indian banking sector: A paradigm shift in growth and financial inclusion in India. In Technology-Driven Business Innovation: Unleashing the Digital Advantage, Volume 1 (pp. 433–439). Cham: Springer Nature Switzerland.

Appendix

I Numerals Used in this Chapter

The numerals in this article follow the Indian numbering system, in which lakh (1,0,000) and crore (1,00,00,000) are commonly used. A conversion with equivalent values in the international numbering system is provided below:

Indian System	International Equivalent
1 lakh (1,00,000)	0.1 million
10 lakh (10,00,000)	1 million
1 crore (1,00,00,000)	10 million
10 crore (10,00,00,000)	100 million
100 crore (100,00,00,000)	1 billion
1,000 crore (1,000,00,00,000)	10 billion
1 lakh crore (1,00,00,00,00,000)	1 trillion

II Abbreviations Used in this Chapter

Abbreviation	Full Form
AEPS	Aadhaar-enabled Payment System
AI	Artificial Intelligence
API	Application Programming Interface
APY	Atal Pension Yojana
BCs	Business Correspondents
BBPS	Bharat Bill Payment System
BSBD	Basic Savings Bank Deposit
CFL	Centre for Financial Literacy
DBT	Direct Benefit Transfer
DBUs	Digital Banking Units
DPI	Digital Public Infrastructure
DPDP Act	Digital Personal Data Protection Act
FI-Index	Financial Inclusion Index
FSDC	Financial Stability and Development Council
FREE AI	Framework for Responsible and Ethical Enablement of AI
IMPS	Immediate Payment Service
IoT	Internet of Things
JAM	Jan Dhan, Aadhaar, Mobile
JLGs	Joint Liability Groups
KCC	Kisan Credit Card
KYC	Know Your Customer
MDR	Merchant Discount Rate

(*Continued*)

Abbreviation	Full Form
ML	Machine Learning
MSMEs	Micro, Small, and Medium Enterprises
NBFCs	Non-Banking Financial Companies
NABARD	National Bank for Agriculture and Rural Development
NDFI	National Digital Financial Infrastructure
NPS	National Pension System
NPCI	National Payments Corporation of India
NSFI	National Strategy for Financial Inclusion
NSFE	National Strategy for Financial Education
PIDF	Payment Infrastructure Development Fund
PMSBY	Pradhan Mantri Suraksha Bima Yojana
PMJDY	Pradhan Mantri Jan Dhan Yojana
PMJJBY	Pradhan Mantri Jeevan Jyoti Bima Yojana
PMMY	Pradhan Mantri MUDRA Yojana
PoS	Point of Sale
PSL	Priority Sector Lending
PSLCs	Priority Sector Lending Certificates
P2P Lending	Peer-to-Peer Lending
RBI	Reserve Bank of India
RBIH	Reserve Bank Innovation Hub
SRO-FT	Self-Regulatory Organization for Fintechs
SDGs	Sustainable Development Goals
SHGs	Self-Help Groups
SMEs	Small and Medium Enterprises
TGFIL	Technical Group on Financial Inclusion and Financial Literacy
TReDS	Trade Receivables Discounting System
ULI	Unified Lending Interface
UPI	Unified Payments Interface

8

Bridging Technology Gaps in Algorithmic Trading: An Integrated Framework for Retail Traders

Neha Parashar and Apoorva Joshi

8.1 Introduction

The evolution of financial markets has been deeply influenced by digital transformation, with algorithmic trading becoming an integral part of modern financial ecosystems. Developed economies have been at the forefront of adopting sophisticated algorithmic trading technologies, but emerging markets are also witnessing rapid advancements in trading automation and digital brokerage solutions (Yan et al., 2022). However, the accessibility and usability of these technologies remain uneven across regions, with disparities in internet penetration, regulatory frameworks, and financial literacy affecting retail trader participation (Vijayagopal et al., 2024). In developed economies like the United States and the United Kingdom, algorithmic trading accounts for a significant share of market transactions driven by high-frequency trading (HFT) and institutional participation (Chlistalla et al., 2011). In contrast, emerging economies, including India, Brazil, and South Africa, have seen gradual but promising growth in algorithmic trading, largely propelled by mobile-based trading platforms and increased regulatory support (SEBI, 2022).

As digital trading platforms continue to expand globally, adapting algorithmic trading technologies to diverse user needs has become a priority. Retail traders in developed markets often have access to high-speed execution, advanced analytics, and colocation services, whereas traders in emerging markets rely more on mobile-first platforms, simplified trading interfaces, and cost-effective brokerage models (Chlistalla et al., 2011). Language barriers, regulatory constraints, and financial education gaps also present additional challenges to improving inclusive participation in algorithmic trading worldwide. Addressing these disparities requires an integrated and accessible framework that can harmonise diverse technology

DOI: 10.1201/9781003591078-11

solutions and ensure equitable access to trading innovations across all user segments (Gomber et al., 2017).

Let us consider the case of India. Bombay Stock Exchange (BSE) was the first stock exchange that was established in India in 1875. It was granted permanent recognition under the Securities Contracts Regulation Act (SCRA) of India in 1957. Since then, an additional 34 stock exchanges were set up, trading various financial instruments and commodity derivatives, which are now reduced to a total of seven stock exchanges operating at present. The other prominent stock exchange in India is the National Stock Exchange (NSE), which was established in 1992, the same year the Securities and Exchange Board of India (SEBI), which is the autonomous market regulator and was established as a statutory body under the provisions of the Securities and Exchange Board of India Act, 1992 (15 of 1992).

Over the period since the inception of stock exchanges, the financial market has witnessed an evolution in technology and trading systems in India (Figure 8.1). Pre-1990, the Open Outcry System existed where traders had to gather physically on the trading floor to buy and sell securities by verbal communication and hand signals inside the trading ring. Such trades were then recorded on paper. In 1990, with advancements in technology, the exchanges adopted the Electronic Trading System known as Bombay Online Trading System (BOLT) in BSE and National Exchange for Automated Trading (NEAT)

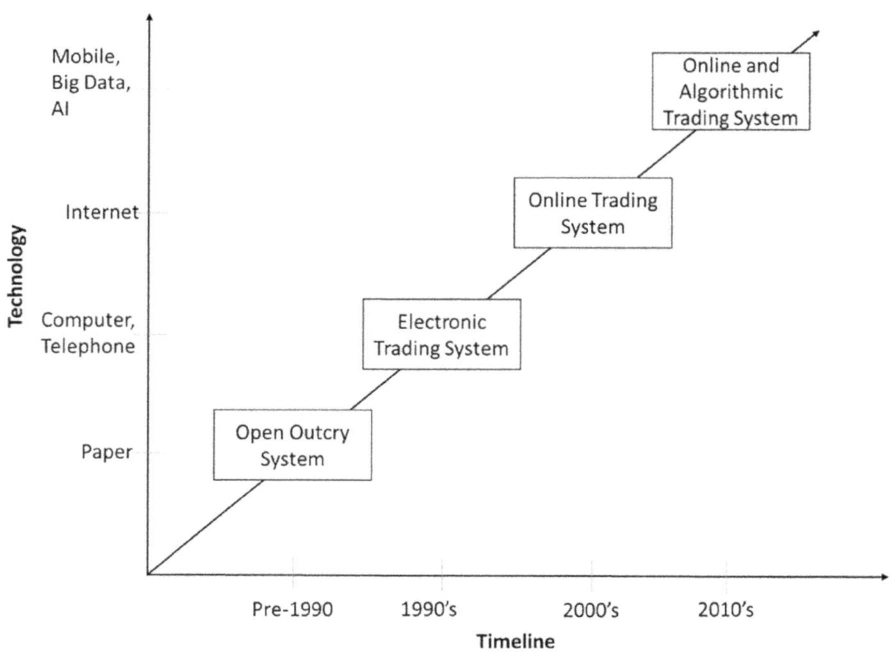

FIGURE 8.1
Evolution of technology and trading systems in India.

in NSE. These electronic trading systems streamlined the trading process and were designed to facilitate efficient and transparent trading of securities on the exchanges. The trading was done using computers and telephones, and even the physical stock certificates were replaced by electronic records held in depositories through dematerialisation in 1996, which helped streamline settlements and reduce risks.

In 2000, SEBI approved the execution of internet-based trades placed through order routing systems. This enabled anyone to place orders by connecting to the broker's internet trading systems, which are then routed for execution to the exchange trading systems and evolved the exchanges towards the era of online trading systems using the internet and advanced software and hardware technologies. The advent of online trading and the democratisation of mobile telephony helped India gain leadership in mobile-based stock trading. SEBI granted approval for the Direct Market Access (DMA) facility for institutional investors in 2008. This allowed clients to access the exchange trading system directly through the broker's infrastructure without the need for manual intervention by the broker. Following this, the exchanges also launched the colocation facilities, enabling the traders and the brokers to set up their servers within the premises of the exchange, which led to low latency in feeds, order execution, and improved security. This laid the foundation for the subsequent adoption of algorithmic trading systems by both institutional investors and retail traders beginning in the 2010s.

The evolution towards the online and algorithmic trading system, the continuous development and improvement in technology, not only enabled India to become a leading market using the mobile mode of trading but also helped in increasing the share of algorithmic trading, which stands at 4.3% in BSE and 14.7% in NSE of all executed trades on these exchanges' cash market, for the financial year 2022–23 (Figure 8.2).

Figure 8.3 shows the participant-wise share in equity derivatives turnover. The "others" category includes the retail individual investors, including the high net-worth individuals among "partnership Finns/LLP, Trust/Society, AIFs, Depository Receipts, PMS clients, Statutory Bodies, VCFs, NBFC, etc." (SEBI, 2022), had a 45.6% share in 2021–22 vs. 41.6% share in 2022–23 at BSE and 47.8 % share in 2021–22 vs. 43% share in 2022–23 at NSE in the cash market. However, in the equity derivatives market, the "other" category comprises "retail and high net-worth individuals (HNIs)" (SEBI, 2022) and has a 14.2% share in 2021–22 vs 21.1% share in 2022–23 at BSE and 33.4% share in 2021–22 vs 34.8% share in 2022–23 at NSE.

In the derivatives market, algorithmic trading is done primarily at the NSE, and the share of algorithmic trading was only 4.4% in 2021–22 vs 4.3% in 2022–23. The overall share of algorithmic trading in the cash and derivative markets has gradually increased over the years, as has the share of retail trades, and there still remains a significant growth opportunity in India. Recently, SEBI "proposed to allow retail investors to participate in algorithmic trading." (ET Bureau, 2024).

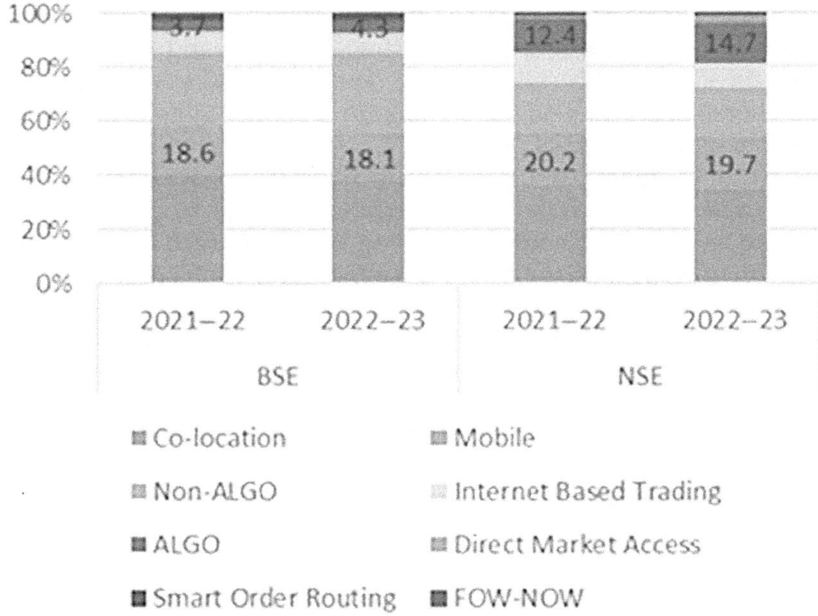

FIGURE 8.2
Mode of Trading in the Cash Market (Data Source: SEBI Annual Report 2022-23 (SEBI, 2022)).

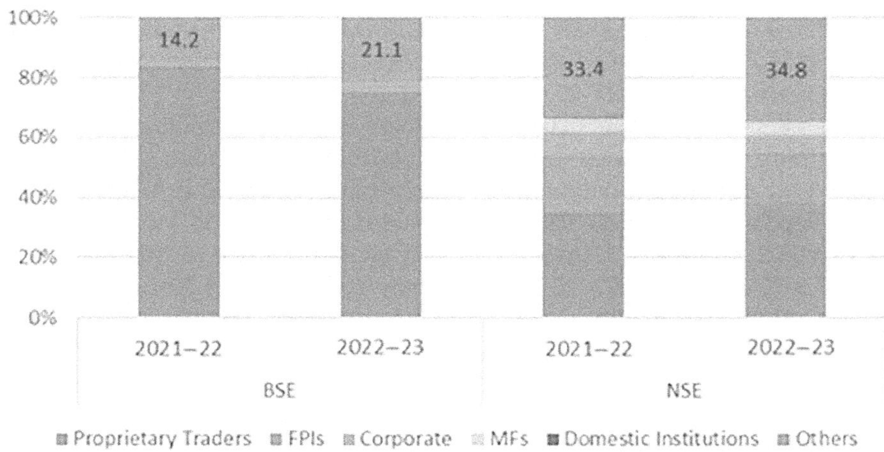

FIGURE 8.3
Participant-wise share in equity derivatives turnover (Data Source: SEBI Annual Report 2022-23) (SEBI, 2022).

The increasing adoption of algorithmic trading by retail investors presents both opportunities and challenges in ensuring accessibility, usability, and inclusivity. Although digital trading platforms have democratized access to financial markets, technological fragmentation and complexity pose barriers to adoption, especially for traders in emerging economies, non-native English speakers, and individuals with limited financial literacy (Fasnacht, 2020). A truly inclusive algorithmic trading framework should address these disparities by integrating user-friendly design principles, multilingual support, mobile adaptability, and cost-effective execution models (Falaiye et al., 2022).

Global regulatory variations impact the accessibility of advanced financial trading systems, including algorithmic trading. The European Union and the United States have well-defined regulations governing digital financial markets and automated trading oversight, while many emerging markets are still in the process of developing clear regulatory frameworks for broader financial innovation, which may influence the adoption of algorithmic trading (IOSCO, 2023). Variations in financial regulations across jurisdictions lead to inconsistencies in compliance burdens and technology adoption rates. An effective integrated framework should, therefore, be modular, allowing regional customization to comply with local regulatory environments while maintaining a core structure that enhances trading efficiency and user experience (Gomber et al., 2017).

Technological equity in digital finance must extend beyond access to trading tools and address the knowledge gap in algorithmic trading. As Aldridge (2010) highlights, the complexities of algorithmic trading and high-frequency strategies create significant barriers for retail traders, who often lack the technical expertise required to develop and manage trading algorithms. This results in an increased reliance on third-party algorithmic solutions, which may not always provide transparency or align with individual risk preferences and market conditions.

Therefore, there is a need to focus on making advanced technology solutions that are not only seamless in their applications but also promote the adoption of algorithmic trading in retail traders efficiently and bridge the gap between technological sophistication and trader inclusivity (Bao et al., 2023). This chapter proposes an integrated framework designed to bridge the technological gap in algorithmic trading faced by retail traders. By consolidating fragmented technology solutions across the pre-trade, trade, and post-trade stages, the framework aims to enhance accessibility, usability, and transparency. More importantly, the design prioritises inclusivity by incorporating features such as multilingual interfaces, explainable AI, mobile-first access, and customisable modules tailored to varying levels of trader experience and digital literacy. In doing so, the framework not only advances technological efficiency but also contributes meaningfully to financial inclusion by lowering entry barriers for underserved and diverse trader populations. It reflects a Diversity, Equity, Inclusion, and Belonging (DEIB) aligned approach to digital finance, ensuring that algorithmic trading platforms are not limited to technically skilled or institutionally privileged users but are adaptable, equitable, and supportive of diverse retail participation in global financial markets.

8.2 Methodology and Framework Design

This section outlines the methodological approach adopted to develop and validate the proposed integrated framework, including its conceptual design process, theoretical underpinnings, survey construction, and analytical techniques.

8.2.1 Design Science Research Method

The Design Science Research (DSR) grid method is used, which provides a foundation for developing a conceptual framework through its six core dimensions, namely, problem description, input knowledge, research process, key concepts, solution description, and output knowledge.(Vom Brocke & Maedche, 2019) It also offers an effective means of communicating the DSR initiative, which could be further worked upon to develop and produce an artefact.

Unlike other methods like portraying design essence (PDE) (Chandra Kruse & Nickerson, 2018), which are built on high-level conceptualization and emphasize capturing design knowledge for sharing with other designers, the DSR grid method is tailored to represent the essential dimensions of a DSR initiative comprehensively. Its high-level visualization capability, adaptability, and integration of key concepts make it suitable for developing a conceptual framework that effectively communicates the scope, objectives, and contributions of a DSR initiative.

The Design Science Research process in this study involved synthesizing literature and practitioner insights to inform input knowledge, identifying and theorizing relationships between design entities during the research process, defining key technical and conceptual constructs, and developing a cohesive solution description. The resulting artefact reflects a clear output knowledge contribution and forms the basis of an integrated framework tailored to the trading lifecycle.

8.2.2 Problem Description

In the following section, the problem is described through a problem statement by positioning it in the problem space. The development of the integrated framework began with identifying the structure of a typical retail

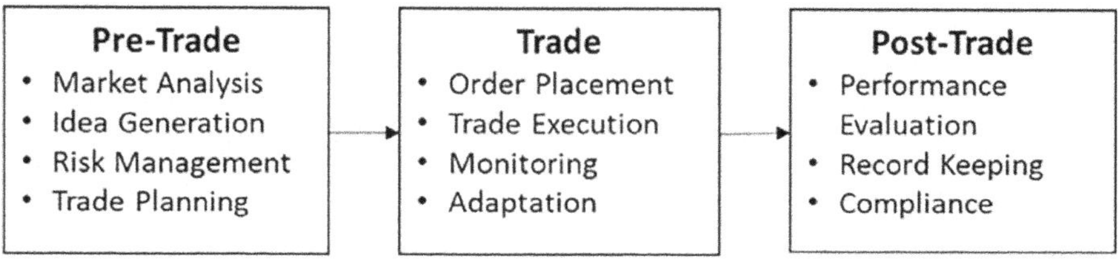

FIGURE 8.4
Trading cycle of a retail trader.

trading cycle and the associated technology gaps across its stages. A standard trading cycle of a retail trader can be divided into three stages, namely, pre-trade, trade, and post-trade (Figure 8.4). Typical pre-trade activities involve market analysis, for which traders use methods like technical analysis, fundamental analysis, sentiment analysis, and quantitative analysis. This leads to idea generation and, consequently, the selection of asset(s) to trade. The trader evaluates the risk and decides the risk management parameters based on his risk tolerance. Finally, trade planning is done, which includes the entry and exit points based on the risk-to-reward ratio and is based on a trading strategy.

After the completion of pre-trade activities, the retail trader places the order in the system, and the trade is executed, after which the trade is monitored. The market behaviour may or may not be as expected by the trader, and therefore, some changes in the trade parameters may be required to adapt to the market conditions. The result of the trade needs to be evaluated, and the trader needs to keep a record of each trade, not only for compliance but also for learning, which are the post-trade activities.

In today's scenario, a trader uses multiple technology solutions and platforms across the trading cycle to perform each activity. Even the traders who have adapted to advanced trading technologies like algorithmic trading have to use different technology solutions because algorithmic trading solutions are only focused on Trade Execution, and they have limitations. A trader's problem is dealing with various separate technology solutions, whether related or completely unrelated. Therefore, there is a need for a multidisciplinary, integrated, and mutually compliant ecosystem of technology solutions that can not only help retail traders but also improve market efficiency and liquidity and have positive policy implications.

8.2.3 Input Knowledge

To support the design of an integrated technology framework, this study draws on established theories of technology ecosystems and cross-domain integration. Technology ecosystems could be understood by breaking them down into their component parts, including product and application technologies, component technologies, support, and infrastructure technologies

(Adomavicius et al., 2008). However, these components are rarely isolated and are often interconnected with other technology domains. The technology domain refers to the individual technologies or fields that make up a broader technology ecosystem. For instance, the ecosystem of Algorithmic trading could be divided into different technologies or fields, like Algorithms, Order Management Systems (OMS), Execution Engines, etc. These areas are generally distinguished by their own standards, technologies, and competitive dynamics. The integration of the domains is essential to the evolution of technology ecosystems. A technology ecosystem's success depends on its individual components' ability to work together seamlessly and adapt to changing market conditions (Adomavicius et al., 2008). The technology domains can be integrated through the creation of standards. The technical specifications for how different technologies should interact with one another are defined by standards. Standards also encourage collaboration and competition among different technology domains since each domain must fulfil the requirements of the standard while also innovating to create better products. The role of standards in technology domains is echoed in the work of Gawer & Cusumano (2014), who describe the rise of platform owners as a key feature of technology ecosystems. Platform owners are firms that control the interfaces and standards around which an ecosystem is built. They provide a centralised point for coordination and collaboration among the different technologies and domains that make up the ecosystem.

The technology domains can be integrated through complementary and substitutive relationships. Complementary relationships between domains manifest themselves when one technology augments the value or usefulness of another technology. Substitutive relationships between domains occur when one technology replaces or competes with another technology. The technology domains can also be integrated through the creation of business models that support collaboration and value-sharing among different firms within the ecosystem (Casadesus-Masanell & Ricart, 2010). By defining how revenues and costs are shared among different players in the ecosystem, business models can encourage complementary relationships and reduce the risks of competition. Through the creation of standards, complementary relationships, substitutive relationships, and business models, different technology domains can work together to create value for consumers and increase the pace of innovation. As technology ecosystems continue to evolve and expand, the ability to effectively integrate different technology domains will remain a critical factor in their success (Adomavicius et al., 2008).

8.2.4 Research Process and Theoretical Foundations

The problem was identified based on input from the retail traders' first-hand experience. Looking at the market potential of the solution to improve the efficacy and efficiency of the retail trader and also provide a thought for new research activities, help build a better technology ecosystem to support algorithmic trading and improve future opportunities for the firms, the DSR approach was chosen to develop a framework. The problem was defined, and the solution was identified through a review of the literature. It was found that for every stage of the trading cycle, there is a technology domain that is operating or has the potential to operate. Robo-Advisor is used and has the potential to operate Pre-trade activities. Algorithmic trading systems, brain–computer interfaces (BCI), and human–machine interfaces (HMI) are partly operating and have the potential to operate trade activities. Robotic process automation (RPA) is also partly operating and has the potential to operate post-trade activities. Together, these technology domains have the collective potential to change the future landscape of trading. The underlying theories in support of the framework are as follows.

Innovation diffusion theory describes how new ideas, technologies, and practices spread within a society or organisation (Wani & Ali, 2015). This theory helps explain how new technologies such as robo-advisors, BCI, HMI, and RPA are adopted and implemented by traders and financial institutions. It also provides insights into the factors that influence the adoption of these technologies, such as relative advantage, compatibility, complexity, trialability, and observability.

Systems integration theory emphasises the need to effectively combine and coordinate different technologies, processes, and functionalities within a system (Rajabalinejad et al., 2020). This theory highlights the importance of integrating algorithmic trading, robo-advisors, BCI, HMI, and RPA into a cohesive and efficient trading ecosystem. It also underscores the significance of considering human factors, such as user experience and usability, when designing and integrating these technologies.

Domain-driven design is an approach to software development that focuses on aligning software design with the domain of the problem being solved (Evans, 2004). It highlights the importance of a shared understanding of the trading domain's concepts, rules, and processes. It also highlights the promotion of collaboration among developers and stakeholders to ensure that the resulting solution is well-suited to the needs of traders and financial firms.

Cognitive load theory focuses on optimising the interaction between humans and systems to enhance performance, safety, and user satisfaction (Sweller, 2011). It highlights that integrated technologies are easy to use, efficient, and aligned with user needs. It also promotes the use of design patterns and user interface design principles that minimise cognitive load and enhance usability.

Complex adaptive systems theory highlights that the algorithmic trading ecosystem has a complex and dynamic nature, considering both technological and human elements (Holland, 1992). As market conditions and user interactions change, the system's adaptability will enable it to learn and adjust accordingly.

8.2.5 Key Concepts

The following concepts form the building blocks of the integrated framework, reflecting both technical capabilities and user-centred considerations relevant to algorithmic trading. System Integration refers to the process of combining different technologies, processes, and functionalities into a cohesive system to enhance efficiency, interoperability, and performance (Madni & Sievers, 2014). Adaptability refers to the ability of a system to adjust and evolve in response to changing market conditions, user requirements, and technological advancements, ensuring long-term viability and effectiveness (Ulanowicz, 2002). User adoption refers to users' acceptance and utilisation of new technologies, considering factors such as ease of use, perceived value, and training requirements for successful implementation (Taherdoost, 2018). Deep Learning is a subset of machine learning that uses neural networks to learn complex patterns and relationships in data, enhancing the predictive capabilities of algorithmic trading systems (Janiesch et al., 2021). Pattern recognition involves identifying recurring patterns in market data using statistical and machine-learning techniques to make informed trading decisions (Bishop & Nasrabadi, 2006). Portfolio management strategies refer to the techniques for managing a portfolio of investments to achieve specific financial goals, often involving diversification, risk management, and asset allocation (Purwanto, 2024). Market efficiency refers to the degree to which stock prices reflect all available information, impacting trading strategies and decision-making processes (Burton, 1989). Liquidity is the ease with which an asset can be bought or sold in the market without affecting its price, influencing trading activities and risk management (Crockett, 2008).

8.2.6 Inclusive Design Principles in Algorithmic Trading

To address barriers to accessibility and adoption among diverse retail traders, the framework integrates inclusive design principles aligned with DEIB objectives. Algorithmic trading platforms have traditionally been designed for institutional investors and experienced traders, often requiring technical expertise in coding, quantitative modelling, and financial analytics (Aldridge, 2010). As digital trading solutions evolve, addressing these complexities is crucial to enhancing inclusivity for retail traders worldwide. However, for retail traders, the barriers to entry remain high, especially in regions with low financial literacy, limited regulatory clarity, and inconsistent technology infrastructure (Vijayagopal et al., 2024). To bridge this gap, the proposed integrated framework adopts inclusive design principles to enhance accessibility, transparency, and adaptability for traders with varying skill levels and technological access. Key inclusive design elements incorporated into the framework include:

User-Centred Human–Machine Interfaces (HMI): The framework prioritises intuitive interfaces that simplify order execution, risk management, and strategy selection. Digital finance advancements emphasise intuitive interfaces that simplify financial service access for a broad range of users. As Gomber et al. (2017) highlight, FinTech-driven digital platforms prioritise ease of use and accessibility, which can extend to algorithmic trading solutions by ensuring that first-time traders and nontechnical users can participate effectively.

Multilingual and Culturally Adaptive Interfaces: As financial technologies evolve, ensuring accessibility across diverse regions remains a challenge. Fasnacht (2020) highlights the importance of adapting financial services to different markets, emphasising the role of digital transformation and co-creation in making financial platforms more inclusive. Algorithmic trading platforms can address these barriers by incorporating language localisation, culturally adapted risk assessment models, and region-specific market data integrations.

Mobile-First Accessibility: In emerging economies, mobile-based trading dominates due to higher smartphone penetration compared to desktop-based trading platforms (Abuelfadl et al., 2016). The framework integrates mobile-friendly execution models, real-time market alerts, and cloud-based accessibility to support traders in resource-constrained environments.

Transparent and Explainable AI (XAI) in Trading Decisions: One of the major challenges retail traders face is trust in algorithmic decision-making. Black-box AI models create opacity, making it difficult for users to understand why a trade is recommended or executed (Bao et al., 2023). The framework incorporates explainable AI (XAI) to enhance user confidence, provide interpretability in model decisions, and allow for real-time user intervention.

Customisation for Risk-Averse and Speculative Traders: Retail traders differ in risk appetite, with some preferring low-risk, long-term investing while others engage in high-frequency speculative trading (Kumar & Lee, 2006). The framework ensures that risk management parameters, automated trading strategies, and portfolio allocations are adaptive to different user profiles, making algorithmic trading accessible to a broader demographic.

By incorporating these inclusive design principles, the framework ensures that algorithmic trading is not limited to a niche group of technically skilled traders but is instead adaptable to diverse users worldwide. Unlike existing retail trading platforms such as MetaTrader, TradingView API integrations, or broker-specific automation platforms like Zerodha's AlgoHub, which predominantly focus on isolated aspects of trade execution or chart-based signal generation, the proposed framework is designed to be holistic and modular. It integrates functionalities across the entire trading lifecycle, pre-trade analysis, trade execution, and post-trade evaluation, within a unified ecosystem. While existing platforms typically assume a certain level of user proficiency in coding, strategy development, or scripting APIs, this framework prioritises inclusivity through explainable AI, multilingual interfaces, and mobile-first design. By combining HMI, brain–computer interfaces (BCI), and robotic process automation (RPA), the framework extends beyond automation to support intuitive interaction, compliance automation, and accessibility for underrepresented or less-experienced traders. This multidimensional integration represents a significant departure from the fragmented, tool-specific approach seen in current platforms, offering instead a customisable and scalable architecture aligned with principles of financial inclusion and DEIB in digital finance.

8.2.7 Solution Description

There is a need for innovative approaches to navigating the dynamic nature of the retail trader's trading cycle that will result in enhanced efficiency, accessibility, and effectiveness. The framework in Figure 8.5 identifies the technology domains that not only have the capability to revolutionise and enhance efficiency and effectiveness for the retail trader's activity in each stage of the trading life cycle but also, if integrated with its diverse yet complementary technologies, can form a cohesive ecosystem for algorithmic trading which will benefit the retail traders.

Robo-Advisor is an intelligent system that can analyse user preferences, risk tolerance, and financial goals to provide personalised investment recommendations and automate portfolio management tasks. It leverages rule-based systems and machine learning algorithms to construct and manage investment portfolios based on individual financial profiles and risk tolerance levels. It has the capability to handle all pre-trade activities like market analysis, idea generation, risk management, and trade planning. The

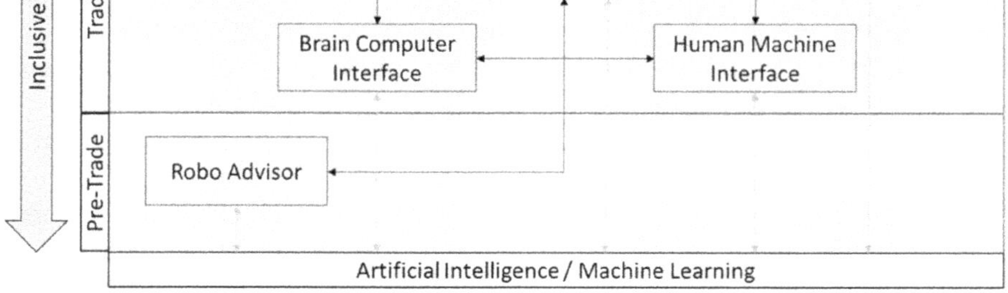

FIGURE 8.5
An integrated framework of technology solutions for algorithmic trading by retail traders.

Algorithmic Trading System, together with the BCI and HMI, can handle and bring efficiency and effectiveness to all trade activities. The Algorithmic Trading System, through its engine, can leverage machine learning and quantitative analysis to generate trading signals based on user-defined strategies and market data. It has shown the capability to utilise statistical and machine learning methodologies, such as time series analysis, natural language processing, and deep learning, for the purpose of detecting patterns and capitalising on market inefficiencies. It can also seamlessly handle all the activities in the Trade stage of the trading cycle. Brain signals can be converted into useful commands using a BCI. This technology, based on electroencephalography (EEG) or other brain imaging techniques, could offer advantages for highly skilled traders seeking faster reaction times and more intuitive control over their strategies. However, ethical considerations and limitations in accuracy and user adoption need to be addressed. HMI can give traders an easy-to-use interface via which they can communicate with the system, track its performance, and comprehend the reasoning behind its suggestions. HMI design plays a crucial role in fostering trust, transparency, and effective communication between humans and the algorithmic system, adhering to principles of cognitive load theory (Sweller, 2011) to minimise user burden. RPA automates repetitive tasks and can address post-trade activities, such as performance evaluation, record keeping, and compliance. This can save resources like time and effort for higher-level decision-making and analysis, improving efficiency and reducing the potential for human error.

The proposed framework integrates advanced technological solutions to address the challenges faced by retail traders across the pre-trade, trade, and post-trade stages of the trading cycle.

8.2.8 Survey Design and Constructs

To validate the framework's usability and acceptability, a structured survey was designed based on the trading cycle, capturing trader experience across three conceptual domains. The survey was designed to evaluate three core constructs: problems faced (PF), perceived solutions (PS), and willingness to use (WS). These constructs were carefully developed based on the framework to align with the three stages of the trading cycle: pre-trade, trade, and post-trade. The questionnaire items, measured on a 5-point Likert scale, aimed to capture respondents' experiences with trading challenges, their perceptions of the proposed solutions, and their willingness to adopt the integrated framework. Table 8.1 shows the details of unobserved variables, observed variables, and the questionnaire items. The complete questionnaire is given as a web appendix.

Several approaches have been established in the literature to assess user usability and acceptability of technological systems. Common models include the Technology Acceptance Model (TAM) (Davis, 1989), which measures perceived usefulness and ease of use; the Unified Theory of Acceptance and

TABLE 8.1

Unobserved variables, observed variables, and questionnaire items

SN	Unobserved Variable	Unobserved Variable Description	Observed Variable	Questionnaire Item
1	Problems Faced (PF)	Challenges encountered by traders during trading cycles. Pre-trade, Trade and Post-trade	PF_PRT_1	I face challenges in analysing markets during pre-trade activities
			PF_PRT_2	Developing and implementing effective trading/investing strategies that align with my investment objectives is difficult for me
			PF_PRT_3	I find it easy to conduct thorough portfolio diversification and asset allocation based on my risk profile
			PF_T_1	Monitoring my open trades/investment portfolio and making timely adjustments in response to market changes is a complex task for me
			PF_T_2	I have no difficulty in maintaining discipline and emotional control during the execution of my trades/changes to my investment portfolio. (Reverse coded)
			PF_T_3	Coordinating and synchronising multiple trading/investing activities (e.g., order placement, risk management) is a complex task
			PF_POT_1	Maintaining accurate and detailed records of my trading/investing activities for compliance and reporting purposes is a significant challenge
			PF_POT_2	I can easily identify and learn from my past trading/investing mistakes and successes to improve my future trading/investing performance. (Reverse coded)
			PF_POT_3	Incorporating the insights gained from post-trade/investment analysis into my future trading/investing strategies is a complex process
2	Perceived Solutions (PS)	Respondents' perceptions of proposed technology solutions during Pre-trade, Trade and Post-trade	PS_PRT_1	The Robo-Advisor's trading/investing strategy development and optimisation features can enhance my ability to create and implement effective trading/investing plans
			PS_PRT_2	The Robo-Advisor's ability to generate personalised trading/investing ideas and asset recommendations cannot help me improve my trading/investing performance. (Reverse coded)
			PS_PRT_3	The Robo-Advisor's portfolio diversification and asset allocation recommendations cannot help me manage my risks more effectively. (Reverse coded)
			PS_T_1	The Algorithmic Trading System's order execution capabilities can help me place and execute trades more efficiently

			PS_T_2	The integration of the Algorithmic Trading System with a Brain-Computer Interface (BCI) cannot enable me to make trading/investing decisions more intuitively and with faster reaction times. (Reverse coded)
			PS_T_3	The Algorithmic Trading System's systematic and disciplined approach can help me maintain consistency in my trading execution/change in investment portfolio, and decision-making
			PS_T_4	The Human-Machine Interface (HMI) cannot provide me with a user-friendly and transparent way to interact with the Algorithmic Trading System. (Reverse coded)
			PS_POT_1	The automation of regulatory compliance and reporting tasks through RPA can significantly reduce the burden and complexity of these post-trade activities
			PS_POT_2	Robotic Process Automation (RPA) cannot help me efficiently evaluate the performance of my trades/change in investment portfolio, and assess the effectiveness of my trading/investing strategies. (Reverse coded)
			PS_POT_3	RPA's ability to automate post-trade/investment activities can free up my time and resources, allowing me to focus on higher-level analysis and strategic decision-making
3	Willingness to Use (WS)	Traders' readiness to adopt the integrated framework.	WS_1	I believe the integrated technology solution would provide me with a competitive advantage in the market compared to using standalone trading platforms and tools
			WS_2	The integrated technology solution, as described in the conceptual framework, does not have the potential to significantly improve my overall trading/investing performance and decision-making. (Reverse coded)
			WS_3	I am not confident that the integrated technology solution would help me address the key problems I face across the pre-trade, trade, and post-trade stages of the trading cycle. (Reverse coded)
			WS_4	The seamless integration of the different technology domains (Robo-Advisor, Algorithmic Trading System, BCI, HMI, RPA) within the framework would not make it a valuable and attractive trading/investing solution for me. (Reverse coded)
			WS_5	I am willing to invest time and effort in learning and adapting to the integrated technology solution, as I expect it to significantly improve my trading/investing outcomes
			WS_6	The enhanced efficiency, effectiveness, and user-friendliness of the integrated technology solution would not encourage me to adopt it as my primary trading/investing platform. (Reverse coded)

(Continued)

TABLE 8.1 (Continued)

Unobserved variables, observed variables, and questionnaire items

SN	Unobserved Variable	Unobserved Variable Description	Observed Variable	Questionnaire Item
			WS_7	The transparency and ease of use provided by the integrated technology solution's user interface would be a key factor in my willingness to use the system
			WS_8	The comprehensive nature of the integrated technology solution, covering all stages of the trading cycle, would not be a key factor in my decision to use it. (Reverse coded)
			WS_9	I would be willing to pay a premium price to access the comprehensive and integrated technology solution for my trading activities
			WS_10	The ability to leverage advanced technologies like AI and machine learning through the integrated technology solution would not be a significant benefit for me. (Reverse coded)
4	Demographic Information	Characteristics of respondents for sample understanding.	DI_1	What is your age? [1] 18-25 years [2] 26-35 years [3] 36-45 years [4] 46-55 years [5] 56 years and above
			DI_2	What is your gender? [1] Male [2] Female [3] Non-binary [4] Prefer not to say
			DI_3	What is your highest level of education? [1] High school or equivalent [2] Bachelor's degree [3] Master's degree [4] Doctoral degree [5] Professional degree (e.g., CFA, CPA)
			DI_4	How many years of experience do you have in trading/investing? [1] Less than 1 year [2] 1-3 years [3] 4-6 years [4] 7-10 years [5] More than 10 years
			DI_5	On average, how frequently do you trade? [1] Daily [2] Weekly [3] Monthly [4] Quarterly [5] Annually
			DI_6	What is your primary investment/trading objective? [1] Capital preservation [2] Income generation [3] Capital growth [4] Speculation [5] Diversification
			DI_7	What is your risk tolerance level? [1] Very low [2] Low [3] Moderate [4] High [5] Very high
			DI_8	Which of the following best describes your trading/Investing style? [1] Fundamental analysis-based [2], Technical analysis-based [3], Quantitative/algorithmic [4], Discretionary [5], Hybrid (combination of approaches)

Use of Technology (UTAUT) (Venkatesh et al., 2003), which incorporates performance expectancy, effort expectancy, and social influence; and the System Usability Scale (SUS) (Brooke, 1996), a ten-item Likert-type scale widely used for evaluating user interfaces.

While these models are effective in general software or system acceptance contexts, they often lack specificity for domain-embedded systems such as algorithmic trading platforms that involve high-stakes financial decision-making and span multiple phases (pre-trade, trade, post-trade). Also, many standard models presume a level of prior familiarity with the technology, which may not be valid for diverse and novice user segments, especially in emerging markets.

In contrast, this study adopts a construct-driven approach by directly aligning questionnaire items with the conceptual stages of the trading cycle and the integrated framework's components. Constructs such as Problems Faced (PF), Perceived Solutions (PS), and Willingness to Use (WS) offer granular insights tailored to the algorithmic trading context. To ensure internal consistency of the survey instrument, Cronbach's alpha was computed for each of the three constructs. The results indicate acceptable to high reliability. Problems Faced (PF): $\alpha = 0.711$; Perceived Solutions (PS): $\alpha = 0.774$; Willingness to Use (WS): $\alpha = 0.851$. These values exceed the commonly accepted threshold of 0.70 (Nunnally & Bernstein, 1994), confirming that the items within each construct measure coherent underlying dimensions. This approach, combined with regression and paired t-test analyses, provides both empirical rigour and conceptual specificity. By averaging Likert-scale responses to form construct scores and opting not to apply dimensionality reduction techniques like PCA, the study maintains interpretability and direct alignment with each stage of the trading framework, making the results more actionable and transparent in the pilot-scale setting. The approach is also scalable and adaptable to further user studies in similar fintech adoption research.

8.2.9 Sample and Demographics

The survey was administered to a pilot sample of retail traders using a snowball sampling method to ensure access to respondents across varying levels of trading experience and backgrounds. The survey used a snowball sampling method, leveraging professional networks to identify and recruit participants. Data collection was conducted through online surveys, ensuring accessibility to a diverse group of respondents across trading expertise levels. A total of 73 participants completed the survey, representing a mix of novice and experienced retail traders. This sample size was deemed appropriate for a pilot study aimed at testing the preliminary usability and acceptability of the framework. The majority of the participants identified as male (78.1%), while females accounted for 21.9% of the respondents. Regarding educational background, most respondents held advanced degrees, with 63% possessing a master's degree, followed by 30.1% with a bachelor's degree, and 5.5%

holding doctoral qualifications. Trading experience varied widely, with 23.3% being novices with less than one year of experience, 28.8% having 1-3 years of experience, and 23.3% being highly experienced with over 10 years in trading. In terms of trading frequency, 31.5% of respondents traded monthly, 21.9% weekly, and 12.3% daily, reflecting a mix of active and less frequent traders. The sample also included a range of risk tolerance levels, with 61.6% identifying as moderate-risk traders, while smaller groups described themselves as high-risk (15.1%) or low-risk (16.4%) traders. This demographic diversity ensured the inclusion of varied perspectives, providing a solid basis for assessing the usability and acceptability of the proposed framework across different trader profiles.

As this was an exploratory pilot study, the target was to collect indicative data for initial empirical validation. According to Krejcie and Morgan's (1970) guidelines for sample size adequacy in social science research, a sample of 73 respondents is sufficient to detect medium effect sizes with basic inferential statistics such as regression and t-tests. The diversity of the respondent pool across age, education, trading experience, and risk tolerance further strengthens the robustness of the pilot findings and supports the preliminary validation of the proposed framework. Table 8.2 shows the demographic profile of survey respondents, and the survey response distribution is shown in Figure 8.6.

The methodological approach adopted in this study integrates principles of Diversity, Equity, Inclusion, and Belonging (DEIB) to ensure that the proposed framework is designed with accessibility and usability in mind for retail traders across different financial and technological backgrounds. While the empirical validation of the framework was conducted among respondents exclusively from India, the study acknowledges that algorithmic trading is a global phenomenon characterised by diverse levels of financial literacy, regulatory environments, and access to digital trading tools. Recognising this, the research methodology has been structured to assess the inclusivity of algorithmic trading technology in ways that can be extended beyond the Indian context.

The survey design prioritised capturing variations in trading behaviour, digital proficiency, and access to financial technology among Indian retail traders. Given that India has a heterogeneous population with disparities in financial education, income levels, and exposure to algorithmic trading, the sample offers insights into the adaptability of digital trading technologies for diverse user segments. However, the findings, while region-specific, provide a foundation for understanding broader challenges related to accessibility and usability that may also be relevant in other emerging and developing markets.

One of the core inclusivity challenges in algorithmic trading is the extent to which traders with different levels of experience and technical proficiency can engage with automated systems. The survey instrument incorporated measures to assess whether traders found existing algorithmic trading solutions accessible, whether they perceived a lack of transparency in

TABLE 8.2

Demographic profile of survey respondents

Demographic Variable	Category	Count (n = 73)
Age	36–45 years	26
	18–25 years	14
	26–35 years	14
	46–55 years	14
	56 years and above	5
Gender	Male	57
	Female	16
Education	Master's degree	46
	Bachelor's degree	22
	Doctoral degree	4
	Professional degree	1
Trading experience	More than 10 years	17
	1–3 years	21
	4–6 years	11
	7–10 years	7
	Less than 1 year	17
Trading frequency	Monthly	23
	Weekly	16
	Daily	9
	Quarterly	12
	Annually	13
Investment objective	Capital growth	28
	Speculation	19
	Income generation	12
	Diversification	8
	Capital preservation	6
Risk tolerance	Moderate	45
	High	11
	Low	12
	Very high	2
	Very low	3
Investing style	Technical analysis-based	20
	Fundamental analysis-based	18
	Hybrid	16
	Quantitative/algorithmic	12
	Discretionary	7

automated decision-making, and whether they believed an integrated framework could improve their ability to participate effectively in financial markets. Global discussions on financial inclusion emphasise the role of digital finance in expanding market access. Digital trading platforms must balance automation with transparency to ensure equitable participation, especially for less-experienced traders navigating increasingly complex financial systems (Gomber et al., 2017).

The study also considered how an integrated trading framework could mitigate barriers to entry for retail traders by taking into account seamless access

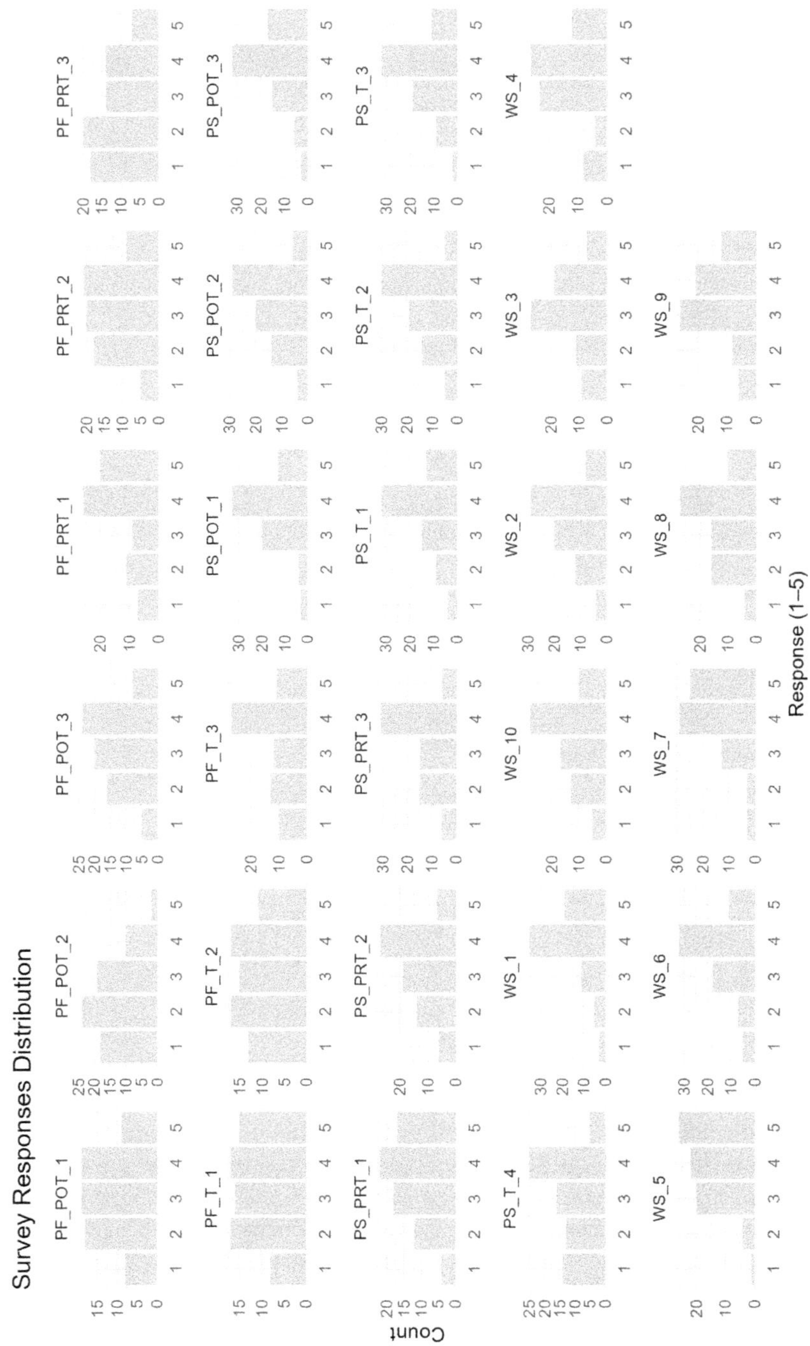

FIGURE 8.6
Survey response distribution.

to different technology solutions, including Robo-Advisors, HMI, and algorithmic trading systems. While the regulatory landscape in India differs from that of other jurisdictions, the need for standardised and adaptable solutions remains a global concern. Regulatory inconsistencies across jurisdictions create disparities in financial market participation, with many countries still working toward establishing comprehensive guidelines for digital and automated trading. As noted by IOSCO (2023), variations in regulatory maturity impact the adoption of financial technologies, which may extend to areas such as algorithmic trading. The methodology of this study highlights the importance of designing trading systems that are not only technically robust but also user-centric and adaptable to various compliance requirements.

8.2.10 Analytical Techniques

A sequence of analytical techniques was used to evaluate the reliability and statistical validity of the constructs used in the study. The collected data were analysed using robust statistical techniques. First, reliability analysis was performed using Cronbach's Alpha to ensure the internal consistency of the constructs. Next, a simple linear regression model (OLS) was used to examine the impact of Perceived Solutions on Willingness to Use, providing evidence of the framework's usability. Finally, a paired t-test compared the mean scores of problems faced and perceived solutions to evaluate the framework's effectiveness in addressing trading challenges.

As a pilot, this study serves as an initial step in validating the usability and user acceptability of the framework, offering empirical insights into its practical application and areas for further refinement. The significant positive relationship between perceived solutions and willingness to use highlights the usability of the framework, while the higher mean scores of perceived solutions relative to problems faced confirm its effectiveness in mitigating trading challenges. These findings are discussed further in the solution description and output knowledge sections. In this study, the resulting conceptual framework is found to be integrated across different technology domains, and therefore, it is referred to as an integrated framework.

A consolidated visual overview of the Design Science Research (DSR) process applied in this study, including problem statement, input knowledge, research process, concepts, solutions, and output knowledge, is provided in Appendix Figure A1.

8.3 Results

This section presents the statistical results obtained from the empirical validation of the proposed framework, including regression and paired t-test outcomes.

8.3.1 Regression Analysis

To empirically validate the usability and user acceptability of the framework, a regression analysis was conducted to assess the impact of perceived solutions (PS) on willingness to use (WS). The analysis provides strong evidence of the framework's relevance and applicability, underscoring its potential to enhance trading efficiency and effectiveness. The regression results, presented in Table 8.3, reveal a significant positive relationship between perceived solutions and willingness to use. The coefficient for PS was estimated at 0.6895 ($p < 0.001$), indicating that for every unit increase in perceived solutions, willingness to use the framework increases by approximately 0.69 units. This highlights the importance of integrated technological solutions in encouraging adoption among retail traders. The R-squared value of 0.367 indicates that the model explains approximately 36.7% of the variation in willingness to use, providing robust support for the framework's usability. The diagnostic plots, displayed in Figure 8.7, validate the assumptions of the regression model. The Residuals vs. Fitted plot confirms the linearity assumption, showing no discernible patterns. The Q–Q plot demonstrates that residuals are approximately normally distributed, while the scale-location plot indicates homoscedasticity, with consistent variance across fitted values. The residuals vs. leverage plot reveals no influential outliers, further affirming the reliability of the model.

8.3.2 Paired *t*-Test Results

The proposed integrated framework aims to address the challenges faced by retail traders by leveraging advanced technological solutions tailored to the trading cycle. To evaluate its effectiveness, a paired t-test was conducted to compare the mean scores of problems faced (PF) and perceived solutions (PS). The results provide empirical evidence supporting the framework's ability to mitigate trading challenges effectively. The paired t-test results, summarised

TABLE 8.3

Regression analysis summary

Term	Estimate	Std. Error	t-value	p-value	Significance
Intercept	1.1715	0.3699	3.167	0.0023	**
Perceived Solutions (PS)	0.6895	0.1075	6.416	1.36e-08	***
Residual Std. Error	0.5704	on 71 df			
Multiple R-squared	0.367				
Adjusted R-squared	0.3581				
F-statistic	41.16	on 1 and 71 df		p = 1.357e-08	

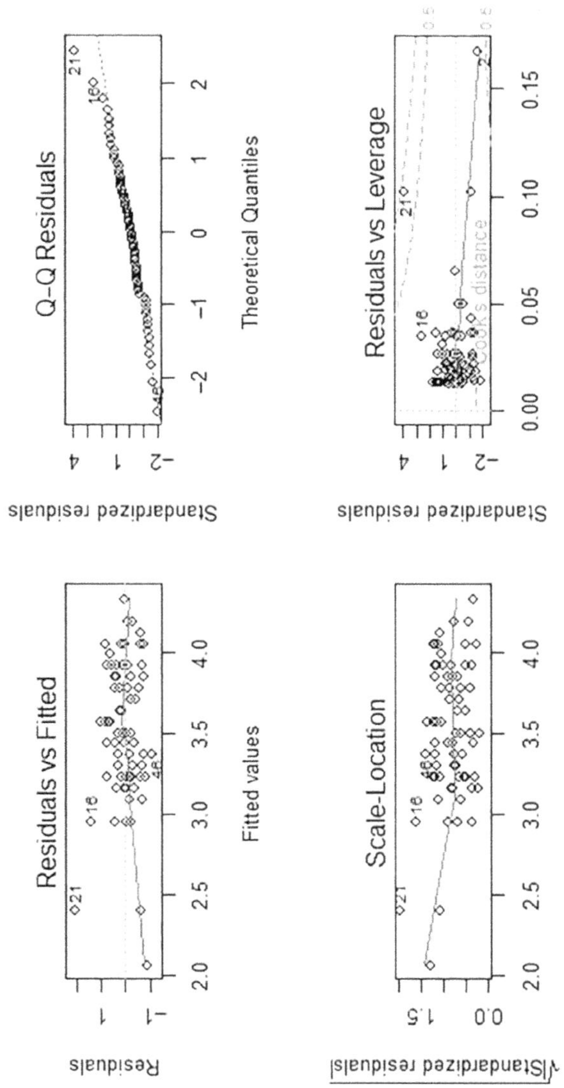

FIGURE 8.7
Regression analysis.

TABLE 8.4

Paired t-test results: problems faced vs. perceived solutions

Statistic	Value
t-statistic	−3.927
Degrees of freedom	72
p-value	0.0002
Mean difference	−0.353
95% Confidence interval	[−0.532, -0.174]

in Table 8.4, reveal a statistically significant difference between the mean scores of problems faced and perceived solutions ($t = -3.927$, $p < 0.001$). The negative mean difference of −0.353 indicates that the perceived solutions significantly outperform the problems faced in addressing trading challenges. The confidence interval for the mean difference, ranging from −0.532 to −0.174, further confirms the robustness of this finding. The visual representation in Figure 8.8 illustrates the higher average score for perceived solutions compared to problems faced, underscoring the framework's effectiveness across the trading cycle. This demonstrates that the proposed solutions align closely with the needs of retail traders and provide comprehensive support across the pre-trade, trade, and post-trade stages. The significant improvement in perceived solutions relative to problems faced highlights the practical utility of the framework in simplifying trading activities, reducing cognitive load, and improving decision-making. These findings establish the framework as an effective tool for overcoming the limitations of existing fragmented technology solutions, ensuring seamless integration and enhanced trader outcomes.

The next section interprets these results in the context of the research questions, existing literature, and practical implications.

8.4 Discussion

8.4.1 Interpretation of Results

The findings from the regression and paired t-test analyses confirm the usability and acceptability of the proposed integrated framework. The regression analysis demonstrated a statistically significant and positive relationship between Perceived Solutions (PS) and Willingness to Use (WS), indicating that retail traders are more inclined to adopt the framework when they perceive the technological solutions as effective. The R-squared value further suggests that a substantial proportion of the variance in willingness to use is explained by perceived solution quality.

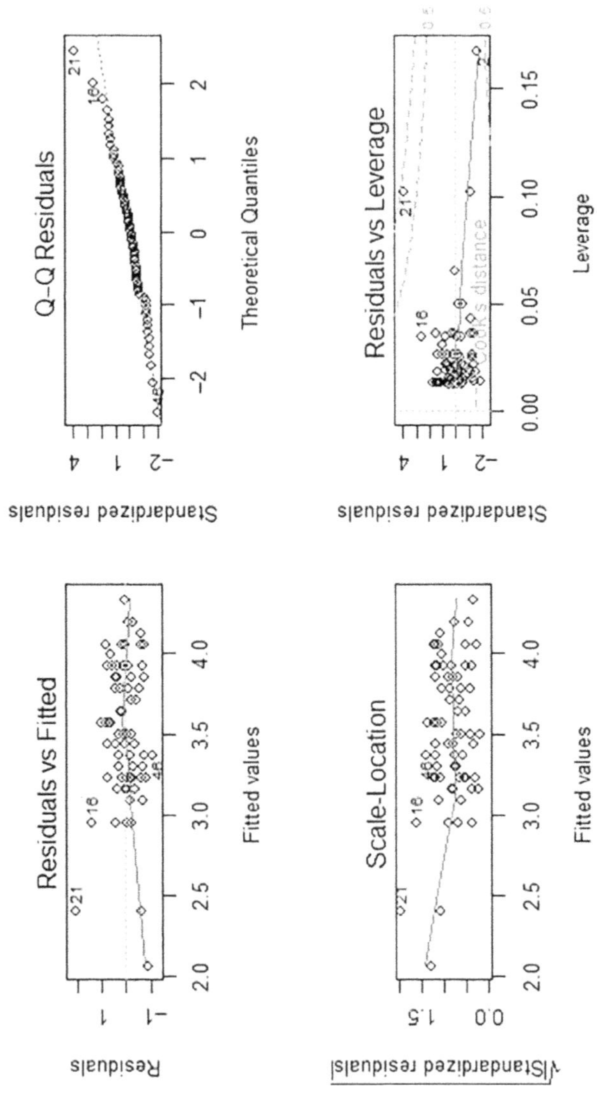

FIGURE 8.8
Mean comparison.

Complementing these findings, the paired t-test results revealed a significant improvement in mean scores from problems faced (PF) to perceived solutions (PS), providing empirical support that the proposed framework addresses key trading challenges. These results highlight that the framework not only resonates with traders' expectations but also effectively aligns with their operational needs across the trading cycle. By consolidating multiple technologies into an accessible structure, the framework simplifies interaction, enhances decision-making, and reduces the fragmentation and inefficiencies associated with existing standalone systems.

8.4.2 Theoretical Contributions

This study contributes to the theoretical understanding of how integrated technological frameworks can enhance algorithmic trading adoption among retail traders. The framework is grounded in innovation diffusion theory, which explains how relative advantage and ease of use drive adoption, both of which are empirically validated in the trader responses. Systems integration theory underpins the cohesive design of the framework, emphasising the need to harmonise distinct technological modules (Robo-Advisors, Algorithmic Trading Systems, BCI, HMI, and RPA) into a unified platform. Cognitive Load Theory supports the design rationale of the framework in minimising information overload, thereby improving usability. Further, complex adaptive systems theory provides a lens through which the adaptive and dynamic behaviour of the framework is conceptualised, as it responds to market conditions and evolving user needs. By combining these theoretical lenses, the framework offers a multidisciplinary model for future research on inclusive, integrated financial technology systems.

8.4.3 Practical and Policy Implications

The framework offers actionable insights for fintech developers, policy regulators, and trading platform providers. For technology developers, it serves as a blueprint for building modular, adaptable, and inclusive platforms that consolidate functionalities from trade planning to post-trade compliance. Emphasis on human-centred design elements such as explainable AI, multilingual interfaces, and mobile-first execution ensures that novice and experienced traders alike can engage effectively with algorithmic trading.

For policymakers and regulators, the framework offers a foundation for guiding the development of algorithmic trading ecosystems that are transparent, equitable, and adaptable to different levels of financial literacy. It aligns with SEBI's proposed agenda of expanding algorithmic trading access to retail participants, while also accommodating evolving regulatory landscapes in other emerging markets.

From a market systems perspective, the framework has the potential to enhance liquidity, reduce operational errors, and improve compliance through automation. Its inclusive design makes it a viable tool for expanding financial participation, thus supporting broader goals of financial inclusion and DEIB in digital finance.

8.4.4 Limitations and Future Research

While the study provides early empirical validation of the framework's usability and acceptability, it is not without limitations. The analysis is based on a pilot survey of 73 respondents, drawn from Indian retail traders using snowball sampling. Although appropriate for exploratory research, this restricts the generalizability of findings across global retail trader populations.

Additionally, the study relies on self-reported perceptions rather than actual trading behaviour. Future studies should employ experimental designs or real-world testing environments to evaluate how the framework influences actual trading performance, decision accuracy, and risk outcomes.

Further research could also explore qualitative insights into user trust, satisfaction, and perceived fairness of algorithm-driven decisions. As financial markets continue to evolve, longitudinal studies assessing the impact of such frameworks on trader success, behavioural adaptation, and market resilience would be valuable. Finally, the inclusion of new technologies, such as blockchain-enabled settlement systems or ESG-focused robo-advisory models, can further extend the framework's utility.

8.5 Conclusion

This study introduces a comprehensive integrated framework of technology solutions designed to address the fragmented and complex nature of retail trading across the pre-trade, trade, and post-trade stages. By leveraging the DSR grid method, the framework integrates robo-advisors, algorithmic trading systems, BCI, HMI, and RPA into a cohesive and adaptable ecosystem. These technological advancements not only enhance efficiency, accessibility, and decision-making capabilities but also ensure that retail traders, regardless of expertise level, can engage with algorithmic trading in a more structured and intuitive manner. The empirical validation through quantitative analysis reinforces the framework's practical relevance, with findings demonstrating a significant positive relationship between PS and WS. The paired t-test results confirm that the framework effectively reduces trading challenges, validating its usability and acceptability in real-world trading environments.

By consolidating diverse technological domains into an integrated and user-centric approach, the framework mitigates the limitations of disparate and inaccessible trading technologies. It fosters a more inclusive and seamless trading experience, helping retail traders navigate the complexities of market analysis, trade execution, and post-trade evaluation without the burden of managing multiple, disconnected platforms. This integration not only enhances individual trading efficiency but also contributes to broader market stability and liquidity, presenting significant implications for financial policymakers, fintech developers, and regulatory authorities. As financial markets continue evolving with advancements in AI-driven automation, real-time data analytics, and cognitive computing, the proposed framework provides a scalable and future-ready solution to meet the needs of diverse retail traders worldwide.

While this study offers a strong foundational model, future research should focus on refining the framework by incorporating larger, more diverse trader populations across various financial markets. Expanding its empirical validation across different regulatory environments and economic contexts will further establish its global applicability and adaptability. Additionally, as AI and neurotechnology continue shaping financial markets, an in-depth examination of regulatory frameworks, compliance standards, and ethical considerations is necessary to ensure that these advancements align with market integrity and trader protection. Addressing concerns related to data privacy, algorithmic transparency, and the ethical use of BCI-driven trading interfaces will be critical in maintaining trust and fairness in automated trading ecosystems. This research paves the way for future innovation in algorithmic trading, bridging the gap between technological sophistication and trader accessibility.

Appendix

These results demonstrate that the framework effectively addresses the challenges faced by retail traders. By integrating technological solutions that align with traders' needs, the framework provides a cohesive and practical approach to overcoming inefficiencies and enhancing performance across the trading cycle. This validation establishes the framework as both a conceptual and practical advancement in algorithmic trading technologies. Figure 8.8 gives the DSR project overview.

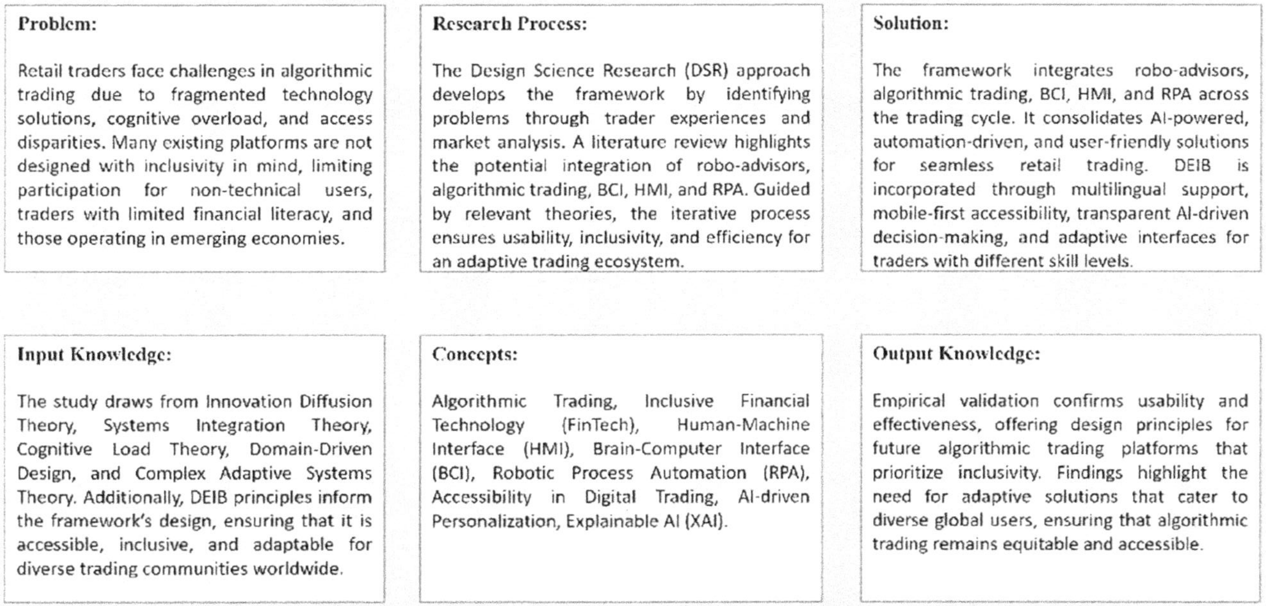

FIGURE A1
DSR project overview.

Data Availability Statement Data are available from the corresponding author upon request.

Funding This research received no external funding

Conflict of interest The authors report no conflicts of interest.

References

Abuelfadl, M., Choi, K. S., & Abbey, B. (2016). Mobile stock trading platforms and individual investors' financial performance. *Annals of Management Science, 5*(1), Article 1. https://digitalscholarship.tnstate.edu/ams/vol5/iss1/1

Adomavicius, G., Bockstedt, J., Gupta, A., & Kauffman, R. J. (2008). Understanding evolution in technology ecosystems. *Communications of the ACM, 51*(10), 117–122. https://doi.org/10.1145/1400181.1400207

Aldridge, I. (2010). *High-frequency trading: A practical guide to algorithmic strategies and trading systems*. Wiley.

Bao, Y., Gong, W., & Yang, K. (2023). A literature review of human–AI synergy in decision making: From the perspective of affordance actualization theory. *Systems, 11*(9), 442. https://doi.org/10.3390/systems11090442

Bishop, C. M., & Nasrabadi, N. M. (2006). *Pattern recognition and machine learning* (Vol. 4, No. 4, p. 738). New York: springer.

Brooke, J. (1996). SUS-A quick and dirty usability scale. Usability evaluation in industry, 189(194), 4–7.

Burton, G. (1989). Is the stock market efficient. *Science,* 243(4896), 1313–1318.

Casadesus-Masanell, R., & Ricart, J. E. (2010). From strategy to business models and onto tactics. *Long Range Planning, 43*(2–3), 195–215. https://doi.org/10.1016/j.lrp.2010.01.004

Chandra Kruse, L., & Nickerson, J. V. (2018). *Portraying Design Essence*. Hawaii International Conference on System Sciences. https://doi.org/10.24251/HICSS.2018.560

Chlistalla, M., Speyer, B., Kaiser, S., & Mayer, T. (2011). High-frequency trading. *Deutsche Bank Research, 7,* 3–4.

Crockett, A. (2008). Market liquidity and financial stability. *Financial Stability Review, 11,* 13–17.

Davis, F. D. (1989). Perceived usefulness, perceived ease of use, and user acceptance of information technology. *MIS Quarterly, 13*(3), 319–340.https://www.jstor.org/stable/249008

ET Bureau. (2024, December 14). Sebi likely to facilitate retail participation in Algo Trading. *The Economic Times*. https://economictimes.indiatimes.com/markets/stocks/news/sebi-likely-to-facilitate-retail-participation-in-algo-trading/articleshow/116305079.cms?from=mdr

Evans, E. (2004). *Domain-driven Design: Tackling Complexity in the Heart of Software.* Addison-Wesley Professional.

Falaiye, T. O., Olutimehin, D. O., Ewim, C. P.-M., & Ibeh, A. I. (2022). Developing an inclusive framework for digital payment systems: Solving barriers to financial inclusion in underserved regions. *International Journal of Social Science Exceptional Research, 2*(1), 143–155. https://doi.org/10.54660/IJSSER.2023.2.1.143-155

Fasnacht, D. (2020). Open innovation in the financial services—the magic bullet. *SSRN Electronic Journal*. https://doi.org/10.2139/ssrn.3684517

Gawer, A., & Cusumano, M. A. (2014). Industry platforms and ecosystem innovation. *Journal of Product Innovation Management*, *31*(3), 417–433. https://doi.org/10.1111/jpim.12105

Gomber, P., Koch, J.-A., & Siering, M. (2017). Digital finance and FinTech: Current research and future research directions. *Journal of Business Economics*, *87*(5), 537–580. https://doi.org/10.1007/s11573-017-0852-x

Holland, J. H. (1992). Complex adaptive systems. *Daedalus*, *121*(1), 17–30.

IOSCO. (2023). *Annual Report 2023*. www.iosco.org/annual_reports/2023/pdf/annualReport2023.pdf

Janiesch, C., Zschech, P., & Heinrich, K. (2021). Machine learning and deep learning. *Electronic Markets*, *31*(3), 685–695. https://doi.org/10.1007/s12525-021-00475-2

Krejcie, R. V., & Morgan, D. W. (1970). Determining sample size for research activities. *Educational and Psychological Measurement*, 30(3), 607-610.

Kumar, A., & Lee, C. M. C. (2006). Retail investor sentiment and return comovements. *The Journal of Finance*, *61*(5), 2451–2486. https://doi.org/10.1111/j.1540-6261.2006.01063.x

Madni, A. M., & Sievers, M. (2014). Systems integration: Key perspectives, experiences, and challenges. *Systems Engineering*, *17*(1), 37–51. https://doi.org/10.1002/sys.21249

Nunnally, J., & Bernstein, I. (1994). Psychometric Theory, 3rd edition (MacGraw-Hill, New York).

Purwanto, B. (2024). Optimal portfolio and the integrated strategy. *Management Analysis Journal*, *13*(2), Article 2. https://doi.org/10.15294/maj.v13i2.8261

Rajabalinejad, M., van Dongen, L., & Ramtahalsing, M. (2020). Systems integration theory and fundamentals. *Safety and Reliability*, *39*(1), 83–113. https://doi.org/10.1080/09617353.2020.1712918

SEBI. (2022). *Annual Report 2022-23*. www.sebi.gov.in/reports-and-statistics/publications/aug-2023/annual-report-2022-23_74990.html

Sweller, J. (2011). Cognitive load theory. In *Psychology of Learning and Motivation* (Vol. 55, pp. 37–76). Elsevier. https://doi.org/10.1016/B978-0-12-387691-1.00002-8

Taherdoost, H. (2018). A review of technology acceptance and adoption models and theories. *Procedia Manufacturing*, *22*, 960–967. https://doi.org/10.1016/j.promfg.2018.03.137

Ulanowicz, R. E. (2002). The balance between adaptability and adaptation. *Biosystems*, *64*(1), 13–22. https://doi.org/10.1016/S0303-2647(01)00170-8

Vijayagopal, P., Jain, B., & Ayinippully Viswanathan, S. (2024). Regulations and fintech: A comparative study of the developed and developing countries. *Journal of Risk and Financial Management*, *17*(8), Article 8. https://doi.org/10.3390/jrfm17080324

Venkatesh, V., Morris, M. G., Davis, G. B., & Davis, F. D. (2003). User acceptance of information technology: Toward a unified view. *MIS Quarterly*, 425-478.

Vom Brocke, J., & Maedche, A. (2019). The DSR grid: Six core dimensions for effectively planning and communicating design science research projects. *Electronic Markets*, *29*(3), 379–385. https://doi.org/10.1007/s12525-019-00358-7

Wani, T. A., & Ali, S. W. (2015). Innovation diffusion theory. *Journal of General Management Research*, *3*(2), 101–118.

Yan, S., Ling, X., Cao, T., Hu, S., Xiong, R., Ye, H., & Zhang, R. (2022). Algorithmic trading and challenges on retail investors in emerging markets. *Journal of Economics, Finance and Accounting Studies*, 4(3), 36–41. https://doi.org/10.32996/jefas.2022.4.3.4

9

Healthcare Equity Through Technology: The eSanjeevani Journey

Arif Perdana and Vijayakumar Bharathi S.

9.1 Introduction

In the vast and diverse landscape of India, where geographical barriers and resource constraints have historically impeded healthcare delivery, digital transformation is quietly reshaping how millions access medical care (Al Dahdah & Mishra, 2023; Faujdar et al., 2020). As the sun rises over remote villages in Ladakh, elderly patients connect with cardiologists in Delhi (Jain et al., 2024); across tribal hamlets in Northeast India, expectant mothers receive specialist guidance without arduous journeys (T. Singh et al., 2023). In desert settlements of Rajasthan, chronic disease management continues uninterrupted despite physical distances (Das et al., 2024; Velan et al., 2024). This transformation is powered by eSanjeevani, India's national telemedicine platform, which has emerged as one of the most significant public health innovations in recent years (Kaladharan et al., 2023; Parameshwarappa & Olickal, 2023).

The challenges that prompted eSanjeevani's development were deeply entrenched in India's healthcare ecosystem. The country has long grappled with severe disparities in medical access, with rural areas facing critical shortages of doctors, especially specialists (R. Singh et al., 2024). Primary healthcare centres often operate with limited resources, whereas district and tertiary hospitals remain perpetually overburdened (Parameshwarappa & Olickal, 2023; Sinha & Rahul, 2025; Upadhyay et al., 2023). For millions of Indians, seeking specialised care has meant undertaking expensive, time-consuming journeys to urban centers, a reality that has kept quality healthcare beyond reach for many vulnerable populations (Dastidar et al., 2022). Moreover, the absence of structured health record systems at the primary and secondary levels has created significant gaps in continuity of care, further complicating treatment journeys for patients with complex or chronic conditions (Renu, 2025).

DOI: 10.1201/9781003591078-12

What distinguishes eSanjeevani from other telemedicine initiatives globally is not merely its technological sophistication, but its remarkable scale and integration within a public healthcare framework (Suhas et al., 2022). Since its launch, the platform has significantly expanded its reach by connecting a vast network of healthcare facilities and professionals to deliver remote medical consultations. It operates through a widespread system of Health & Wellness Centers (HWCs) and hub hospitals supported by a large pool of telemedicine practitioners. This extensive ecosystem has enabled millions of virtual consultations, reinforcing the role of digital health solutions in improving access to medical care (Arora et al., 2024; Dastidar et al., 2022). This extraordinary position eSanjeevani is the world's largest telemedicine network within a primary healthcare system, a testament to India's capacity to implement digital health solutions at the population scale.

The platform's dual-modality approach addresses diverse healthcare needs through two distinct models: eSanjeevani Ayushman Bharat—Health and Wellness Centers (AB-HWC), which facilitates doctor-to-doctor consultations, and the eSanjeevani outpatient department (OPD), which enables direct patient-to-doctor interactions (Dastidar et al., 2022). The former operates on a hub-and-spoke model, allowing community health officers at primary centres to connect patients with specialists at district hospitals, whereas the latter permits individuals to seek medical advice directly from their homes via web or mobile interfaces. This flexibility has proven to be particularly valuable in responding to various healthcare contexts across India's heterogeneous landscape.

The eSanjeevani platform contributes significantly to healthcare inclusivity by providing accessible telemedicine services to underserved populations (Renu, 2025; Suhas et al., 2022; Upadhyay et al., 2023). This platform has broadened access to medical expertise, particularly for groups that have historically encountered greater challenges in obtaining healthcare. The data revealed that a significant share of users were women and older adults, highlighting its role in reducing barriers and fostering more inclusive healthcare delivery. By eliminating travel requirements and associated costs, eSanjeevani reduced both financial and logistical impediments to seeking medical attention, particularly for rural populations and those with limited mobility.

The COVID-19 pandemic has served as a critical inflection point for platform adoption. What began as a modest initiative in November 2019 expanded rapidly into a vital component of India's pandemic response strategy. As healthcare systems worldwide struggled with unprecedented demands, eSanjeevani demonstrated remarkable adaptability, scaling from a few thousand pre-pandemic consultations to over 75,000 daily sessions at its peak[1]. This rapid expansion underscored the platform's robust cloud-based infrastructure and capacity to function effectively under extreme pressure.

Beyond its immediate impact on healthcare accessibility, eSanjeevani represents a significant advancement in India's broader digital health architecture. Its integration with the Ayushman Bharat Digital Mission (ABDM) and alignment with electronic health record systems signals a shift toward a more connected and interoperable healthcare ecosystem (R. Singh et al., 2024). The platform's incorporation of AI-driven language processing, automated prescription translations, and clinical decision support tools further positions it at the forefront of digital health innovations.

This chapter is guided by the central research question: How has eSanjeevani's comprehensive approach to telemedicine, encompassing technological infrastructure, service delivery models, social inclusion strategies, and transformed healthcare accessibility in India, and what implications does this transformation hold for digital health initiatives in other resource-constrained environments? By examining eSanjeevani's evolution from its conceptual foundations to its nationwide implementation, we aimed to understand how its cloud-based architecture, security frameworks, artificial intelligence (AI) integration, and interoperability have collectively enabled it to address long-standing healthcare disparities while adapting to emerging challenges.

By exploring this question, we aimed to extract insights that extend beyond India's specific context, offering valuable perspectives for healthcare systems worldwide. As digital health technologies continue to evolve, eSanjeevani is a compelling example of how thoughtful implementation at scale can bridge longstanding gaps in healthcare accessibility. Its journey from concept to nationwide deployment illustrates the potential of telemedicine to transform healthcare delivery, particularly in settings where traditional infrastructure falls short. Through this examination, we seek to understand not just what eSanjeevani has accomplished but what its success portends for the future of global healthcare delivery.

The remainder of this chapter is organised as follows. First, we examined the evolution of eSanjeevani from its conceptualization to its current status as the world's largest telemedicine network, highlighting key developmental milestones. Second, we analyse the robust technological infrastructure that powers the platform, focusing on the cloud architecture, security protocols, AI integration, and system interoperability. Finally, we evaluated eSanjeevani's impact on healthcare inclusion across India, particularly for rural populations, women, elderly citizens, and other vulnerable groups, demonstrating how digital transformation can meaningfully address healthcare inequities in developing economies.

9.2 Overview of eSanjeevani

India's healthcare system has long struggled with accessibility challenges, particularly in rural and remote areas, where the shortage of doctors, especially specialists, has severely impacted service delivery. District and tertiary hospitals remain overburdened because of the limited availability of primary level (R. Singh et al., 2024; Sinha & Rahul, 2025; Upadhyay et al., 2023). Patients seeking specialist care often have to travel long distances, leading to treatment delays and higher costs. The lack of a structured system for maintaining health records at primary and secondary levels further exacerbates these challenges, creating significant gaps in the continuity of care.

Recognizing these issues, the Government of India launched eSanjeevani, a national telemedicine platform designed to integrate digital solutions into healthcare delivery (Upadhyay et al., 2023). The goals were to enhance accessibility, reduce dependency on physical infrastructure, and ensure universal health coverage. eSanjeevani provides a hub-and-spoke model for doctor-to-doctor consultations (eSanjeevani AB-HWC) and patient-to-doctor model (eSanjeevani OPD) for remote consultations. By leveraging telemedicine, this initiative bridges the gap between healthcare providers and patients, offering timely medical advice without geographical constraints.

9.2.1 History and Evolution of eSanjeevani

eSanjeevani was conceptualised to address India's persistent healthcare disparities, particularly in rural and remote areas, where access to specialised medical care remains a significant challenge (Kaladharan et al., 2023; Upadhyay et al., 2023). The initiative emerged in response to structural inefficiencies in the healthcare system, including an acute shortage of specialist doctors outside urban centres and an overwhelming burden on tertiary hospitals. By leveraging India's extensive public health infrastructure, the government envisioned a scalable telemedicine solution that could bridge the gap between healthcare providers and patients, ensuring that medical expertise efficiently reached underserved populations. The initial phase focused on identifying key healthcare gaps, defining a digital solution concept, and establishing a framework for implementation.

The first implementation phase materialised in November 2019 with the launch of the eSanjeevani AB-HWC in Andhra Pradesh (Dastidar et al., 2022). Building on a hub-and-spoke model, the system enabled Community Health Officers (CHOs) at primary health centres to facilitate virtual consultations between patients and specialists at district hospitals and medical colleges. This structured approach improves medical accessibility by providing real-time consultations, electronic prescriptions, and referral services, significantly reducing the need for patients to travel long distances for specialised care. The success of the initial pilot study demonstrated the feasibility of integrating telemedicine into India's public healthcare framework and laid the foundation for its expansion.

The COVID-19 pandemic in 2020 accelerated the urgency for remote healthcare solutions, leading to the rapid launch of the eSanjeevani OPD in April of that year (Iswarya & Shobana, 2024). This direct-to-patient teleconsultation service allows individuals to connect with doctors from their homes through web portals and mobile applications. The initial deployment involved a single OPD per state; however, as demand surged, the platform was scaled to include multiple specialty OPDs, covering domains such as mental health, paediatrics, and chronic disease management. The service ensured continuity of care during lockdowns, mitigating disruptions in healthcare access, while alleviating pressure on already stretched hospital resources.

As adoption grew, eSanjeevani transitioned from a pandemic response measure to a long-term component of India's health care strategy. The platform underwent systematic expansion, integrating state health departments and evolving into a critical element of India's Digital Health Mission. Rather than being developed specifically for non-communicable diseases (NCDs), eSanjeevani was conceived as a comprehensive telemedicine solution initially designed to address COVID-19 pandemic challenges and provide general healthcare access. The implementation of eSanjeevani across thousands of HWCs facilitated decision support for healthcare professionals, particularly in semi-urban and rural areas, where medical expertise remains scarce. The platform's multilingual interface and optimization for low-bandwidth environments further enhanced its accessibility, ensuring that the technological limitations did not impede its effectiveness.

India faces a significant NCD burden, with cardiovascular diseases, diabetes, cancer, and chronic respiratory diseases accounting for approximately 60% of national deaths and disproportionately affecting underserved populations[2]. Digital health equity principles position telemedicine platforms like eSanjeevani as critical solutions for bridging healthcare access gaps. While initially deployed for pandemic response, eSanjeevani's unified digital infrastructure enables comprehensive management of both communicable and noncommunicable diseases, providing essential chronic care services including regular monitoring, medication adjustments, and lifestyle counseling to remote and rural populations previously lacking specialist access.

Recognizing the need for greater diagnostic capabilities in remote consultations, Sanjeevani introduced telediagnosis in March 2023. By integrating Point-of-Care Diagnostic devices (PoCDs), healthcare workers can conduct essential clinical tests remotely, with results instantly available for specialist review. This advancement has enabled more precise medical decision-making, particularly in managing chronic diseases and routine health check-ups. The integration of remote diagnostics has marked a significant leap in telemedicine, improving consultation efficacy and expanding the scope of services that could be delivered virtually (see Figure 9.1).

The incorporation of AI further transformed the operational efficiency of eSanjeevani. AI-driven enhancements facilitate clinical decision making, automated administrative workflows, and introduce predictive analytics to optimize patient management (Gupta et al., 2025; Pillai, 2023). These capabilities support the transition from reactive healthcare delivery to a more data-driven and preventive model. AI-assisted recommendations improve

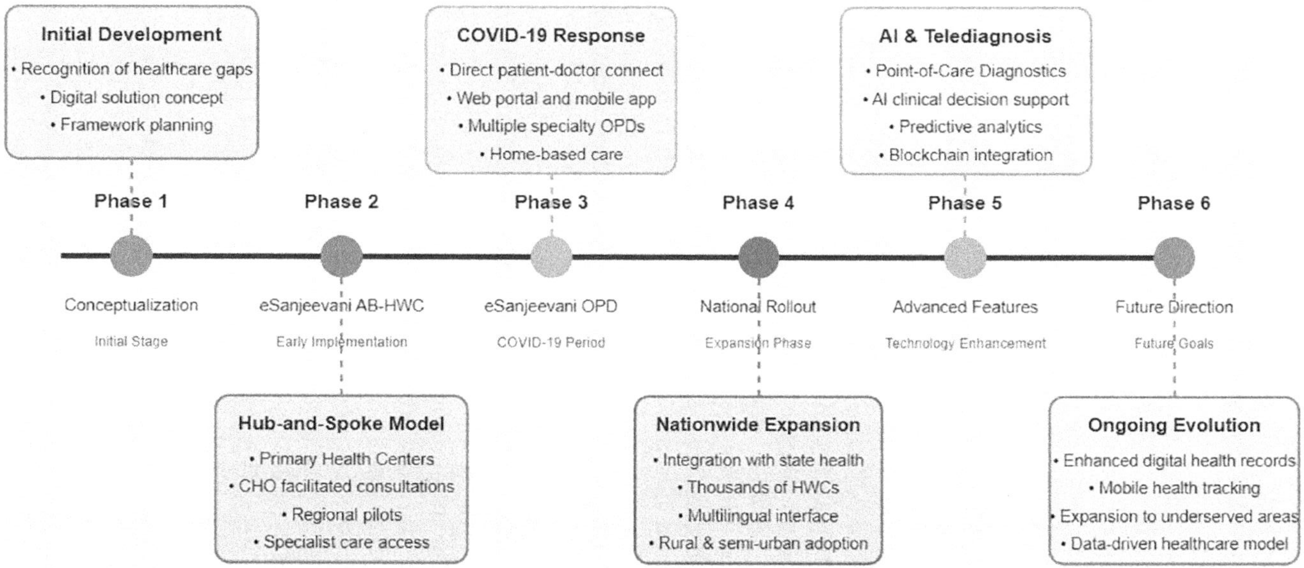

FIGURE 9.1
eSanjeevani historical timeline.

diagnostic accuracy, while automation streamlines scheduling and documentation processes, allowing healthcare providers to focus more on patient care. The platform's ongoing AI integration is expected to play a critical role in refining healthcare delivery and expanding personalised medicine approaches. Figure 9.1 shows an overview of the e-Sanjeevani historical timeline.

By 2024, eSanjeevani had facilitated over 276 million consultations, establishing itself as the world's largest telemedicine network within the primary healthcare system. The service operates across 127,499 HWCs (spokes) and 16,211 hub hospitals, with 218,489 telemedicine practitioners providing remote medical care (Arora et al., 2024; Dastidar et al., 2022). Its widespread adoption underscored its impact on healthcare accessibility, particularly among marginalised groups, women accounted for 57% of users and senior citizens represented 12%, illustrating its role in fostering healthcare inclusivity[3].

Future developments aim to further enhance a platform's capabilities and security. Planned initiatives include the integration of blockchain-based secure health data management, ensuring that patient records remain tamper-proof, while facilitating seamless data sharing across healthcare providers. Additionally, mobile-integrated health tracking enables patients to monitor their health metrics in real time, bridging the gap between teleconsultations and proactive health management. Expanding the platform's reach into underserved regions remains a key priority, with ongoing efforts to strengthen the digital infrastructure and improve awareness of telemedicine services.

9.3 eSanjeevani Technological Infrastructure

Following widespread disruptions in global healthcare, India developed a digital solution that has significantly changed how millions access medical services. Although the concept of telemedicine has been widely discussed in international forums, few countries have successfully implemented it on a national scale until the introduction of eSanjeevani. This platform utilizes smartphones and internet connectivity to facilitate online consultations and deliver healthcare services remotely. In addition, it integrates mobile technology to provide accessible health education, empowering both patients and healthcare providers (Chawhan et al., 2023).

eSanjeevani represents more than just technological advancement; it signifies a fundamental shift in how healthcare can be delivered in resource-limited settings. By creating a digital infrastructure that balances accessibility with security and scalability with personalization, the platform challenges traditional assumptions regarding the feasibility of remote healthcare. Its design provides key insights for organizations aiming to implement large-scale digital solutions, particularly in emerging economies, where infrastructure constraints often pose significant obstacles to technological adoption.

9.3.1 Cloud-Based Infrastructure for Scalability and Reliability

The effectiveness of eSanjeevani as a national telemedicine platform is largely attributed to its cloud-based infrastructure, which ensures scalability and uninterrupted services. The eSanjeevani OPD telemedicine system integrates both web-based and Android-based applications, enabling seamless doctor-patient consultations (Kaladharan, 2023). Developed by the Center for Development of Advanced Computing (C-DAC) Mohali, the platform operates as a centrally managed telemedicine solution, utilizing cloud servers to efficiently handle consultations, user data, and video communication (A. Singh et al., 2023). Built on .NET Core, eSanjeevani leveraged cloud infrastructure to enhance reliability and scalability, ensuring stable performance under varying demand conditions (Wadali et al., 2020). .NET Core, an open-source framework developed by Microsoft, supports the development of high-performance applications across multiple platforms, including the web, mobile, desktop, microservices, and cloud-based environments.

The platform's architecture was designed to dynamically allocate resources based on demand, a critical feature during the COVID-19 pandemic, when consultation volumes increased significantly. C-DAC enables eSanjeevani to provide secure, video-based clinical consultations directly to patients' homes and streamline access to medical care (Parameshwarappa & Olickal, 2023). According to reports from the National Health Authority, the system is capable of handling over one million consultations per day, ensuring continuous service, even during peak demand periods.

A major advantage of eSanjeevani's cloud deployment is its elasticity, which allows it to support simultaneous connections from thousands of endpoints, including Health and Wellness Centers (HWCs) and individual users. This setup reduces the latency in video consultations and enhances the overall user experience. In addition, cloud hosting simplifies system-wide updates and feature enhancements. The transition to eSanjeevani 2.0 in 2023 introduced several new functionalities without disrupting the existing services (Arora et al., 2024). The platform's reliability is further strengthened through partnerships with cloud service providers, such as Microsoft Azure, which enhances performance and data management through cloud-based and AI-driven optimizations.

9.3.2 Ensuring Data Security and Privacy

Managing sensitive medical data at a national level requires robust security protocols. eSanjeevani employs a multilayered security framework to safeguard patient confidentiality while adhering to India's data protection regulations. Teleconsultations are conducted through encrypted channels, ensuring that video and text communication between patients and healthcare providers remains secure. The platform also incorporates user authentication measures such as mobile-based OTP verification and health ID integration, thus preventing unauthorised access. In addition, eSanjeevani integrates a DICOM viewer, which can function independently or alongside a DICOM/PACS server, maintaining data security through encryption, access controls, and compliance with healthcare standards. This setup ensures a secure and flexible approach to managing medical imaging (Wadali et al., 2020). A DICOM viewer enables the visualization and analysis of medical images, whereas a Picture Archiving and Communication System (PACS) facilitates centralised storage, retrieval, and sharing. Together, these tools streamline medical imaging workflows, while maintaining efficiency, interoperability, and data security across healthcare facilities.

Data privacy was further strengthened through the alignment of eSanjeevani with ABDM. Since its integration in June 2022, the platform has allowed users to create and manage Ayushman Bharat Health Accounts (ABHA), linking teleconsultation records such as prescriptions and diagnostic reports to a secure digital repository (Kamath et al., 2025). This system ensures that the patient data remain under control and are accessible only through consent-based mechanisms. Unlike conventional health records, which are often fragmented across healthcare providers, this integration facilitates seamless and secure access while maintaining privacy protection.

To further enhance data security, eSanjeevani incorporated blockchain technology to ensure the integrity of the health records. As the volume of digital health data continues to grow, blockchain provides an additional layer of security, supporting data privacy and maintaining user trust in digital healthcare systems (Hazra & Bora, 2025). The platform's backend infrastructure is protected by government firewalls, and regular security audits are conducted to identify potential vulnerabilities and enhance system defenses. Compliance with India's national telemedicine guidelines ensures that eSanjeevani follows the best practices in data handling and storage. Collectively, these measures reinforce the platform's ability to provide a secure and reliable telemedicine service, while maintaining public confidence in digital healthcare.

9.3.3 Integrating AI and Automation for Enhanced Service Delivery

A key feature of eSanjeevani 2.0 is the integration of AI and automation to enhance efficiency and accessibility in teleconsultations (Gupta et al., 2025; Pillai, 2023). One of the most notable advancements is the use of AI-driven language processing, which enables multilingual interaction. The platform also includes improved audio-video connectivity, the ability to attach past consultation records, prescription previews and synchronization, and a multilingual dashboard that supports 13 languages with customizable font sizes (Gupta et al., 2025).

eSanjeevani incorporates AI of Medical Things (AIoMT) technologies, utilizing IoT-based health sensing tools, cloud- and edge-integrated IoT networks with AI, and AR/VR capabilities. Machine learning, deep learning models, and natural language processing support teleconsultation and remote communications. In addition, the platform is built on a cloud-based architecture and operates on an open-source technology stack for audio-video consultations (Pillai, 2023). With the integration of Azure OpenAI services, eSanjeevani provides real-time translation and transcription, helping bridge communication barriers between doctors and patients who speak different languages. This feature is particularly beneficial for India's linguistically diverse healthcare landscape.

AI has also been applied to automated prescription translations, allowing patients to download prescriptions in their native language. This improves medication adherence by ensuring that the patients fully understand their treatment instructions[4]. Another significant advancement was the introduction of speech-to-text transcription during consultations. By leveraging cognitive services, the platform can transcribe doctor-patient interactions, enhance documentation, and reduce the need for manual note-taking. These transcriptions also support quality assurance efforts by ensuring that consultations align with the medical guidelines.

Beyond documentation and translation, AI is being explored for supporting clinical decisions. Efforts are underway to develop AI-powered symptom triaging in which patients interact with a chatbot before their consultation to record symptoms and identify potential emergencies. AI-driven diagnostic assistance is also in development, offering clinical decision support to doctors and helping standardize care quality. Initial studies on eSanjeevani 2.0 suggest that these AI-driven enhancements improve consultation efficiency by reducing incomplete patient histories and minimizing connectivity issues.

Despite these benefits, scaling AI integration is challenging. Ensuring the accuracy of automated translations, maintaining physician oversight, and adhering to regulatory standards are critical considerations. The development team continues to refine these AI capabilities with input from medical professionals to ensure that AI complements rather than replaces clinical expertise. As AI functionalities expand, maintaining transparency and user trust will remain central to their successful implementation.

9.3.4 Digital Health Records and System Interoperability

eSanjeevani functions as part of India's broader digital health ecosystem, rather than as a standalone service. Its interoperability with national health databases and electronic health records (EHRs) enables a more integrated and coordinated approach to patient care. The platform is linked to ABDM, allowing seamless data exchange. This integration ensured that a patient's teleconsultation history, prescriptions, and laboratory results were securely connected to their ABHA. By facilitating access to a comprehensive patient record, the system minimizes redundancy, enhances diagnostic accuracy, and improves the continuity of care. For instance, eSanjeevani incorporates tele-spirometry for early detection and management of respiratory conditions, integrates EHRs to automatically log spirometry data, and provides a virtual asthma self-management education program led by Certified Asthma Educators. In addition, it employs an EHR-based SMART Asthma Action Plan template to support treatment planning (De Gardner et al., 2025).

In addition to the ABDM, eSanjeevani supports multiple national health initiatives. It was adapted for use by the Ministry of Defense, offering telehealth services to armed force personnel and retired service members. The platform is also a core component of Tele-MANAS, India's National Telemental Health Program (Chakraborty et al., 2025; Prakash, 2025). Through this initiative, eSanjeevani facilitates remote psychiatric consultations and expands access to mental health services across the country. These integration positions are central elements in India's evolving digital healthcare infrastructure.

From a technical standpoint, eSanjeevani complies with global interoperability standards, including HL7 FHIR (Fast Healthcare Interoperability Resources), ensuring that health data generated on the platform can be accessed and utilised by other health IT systems (Thapliyal et al., 2024). The use of ABHA IDs in teleconsultations enhances data continuity by enabling secure sharing of medical records across public and private healthcare providers. Additionally, the platform's cloud-based electronic record-keeping system allows physicians to retrieve prior consultation histories, facilitating better clinical decision-making while reducing unnecessary repetition of medical assessments.

9.3.5 The Future of eSanjeevani's Digital Evolution

As eSanjeevani continues to evolve, the focus will be on enhancing its digital infrastructure while maintaining security, scalability, and user centricity. The planned expansion of AI functionalities, improved interoperability with private healthcare providers, and further integration with insurance schemes will shape the future trajectory of the platform. Given its role in national healthcare delivery, ongoing regulatory oversight and physician engagement are critical in ensuring that technological advancements align with clinical best practices (Renu, 2025; Suhas et al., 2022; Upadhyay et al., 2023).

Telemedicine has emerged as a transformative force in healthcare, and eSanjeevani exemplifies how digital platforms can bridge accessibility gaps on a population-scale (Choudhary et al., 2024; Kaladharan et al., 2023). Its robust cloud architecture, stringent data security measures, AI-driven innovations, and seamless interoperability have positioned it as a digital health transformation model. Moving forward, its continued success will hinge on balancing technological advancements with the foundational principles of trust, security, and equitable access to health care.

9.4 The Technology Powering e-Sanjeevani's Telemedicine Revolution

E-Sanjeevani represents a significant leap in India's digital healthcare strategy, offering a robust and scalable telemedicine platform. The system was built on a cloud-based architecture, ensuring accessibility and operational efficiency across diverse geographical regions. By leveraging secure government-backed data centres, e-Sanjeevani maintains high levels of security and reliability. The platform operates on a modular framework, allowing seamless integration with other digital health initiatives, such as the ABDM and EHRs (Rajendran & Chandrashekar, 2024; R. Singh et al., 2024; Thapliyal et al., 2024). This interconnected approach fosters continuity of care, enabling healthcare professionals to access patient history and provide informed consultations.

At its core, e-Sanjeevani is designed as a browser-based application, eliminating the need for software installation and ensuring a user-friendly experience. It incorporates real-time video conferencing, secure data exchange, and electronic prescriptions within a streamlined interface. The cloud-native design of the system ensures scalability, allowing it to accommodate surges in demand, such as those witnessed during the COVID-19 pandemic. The integration of Application Programming Interfaces (APIs) enables interoperability with other health applications, enhances efficiency, and minimizes redundancy in patient data management.

9.4.1 Doctor-to-Doctor and Patient-to-Doctor Consultation Models

The doctor-to-doctor mode facilitates teleconsultations between frontline health workers and specialists in higher-tier hospitals (Dash et al., 2021; Renu, 2025). This feature is particularly impactful in rural areas, where primary healthcare providers, such as nurses and community health workers, require expert guidance for chronic disease management and maternal care. The remote consultation model helps reduce stigma associated with certain conditions by enabling discreet access to specialist care without requiring patients to visit specialised clinics where their conditions might become publicly visible. The consultation process followed a structured workflow in which patient vitals and medical history were recorded at HWCs before being reviewed by specialists in tertiary hospitals. This enables structured clinical decision making and improved patient outcomes.

In contrast, the patient-to-doctor mode allows individuals to connect directly with healthcare providers via smartphones or computers (Gupta et al., 2025; V. K. Sahu & Dave, 2022). This direct access model significantly reduces economic barriers for lower-income patients by eliminating travel costs, accommodation expenses, and lost wages associated with hospital visits, while the free-to-use platform ensures healthcare accessibility regardless of economic status. The platform is designed for high-volume usage by employing an intelligent queue-management system that optimizes consultation efficiency. Patients can register using a simple interface, select specialties, and enter a virtual waiting room before connecting to an available doctor. Electronic prescriptions generated through the platform enable patients to collect medicines from designated pharmacies, thereby reducing the need for physical visits.

9.4.2 Enhancing Chronic Disease Management with Remote Monitoring

One of the most important applications of e-Sanjeevani is in the management of chronic diseases, such as diabetes, hypertension, and cardiovascular conditions (Rajendran & Chandrashekar, 2024; Thapliyal et al., 2024). The platform enables continuous monitoring through regular virtual check-ins, preventing complications associated with poor adherence to treatment plans. Health workers stationed in rural HWCs use the doctor-to-doctor mode to relay patient vitals, including blood pressure and glucose levels, to specialists. This model ensures that patients receive timely adjustments to their treatment regimens, without the logistical burden of frequent hospital visits.

To further enhance remote chronic disease management, e-Sanjeevani integrates India's digital health ecosystem, allowing structured documentation of patient data. Teleconsultations were documented within the EHRs to ensure seamless follow-up care. Some states have also introduced specialty teleclinics, in which endocrinologists and cardiologists conduct virtual consultations for patients with chronic diseases referred from primary care centres. The system's ability to facilitate expert-driven interventions at the grassroots level significantly improves long-term disease management and patient adherence to prescribed treatment.

9.4.3 Telemedicine for Maternal and Child Health Services

Maternal and child health care is another domain in which e-Sanjeevani has demonstrated a substantial impact. This platform enables teleconsultations between pregnant women in remote areas and gynaecologists at higher-tier hospitals, ensuring comprehensive antenatal care (T. Singh et al., 2023). Community health workers use the system to discuss ultrasound reports, laboratory results, and pregnancy-related symptoms with specialists, allowing early identification of high-risk cases. This minimizes the need for long-distance travel, ensuring that expectant mothers receive timely intervention without disrupting their daily lives.

In paediatric care, e-Sanjeevani provides a mechanism for virtual consultations on immunization schedules, nutritional guidance, and general paediatric conditions (Malviya et al., 2025; Vashisht et al., 2024). Newborns presenting with symptoms of jaundice or respiratory distress can be evaluated remotely with doctors advising on further management or referrals to neonatal units. Some states have implemented dedicated telepaediatric OPDs to streamline child healthcare consultations and to improve access to specialist care in underserved regions. Although telemedicine cannot fully replace in-person examinations for maternal and child health, it serves as a critical adjunct that enhances accessibility and promotes early detection of complications.

9.4.4 Mental Health Support and the Integration of Tele-MANAS

Mental health care remains one of the most significant areas where e-Sanjeevani has made strides, particularly in light of the growing awareness of psychological well-being (Choudhary et al., 2024). The government's Tele-MANAS initiative, launched in 2022, is integrated with e-Sanjeevani and offers a multi-tiered mental health support system. While initial counselling is provided via a phone helpline, individuals requiring specialised psychiatric consultations are referred to e-Sanjeevani for video-based sessions with mental health professionals. This model ensures that individuals in remote or underserved areas receive expert psychiatric care without the stigma often associated with visiting mental health institutions (Suhas et al., 2022).

Telepsychiatry services under e-Sanjeevani have proven effective in bridging gaps in access, particularly in small towns and rural regions, where psychiatrists are scarce (Chakraborty et al., 2025). The platform enables structured therapy sessions, medication management, and follow-up consultations (Prakash, 2025). By allowing families to participate in therapy sessions remotely, e-Sanjeevani also provides a supportive environment for individuals dealing with mental health challenges. The National Institute of Mental Health and Neurosciences (NIMHANS) has played a crucial role in expanding Tele-MANAS by integrating AI-driven mental health screening and support tools, enabling the early detection of high-risk individuals, particularly those at risk of self-harm or suicide. AI models, such as Mental-Llama, have been piloted to assist mental health professionals by offering real-time, contextualised assessments, and facilitating crisis interventions (Chakraborty et al., 2025). These AI-driven systems help mitigate India's shortage of trained mental health professionals by acting as triage mechanisms and directing patients to appropriate care pathways based on risk levels.

Furthermore, the integration of generative AI in tele-MANAS has enabled AI-assisted chatbots and automated mental health monitoring systems to enhance the scalability of crisis support services (Chakraborty et al., 2025). AI-driven chatbots provide initial psychological first aid, reducing the burden on human counsellors while ensuring timely intervention. By leveraging language models trained to understand regional dialects and cultural nuances, Tele-MANAS has improved accessibility for non-English speakers and marginalised communities, ensuring inclusivity in mental healthcare.

During crises such as the COVID-19 pandemic, AI-enhanced Tele-MANAS services have played a pivotal role in providing remote mental health assistance to vulnerable populations, including students, frontline workers, and individuals facing social isolation (Chakraborty et al., 2025; Gupta et al., 2025; Prakash, 2025). Additionally, the initiative has been aligned with India's broader digital health strategies, such as the Ayushman Bharat Digital Mission and IndiaAI Mission, to enhance data-driven mental health policymaking and improve long-term mental health outcomes through predictive analytics and real-time monitoring.

9.4.5 Adapting to Public Health Emergencies: The COVID-19 Catalyst

The COVID-19 pandemic has significantly accelerated the adoption of telemedicine in India, positioning e-Sanjeevani as an essential public health tool. During lockdowns, when hospitals experience severe strain due to rising patient loads, the platform plays a critical role in managing COVID-positive individuals under home isolation (Dash et al., 2021). Through virtual consultations, healthcare providers monitored symptoms, advised on oxygen saturation levels, and identified early indicators of hospital admission. In addition to COVID-19 management, e-Sanjeevani facilitated access to routine medical care, ensuring that non-COVID patients received necessary consultations despite disruptions in outpatient services. This approach helped reduce exposure risks and alleviate pressure in overwhelmed hospitals (Raj et al., 2024).

The e-Sanjeevani was supported by an integrated digital health ecosystem that played a crucial role in India's pandemic response. Key digital tools include Aarogya Setu for contact tracing and exposure notifications, COWIN for vaccination registration and certification, Quarantine Watch for monitoring isolated individuals through geo-tagged images, COVA for verified pandemic-related information, and GoK Direct for official updates via WhatsApp. This ecosystem allows for remote patient monitoring, early disease detection using symptom-tracking algorithms, support for national vaccination efforts through digital verification, and reduced hospital congestion through virtual consultations. Collectively, these tools transformed India's healthcare delivery infrastructure during the crisis (V. K. Sahu & Dave, 2022).

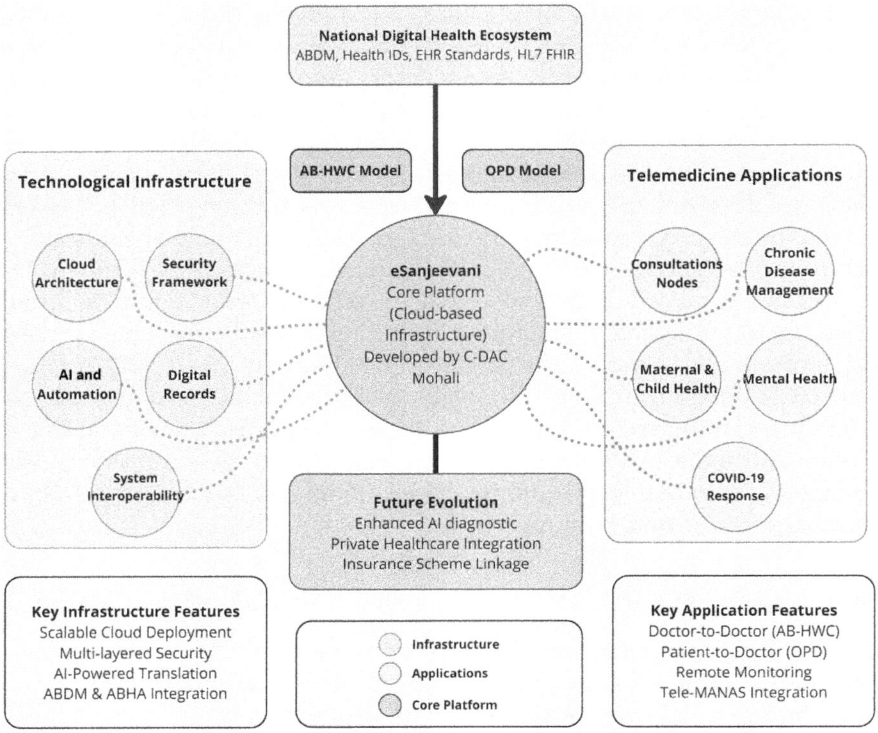

FIGURE 9.2
The connection between eSanjeevani's technological framework, telemedicine applications, and the essential features of its infrastructure and functionalities.

The scalability of e-Sanjeevani became evident as its capacity expanded rapidly during the pandemic (Hazra & Bora, 2025). While initially serving a limited number of patients, the platform grew to accommodate more than 75,000 consultations per day, at its peak. The government mobilised additional healthcare professionals, including retired military doctors, to meet rising demand. AI-driven enhancements such as automated triage and symptom assessment tools further streamlined patient flow and improved consultation efficiency.

The pandemic has underscored the long-term viability of telemedicine as a central component of healthcare services. With telemedicine guidelines firmly in place, e-Sanjeevani continues to expand its capabilities. Future developments are expected to include AI-assisted diagnostics, automated case documentation, and predictive analytics for personalised medical care, reinforcing their role in India's evolving healthcare landscape. Figure 9.2 shows the link between the eSanjeevani technological infrastructure, telemedicine applications, and key infrastructure and application features.

9.5 eSanjeevani's Alignment with WHO Health System Building Blocks

eSanjeevani, India's national telemedicine platform, demonstrates a comprehensive approach to health system strengthening that aligns strategically with the World Health Organization's six core building blocks. This digital health intervention exemplifies how technological innovation can simultaneously reinforce multiple components of health systems architecture while addressing persistent challenges in healthcare delivery.

9.5.1 Service Delivery Enhancement

The platform fundamentally transforms service delivery by creating a dual-modal approach that extends healthcare reach without compromising quality. Through the AB-HWC variant, eSanjeevani establishes a hub-and-spoke model connecting over 127,499 Health and Wellness Centres with 16,211 specialist hubs (Arora et al., 2024), effectively democratizing access to expert consultation. This configuration enables real-time specialist support for primary care providers, transforming isolated rural clinics into digitally-connected healthcare nodes. The patient-to-doctor OPD variant further diversifies service delivery by providing direct-access teleconsultations, eliminating geographical barriers and reducing the traditional burden on tertiary care facilities (Dastidar et al., 2022). The platform's capacity to handle over 1 million consultations daily during peak periods demonstrates robust service delivery infrastructure that maintains quality while achieving unprecedented scale.

9.5.2 Health Workforce Optimization

eSanjeevani addresses workforce distribution challenges by digitally extending specialist expertise to underserved regions. With more than 218,000 healthcare practitioners engaged in the digital health network, the platform establishes a technologically-empowered medical workforce that overcomes spatial limitations (Arora et al., 2024). This enables urban specialists to serve multiple rural locations simultaneously, amplifying human resource capacity. The system enhances clinical capabilities through technology-supported decision-making tools, enabling primary care providers to deliver sophisticated care via remote specialist guidance (Renu, 2025). Integrated training programs develop teleconsultation competencies among providers, creating a digitally-proficient workforce essential for modern healthcare transformation (Gupta et al., 2025).

9.5.3 Health Information Systems Integration

The platform demonstrates sophisticated health informatics design through seamless integration with the ABDM, facilitating continuous information exchange between virtual consultations and patient health documentation. eSanjeevani's cloud-native architecture supports immediate data collection, secure storage, and rapid access, enabling clinical decision-making based on comprehensive evidence while ensuring care continuity among healthcare providers (R. Singh et al., 2024). The platform's compatibility with ABDM digital health repositories allows teleconsultation results to be incorporated into patients' ongoing medical histories, strengthening coordinated care delivery (Kamath et al., 2025). Sophisticated analytical features within eSanjeevani 2.0, encompassing AI-powered clinical insights and service quality assessment, convert standard patient encounters into actionable health data that supports both personalised treatment and broader public health planning (Gupta et al., 2025).

9.5.4 Medical Products and Technologies Access

Although eSanjeevani cannot physically distribute medical supplies, it substantially enhances accessibility through smart prescription coordination and streamlined referral processes. The platform's digital prescription framework, augmented by AI-driven multilingual capabilities, guarantees patients obtain comprehensible treatment instructions in their native language (Pillai, 2023). The system's clinical assessment and referral functions assist in determining when patients need specialised medical equipment or procedures, enabling prompt and appropriate access to critical healthcare services (De Gardner et al., 2025). Since March 2023, the incorporation of Point-of-Care Diagnostic devices has allowed healthcare personnel to perform vital diagnostic tests at remote locations, with findings immediately accessible for specialist evaluation (Arora et al., 2024).

9.5.5 Financing Mechanisms

eSanjeevani enhances health system financial sustainability through no-cost consultation services, substantially lowering economic barriers to medical care access. The platform markedly reduces patients' direct healthcare expenses by removing transportation costs and minimizing income loss from time away from work (Sahu et al., 2024). From a healthcare system perspective, telemedicine offers economically efficient service delivery, with research demonstrating that teleconsultations eliminate the need for extensive travel and prevent significant transportation-related expenditures for patients (Sahu et al., 2024). Connectivity with Ayushman Bharat insurance programs via ABDM establishes opportunities for telemedicine services to be included within current healthcare financing frameworks, thereby strengthening economic protection for disadvantaged communities (Kamath et al., 2025).

9.5.6 Leadership and Governance Strengthening

eSanjeevani strengthens healthcare financing models by offering complimentary teleconsultation services, dramatically reducing economic obstacles to medical care. The platform substantially diminishes patients' personal healthcare costs by eliminating travel expenses and preventing productivity losses associated with medical visits (Sahu et al., 2024). From an institutional standpoint, digital health delivery provides cost-efficient healthcare provision, with evidence showing that virtual consultations remove the burden of long-distance journeys and associated financial hardships for patients (Sahu et al., 2024). Integration with Ayushman Bharat insurance frameworks through ABDM creates pathways for incorporating telemedicine into established healthcare funding systems, thereby expanding financial safeguards for marginalised populations (Kamath et al., 2025).

9.6 The Impact of eSanjeevani on Health Inclusion in India

India's healthcare landscape has long been characterised by significant disparities, particularly in access to quality medical care, between urban and rural populations. Historically, patients in remote villages and tribal regions have struggled to access specialist services, relying on overburdened primary health centres with limited resources (De Gardner et al., 2025). The launch of eSanjeevani, India's national telemedicine initiative, represents strategic intervention aimed at reducing these disparities. Sanjeevani, India's National Telemedicine Service, has facilitated over 30 million teleconsultations, indicating significant uptake of virtual care (Dastidar et al., 2022). Designed to connect patients in underserved areas with healthcare professionals via digital platforms, eSanjeevani has made substantial progress in democratizing access to medical services. Its impact is especially pronounced in rural and remote communities, among women and vulnerable populations, and in mitigating systemic health care disparities.

9.6.1 Reaching Rural and Remote Populations

A key measure of eSanjeevani's impact is its expansion into rural and remote areas where access to healthcare services has historically been limited (Raj et al., 2024). The platform has been integrated into over 115,000 Health & Wellness Centers (HWCs), serving as primary healthcare facilities in villages and small towns. Through a doctor-to-doctor teleconsultation model, general practitioners in these centres can consult specialists in urban hospitals, enabling rural patients to receive expert medical advice without the need for long-distance travel (Renu, 2025).

Before telemedicine, specialised healthcare required patients to travel significant distances, often resulting in financial strain and a long, time-consuming journey. eSanjeevani has reduced these barriers by allowing digital consultations. For instance, a dermatology consultation that previously required a full day of travel can now be completed in less than 10 min via video call, reducing both time and cost for patients (P. Sahu et al., 2024). These benefits extend beyond individual convenience. By shifting non-urgent consultations online, eSanjeevani has helped reduce overcrowding in urban hospitals, allowing them to focus on critical cases while ensuring timely diagnoses for rural patients. A teleophthalmology initiative using eSanjeevani reported that 11.6% of patients required surgical intervention and were referred accordingly, while 57% of cases were managed remotely, eliminating the need for in-person visits. Without telemedicine, many of these conditions may have remained undiagnosed or only received attention after significant delays.

This platform has also been particularly effective in regions with geographical challenges (Dastidar et al., 2022). In Ladakh, patients were able to access specialised cardiology and oncology consultations from experts based in Delhi, overcoming the logistical barriers that previously made such care inaccessible. Similarly, in the tribal areas of Northeast India and remote desert settlements in Rajasthan, eSanjeevani's integration into the local healthcare infrastructure has increased access to specialist consultations. One study found that 7,062 patients used the platform for dermatology-related video consultations, with 56% successfully completing their sessions. The average patient age was 32 years, and 60% of the participants were women. Notably, 88% of the users were from rural areas. On average, each teleconsultation saved patients from traveling approximately 459 km and spending approximately 482 rupees on travel expenses. The consultations lasted just over nine minutes, and most patients recovered after their virtual appointments, avoiding the need for an in-person visit (Sahu et al., 2024). The service has also been extended to island regions, such as the Andaman and Nicobar Islands, as well as conflict-prone areas in Jammu and Kashmir, demonstrating its ability to reach diverse and challenging locations.

In addition to geographic coverage, eSanjeevani helps to address systemic disparities in healthcare access. Medical specialists are often concentrated in urban hospitals, which limits their availability to rural populations. By digitally connecting specialists with patients in underserved areas, the platform helped reduce this gap and ensured that high-quality medical expertise was more evenly distributed. Moreover, eSanjeevani operates as a free service, eliminating financial barriers that may prevent low-income households from seeking medical care. By removing the costs associated with travel and private consultations, the platform has encouraged broader healthcare participation among socioeconomically disadvantaged groups.

9.6.2 Inclusion of Women and Vulnerable Populations

Telemedicine plays a crucial role in addressing health care barriers for populations facing social and logistical challenges. The usage data from eSanjeevani highlight its impact, particularly among women, who account for more than 57% of consultations on the platform (P. Sahu et al., 2024). In many communities, women prioritize their families' health over their own and face mobility restrictions due to cultural norms. eSanjeevani allows them to consult medical professionals from home or local centres, providing easier access to healthcare without societal limitations. Singh et al. (2023) found that 3,219 patients were treated over ten months, with 71.5% of cases related to gynaecological concerns and 29% involving early pregnancy complications. The study also noted that teleconsultations reduce unnecessary hospital visits for non-emergency cases and alleviate pressure on tertiary healthcare facilities (De Gardner et al., 2025).

Further research underscores the role of digital health platforms in providing critical support to expectant mothers, new parents, and caregivers as well as improving healthcare access for rural and tribal populations, including the elderly (Renu, 2025). Suhas et al. (2022) highlighted that eSanjeevani is particularly beneficial for individuals requiring mental health support, including women, children, adolescents, transgender individuals, migrant workers, institutionalised persons, and marginalised communities. The platform offers free mental health consultations, making professional care accessible from home or nearby wellness centres.

Elderly patients who often struggle with mobility issues also benefit significantly from telemedicine. Approximately 12% of consultations on eSanjeevani involve senior citizens, enabling them to receive timely medical attention and reducing the risk of worsening health conditions due to delays in care. In remote areas, mobile medical units equipped with telemedicine capabilities further extend healthcare services to tribal populations, thereby ensuring access to essential medical support. While specific demographic data on caste and ethnicity are not publicly available, the government has emphasised efforts to reach vulnerable groups, aiming to close long-standing healthcare access gaps. Additionally, the involvement of community health workers in assisting patients with telemedicine platforms has helped increase adoption, particularly among individuals with limited digital literacy. Figure 9.3 provides an overview of the impact of eSanjeevani on health care inclusion in India.

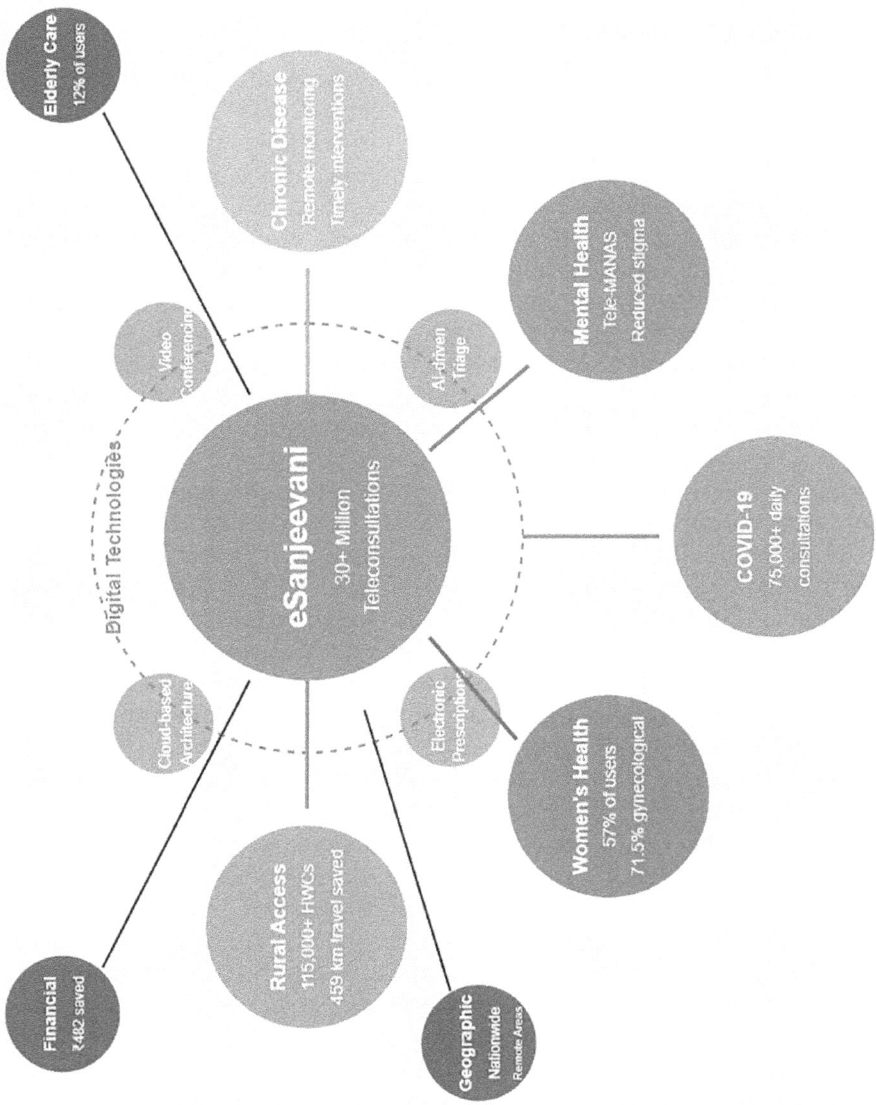

FIGURE 9.3
eSanjeevani impact on health inclusion in India.

TABLE 9.1

Policy Recommendations for Health Inclusion in India

Policy Area	Recommendation	Source
Electronic health records (EHR)	Implement standardised EHR with interoperability and data privacy measures	EHR Guidelines[6]
Data interoperability	Adopt global health informatics standards like HL7 and SNOMED CT for data exchange	
Health data privacy	Enforce strong authentication, access control, and encryption for health data	
Integration with e-Governance	Link health records with Aadhaar and other government identifiers for seamless access	
Infrastructure for health inclusion	Strengthen IT infrastructure at primary health centres for digital health adoption	Guidelines for Telemedicine Services[7]
Telemedicine expansion	Scale up telemedicine services under Ayushman Bharat using the Hub and Spoke model	
Training and capacity building	Provide telemedicine and digital health training to healthcare providers	User Guide for Doctors[8]
Public awareness	Educate citizens on using telemedicine and digital health platforms	eSanjeevani 2.0 Policy[9]

9.6.3 Future Policy Directions for Digital Health Inclusion

As eSanjeevani continues to redefine healthcare accessibility in India, it is important to establish a robust policy framework that ensures the long-term sustainability, security, and effectiveness of telemedicine and digital health initiatives. While the platform has made significant strides in bridging healthcare gaps, targeted policy interventions can further enhance its impact, ensuring that no section of society remains underserved. Table 9.1 presents the policy recommendations align with India's National Digital Health Blueprint, which are drawn from the guideline documents released by the ministry of health and family welfare, Government of India[5]. It outlines strategic steps to strengthen health inclusion through digital means in India.

9.7 Critical Challenges and Limitations

Despite its remarkable achievements, eSanjeevani faces significant implementation challenges that highlight the complexities of digital health transformation in resource-constrained settings. These limitations underscore the gap between technological potential and ground-level realities.

9.7.1 Digital Divide and Access Inequities

The platform's effectiveness remains constrained by persistent digital inequalities that paradoxically exclude those who could benefit most from telemedicine services. Rural communities with limited internet penetration, particularly tribal and remote populations, face connectivity barriers that prevent consistent platform utilization (Raj et al., 2024). Research indicates that awareness levels remain disturbingly low, with studies documenting that only 2.2% of rural respondents were familiar with teleconsultation services (Parameshwarappa & Olickal, 2023). This awareness gap perpetuates existing healthcare inequities, as digitally literate urban populations increasingly benefit from telemedicine while underserved rural communities remain excluded. The requirement for smartphone access and basic digital literacy creates additional barriers for elderly patients and economically disadvantaged populations (Upadhyay et al., 2023).

9.7.2 Quality Assurance and Clinical Limitations

Teleconsultation inherently limits clinical assessment capabilities, potentially compromising diagnostic accuracy for conditions requiring physical examination. The absence of tactile assessment, direct vital sign measurement, and comprehensive physical evaluation may lead to misdiagnosis or delayed recognition of serious conditions (Choudhary et al., 2024). Provider concerns about liability and diagnostic confidence in virtual settings can result in conservative treatment approaches or unnecessary referrals, potentially undermining cost-effectiveness (Arora et al., 2024). The challenge of maintaining therapeutic relationships and clinical empathy through digital interfaces may affect patient satisfaction and treatment adherence, particularly for complex chronic conditions requiring ongoing support (Suhas et al., 2022).

9.7.3 Infrastructure Dependencies and Sustainability

The platform's effectiveness remains hostage to unreliable technological infrastructure, particularly in regions where it could provide greatest benefit (Raj et al., 2024). Power outages, network instability, and equipment failures disproportionately affect rural healthcare facilities, creating service disruptions that undermine patient confidence and provider adoption (Sinha & Rahul, 2025). The substantial ongoing investment required for infrastructure maintenance, software updates, and cybersecurity measures raises questions about long-term financial sustainability, particularly as utilization scales (Hazra & Bora, 2025). Integration complexities with existing health information systems create technical challenges that may require significant resources to resolve effectively (Thapliyal et al., 2024).

9.7.4 Human Resource and Training Challenges

Many healthcare providers lack adequate training in teleconsultation best practices, affecting service quality and patient safety (Arora et al., 2024). The transition from traditional face-to-face interactions to digital communication requires skill development that may not be adequately addressed in current medical education curricula (Renu, 2025). Provider resistance to technology adoption, particularly among experienced practitioners, can limit platform effectiveness and create inconsistent service quality across different facilities (Upadhyay et al., 2023).

These challenges illuminate the complex interplay between technological innovation and health system realities, emphasizing that digital health solutions require comprehensive ecosystem approaches addressing infrastructure, training, awareness, and quality assurance to achieve their transformative potential.

9.8 Conclusion

eSanjeevani represents a watershed moment in the evolution of digital healthcare delivery, particularly for nations facing resource constraints and accessibility challenges. The journey from a modest pilot initiative to the world's largest telemedicine network within a primary healthcare system demonstrates the transformative potential of thoughtfully designed digital interventions. The platform's success stems not only from technological sophistication but also from its holistic integration across India's healthcare ecosystem, bridging gaps between urban specialists and rural patients through accessible digital pathways.

Looking forward, eSanjeevani's continued evolution will likely centre on deepening AI capabilities, strengthening blockchain-based security frameworks, and expanding mobile health-tracking features. The incorporation of these advancements promises to further enhance personalised care while maintaining scalability, which has defined the success of the platform. As healthcare systems worldwide increasingly recognize telemedicine as a core component rather than a supplementary service, eSanjeevani provides valuable lessons about balancing technological innovation with equity considerations.

Perhaps most significantly, eSanjeevani challenges conventional assumptions regarding digital healthcare deployment in developing economies. This demonstrates that, with appropriate infrastructure design, security protocols, and user-centric interfaces, telemedicine can thrive even in settings with connectivity challenges and varying levels of digital literacy.

As countries worldwide seek solutions to healthcare disparities, eSanjeevani stands as compelling evidence that digital transformation, when mindfully implemented, can advance not only technological innovation, but also fundamental healthcare equity. The platform's legacy may ultimately be measured not only in consultations delivered, but also in its contribution to reimagining healthcare access for underserved populations globally.

Notes

1 https://pib.gov.in/PressReleasePage.aspx?PRID=1748652
2 www.shankariasparliament.com/current-affairs/non-communicable-diseases
3 https://pib.gov.in/PressReleasePage.aspx?PRID=1899855
4 www.microsoft.com/en-in/aifirstmovers/esanjeevani
5 https://esanjeevani.mohfw.gov.in/
6 https://esanjeevani.mohfw.gov.in/assets/guidelines/ehr_guidlines.pdf
7 https://esanjeevani.mohfw.gov.in/assets/guidelines/Guidelines_for_Telemedicine_Services.pdf
8 https://esanjeevani.mohfw.gov.in/assets/guidelines/Telemedicine_Practice_Guidelines.pdf
9 https://esanjeevani.mohfw.gov.in/assets/guidelines/esanjeevani2.0_Private_Policy.pdf

References

Al Dahdah, M., & Mishra, R. K. (2023). Digital health for all: The turn to digitized healthcare in India. *Social Science & Medicine, 319*, 114968. https://doi.org/10.1016/j.socscimed.2022.114968

Arora, S., Huda, R. K., Verma, S., Khetan, M., & Sangwan, R. K. (2024). Challenges, barriers, and facilitators in telemedicine implementation in India: A scoping review. *Cureus*. https://doi.org/10.7759/cureus.67388

Chakraborty, T., Sinha Deb, K., Kulkarni, H., Masud, S., Math, S. B., Oke, G., Sagar, R., & Sharma, M. (2025). The promise of generative AI for suicide prevention in India. *Nature Machine Intelligence, 7*(2), 162–163. https://doi.org/10.1038/s42256-025-00992-1

Chawhan, A., Thakrar, D., & Pinto, L. (2023). Inhaler devices and their challenges—Helping patients use inhalers. *Lung India, 40*(4), 303–305. https://doi.org/10.4103/lungindia.lungindia_24_23

Choudhary, S., Dutt, S., Torous, J., & Mehta, U. M. (2024). Bridging the mental health gap: The scope, challenges, and future of digital psychiatry in India. *Asian Journal of Psychiatry, 101*, 104215. https://doi.org/10.1016/j.ajp.2024.104215

Das, A. K., Srivastava, A. K., Ghosh, S., Bhargava, R., Gupta, R., & Singh, R. R. (2024). The adequacy of health system measures in reducing vulnerability to COVID-19 among the health care providers working in primary health care in Rajasthan, India: A cross-sectional Study. *Journal of Health Management, 26*(2), 225–237. https://doi.org/10.1177/09720634241227310

Dash, S., Aarthy, R., & Mohan, V. (2021). Telemedicine during COVID-19 in India—A new policy and its challenges. *Journal of Public Health Policy, 42*(3), 501–509. https://doi.org/10.1057/s41271-021-00287-w

Dastidar, B. G., Suri, S., Nagaraja, V. H., & Jani, A. (2022). A virtual bridge to universal healthcare in India. *Communications Medicine, 2*(1), 145. https://doi.org/10.1038/s43856-022-00211-7

De Gardner, D., Tonweber, L., Flynn, S., Gibson, S., & Patel, M. (2025). Virtual asthma self-management education program offered by certified asthma educators and digital platform. *Journal of Allergy and Clinical Immunology, 155*(2), AB107. https://doi.org/10.1016/j.jaci.2024.12.340

Faujdar, D. S., Sahay, S., Singh, T., Kaur, M., & Kumar, R. (2020). Field testing of a digital health information system for primary health care: A quasi-experimental study from India. *International Journal of Medical Informatics, 141*, 104235. https://doi.org/10.1016/j.ijmedinf.2020.104235

Gupta, R., Priya, M. P., Dash, N., Singh, A., Das, L., Arora, A., Sahu, P., Vashisht, K. R., Eragam, A., Singh, P., Singh, K., Agarwal, A., & Saikia, B. (2025). Evolution of India's National teleconsultation platform e-Sanjeevani: A comparative analysis of versions 2.0 and 1.0, with a preliminary report from the state of Haryana. *Health and Technology, 15*(1), 153–160. https://doi.org/10.1007/s12553-024-00907-x

Hazra, S., & Bora, K. S. (2025). Capitalization of digital healthcare: The cornerstone of emerging medical practices. *Intelligent Pharmacy*, S2949866X24001229. https://doi.org/10.1016/j.ipha.2024.12.002

Iswarya, B., & Shobana, K. (2024). Impact of telehealth during pandemic in remote locations. In J. M. Chatterjee, R. Sujatha, & S. K. Saxena (Eds.), *Role of Artificial Intelligence, Telehealth, and Telemedicine in Medical Virology* (pp. 149–160). Springer Nature Singapore. https://doi.org/10.1007/978-981-97-2938-8_7

Jain, S., Arora, S., Chauhan, A., Agarwal, A., Saikia, B., & Singh, M. (2024). Super-specialty medical teleconsultations to remote areas of Ladakh, India via E-Sanjeevani under hub-and-spoke model: A pilot study. *Telehealth and Medicine Today, 9*(2). https://doi.org/10.30953/thmt.v9.471

Kaladharan, S., Dhanya, M., Drisya, R., & Raj, M. B. (2023). Intention to use eSanjeevani-OPD App: An empirical investigation using health belief model. *2023 Advanced Computing and Communication Technologies for High Performance Applications (ACCTHPA)*, 1–6. https://doi.org/10.1109/ACCTHPA57160.2023.10083374

Kamath, R., Banu, M., Shet, N., Jayapriya, V. R., Lakshmi Ramesh, V., Jahangir, S., Akthar, N., Brand, H., Prabhu, V., Singh, V., & Kamath, S. (2025). Awareness of and challenges in utilizing the ayushman bharat digital mission for healthcare delivery: Qualitative insights from university students in Coastal Karnataka in India. *Healthcare, 13*(4), 382. https://doi.org/10.3390/healthcare13040382

Malviya, R., Karakuş, S., & Roy, M. (Eds.). (2025). *Embedded system for biomedical applications: Industry perspectives* (First edition). C&H/CRC Press.

Parameshwarappa, P. M., & Olickal, J. J. (2023). Telemedicine awareness and the preferred digital healthcare tools: A community-based cross-sectional study from

Rural Karnataka, India. *Indian Journal of Community Medicine, 48*(6), 915–919. https://doi.org/10.4103/ijcm.ijcm_770_22

Pillai, A. P. S. (2023). AIoMT-assisted telemedicine: A case study of eSanjeevani telemedicine service in India. In *Handbook of Security and Privacy of AI-Enabled Healthcare Systems and Internet of Medical Things*. CRC Press.

Prakash, O. (2025). Tackling gender disparities in physician suicide: Insights from India. *BMJ*, q2346. https://doi.org/10.1136/bmj.q2346

Raj, A., Valsala, P., & Unnikrishanan, R. (2024). Technological and sociocultural barriers to e-sanjeevani as a parallel means of health care: A narrative review. *2024 5th International Conference on Innovative Trends in Information Technology (ICITIIT)*, 1–4. https://doi.org/10.1109/ICITIIT61487.2024.10580209

Rajendran, S. R., & Chandrashekar, B. S. (2024). The essence of telemedicine in Health 4.0: A futuristic approach. In N. Wickramasinghe (Ed.), *Advances in Medical Technologies and Clinical Practice* (pp. 331–358). IGI Global. https://doi.org/10.4018/979-8-3693-9641-4.ch012

Renu, V. (2025). Revolutionizing healthcare: Unleashing the power of digital health. In *Leveraging Metaverse and Analytics of Things (AoT) in Medical Systems* (pp. 1–13). Elsevier. https://doi.org/10.1016/B978-0-443-24049-2.00009-1

Sahu, P., Vashisht, K. R., Agarwal, A., Gupta, R., Garg, R., & Saikia, B. (2024). Navigating dermatological care: Experience with assisted teledermatology practice on e-Sanjeevani platform. *Journal of the European Academy of Dermatology and Venereology, 38*(12), 2311–2313. https://doi.org/10.1111/jdv.20181

Sahu, V. K., & Dave, S. (2022). Continuum of care through patient relationship management approach in Indian public healthcare system. In *Digital Innovation for Healthcare in COVID-19 Pandemic: Strategies and Solutions* (pp. 173–188). Elsevier. https://doi.org/10.1016/B978-0-12-821318-6.00010-4

Singh, A., Agarwal, A., Thakur, G., Goel, S., & Singh, M. (2023). Role of telemedicine in obstetrics and gynecology: An experience at tertiary care center. *Expert Review of Medical Devices, 20*(12), 1251–1256. https://doi.org/10.1080/17434440.2023.2264768

Singh, R., Raj, R. S., & Radha. (2024). Ensuring health for all: Examining the role of digital health in India. In S. K. Singh (Ed.), *Intersecting Realities of Health Resilience and Governance in India: Emerging Domestic and Global Perspectives* (pp. 201–227). Springer Nature Singapore. https://doi.org/10.1007/978-981-97-9096-8_11

Singh, T., Kaur, R., Kant, S., Mani, K., Yadav, K., & Gupta, S. K. (2023). Maternal healthcare services in a rural area of Haryana during the COVID-19 pandemic: A community-based study. *Indian Journal of Community Medicine, 48*(5), 715–720. https://doi.org/10.4103/ijcm.ijcm_43_23

Sinha, N., & Rahul, E. (2025). India's digital health transformation: Advancements and challenges in telemedicine. *Medicon Medical Sciences*. https://doi.org/10.55162/MCMS.08.271

Suhas, S., Kumar, C., Math, S., & Manjunatha, N. (2022). E-sanjeevani: A pathbreaking telemedicine initiativefrom India. *Journal of Psychiatry Spectrum, 1*(2), 111. https://doi.org/10.4103/jopsys.jopsys_8_21

Thapliyal, K., Thapliyal, M., & Thapliyal, D. (2024). Digital health technologies enhancing human life. In N. Wickramasinghe (Ed.), *Advances in Medical Technologies and Clinical Practice* (pp. 139–176). IGI Global. https://doi.org/10.4018/979-8-3693-9641-4.ch005

Upadhyay, N., Kamble, A., & Navare, A. (2023). Virtual healthcare in the new normal: Indian healthcare consumers adoption of electronic government telemedicine service. *Government Information Quarterly*, *40*(2), 101800. https://doi.org/10.1016/j.giq.2022.101800

Vashisht, K. R., Gupta, R., Sahu, P., Mandula, P. P., Dash, N., Eragam, A., Saikia, B., & Agarwal, A. (2024). Managing outbreak of community-onset paediatric impetigo in underserved areas of North India via teledermatology: A tertiary care centre's experience. *Indian Journal of Dermatology, Venereology and Leprology*, *91*, 253–254. https://doi.org/10.25259/IJDVL_1102_2023

Velan, D., Mohandoss, H., Valarmathi, S., Sundar, J. S., Kalpana, S., & Srinivas, G. (2024). Digital health in your hands: A narrative review of exploring Ayushman Bharat's digital revolution. *World Journal of Advanced Research and Reviews*, *23*(3), 1630–1641. https://doi.org/10.30574/wjarr.2024.23.3.2762

Wadali, J. S., Sood, S. P., Kaushish, R., Syed-Abdul, S., Khosla, P. K., & Bhatia, M. (2020). Evaluation of free, open-source, web-based DICOM viewers for the Indian National Telemedicine Service (eSanjeevani). *Journal of Digital Imaging*, *33*(6), 1499–1513. https://doi.org/10.1007/s10278-020-00368-4

10

Operationalising Diversity, Equity, Inclusion, and Belonging in the Foundations of Digital Infrastructure

Arif Perdana

10.1 Introduction

The accelerating digitisation of economies, services, and governance has elevated digital technology from a tool of convenience to a critical infrastructure for economic inclusion, civic participation, and social cohesion (G. Y. Gao et al., 2024; Manzoor & Vimarlund, 2018; McClung & Linton, 2024). Yet, as digital systems increasingly mediate everyday life, a persistent tension has emerged: the same technologies that promise empowerment often reproduce structural inequities (Buolamwini & Gebru, 2018; Martin, 2022; Xiong & Kim, 2025). Diversity, Equity, Inclusion, and Belonging (DEIB) has thus become central to contemporary debates on the governance, design, and deployment of digital systems (Capel & Brereton, 2023; Chen, 2023; Margetis et al., 2021). What was once framed as an ethical aspiration, ensuring that digital transformation includes historically marginalised populations, is now recognised as an operational imperative for resilient innovation and sustainable development.

At its core, DEIB in digital technology encompasses the design of systems, structures, and institutional practices that foster equitable access, representative participation, and meaningful agency across intersecting identities (e.g., gender, class, race, ability, geography, and beyond) (Dolata et al., 2022; Floridi et al., 2021; Martin, 2022). This includes, but is not limited to, closing gender gaps in internet access, ensuring accessibility for persons with disabilities, preventing algorithmic bias, and creating digital cultures where marginalised voices are seen, heard, and valued. These goals are not peripheral to technological advancement; instead, they shape who benefits from innovation, who is excluded, and how power is distributed in the digital age.

Despite widespread normative commitments to DEIB, global disparities persist. As of 2022, 2.7 billion people who are predominantly from rural

 DOI: 10.1201/9781003591078-13

areas, low-income countries, and marginalised communities remain offline[1]. Women are systematically less likely to own mobile devices, access the internet, or participate in online economies[2]. Persons with disabilities encounter inaccessible interfaces; LGBTQIA+ users face online harassment and algorithmic invisibility (Abreu & Kenny, 2018; Hendricks et al., 2020; Olawade et al., 2025). These inequities are not only reflections of broader structural injustice but are often amplified by digital systems themselves.

In response, international organisations, governments, and private sector actors have launched a growing number of interventions aimed at embedding DEIB principles into digital environments (Lillevik, 2025). These range from telemedicine platforms serving rural populations in India (R. Gupta et al., 2025), to blockchain-enabled aid disbursement systems in Afghanistan (Bharathi et al., 2025), to inclusive financial tools for unbanked users in Latin America (Tariq, 2024). At the same time, legal frameworks such as the European Union's AI Act[3] and participatory civic platforms like Meu Rio[4] signal a shift toward institutionalizing digital inclusion as a right, not a privilege.

Yet the question remains, what transforms DEIB from abstract commitment into material practice? While strategies abound (e.g., diversity hiring, inclusive product design, infrastructure investments, regulatory standards) less is known about how these interventions intersect, what conditions enable their success, and how they can be systematically scaled across sectors and geographies. Existing literature tends to isolate either the technological or sociopolitical dimensions of inclusion, rarely addressing their co-constitution in shaping digital equity outcomes. Furthermore, the dominant analytical lens remains Western-centric, despite the growing leadership of Global South actors in advancing inclusion through localised models of digital innovation.

This chapter seeks to advance a more integrated understanding of DEIB in digital technology by analysing a diverse set of global initiatives that operationalise inclusion through infrastructure, policy, design, and governance. It aims to surface the structural, contextual, and institutional enablers of inclusive digital transformation, offering theoretical insights and practical lessons that cut across sectors and regions. The central research question guiding this paper is: *How can DEIB principles be embedded into the architectures, governance models, and institutional practices of digital systems in ways that produce equitable outcomes across diverse sociotechnical contexts?*

We draw on over a dozen case studies spanning healthcare, finance, education, civic tech, platform labour, and assistive technologies to address this question. These cases are situated in varied geographies, from India and Kenya to Brazil and Afghanistan, and reflect a spectrum of institutional arrangements, technological models, and inclusion strategies. Through this comparative analysis, we move beyond access metrics to interrogate how belonging, representation, and power operate in digital environments, and how they might be restructured.

The rest of the paper is structured as follows. Section 10.2 provides a global overview of the institutional landscape of DEIB in digital and IT sectors, highlighting emerging trends and persistent gaps. Section 10.3 analyses real-world applications across five thematic areas (i.e., foundational infrastructure, inclusive finance, digital skills, assistive and representational technologies, and algorithmic governance), demonstrating how DEIB has been implemented in practice. Section 10.4 synthesises key lessons, emphasizing cross-cutting themes such as participatory design, governance alignment, ecosystem thinking, and psychological safety. Section 10.5 examines the policy and regulatory pathways inclusive digital systems at scale. Finally, Section 10.6 explores future trajectories, outlining how inclusion can be embedded into emerging digital architectures and innovation pipelines from the outset. Through this structure, the paper builds a conceptual foundation for reimagining digital transformation as a vehicle for justice, not just growth.

10.2 Global Trends in DEIB within Digital and IT Sectors

Digital transformation has emerged as both an enabler of opportunity and a reproducer of inequality (Bera et al., 2023; Chandana et al., 2024; Eichenseer et al., 2025; Fernandez-Vidal, 2022). Within this duality, global efforts to institutionalise DEIB in digital environments have gained prominence among policymakers, development agencies, and industry actors (Abdelhalim et al., 2024; Marabelli et al., 2023; Rahimi et al., 2024). These initiatives reflect a growing consensus: equitable digital access and participation are not peripheral concerns but central to sustainable development, economic inclusion, and human rights in the 21st century. Yet realizing this vision requires more than strategy, it demands tangible, grounded interventions that reshape how digital systems function in practice.

Multilateral institutions have been at the forefront of framing digital inclusion as a foundational pillar of global development. The United Nations' 2030 Agenda embeds digital access into the Sustainable Development Goals (SDGs)[5], with Target 9.c explicitly calling for universal and affordable internet access in the least developed countries. The UN Secretary-General's digital cooperation roadmap reaffirms this agenda, asserting that rights such as privacy, access, and freedom of expression must be protected online with the same vigour as offline.

Parallel to UN efforts, coalitions such as the World Economic Forum's EDISON Alliance have mobilised multi-stakeholder actions across 127 countries, supporting over 320 digital inclusion projects aimed at reaching one billion underserved individuals by 2025[6]. The International Telecommunication Union (ITU) similarly advances initiatives to close the gender digital divide and expand affordable broadband access in low-income regions[7]. At the national level, numerous governments have adopted digital inclusion frameworks, which often combine infrastructure expansion with digital literacy campaigns. Corporations, too, have intensified internal DEIB programming, recognizing the need for inclusive representation in technological development (Agnihotri & Bhattacharya, 2024; Kondra et al., 2025).

These efforts reflect a shared acknowledgment in which digital connectivity is no longer a luxury. Rather, it is a precondition for full participation in economic, civic, and cultural life. The framing of digital inclusion as a right, and not merely as access to a service, has gained normative legitimacy across sectors. This shift in thinking invites a broader interrogation of whose needs digital systems are designed to meet, and how DEIB principles can be embedded not just in policy but in lived experience.

Despite these ambitious programs, significant disparities persist across regions, demographic groups, and types of digital engagement. As of 2022, approximately one-third of the global population, equivalent to 2.7 billion people, remained offline[8]. The geographic distribution of this exclusion reveals deeper structural divides. While 81% of urban residents globally have internet access, only 50% of rural populations are connected (Fellah, 2024). In Sub-Saharan Africa, while 84% of the population lives in areas with 3G coverage and 63% within 4G range, only 22% actually use mobile internet services. This situation highlights a significant gap between coverage and usage. Rural connectivity is especially limited, with digital infrastructure access in some areas falling below 25%. This reflects persistent regional disparities in affordability, access to devices, and digital literacy[9].

Gender-based inequities in digital access remain significant. Men are more likely to be internet users than women, and this imbalance becomes even more pronounced in regions where connectivity is generally low[10]. In places like sub-Saharan Africa, the gap between male and female internet use is especially stark. Beyond gender, other marginalized groups, such as people with disabilities, indigenous communities, and ethnic minorities, also encounter distinct challenges (Anshari et al., 2024). These include the absence of content in local languages, user interfaces that are not designed with accessibility in mind, and the high cost of data or digital devices, all of which limit their ability to fully participate in the digital world (Shaban, 2024; Subramaniam & Masron, 2025).

These digital inequities are not merely reflections of offline inequality; they often reinforce and exacerbate them. For example, limited digital access can constrain access to education, health services, financial tools, and political participation, thereby entrenching cycles of exclusion. Accordingly, digital equity must be pursued not only as an ethical imperative but also as a structural correction to historically embedded disparities (Dignum, 2019; Floridi, 2021; Floridi et al., 2021).

Scholarly and practitioner discourse on the digital divide has evolved considerably. Earlier definitions focused primarily on access to hardware and connectivity (Anshari et al., 2024). However, contemporary analyses conceptualise digital inclusion as a multi-dimensional phenomenon. In addition to access, digital inclusion encompasses digital literacy, meaningful usage, content relevance, and the capacity to derive socioeconomic benefits from digital tools (David et al., 2025). This shift has led to more comprehensive frameworks. One such approach, the "Five A's" model, articulates digital inclusion across five domains: Availability (of infrastructure), Affordability (of services and devices), Access to devices, digital Abilities (skills), and Accessible design (United Nations, 2023). This framework calls attention to the interdependence of infrastructural, economic, cognitive, and design-based barriers.

Moreover, an intersectional perspective has become central in analysing digital exclusion (Shaban, 2024). Intersectionality highlights how overlapping identities, such as gender, socioeconomic status, geographic location, and disability, compound disadvantage. A rural woman with limited education, for instance, may face multiple, interlocking barriers to digital participation (Ibrahim et al., 2025). Accordingly, effective interventions must address systemic and structural drivers of exclusion rather than treating digital disparities as isolated phenomena.

Furthermore, the human rights framing of digital inclusion stresses the importance of agency and safety in digital environments. Beyond connectivity, meaningful digital participation entails protection from surveillance, cyber harassment, and algorithmic bias, as well as the ability to contribute to and shape digital ecosystems (Rodrigues, 2020). In parallel with policy interventions, organisational actors in the tech sector have increasingly integrated DEIB principles into their internal operations and product development (Agnihotri & Bhattacharya, 2024; Kondra et al., 2025). A growing number of firms have adopted diversity benchmarks, inclusive hiring practices, and equity audits (Agnihotri & Bhattacharya, 2024; Hofeditz et al., 2022; Van Den Broek et al., 2021). These initiatives reflect the recognition that the composition of teams, especially those involved in product design and algorithm development, significantly affects whether technologies are inclusive or exclusionary.

The concept of "belonging" has gained traction as a vital component of DEIB within both organisational and digital community contexts (Devine & Ash, 2022). Emerging research suggests that belonging, defined as the perception of being accepted, respected, and valued, can have significant performance implications (Allen et al., 2021). One study, for example, found that a high sense of belonging among underrepresented employees was correlated with over a 50% increase in job performance (Carr et al., 2019).

In digital spaces, we argue that belonging also influences participation rates among marginalised users (Carter et al., 2023). When individuals encounter hostility, discrimination, or invisibility in online environments, they may disengage, perpetuating underrepresentation in digital cultures. Consequently, digital inclusion is not solely a question of access but also of culture. Inclusion must be cultivated through respectful design, equitable moderation practices, and the amplification of diverse voices.

Global trends in digital inclusion and DEIB reveal a complex, dialectical dynamic. On one hand, there is unprecedented global mobilisation around the principles of equitable access, inclusive design, and representative participation in digital economies. Policymakers, international organisations, and corporations have embraced a multi-faceted approach to addressing digital disparities, investing in infrastructure, skills development, and inclusive culture-building. On the other hand, the persistence of structural inequalities across gender, geography, ability, and income levels highlights the limitations of current interventions. These disparities underscore the need for sustained, context-sensitive, and innovation-driven responses. Without addressing underlying power dynamics, both online and offline, digital inclusion efforts risk becoming superficial or selectively beneficial (Kordzadeh & Ghasemaghaei, 2022; Nishant et al., 2024; Ntoutsi et al., 2020).

As the next section illustrates, meaningful progress requires not just vision but execution. Real-world applications, spanning health, finance, urban safety, education, and algorithmic governance, demonstrate how DEIB principles can be operationalised at scale. These cases move beyond abstract commitments to deliver structural inclusion through digital design, regulation, and community-led innovation. The future of equitable digital transformation will depend on how well global intentions are translated into local impact.

10.3 Real-World Applications of Digital Technology Advancing DEIB

Digital technology can entrench exclusion or unlock empowerment, it depends on how it is built, governed, and deployed. This section showcases real-world initiatives where digital tools have been mobilised not just to deliver services, but to reimagine who benefits from them. From remote healthcare and inclusive finance to civic tech and algorithmic fairness, each case reveals how technology, when grounded in principles of DEIB, can transform systems of access, participation, and accountability. These examples offer more than innovation; they provide a blueprint for digital transformation rooted in justice and structural inclusion.

10.3.1 Foundational Access and Infrastructure for Equity

Inclusion in the digital age begins not with innovation for the elite but with infrastructure for the underserved. Around the world, governments and civil society actors are using digital platforms to rebalance access to healthcare, utilities, and public spaces. The logic is simple but profound: when foundational access is prioritised, when underserved geographies and marginalised populations are placed at the centre of service design, technology becomes a tool for equity, not exclusion.

Three cases namely eSanjeevani in India, MajiVoice in Kenya, and Safetipin in urban India, offer critical lessons in how digital transformation can be mobilised not merely to optimise services but to reconfigure who benefits from them. Though the sectors differ (i.e., healthcare, water services, and urban safety), their shared focus on foundational access reveals a blueprint for inclusive digital governance.

10.3.1.1 eSanjeevani: Remote Healthcare as Public Infrastructure

India's eSanjeevani, a government-run telemedicine platform, was not designed for early adopters in metro cities (R. Gupta et al., 2025). Its mission was, and remains, bolder: to bridge a structural inequity wherein 70% of the population lives in rural areas while 80% of doctors are based in urban centres (R. Gupta et al., 2025; Suhas et al., 2022). Operationalised under the Digital India initiative, eSanjeevani scales healthcare access by offering free digital consultations, either through a hub-and-spoke model that connects rural clinics to urban specialists or via a direct-to-consumer outpatient module (eSanjeevaniOPD) (Jain et al., 2024; Kaladharan et al., 2023; Wadali et al., 2020).

By early 2022, the platform had crossed 30 million consultations, the majority coming from rural India (R. Gupta et al., 2025). The uptake is not merely a metric of volume; it is a validation of latent demand in underserved communities. Where healthcare infrastructure is thin, digital infrastructure, if designed inclusively, can step in as a substitute. Crucially, eSanjeevani is integrated with India's national digital health mission, enabling patients to generate digital health IDs and access prescriptions and follow-up care, creating continuity in an otherwise fragmented system.

However, the rollout also exposed structural gaps (Kaladharan et al., 2023; Raj et al., 2024). Internet connectivity, digital literacy, and cultural scepticism toward remote consultation were significant hurdles. India's policy response, most notably, the 2020 Telemedicine Practice Guidelines, was pivotal in legitimizing the service. Equally important was the political signalling: the inclusion of eSanjeevani under the Ayushman Bharat insurance umbrella sent a message of state-backed trust. These policy moves reveal that inclusive infrastructure must be supported by regulatory clarity and public investment, not just innovation. eSanjeevani's impact lies not in novelty, but in scale and intentionality. It reframes telemedicine not as a market convenience, but as a public good. In doing so, it advances digital equity by redefining what it means to access health services in the 21st century.

10.3.1.2 MajiVoice: Feedback Loops for Public Accountability

Where eSanjeevani uses technology to deliver services at scale, Kenya's MajiVoice uses it to hold service providers accountable (Georgiadou et al., 2014). Developed initially for Nairobi's water utility, MajiVoice enables citizens to report problems (e.g., leaks, outages, or billing issues) via SMS, web portal, or utility offices (Murthy et al., 2018). Each complaint is logged, tracked, and required to be resolved within a set timeframe, with escalation mechanisms if deadlines are missed. This is more than digitised customer service; it's infrastructure for civic participation.

Before MajiVoice, customer complaints in Kenya's water sector were often ignored or lost in opaque bureaucracies (Murthy et al., 2018). The introduction of a digital, auditable system brought transparency to the forefront. World Bank evaluations show that complaint resolution rates jumped from significantly in Nairobi, and repair responsiveness improved (*Civic Tech in the Global South*, 2017). Importantly, the volume of complaints doubled, not because services declined, but because people trusted that their grievances would no longer be ignored.

MajiVoice also had redistributive consequences. It gave voice to low-income residents in informal settlements, areas traditionally neglected by utilities. Community groups began using complaint data to advocate for improvements in their neighbourhoods. The platform became a tool not just for feedback, but for local activism and participatory governance (Salim & Wangusi, 2014). One reason MajiVoice succeeded where others stalled is its integration into regulatory contracts. Utilities' licenses became conditional on complaint responsiveness, aligning incentives with inclusivity. The government and donors ensured that the platform remained open-source and simple enough for users without smartphones. These institutional safeguards underscore a broader principle: digital platforms do not create accountability by themselves; they need governance frameworks that embed consequences and reward responsiveness (Chuene & Mtsweni, 2015; Georgiadou et al., 2014; Murthy et al., 2018).

10.3.1.3 Safetipin: Crowdsourcing Urban Safety for Women

If eSanjeevani addresses bodily health and MajiVoice ensures infrastructure integrity, Safetipin tackles the right to public space, especially for women (S. Gupta et al., 2022). Designed as a crowdsourced safety mapping tool, Safetipin allows users to conduct "safety audits" of urban areas, rating spaces on lighting, visibility, and security (Le, 2022; Viswanath & Basu, 2015). The resulting maps inform both individual mobility decisions and city-level interventions.

The data has been transformative. In New Delhi, Safetipin audits led to the installation of thousands of streetlights and the redesign of police patrol routes (Safetipin, 2018). Within three years of its launch, the number of unlit areas in the city dropped by 63%. The implications go beyond illumination. Women who once avoided night-time travel reported feeling safer, more confident, and freer to pursue work or education opportunities (Manazir et al., 2019). Safetipin's inclusive design is central to its impact. It collaborated with marginalised women, including those in informal settlements, to ensure that their lived experiences shaped urban policy. The app's data is time-stamped, transparent, and open to public scrutiny. It even includes escalation features if authorities fail to act on flagged issues. Here, inclusion is both epistemic and material: whose knowledge counts in planning a city, and whose safety is prioritised in its design? Safetipin answers both by democratizing data and distributing accountability. The platform exemplifies how urban safety, often framed as a policing issue, can be reimagined through design justice and citizen-led tech.

10.3.2 Inclusive Finance and Economic Empowerment

The promise of fintech lies not only in innovation but in inclusion, especially for the billions left on the margins of formal finance. From South Asia to Latin America, digital platforms are redrawing the map of economic participation. They are reframing what it means to "bank the unbanked," extend credit, and enable livelihoods. Cases such as bKash in Bangladesh, HesabPay in Afghanistan (Bharathi S et al., 2025), Nubank in Brazil, Kasikornbank in Thailand (Kasikornbank, 2025), and Rappi across Latin America reveal a shared trajectory: leveraging technology to embed DEIB into financial systems that have long privileged the few over the many.

10.3.2.1 Mobile Finance in Fragile Economies: bKash and HesabPay

In Bangladesh, bKash exemplifies a mobile-first strategy that has scaled access to finance at an unprecedented pace (Islam et al., 2025). Launched in 2011, bKash targeted a population where fewer than half of adults held a formal bank account. What set bKash apart was not just its simplicity, a mobile wallet operable via basic phones, but its infrastructure: a vast agent network that now exceeds 400,000, including in remote villages. This last-mile presence allowed garment workers, rural farmers, and domestic migrants to transact digitally, often for the first time (Nandhakumar, 2023).

Critically, bKash became more than a wallet; it became a channel for empowerment (Mahmud, 2024). Government-to-person (G2P) transfers, wages, and remittances flowed directly into accounts that users could control. Women, often constrained by mobility and social norms, gained a measure of financial autonomy through mobile access. For the poor, digital transactions meant less reliance on informal lenders and greater access to micro-loans, as bKash partnered with banks to link transaction histories with credit eligibility.

In Afghanistan, HesabPay represents fintech inclusion under the most constrained conditions: political instability, economic collapse, and acute gender-based restrictions (Bharathi S et al., 2025). Here, access to finance, particularly for women, has become a human rights issue. Against this backdrop, HesabPay emerged as a local digital wallet designed to facilitate both aid distribution and everyday commerce. Developed in collaboration with the World Food Programme, the platform has been instrumental in delivering digital cash assistance to women, bypassing traditional channels that required male intermediaries or travel to urban banks (Algorand Foundation, 2022).

HesabPay's significance is not just functional; it is political. Women receive aid directly on mobile phones and redeem it at approved merchants, granting them agency over household spending. The platform uses blockchain to ensure transparency, protect user data, and track funds, critical in a context where trust is fragile and fraud risks are high. With over 1,000 merchants now onboard and expanding coverage into rural areas, HesabPay demonstrates how digital finance, when designed for local realities, can anchor inclusion even amidst systemic disruption (Bharathi S et al., 2025).

10.3.2.2 Digital Banking with a Mission: Nubank and Kasikornbank

While bKash and HesabPay respond to financial exclusion at the edge of stability, Nubank in Brazil and Kasikornbank in Thailand operate in comparatively mature ecosystems (Au, 2024; Kasikornbank, 2025). Yet their interventions are no less transformative. Nubank, now the largest digital bank in Latin America, was born out of a frustration with exclusionary legacy banking[11]. High fees, limited credit access, and bureaucratic inertia had locked out millions (Calomiris & Haber, 2014; King, 2014). Nubank flipped the model: no branches, no paperwork, no fees. Instead, a mobile-first experience built for scale. Initially appealing to urban millennials, Nubank rapidly expanded its reach to include rural users, informal sector workers, and others underserved by traditional institutions (Kawamoto et al., 2023; Quintero & Quintero, 2023).

Its inclusion impact is measurable: by 2020, over 48 million users had joined, many of them previously unbanked[12]. Nubank offered not just accounts but tools for financial health, alerts, credit education, and data-driven approval models that looked beyond conventional credit scores. This opened lending to women, gig workers, and low-income clients often deemed "unprofitable" by traditional banks. Nubank's customer-centric model fostered trust in segments historically distrustful of banks, a lesson in the power of intuitive design, transparent fees, and consistent service.

In contrast, Kasikornbank (KBank) in Thailand illustrates how a legacy institution can infuse DEIB principles into digital transformation (Paisarn & Intarawong, 2019). KBank brands itself as a "Bank of Sustainability," embedding inclusion within a broader environmental, social, and governance (ESG) strategy (Kasikornbank, 2015, 2018). Its commitment extends beyond marketing. The LINE BK platform, a partnership with a popular messaging app, created a social banking model aimed at bringing unbanked Thais into the fold. With over 2.5 million users and half a million borrowers (30% previously unqualified elsewhere), LINE BK signals what is possible when banking is embedded in everyday digital behaviour (Banchongduang, 2025; Line, 2020; Line BK, 2023).

KBank's inclusive banking is underpinned by parallel efforts in sustainability. It has pledged over THB 200 billion (USD 6 billion) in green financing by 2030 and has already funded projects in renewable energy, low-carbon industries, and climate-resilient agriculture (Indonesia Business Post, 2024, 2024; Kasikornbank, 2021, 2025). This dual strategy (i.e., advancing environmental goals while ensuring financial access) positions KBank as a model for holistic ESG integration. The bank's approach suggests that equity and environmental stewardship are not competing objectives but reinforcing ones.

10.3.2.3 Platforms and Precarity: Rappi's Double-Edged Inclusion

If bKash, HesabPay, Nubank, and KBank show the potential of fintech to deepen financial participation, Rappi reveals the limits, and trade-offs, of platform-driven inclusion. As a Latin American "super-app" (Zhong, n.d.). It offers on-demand delivery, Rappi has enabled tens of thousands of people (i.e., many migrants and youth with no formal employment opportunities) to earn income (Yohanna Sánchez et al., 2024). Its model requires minimal entry: a smartphone, ID, and transport. For Venezuelan refugees in Colombia, for instance, Rappi offered a critical foothold in an unfamiliar labour market (Brown, 2025).

Yet Rappi's contribution to inclusion is more ambiguous. While it creates access to income, it often does so under conditions of insecurity: no benefits, algorithmic management, and income volatility[13]. Women couriers face safety risks; older workers struggle with digital navigation; and low pay after accounting for expenses has sparked protests (Pires, 2024; Strano, 2020). From a DEIB perspective, Rappi advances diversity and a measure of inclusion, but equity and belonging remain unresolved (Bernier, 2023; Foggin & Martins, 2024). Workers are rarely treated as stakeholders. Without regulatory guardrails, such as portable benefits or baseline wages, the gig economy can entrench precarity even as it expands participation.

Still, Rappi's model offers openings for deeper inclusion. With the right partnerships, it could transition gig work from stopgap to springboard. Pilot programs connecting rural farmers to urban buyers via Rappi's platform suggest new roles beyond delivery: digital intermediation that boosts livelihoods (Loukos & Arathoon, 2024). The challenge is clear: economic inclusion cannot rest on access alone, it must also account for the quality, stability, and dignity of that participation.

10.3.3 Empowerment through Digital Skills, Learning, and Market Access

Across Africa and other emerging regions, the promise of digital transformation often obscures a more sobering reality: the benefits of connectivity and online platforms are not equally distributed. In many rural communities, women remain excluded from both the digital economy and its accompanying infrastructure. This exclusion in which rooted in a combination of social norms, limited access to technology, and underdeveloped infrastructure, represents a critical blind spot in digital development. The work of initiatives like Tech Herfrica and global trends in inclusive online education signal a turning point, highlighting a new paradigm for economic inclusion: one where empowerment stems not just from access to digital tools, but from the deliberate pairing of skills, context-sensitive learning, and meaningful market linkages.

10.3.3.1 From the Margins to the Market: Tech Herfrica's Holistic Inclusion Model

Tech Herfrica, founded in Nigeria in 2023, operates with a clear mission: to dismantle the structural barriers that keep rural African women on the periphery of the digital and financial systems[14]. Its model is intentionally multidimensional. Recognizing that providing internet-enabled devices without digital literacy, or financial literacy without access to formal financial institutions, results in limited impact, the initiative adopts an integrated capacity-building approach.

The EquipHer4Growth program exemplifies this. Delivered in indigenous languages and grounded in local contexts, it offers training in digital navigation, smartphone use, budgeting, digital payments, and microfinance. This instructional design ensures that rural women in which many of whom have limited formal education, are not left behind in the push for digital transformation. What sets Tech Herfrica apart is not just the technical skills it imparts, but how these skills are translated into tangible economic opportunities.

The second arm of the initiative, HerLocal Market, bridges the gap between skill acquisition and economic participation. Through a bespoke e-commerce platform, rural women can showcase agricultural produce, handicrafts, and homemade products to buyers beyond their immediate geographic area. This intervention addresses two longstanding problems: market isolation and information asymmetry. By digitizing access to markets, HerLocal Market enables women to command better prices, reduce post-harvest losses, and maintain ownership over their economic output.

This dual-program structure (i.e., literacy plus market access), has generated notable outcomes. Within a year, over 4,000 women have participated, with many reporting not only higher incomes but also greater autonomy and social influence within their communities. Some have launched micro-enterprises. Others have streamlined their farming operations through mobile payments and price-checking apps. In these ways, Tech Herfrica extends beyond simple empowerment rhetoric; it reconfigures the socio-economic fabric in which rural women operate.

10.3.3.2 Online Education as a Ladder to Inclusion

While Tech Herfrica represents a hyperlocal, community-rooted solution, the broader expansion of inclusive online learning platforms is also shifting the landscape of women's empowerment globally. The acceleration of digital education during the COVID-19 pandemic catalysed a wave of participation from women, particularly those for whom traditional educational avenues had long been out of reach. Between 2019 and 2021, the percentage of female learners on platforms like Coursera rose from 38% to 45%. The increase was even more pronounced in STEM fields, where female enrolment jumped from 31% to 38%.

This growth is not merely statistical. It signals a rebalancing of opportunity. Online education offers flexibility, which is crucial for women balancing domestic responsibilities or constrained by social mobility limitations. It allows asynchronous learning, minimises safety risks associated with travel, and often reduces financial burdens linked to physical attendance. In conservative settings or conflict-affected areas, digital learning may be the only viable option for women to pursue formal education or professional certification.

Beyond accessibility, these platforms are increasingly designed with inclusion in mind. Features such as multilingual content, offline access, and gender-sensitive pedagogical designs are now more common. Initiatives like UN Women's digital skills camps and Google's Women Will program further reinforce the ecosystem by targeting women in low-connectivity regions and providing not just skills but pathways to employment or entrepreneurship.

10.3.4 Representation, Accessibility, and Belonging in Digital Spaces

The digital age was meant to flatten barriers. Yet, for many, the architecture of the internet continues to reproduce offline exclusions, particularly for those with disabilities and marginalised identities. While design teams frequently centre the average user, such an archetype often ignores those at the margins: the blind user navigating a website, the wheelchair user planning a city trip, or the LGBTQIA+ youth seeking a safe space to talk. Without targeted interventions, digital spaces risk becoming mirrors of the inequities they were meant to transcend. Fortunately, a growing ecosystem of assistive technologies and inclusive digital communities is redefining what it means to participate, belong, and thrive online.

10.3.4.1 Making the Invisible Visible: Assistive Technologies in Daily Life

Tools like *Be My Eyes*[15], *Voiceitt*[16], *Seeing AI*[17], and *Wheelmap*[18] show how technology can accommodate and empower. Be My Eyes connects blind and low-vision individuals with sighted volunteers for real-time visual assistance. The addition of "Be My AI," powered by GPT-4, has pushed this even further, offering users autonomous access to visual interpretation. Whether identifying medication labels or navigating a busy street, the app turns moments of dependency into acts of independence. Similarly, Voiceitt offers a rare technological bridge for people with non-standard speech, translating their words into real-time audio or text. In doing so, it addresses one of the most persistent barriers in physical and virtual spaces: the ability to be heard and understood. Rather than asking users to fit into pre-existing systems, Voiceitt reshapes those systems to listen more closely.

Wheelmap takes on a different but equally critical challenge: mobility in physical space. It maps out wheelchair-accessible locations through crowdsourced reviews, ranging from cafés and train stations to public restrooms. Users benefit from the map and actively contribute to it, cultivating a sense of shared responsibility and collective knowledge. Seeing AI, developed by Microsoft, embodies another layer of inclusive design. It reads text aloud, recognises faces, and even describes scenes to blind users. What distinguishes it is its iterative design, which is built and improved with constant feedback from the community it serves. In this model, users are not just recipients of aid but co-creators of technological solutions.

10.3.4.2 From Safety to Solidarity: Digital Communities for LGBTQIA+ Users

The need for inclusion extends beyond disability. In the digital world, representation and psychological safety are paramount, especially for LGBTQIA+ individuals who may face discrimination in their offline lives. Platforms like *TrevorSpace*[19], *Voda*[20], and *MindOut*[21] have emerged to fill this void. TrevorSpace, a moderated community for LGBTQIA+ youth, provides more than just a chatroom. It is a refuge, a space where identity is not questioned but affirmed. For many young users, it is the first place they can express themselves authentically, access mental health resources, and build supportive relationships.

Voda takes a more therapeutic approach. Designed by LGBTQIA+ psychotherapists, the app offers guided meditations, self-help resources, AI-powered journaling, and modules on topics like queer shame, coming out, and gender dysphoria. Crucially, it uses voices and language that reflect the lived experiences of its users. Rather than adapting generic tools, Voda crafts an entirely bespoke experience, recognizing the intersectional mental health needs of LGBTQIA+ individuals. MindOut, based in the UK, extends this approach by providing online and offline support services. Peer groups, advocacy, and counselling are explicitly offered by and for LGBTQIA+ people, making mental health care not just accessible but also contextually meaningful. Their live chat service, accessible globally, reinforces the principle that digital inclusion is not a one-size-fits-all solution; it must reflect the nuanced realities of its users.

10.3.4.3 Language as Infrastructure: The Case for Localised Platforms

Inclusivity is not only about who is seen or heard, but also about which languages and literacies are accommodated. The JioPhone initiative in India illustrates how linguistic accessibility can shape digital participation (James, 2020; Mukherjee, 2019). Through an affordable 4G phone with voice-based internet in multiple Indian languages, JioPhone brings non-English-speaking and often semi-literate users online. Voice assistants and simplified interfaces further reduce barriers. This localised design approach disrupts the dominance of English-centric interfaces, acknowledging that the digital divide often correlates with language exclusion. By tailoring technology to cultural and linguistic contexts, JioPhone allows users to interact with digital content in ways that feel natural and intuitive (Mukherjee, 2019).

10.3.5 Digital Rights, Governance, and Algorithmic Fairness

In the era of artificial intelligence, digital public infrastructure holds transformative potential. Yet, as states and institutions race to deploy sophisticated systems, the urgency of embedding equity, transparency, and governance at their core becomes paramount. Nowhere is this tension more visible than in the interplay between digital identification systems, civic technology platforms, and algorithmic regulation. The cases of Aadhaar, Mojaloop, Ushahidi, Meu Rio, and the evolving global regulatory frameworks for algorithmic fairness provide a blueprint for rethinking how digital rights can be safeguarded without undermining innovation.

10.3.5.1 Aadhaar: Identity at Scale and Its Discontents

India's Aadhaar project is one of the most ambitious digital identity initiatives ever attempted. Launched in 2009, Aadhaar assigns each resident a unique 12-digit number linked to biometric and demographic data (Dattani, 2020). The aim was to streamline public service delivery and expand inclusion in a country where millions lacked formal identification. Over time, Aadhaar evolved from a voluntary system to a prerequisite for essential services such as welfare transfers, bank accounts, and mobile connectivity. The government positioned it as the backbone of its digital welfare infrastructure, anchored by the JAM trinity: Jan Dhan (banking access), Aadhaar (identity), and Mobile (connectivity) (Goel, 2021).

The benefits of Aadhaar are clear. It enabled direct benefit transfers at scale, reducing leakages and fraud. It created a portable identity for internal migrants and helped digitise India's vast welfare apparatus (Bhatia & Bhabha, 2017; Chaudhuri & König, 2018). Yet, its integration into daily life raised structural concerns. Biometric authentication failures sometimes denied access to food or pensions. These cases, though statistically rare, disproportionately impacted the poorest, in which precisely the population Aadhaar aimed to serve.

A more considerable concern lies in governance. Aadhaar expanded in the absence of a strong data protection law. Legal and civil society critiques focused on surveillance risks and insufficient safeguards against misuse (Gopichandran et al., 2020). The Supreme Court's 2018 ruling curtailed its use by private firms and mandated voluntary consent, but implementation gaps remain. Globally, Aadhaar continues to influence digital ID systems. Its lesson is clear in which digital infrastructure must be embedded in legal and ethical frameworks that protect rights while enabling inclusion. Without that balance, scale alone cannot deliver trust (Gopichandran et al., 2020; Raju et al., 2017; Singh, 2021).

10.3.5.2 Mojaloop: Interoperability as a Right, Not a Feature

Mojaloop offers a fundamentally different vision from Aadhaar's centralised architecture. Built with backing from the Bill & Melinda Gates Foundation, Mojaloop is an open-source platform designed to power interoperable, real-time payments among banks, mobile money providers, and fintech players[22]. Its core proposition is straightforward: make digital financial services universally accessible, especially for the unbanked and underbanked in emerging economies(International Monetary Fund, 2021).

At its heart, Mojaloop acts as a digital public utility. It provides a transaction switch, directory services, and built-in compliance tools to ensure secure, efficient, and inclusive transactions (Abel, 2024). But Mojaloop is more than a technical platform, it's a challenge to the dominance of proprietary systems. By embracing open standards, it reduces vendor lock-in and supports modular, locally governed implementations. This is especially valuable for countries seeking financial data sovereignty and resilience (Nawrocki, 2024).

In fragmented financial ecosystems, Mojaloop serves as connective tissue (Abel, 2024; Khairnar, 2022; Nawrocki, 2024). It empowers governments and central banks to design payment systems that reflect national priorities, including support for real-time settlements and integration with central bank digital currencies. Importantly, its decentralised design ensures that a single provider or centralised authority does not constrain innovation (Khairnar,

2022). As digital payments become the primary mode of delivering public services, from welfare to remittances, interoperability becomes critical. Mojaloop reframes this not as a technical feature but as a civic imperative. The ability to transact across systems is foundational to digital citizenship. In that sense, Mojaloop is not just infrastructure, it is policy embedded in code, enabling access, inclusion, and self-determination in the digital economy (Abel, 2024; Khairnar, 2022; Nawrocki, 2024).

10.3.5.3 Ushahidi and Meu Rio: Civic Tech for Participatory Accountability

While Aadhaar and Mojaloop focus on identity and financial access, civic technology platforms like Ushahidi and Meu Rio target the democratic process. Ushahidi, launched in Kenya during the 2008 post-election crisis, offered a novel solution to an urgent problem on how to document violence when official channels were silent (Marsden, 2013). Citizens submitted reports via SMS and internet, which were mapped in real time to identify conflict zones. This crowdsourced approach shifted the dynamics of information, placing the power to report, interpret, and respond into the hands of everyday people. Since then, Ushahidi has evolved into a global civic infrastructure (Hirata et al., 2018; Pánek et al., 2017). It has supported disaster response in Haiti (H. Gao et al., 2011), monitored nuclear fallout in Japan (Hoetzlein, 2012), and documented human rights violations in Syria (Macdonell, 2015). The underlying model remains consistent to reduce barriers to civic participation and harness distributed networks to produce real-time accountability.

Meu Rio, operating in Brazil, takes a more institutional approach. Its digital platform helps residents of Rio de Janeiro engage directly with local governance[23]. Citizens can track decisions, launch campaigns, and pressure officials through tools like Panela de Pressão, automating emails, tweets, and calls to elected representatives (Bintrim, 2014). This has led to measurable policy outcomes, from halting school closures to protecting public spaces. Both platforms challenge the idea that democracy is confined to elections or legislative halls. They demonstrate that civic power can be continuous and distributed (Omydar Network, 2018). Still, their success depends on enabling conditions: digital access, political receptivity, and institutional safeguards. As digital democracy scales, the question is whether civic tech can preserve its grassroots integrity without becoming another layer of bureaucracy.

10.3.5.4 Algorithmic Fairness: From Principles to Regulation

As digital systems mature, questions of equity shift from access to outcomes. Nowhere is this more critical than in the realm of algorithmic decision-making

(Future of Privacy Forum, 2017; Helberger et al., 2020). Algorithms increasingly mediate high-stakes domains: creditworthiness, job recruitment, healthcare triage, and even criminal sentencing. Left unchecked, these systems can replicate and amplify existing biases, often under the guise of objectivity. The imperative for algorithmic fairness, therefore, is no longer theoretical; it is regulatory (Perdana et al., 2025).

The European Union's AI Act represents the most comprehensive effort to date[24]. Passed in 2024, it categorises AI systems by risk level, with high-risk systems subject to stringent conditions. These include requirements for bias mitigation in training data, transparency of decision-making processes, mandatory human oversight, and ongoing post-market monitoring. The Act underscores that fairness is not a peripheral concern but a regulatory obligation, enforced through fines and audits.

The United States has taken a more decentralised route. While lacking federal legislation akin to the AI Act, the White House's Blueprint for an AI Bill of Rights articulates core principles, safety, non-discrimination, transparency, privacy, and human fallback mechanisms[25]. Although non-binding, it provides a moral compass for agencies and companies navigating ethical dilemmas. Singapore's Model AI Governance Framework complements these efforts by offering practical guidance to businesses on implementing fairness, proportionality, and accountability in AI deployment[26]. Figure 10.1 presents the overview of digital technology applications in DEIB.

These frameworks are converging around a shared understanding: that algorithms must be transparent, contestable, and grounded in human rights. Still, formidable challenges remain. Fairness is notoriously difficult to define across contexts (Barocas et al., 2023; Buijsman, 2024; Dolata et al., 2022). Enhancing algorithmic equity can compromise predictive accuracy, raising trade-offs between ethical and business goals. Proprietary systems often resist scrutiny, invoking intellectual property protections. Moreover, regulators, especially in the Global South, often lack the technical expertise to audit these systems effectively (Perdana et al., 2025).

10.4 Synthesizing Key Insights and Lessons Learned

Digital transformation presents a critical inflection point: technology can reinforce exclusion or become a lever for justice. Examining cases across healthcare, finance, civic participation, education, and algorithmic governance reveals that inclusion requires intentional design, contextual adaptation, and governance structures centered on marginalised communities.

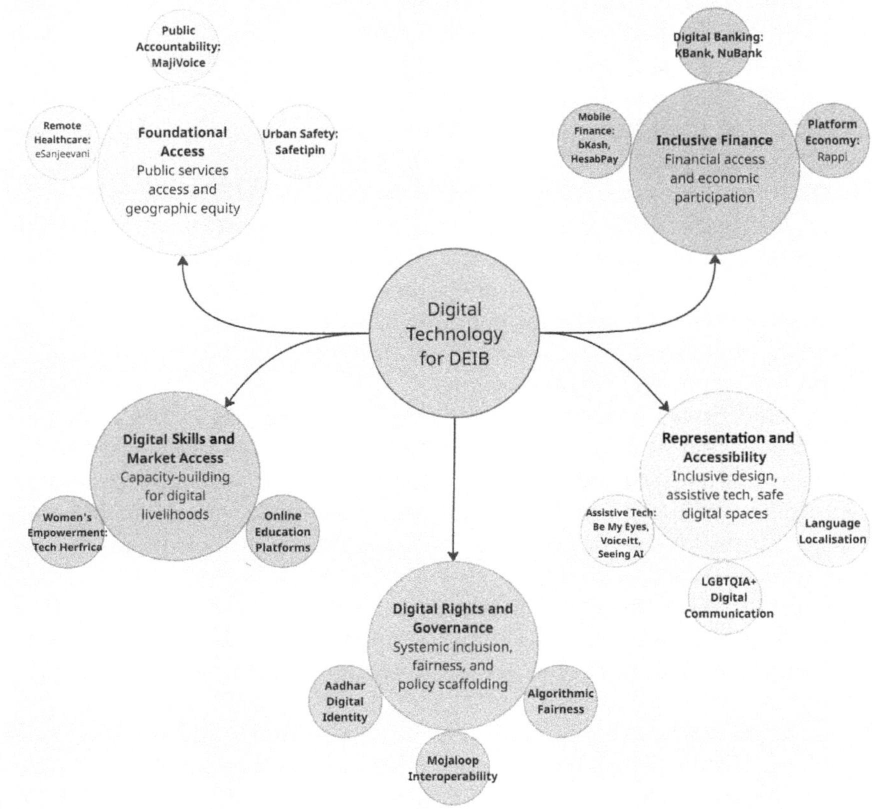

FIGURE 10.1
Digital technology applications in DEIB.

10.4.1 Infrastructure First: Systemic Foundations

Transformative digital initiatives begin with foundational infrastructure that reaches underserved populations, not just physical infrastructure but institutional, legal, and service delivery architectures. eSanjeevani demonstrated how telemedicine can bridge structural inequities when designed as public infrastructure integrated with broader health systems and policy frameworks (R. Gupta et al., 2025; Raj et al., 2024). Similarly, platforms like MajiVoice and bKash created digital channels for civic participation and financial empowerment (Georgiadou et al., 2014; Murthy et al., 2018; Nandhakumar, 2023). Digital equity requires practical infrastructure that meets users where they are, designing for context-specific constraints and embedding technologies within support ecosystems. This challenges the "innovation-first" mindset, prioritizing accessibility, reliability, and interoperability over novelty.

10.4.2 Trust and Participatory Design: Accountability as a Feature

The most inclusive digital platforms elevate users from passive recipients to active co-creators. Safetipin transformed women's experiential knowledge into urban policy, while assistive technologies like Be My Eyes incorporated continuous feedback from disability communities (Le, 2022; Sullivan, 2025). MajiVoice's increased complaint reporting indicated growing trust in the system's responsiveness (Georgiadou et al., 2014; Murthy et al., 2018). Meaningful representation throughout development is essential. When organisations lack internal diversity, they must establish structured mechanisms for engaging marginalised communities as compensated design partners. The financial success of inclusive initiatives like Nubank demonstrates that user-centered design is both ethical and economically viable.

10.4.3 Governance and Regulation: Political Economy of Digital Equity

Digital technologies require governance structures that incentivise responsiveness and penalise exclusion. MajiVoice succeeded because it embedded performance metrics into regulatory contracts. Similarly, the European Union's AI Act represents a shift from voluntary ethics to enforceable standards. Aadhaar's evolution shows how digital identity systems can become exclusionary without robust safeguards. India's Supreme Court intervention demonstrated how governance can balance innovation with rights protection. Organisations must move beyond self-regulation toward transparent standards, independent audits, and formal recourse mechanisms, recognizing governance as a continuous rather than one-time implementation.

10.4.4 Interoperability as a Right

Interoperability emerges as a fundamental right across cases. Mojaloop offers a open-source, decentralised financial infrastructure model that challenges proprietary systems. eSanjeevani's integration with digital health IDs enables continuity of care across fragmented systems. When financial services communicate across platforms, users gain freedom to choose providers based on value rather than network effects. Inclusive design must prioritise open standards, data portability, and ecosystem integration, moving beyond competitive advantage through lock-in toward value creation through participation.

10.4.5 Ecosystemic Thinking: Beyond Skills Training

Tech Herfrica's initiatives reveal that digital empowerment requires end-to-end systems connecting capacity-building to economic outcomes. Successful inclusion adapts to local realities rather than imposing external models.

HesabPay's impact in Afghanistan stemmed from recognizing gender-based constraints and designing alternative authentication mechanisms (Bharathi et al., 2025). Skills must be matched with platforms, platforms with market access, and digital interfaces with local language and cultural context. JioPhone's voice-first approach recognised that text-based interfaces exclude millions with limited literacy (James, 2020). bKash's agent network bridged digital and physical worlds where smartphone penetration was limited (Nandhakumar, 2023).

10.4.6 Representation and Psychological Safety

Assistive technologies like Be My Eyes and Voiceitt demonstrate that inclusion means redefining participation on users' terms. Digital platforms excel at scale, but numbers alone don't constitute meaningful inclusion. Rappi's experience shows that while it expanded economic participation, the quality of that participation, characterised by precarity, fell short of genuine empowerment (Zhong, n.d.). Platforms for LGBTQIA+ mental health highlight that inclusion is also emotional. Representation requires psychological safety, creating spaces where users are seen, heard, and understood. JioPhone's multilingual voice access affirms that language is infrastructure, not an afterthought.

10.4.7 From Access to Empowerment

As digital adoption expands globally, the frontier shifts from basic access to equitable outcomes. The EU, US, and Singapore are developing frameworks that look beyond procedural fairness to substantive results, recognizing that "neutral" systems can produce discriminatory impacts if they encode historical biases. This outcomes focus requires sophisticated approaches to design and evaluation, examining whether services produce equitable benefits across demographic groups. Kasikornbank's integration of financial inclusion with environmental sustainability exemplifies this holistic perspective.

10.4.8 Centering Justice in Digital Transformation

Digital technologies can either entrench exclusion or enable empowerment depending on how they're designed, governed, and deployed. When digital transformation centres justice, prioritizing historically marginalised communities, it can catalyse systemic change beyond technological adoption. This justice-cantered approach requires asking different questions: Who defines the problem? Whose knowledge counts? Who benefits? Who bears risks? Who has power to modify systems? Organisations must develop new structures for community participation, cross-sector collaboration, and continuous learning. As digital technologies become increasingly embedded in critical systems, these lessons take on greater urgency. DEIB is not an optional layer but the architecture on which digital systems must be built. The path forward requires translating these insights into operating principles: designing from the margins, embedding feedback as core functionality, linking inclusion to accountability, building ecosystems instead of isolated products, and regulating for equity rather than merely mitigating risk.

10.5 Policy and Regulatory Pathways to Digital Inclusion

As digital technologies become embedded in the daily lives of billions, policymakers and regulators worldwide are adopting frameworks that not only expand access but also embed DEIB principles into digital ecosystems. These frameworks are increasingly sophisticated, moving beyond infrastructure provision to address affordability, literacy, representation, and safe participation.

At the international level, global agreements such as the United Nations Sustainable Development Goals (SDGs) have become reference points for inclusive digital development. SDG 9 (Industry, Innovation, and Infrastructure) and SDG 5 (Gender Equality) call for universal internet access and gender empowerment through technology. Countries have responded by aligning national ICT policies with these targets (Barikzai et al., 2024, 2025). Organisations such as the Broadband Commission for Sustainable Development, backed by the UN and ITU, promote the collection of sex-disaggregated data and advocate for closing the gender digital divide (Broadband Commission for Sustainable Development, 2018). Additionally, nations have implemented inclusive digital policy design, such as Rwanda's approach to increasing women's participation in tech[27] or Malaysia's use of telecentres to improve rural connectivity[28].

National governments are increasingly adopting digital inclusion strategies that span infrastructure development, access subsidies, and educational reforms (Barikzai et al., 2024). Common initiatives include rural broadband expansion, community Wi-Fi, and licensing requirements that oblige mobile operators to cover remote areas. Subsidies targeting marginalised groups are also becoming widespread, India's "Digital Beti" program, for example, provides devices and data to school-aged girls[29]. Many countries are also integrating digital literacy into school curricula to build long-term capacity.

In some cases, pilot programs have informed broader policy moves. Kenya's success with MajiVoice, led the government to mandate mobile accessibility and citizen input mechanisms in new e-governance initiatives (Georgiadou et al., 2014; Murthy et al., 2018). In Bangladesh, the central bank's decision to promote financial inclusion via nominal-fee savings accounts and mobile financial services laid the groundwork for bKash, now a globally recognised mobile money platform (Islam et al., 2025). On the legislative front, certain jurisdictions are codifying digital rights into law. These bills articulate principles such as equal access and non-discrimination, which can serve as a legal basis for redress, for instance, when algorithmic systems disproportionately disadvantage minority groups. The European Union's Web Accessibility Directive, which requires public sector digital assets to comply with international accessibility standards, exemplifies a rights-based approach to digital inclusion[30].

Financial and telecommunications regulators are also adapting their mandates. In the finance sector, central banks and supervisory bodies are creating enabling conditions for fintech, microfinance, and mobile money. Proportional Know-Your-Customer (KYC) regimes, such as India's Aadhaar-enabled eKYC, have significantly expanded access to formal financial services by allowing individuals with minimal documentation to open accounts (Algorand Foundation, 2022; Bharathi et al., 2025). These efforts are often paired with updated consumer protection measures that cover data privacy, fraud, and pricing transparency for digital products.

Telecom regulators are working to reduce the cost of internet access through competition policy, spectrum management, and the deployment of universal service funds to connect underserved regions. Service quality standards in low-income or remote areas are being enforced more strictly to ensure equity in digital service delivery. Regulators in some jurisdictions also respond to emerging issues in the gig economy. For instance, labour ministries in Brazil and Colombia have begun to debate legal protections for platform workers, aiming to ensure that digital inclusion encompasses fair and equitable participation in new forms of work (Bernier, 2023; Foggin & Martins, 2024).

Global organisations contribute to this policy landscape by developing tools, frameworks, and peer learning platforms. The World Bank's Digital Development Pathways help governments design tailored interventions based on their stage of digital maturity[31]. The OECD's policy guidance on women's digital empowerment encourages states to use fiscal tools, such as tax incentives for women-led tech firms, to address gender disparities (OECD, 2022). The International Labour Organisation (ILO) has turned its attention to platform economies, producing recommendations to safeguard workers while maximizing the inclusive potential of gig work[32]. Figure 10.2 presents the proposed framework for inclusive technology design and policy.

One emerging area of focus is the promotion of Digital Public Goods (DPGs), such as, open-source platforms, software, and data standards that countries can adopt to accelerate inclusion (Khairnar, 2022; Wadali et al., 2020). For instance, the Modular Open-Source Identity Platform (MOSIP) enables the development of inclusive digital ID systems, ensuring that refugees, stateless individuals, and other marginalised populations can be issued secure digital

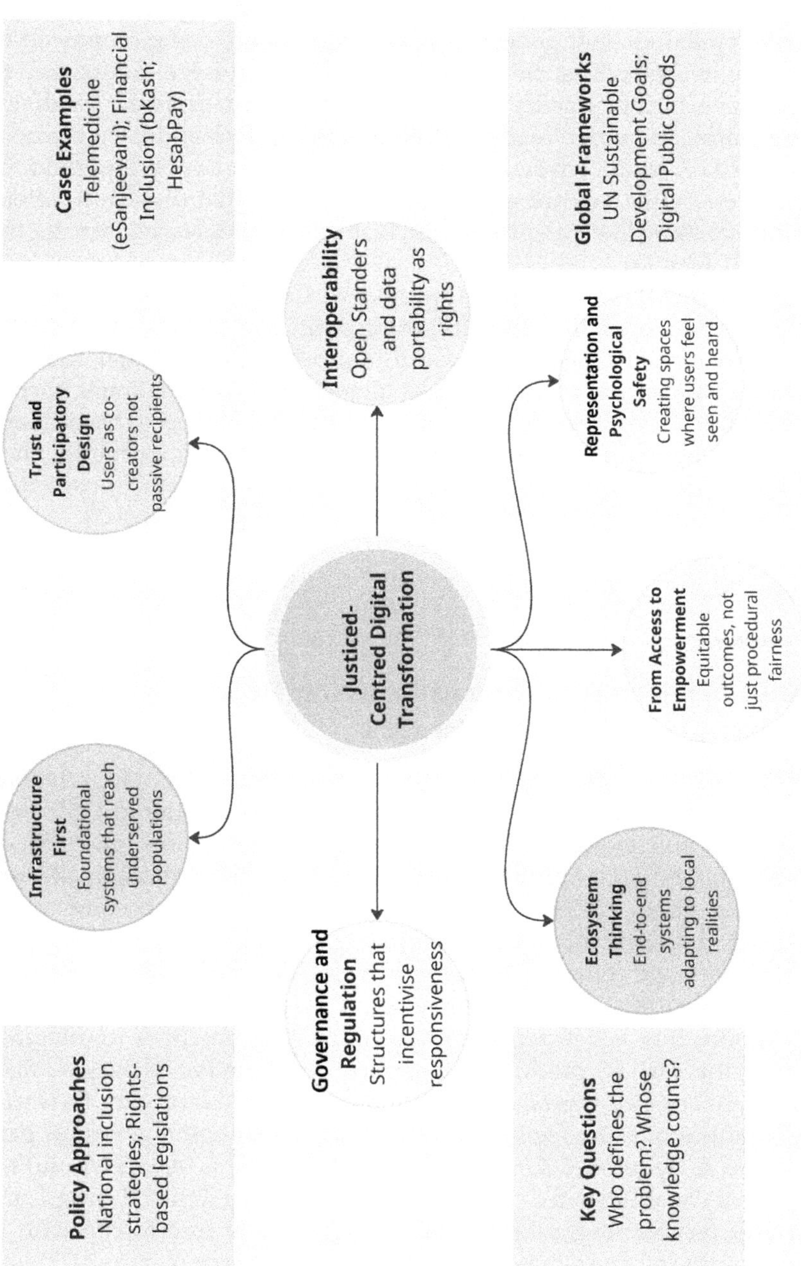

FIGURE 10.2
A Framework for inclusive technology design & policy.

credentials[33]. Policy toolkits accompany many DPGs to help governments design inclusive rollouts.

Workplace inclusion in the technology sector is also gaining attention. While not strictly regulatory, soft governance mechanisms are being employed to shape corporate behaviour. Some governments incentivize companies to adopt inclusive hiring practices, such as procurement preferences, diversity benchmarks, or public reporting requirements. Tech industry councils in countries like Canada have also set gender inclusion targets and monitor progress. These initiatives are grounded in the belief that diverse development teams are more likely to produce inclusive technologies, reinforcing the broader DEIB agenda.

Across these efforts, a few patterns are evident. Countries making headway on digital inclusion often demonstrate strong political commitment, typically through national digital inclusion task forces or cross-ministerial coordination. They establish policy frameworks aligned with international norms, use tiered or sandbox regulatory approaches to balance innovation with inclusion, and maintain feedback loops with civil society. Importantly, they frame digital inclusion not merely as a tool for economic growth, but as a fundamental right, integral to full participation in contemporary society.

10.6 Future Trajectories: Operationalizing DEIB in Emerging Digital Landscapes

While past and current practices have highlighted the structural foundations of inclusive technology design, we argue that the next frontier in DEIB will involve embedding inclusion into the evolving architectures, governance models, and operational cultures of digital systems (Floridi, 2021; Martin, 2022; Perdana et al., 2025). As technological ecosystems become more decentralised, data-driven, and cross-border, DEIB will no longer be a peripheral concern but a central organizing principle for innovation and policy alignment (Kondra et al., 2025; Rahimi et al., 2024).

A key opportunity lies in reconfiguring innovation pipelines to integrate inclusion at the earliest product and service development phases. Unlike prior efforts that treated accessibility and representation as add-ons, forward-looking organisations are beginning to treat DEIB as a baseline design parameter (Capel & Brereton, 2023; Hofeditz et al., 2022). This includes building organisational capabilities for "inclusion impact assessments" during early ideation and prototyping, where teams systematically interrogate who is likely to be excluded and where design bias might emerge (Chen, 2023; Van Den Broek et al., 2021). Unlike participatory co-design processes that focus on user voice during development (Safetipin: Viswanath & Basu, 2015; Be My

Eyes: Sullivan, 2025), these assessments anticipate structural exclusion before users engage, especially in emerging domains like AI, biometric ID systems, and ambient computing.

In parallel, new technical standards and institutional norms are forming around inclusive innovation. For example, there are early moves toward industry-wide certifications for "inclusive AI" tools, focusing on explainability, fairness, and accessibility (Barocas et al., 2023; Buijsman, 2024; Helberger et al., 2020). These mechanisms, analogous to GDPR in privacy or ISO standards in cybersecurity, signal a shift from isolated best practices to shared accountability infrastructures (Buijsman, 2024; Perdana et al., 2025). They also reduce the burden on individual organisations to create inclusion frameworks from scratch while increasing the reputational cost of exclusionary systems.

The global expansion of digital markets also creates opportunities to redistribute where and how inclusion is defined. While much of the inclusion discourse has historically originated in OECD contexts, countries in the Global South are increasingly influencing the direction of digital DEIB through homegrown models and south-south knowledge exchange (Bharathi S et al., 2025; Islam et al., 2025; Khairnar, 2022). This shift is not just about exporting solutions like Aadhaar or M-Pesa, but about redefining global norms through reciprocal technical and regulatory dialogue (Abel, 2024; Nawrocki, 2024).

In this evolving landscape, funders, investors, and development agencies are beginning to recalibrate their risk and return frameworks. Some are embedding DEIB metrics into investment theses and grant conditions, requiring measurable inclusion outcomes, such as reach among underrepresented demographics or percentage of localised content. These metrics incentivise digital innovators to build for populations outside the typical addressable market. More importantly, they reframe inclusion not as a cost centre but as a proxy for resilience, relevance, and long-term value generation (Dignum, 2019; Floridi, 2021).

Another significant frontier is infrastructure modularity. Whereas earlier digital inclusion efforts focused on centralised infrastructure delivery (e.g., Aadhaar: Singh, 2021; Raju et al., 2017), the future points to more distributed and adaptive approaches. This includes modular open-source platforms (e.g., Mojaloop: Abel, 2024), edge computing for remote areas, and decentralised identity systems (e.g., MOSIP: Khairnar, 2022), all of which allow more agile adaptation to diverse user needs. Unlike Section 4's emphasis on interoperability as a right, here the focus is on modularity as a design strategy for inclusion.

The internal cultures of technology organisations are also likely to change. While the role of participatory design and representation has been emphasised (Safetipin: Viswanath & Basu, 2015; Be My Eyes: Sullivan, 2025), the next phase of workplace DEIB will involve integrating inclusion into decision rights, performance evaluation, and strategic planning processes (Agnihotri & Bhattacharya, 2024). This means moving beyond mentorship and hiring targets toward revising incentive structures, procurement policies, and R&D agendas to explicitly account for inclusion metrics (Allen et al., 2021; Carr et al., 2019; Devine & Ash, 2022).

Finally, cross-sectoral collaboration will become more experimental and iterative. Sandboxed collaborations between regulators, civil society actors, and technology firms, especially in areas like social protection delivery, digital labour, and algorithmic oversight, will serve as laboratories for evolving inclusive governance models (Meu Rio: Bintrim, 2014; Ushahidi: Marsden, 2013). These are not merely pilot programs, but structured spaces for stress-testing new rules, tools, and relationships before codifying them at scale.

In sum, the next chapter of DEIB in digital systems will be defined not just by what gets built, but by how innovation is structured, funded, and governed. Moving from ideals to operations, from case-based interventions to system-wide norms, and from centralised infrastructure to modular, pluralistic architectures, digital inclusion will increasingly be shaped by the ability to embed equity into the DNA of technological and institutional design (see, Table 10.1 for the summary). The challenge is not simply expanding access, but building digital futures in which inclusion is the default rather than the afterthought.

10.6.1 Digital DEIB and Political Trajectories: The Double-Edged Nature of Technological Intervention

The relationship between digital DEIB initiatives and political governance reveals a fundamental tension that demands critical examination. While platforms like TrevorSpace and MindOut create spaces for psychological safety among LGBTQIA+ communities, their digital traces simultaneously generate data that can be weaponised by conservative or authoritarian governments. In contexts like Indonesia, where nationalist and religious conservative movements exert significant influence, the same technologies that enable marginalised voices may inadvertently provide surveillance infrastructure for discriminatory policies.

This paradox extends beyond individual platforms to systemic questions of digital governance. Digital financial inclusion through platforms like HesabPay in Afghanistan demonstrates how technology can preserve agency under restrictive regimes, yet these same systems require careful design to prevent becoming tools of control. The challenge intensifies when considering ethnic minorities such as Papuans in Indonesia, where digital engagement might simultaneously offer economic empowerment and expose communities to increased monitoring.

Technology companies thus occupy a precarious position as inadvertent political actors. Their design choices, data policies, and cooperation with state authorities can either reinforce democratic participation or enable

TABLE 10.1

Embedding DEIB as a central organizing principle

Key Dimension	Core Concept	Implementation Approach
Early Development	Inclusion at the earliest phases of product and service development	Inclusion impact assessments during ideation and prototyping that anticipate structural exclusion before user engagement
Technical Standards	Industry-wide certifications for inclusive tools	Shared accountability infrastructures focusing on explainability, fairness, and accessibility (like GDPR for privacy)
Global Expansion	Redistributing where and how inclusion is defined	South-South knowledge exchange moving beyond Silicon Valley models toward plural, context-specific epistemologies
Funding Recalibration	Embedding DEIB metrics into investment frameworks	Requiring measurable inclusion outcomes like reach among underrepresented demographics; reframing inclusion as strategic value not cost
Infrastructure Modularity	Distributed and adaptive approaches to infrastructure	Modular open-source platforms, edge computing, and decentralised identity systems allowing tailoring to localised constraints
Organisational Culture	Integration into decision rights and evaluation	Moving beyond mentorship and hiring targets toward revised incentive structures and procurement policies with inclusion metrics
Cross-Sectoral Collaboration	Experimental and iterative partnerships	Sandboxed collaborations between regulators, civil society, and tech firms for prototyping under uncertainty rather than merely scaling known solutions

authoritarian overreach. The cases examined reveal that progressive digital policies do not automatically translate into progressive governance; rather, they require active safeguarding through technical design, regulatory frameworks, and corporate accountability mechanisms. As digital systems become more pervasive, the responsibility for protecting vulnerable populations extends beyond government policy to encompass the fundamental architecture of digital platforms themselves.

10.7 Conclusion

The future of inclusive digital transformation depends not on the novelty of tools, but on the coherence between intent, infrastructure, and institutional design. Across diverse cases, one insight remains constant: meaningful inclusion emerges when technologies are shaped by those who have been historically excluded. Whether through localised financial platforms in fragile economies, telemedicine in rural clinics, or safety apps co-designed with marginalised women, the architecture of digital systems must be informed by the lived experiences of those they seek to serve.

This study reframes DEIB not as a set of checklist items, but as a systemic approach to rethinking digital participation, governance, and innovation. Inclusion cannot be retrofitted; it must be foundational. That requires changes to funding models, regulatory expectations, product design cultures, and metrics of success. It also requires a redistribution of epistemic authority: recognizing that solutions do not only emerge from labs and boardrooms, but from community-led innovations and context-specific knowledge systems.

The analysis challenges the linear view of progress that equates digital expansion with equity. Instead, it posits that inclusion is about the quality of participation, the fairness of outcomes, and the responsiveness of systems. As digital infrastructures evolve, the risk is not just of exclusion but of deepening dependency on systems that do not recognise or protect all users. Avoiding this future means embedding equity into the DNA of digital governance, moving from projects that include, to systems that belong to all. Justice is not an outcome of digital transformation; it must be its foundation.

Notes

1 2.7 Billion People Still Offline — Despite progress, 2.7B people lack internet access, showing persistent global digital divide. www.un.org/en/desa/27-billion-people-still-left-offline
2 Explainer on building an equitable digital future, focusing on gender equality and inclusive access. www.unwomen.org/en/news-stories/explainer/2023/02/power-on-how-we-can-supercharge-an-equitable-digital-future
3 Information hub on the EU's AI Act: rules for trustworthy AI, risk classification, and governance. https://artificialintelligenceact.eu/
4 Civic tech movement mobilizing Rio de Janeiro citizens to influence public policy. www.meurio.org.br/
5 Framework for the 17 Sustainable Development Goals. https://sdgs.un.org/2030agenda
6 WEF initiative accelerating digital inclusion worldwide. www.edisonalliance.org/home
7 Backgrounder on the global gender gap in digital access and skills. www.itu.int/en/mediacentre/backgrounders/Pages/bridging-the-gender-divide.aspx
8 Same report on 2.7B people offline (see #1). www.un.org/en/desa/27-billion-people-still-left-offline
9 Case studies from Africa showing digital adoption driving development. www.worldbank.org/en/results/2024/01/18/digital-transformation-drives-development-in-afe-afw-africa

10 Global stats on women's and men's digital access and skills gaps. www.itu.int/itu-d/reports/statistics/2023/10/10/ff23-the-gender-digital-divide/
11 How Nubank became the world's largest digital bank. https://thefinancialbrand.com/news/fintech-banking/how-nubank-became-the-worlds-biggest-digital-bank-131658
12 Nubank's approach to inclusion and digital banking in Latin America. https://international.nubank.com.br/company/financial-inclusion-and-digital-transformation-the-future-of-banking-in-our-region/
13 How Rappi used Amplitude analytics to scale digital services. https://amplitude.com/case-studies/rappi
14 NGO advancing digital and financial access for African women. www.techherfrica.org/
15 App connecting blind/low-vision users with volunteers for visual help. www.bemyeyes.com/
16 Speech recognition for people with non-standard speech patterns. www.voiceitt.com/
17 App describing the world for visually impaired users. www.seeingai.com/
18 Collaborative map for wheelchair accessibility worldwide. https://wheelmap.org/
19 Global online community for LGBTQ+ youth. www.trevorspace.org/
20 AI platform helping water utilities predict pipe failures. www.voda.co/
21 UK LGBTQ+ mental health support organization. https://mindout.org.uk/
22 Open-source platform enabling interoperable digital financial services. https://mojaloop.io/
23 Social design case on citizen engagement via Meu Rio. https://foossa.com/meu-rio
24 Same EU AI Act site (see #3). https://artificialintelligenceact.eu/
25 Framework of five principles for rights-respecting AI. https://bidenwhitehouse.archives.gov/ostp/ai-bill-of-rights/
26 Practical guide for responsible AI deployment. www.pdpc.gov.sg/help-and-resources/2020/01/model-ai-governance-framework
27 Rwanda's leadership on gender equality through technology. www.rwandainsweden.gov.rw/info/info-details/rwanda-a-global-leader-on-womens-empowerment-using-innovation-and-technology-to-lead-the-way-for-gender-equality
28 Official page on Malaysia's digital transformation programs. www.malaysia.gov.my/portal/content/30631
29 Initiative empowering women with digital literacy. https://literacyindia.org/digital-beti/
30 Standards ensuring accessibility of EU digital services. https://digital-strategy.ec.europa.eu/en/policies/web-accessibility-directive-standards-and-harmonisation
31 Overview of Bank's programs to boost global digital inclusion. www.worldbank.org/en/topic/digital
32 Digital Labour Platforms — ILO research on gig platforms' impact on work and rights. www.ilo.org/digital-labour-platforms
33 Modular Open Source Identity Platform supporting digital ID systems. www.mosip.io/

References

Abdelhalim, E., Anazodo, K. S., Gali, N., & Robson, K. (2024). A framework of diversity, equity, and inclusion safeguards for chatbots. *Business Horizons, 67*(5), 487–498. https://doi.org/10.1016/j.bushor.2024.03.003

Abel, M. (2024, September 30). The Mojaloop moment: Expanding financial inclusion. *Gates Foundation.* https://www.gatesfoundation.org/ideas/articles/digital-payments-financial-inclusion-mojaloop

Abreu, R. L., & Kenny, M. C. (2018). Cyberbullying and LGBTQ youth: A systematic literature review and recommendations for prevention and intervention. *Journal of Child & Adolescent Trauma, 11*(1), 81–97. https://doi.org/10.1007/s40653-017-0175-7

Agnihotri, A., & Bhattacharya, S. (2024). *Artificial Intelligence for Hiring and Induction: The Unilever Experience.* SAGE Publications: SAGE Business Cases Originals. https://doi.org/10.4135/9781071921470

Algorand Foundation. (2022, December 21). Afghan E-payment solution HesabPay successfully migrates to algorand blockchain through grant funding. *PR Newswire.* https://www.prnewswire.com/news-releases/afghan-e-payment-solution-hesabpay-successfully-migrates-to-algorand-blockchain-through-grant-funding-301629061.html

Allen, K.-A., Kern, M. L., Rozek, C. S., McInerney, D. M., & Slavich, G. M. (2021). Belonging: A review of conceptual issues, an integrative framework, and directions for future research. *Australian Journal of Psychology, 73*(1), 87–102. https://doi.org/10.1080/00049530.2021.1883409

Anshari, M., Almunawar, M. N., & Ordóñez De Pablos, P. (Eds.). (2024). *Impacts of Digital Technologies Across Generations:* IGI Global. https://doi.org/10.4018/979-8-3693-6366-9

Au, A. (2024). Neobanks in emerging markets: A risk assessment. *Humanities and Social Sciences Communications, 11*(1), 655. https://doi.org/10.1057/s41599-024-03138-7

Banchongduang, S. (2025, February 13). Line BK targets double-digit loan gain. *Bangkok Post.* https://www.bangkokpost.com/business/general/2960081/line-bk-targets-double-digit-loan-gain

Barikzai, S., Bharathi S, V., & Perdana, A. (2024). Challenges and strategies in e-learning adoption in emerging economies: A scoping review. *Cogent Education, 11*(1), 2400415. https://doi.org/10.1080/2331186X.2024.2400415

Barikzai, S., Bharathi S, V., & Perdana, A. (2025). Digital learning initiatives forging inclusive education in post-conflict nations. *Cogent Education, 12*(1), 2457904. https://doi.org/10.1080/2331186X.2025.2457904

Barocas, S., Hardt, M., & Narayanan, A. (2023). *Fairness and machine learning: Limitations and opportunities.* The MIT Press.

Bera, S., Yao, Y., Palit, A., & Rahut, D. (2023). *Digital Transformation for Inclusive and Sustainable Development in Asia.* Asian Development Bank Institute.

Bernier, M. (2023, July 22). What does Colombia need more: Rappi or Labor Reform? *Econlog Post.* https://www.econlib.org/what-does-colombia-need-more-rappi-or-labor-reform/

Bharathi S, V., Perdana, A., & Barikzai, S. (2025). Digital innovation at the intersection of financial inclusion and humanitarian aid: HesabPay's journey in Afghanistan. *Journal of Information Technology Teaching Cases*, 20438869251325867. https://doi.org/10.1177/20438869251325867

Bhatia, A., & Bhabha, J. (2017). India's Aadhaar scheme and the promise of inclusive social protection. *Oxford Development Studies, 45*(1), 64–79. https://doi.org/10.1080/13600818.2016.1263726

Bintrim, R. (2014, November 5). Civic Innovator: Alessandra Orofino. *Americas Quarterly*. https://www.americasquarterly.org/fulltextarticle/civic-innovator-alessandra-orofino/

Broadband Commission for Sustainable Development. (2018). *Working Group on the Digital Gender Divide: Bridging the gender gap in Internet and broadband access and use: Progress Report*. https://www.broadbandcommission.org/Documents/publications/DigitalGenderDivideProgressReport2018.pdf

Brown, R. (2025, January 6). Colombia's First Unicorn Keeps Delivering. *Americas Quarterly*. https://www.americasquarterly.org/article/colombias-first-unicorn-keeps-delivering/

Buijsman, S. (2024). Navigating fairness measures and trade-offs. *AI and Ethics, 4*(4), 1323–1334. https://doi.org/10.1007/s43681-023-00318-0

Buolamwini, J., & Gebru, T. (2018). Gender Shades: Intersectional Accuracy Disparities in Commercial Gender Classification. *Proceedings of the 1st Conference on Fairness, Accountability and Transparency*.

Calomiris, C. W., & Haber, S. H. (2014). *Fragile by design: The political origins of banking crises and scarce credit*. Princeton University Press.

Capel, T., & Brereton, M. (2023). What is human-centered about human-centered AI? A map of the research landscape. *Proceedings of the 2023 CHI Conference on Human Factors in Computing Systems*, 1–23. https://doi.org/10.1145/3544548.3580959

Carr, E. W., Reece, A., Kellerman, G. R., & Robichaux. (2019, December 16). The value of belonging at work. *Harvard Business Review*. https://hbr.org/2019/12/the-value-of-belonging-at-work

Carter, B. M., Sumpter, D. F., & Thruston, W. (2023). Overcoming marginalization by creating a sense of belonging. *Creative Nursing, 29*(4), 320–327. https://doi.org/10.1177/10784535231216464

Chandana, C., Sarkar, A., Deshmukh, K., Kulkarni, P., Bikash Acharjee, P., & Lourens, M. (2024). Analysing employee management using machine learning techniques and solutions in human resource management. In *2024 4th International Conference on Innovative Practices in Technology and Management (ICIPTM)*, 1–6. https://doi.org/10.1109/ICIPTM59628.2024.10563736

Chaudhuri, B., & König, L. (2018). The Aadhaar scheme: A cornerstone of a new citizenship regime in India? *Contemporary South Asia, 26*(2), 127–142. https://doi.org/10.1080/09584935.2017.1369934

Chen, Z. (2023). Ethics and discrimination in artificial intelligence-enabled recruitment practices. *Humanities and Social Sciences Communications, 10*(1), 567. https://doi.org/10.1057/s41599-023-02079-x

Chuene, D., & Mtsweni, J. (2015). The adoption of crowdsourcing platforms in South Africa. *2015 IST-Africa Conference*, 1–9. https://doi.org/10.1109/ISTAFRICA.2015.7190561

Civic Tech in the Global South: Assessing Technology for the Public Good (with Peixoto, T., & Sifry, M. L.). (2017). The World Bank and Personal Democracy Press.
Dattani, K. (2020). "Governtrepreneurism" for good governance: The case of Aadhaar and the India Stack. *Area*, *52*(2), 411–419. https://doi.org/10.1111/area.12579
David, L. K., Wang, J., Brooks, W., & Angel, V. (2025). Digital transformation and socio-economic development in emerging economies: A multinational analysis. *Technology in Society*, *81*, 102834. https://doi.org/10.1016/j.techsoc.2025.102834
Devine, P. G., & Ash, T. L. (2022). Diversity training goals, limitations, and promise: A review of the multidisciplinary literature. *Annual Review of Psychology*, *73*(1), 403–429. https://doi.org/10.1146/annurev-psych-060221-122215
Dignum, V. (2019). *Responsible Artificial Intelligence*. Springer International Publishing. https://doi.org/10.1007/978-3-030-30371-6
Dolata, M., Feuerriegel, S., & Schwabe, G. (2022). A sociotechnical view of algorithmic fairness. *Information Systems Journal*, *32*(4), 754–818. https://doi.org/10.1111/isj.12370
Eichenseer, P., Hans, L., & Winkler, H. (2025). A data-driven machine learning model for forecasting delivery positions in logistics for workforce planning. *Supply Chain Analytics*, *9*, 100099. https://doi.org/10.1016/j.sca.2024.100099
Fellah, A. (2024, December 20). Wi-Fi and cellular: A pragmatic perspective to convergence (Analyst Angle). *RCRWirelessNews*. https://www.rcrwireless.com/20241220/5g/wi-fi-convergence
Fernandez-Vidal, J., Jorge, Antonio Perotti, Francesco, Gonzalez, Reyes, Gasco. (2022). Managing digital transformation: The view from the top. *Journal of Business Research*, *152*, 29–41. https://doi.org/10.1016/j.jbusres.2022.07.020
Floridi, L. (Ed.). (2021). *Ethics, Governance, and Policies in Artificial Intelligence* (Vol. 144). Springer International Publishing. https://doi.org/10.1007/978-3-030-81907-1
Floridi, L., Cowls, J., Beltrametti, M., Chatila, R., Chazerand, P., Dignum, V., Luetge, C., Madelin, R., Pagallo, U., Rossi, F., Schafer, B., Valcke, P., & Vayena, E. (2021). *An Ethical Framework for a Good AI Society: Opportunities, Risks, Principles, and Recommendations* (pp. 19–39). https://doi.org/10.1007/978-3-030-81907-1_3
Foggin, S., & Martins, L. (2024, January 30). Rappi drivers say a public defender's office for gig workers is useless, not neutral. *Rest Of World*. https://restofworld.org/2024/rappi-mediator-service/
Future of Privacy Forum. (2017). *Unfairness by Algorithm: Distilling the Harms of Automated Decision Making*. FPF.ORG.
Gao, G. Y., Lyu, J., & Cheung, C. M. K. (2024). AI recruiting and workplace diversity, equity, and inclusion: A literature analysis. *Pacific-Asia Conference on Information Systems*.
Gao, H., Barbier, G., & Goolsby, R. (2011). Harnessing the crowdsourcing power of social media for disaster relief. *IEEE Intelligent Systems*, *26*(3), 10–14. https://doi.org/10.1109/MIS.2011.52
Georgiadou, Y., Lungo, J. H., & Richter, C. (2014). Citizen sensors or extreme publics? Transparency and accountability interventions on the mobile geoweb. *International Journal of Digital Earth*, *7*(7), 516–533. https://doi.org/10.1080/17538947.2013.782073

Goel, A. (2021). Jan Dhan- Aadhaar- mobile trinity: Issues and prospects. *MUDRA: Journal of Finance and Accounting, 8*(1), 120–137. https://doi.org/10.17492/jpi.mudra.v8i1.812107

Gopichandran, V., Ganeshkumar, P., Dash, S., & Ramasamy, A. (2020). Ethical challenges of digital health technologies: *Aadhaar*, India. *Bulletin of the World Health Organization, 98*(4), 277–281. https://doi.org/10.2471/BLT.19.237123

Gupta, R., Priya, M. P., Dash, N., Singh, A., Das, L., Arora, A., Sahu, P., Vashisht, K. R., Eragam, A., Singh, P., Singh, K., Agarwal, A., & Saikia, B. (2025). Evolution of India's National teleconsultation platform e-Sanjeevani: A comparative analysis of versions 2.0 and 1.0, with a preliminary report from the state of Haryana. *Health and Technology, 15*(1), 153–160. https://doi.org/10.1007/s12553-024-00907-x

Gupta, S., Janicki, S., Casula, P., & Parvin, N. (2022). Rethinking Safe Mobility: The Case of Safetipin in India. *International Conference on Information & Communication Technologies and Development 2022,* 1–6. https://doi.org/10.1145/3572334.3572392

Helberger, N., Araujo, T., & de Vreese, C. H. (2020). Who is the fairest of them all? Public attitudes and expectations regarding automated decision-making. *Computer Law & Security Review, 39*, 105456. https://doi.org/10.1016/j.clsr.2020.105456

Hendricks, K., Tsibolane, P., & Van Belle, J.-P. (2020). Cyber-harassment victimization among South African LGBTQIA+ Youth. In M. Hattingh, M. Matthee, H. Smuts, I. Pappas, Y. K. Dwivedi, & M. Mäntymäki (Eds.), *Responsible Design, Implementation and Use of Information and Communication Technology* (Vol. 12067, pp. 135–146). Springer International Publishing. https://doi.org/10.1007/978-3-030-45002-1_12

Hirata, E., Giannotti, M. A., Larocca, A. P. C., & Quintanilha, J. A. (2018). Flooding and inundation collaborative mapping – use of the Crowdmap/Ushahidi platform in the city of Sao Paulo, Brazil. *Journal of Flood Risk Management, 11*(S1). https://doi.org/10.1111/jfr3.12181

Hoetzlein, R. C. (2012). Visual communication in times of crisis: The Fukushima Nuclear Accident. *Leonardo, 45*(2), 113–118. https://doi.org/10.1162/LEON_a_00276

Hofeditz, L., Clausen, S., Rieß, A., Mirbabaie, M., & Stieglitz, S. (2022). Applying XAI to an AI-based system for candidate management to mitigate bias and discrimination in hiring. *Electronic Markets, 32*(4), 2207–2233. https://doi.org/10.1007/s12525-022-00600-9

Ibrahim, S., Marcella, R., & MacLennan, A. (2025). Investigating intersectionality and its influence on information behaviours of women and immigrant digital entrepreneurs in Nigeria: Overcoming social inequalities through information strategies. *Journal of Librarianship and Information Science,* 09610006251329031. https://doi.org/10.1177/09610006251329031

Indonesia Business Post. (2024, October 18). *Kasikornbank targets THB200 billion in green financing by 2030.* https://indonesiabusinesspost.com/2951/Politics/kasikornbank-targets-thb200-billion-in-green-financing-by-2030

International Monetary Fund. (2021). *The Global Informal Workforce.* IInternational Monetary Fund. https://doi.org/10.5089/9781513575919.071

Islam, Q., Brishty, S., & Islam, Q. (2025). *bKash: Revolutionizing Financial Inclusion and Sustainable Development in Bangladesh.* SAGE Publications: SAGE Business Cases Originals. https://doi.org/10.4135/9781071959978

Jain, S., Arora, S., Chauhan, A., Agarwal, A., Saikia, B., & Singh, M. (2024). Super-specialty medical teleconsultations to remote areas of Ladakh, India via E-Sanjeevani under hub-and-spoke model: A pilot study. *Telehealth and Medicine Today*, *9*(2). https://doi.org/10.30953/thmt.v9.471

James, J. (2020). The smart feature phone revolution in developing countries: Bringing the internet to the bottom of the pyramid. *The Information Society*, *36*(4), 226–235. https://doi.org/10.1080/01972243.2020.1761497

Kaladharan, S., Dhanya, M., Drisya, R., & Raj, M. B. (2023). Intention to use eSanjeevani-OPD App: An empirical investigation using health belief model. *2023 Advanced Computing and Communication Technologies for High Performance Applications (ACCTHPA)*, 1–6. https://doi.org/10.1109/ACCTHPA57160.2023.10083374

Kasikornbank. (2015). *Bank of Sustainability*. Kasikornbank.

Kasikornbank. (2018). *KASIKORNBANK Sustainability Bond Framework*. Kasikornbank. https://www.kasikornbank.com/en/sustainable-development/sustainability-bond/SustainableBondFramework/KBank%20Sustainability%20Bond%20SPO%20Update%20Final.pdf

Kasikornbank. (2021, December 16). *KBank with 2 partners in extending loan to Green Yellow (Thailand)*. Kasikornbank. https://www.kasikornbank.com/en/news/pages/syndication-loan-green-yellow.aspx

Kasikornbank. (2025). *Investor Presentation as of 4Q24*.

Kawamoto, C. T., Spers, R. G., Fleury, A. L., Feldmann, P. R., & Yoshida, N. D. (2023). Determinants of success of mobile payments as innovations: An exploratory study based on the extant literature, the M-Pesa, Alipay, and Nubank cases, and the opinion of experts. *Future Business Journal*, *9*(1), 93. https://doi.org/10.1186/s43093-023-00272-7

Khairnar, S. (2022, July 13). Mojaloop: The open source software powering payments for the unbanked. *Fintech Futures*. https://www.fintechfutures.com/baas/mojaloop-the-open-source-software-powering-payments-for-the-unbanked

King, B. (2014). *Breaking banks: The innovators, rogues, and strategists rebooting banking*. Wiley. https://doi.org/10.1002/9781118958247

Kondra, S., Medapati, S., Koripalli, M., Chandra Nandula, S. R. S., & Zink, J. (2025). AI and Diversity, Equity, and Inclusion (DEI): Examining the potential for AI to mitigate bias and promote inclusive communication. *Journal of Artificial Intelligence and Machine Learning*, *3*(1). https://doi.org/10.55124/jaim.v3i1.249

Kordzadeh, N., & Ghasemaghaei, M. (2022). Algorithmic bias: Review, synthesis, and future research directions. *European Journal of Information Systems*, *31*(3), 388–409. https://doi.org/10.1080/0960085X.2021.1927212

Le, T. (2022). Crowdsourcing women's experiences of space: Empowerment, (in)visibility, and exclusions – A critical reading of safetipin map. *Platform: Journal of Media and Communication*, 43–55. https://doi.org/10.46580/p62073

Lillevik, W. (2025). Digital leadership and diversity, equity and inclusion. In J. M. Munoz (Ed.), *Digital Leadership* (pp. 129–142). Edward Elgar Publishing. https://doi.org/10.4337/9781035321247.00016

Line. (2020). *Introducing LINE BK, Thailand's First 'Social Banking' Platform*. Line. https://linecorp.com/en/pr/news/global/2020/65

Line BK. (2023, July 19). *LINE BK Reports Strong Growth in First Half of 2023 Company Sets Sights on Provincial Market Expansion and Insurance Broker Market Entry in*

Q3. www.linebk.com/en/news/detail/line-bk-reports-strong-growth-in-first-half-of-2023-company-sets-sights-on-provincial-market-expansion-and-insurance-broker-market-entry-in-q3/

Loukos, P., & Arathoon, L. (2024). *Landscaping the agritech ecosystem for smallholder farmers in Latin America and the Caribbean*. Inter-American Development Bank IDB Lab.

Macdonell, C. (2015). Ushahidi: A crisis mapping system. *ACM SIGCAS Computers and Society*, *45*(2), 38–38. https://doi.org/10.1145/2809957.2809969

Mahmud, J. (2024). Digital payments and economic growth: Analyzing the contribution of bKash to Bangladesh's GDP. *International Journal of Research and Innovation in Applied Science*, *IX*(II), 55–63. https://doi.org/10.51584/IJRIAS.2024.90207

Manazir, S. H., Govind, M., & R, R. (2019). My Safetipin mobile phone application: Case study of E-participation platform for women safety in India. *Journal of Scientometric Research*, *8*(1), 47–53. https://doi.org/10.5530/jscires.8.1.7

Manzoor, M., & Vimarlund, V. (2018). Digital technologies for social inclusion of individuals with disabilities. *Health and Technology*, *8*(5), 377–390. https://doi.org/10.1007/s12553-018-0239-1

Marabelli, M., Zaza, S., Masiero, S., Li, J. (Lydia), & Chudoba, K. (2023). Diversity, Equity and Inclusion in the AIS: Challenges and opportunities of remote conferences. *Information Systems Journal*, *33*(6), 1370–1395. https://doi.org/10.1111/isj.12458

Margetis, G., Ntoa, S., Antona, M., & Stephanidis, C. (2021). Human-centered design of artificial intelligence. In G. Salvendy & W. Karwowski (Eds.), *HANDBOOK OF HUMAN FACTORS AND ERGONOMICS* (1st ed., pp. 1085–1106). Wiley. https://doi.org/10.1002/9781119636113.ch42

Marsden, J. (2013). Stigmergic self-organization and the improvisation of Ushahidi. *Cognitive Systems Research*, *21*, 52–64. https://doi.org/10.1016/j.cogsys.2012.06.005

Martin, K. (2022). *Ethics of Data and Analytics: Concepts and Cases* (1st ed.). Auerbach Publications. https://doi.org/10.1201/9781003278290

McClung, K. T., & Linton, D. M. (2024). *An Introduction to Inclusive Healthcare Design* (1st ed.). Routledge. https://doi.org/10.4324/9781003414902

Mukherjee, R. (2019). Jio sparks Disruption 2.0: Infrastructural imaginaries and platform ecosystems in 'Digital India.' *Media, Culture & Society*, *41*(2), 175–195. https://doi.org/10.1177/0163443718818383

Murthy, S. L., Shemie, D., & Bichai, F. (2018). The role of adaptation in mobile technology innovation for the water, sanitation and hygiene sector. *Water Practice and Technology*, *13*(1), 143–156. https://doi.org/10.2166/wpt.2018.002

Nandhakumar, J. (2023, September 6). How bKash became king: Three steps to balance purpose with profit. *Finance and Market WBS*.

Nawrocki, T. (2024, September 13). Interledger steps up to foster cross-border payments in 130 countries. *Payments Journal*. https://www.paymentsjournal.com/interledger-steps-up-to-foster-cross-border-payments-in-130-countries/

Nishant, R., Schneckenberg, D., & Ravishankar, M. (2024). The formal rationality of artificial intelligence-based algorithms and the problem of bias. *Journal of Information Technology*, *39*(1), 19–40. https://doi.org/10.1177/02683962231176842

Ntoutsi, E., Fafalios, P., Gadiraju, U., Iosifidis, V., Nejdl, W., Vidal, M., Ruggieri, S., Turini, F., Papadopoulos, S., Krasanakis, E., Kompatsiaris, I., Kinder-Kurlanda, K., Wagner, C., Karimi, F., Fernandez, M., Alani, H., Berendt, B., Kruegel, T., Heinze, C., … Staab, S. (2020). Bias in data-driven artificial intelligence systems—An introductory survey. *WIREs Data Mining and Knowledge Discovery*, *10*(3), e1356. https://doi.org/10.1002/widm.1356

OECD. (2022). *Gender Equality and the Empowerment of Women and Girls:DAC Guidance for Development Partners*. OECD. https://www.oecd.org/en/publications/2022/05/gender-equality-and-the-empowerment-of-women-and-girls_9fbdf09e.html

Olawade, D. B., Bolarinwa, O. A., Adebisi, Y. A., & Shongwe, S. (2025). The role of artificial intelligence in enhancing healthcare for people with disabilities. *Social Science & Medicine*, *364*, 117560. https://doi.org/10.1016/j.socscimed.2024.117560

Omydar Network. (2018, February 13). How can civic technology transform Brazil? *Medium*. https://omidyarnetwork.medium.com/how-can-civic-technology-transform-brazil-392764f92c85

Paisarn, P., & Intarawong, W. (2019). *Strategic Leadership and Employee Engagement: The Antecedent of Performance of Kasikornbank Public Company Limited*. The International Academic Multidisciplines Research Conference.

Pánek, J., Marek, L., Pászto, V., & Valůch, J. (2017). The crisis map of the Czech Republic: The nationwide deployment of an Ushahidi application for disasters. *Disasters*, *41*(4), 649–671. https://doi.org/10.1111/disa.12221

Perdana, A., Arifin, S., & Quadrianto, N. (2025). Algorithmic trust and regulation: Governance, ethics, legal, and social implications blueprint for Indonesia's central banking. *Technology in Society*, *81*, 102838. https://doi.org/10.1016/j.techsoc.2025.102838

Pires, T. (2024, February 24). Dispute between apps and delivery workers to be ruled by the Supreme Court; decision will have an impact on the job market. *BrasildeFato*. https://www.brasildefato.com.br/2024/02/12/dispute-between-apps-and-delivery-workers-to-be-ruled-by-the-supreme-court-decision-will-have-an-impact-on-the-job-market/

Quintero, R. V. B., & Quintero, F. B. (2023). Fintech and consumer expectations: A global perspective. In G. Giannattasio, E. Kongar, M. Dabić, C. Desmond, M. Condry, S. Koushik, & R. Saracco (Eds.), *IEEE Technology and Engineering Management Society Body of Knowledge (TEMSBOK)* (1st ed., pp. 21–52). Wiley. https://doi.org/10.1002/9781119987635.ch2

Rahimi, S. A., Shrivastava, R., Brown-Johnson, A., Caidor, P., Davies, C., Idrissi Janati, A., Kengne Talla, P., Madathil, S., Willie, B. M., & Emami, E. (2024). EDAI framework for integrating equity, diversity, and inclusion throughout the lifecycle of AI to improve health and oral health care: Qualitative study. *Journal of Medical Internet Research*, *26*, e63356. https://doi.org/10.2196/63356

Raj, A., Valsala, P., & Unnikrishanan, R. (2024). Technological and sociocultural barriers to e-sanjeevani as a parallel means of health care: A narrative review. *2024 5th International Conference on Innovative Trends in Information Technology (ICITIIT)*, 1–4. https://doi.org/10.1109/ICITIIT61487.2024.10580209

Raju, R. S., Singh, S., & Khatter, K. (2017). *Aadhaar Card: Challenges and Impact on Digital Transformation* (Version 1). arXiv. https://doi.org/10.48550/ARXIV.1708.05117

Rodrigues, R. (2020). Legal and human rights issues of AI: Gaps, challenges and vulnerabilities. *Journal of Responsible Technology, 4,* 100005. https://doi.org/10.1016/j.jrt.2020.100005

Safetipin. (2018). *Delhi: A Safety Assessment*. Safetipin. https://safetipin.com/wp-content/uploads/2016/01/delhi_a_safety_assessment_2016.pdf

Salim, A., & Wangusi, N. (2014). Mobile phone technology: An effective tool to fight corruption in Kenya. *Proceedings of the 15th Annual International Conference on Digital Government Research,* 300–305. https://doi.org/10.1145/2612733.2612772

Shaban, A. (2024). Digitalization and exclusion—Digital divides and development. In A. Shaban (Ed.), *Digital Geographies—Theory, Space, and Communities* (pp. 255–496). Springer Nature Singapore. https://doi.org/10.1007/978-981-97-4734-4_4

Singh, P. (2021). Aadhaar and data privacy: Biometric identification and anxieties of recognition in India. *Information, Communication & Society, 24*(7), 978–993. https://doi.org/10.1080/1369118X.2019.1668459

Strano, S. (2020, July 1). Bumpy Ride: Why Brazil's Delivery Workers Are Fed Up. *Americas Quarterly.* https://www.americasquarterly.org/article/bumpy-ride-why-brazils-delivery-workers-are-fed-up/

Subramaniam, Y., & Masron, T. A. (2025). Digital technologies, poverty and microfinance in developing countries. *Journal of Strategy and Management, 18*(1), 110–122. https://doi.org/10.1108/JSMA-06-2023-0134

Suhas, S., Kumar, C., Math, S., & Manjunatha, N. (2022). E-sanjeevani: A pathbreaking telemedicine initiative from India. *Journal of Psychiatry Spectrum, 1*(2), 111. https://doi.org/10.4103/jopsys.jopsys_8_21

Sullivan, M. (2025, April 9). "Be My Eyes" app connects blind users with volunteers to help with visual tasks. *CBS News.* https://www.cbsnews.com/boston/news/cape-cod-be-my-eyes-hot-rod-racing/

Tariq, M. U. (2024). Innovative strategies for enhancing SME competitiveness in emerging economies. In R. Perez-Uribe, D. Ocampo-Guzman, & L. J. Lozano-Correa (Eds.), *Advances in Business Strategy and Competitive Advantage* (pp. 151–172). IGI Global. https://doi.org/10.4018/979-8-3693-4046-2.ch007

United Nations. (2023). *Promoting Local Innovation for Inclusion of People in Vulnerable Situations and Leaving No One Behind*. United Nations.

Van Den Broek, E., Sergeeva, A., Universiteit Amsterdam, Huysman Vrije, M., & Universiteit Amsterdam. (2021). When the machine meets the expert: An ethnography of developing AI for hiring. *MIS Quarterly, 45*(3), 1557–1580. https://doi.org/10.25300/MISQ/2021/16559

Viswanath, K., & Basu, A. (2015). SafetiPin: An innovative mobile app to collect data on women's safety in Indian cities. *Gender & Development, 23*(1), 45–60. https://doi.org/10.1080/13552074.2015.1013669

Wadali, J. S., Sood, S. P., Kaushish, R., Syed-Abdul, S., Khosla, P. K., & Bhatia, M. (2020). Evaluation of free, open-source, web-based DICOM viewers for the Indian National Telemedicine Service (eSanjeevani). *Journal of Digital Imaging, 33*(6), 1499–1513. https://doi.org/10.1007/s10278-020-00368-4

Xiong, Y., & Kim, J. K. (2025). Who wants to be hired by AI? How message frames and AI transparency impact individuals' attitudes and behaviors toward companies using AI in hiring. *Computers in Human Behavior: Artificial Humans, 3,* 100120. https://doi.org/10.1016/j.chbah.2025.100120

Yohanna Sánchez, D., Maldonado, O. J., Agudelo-Londoño, S., Hernández, M., Hernández, L. J., Suárez-Morales, Z. B., Mantilla, L., & PLADDS team. (2024). Infrastructuring platform delivery work: Exclusions, coercions and resistance in delivery platforms' migrant work in Bogotá, Colombia. *Tapuya: Latin American Science, Technology and Society*, *7*(1), 2343161. https://doi.org/10.1080/25729861.2024.2343161

11

Corporate Contribution to SDGs: A Focus on Diversity, Equity, Inclusion and Environment Stewardship

Shaji Joseph and Vijayakumar Bharathi S.

11.1 Introduction

At a time when global challenges increasingly define business decisions, organisations must align their goals and strategies with social and environmental responsibilities. This research paper aims to understand how large business organisations incorporate their sustainability practices to align with the United Nations Sustainable Development Goals (SDGs). This paper examines the sustainable strategies, practices and innovations of business organisations to meet the SDGs especially that relate to DEI (Diversity, Equity and Inclusivity) and, at the same time, maintain a competitive advantage in a rapidly evolving global market. In 2013, the government of India enacted and made Corporate Social Responsibility (CSR) contributions mandatory for business organisations in an effort to expand the governments welfare programs (Bihari & Shajahan, 2023). The amendments had brought in factors such as gender equality, workplace diversity, social inclusion and accessibility. With the Sustainable Development Goals (SDG) introduction in 2015, governments and international bodies are looking for greater transparency and accountability from business organisations towards their DEI commitments (Bhimavarapu et al., 2022.

At the Historic UN summit in September 2015, the UN adopted the 17 SDGs. These goals incorporate values of social development, economic growth, and environmental sustainability (Hák et al., 2016). The target year for achieving these goals is set for 2030. Each nation must undertake a national framework for achieving the SDGs (Ranalder, 2024). Given the enormity of their size and the influence they hold, business organizations have a critical role in achieving SDG goals (Joseph & Kulkarni, 2020). Today, all the listed companies in India are mandated to report their sustainability practices with a

DOI: 10.1201/9781003591078-14

reasonable assurance (Mahajan, 2022). Companies must align their activities to SDGs as each government prepares for the 2030 target (Beisheim, 2023). A major part of the SDG achievement is related to ensuring DEI commitments in the organisations. Globally the #MeToo, BLM (Black lives matter) and LGBTQIA+ rights saw its reverberations in the corporate strategies. In India, inclusion of caste-based hiring or exclusive hiring form rural areas became a trend among some companies to ensure DEI factors.

Technology plays a crucial role in ensuring DEI. Kyoto Protocol first discussed technological transfer for sustainability (Dionisio et al., 2024). In response, several Indian companies have introduced digital technologies for social and environmental sustainability. For example, ITC's e-choupal helps farmers connect with the market, and the JioKrishi of Reliance Industries created a data-driven farmer ecosystem by facilitating soil condition analysis, irrigation needs assessment, education and training, and expert consultation. This and such initiatives are a major step towards including the rural and marginalised society to the mainstream economy.

Business organisations have been at the forefront of leveraging digital technologies to help people across the globe reduce poverty, inequality, and environmental degradation (Hong et al., 2024). Integrating digital technologies fosters innovation, competitiveness, and the creation of sustainable and equitable solutions, contributing to the overall progress towards the UN's 2030 Agenda for Sustainable Development (Kaur et al., 2023).

The current study provides a benchmark for other companies planning to implement SDG activities. It highlights the diverse activities of companies, indicating the SDGs where business organizations are putting their money and areas where there is a need for more involvement. It also focuses on the sustainable technologies companies invest in, providing insights into how corporations integrate SDG goals and targets into their strategies, operations, and reporting structures. The alignment of corporate social responsibility practices with the SDGs fosters innovation and competitiveness, contributing to a sustainable and equitable future (Berrone et al., 2023).

Overall, the study provides critical insights into how corporations integrate SDG goals and targets into their strategies, operations, and reporting structures, augmenting investors, statutory and regulatory bodies, and policymakers in evaluating the impact and effectiveness of corporate sustainability initiatives in addressing persistent societal and environmental challenges. This paper categorizes the technologies reported in their annual sustainability reports into social, environmental, profit, and governance topics. This comprehensive approach provides a detailed understanding of how businesses leverage digital technologies to drive sustainable development and achieve their SDG goals.

Based on the context set in the previous paragraphs, this research aims to

- *Identify and categorize the diverse activities that companies report as SDG-related initiatives,* providing a benchmark for other organizations planning to implement SDG activities and
- *Explore the digital technologies companies' role in supporting* their SDG integration efforts.

11.2 Literature Review

Sustainability reporting has gained widespread acceptance among business organizations and governments, serving as a valuable tool for stakeholders to strategise and collaborate (Friske et al., 2023; Mugoni et al., 2024). The Sustainable Development Goals (SDGs) have become a crucial framework for companies to communicate their Diversity, Equity, and inclusivity programs (Raman et al., 2023; Lafont-Torio et al., 2024). In recent years, there has been a significant increase in companies voluntarily publishing their sustainability practices, driven in part by the growing importance of SDG-2030. This trend has created a sense of compulsion for organizations to publish their reports, highlighting the need for a comprehensive approach to sustainability reporting (Friske et al., 2023).

The subsequent paragraphs will review the relevant literature to identify the gaps in understanding how businesses adopt and implement the SDG framework.

11.2.1 DEI and Sustainability Reporting by Companies

A recent study by Arun and Charumathi (2024) explored 12 different topics that are included to promote DEI. They include sexual harassment policies, inclusion of marginalised communities, talent, and leadership development, employee well-being through community development, sustainable workplace, gender diversity, employees' associations for gender equity and equal rights, cultivating diversity at workplace, ensuring human rights, improving board diversity, higher remuneration of for board members, are some of these factors. Since the publication of Social responsibility of the business mean by Howard Bowen in 1953, CSR has gone through different phases and today DEI is the dominant factors. Today to remain competitive business has to make CSR part of its business strategy (Carroll, 2021). Diversity include factors such as gender, age, education, status, caste, and class. Most studies focus only on gender aspects (Gaur 2025). Sreedhar and Nayak (2024) found in their study that DEI are most evidently found in the area of hiring and retaining employees, engaging and supporting employee relationships, creating culturally relevant programs and policies, and change strategies.

11.2.2 Business Organisation's Response to Sustainable Development Goals

With the introduction of SDGs in 2015, business organizations are forced to focus on corporate social responsibility (CSR) to create business excellence through sustainability practices (Bennich et al., 2020; Giri & Chaparro, 2023). A meta-analysis on CSR and DEI investment in healthcare observed that while much attention is paid to the medical aspects of SDG 3, very little investment is made in financing healthcare programs (Kuzey et al., 2021). Some of the gaps identified are the lack of policy innovation, integrated monitoring, and evaluation (Bennich et al., 2020; Makarenko et al., 2021), lack of funding and research collaboration (Sweileh (2020), lack of attention paid to non-financial reporting and the lack of education on SDGs (Pizzi et al. (2020), and a general lack of academic interest (Siti & Rusnah, 2020). Most sustainability research is conducted bottom-up, while the top-down approach is ignored. This results in a large-scale ignoring of how the business organizations respond to DEI commitments. Politically, the DEI have generated tremendous interest among leaders. However, they largely remain at a discursive level and seldom get reflected in creating rules and institutions that can create long-term change in society (Biermann et al., 2022). Gender and sexuality, along with health, are areas where researchers have been focusing their attention (Majeedullah et al., 2016). Pizzi et al. (2021) studied the SDG performance readiness of Italian firms and focused on the governance framework that enables reporting of non-financial performance. Datta and Goyal (2022) researched the state of reporting in different nations and identified firm-level, national, and global-level determinants of SDG reporting by business firms. Erin et al. (2022) studied the factors that prevent business organisations from engaging in SDG activities. Emma and Jennifer (2021) looked at companies' reports and asked whether the companies are interested in SDGs or engage in sustainable practices that bring profit. However, very few studies focus on companies' sustainability reporting that map to the SDGs in different sectors, to which this paper contributes.

11.2.3 The Pervasive Nature of Sustainable Technologies

Sustainable technologies have emerged as pervasive forces shaping the contemporary landscape, infiltrating diverse sectors and redefining how we approach development (Cecere et al., 2014). From renewable energy sources like solar and wind power to advanced waste management systems and eco-friendly transportation solutions, the influence of sustainable technologies extends far beyond mere environmental considerations (Krishnamurthy et al., 2017). Its pervasive nature is evident in its transformative impact on industries, emphasising integrating socially responsible practices and ecological stewardship (Duan et al., 2024; Balashova & Maiorova, 2021). In the digital realm, sustainable technologies foster sustainable development goals (SDGs) (Asopa et al., 2021). As societies worldwide increasingly recognize the urgent need for sustainable practices, these technologies have become integral across sectors, driving innovation and reshaping the global economic landscape towards a more environmentally conscious and socially responsible future (Kulkarni et al., 2024). Prakash et al. (2024) studied how organisations are using technologies to extend DEI as part of their CSR activities. The use of AI by many companies have improved diversity and reduced biases in recruiting and retention of employees (Kondra et al., 2025).

11.2.4 Alignment of Corporate Practices with the SDGs

The sustainable development goals reported by different companies and sectors vary greatly (Van Zanten & van Tulder, 2021). While a manufacturing company focuses on zero hunger, clean water and sanitation, responsible consumption and production, an information technology company may focus on quality education, gender equality, and industry innovation and infrastructure (Joseph & Kulkarni, 2020). A third set of companies may focus on affordable, clean energy and climate action. The focus of companies differs from industry to industry. Several factors influence this decision, ranging from the values of the founders/leaders of the company, the focus the particular government has, the pressure from investors, and the need to create a brand identity (Hatayama, 2022). While a pharma company might focus on good health and well-being, a manufacturing company might focus on infrastructure, urban planning and similar goals.

11.3 Methodology

The research collected secondary data from the sustainability reports of 40 companies operating in India from five different sectors (Automobiles (AM), six in infrastructure (INF), ten in information technology (IT), seven in pharmaceuticals (PHR), and six in petrochemicals (PCH)). A similar study has been conducted by Sadiq et al. (2023). We mapped the SDG activities of these companies to 15 of the 17 SDGs. We did not include the last two goals are more for the nation states (Figure 11.1). At the initial stage, we elicited data from the voluminous reports on SDG-specific activities and sustainable technological innovation published by listed companies. The researchers then categorized the data under people, profit, and planet. In the next level, we coded this data with the help of NVIVO-12.

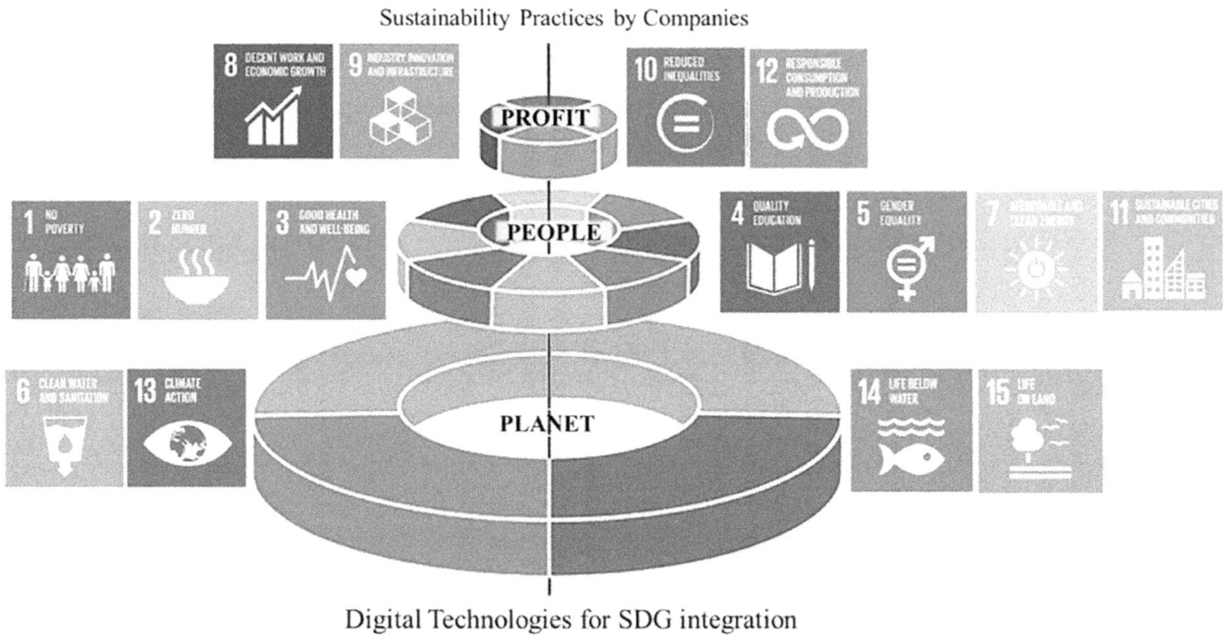

FIGURE 11.1
Thematic representation of SDGs and the study objectives (adapted from https://commons.wikimedia.org/wiki/File:SDG_wedding_cake.jpg).

The researchers do not claim 100% data accuracy as it is based on companies' self-prepared reports. The researchers followed a two-level authentication to ensure that the categories under which data is collected are correct. At the first level, the research assistants read through the voluminous reports of the companies, picked out SDG activities, and categorized them according to the four criteria identified. It was further validated by two academic experts who reviewed the reports. It is generally assumed that the reports of these companies in the public domain have a reasonable assurance certificate; hence, the researchers assumed that the data they accessed was genuine. The research process is provided in Figure 11.2.

11.4 Analysis and Findings

This section comprises two broad topics. The first topic, presented in sub-section 4.1, examines and groups the varied actions that businesses describe as SDG-linked efforts, offering a reference point for other entities aiming to engage in SDG-related work (this topic addresses the first objective of our study.). In sub-section 11.4.2, we explore how digital technologies that companies invest in contribute to their efforts in integrating the SDGs (this topic addresses the second objective of the study)

11.4.1 Alignment of Company Sustainable Practices to SDGs

We mapped the SDG activities of companies to 15 of the 17 SDGs, excluding SDG 16 and SDG 17, due to their more strategic and global nature and the lack of activities reported by the companies. We identified over 543 activities from the 40 companies surveyed (see Appendices 11.1 and 11.2). While some companies reported activities across all 15 SDGs, others focused on a few selected SDGs. Figure 11.3 presents the consolidated data by the number of activities of the companies across SDGs that include Diversity, Equity and Inclusivity programs.

In a bird's eye view, Figure 11.3 shows that the automobile sector activities are centred around SDGs 3, 6, 7, 10, 12, and 13 (good health, clean water, affordable and clean energy, reduced inequalities, responsible consumption and production and climate action). Activities reported by infrastructure companies focus on SDGs 3, 6, 8, 9, and 13 (good health, clean water, decent work, industry innovation, and climate action). IT company's activities are widespread around SDGs 3, 4, 5, 6, 8, 9, 10, 13, and 15 (good health, quality education, gender equality, clean water and sanitation, decent work and economic growth, industry innovation and infrastructure, reduced inequalities, climate action and life on land). Pharmaceutical company's activities

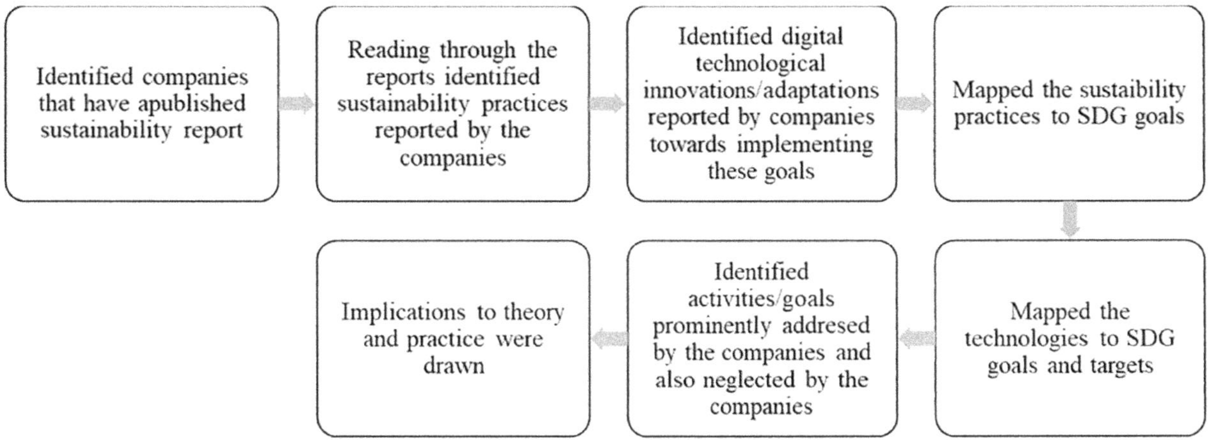

FIGURE 11.2
The flow chart depicting the research process.

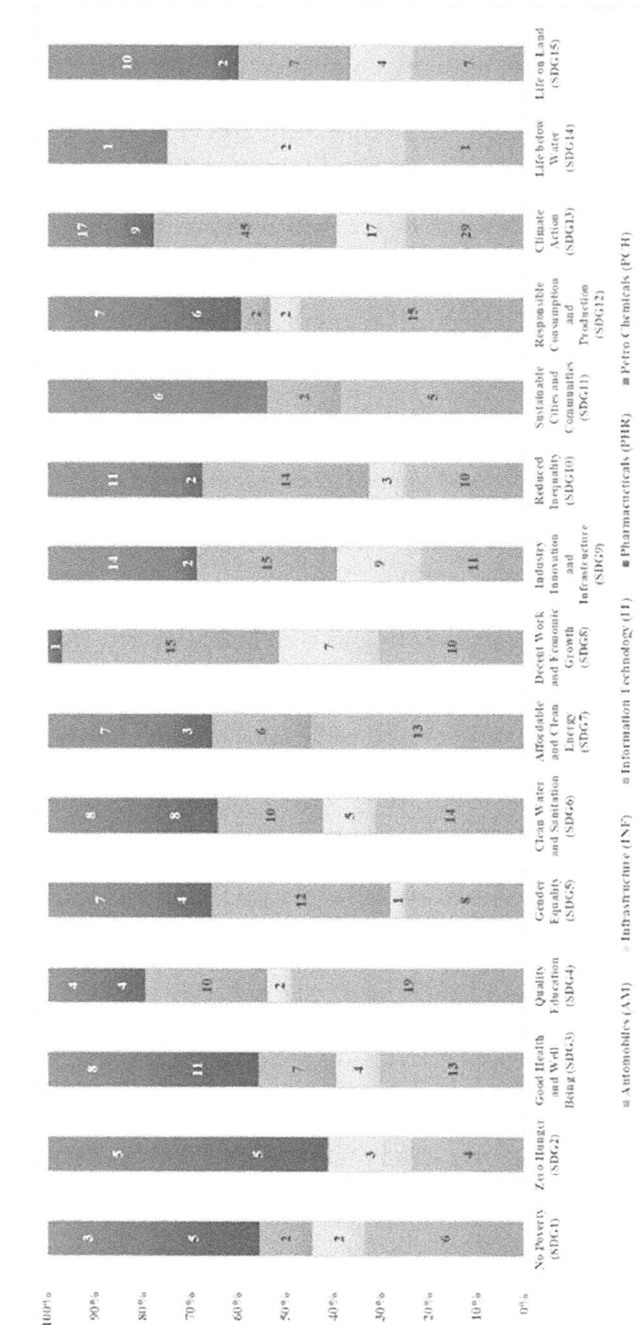

FIGURE 11.3
Number of SDG activities across the select Industry sectors.

are limited to SDGs 3, 6, and 13 (good health and wellbeing, clean water and sanitation and climate action). In contrast, petrochemical companies' activities are set on SDGs 3, 6, 9, 10, and 13 (good health and wellbeing, clean water and sanitation, industry innovation and infrastructure, reduced inequalities and climate action). In all these activities, the focus is to improve gender positions, reduce rural–urban disparity, and include everyone in the process of development, thereby organisations are aiming to extend the DEI principles through SDG reporting.

We also observed that companies across the different sectors favour specific goals over others. For example, most companies report good health (SDG3), quality education (SDG4), climate action (SDG13), and gender equality (SDG5). In the subsequent paragraphs, we report all five sectors studied through analysis of the reports of all five sectors studied with the help of charts.

For the automobile sector (Figure 11.4), SDGs 1, 2, 11, 14, and 15 (no poverty, zero hunger, sustainable cities and communities, life below water, and life on land) are the least prioritised goals. However, many companies reported activities related to SDGs 3, 4, 5, 6, 7, and 13 (good health and well-being, quality education, gender equality, clean water and sanitation, affordable and clean energy, and climate action).

In the infrastructure sector (Figure 11.5), almost all companies reported on SDGs 3, 8, 9, and 13 (good health and well-being, decent work and economic growth, industry innovation and infrastructure, and climate action). However, goals 1, 2, 4, 10, 12, 14, and 15 (no poverty, zero hunger, quality education, reduced inequalities, responsible consumption, life below water, and life on land) saw limited contributions.

For the IT sector (Figure 11.6), we studied 10 companies. Most reported on SDG 13, with other prominently reported goals being SDGs 3, 4, 5, 6, 8, 9, and 10 (good health and well-being, quality education, gender equality, clean water and sanitation, decent work and economic growth, industry innovation, and reduced inequalities). Very few activities were reported under SDGs 1, 7, 11, and 15 (no poverty, affordable and clean energy, sustainable cities and communities, and life on land). SDGs 2 (zero hunger) and 14 (life below water) were not reported by any IT companies surveyed.

Figure 11.7 presents the SDG activities of pharmaceutical companies. None of the seven companies surveyed reported activities under SDG 11 (sustainable cities and communities). The most popular SDGs for this sector are SDGs 1, 3, 6, and 13 (no poverty, good health and well-being, clean water and sanitation, and climate action).

Figure 11.8 shows six petrochemical companies. This sector reported activities on all SDGs except SDG 8 (decent work and economic growth). Few companies reported on SDGs 1 and 14 (no poverty and life below water). Most companies in this sector reported activities under SDGs 5, 6, 9, 13, and 15 (gender equality, clean water and sanitation, industry innovation and infrastructure, climate action, and life on land).

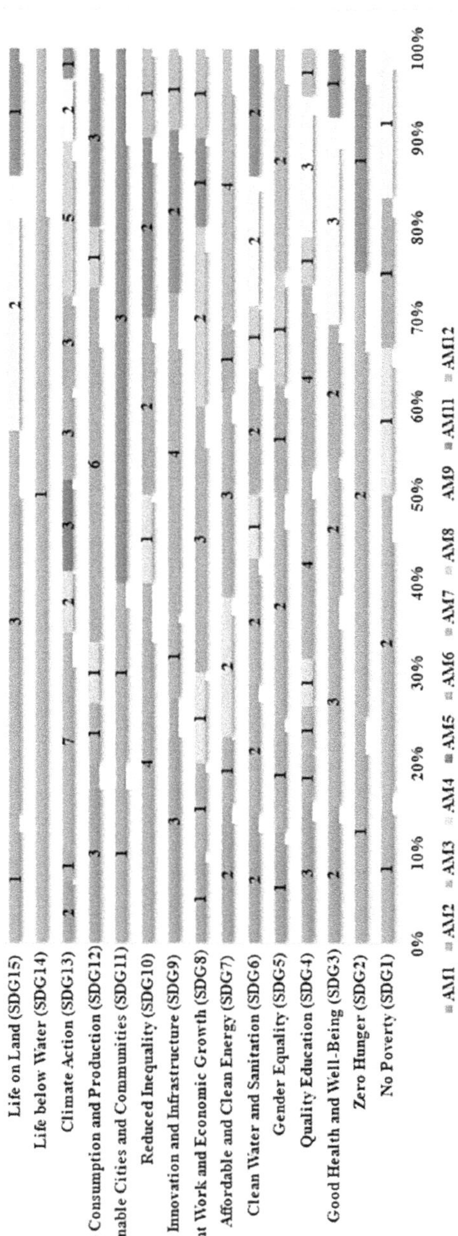

FIGURE 11.4
Number of activities mapped to SDG for the automobile sector.

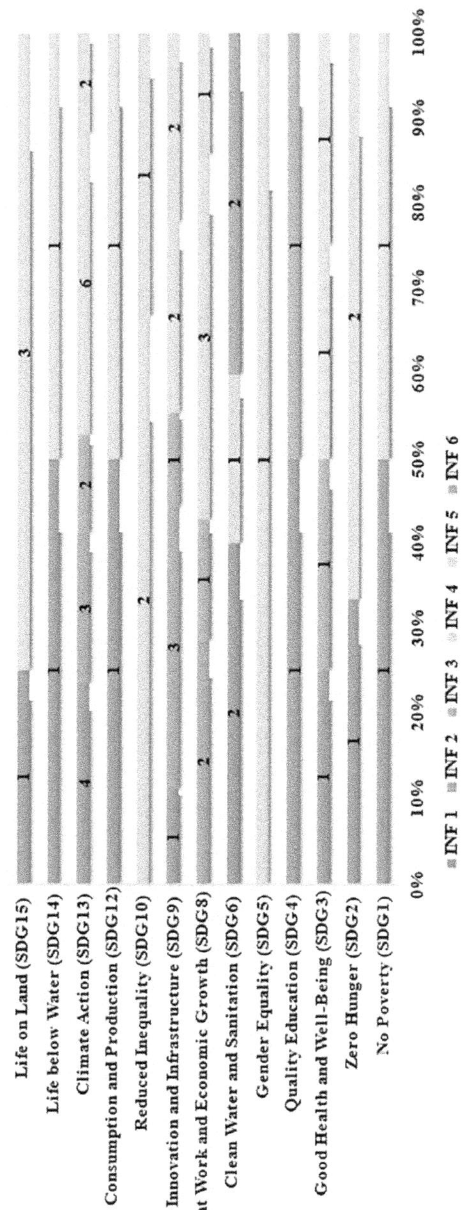

FIGURE 11.5
Number of activities mapped to SDG for the infrastructure sector.

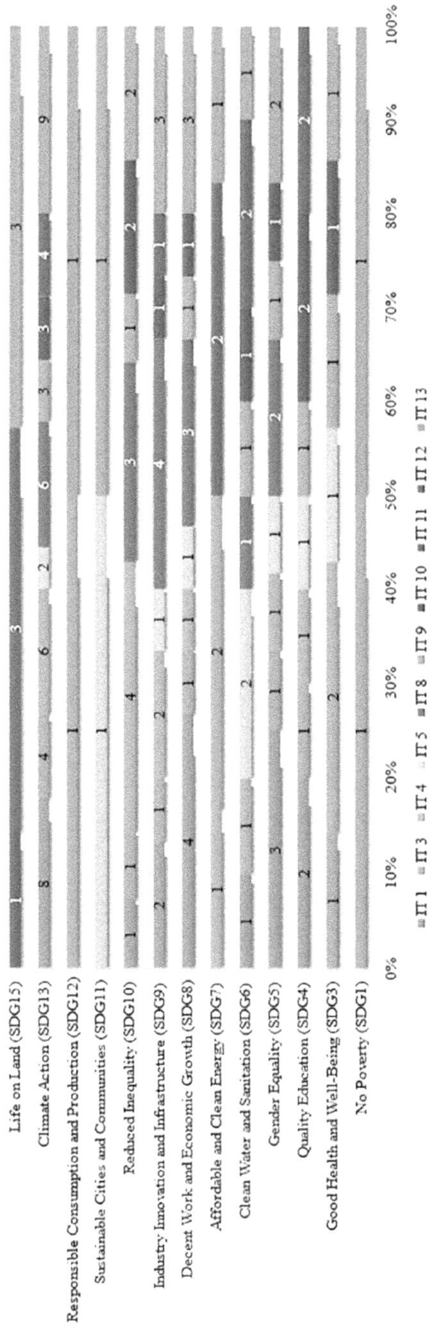

FIGURE 11.6
Number of activities mapped to SDGs for IT sector.

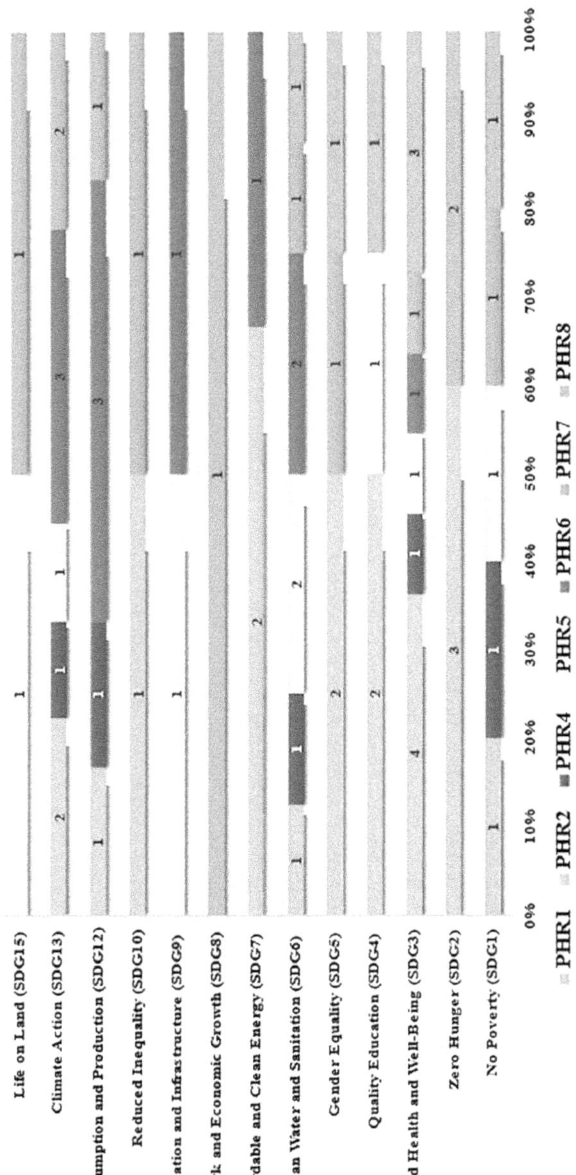

FIGURE 11.7
Number of activities mapped to mapped to SDGs for the pharma sector.

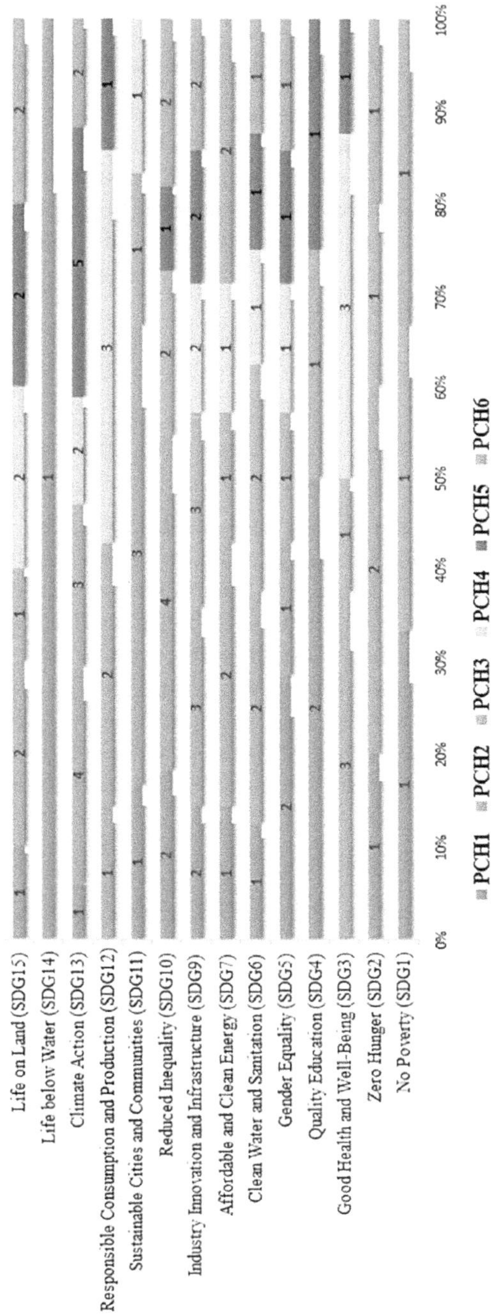

FIGURE 11.8
Number of activities mapped to SDGs for the petrochemical sector.

Based on the number of activities sectoraly mapped with the SDG, in Table 11.1, we list the various activities.

11.4.2 Digital Technologies Aiding in Integrating the SDGs

We analysed the digital technologies used by these 40 companies in order to extend their sustainability practices. We identified 200 instances of digital technology these companies use from a people, planet and profit perspective in their sustainability journey. Digital technology is used at every level whether it is an application that connects people to the market or a high-end AI tool that detects the pH factor in the soil or measures the carbon dioxide inside the workspace (Tables 11.2 and 11.3).

11.5 Discussion

The alignment of Corporate Social Responsibility (CSR) and DEI activities with the United Nations SDGs is crucial to achieving sustainable and inclusive development. This alignment fosters innovation, competitiveness, and collaboration between businesses, governments, non-governmental organisations, and communities. It ensures that their contributions to society are consistent with global development priorities, enhancing their reputation and credibility. Additionally, this alignment helps companies identify and address social, economic, and environmental challenges more effectively, reducing their negative impact on the environment and society.

11.5.1 Implications to Policymakers

Policymakers play a vital role in aligning DEI activities with SDGs. They can create an enabling environment for companies to adopt sustainable practices. For instance, the Indian government has incorporated the SDGs into its development agenda, making them a guiding framework for policy formulation. The alignment of DEI activities with SDGs is particularly significant in the Indian context, where economic growth and social development take priority. By embracing the SDGs as a guiding framework, companies can integrate social, economic, and environmental considerations into their DEI strategies. This alignment also underscores the need for more significant association between the corporate and the global community in pursuit of the SDGs, ultimately fostering a more sustainable and equitable future for the world.

TABLE 11.1

Details of the sustainable practices reported by the companies

SDG	Company ID	Description of the initiatives
SDG 1 No Poverty	*AM (2, 3, 4, 7, 9) INF (1, 4); IT (3, 13); PHR (1, 4, 5, 7, 8); PCH (1, 3, 6)*	a) Project Jeevika for skilling young girls and women to help them out of the poverty cycle, b) Self-help groups for women entrepreneurship development, c) Providing impact training for disadvantaged youth, d) Creating zero-carbon villages to increase the rural income, and e) provided shelters for migrant workers, especially during the COVID-19 lockdown period, and raise fund under the employee giving program. Programs aim to include everyone in the process of development and achieve inclusivity
SDG 2 Zero Hunger	*AM (2, 3, 11) INF (1, 5); PHR (1, 8); PCH (1, 3, 6)*	a) Providing mid-day meals through schools, b) Planting fruit trees to make unlimited fruits to the poor communities, c) Seminars on food loss reduction, d) Rationing to the rural areas, e) helping the poor to avail government schemes such as Atal Aadhaar Yojana and other local municipal schemes, f) Connecting needy people with food suppliers through a mobile application built by the company, g) Helping farmers to increase productivity through the help of 5G technology and adopt suitable agricultural practices, and h) Monitoring the food production process through drones. Most companies had some or other activities to report under this goal. Programs aim to include everyone in the process of development and achieve inclusivity
SDG 3 Good Health	*AM (1, 2, 6, 7, 9, 11) INF (1,3, 4, 5); IT (3, 4, 5, 9, 10, 13); PHR (1, 4, 5, 6, 7, 8); PCH (2, 3, 4, 5)*	a) Global Safety System (SOS), b) Responsible Mining Assurance, c) Project Arogya, d) Project Khelo, e) Project Shiksha, f) Water recycling plants, g) Online wellness initiative such as Dil Se, h) Providing social security measures for the elderly, i) Engaging employees in sports activities, j) Malnutrition treatment centres, k)LIFE projects to improve the quality of life, l) Providing job specific personal protective Equipment, ensuring daily sanitation and daily health screening programs at labour camps, m) Providing COVID care and isolation wards, n) Organising emotional wellbeing programs such as Thriving mind, o) Mindful Moment sessions, p) MCare, IoT based health monitoring activities, q) Family matters on parenting and building relationships, r) Program for employee wellness and experience, s) Heart care, t) Creating a digital nerve centre for cancer care, and u) Many more. Companies also reported on health initiatives. All the activities have a focus on to include a large number of people under health cover

(Continued)

TABLE 11.1 (Continued)

Details of the sustainable practices reported by the companies

SDG	Company ID	Description of the initiatives
SDG 4 Quality Education	*AM (1, 2, 3, 4, 6, 7, 8, 9, 12) INF (1, 3); IT (1, 3, 4, 5, 9, 10, 11); PHR (1, 5, 8); PCH (1, 2, 5)*	a) Partnering with FIRST-an organisation helping to build future engineers and STEM education, b) ensuring through Project Shiksha that no children in the vicinity of the company go uneducated, c) Project Jeevika to ensure basic training for productive employment. d) Developing a six-semester program to equip children to hone their skills and talents at Hyundai Dream Center. e) Supporting thousands of children through the program Nanhi Kali, Mahindra Pride Classrooms, f) Project Prerna to empower women through agricultural training, g) Training workforce of suppliers and other partners, h) partnering with the government's *Skill India* scheme, i) Building school infrastructure, helping kids chase their dreams (a finishing school program for class XII kids, j) Recognising meritorious students, k) Prepare youth for future though digital and English language education, l) Pledging $100 million for creating learning solutions to kids, m) Encouraging kids to be the change they want to see, n) After school support to school children, o) providing holistic development programs, p) Providing scholarship and mentoring to kids, q) Organising adult literacy programs, r) vocational education, and s) Creating learning excellence centres in the rural areas through projects such as Sahapedia. Education program aim to achieve equity in the society
SDG 5 Gender Equality	*AM (1, 2, 3, 7, 8, 12) INF (4); IT (1, 3, 4, 5, 9, 10, 13); PHR (1, 5, 8); PCH (1, 2, 5)*	a) Identifying high-potential girl children and sponsoring them for higher education; b) Project Jeevika for vocational training for women; c) project Ek Pahal to train women drivers d) Equal opportunity programs while recruiting; e) Breaking the bias program to improve gender equality, f) breaking the glass ceiling by promoting more women in the higher management, g) Project Kompass to help women to be decision-makers, h) Aadya a platform for women to connect, i) Conversing, collaborating, and promoting women self-help group, j) Project Insight for career development for middle-aged women, h) Pivot Program for women career development, i) executive development for women employees, j) Creating inclusive workplace, k) reservation form women in the company leadership; l) Creating diversity councils, m) Residential workshop from women in leadership, n) ensuring 50% women in the workplace, and o) Project ASPIRE formed a women's leadership program. These programs aim to ensure equity in the society

TABLE 11.1 (Continued)

Details of the sustainable practices reported by the companies

SDG	Company ID	Description of the initiatives
SDG 6 Clean Water and Sanitation	*AM (1, 2, 3, 4, 7, 8, 9, 11) INF (1, 5, 6); IT (1, 4, 5, 8, 9, 10, 12, 13); PHR (1, 4, 5, 6, 7, 8); PCH (1, 2, 3, 4, 5, 6)*	a) Has set up many RO water filters and toilets in schools across the nation, b) Supported project Namami Gange to clean up rivers, c) Efforts are made to improve the quality of water and create a better ecosystem of water management, d) Water ATMs installed for potable water for local communities, e) Recycling of water by companies, innovate on dry washing technology for car cleaning, f) Developing water stewardship, g) innovate vehicle manufacturing with reduced water consumption, h) Decarbonisation program, i) Providing water budgeting exercises to employees, j) Being part of cleanliness drives, k) placement of dustbins on roads and other public places, l) Installing green water purifier plants, m) Using solar energy for water management, n) developing water resilience for plants, o) Reduce the use of fresh water in the factories, p) Bottling plants to measure the groundwater enrichment, q) rainwater harvesting, r) Recycling sewage water for washroom usage
SDG 7 Affordable and clean energy	*AM (1, 2, 4, 6, 7, 12); IT (4, 9, 12, 13); PHR (2, 6); PCH (1, 2, 3, 4, 6)*	a) Innovations in EV batteries, b) Tripple action ZERO to reach Carbon Neutrality, c) Rout Zero a global coalition to covert all cars to zero emission by 2040, d) Project Arush focusing on solar powered streetlights in villages, e) Replacing old bulbs with LED bulbs, f) Innovating on car engines to reduce carbon monoxide, g) Hydrocarbons and nitrogen emissions, h) Building zero carbon lodging villages, i) Hydrogen to you campaign to acceleration the transition to hydrogen society, j) Installing polycarbonate skylights to reduce carbon, k) Effort to reduce Scope 1 emissions by companies, l) Installing the 'weather O meter an energy efficient liquiair cooling technique for chillers, m) Installing high Volume low speed ventilation fans, increasing the use of solar power in manufacturing vehicles by Auto mobile companies, n) Increasing the use of rail transportation of goods, o) Roof top solar installations, p) Refineries gearing up to meet the Euro VI standards, q) achieving NetZero emission, r) Zero waste, asset reuse programs, s) computer manufacturers moving to power their devises using solar power, t) Biogas plants, collaborating with CDP and RE100, u) Investing in green infrastructure, w) more efficient operations, and x) greater adoption of green IT and renewable energy

(Continued)

TABLE 11.1 (Continued)

Details of the sustainable practices reported by the companies

SDG	Company ID	Description of the initiatives
SDG 8: Decent work and economic growth	*AM (1, 2, 4, 7, 8, 11, 12); INF (2, 3, 4, 5); IT (1, 3, 4, 5, 8, 9, 10, 13); PHR (8);*	a) Electric vehicles. b) The project Jeevika provides professional skills training to thousands of youth to enable them to get good jobs; c) Training youth for motor vehicle mechanics and develops almost 3.5 million Indians, d) Funding India to develop trained technicians, e) Some also reported on initiating projects that ensure quality education, f) Rural infrastructure development and livelihood development. g) Some also reported providing inclusive workplaces to facilitate the entrance of LGBTQIA+ members into the workforce. h) Many companies have in their code fair employment practice clearly mentioned. I) Some reported setting the benchmark for better employee compensation, j) Creating a safe workplace with zero fatalities, and k) Some logistics companies reported creating safe ports across India. Companies also reported on Zero Tolerance for Retaliation and l) Prohibition on Human Trafficking, Forced Labor and Child Labor. M) Another reported on the commitment to deliver future-ready skills development for workers in our supply chain, n) Start-up challenges being organised by companies, and o) Companies have reported on their intrapreneurship activities to take development to the community where they operate. This goal aim to bring in diversity, equity and inclusivity through various activities
SDG 9 Industry innovation and infrastructure	*AM (1, 2, 7, 11, 12); INF (1, 2, 3, 4, 5); IT (1, 3, 4, 5, 8, 10, 11, 13); PHR (8); PCH (1, 2, 3, 4, 5, 6)*	a) Building the car with inbuilt power backup, b) Inventing a unique cooling agent that changes the liquid vapour to reduce the charging time for EV vehicles, c) Expanding its domestic hydrogen charging infrastructure and increase the supply of FCEVs in Saudi Arabia while securing global competitiveness in robust hydrogen tanks and vehicle weight reduction. d) Automotive companies align with India's Start-up India and Digital India initiatives. e) Some also fund 3D platforms and A.R. to give a better customer experience. f) Some companies reported technological improvements in logistics and supply chain processes. g) There are also many innovations in IT and robotics to optimise production and reduce carbon emissions. h) Harmonization and digitisation of the HR process have given smooth management of employees within the organisations. i) Companies also reported investing in responsible AI. j) innovations in agricultural development (lift irrigation program, assist employees to get governments affordable housing projects)

TABLE 11.1 (Continued)

Details of the sustainable practices reported by the companies

SDG	Company ID	Description of the initiatives
SDG 10 Reduce inequalities	*AM (2, 4, 7, 11, 12); INF (4, 5); IT (1, 3, 4, 8, 9, 10, 13); PHR (1, 7); PCH (1, 2, 3, 5, 6)*	a) Organizing wellness sessions for employees, b) ensuring diversity in the workplace and providing equal opportunities, c) Office Kirari for a fulfilling life, d) Leave no one behind attitude as an organisational culture, ensuring respect, equal opportunities, teamwork, and e) Treating everyone equally regardless of their ethnicity, race, gender, disability, ideology, religion, nationality, sexual orientation, social background, or political beliefs in the organisation, f) Penalties for discriminatory behaviour, g) Having more than 45% female employees, h) Having affirmative action programs for minority and women, i) Project Enable to strengthen inclusiveness, j) Project Khelo to support Para-athletes, k) Promote 'Respect for the individual and respect for Human Rights' to include LGBTQIA+, l) Helping the unbanked people to become more bank-friendly, m) Focused hiring and retention of people with disabilities. Most of these activities aim to bring in values of DEI through strategic activities
SDG 11 Sustainable cities and communities	*AM (2, 6, 11); IT (5, 9); PCH (1, 2, 3, 4)*	a) Mass awareness campaigns in cities on environmental conservation and personal safety; b) Projects that use crowdsourcing activities to future-proof and personal safety; c) Projects that use crowdsourcing activities to future-proof the cities. d) Another company contributed to creating a zero-fatality corridor in the Mumbai–Pune expressway. e) Yet another company has pushed initiatives towards zero emissions, fatalities, and inequality. f) It is also noted that encouraging local sourcing of raw materials, engaging local contractors for housekeeping and security services, and adopting rooftop solar panels g) Disaster management training, introducing new mobility system, h) Hybrid drone to avert disasters, i) Technology companies reported innovating technologies that are zero-emission or creating ultralow emission zones. j) Creating resilient cities to protect against major catastrophes, green buildings, k) Using of renewable energy, sustainable transportation, vehicle sharing initiatives, e-waste disposal programs, and reducing paper and printing in offices are some other initiatives

(Continued)

TABLE 11.1 (Continued)

Details of the sustainable practices reported by the companies

SDG	Company ID	Description of the initiatives
SDG 12 Responsible consumption and production	*AM (1, 2, 4, 7, 8, 11); INF (1, 4); IT (9, 13): PHR (1, 4, 6, 7); PCH (2, 3, 4, 5)*	a) One such initiative is where they launched plant-based materials for vehicle manufacturing, such as using coffee chaff to reinforce headlamp housing, b) Many companies have reported that they use a combination of grid electricity, natural gas, and solar power, c) Encourage women's self-help groups to upcycle waste materials to produce handicrafts, d) Sustainable supply chain is another initiative they have reported, i) Some companies reported that all their products are from scrapped iron to reduce the use of iron significantly, ii) some companies also reported that they manage cradle to grave the cradle-to-grave lifecycle of their products, e) Installation of sewage treatment at the plant has reduced water consumption, f) Advanced foam washing is used to reduce water consumption, g) Another company reported creating a culture of a recycle-based society from a throwaway society, h) Yet another company reported managing almost 95% of cargo loading and port-related waste through the 5R principle (Reuse, Reprocess, Recycle and Recover). Some ports in India have reported zero waste to landfill (AWL) and zero hazardous waste to landfill-certified ports, i) Construction companies have reported using crushed sand instead of natural sand, j) Companies are digitising internal processing to reduce paper usage, k) Data analysis predicts the future need to minimise wastage, l) A company reported saving 13.9 million metric tons of carbon emission during the 2021 period in this way, m) Companies also report packaging from recycled or renewable materials, n) A new area where companies have reported initiatives is in the area of e-waste management. In summary, there is a move towards creating a circular economy
SDG 13 Act for the climate	*AM (1, 2, 3, 4, 5, 6, 7, 8, 9, 11, 12); INF (1, 2, 3, 4, 5); IT (1, 3, 4, 5, 8, 9, 10, 12, 13); PHR (1, 4, 5, 6, 7); PCH (1, 2, 3, 4, 5, 6)*	a) Companies reported their participation with the governments in reducing greenhouse gas emissions and initiatives to plant more trees as carbon sinks, b) Some also reported their partnership with stakeholders to reduce waste and engage in climate action activities, c) Automotive companies are targeting 2050 as the year for achieving carbon neutrality through adopting Electric Vehicles and sustainable fuel cell manufacturing, d) There are also efforts to reclaim decertified lakes and grasslands, plant

TABLE 11.1 (Continued)

Details of the sustainable practices reported by the companies

SDG	Company ID	Description of the initiatives
		1 million trees, rainwater harvesting schemes, etc. Another company reported on installing CNG and intelligent hybrid technology to minimise carbon emissions, e) Another initiative is to create awareness through education on environmental conservation, f) The launch of the Eco cycle and e-Power are other initiatives reported in this direction, g) Introducing a detailed series of hybrid buses in cities and a Starbus Fuel Cell bus, h) Some also reported on hydrogen fuel cells for their vehicles, i) Avenue and median plantations along the national highways and reduced water usage for train washing are also reported, j) Another large-scale initiative was using smart meters to reduce carbon footprint, k) Migrating to a greener cloud, eco-innovation challenges, significant nature-based carbon removal (Tree planting), sourcing a significant chunk of electricity requirement from alternate sources, L) Most companies declared their commitment to reach carbon neutrality by 2050, m) Dell's net zero by 2050 and KPMG Climate IQ are such initiatives, n) Many have also reported the installation of solar panels on the rooftop
SDG 14 Life underwater	*AM (3); INF (1, 4); PCH (1)*	a) Establishing a laboratory for marine environmental monitoring assessment, b) working to improve biodiversity and fresh water, ocean, wetland and forest ecosystem restoration are some other activities reported in this section
SDG 15: Life on earth	*AM (2, 6, 9, 11); INF (1, 4); IT (10, 12, 13); PHR (5, 7); PCH (1, 2, 3, 4, 5, 6)*	a) Many companies have reported activities on tree plantation and forest regeneration activities, b) Support forest guards and rangers and equip them with motorcycles to stop illegal poaching; another company reported off and equipped them with motorcycles to stop illegal poaching; another company reported preserving over 85 species to ensure biodiversity, c) It is also reported of activities to desalinate deserts, d) Another company reported their initiative to protect Olive Ridley Turtles, e) Protecting and preserving mangroves and Casuarina plantations in another initiative, f) Another one reported on conducting impact assessment to ensure map the ecosystem biodiversity

TABLE 11.2

Digital technologies developed or implemented by companies (With a focus on People and Profit)

Company	Digital Technology used	Application	SDGs and SDG Targets
AM1	Mustang Mach-E Cart	Checkout commerce platform in the U.S. and Europe, providing an end-to-end online experience that includes financing, trade-in appraisal, accessories	SDG 9 Targets 9.5 and 9C
AM11	Dress Up Paint	Paint removal tech that will allow the consumers to switch the colour of their car	SDG 9, 12 Target 9.4, 12.1 and 12.5
	Community-Based Technology	Considering the quality of life and improving health, the company launched technologies in rural areas to ensure better inclusivity of all	SDG 6, 8 and 12 Targets: 6.3 8.3,12,2
	Mobility Service Platform:	Considering the customer with low financial ability and the requirement, AM 11 came up with a Mobility Service Platform where customers can pick cars for a fixed tenure on lease. This helps in bringing in an equitable access to mobility services	SDG 12 Trgets: 12.1, 12.11
AM3	Just in Time (JiT) inventory system and Electronic Data Interchange (EDI)	Helps organisations for effectively management of resources of the organization and reduce waste	SDG 9 Targets: 9.4, 9C
AM4	Remote smart parking assist and advanced head- up	It helps improve consumer experience. Also helps with space optimisation	SDG 9 Targets: 9.1
	Open Innovation Center	Allowed start-ups to approach the organization to partner and work on technologies such as future mobility and artificial intelligence (Bring n inclusivity in the society)	SDG 9 Targets 9.1, 9.3
AM7	Idling Stop (Engine Auto Stop-Start System)	This technology helps to fuel savings by switching off the vehicle engine when not in use and instantly turns it back on when you need to start it again	SDG 12, 13 Targets: 12.2, 13.1
	K series engines	It helps to reduce losses and improve fuel efficiency	SDG 12, 13 Targets: 12.2, 13.1
	S-CNG	S-CNG vehicles come with an intelligent Injection system that provides information about an optimum ratio during combustion, thereby ensuring better and consistent performance along with high fuel efficiency	SDG 9 Targets 9.1, 9B
AM8	Machine learning	For tracing, monitoring and analysing their green energy management	SDG 7, 9 Targets: 9B, 7B

TABLE 11.2 (Continued)

Digital technologies developed or implemented by companies (With a focus on People and Profit)

Company	Digital Technology used	Application	SDGs and SDG Targets
AM9	E-Dukan and Industry 4.0	This platform is applied for the digital enablement of its channel partners and retailers for spare parts management. The platform evangelises the company's efforts towards addressing climate change and sustainability and contributes towards NetZero. This technology help inclusion of rural farmers to the mainstream markets	SDG 12 Targets: 12.7
Infra1	Smart(e)PIC	It is an IoT-enabled port community system integrating its internal and external stakeholders, ensuring sustainable and eco-friendly cargo management and asset tracking. It empowers its stakeholders to manage its smart logistic management system in an eco-friendly manner	SDG 12 Target:12.7
Infr2	Robots, VTOL Drones	Application of VTOL (vertical take-off and landing aircraft) drones and delivery robots for near future transportation for last mile connectivity and environmentally sustainable transportation	SDG 11 Target: 11.2
Infra3	Program *'SHIELD'* LTTS i-BEAMS	LTTS i-BEAMS is a modular system of system platforms to unify campus-wide operations under one platform. Built-in with high-end energy analysis and fault diagnostic for energy conservation and net-zero compliance	SDG 7 (7.3, 7.b SDG 9 (9.1, 9.4)
Infra5	Blockchain	Help provide end-to-end contracting and supply chain in the construction industry	SDG 12 Targets: 11.b
	SAP Analytics Cloud and SAP BW/4HANA	These tools help access easy information on business performance	SDG 12 Targets: 11.b
IT1	Fire Compass	To discover vulnerabilities to protect people against cyberattacks	SDG 8 Target: 8. 7, 8.8
IT4	Dell EMC PowerEdge	Optimise energy consumption, maximise performance, and support climate goals with servers validated by recognised eco-labels	SDG 7 Target: 7.b
PCH2	Learning Management System	Helps employees learn about small changes in the workplace to reduce accidents	SDG 8 Targets: 8.8

TABLE 11.3

Digital technologies developed or implemented by companies (with focus on planet)

Company	Digital Technology	Usage	SDG goals and target ID
AM1	Geothermal Cooling System	Geothermal energy, while reducing the cost of heating systems, also helps preserve our natural resources and lessens our dependency on fossil fuels	SDG 7 Target: 7.2, 7B
AM11	E-Drive (Advanced Automotive Technology)	It is an effort to localise the e-drive transmission system in their green vehicles to reach carbon neutrality	SDG 9 Targets 9.2, 9B
	Self-charging Hybrid Electric Technology	Electricity gets generated as you drive the car	SDG 7, 9 Targets: 7.3, 9.5
AM12	"Factory goTOzero – Zero Impact	This project aims at decarbonisation and reduction of the environmental impact of retailers worldwide and to achieve NetZero	SDG 7, 9 Targets 7.3, 9.1
	ICE vehicles	It is an effort towards moving to create futuristic EV vehicles and has invested heavily into this technology	SDG 7,9 Targets: 7.3, 9.1, 9.5
AM3	Low-pollution CVCC engine	Help reduce carbon monoxide, hydrocarbon, and nitrogen oxide emissions	SDG 7.3 Targets 13.B
	Triple Action to ZERO	To reach carbon neutrality, clean energy, and resource circulation	SDG 7,9 Targets: 7.3, 9.1, 9.5
AM4	Zero carbon lodging village	It is an effort to increase the income of the nearby low-income villages	SDG 11 Target 11b
	Ecological restoration technology	This is a technology to help in their green zone project to prevent desertification in low-income nations	SDG 15 Target: 15.3
	Fuel cell electric vehicles (FCEV)	To reduce the dependency on nonrenewable sources of energy and promote hydrogen fuel in the future for its vehicles	SDG 7 Target 7.2
AM7	Hybrid vehicles and EVs	For environment stewardship	SDG 7 Target 7.2
	Eco-Cool	reduced the complexity of air conditioning in cars in a very eco-friendly way by using cold storage material, thus keeping the cabin cool while the engine is shut down	SDG 7 Target. 7.3
	Ene-Charge	uses stored electricity to power electrical equipment such as the car's audio system and meters	SDG 7 Target: 7.3

TABLE 11.3 (Continued)

Digital technologies developed or implemented by companies (with focus on planet)

Company	Digital Technology	Usage	SDG goals and target ID
AM9	E-Mobility	Vehicles with 100% renewable energy	SDG 7, 13 Targets 7.2, 13b
	Fleet Edge, a connected vehicle platform, E- E-Dukaan (app to connect with the channel partners), Bandhu (app for better customer care), E-Guru (to connect with the channel partners and create business opportunity and economic growth)	Have introduced a series of technological innovations For environmental and social sustainability	SDG 12 Targets: 12.7
Infra1	Simplified Greenhouse Gas (GHG) Emissions Calculator	To help small businesses develop a corporate-wide inventory and establish a plan to ensure GHG data consistency as they track progress towards reaching an emissions reduction goal	SDG 13 Targets 13. 3
	Tool for the Reduction and Assessment of Chemical and Other Environmental Impacts (TRACI)	Examines the potential impacts of raw material usage and chemical releases resulting from production processes	SDG 13 Targets 13. 3
Infra2	Cryogenic technology	Makes large volume transportation of hydrogen possible and reduces CO_2 emission	SDG 7
Infra4	Next-gen digital technologies – IoT, AI/ML	This is an effort to bring technology to everyone and help the proliferation of innovation and entrepreneurship	SDG 9 Target 9.2
	Solar Blinker and Solar lights	To reduce power consumption by adopting LED lights in place of Sodium vapour lights	SDG 7, 13
IT10	EMS data, regular auditing, and AI-based tracking	To reduce carbon footprint and energy consumption	SDG 13 Target 9.2
IT13	Cloud migration	Reduced On-prem infrastructure and thereby reduced CO2 emissions greatly	SDG 13 Target 13 b
	Eco-meter	This is a tool to help the Automotive sector to improve fuel efficiencies and reduce emissions	SDG 13 Target 13 b
IT9	Climate IQ	A multi-industry risk management tool that lets businesses identify, assess, and manage their physical and transition risks related to climate change	SDG 13 Target 13b

(Continued)

TABLE 11.3 (Continued)

Digital technologies developed or implemented by companies (with focus on planet)

Company	Digital Technology	Usage	SDG goals and target ID
PCH1	Advanced recycling technology	Effectively transforms plastic waste into the raw materials that are used in the process of making virgin-quality plastic and other valuable products	SDG 12 Target 12.3
	Low carbon solutions	Business unit to advance the development and deployment of these technologies and projects, including CCS, hydrogen and advanced biofuels, breakthrough energy efficiency processes, advanced energy-saving materials, and other technologies	SDG 13 Target 13b
PCH3	Volatile Organic Compound (VOC)	Emission monitoring and leak detection	SDG 9 Target 9.1
	370 TPA Green Hydrogen plant	To provide green hydrogen, meeting the partial refining process requirement in alignment with the National Green Hydrogen Mission	SDG 7 Target 2
PCH4	TERI Digital Transformation Integrated Management System (IMS)	Use digital technologies for environmental monitoring continuously	SDG 12
	Leveraging Robots	To clean oil sludge at refineries, oil water separator (OWS) sumps	SDG12 Target: 12.4
PCH5	Catalytic Gasification Technology	This technology can convert a variety of carbonaceous feedstocks like coal, biomass, etc. into hydrogen and syngas	SDG 7

11.5.2 Implications for Companies

Initiatives such as climate action (SDG13), clean water and sanitation (SDG6), and life on land (SDG15), drive businesses to adopt more sustainable practices. These practices include reducing carbon footprints, managing water resources responsibly, and preserving biodiversity. By integrating these goals, companies can contribute to mitigate adverse environmental impacts, contribute to climate resilience, and promote ecological sustainability. For instance, companies can invest in renewable energy projects, reduce waste through circular economy practices, and support conservation efforts. These actions enhance environmental stewardship and improve corporate reputations and compliance with environmental regulations.

From a social perspective SDGs addresses issues such as poverty alleviation (SDG1), gender equality (SDG5), and decent work and economic growth (SDG8). Companies can contribute to social well-being by ensuring fair labour practices, supporting local communities, and fostering inclusive economic growth. For example, CSR initiatives may involve educational programs, healthcare services, and skill development for marginalised communities, thus enhancing social equity and inclusion. Additionally, promoting gender equality within corporate structures and supply chains helps to empower women and reduce gender disparities (Hazlett et al., 2007).

Pharmaceutical companies should ensure that their supply chains are transparent and sustainable, addressing issues like counterfeit medicines and environmental impact. Pharmaceutical companies can work to increase access to medicines, particularly in low-income countries, by developing affordable treatments and improving distribution networks. Pharmaceutical companies can invest in healthcare infrastructure, such as hospitals and clinics, to improve healthcare services and access to medicines. Pharma companies mainly focus on SDG 1, 3, 6, and 13 (no poverty, good health and well-being, clean water and sanitation and climate action).

The automotive industry can focus on developing electric vehicles and sustainable manufacturing practices to reduce emissions and environmental impact. They should ensure their supply chains are transparent and sustainable, addressing issues like labour practices and environmental impact. To protect drivers and passengers, automotive companies can invest in safety and security features, such as advanced driver-assistance systems and cybersecurity measures. Automotive companies can invest in infrastructure development, such as charging stations and public transportation systems, to support the transition to electric vehicles. Currently, there is an increased focus on no poverty (SDG 1), gender equality (SDG 5) and clean water (SDG 6).

Infrastructure companies can focus on developing sustainable infrastructure, such as green buildings and renewable energy systems, to reduce environmental impact. They can invest in transportation systems, such as public transportation and logistics networks, to improve connectivity and reduce emissions. Infrastructure companies can invest in water and sanitation systems to improve access to clean water and sanitation services. Infrastructure companies can invest in disaster risk reduction measures, such as flood protection systems and earthquake-resistant structures, to protect communities from natural disasters. Given their impact on land and water, it is imperative that they contribute more to protect the land and ocean and various flora and found on it (SDGs 14,15).

IT companies can focus on developing digital infrastructure, such as cloud computing and data centres, to support the growth of digital technologies. IT companies are one of the fastest sectors in India and contribute significantly to the nation's GDP. It is important that they contribute more towards achieving no poverty and zero hunger. With the increasing stress given to smart cities, they also can contribute more towards sustainable cities and communities (SDG11) and reduce inequality in the workplace by creating more equitable workplaces (SDG10).

Petrochemical industries have a direct relation to environmental goals. Hence, they should focus more on life in SDGs 13, 14, and 15. Companies can contribute to achieving the SDGs and drive sustainable growth and development by focusing on these areas.

The research identified SDGs 1, 2, 11, and 14 as the goals in which corporates are least engaged. This could be because the target beneficiary is large and the investment required is enormous. Single organisations may be unable to contribute significantly to reducing poverty, hunger, and urban development. Companies can augment technologies to collaborate to ensure the fulfilment of SDGs that are less explored by the business houses. This requires a government to mediate this collaboration process and create an enabling environment. Overall, the strategic alignment of CSR activities with SDGs enables companies to contribute meaningfully to global sustainability efforts, driving systemic change. This approach enhances businesses' environmental and social footprint and aligns their operations with broader international sustainability frameworks.

Digital technologies extend and support organisations' sustainability initiatives that address social, economic, and environmental areas. However, most of the technologies address environmental issues. There were technologies such as e-choupal to provide real-time market information to farmers, community-based technology to provide health tips to people, E-dukan, Smart e-PIC, Program SHIELD, Firecompas and LMS to reduce accidents, protect from frauds, and help business to procure at affordable prices. However, these digital interventions are far too few compared to environment-related technologies. The researchers felt that business organisations could leverage the digital transformation that is taking place in order to extend more sustainable practices.

11.6 Conclusion

This research has been advantageous personally as it helped me understand the nuances of sustainability reporting. It was indeed an eye-opener as it helped me understand how various companies prioritise different SDGs based on their core competence and the impact they create on society and the environment. It also enabled me to understand how companies incorporate the values of DEI in the CSR activities. While IT companies focus on education, petrochemical companies prioritise climate action. Auto-manufacturing companies engage in various activities as their impact is more visible than others. The research documented companies' social and environmental contributions and mapped them to 15 SDGs. The paper also documented the sustainable technologies companies use that facilitate SDG attainment.

Since business organisations depend heavily on society and the environment for their survival, it is only apt to say that they are responsible for contributing to sustainable development. SDGs provide a comprehensive plan to tackle societal and environmental problems through the 169 targets categorised under the 17 goals. Aligning their practices with SDGs helps organisations focus and create significant contributions to sustainable development. This will also help organisations to create long-term value by fostering innovation, enhancing reputation and mitigating risks associated with social and environmental issues. Prioritising activities along SDG also helps organisations to ensure inclusivity, equity, and justice.

This paper endeavours to list activities and technologies used to extend sustainable development. This is the first study documenting both sustainable practices and technologies enabling these practices. This paper can be furthered by expanding the scope to all the sectors. MSME is another area where reporting is still in its initial stage. MSMEs have a significant role in ensuring sustainability. Since they are the primary producers of goods and services that larger organisations use, they are the main contributors to the CO_2 emission. Larger companies look at the MSMEs for cheap goods and services. They are also alleged to be exploiting workers and society. Hence, measuring and documenting their contribution to sustainable development is essential.

References

Arun, P., & Charumathi, B. (2024). Uncovering DEI disclosure on corporate annual reports through unsupervised machine learning and text mining. In *Diversity, Equity And Inclusion* (pp. 299–347). Routledge.

Asopa, P., Purohit, P., Nadikattu, R. R., & Whig, P. (2021). Reducing carbon footprint for sustainable development of smart cities using IoT. In *2021 Third International Conference on Intelligent Communication Technologies and Virtual Mobile Networks (ICICV)*. 10.1109/ICICV50876.2021.9388466

Balashova, E., & Maiorova, K. (2021). Transforming industrial value creation in aspect of sustainable technology digitialization. *E3S Web of Conferences, 258*, 12006. https://doi.org/10.1051/e3sconf/202125812006

Beisheim, M. (2023). Analysing political will as a critical element of the Mid-term review of the 2030 Agenda and the SDGs. *SWP Research Paper, 7*. https://doi.org/10.18449/2023RP07

Bennich, T., Weitz, N., & Carlsen, H. (2020). Deciphering the scientific literature on SDG interactions: A review and reading guide. *The Science of the Total Environment, 728*(138405), 138405. https://doi.org/10.1016/j.scitotenv.2020.138405

Berrone, P., Rousseau, H. E., Ricart, J. E., Brito, E., & Giuliodori, A. (2023). How can research contribute to the implementation of sustainable development goals? An interpretive review of SDG literature in management. *International Journal of Management Reviews, 25*(2), 318–339. https://doi.org/10.1111/ijmr.12331

Bhimavarapu, V. M., Rastogi, S., & Abraham, R. (2022). The influence of transparency and disclosure on the valuation of banks in India: The moderating effect of environmental, social, and governance variables, shareholder activism, and market power. *Journal of Risk and Financial Management, 15*(12), 612. https://doi.org/10.3390/jrfm15120612

Biermann, F., Hickmann, T., Sénit, C.-A., Beisheim, M., Bernstein, S., Chasek, P., Grob, L., Kim, R. E., Kotzé, L. J., Nilsson, M., Ordóñez Llanos, A., Okereke, C., Pradhan, P., Raven, R., Sun, Y., Vijge, M. J., van Vuuren, D., & Wicke, B. (2022). Author correction: Scientific evidence on the political impact of the sustainable development goals. *Nature Sustainability, 6*(3), 344–344. https://doi.org/10.1038/s41893-022-00938-0

Bihari, A., & Shajahan, P. K. (2023). Changing CSR practices of corporates-a study of institutionalization of mandated corporate social responsibility in India. *International Journal of Law and Management, 65*(2), 105–124. https://doi.org/10.1108/IJLMA-09-2022-0198

Carroll, A. B. (2021). Corporate social responsibility: Perspectives on the CSR construct's development and future. *Business & Society, 60*(6), 1258–1278.

Cecere, G., Corrocher, N., Gossart, C., & Ozman, M. (2014). Technological pervasiveness and variety of innovators in green ICT: A patent-based analysis. *Research Policy, 43*(10), 1827–1839. https://doi.org/10.1016/j.respol.2014.06.004

Datta, S., & Goyal, S. (2022). Determinants of SDG reporting by businesses: A literature analysis and conceptual model. *Vision*, 09722629221096047.

Dionisio, M., De Souza Junior, S. J., Paula, F., & Pellanda, P. C. (2024). The role of digital social innovations to address SDGs: A systematic review. *Environment, Development and Sustainability, 26*(3), 5709–5734. https://doi.org/10.1007/s10668-023-03038-x

Duan, W., Khurshid, A., Khan, K., & Calin, A. C. (2024). Transforming industry: Investigating 4.0 technologies for sustainable product evolution in china through a novel fuzzy three-way decision-making process. *Technological Forecasting and Social Change, 200*(123125), 123125. https://doi.org/10.1016/j.techfore.2023.123125

Emma, G.-M., & Jennifer, M.-F. (2021). Is SDG reporting substantial or symbolic? An examination of controversial and environmentally sensitive industries. *Journal of Cleaner Production, 298*(126781), 126781. https://doi.org/10.1016/j.jclepro.2021.126781

Erin, O. A., Bamigboye, O. A., & Oyewo, B. (2022). Sustainable development goals (SDG) reporting: An analysis of disclosure. *Journal of Accounting in Emerging Economies, 12*(5), 761–789. https://doi.org/10.1108/jaee-02-2020-0037

Friske, W., Hoelscher, S. A., & Nikolov, A. N. (2023). The impact of voluntary sustainability reporting on firm value: Insights from signaling theory. *Journal of the Academy of Marketing Science, 51*(2), 372–392. https://doi.org/10.1007/s11747-022-00879-2

Gaur, S. P. (2025). Equity and inclusion of women in Top Indian Organisations: Imperatives for leadership towards a responsible world. In *Building a Resilient and Responsible*

World: Psychological Perspectives from India (pp. 181–219). Singapore: Springer Nature Singapore.

Giri, F. S., & Chaparro, T. S. (2023). Measuring business impacts on the SDGs: A systematic literature review. *Sustainable Technology and Entrepreneurship*, 100044.

Hák, T., Janoušková, S., & Moldan, B. (2016). Sustainable development goals: A need for relevant indicators. *Ecological Indicators, 60*, 565–573. https://doi.org/10.1016/j.ecolind.2015.08.003

Hatayama, H. (2022). The metals industry and the sustainable development goals: The relationship explored based on SDG reporting. *Resources, Conservation, and Recycling, 178*(106081), 106081. https://doi.org/10.1016/j.resconrec.2021.106081

Hazlett, S.-A., McAdam, R., & Murray, L. (2007). From quality management to socially responsible organisations: The case for CSR. *International Journal of Quality & Reliability Management, 24*(7), 669–682. https://doi.org/10.1108/02656710710774665

Hong, X., Chen, Q., Man, D., Shi, C., & Wang, N. (2024). The impact of digitalization on the rich and the poor: Digital divide or digital inclusion? *Technology in Society, 102634*, 102634. https://doi.org/10.1016/j.techsoc.2024.102634

Joseph, S., & Kulkarni, A. V. (2020). Creating sustainable contribution to the environment: Case studies from MSMEs in Pune. *International Journal of Social Ecology and Sustainable Development (IJSESD), 11*(4), 1-14.

Kaur, J., Kaur, K., & Singh, R. (2023). Adopting technology for sustainable development: Reflections on innovative ecosystem. In *Fostering Sustainable Development in the Age of Technologies* (pp. 93–111). Emerald Publishing Limited. https://doi.org/10.1108/978-1-83753-060-120231009

Kondra, S., Medapati, S., Koripalli, M., Nandula, S. R. S. C., & Zink, J. Z. (2025). AI and Diversity, Equity, and Inclusion (DEI): Examining the Potential for AI to Mitigate Bias and Promote Inclusive Communication. *Journal of Artificial intelligence and Machine Learning, 3*(1), 1–8.

Krishnamurthy, S., Joseph, S., Pradhan, V., & Rao, P. (2017). Empowering women of rural India for renewable energy adoption–An exploratory factor analysis. *Indian Journal of Science and Technology, 10*(37), 1–10.

Kulkarni, A. V., Joseph, S., & Patil, K. P. (2024). Artificial intelligence technology readiness for social sustainability and business ethics: Evidence from MSMEs in developing nations. *International Journal of Information Management Data Insights, 4*(2), 100250. https://doi.org/10.1016/j.jjimei.2024.100250

Kuzey, C., Uyar, A., Nizaeva, M., & Karaman, A. S. (2021). CSR performance and firm performance in the tourism, healthcare, and financial sectors: Do metrics and CSR committees matter? *Journal of Cleaner Production, 319*(128802), 128802. https://doi.org/10.1016/j.jclepro.2021.128802

Lafont-Torio, J., Martín, J. M. M., Fernández, J. A. S., & Soriano, D. R. (2024). Perceptions of progress toward achieving the sustainable development goals: Insights from cooperative managers. *Sustainable Technology and Entrepreneurship, 3*(1), 100055.

Mahajan, R. (2022). Sustainability reporting in India: A critical assessment of business responsibility reports of the top 100 companies. In *ICRMAT* (pp. 27–36). doi:10.15439/2022M7908

Majeedullah, A., Wied, K., & Mills, E. (2016). Gender, sexuality and the sustainable development goals: A meta-analysis of mechanisms of exclusion and avenues for inclusive development. *Institute of Development Studies*. Available at https://rb.gy/wxisyb *Retrieved June 25, 2024*

Makarenko, I., Plastun, A., Situm, M., Serpeninova, Y., & Sorrentino, G. (2021). Metaanalysis of the literature related to SDG 3 and its investment. *Public and Municipal Finance, 10*(1), 119–137. http://dx.doi.org/10.21511/pmf.10(1).2021.10

Mugoni, E., Kanyepe, J., & Tukuta, M. (2024). Sustainable supply chain management practices (SSCMPS) and environmental performance: A systematic review. *Sustainable Technology and Entrepreneurship*, 3 (1), 100050.

Pizzi, S., Caputo, A., Corvino, A., & Venturelli, A. (2020). Management research and the UN sustainable development goals (SDGs): A bibliometric investigation and systematic review. *Journal of Cleaner Production, 276*(124033), 124033. https://doi.org/10.1016/j.jclepro.2020.124033

Pizzi, S., Rosati, F., & Venturelli, A. (2021). The determinants of business contribution to the 2030 agenda: Introducing the SDG reporting score. *Business Strategy and the Environment, 30*(1), 404–421. https://doi.org/10.1002/bse.2628

Prakash, T. M., Rao, N. V. J., & Das, S. K. (2024). Combining technical competency and DEI for sustainable workplaces: Case of human capital at non-ferrous value-added products in Western Odisha, *International Journal of Innovative Research and Practices*, 12/6, 106–112.

Raman, R., Nair, V. K., Shivdas, A., Bhukya, R., Viswanathan, P. K., Subramaniam, N., & Nedungadi, P. (2023). Mapping sustainability reporting research with the UN's sustainable development goal. *Heliyon, 9*(8), 1–24. https://doi.org/10.1016/j.heliyon.2023.e18510

Ranalder, L., Hidalgo, L. G., Jones-Langley, J., Vener, J., & Tollin, N. (2024). *Local Action for Global Goals: An Opportunity for Enhancing Nationally Determined Contributions1*. Retrieved on 25 June 2024 from https://findresearcher.sdu.dk/ws/portalfiles/portal/256310516/un-habitat_ndcanalysis-technicalbrief.pdf

Sadiq, M., Ngo, T. Q., Pantamee, A. A., Khudoykulov, K., Thi Ngan, T., & Tan, L. P. (2023). The role of environmental social and governance in achieving sustainable development goals: Evidence from ASEAN countries. *Economic Research-Ekonomska Istraživanja, 36*(1), 170–190. https://doi.org/10.1080/1331677x.2022.2072357

Siti, N. M., & Rusnah, M. (2020). Sustainable business practices and financial performance during pre and post-SDG adoption periods: A systematic review. *Journal of Sustainable Finance & Investment, 11*(4), 291–309. https://doi.org/10.1080/20430795.2020.1727724

Sreedhar, V. N., & Nayak, P. (2024). Perspective study on identification of high-impact processes for advancing Diversity, Equity and Inclusion (DEI) in Indian organizations. *Human Systems Management, 43*(2), 165–180.

Sweileh, W. M. (2020). Bibliometric analysis of scientific publications on "sustainable development goals" with emphasis on "good health and wellbeing" goal (2015–2019). *Global Health, 16*(68), 1–13. https://doi.org/10.1186/s12992-020-00602-2

van Zanten, J. A., & van Tulder, R. (2021). Improving companies' impacts on sustainable development: A nexus approach to the SDGS. *Business Strategy and the Environment, 30*(8), 3703–3720. https://doi.org/10.1002/bse.2835

APPENDIX 11.1

Master list showing the number of activities across company types and SDGs

Code	Type of Company	SDG1	SDG2	SDG3	SDG4	SDG5	SDG6	SDC7	SDG8	SDG9	SDG10	SDG11	SDG12	SDG13	SDG14	SDG15	TOTAL (mapped per Company)
AM1	F-MNC			2	3	1	2	2	1	3			3	2			**19**
AM2	I-MNC	1	1	3	1	1	2	1	1	1	4	1	1	1		1	**20**
AM3	F-MNC	2	2		1	2	2							7	1		**17**
AM4	F-MNC	1			1		1	2	1		1		1	2			**10**
AM5	F-MNC													3			**3**
AM6	I-MNC			2	4			3				1		3		3	**16**
AM7	F-MNC	1		2	4	1	2	1	3	4	2		6	3			**29**
AM8	I-MNC				1	1	1		2				1	5			**11**
AM9	I-MNC	1		3	3		2							2		2	**13**
AM11	F-MNC		1	1			2		1	2	2	3	3	1		1	17
AM12	F-MNC				1	2		4	1	1	1						10
INF1	I-MNC	1	1	1	1		2			1			1	4	1	1	14
INF2	F-MNC								2	3				3			8
INF3	I-MNC			1	1				1	1				2			6
INF4	I-MNC	1		1		1			3	2	2		1	6	1	3	21
INF5	I-MNC		2	1			1		1	2	1			2			10
INF6	I-MNC						2										**2**
IT 1	F-MNC				2	3	1		4	2	1			8			21
IT 3	F-MNC	1		1	1	1			1	1	1			4			11
IT 4	F-MNC			2	1	1	1	1	1	2	4			6			19
IT 5	F-MNC			1	1	1	2		1	1		1		2			10
IT 8	I-MNC					2	1		3	4	3			6			**19**
IT 9	I-MNC			1	1	1	1	2	1		1	1	1	3			13
IT 10	F-MNC			1	2	1	1		1	1	2			3		1	13

(*Continued*)

APPENDIX 11.1

Master list showing the number of activities across company types and SDGs

Code	Type of Company	SDG1	SDG2	SDG3	SDG4	SDG5	SDG6	SDC7	SDG8	SDG9	SDG10	SDG11	SDG12	SDG13	SDG14	SDG15	TOTAL (mapped per Company)
IT 11	I-MNC				2					1							3
IT 12	I-MNC						2	2						4		3	11
IT 13	I-MNC	1		1		2	1	1	3	3	2		1	9		3	27
PHR1	F-MNC	1	3	4	2	2	1				1		1	2			17
PHR2	I-MNC							2									2
PHR4	I-MNC	1		1			1						1	1			5
PHR5	I-MNC	1		1	1		2			1				1		1	8
PHR6	F-MNC			1			2	1		1			3	3			**11**
PHR7	F-MNC	1		1		1	1				1		1	2		1	**9**
PHR8	I-MNC	1	2	3	1	1	1		1								**10**
PCH1	F-MNC	1	1		2	2	1	1		2	2	1		1	1	1	**16**
PCH2	I-MNC		2	3	1	1	2	2		3	4	3	1	4		2	**28**
PCH3	I-MNC	1	1	1		1	2	1		3	2	1	2	3		1	**19**
PCH4	I-MNC			3		1	1	1		2		1	3	2		2	**16**
PCH5	I-MNC			1	1	1	1			2	1		1	5		2	**15**
PCH6	F-MNC	1	1			1	1	2		2	2			2		2	**14**
Total (mapped per Goal)		**18**	**17**	**43**	**39**	**32**	**45**	**29**	**33**	**51**	**40**	**13**	**32**	**117**	**4**	**30**	***543***

APPENDIX 11.2

Summary of the number of activities across company types and SDGs

No. of Companies	Industry	SDG1	SDG2	SDG3	SDG4	SDG5	SDG6	SDG7	SDG8	SDG9	SDG10	SDG11	SDG12	SDG13	SDG14	SDG15	Total
11	AM	6	4	13	19	8	14	13	10	11	10	5	15	29	1	7	**165**
6	INF	2	3	4	2	1	5	0	7	9	3	0	2	17	2	4	**61**
10	IT	2	0	7	10	12	10	6	15	15	14	2	2	45	0	7	**147**
7	PHR	5	5	11	4	4	8	3	1	2	2	0	6	9	0	2	**62**
6	PCH	3	5	8	4	7	8	7	0	14	11	6	7	17	1	10	**108**
40	**Total**	**18**	**17**	**43**	**39**	**32**	**45**	**29**	**33**	**51**	**40**	**13**	**32**	**117**	**4**	**30**	543

Part IV

Workforce Transformation and Digital Capability Building

12

Empowered by Diversity: Building Inclusive Tech Workforces through DEIB

Rajwinder Kaur and Tanuj Negi

12.1 Introduction

Diversity, Equity, Inclusion, and Belonging (DEIB) are fundamental principles that aim to create fair and supportive environments where individuals from all backgrounds feel valued and empowered. In the tech industry, DEIB is not just a moral imperative but a business necessity. Diversity brings together varied perspectives and experiences, fostering creativity and innovation critical to solving complex technological challenges. Equity ensures that all employees have access to opportunities and resources needed for success, while inclusion builds environments where everyone feels respected and engaged. Belonging, often overlooked, emphasises emotional and psychological safety, ensuring employees feel accepted and connected within their teams and organisations.

DEIB has emerged as a crucial element in addressing workforce disparities in the global IT sector. Despite being a hub of innovation, the tech industry has historically struggled with the underrepresentation of women, minorities, and neurodiverse individuals. This lack of diversity perpetuates social inequities and limits the industry's ability to leverage the full spectrum of human talent. By cultivating inclusive environments, organisations that embrace DEIB principles can drive innovation, improve employee engagement, and achieve better business outcomes.

12.1.1 Problem Statement

Despite widespread recognition of the importance of DEIB, the tech industry continues to face significant challenges in creating a truly diverse and inclusive workforce. Unconscious bias often shapes hiring and promotion decisions, leading to inequitable representation at all levels. Women, racial minorities, and individuals from nontraditional backgrounds frequently encounter barriers to entry and advancement. Cultural and systemic

DOI: 10.1201/9781003591078-16

factors exacerbate these challenges, such as workplace stereotypes, limited mentorship opportunities, and lack of inclusive policies. Furthermore, the rapid pace of technological innovation often prioritises technical skills over fostering inclusive practices, creating environments where underrepresented groups feel marginalised.

These persistent issues hinder individual potential and constrain organisational growth and innovation. To address these challenges, organisations must rethink traditional approaches to recruitment, leadership, and workplace culture, adopting strategies rooted in DEIB principles.

12.1.2 Research Questions

This chapter seeks to explore key questions that can guide organisations in building diverse and inclusive tech workforces:

1. *What theoretical frameworks can guide the recruitment of diverse talent?:* Identifying frameworks that address bias and promote equitable hiring practices is crucial to diversifying the workforce.
2. *How can organisations conceptualise a culture of belonging in tech spaces?:* Examining the role of organisational culture and policies in fostering psychological safety and engagement for all employees.
3. *What leadership models foster inclusivity and mitigate bias?:* Analysing leadership styles and practices prioritising equity, promoting inclusive decision-making, and addressing systemic inequalities.

12.1.3 Purpose

This chapter theoretically examines the practices and policies necessary for cultivating inclusive tech workforces globally. Drawing on insights from DEIB theories, leadership models, and organisational culture frameworks, it aims to equip readers with a deeper understanding of navigating and addressing diversity and inclusion challenges in the tech industry. By integrating these perspectives, the chapter offers a foundation for reimagining recruitment, management, and leadership strategies to build equitable and innovative workplaces.

This exploration highlights the critical role of theoretical insights in shaping practical solutions and empowering organisations to foster DEIB in a rapidly evolving global tech landscape. The remainder of this chapter is structured as follows. Section 12.2 presents the theoretical frameworks underpinning DEIB, including insights from leadership models and organisational culture theories. Section 12.3 explores the conceptualisation of diversity and inclusion within tech workforces, highlighting the impact of cognitive and implicit biases on talent management. Section 12.4 discusses best practices and showcases noteworthy DEIB initiatives from leading technology organisations. Section 12.5 provides a comprehensive discussion, drawing out theoretical and practical implications and identifying future research directions. Finally, Section 12.6 concludes the chapter by summarising key findings and emphasising the strategic importance of DEIB in building inclusive, innovative, and sustainable tech workforces.

12.2 Theoretical Frameworks

DEIB is a multifaceted domain supported by many theories, frameworks, and inspirational models. To gain a comprehensive understanding of DEIB, the following subsections delve into select DEIB theories, inclusive leadership models/frameworks, and organisational culture frameworks.

12.2.1 DEIB Theories: A Multidimensional Understanding

DEIB theories can be categorised based on various dimensions, such as their primary focus, methodological approach, disciplinary origin, level of analysis, and practical application (see Figure 12.1).

By examining these theories through multiple lenses, managers and leaders can comprehensively understand the complex issues surrounding DEIB. For example, *Social Psychology* offers insights into individual-level processes through theories like Social Identity Theory and Stereotype Threat Theory. Conversely, *Sociological theories* such as Intersectionality Theory and Critical Race Theory examine systemic inequalities at a societal level.

In the subsequent section, we present a brief commentary utilising a multidimensional classification framework for DEIB theories. By considering the overlapping and intersecting themes within these classifications, the field of DEIB continues to evolve, deepening our understanding and advancing the pursuit of justice and inclusivity across various societal contexts.

A classification by focus organises DEIB theories into individual, group, and organisational levels. *Individual-level* theories delve into personal experiences and biases, as exemplified by Social Identity Theory (Tajfel & Turner, 1979), which explores self-concept derived from group membership, and Implicit Bias Theory (Banaji & Greenwald, 1998), which highlights unconscious attitudes influencing behaviour. Stereotype Threat Theory (Steele & Aronson, 1995) examines how performance is negatively impacted when individuals fear conforming to stereotypes.

At the *group level*, theories like social dominance theory (Sidanius & Pratto, 1999) address the maintenance of hierarchical structures. Intersectionality theory (Carbado et al., 2013) uncovers how intersecting identities shape experiences of privilege and discrimination. Critical race theory (Bell, 1992),

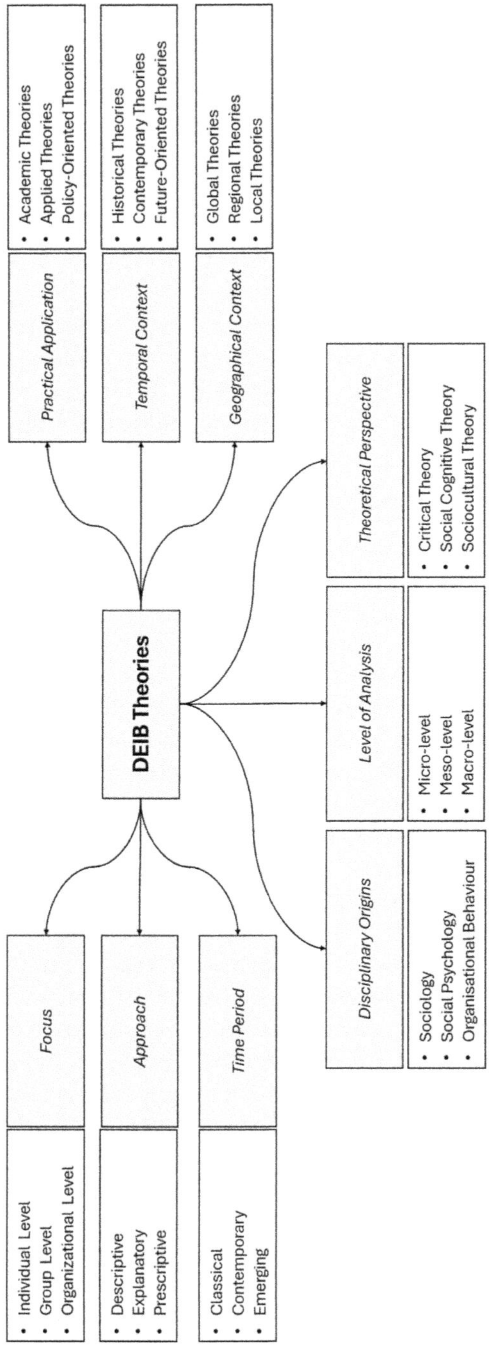

FIGURE 12.1
An informative classification scheme for DEIB theories.

focusing on the systemic role of race, offers critical insights into legal and social inequities. Diversity management theory provides frameworks for implementing inclusive practices at the organisational level, while organizational culture theory (Schein, 2004) examines shared organisational values. Equity theory (Adams, 1965) further investigates perceptions of fairness in workplace exchanges.

DEIB theories can also be categorised by their approach. *Descriptive theories*, such as Social Identity Theory (Tajfel & Turner, 1979) and Implicit Bias Theory (Banaji & Greenwald, 1998), provide a foundational understanding of behaviours and attitudes. *Explanatory theories*, including Stereotype Threat Theory (Steele & Aronson, 1995) and Social Dominance Theory (Sidanius & Pratto, 1999), delve into causative mechanisms behind observed phenomena. *Prescriptive theories* like Equity Theory (Adams, 1965) offer actionable strategies for fostering inclusivity and fairness.

When classified by time period, DEIB theories span classical, contemporary, and emerging categories. *Classical theories*, such as Realistic Conflict Theory (Sherif, 1966), examine the role of intergroup competition in shaping behaviours, while Relative Deprivation Theory (Stouffer et al., 1949) investigates perceived inequality as a driver of social unrest. The Contact Hypothesis (Allport, 1954) suggests increased intergroup contact can reduce prejudice and discrimination.

Contemporary theories include Intersectionality Theory (Carbado et al., 2013) and Critical Race Theory (Bell, 1992), which dissect current socio-legal inequities. *Emerging theories* like Postcolonial Theory (Said; Spivak) and Disability Studies (Butler; Davis) expand the DEIB discourse by addressing the legacies of colonialism and the lived experiences of marginalised communities, respectively.

The disciplinary origins of DEIB theories reveal a rich tapestry of interdisciplinary contributions. Social Identity Theory (Tajfel & Turner, 1979), rooted in *Social Psychology*, investigates group categorisation and self-concept. Critical Pedagogy (Freire, 1996; Giroux, 2004), originating from *education*, challenges traditional frameworks to promote social justice. *Sociology* contributes to Intersectionality Theory (Carbado et al., 2013) and Critical Race Theory (Bell, 1992), illuminating the systemic interplay of power and oppression.

Organisational behaviour offers practical insights through Equity Theory (Adams, 1965), emphasising strategies for inclusivity and fairness. Furthermore, *Communication Studies*, like Rhetorical Theory provided by Burke and Derrida (refer to Olson, 1990; Wolin, 2001), analyses how discourse perpetuates or challenges dominant ideologies.

Analysing DEIB theories by their level of analysis reveals *micro, meso,* and *macro-level* perspectives. *Micro-level theories* like Implicit Bias (Banaji & Greenwald, 1998) and Stereotype Threat (Steele & Aronson, 1995) focus on individual processes, examining how unconscious attitudes and stereotype-induced stressors impact behaviour.

Meso-level theories, such as Intersectionality Theory (Carbado et al., 2013), address group dynamics and the compounded effects of intersecting identities. *Macro-level theories*, including Critical Race Theory (Bell, 1992), analyse structural and institutional inequalities, providing a lens to interrogate societal power dynamics.

From a theoretical perspective, DEIB theories adopt various lenses, including *critical, social-cognitive,* and *sociocultural theories*. *Critical perspectives*, represented by Intersectionality (Carbado et al., 2013) and Critical Race Theory (Bell, 1992), scrutinise power structures and advocate for transformative change. *Social cognitive* approaches, such as Stereotype Threat Theory (Steele & Aronson, 1995), emphasise cognitive processes that shape behaviour. *Sociocultural frameworks* like Social Identity Theory (Tajfel & Turner, 1979) explore how cultural and social affiliations shape individual and group identity.

Geographical and temporal contexts further refine the classification of DEIB theories. *Global theories*, such as Social Identity Theory (Tajfel & Turner, 1979), possess universal applicability, whereas *regional theories*, like Latin American Dependency Theory, address context-specific socio-economic dynamics (Frank, 1967).

Local theories, including Indigenous Knowledge Systems (Deloria, 1999), prioritise marginalised communities' cultural and historical particularities. Similarly, *historical theories* examine past events' influence on present dynamics, while *future-oriented theories* like Post-Humanism (Haraway, 1985; Braidotti, 2019) anticipate the implications of technological and societal transformations.

Finally, the practical applications of DEIB theories underscore their relevance in academia, policy, and practice. *Academic theories* provide foundational insights into social phenomena, while *applied theories*, such as Equity Theory (Adams, 1965), offer tangible strategies for organisational change. *Policy-oriented theories* like Critical Race Theory (Bell, 1992) and Intersectionality Theory (Carbado et al., 2013) shape legislative and societal approaches to combat discrimination and foster equity.

12.2.2 Insights from Inclusive Leadership Frameworks and Models

Inclusive leadership prioritises the inclusion and empowerment of all individuals, regardless of their background or identity. Inclusive leaders create environments where everyone feels valued and respected and can contribute their unique perspectives. They are open and accessible, fostering psychological safety and empowering team members. Inclusive leaders challenge biases and discrimination by prioritising equity and fairness and developing cultural competence. This leadership style has been linked to numerous benefits, including increased employee engagement, job satisfaction, and organisational performance (Herring, 2008).

In the following subsections, we review three relevant frameworks from leadership theory that offer advice on issues related to DEIB.

12.2.2.1 Servant Leadership

Servant leadership, a philosophy rooted in the idea of serving others, is a leadership approach that prioritises the needs of followers over the leader's self-interest (Greenleaf, 1970). Servant leaders focus on empowering and developing their team members, fostering a sense of community and purpose. Key characteristics of servant leadership include listening, empathy, healing, awareness, persuasion, conceptualisation, foresight, stewardship, commitment to the growth of people, and building community (Spears, 2002).

Servant leadership aligns closely with DEIB principles. By prioritising the needs of others and fostering a sense of community, servant leaders can create inclusive and equitable work environments (Spears, 2002). This approach can help to break down barriers, reduce bias, and promote diversity of thought (Northouse, 2018). Servant leaders often empower their team members, giving them the autonomy and support to contribute their unique perspectives and skills (Spears, 2002). This can lead to increased innovation, creativity, and a stronger employee sense of belonging.

12.2.2.2 Transformative Leadership

Transformational leadership, a theory developed by Burns (1978) and further popularised by Bass (1985), focuses on inspiring and motivating followers to achieve extraordinary results. Transformational leaders inspire their followers through idealised influence, inspirational motivation, intellectual stimulation, and individualised consideration.

Transformational leadership aligns well with DEIB principles. By inspiring and motivating followers, transformational leaders can create a sense of purpose and shared vision, which can be particularly powerful in fostering a culture of inclusion and belonging (Bass & Riggio, 2006). They can also challenge the status quo and encourage innovation, leading to more equitable and inclusive practices (Avolio & Bass, 1991). Additionally, by providing individualised consideration, transformational leaders can recognise and value the unique contributions of each team member, regardless of their background or identity (Bass, 1985).

12.2.2.3 Positive Leadership

Positive leadership, a relatively new field of study, emphasises the importance of fostering positive emotions, behaviours, and outcomes. Key principles include cultivating positive emotions, building strong relationships, encouraging positive behaviours, and creating a positive organisational culture (Luthans et al., 2006).

Positive leadership aligns with DEIB principles by fostering a positive work environment where everyone feels valued and respected. By emphasising strengths, well-being, and optimism, positive leadership can contribute to a more inclusive and equitable workplace (Luthans et al., 2006). Additionally, by building strong relationships and promoting positive behaviours, positive leadership can help to break down barriers and reduce bias, leading to a more diverse and inclusive organisation (Luthans et al., 2006).

12.2.3 Insights from Organizational Culture Frameworks and Theories

Organisational culture frameworks offer valuable insights into the shared values, beliefs, and behaviours that shape an organisation's climate. By understanding these cultural dynamics, leaders can identify barriers to DEIB and implement strategies to foster more inclusive environments. Models like Edgar Schein's three-level model (Schein, 2004) help to uncover the underlying assumptions and values that influence organisational behaviour. By recognising and addressing implicit biases and power dynamics, leaders can promote psychological safety, encourage open communication, and tailor DEIB initiatives to the organisation's needs.

Leaders can create more inclusive, equitable, and diverse organisations by leveraging insights from organisational culture frameworks. Such frameworks can also help identify cultural barriers and promote a culture of inclusivity. By understanding the underlying assumptions and values that shape organisational behaviour, leaders can tailor DEIB initiatives to their organisation's specific needs and measure their impact.

We present insights from organisational culture frameworks that may be relevant for managers and leaders focusing on DEIB issues.

12.2.3.1 Edgar Schein's Organisational Culture Model

Edgar Schein's model of organisational culture provides a framework for understanding the layers of culture within an organisation. This model identifies three levels: *artefacts, espoused values,* and *underlying assumptions* (Schein, 2004). Artifacts are the visible elements of culture, such as dress codes, office layouts, and company logos. Espoused values are the stated beliefs and values of the organisation. Underlying assumptions, the deepest level of culture, are unconscious beliefs and values that shape behaviour and decision-making.

Schein's model is particularly relevant to DEIB initiatives. By understanding the underlying assumptions of an organisation's culture, leaders can identify potential biases and barriers to inclusion. For example, if an organisation's underlying assumptions are rooted in traditional gender roles or racial stereotypes, promoting diversity and equity may be challenging.

Addressing these assumptions can help organisations create more inclusive and equitable workplaces (Schein, 2004). Additionally, by examining the organisation's artefacts and espoused values, leaders can identify areas where changes may be needed to promote a more inclusive culture. By aligning these elements with DEIB principles, organisations can create a more welcoming and supportive environment for all employees.

12.2.3.2 Geert Hofstede's Cultural Dimensions Theory

Hofstede's cultural dimensions theory provides a framework for understanding cultural differences across countries and regions (Hofstede, 2001). This theory identifies six dimensions: *the Power Distance Index (PDI), Individualism vs Collectivism (IDV), Masculinity vs Femininity (MAS), Uncertainty Avoidance Index (UAI), Long-Term Orientation vs Short-Term Normative Orientation (LTO),* and *Indulgence vs Restraint (IND).*

Hofstede's model can be applied to DEIB initiatives by helping organisations understand and navigate cultural differences. Organisations can create more inclusive and equitable work environments by recognising and respecting cultural differences. Additionally, by understanding the cultural values of different groups, organisations can tailor their DEIB strategies to be more effective. For example, in a collectivist culture, it may be important to emphasise teamwork and collaboration, while in an individualistic culture, it may be important to recognise and reward individual contributions (Hofstede, 2001).

12.2.3.3 Aperian's GlobeSmart

Aperian's GlobeSmart is a commercial tool for understanding and navigating cultural differences in global business. By providing insights into cultural dimensions such as *individualism vs. collectivism, power distance,* and *uncertainty avoidance,* GlobeSmart helps individuals develop intercultural competence and build stronger relationships with colleagues from diverse backgrounds (see also: https://aperian.com/).

For organisations, GlobeSmart can be a valuable asset in promoting DEIB initiatives. Using GlobeSmart to train employees on cultural differences, organisations can foster a more inclusive and respectful workplace. This can lead to improved communication, collaboration, and innovation. Additionally, GlobeSmart can help organisations identify and address cultural biases hindering DEIB efforts. Organisations can create a more equitable and diverse workplace by equipping employees with the knowledge and skills to navigate cultural differences effectively. Based on the above, Table 12.1 provides a summary of this section

TABLE 12.1

Summary of key theories, leadership models, and organizational culture frameworks relevant to DEIB. Source: Compiled by Authors

Theory/Model	Area	Focus	Relevance to DEIB
Social Identity Theory (Tajfel & Turner, 1979)	DEIB Theory (Individual Level)	Group membership shapes self-concept and behaviour	Explains in-group/out-group biases in workplaces
Implicit Bias Theory (Banaji & Greenwald, 1998)	DEIB Theory (Individual Level)	Unconscious attitudes influencing judgments	Reveals hidden biases affecting talent management
Stereotype Threat Theory (Steele & Aronson, 1995)	DEIB Theory (Individual Level)	Anxiety caused by fear of confirming stereotypes	Highlights barriers faced by marginalised groups
Social Dominance Theory (Sidanius & Pratto, 1999)	DEIB Theory (Group Level)	Maintenance of group-based hierarchies	Explains systemic resistance to inclusion
Intersectionality Theory (Crenshaw; Carbado et al., 2013)	DEIB Theory (Group Level)	Overlapping identities create unique experiences	Supports multifaceted DEIB interventions
Critical Race Theory (Bell, 1992)	DEIB Theory (Macro Level)	Systemic racism embedded in laws and institutions	Informs policy reforms for racial equity
Diversity Management Theory	DEIB Theory (Organizational Level)	Strategies for managing diverse talent pools	Offers frameworks for DEIB organisational practices
Organisational Culture Theory (Schein, 2004)	DEIB Theory (Organizational Level)	Shared assumptions, values, and norms in organisations	Explains culture's role in inclusion/exclusion
Equity Theory (Adams, 1965)	DEIB Theory (Organizational Level)	Perceptions of fairness in exchanges	Emphasises the importance of equitable treatment
Postcolonial Theory (Said; Spivak)	Macro	Effects of colonial histories on societies and identities	Broadens DEIB conversations beyond Western frameworks
Servant Leadership (Greenleaf, 1970)	Inclusive Leadership Framework	Prioritising follower needs and growth	Empowers diverse employees and fosters belonging
Transformational Leadership (Bass, 1985)	Inclusive Leadership Framework	Inspiring and motivating followers toward change	Drives cultural shifts toward inclusivity
Positive Leadership (Luthans et al., 2006)	Inclusive Leadership Framework	Fostering positive emotions and strengths	Creates positive, inclusive organisational environments
Edgar Schein's Organizational Culture Model (2004)	Organisational Culture Framework	Artifacts, espoused values, and underlying assumptions	Diagnoses cultural biases affecting DEIB
Hofstede's Cultural Dimensions Theory (2001)	Organisational Culture Framework	National culture dimensions (e.g., power distance)	Tailors DEIB initiatives to cultural contexts
GlobeSmart (Aperian Global)	Organisational Culture Tool	Cultural profiles and intercultural competence	Enhances cultural intelligence for global DEIB efforts

12.3 Conceptualising Diversity and Inclusion in Tech Workforces

Having established the theoretical foundations of DEIB through social, organisational, and leadership lenses, it is crucial to connect these frameworks to the practical realities within tech organisations. Theories such as Social Identity Theory and Implicit Bias Theory underscore how individual perceptions and unconscious attitudes influence behaviours in workplace settings. Building on these insights, Section 12.3 delves into how cognitive and implicit biases manifest in talent management practices and organisational culture, shaping the lived experiences of diverse employees. This practical exploration aims to operationalise the earlier theoretical concepts, bridging the gap between abstract frameworks and tangible workplace dynamics.

12.3.1 Cognitive and Implicit Biases

Cognitive biases are systematic errors in thinking that can influence our judgments and decisions. They arise from various factors, including heuristics, emotions, and social pressures. For example, confirmation bias, the tendency to seek information that confirms existing beliefs, can lead to biased decision-making (Nickerson, 1998).

Similarly, the Dunning–Kruger effect, the tendency for people with low ability to overestimate their competence, can hinder learning and growth (Kruger & Dunning, 1999). By understanding these biases, managers can make more informed and rational decisions. Numerous studies have explored the impact of cognitive biases on various aspects of human behaviour, including decision-making, problem-solving, and social interactions (Kahneman, 2011).

On the other hand, *implicit bias* refers to unconscious attitudes and stereotypes that affect our understanding, actions, and decisions. These biases are often subtle and operate outside of our conscious awareness. They can lead to discriminatory behaviour, even when managers and leaders have no intention of being biased. For example, earlier studies have shown that implicit racial bias can lead to racial disparities in criminal justice, healthcare, and employment (Banaji & Greenwald, 1998). Similarly, implicit gender bias can lead to gender disparities in education, leadership, and STEM fields (Moss-Racusin et al., 2012). Understanding implicit bias is crucial for promoting fairness, equity, and inclusion.

12.3.1.1 Unconscious Biases and Talent Management

Cognitive biases and implicit biases play a significant role in shaping talent management and development practices. Confirmation bias, for instance, can lead to biased performance evaluations, as individuals may seek information that confirms their pre-existing beliefs about an employee's abilities (Nickerson, 1998). Similarly, the halo effect, where a positive impression in one area influences perceptions in others, can lead to biased promotion decisions (Thorndike, 1920).

Implicit bias, often rooted in unconscious stereotypes and associations, can exacerbate these issues. For example, implicit racial or gender biases can influence hiring decisions, performance reviews, and opportunities for advancement. Research has shown that individuals with stereotypically "masculine" names may be more likely to be hired for leadership positions, even if their qualifications are identical (Moss-Racusin et al., 2012).

12.3.1.2 Addressing DEIB Issues Observed in Talent Management Practices

To effectively address talent management issues related to unconscious bias, organisations should adopt a multifaceted approach:

1. *Education and Training*: Implement unconscious bias training programs to educate employees about the nature and impact of bias (Banaji & Greenwald, 1998). Provide training on inclusive leadership and effective communication.
2. *Diverse Hiring Practices*: Use anonymous resume reviews to eliminate bias based on name or demographic information. Implement structured interview processes to ensure fair and consistent evaluation of candidates. Diversify hiring panels to include individuals from diverse backgrounds.
3. *Performance Management:* Develop objective performance metrics to reduce subjective bias in evaluations. Provide regular feedback and coaching to help employees develop their skills and address performance gaps.
4. *Mentorship and Sponsorship Programs:* Create mentorship and sponsorship programs to support the development of underrepresented employees.
5. *Data-driven decision-making:* Use internal and external data to identify and address bias in hiring, promotion, and compensation practices.

12.3.1.3 Building a Culture of Belonging

Fostering a sense of belonging is crucial for creating inclusive and high-performing organisations. This involves creating environments where employees feel valued, respected, and connected to the organisation.

12.3.2 Psychological Safety

A key aspect of fostering belonging is creating a psychologically safe environment. This involves creating a space where employees feel comfortable sharing ideas, taking risks, and learning from mistakes without fear of negative consequences. Psychological safety can be fostered through open communication, active listening, and a culture of trust and respect (Edmondson, 2019).

12.3.3 Inclusive Policies and Practices

Organisations can foster a sense of belonging by implementing inclusive policies and practices. This includes:

1. Flexible Work Arrangements: Offering flexible work arrangements can help employees balance work and personal commitments, increasing job satisfaction and a stronger sense of belonging (Miller & Giblin, 2023).
2. Diversity and Inclusion Training: Training on diversity, equity, and inclusion can help employees understand and appreciate differences, leading to more inclusive and respectful workplaces (Ely et al., 2011).
3. Mentorship and Sponsorship Programs: These programs can help employees develop their skills, advance their careers, and build relationships with colleagues from diverse backgrounds (Allen et al., 2004).

12.3.4 Employee Engagement

Engaged employees are likelier to feel a sense of belonging to their organisation. Organisations can foster employee engagement by:

1. Recognising and Rewarding Employees: Recognising and rewarding employees for their contributions can boost morale and motivation (Amabile & Kramer, 2011).
2. Providing Opportunities for Growth and Development: Offering opportunities for professional development can help employees feel valued and invested in their careers (Spreitzer, 2007).
3. Encouraging Employee Voice: Creating channels for employees to share their ideas and feedback can help to foster a sense of ownership and belonging (Bakker & Demerouti, 2007).

12.4 Best Practices and Noteworthy Cases

A comprehensive examination of successful DEIB strategies employed by global tech giants and regional firms reveals several key principles. A fundamental step is thoroughly assessing the organisation's cultural landscape and identifying areas ripe for improvement. Transparency is paramount; companies should openly communicate their DEIB goals and progress to all employees. Fostering a sense of ownership and ensuring relevant initiatives require active employee involvement from diverse backgrounds.

Creating a psychologically safe environment where employees feel comfortable sharing concerns and opinions is crucial. A growth mindset, encouraging risk-taking and learning from failures, fosters a culture of innovation. Regular feedback mechanisms, soliciting input from employees and acting on their suggestions, ensure the effectiveness and relevance of DEIB initiatives.

We now present four cases of innovative DEIB initiatives in technology companies.

12.4.1 Amazon's Rekindle Program

Amazon's Rekindle program is a valuable initiative to support women re-entering the tech workforce after a career break of at least 12 months. By offering mentorship, on-the-job training, and interview preparation, the program addresses the challenges faced by women who take career breaks, including skill gaps and perceived employment barriers. Given Amazon's global workforce of over 1.5 million, Rekindle likely reaches hundreds to thousands annually.

In addition to Rekindle, Amazon's WoW (Women@Work) network provides ongoing support and development opportunities for women throughout their careers. It fosters connections between participants and key figures within Amazon's tech community, including leaders and recruiters.

However, it must be noted that the Rekindle program's scope is currently limited to women, raising questions about whether similar support is available for men returning from career breaks. Additionally, while the 12-month career break threshold is a standard benchmark, it may not adequately address the needs of women who have been out of the workforce for extended periods. Finally, the program's long-term impact and the extent to which it fosters ongoing career development for participants remain unclear.

According to Amazon's diversity and inclusion report (Edison International, 2022), women now represent 43.7% of Amazon's global tech workforce, showing incremental growth supported by programs like Rekindle. (www.aboutamazon.com/news/workplace/our-workforce-data)

Information primarily sourced from: www.amazon.jobs/content/en/career-programs/rekindle

12.4.2 UnlimITed at Globant

Globant's commitment to fostering a diverse and inclusive work environment extends beyond physical disabilities. Their UnlimITed program equips individuals with disabilities with the skills and support needed to thrive in the IT industry, offering tailored educational programs and ensuring a smooth integration through accessibility initiatives. This program aligns with their broader "Be Kind" initiative, emphasising social responsibility and inclusivity across various aspects of their operations (see also https://stayrelevant.globant.com/en/be-kind/).

Furthermore, their collaboration with AutismoTech (see also: https://www.autismotech.com/), a hackathon event focused on neurodivergent individuals for IT careers, demonstrates their commitment to expanding their talent pool and fostering a culture that embraces diverse perspectives. While details regarding the specific training modules, accessibility modifications, and long-term outcomes of UnlimITed would be valuable for a comprehensive evaluation, Globant's efforts represent a significant step towards a more inclusive and innovative tech sector.

12.4.3 SAP Embracing Neurodivergence

SAP, a prominent name in enterprise software, actively seeks to recruit neurodivergent candidates, particularly those on the autism spectrum (Hennekam & Follmer, 2024). Their "Autism at Work" program offers a comprehensive approach to attract, integrate, and empower these individuals within the company. Through dedicated career pages and outreach initiatives, SAP aims to connect with talented neurodivergent professionals who may excel in areas like data analysis, software development, and quality assurance. According to Austin and Pisano (2017), neurodiverse employees are 30% more productive on specific innovation tasks than their neurotypical peers, validating the impact of the Autism at Work initiative.

The program goes beyond just sourcing talent. It recognises that adjustments may be needed to create a genuinely inclusive environment. New hires are introduced to a "support circle" consisting of an Autism at Work buddy, mentor, and coach. On-the-job training and alternative interview processes cater to the unique strengths and communication styles of neurodivergent individuals. This holistic approach fosters a sense of belonging and empowers them to reach their full potential within SAP. While specifics regarding the program's long-term effectiveness and integration across all SAP roles would be valuable, their efforts showcase a commitment to building a diverse and neuro-inclusive workforce, potentially leading to a more innovative and successful company. SAP's Autism at Work program, launched in 2013, hires autistic individuals, targeting 1% of its ~80,000 workforce (~650 employees) by 2020 (SAP, 2016). As per the SAP official website today, SAP has over 160 employees with autism in 14 countries, across 28 locations and in 25+ job types

Information primarily sourced from: https://jobs.sap.com/content/Autism-at-Work/

12.4.4 Basecamp: The Remote Company

Basecamp's 100% remote work model provides a unique approach to fostering DEIB. By eliminating the traditional office setting, the company empowers employees to work in a way that best suits their needs and preferences. This remote-first culture can be particularly beneficial for individuals with disabilities or neurodivergent conditions, as it allows them to work in quieter, less stimulating environments. Additionally, flexible work arrangements enable employees to balance work and family commitments, promoting better work-life balance and mental health.

Furthermore, a globally distributed workforce can bring diverse perspectives and experiences together, leading to more innovative solutions. Remote work can also minimise biases based on appearance, age, or social status, as individuals are evaluated solely on their work. By fostering a sense of belonging through strong communication, virtual team-building activities, and transparent company culture, Basecamp demonstrates a commitment to creating a workplace where everyone feels valued and empowered, regardless of location or background.

Information primarily sourced from: https://basecamp.com/articles/how-basecamp-became-a-remote-company.

12.5 Discussion

This chapter's findings and theoretical underpinnings underscore DEIB's multifaceted challenges and opportunities in the global tech industry. We examine key frameworks and leadership models to reveal how organisations can systematically embed DEIB principles to create inclusive, equitable, and innovative workplaces.

12.5.1 Theoretical Implications

The chapter's exploration of DEIB theories emphasises that diversity and inclusion are not isolated phenomena but operate across micro, meso, and macro levels. At the individual level, theories like Social Identity Theory (Tajfel & Turner, 1979) and Implicit Bias Theory (Banaji & Greenwald, 1998) illuminate how unconscious biases and group identities influence perceptions, interactions, and decision-making. However, addressing individual biases alone is insufficient. Organisational-level frameworks, such as Diversity Management Theory and Schein's Organizational Culture Model, highlight the need for systemic interventions to address structural inequities.

Furthermore, integrating Critical Race Theory (Bell, 1992) and Intersectionality Theory (Carbado et al., 2013) broadens the understanding of power dynamics and interconnected identities, offering organisations the tools to address systemic exclusion. These frameworks contribute to a holistic approach, balancing individual, group, and institutional strategies for DEIB advancement. Hence, it is crucial to apply these theoretical insights to DEIB practices.

Theoretical frameworks offer critical guidance for designing and implementing effective DEIB strategies. For example, Social Identity Theory suggests that individuals' self-concepts are deeply tied to group memberships, often leading to in-group favouritism and out-group biases. Organisations can apply this insight by creating employee resource groups (ERGs) that foster a sense of belonging across diverse identity categories, implementing cross-functional team structures to encourage intergroup collaboration, and designing training programs to reduce in-group bias awareness.

Similarly, Intersectionality Theory emphasises that individuals experience unique and compounded forms of discrimination based on the intersection of multiple identities (e.g., race, gender, ability). Organisations can apply this by ensuring that DEIB policies are not "one-size-fits-all" but instead address the layered experiences of marginalised groups. This can include conducting intersectional pay equity audits, tailoring mentorship programs for women of colour or neurodivergent individuals, and designing inclusive leadership pipelines that recognize complex identity intersections.

12.5.2 Practical Insights for Tech Workforces

The case studies of Amazon, Globant, SAP, and Basecamp illustrate best practices for fostering inclusive cultures within technology organisations. Each initiative—whether addressing women's re-entry into the workforce, neurodivergent recruitment, or flexible remote work—serves as a critical exemplar of tailored strategies for overcoming DEIB barriers. However, several key insights emerge:

Inclusive Leadership: Leadership approaches like servant leadership (Greenleaf, 1970) and transformational leadership (Bass, 1985) emerge as pivotal enablers of DEIB. Servant leaders emphasise empowerment, while transformational leaders inspire cultural change and inclusivity.

Leaders must prioritise psychological safety (Edmondson, 2019) to foster a culture of open dialogue and innovation.

Addressing Unconscious Bias: The chapter demonstrates that implicit biases influence talent management processes, such as recruitment, performance evaluation, and advancement. Strategies such as anonymous resume reviews, structured interviews, and mentorship programs are critical for mitigating these biases. However, organisations must complement these measures with ongoing education, training, and data-driven decision-making.

Belonging and Psychological Safety: This work's unique contribution is its focus on belonging, which addresses employees' emotional and psychological needs. Policies fostering flexible work, employee engagement, and voice mechanisms create inclusive environments where employees feel connected and valued.

Tailoring DEIB to Organisational Contexts: DEIB frameworks like Hofstede's Cultural Dimensions highlight that effective strategies must align with cultural and contextual realities. For global tech organisations, sensitivity to regional and organisational nuances ensures that initiatives are relevant and impactful.

12.5.3 Contributions to Organisational Practice

This chapter contributes to practice by offering a interventions for integrating DEIB principles into organisational culture, leadership, and talent management systems. Key takeaways for practitioners include:

- Adopting inclusive leadership models to champion equity and belonging.
- Systematically addressing **biases** through policy, education, and technology.
- Leveraging organisational culture frameworks to align shared values with DEIB objectives.
- Promoting psychological safety and fostering employee voice to build inclusive cultures.

While the presented best practices provide actionable insights, organisations must approach DEIB as iterative. Continuous evaluation, employee feedback, and adaptability are essential for sustained progress.

12.5.4 A Roadmap for Organisations to Build and Sustain DEIB Initiatives

To support organisations in operationalising DEIB principles, we propose an integrated strategy roadmap that aligns theory with actionable practice. This roadmap outlines a phased approach tailored to the varying maturity levels of organisations on their DEIB journey. Each phase includes key objectives, strategic actions, insights from relevant literature, and expected deliverables. The roadmap emphasises leadership commitment, structural integration, and long-term sustainability. Table 12.2 presents the detailed framework across four progressive phases.

This phased roadmap provides organisations with a structured yet flexible path to embed DEIB into core operations. Aligning strategic intent with measurable outcomes enables long-term cultural transformation and sustained impact.

12.5.5 Limitations and Future Research Directions

Despite the growing attention to DEIB in organisations, current initiatives often face significant limitations. Many DEIB programs remain performative rather than transformational, lacking sustained leadership commitment or rigorous impact evaluation. Additionally, while many initiatives target visible diversity dimensions (e.g., gender, race), they often underemphasise intersectionality, neurodivergence, and less visible aspects of diversity. A further limitation is that metrics for measuring belongingness and inclusion often remain subjective and vary widely across organisations, making it difficult to benchmark progress or establish best practices.

Future research could address these gaps by:

- **Developing standardised metrics for measuring belonging and inclusion** that are comparable across industries and geographies.
- **Exploring intersectional outcomes** more deeply, particularly the experiences of individuals with overlapping marginalised identities (e.g., women of colour with disabilities) in tech environments.
- **Evaluating the long-term sustainability** of DEIB programs through longitudinal, multi-year studies rather than short-term assessments.
- **Investigating the unintended consequences** of DEIB initiatives, such as backlash effects or resistance among dominant groups, to develop more resilient implementation strategies.
- **Studying the role of emerging technologies** (e.g., AI-driven recruitment platforms) in mitigating or exacerbating biases, offering guidance on ethical tech design for DEIB purposes.

12.6 Conclusion

This chapter has comprehensively examined DEIB within the global tech industry. Integrating theoretical frameworks, leadership models,

TABLE 12.2

DEIB Strategy Roadmap, Source: Compiled by authors based on the work of

Phase (Time Frame Months)	Objective	Key Actions	Insights from Hogan et al., 2023	Deliverables
1. **Initiation and Strategic Commitment (1–3)**	Secure leadership alignment and assess organisational readiness	- Appoint Chief Diversity Officer (CDO) with C-suite access - Align DEIB with org strategy (ESG, talent) - Conduct equity audits and climate surveys - Host listening sessions- Form DEIB steering committee - Draft DEIB charter	- CDOs must negotiate autonomy - Trust-building via transparency is critical	- DEIB leader JD and governance model - Gap analysis report
2. **Planning and Infrastructure (4–9)**	Build systems for sustainable DEIB integration	- Define SMART goals (e.g., 30% diverse leaders) - Develop a logic model (e.g., mentorship → retention) - Revise HR policies (recruitment, promotion) - Launch mandatory training - Secure DEIB budget (2–5% of HR) - Fund ERGs with plans	- Integrate DEIB into performance systems to avoid fatigue	- Strategic DEIB plan with KPIs - Updated HR policies and training
3. **Implementation and Cultural Embedding (10–18)**	Execute interventions and foster an inclusive culture	- Roll out pay equity audits, mentorship, accessibility - Supplier diversity (20% diverse vendors) - Launch DEIB dashboards and pulse surveys - Establish community partnerships - Public DEIB reporting	- Link DEIB metrics to leadership incentives	- DEIB scorecard (baseline vs. progress) - Supplier diversity audit
4. **Sustainment and Scaling (19+)**	Institutionalize DEIB into organisational DNA	- Embed DEIB in JD, leadership, M&A - Annual DEIB impact benchmarking - AI sentiment tools for early detection - Iterate underperforming programs - Sponsorships for high-potential talent - DEIB board oversight	- DEIB must shift from project-based to core operations	- Updated leadership competency model - Multi-year community engagement strategy

Hogan *et al.* (2023)

and organisational culture theories highlights actionable pathways for organisations to address workforce inequities and foster inclusive, equitable, and innovative workplaces.

Theoretical insights, such as Social Identity Theory, Intersectionality Theory, and Organizational Culture Models, emphasise that DEIB challenges are deeply rooted in individual behaviours, systemic barriers, and cultural norms. The interplay of these elements requires a multi-level approach that balances individual-level interventions with organisational and societal reforms. Moreover, inclusive leadership, mainly through servant and transformational leadership, emerges as a catalyst for driving cultural change, mitigating biases, and fostering psychological safety in teams.

The discussion of successful initiatives by organisations such as Amazon, Globant, SAP, and Basecamp demonstrates that tailored DEIB strategies—addressing gender equity, neurodivergence, and flexible work environments—can yield significant organisational benefits, including increased innovation, employee engagement, and retention. However, these cases also underscore the need for organisations to continuously monitor and evaluate the impact of DEIB programs to ensure sustained progress.

A key contribution of this chapter is the emphasis on fostering a culture of belonging. Beyond recruitment and representation, the chapter stresses the importance of creating psychologically safe environments where all employees feel respected, valued, and empowered to contribute their unique perspectives. This focus aligns DEIB with the broader goals of employee well-being, organisational performance, and business sustainability.

12.6.1 Looking Ahead

As the tech industry continues to evolve in response to global challenges, rapid innovation, and increasing workforce diversity, organisations must approach DEIB as an ongoing and adaptive process. By embracing inclusive leadership, addressing systemic biases, and cultivating cultures of belonging, organisations can unlock the full potential of their diverse talent pools. The road ahead requires commitment, intentionality, and collaboration across all organisational levels to drive meaningful, measurable change.

Therefore, fostering DEIB in the tech sector is not merely a moral imperative but a strategic necessity. Organisations prioritising these principles are better equipped to address societal inequities, enhance employee satisfaction, and drive long-term innovation and growth. This chapter offers a foundational blueprint for reimagining workforce strategies that are inclusive, equitable, and sustainable in the face of an ever-changing global landscape.

Declaration

The authors confirm that artificial intelligence (AI) tools were used to enhance the grammar, sentence structure, and readability of this manuscript. The use of AI was limited to language refinement and did not influence the originality, conceptual framework, analysis, or intellectual content of the work. The ideas, arguments, and findings presented remain the sole contributions of the authors. The authors are responsible for the manuscript's accuracy, integrity, and originality.

References

Adams, J. S. (1965). Inequity in social exchange. In L. Berkowitz (Ed.), *Advances in Experimental Social Psychology* (Vol. 2, pp. 223–267). Academic Press.

Allen, T. D., Eby, L. T., Poteet, M. A., Lentz, E. J., & Magley, V. J. (2004). Work-family boundary management: A qualitative analysis. *Journal of Vocational Behavior, 64*(1), 48–77. https://doi.org/10.1016/S0001-8791(03)00044-6

Allport, G. W. (1954). *The Nature of Prejudice*. Addison-Wesley.

Amabile, T. M., & Kramer, S. J. (2011). *The Progress Principle: Using Small Wins to Ignite Work Joy, Engagement, and Creativity*. Harvard Business Review Press.

Austin, R. D., & Pisano, G. P. (2017). Neurodiversity as a competitive advantage. *Harvard Business Review, 95*(3), 96–103.

Avolio, B. J., & Bass, B. M. (1991). *The Full Range Leadership Development Program: Facilitator's Guide*. Mind Garden.

Bakker, A. B., & Demerouti, E. (2007). Job demands-resources model: State of the art. *Journal of Occupational Health Psychology, 12*(3), 279–285. https://doi.org/10.1037/1076-8998.12.3.279

Banaji, M. R., & Greenwald, A. G. (1998). Implicit prejudice. *Current Directions in Psychological Science*, 7(2), 100–103.

Bass, B. M. (1985). *Leadership and Performance Beyond Expectations*. McGraw-Hill.

Bass, B. M., & Riggio, R. E. (2006). *Transformational leadership* (2nd ed.). Lawrence Erlbaum Associates.

Bell, D. A. (1992). *Faces at the Bottom of the Well: The Permanence of Racism*—Basic Books.

Braidotti, R. (2019). The contemporary posthumanities. *Higher Education in the World 7*, 133.

Burns, J. M. (1978). *Leadership*. Harper & Row.

Carbado, D. W., Crenshaw, K. W., Mays, V. M., & Tomlinson, B. (2013). Intersectionality: Mapping the movements of a theory. *Du Bois Review: Social Science Research on Race, 10*(2), 303–312. https://doi.org/10.1017/S1742058X13000349

Deloria, V. (1999). *Red Earth, White Lies: Native Americans and the Myth of Scientific Fact*. Fulcrum Publishing.

Edison International. (2022). *2022 diversity, equity & inclusion report: The power of our people*. Edison International. https://s3.amazonaws.com/cms.ipressroom.com/405/files/202210/eix-2021-diversity-equity-and-inclusion-report.pdf

Edmondson, A. C. (2019). *The Fearless Organization: Creating Psychological Safety in the Workplace for Learning, Innovation, and Growth*. Penguin Random House.

Ely, R. J., Ibarra, H., & Kolb, L. M. (2011). *Teams at the Top: The Leadership Advantage in Diverse Organizations*. Harvard Business Press.

Frank, A. G. (1967). *Capitalism and underdevelopment in Latin America: Historical studies of Chile and Brazil*. Monthly Review Press.

Freire, P. (1996). Pedagogy of the Oppressed (revised). *New York: Continuum, 356*, 357–358.

Giroux, H. A. (2004). Critical pedagogy and the postmodern/modern divide: Towards a pedagogy of democratisation. *Teacher Education Quarterly, 31*(1), 31–47.

Greenleaf, R. K. (1970). *The Servant Leader*. Robert K. Greenleaf Center.

Haraway, D. (1985). Manifesto for cyborgs: Science, technology, and socialist feminism in the 1980s. *Socialist Review, 80*, 65.

Hennekam, S., & Follmer, K. (2024). Neurodiversity and HRM: A practice-based review and research agenda. *Equality, Diversity and Inclusion: An International Journal, 43*(7), 1119–1129.

Herring, C. (2018). *Leading with Diversity: Creating Inclusive Workplaces*. Routledge.

Hofstede, G. (2001). Culture's Consequences: Comparing Cultures Across Nations (2nd ed.). Sage Publications.

Hogan, T. H., O'Rourke, B. P., Weeks, E., Silvera, G. A., & Choi, S. (2023). Top-level leaders and implementation strategies to support organisational diversity, equity, inclusion, and belonging (DEIB) interventions: A qualitative study of top-level DEIB leaders in healthcare organisations. *Implementation Science, 18*(1), 59.

Kahneman, D. (2011). *Thinking, Fast and Slow*. Farrar, Straus and Giroux.

Kruger, J., & Dunning, D. (1999). Unskilled and unaware of it: How difficulties in recognising one's own incompetence lead to inflated self-assessments. *Journal of Personality and Social Psychology, 77*(6), 1121–1134.

Luthans, F., Avolio, B. J., Avey, J. B., & Peterson, S. J. (2006). *Positive Organisational Behavior: Developing the Strengths and Virtues of Individuals and Organisations*. American Psychological Association.

Miller, C. S., & Giblin, J. (2023). Improving job satisfaction and belonging through flexible work and leadership cohorts. *Advances in Developing Human Resources*. Advance online publication. https://doi.org/10.1177/15234223231212675

Moss-Racusin, C. A., Dovidio, J. F., Brescoll, V. L., Graham, M. J., & Handelsman, J. (2012). Science faculty's subtle gender biases favor male students. *Proceedings of the National Academy of Sciences*, 109(41), 16474–16479. https://doi.org/10.1073/pnas.1211286109

Nickerson, R. S. (1998). Confirmation bias: A ubiquitous phenomenon with devastating consequences. *Review of General Psychology, 2*(2), 175–220.

Northouse, P. G. (2018). *Leadership: Theory and Practice* (8th ed.). Sage Publications.

Olson, G. A. (1990). Jacques Derrida on rhetoric and composition: A conversation. *Journal of Advanced Composition, 10*(1), 1–21. http://www.jstor.org/stable/20865695

SAP. (2016). *Autism at Work: Creating opportunities for Neurodiverse Talent*. SAP News. https://news.sap.com/2016/05/autism-at-work-creating-opportunities/
Schein, E. H. (2004). *Organisational Culture and Leadership* (4th ed.). Jossey-Bass.
Sherif, M. (1966). In common prejudice. *Scientific American, 214*(4), 28–33.
Sidanius, J., & Pratto, F. (1999). *Social dominance: An intergroup theory of social hierarchy and oppression.* Cambridge University Press. https://doi.org/10.1017/CBO9781139175043
Spears, L. C. (2002). *Reflections on Leadership: How to be a Servant-Leader*. John Wiley & Sons.
Spreitzer, G. M. (2007). The path to meaningfulness in work: A conceptual framework. *Academy of Management Review, 32*(2), 464–478. https://doi.org/10.5465/AMR.2007.22650413
Steele, C. M., & Aronson, J. (1995). Stereotype threat and the intellectual test performance of African Americans. *Journal of Personality and Social Psychology*, 69(5), 797–811. https://doi.org/10.1037//0022-3514.69.5.797
Stouffer, S. A., Suchman, E. A., DeVinney, L. C., Star, S. A., & Williams, R. M. (1949). *The American soldier: Adjustment during army life.* Princeton University Press.
Tajfel, H., & Turner, J. C. (1979). An integrative theory of intergroup conflict. In W. G. Austin & S. Worchel (Eds.), *The Social Psychology of Intergroup Relations* (pp. 33–47). Monterey, CA: Brooks/Cole.
Thorndike, E. L. (1920). A constant error in psychological ratings. *Journal of Applied Psychology*, 4(1), 25–29.
Wolin, R. (2001). *The rhetorical imagination of Kenneth Burke*. University of South Carolina Press.

13

The Citizen Development Culture: Cultivating an Inclusive and Empowered Digital Workforce

Sumant Devasthali and Manisha Sharma

13.1 Introduction

In today's business landscape, the technology plays a central role in driving operational efficiency, innovation, and competitive advantage. Traditionally, the responsibility of defining and executing the IT strategies has been centralized within the IT departments, typically under the direction of the Chief Technology Officer (CTO). However, this model is shifting toward a more decentralized approach to the technological development. This evolution reduces the organizational over-reliance on the IT teams and promotes broader employee involvement in their digital innovation (Nimje, 2024). Advances in the digital enablers have empowered the cross functional employees to actively participate in the design and deployment of digital solutions (Rokis & Kirikova, 2022).

Low-code/no-code (LCNC) platforms have emerged as transformative tools that enable the employees across diverse business functions to contribute directly to an organization's digital assets, regardless of their formal technical background (Silva et al., 2023). Offered by a wide range of vendors, these platforms encompass various technologies, including the robotic process automation (RPA) and the AI-powered code generators. By utilizing the LCNC tools, business-oriented employees can assume the role of 'citizen developers', thereby accelerating and scaling the IT-driven innovation across the enterprise. Moreover, the LCNC platforms foster a stronger collaboration between the IT and the business units (Shridhar, 2021). They empower business teams to conceptualize and articulate the solution wireframes, which IT professionals can then refine and implement efficiently.

This collaborative model promotes an inclusive digital environment, where employees from across the organization contribute with their domain-specific expertise to drive the organizational growth (Guthardt et al., 2024). Notably,

DOI: 10.1201/9781003591078-17

this inclusiveness extends opportunities to underrepresented groups, allowing a wider talent base to participate in shaping the digital future of the organization. Ultimately, the integration of the LCNC solutions enables businesses to cultivate an agile, inclusive workplace and embed a culture of innovation and technological empowerment at all the organizational levels.

While the LCNC platforms offer significant advantages to businesses, their growing adoption also raises critical questions about the long-term implications for business agility, workforce dynamics, and the strategic planning. Despite its widespread uptake across industries, a structured understanding of the broader organizational impact of LCNC remains limited (Luo et al., 2021). To address this gap, the present study investigates the following research questions:

RQ1: How do LCNC platforms impact the business agility, and the workforce transformation?

RQ2: What are the future implications and the strategic planning considerations for organizations to effectively leverage the Citizen Development phenomenon?

This study adopts a Systematic Literature Review (SLR) methodology to synthesize the insights from peer-reviewed academic literature and industry reports. Section 13.2 details the research design and the article selection criteria. Section 13.3 presents key findings, organized into three thematic areas namely *'Conceptual Foundations'*, *'Industry Applications and Business Implications'*, and *'Future-Proofing and Strategic Planning'*. Section 13.4 contextualizes these findings and highlights their theoretical contributions and practical relevance. Finally, Section 13.5 summarizes the key takeaways and the future readiness areas.

13.2 Methods

This study employed a Systematic Literature Review (SLR) methodology to synthesize the existing insights on the Low-Code/No-Code (LCNC) platforms and their implications (see Figure 13.1). Following the established SLR framework proposed by Tranfield (2003), a structured process was applied, encompassing peer-reviewed journal articles, conference proceedings, and high-impact industry reports sourced from the Scopus, the Web of Science, and reputable web based publications. A systematic search was conducted using predefined keywords such as 'Low-Code Development', 'No-Code Platforms', 'Citizen Development', and 'Digital transformation'. The search

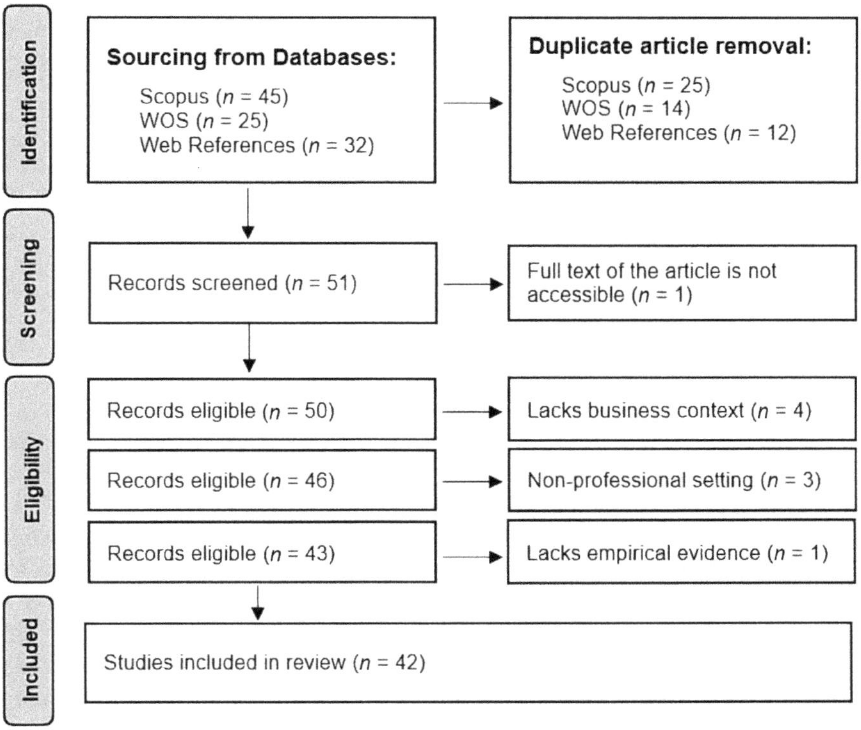

FIGURE 13.1
Identification of studies from research databases.

strategy incorporated Boolean operators and thematic filters to ensure the inclusion of relevant literature. The Inclusion criteria were restricted to studies published in English between 2018 and 2024 that focused on LCNC applications within the business and organizational contexts. Studies lacking empirical contributions or focusing on LCNC in nonprofessional settings were excluded.

The initial search yielded 102 articles. After removing the duplicates and applying the relevant filters, 51 articles remained. Full-text screening further narrowed this into a final corpus of 42 studies. The accompanying diagram illustrates the systematic review process used to select these studies.

These articles were categorized into three thematic areas namely: 'Conceptual Foundations', which covered definitions and core principles of LCNC platform; 'Industry Applications and Business Implications', which explored the adoption patterns across industries; and 'Future-Proofing and Strategic Planning' which addressed topics such as the governance, workforce shifts, and the long-term strategic role of LCNC in business transformations.

TABLE 13.1

Summary of selected 42 papers

Themes	Type of Source				
	Scientific Journal	Conference articles	Edited books	Web Articles	Total
Conceptual foundations	12	2	2	3	19
Industry applications and business implications	8	1	1	5	15
Future proofing and strategic planning	4	1		3	8
Total	24	4	3	11	42

The following Table 13.1 summarizes the selected literature by thematic focus and publication source.

To synthesize the data, qualitative coding and thematic clustering methods were employed to ensure the consistency in aggregating key findings (Guest & McLellan, 2003). A narrative synthesis approach was further adopted to interpret the broader patterns, including the emerging trends, shifts in workforce roles, and key organizational challenges (Popay et al., 2006). This layered methodology enhanced the credibility of the insights and offered a coherent understanding of the significance of the LCNC platforms in business transformations.

13.3 Results

The systematic literature review revealed three overarching themes that define the evolving role of the Low-Code/No-Code (LCNC) platforms: Conceptual Foundations, Industry Applications and Business Implications, and Future-Proofing and Strategic Planning. These themes were derived through a systematic process of qualitative coding and thematic clustering (Guest & McLellan, 2003), which enabled the recognition of recurring patterns and concepts across the selected studies. This process was further guided by the synthesis strategies established in prior scholarly work on LCNC platforms and digital transformation (Kulkarni, 2021; Velásquez et al., 2024). A narrative synthesis approach (Popay et al., 2006) was further employed to interpret these themes contextually, enabling a cohesive understanding of LCNC's role across different organizational settings and industry verticals.

The **Conceptual Foundations** theme underscores LCNC's role in democratizing the software development by enabling citizen developers to create functional applications with minimal coding expertise. Research highlights the potential of LCNC tools to reduce the IT backlogs, enhance organizational agility, and lower development costs. However, concerns persist around scalability, data security, and governance—particularly in large-scale enterprise environments.

The theme of **Industry Applications and Business Implications** illustrates LCNC's transformative impact across multiple sectors. Within IT workflows, the LCNC platforms promote the collaboration between business users and professional developers. In the industrial manufacturing, they support the process automation and drive digital transformation. For small and medium-sized enterprises (SMEs), LCNC solutions offer the cost-effective innovation without the need for a heavy reliance on the external IT vendors. The reviewed studies suggest that LCNC adoption accelerates time-to-market, boosts operational agility, and improves resource efficiency.

Finally, the **Future-Proofing and Strategic Planning** theme addresses the long-term organizational implications of the LCNC adoption. Younger workforce cohorts, particularly the Gen Z professionals, are quick to adopt LCNC tools as part of their daily workflows. Yet, challenges related to the IT governance, legacy system integration, and enterprise-wide security remain significant. LCNC is also recognized as an enabler of the agile experimentation, which allows organizations to prototype and test new solutions with minimal risk. Long-term success, however, requires robust strategies to manage the compliance, scalability, and the governance process.

Building on these synthesized findings, the subsequent analysis is structured around three identified themes. Each theme provides a lens to examine critical dimensions of LCNC adoption, including the foundational principles, sectoral use cases, and strategic implications for the future of the business and workforce transformation.

13.3.1 Conceptual Foundations

Core Concepts: LCNC and Citizen Development

Low-code and no-code (LCNC) platforms are reshaping the software development landscape by empowering the nontechnical and semitechnical employees to contribute actively to the application development (Hoogsteen & Borgman, 2022). These platforms offer visual development environments, where users can design applications through intuitive drag-and-drop interfaces, configure workflows, and automate business processes—all with minimal or no coding expertise.

No-code platforms are typically tailored for business users with limited to no programming background, whereas low-code platforms provide greater customization capabilities for users with some technical proficiency (Jin & Pan, 2022). Together, these technologies bridge the gap between the business requirement and its technical execution, by democratizing the software development and reducing the dependence on IT teams. This shift has given rise to the phenomenon of **citizen development**, wherein employees outside of the IT function assume the responsibility for building and maintaining applications. Citizen development is increasingly recognized as a strategic enabler of digital transformation (Lebens et al., 2021). Gartner analysts have emphasized its role in accelerating the development cycles, lowering costs, and expanding the pool of digital innovators within organizations.

By leveraging LCNC tools, organizations can scale the enterprise-grade applications efficiently while remaining agile in responding to evolving business needs (Muhammad et al., 2024). Beyond operational efficiency, the LCNC platforms also promote inclusivity by enabling employees from various departments—regardless of their technical background—to engage in digital innovation. The ability to rapidly build, adapt, and deploy applications, fosters the cross-functional collaboration, enhances productivity, and cultivates a culture of experimentation (Kulkarni, 2021). As adoption continues to expand, organizations are increasingly relying on the diverse, multidisciplinary teams to design the digital solutions that reflect the needs of both the workforce and the client base.

Redefining IT–Business Collaboration

The integration of LCNC platforms is redefining the IT workflows and transforming the dynamics of business–IT collaboration. These platforms introduce an agile, decentralized approach to the application development, enabling more responsive and iterative innovation cycles. Traditionally, business units would articulate their technology needs and submit them to the IT departments, which would then engage in prolonged development processes (Binzer & Winkler, 2022). This centralized model often resulted in delayed deliveries, with many applications becoming misaligned with evolving business needs before deployment.

LCNC platforms mitigate such inefficiencies by empowering the business users to participate directly in application development. Through visual, drag-and-drop interfaces and preconfigured logic, the employees from various departments can rapidly develop applications tailored to their immediate needs (Bhattacharyya & Kumar, 2023). This not only alleviates the workload of the IT departments but also shifts their focus toward more complex tasks, such as the system architecture, security, and enterprise integration. The outcome is a more collaborative and adaptive development environment where the business and IT teams co-create solutions in real time.

While both low-code and no-code platforms streamline the application development, they serve distinct roles within the organizations. No-code platforms are primarily designed for the non-technical users, enabling them to create applications using prebuilt components and automated workflows (Muhammad et al., 2024). In contrast, low-code platforms offer the enhanced flexibility, allowing developers and technically proficient users to customize their applications with minimal coding effort. This distinction enables the organizations to strategically adopt the right tools based on user capabilities, thereby balancing ease of use with scalability and customization.

By embracing LCNC tools, organizations foster a more inclusive digital ecosystem that encourages a collaboration between the IT and business stakeholders. This paradigm shift repositions the IT departments from traditional gatekeepers to strategic enablers, responsible for the governance, security, and digital alignment—while empowering a broader workforce to drive the innovation (Kulkarni, 2021; Myles Suer, 2024).

13.3.2 Industry Applications and Business Implications

Business Impact of Low-Code and No-Code Platforms

The low-code and no-code (LCNC) platforms are significantly reshaping how businesses approach the software development, primarily by closing the traditional gap between business teams and the IT department (Bock & Frank, 2021b). Historically, software development was the exclusive domain of IT professionals, requiring the advanced programming skills, specialized tools, and considerable time and resources. The emergence of LCNC platforms has democratized this process by enabling the business users to build tailored software solutions without needing an extensive technical expertise (Woo, 2020). This shift not only reduces the development burden on the IT teams but also ensures that, applications are directly guided by the insights of the employees who are closest to operational processes and customer interactions. As a result, organizations benefit from faster development cycles, enhanced alignment with business needs, and increased responsiveness to change.

A key strategic advantage of LCNC adoption lies in its potential to mitigate the global shortage of skilled software developers (Bernsteiner et al., 2022). While the demand for customized digital solutions continues to rise, the availability of qualified IT professionals remains limited. LCNC platforms help bridge this gap by expanding the pool of contributors to include the non-technical staff—often referred to as the citizen developers—thereby accelerating the pace of digital transformation (Schwinger et al., 2023). Moreover, the cloud-native architecture of many LCNC solutions enhances their scalability, flexibility, and accessibility. Unlike traditional development approaches, which often depend on a complex on-premises infrastructure, the cloud-based LCNC tools enable the remote deployment and iterative updates, allowing organizations to respond quickly to the evolving market dynamics (Sufi, 2023). These platforms also enable organizations to modernize their legacy systems, automate workflows, and enhance collaboration across departments, while driving the efficiency and fostering the agile and inclusive digital workforce (Myles Suer, 2024).

Empowering Small and Medium Businesses (SMBs)

In today's resource-constrained landscape, small and medium businesses (SMBs) face considerable challenges in meeting their technological needs while managing associated costs and timelines. Traditional software development often necessitates the specialized IT expertise, which can result in delays due to the stretched internal resources or costly outsourcing involved (Myles Suer, 2024). The rise of citizen development is reshaping how the SMBs approach digital transformation. Industry cloud solutions now offer ready-to-use templates that simplify the operational automation and enable rapid deployment with minimal customization (Elshan, Dickhaut, et al., 2023). Citizen development allows business users to leverage prebuilt modules, drag-and-drop interfaces, and automation tools to build customized applications for the customer engagement, internal process management, and workflow optimization—enhancing both the agility and efficiency. One of its key advantages lies in bypassing the lengthy IT queues, allowing critical applications to be developed and deployed faster (Elshan, Ebel, et al., 2023). This is particularly valuable for the SMBs, which often lack the dedicated IT staff and face skill issues that hinder responsiveness and competitiveness (Sahay et al., 2020).

The cost-effectiveness of doing in-house development through LCNC platforms makes technology adoption more attainable for SMBs, by reducing operational expenses and improving process efficiency. Beyond cost and speed, the citizen development fosters innovation and autonomy by enabling employees—who best understand the daily workflows—to design solutions that directly reflect the operational realities (Bies et al., 2022). This empowerment nurtures a culture of experimentation and continuous improvement, allowing the SMBs to iterate quickly without relying on the external development teams. Developing tailored internal applications also boosts productivity, reduces inefficiencies, and minimizes the dependency on third-party tools (Johannes Hintsch, 2022).

However, the widespread adoption of LCNC platforms introduces critical considerations around security, governance, and scalability (Elshan, Dickhaut, et al., 2023). To sustain innovation while mitigating risk, SMBs must ensure that the citizen development efforts align with organizational security protocols and their long-term strategic objectives.

Impact on Industrial Manufacturing

The rise of the citizen development in industrial manufacturing highlights the transformative potential of the LCNC platforms in addressing the operational inefficiencies. Manufacturing firms often grapple with rigid enterprise software, intricate workflows, and rapidly evolving production requirements (Zhang et al., 2021). Traditionally, operators, engineers, and integration specialists—despite possessing the deep domain knowledge, relied on the IT departments for their digital solutions. This dependency frequently resulted in delays and misalignments between the technical outputs and operational needs. LCNC platforms mitigate these challenges by enabling the nontechnical employees to design and adapt digital tools that directly reflect their on-the-ground insights (Elshan, Dickhaut, et al., 2023).

In the dynamic manufacturing environments, where maintaining efficiency, compliance, and profitability demands a constant adaptation; conventional systems such as Manufacturing Execution Systems (MES) and Enterprise Resource Planning (ERP) often prove to be rigid and resource-intensive to adjust quickly (Sanchis et al., 2019). LCNC platforms introduce a more agile approach, allowing the frontline teams to refine the existing ERP capabilities, integrate external functionalities, and implement digital enhancements without requiring extensive coding expertise.

On the shop floor, LCNC tools are increasingly used to automate manual processes, improve quality control, and boost production efficiency. Engineers and technicians can develop applications that embed logic-based automation, interface with IoT devices, and leverage real-time operational data (Waszkowski, 2019). For example, digital root cause analysis tools can automate the data collection and documentation, ensuring a faster and more effective corrective action. Similarly, dynamic digital work instructions adapt to the evolving production conditions, reducing the human error and enhancing the responsiveness (Martinez & Pfister, 2023). In quality assurance, no-code platforms support AI-driven defect detection, by enabling automated inspections through sensors or the computer vision, which reduces waste and ensures the compliance with industry standards.

The strategic value of LCNC adoption in the manufacturing extends well beyond productivity gains. By equipping the frontline workers, these platforms enhance organizational agility and ensure production workflows remain responsive to the market dynamics (Moreira-Filho et al., 2024). Reducing dependence on the IT teams allows technical resources to be reallocated to mission-critical initiatives, while citizen developers address the routine operational challenges. This decentralization of digital innovation enables solutions to originate from those who possess the direct process knowledge, rather than being solely driven by the centralized IT units (Luo et al., 2021). This fosters a culture of continuous improvement, empowering the employees across hierarchical levels to prototype, refine, and deploy context-relevant digital tools that builds a more inclusive and empowered workforce (Cabot, 2020).

While the manufacturing illustrates the profound benefits of LCNC platforms, their applicability extends across industries, in varying degrees and based on sector-specific needs and digital maturity. Industries are witnessing increasing use and tailoring of LCNC platforms for industry-specific use cases, empowering nontechnical professionals to drive innovation from within. This momentum is evident across a range of sectors, where complex workflows and evolving operational demands benefit from decentralized digital solutions (Martinez & Pfister, 2023).

13.3.3 Future Proofing and Strategic Planning

LCNC Adoption: Challenges and IT Governance

While the citizen development opens new avenues for innovation, it also introduces critical challenges that must be managed thoughtfully. Key concerns include the security vulnerabilities, integration difficulties, and governance gaps—all of which can undermine the enterprise goals if not addressed (Elshan, Ebel, et al., 2023). A well-defined citizen development strategy mandates a strategic oversight from the central IT team, to mitigate these risks while maintaining the security, compliance, and operational efficiency (Aggarwal, 2023).

Yet, few limitations can remain. Many LCNC tools rely on standardized modules and templates, which, while being useful for automating routine tasks, often lack the flexibility needed for complex enterprise solutions. These include scenarios requiring system integrations with enterprise systems, custom extension logic, or the AI-driven functionality (Overeem et al., 2021). Another major concern is the vendor lock-in. Applications built on the proprietary LCNC platforms are difficult to migrate to alternative environments, posing risks to the long-term adaptability and sustainability.

In addition to the technical and governance-related limitations, few broader organizational concerns also persist. A lack of formal IT oversight can increase the risk of security breaches, compliance failures, and data privacy issues (Cabot, 2020). The emergence of 'shadow IT'—where applications are developed outside of central IT's purview—can lead to a fragmented and unregulated digital ecosystem. Addressing these risks requires clear enterprise-wide policies to harness citizen development, along with continuous IT monitoring and alignment of citizen-built tools with the broader IT architecture (Alamin et al., 2023).

A recurring debate centres on the impact of the LCNC platforms on professional software developers. While these platforms empower the nontechnical employees, they do not replace the experienced IT professionals (Zolotas et al., 2018). Instead, the role of the IT professionals shifts from application development to higher-order areas such as the enterprise architecture, cybersecurity, and regulatory compliance. IT professionals thus become the key enablers of digital transformation, guiding and supporting citizen developers to ensure an alignment with the firm's strategic goals. Organizations that strike an effective balance between the decentralized innovation and the centralized IT strategy can create resilient foundation for modern innovative businesses (Brüggemann, 2023).

LCNC and the Agile Enterprise

The adoption of low-code/no-code (LCNC) platforms is reshaping how organizations approach the innovation, growth, and experimentation. By empowering nonprogrammers across different functions, these platforms decentralize the software creation and promote greater inclusivity and agility

(Kass et al., 2022). Employees with deep operational knowledge are now able to craft tailored digital solutions that address business needs directly, thus expanding the developer base through citizen participation. Empirical studies show that the organizations leveraging LCNC for customer-facing applications report accelerated deployment cycles and measurable gains in business performance (Bock & Frank, 2021a). Reflecting this shift, Gartner estimated that by 2024, 80% of software development would occur outside of the traditional coding environments (Paul Vincent, 2019).

LCNC platforms enable experimentation in several ways. First, they facilitate rapid digital transformation by allowing the domain experts to build applications without requiring coding proficiency, thereby enhancing the responsiveness to market shifts and regulatory updates (Daniel et al., 2020). Second, the intuitive visual interfaces and robust integration capabilities of LCNC platforms enable the rapid extension of enterprise solutions with minimal technical complexity (Ihirwe et al., 2020). Third, development costs and timelines are significantly reduced, making it feasible to pilot and refine solutions with minimal risk. Furthermore, LCNC tools support iterative prototyping, enabling a real-time feedback and user-centred innovation (Jacinto et al., 2020).

The evolution of LCNC is also redefining the time intensive software development cycles. Traditional coding environments often involve long lead times and a burden of legacy system maintenance (Khorram et al., 2020). In contrast, LCNC platforms enable development speeds up to three times faster, reduce manual errors, and alleviate maintenance workloads. Although once perceived as suitable only for basic applications, the contemporary LCNC tools are increasingly capable of supporting enterprise-grade solutions, including those with AI intelligence, cross-platform compatibility, and legacy system interfaces (Maiya, 2020; Zohuri, 2024). Notably, McKinsey reports suggest that LCNC could automate up to 45% of the routine tasks, highlighting their impact on the business productivity (Goel, Vivek, 2022).

By lowering the dependence on centralized IT teams, the LCNC platforms foster greater organizational autonomy and agility. Business users can independently modify applications, allowing enterprises to stay aligned with the shifting customer expectations and operational realities (Binzer & Winkler, 2022). As experimentation becomes a cornerstone of innovation, LCNC platforms prove essential to enabling rapid iteration, continuous learning, and scalable transformation of businesses.

Fostering Inclusivity through LCNC Platforms

Low-code/no-code (LCNC) technologies are transforming digital accessibility by reducing the long-standing barriers that have excluded individuals with disabilities, marginalized communities, and non-English speakers from a meaningful participation in the digital domain. By enabling users to create, adapt, and deploy digital solutions without advanced technical expertise,

LCNC platforms foster a more inclusive digital ecosystem which unfolds across several critical dimensions of diversity:

Self-Advocacy Through Technology: LCNC platforms empower individuals with disabilities to independently develop applications tailored to their unique accessibility needs (Gagik, 2023). This capability promotes digital autonomy and reduces a reliance on one-size-fits-all systems; thus, enabling users to shape their digital environments and enhance participation in online spaces.

Embedded Accessibility Standards: Many LCNC tools now integrate accessibility standards directly into the development environment, making inclusive design a default feature rather than an afterthought (Kerv Digital, 2024). This built-in compliance ensures that applications are more likely to meet accessibility best practices from inception, fostering equitable engagement for a broader range of users.

Economic Inclusion: The affordability of LCNC platforms often offered through freemium models or low-cost entry tiers; provides access to individuals and organizations with limited financial resources (Kurtzman, 2022). This economic accessibility is vital for narrowing the digital divide and encouraging participation in digital innovation among underserved populations.

Bridging Language Barriers: Traditional development tools often privilege English, limiting global accessibility. In contrast, LCNC platforms with multilingual support enable users to build applications in their native languages (Meegle Editor, 2025). True localization features allow for the development of culturally and linguistically relevant solutions, expanding global participation.

LCNC for the Digital Native Workforce

The entry of the Digital-native workforce into modern organizations signals a paradigm shift in the workplace expectations and digital transformation priorities. Unlike prior generations, Digital-natives value flexibility and digital autonomy, seeking careers that prioritize impact and innovation (Jayatissa, 2023). Having matured in a fully digital environment particularly shaped by the pandemic; their expectations include intuitive, self-sufficient technologies that enhance the creativity and productivity. LCNC platforms align well with these needs by democratizing the software development to build tailored digital solutions.

As the first generation raised entirely in the digital era, the Digital natives are naturally adept at navigating the technological ecosystems. According to the Global Web Index, 98% of Digital natives own smartphones and spend up to eight hours daily online, while engaging with self-directed and collaborative digital tools (Wandhe, 2024). Early exposure to basic programming through school curricula has introduced them to structured problem-solving, though the access to formal technical education remains uneven. LCNC platforms bridge this skills gap, allowing young professionals to automate workflows, and engage in digital solutioning without any advanced coding knowledge. This accessibility broadens their participation in the enterprise innovation and fosters digital inclusivity. Digital-natives' familiarity with drag-and-drop builders, AI-assisted content tools, and platforms like YouTube makes them especially receptive to the LCNC paradigm (Schroth, 2019).

Beyond enhancing workplace productivity, the LCNC platforms are reshaping the creator economy. Digital-native professionals are leveraging these tools to launch digital ventures, develop websites, and monetize knowledge; often without significant capital or formal tech training. The integration of AI, blockchain, and automation further expands opportunities for ventures in NFTs, decentralized apps, and AI-enabled services. This entrepreneurial engagement highlights LCNC's potential to fuel inclusive innovation (Elshan, Dickhaut, et al., 2023).

As the Digital-native workforce continues to shape the evolving world of work, the convergence of LCNC and AI represents a strategic inflection point. Understanding this shift is essential for the organizations aiming to remain competitive, foster innovation, and attract the next generational digital talent.

13.4 Discussion

In an era of rapid disruption, businesses must embrace digital transformation to stay competitive. Traditionally, this has involved top-down strategies such as business model innovation, complex technology deployments and strategic market shifts (Bhattacharyya & Kumar, 2023). However, alongside or even in place of these traditional strategies, a bottom-up lever of change is gaining a momentum; the **LCNC-driven digital democratization** (Myles Suer, 2024). By empowering employees at all levels, LCNC fosters an inclusive, skills-oriented transformation model. Citizen development bridges the technical and nontechnical domains, thereby extending software creation beyond IT departments. This not only accelerates digital initiatives but also nurtures a collaborative, innovation-driven organizational culture (Zhang et al., 2021). However, for this democratization to succeed, robust governance is essential to ensure alignment with enterprise security, compliance, and strategic objectives.

The convergence of LCNC with artificial intelligence (AI) is poised to further reshape business productivity and innovation. AI-powered tools like ChatGPT and generative systems are reducing barriers to digital innovation, enabling users to generate code, automate workflows, and build intelligent systems with minimal technical background (Voelz et al., 2023). This integration is particularly transformative for traditionally automation-resistant sectors such as manufacturing and logistics (Bies et al., 2022; Sanchis et al., 2019). According to OpenAI, up to 80% of U.S. workers experienced automation of at least 10% of their tasks, with some reporting up to 50%. Rather than replacing jobs, this shift reorients human roles toward higher-value functions by emphasizing creativity, critical thinking, and strategic input (Elshan, Ebel, et al., 2023). This trend is expected to accelerate digital transformation, particularly in sectors slow to adopt automation, ensuring that businesses remain agile and innovation-ready (Maiya, 2020).

Importantly, the convergence of LCNC and AI is also breaking down structural barriers for the historically marginalized groups, making digital participation more accessible across lines of ability, language, and socioeconomic status. By narrowing the digital divide and enabling broader participation in innovation, these technologies contribute to a more equitable and inclusive digital economy. Organizations that embrace this shift will not only enhance productivity and inclusivity but also position themselves for sustained competitive advantage and leadership in the digital era.

13.5 Conclusion

The adoption of low-code/no-code (LCNC) platforms is redefining how organizations approach software development, digital transformation, and workforce inclusivity (Richardson, 2016). By democratizing application development, LCNC tools empower a broader range of employees—beyond the traditional IT teams to collaborate, innovate, and rapidly deliver user-centred solutions. This shift bridges the gap between business and technology units, enhancing agility and reducing reliance on specialized developers.

More than just the tools for productivity, LCNC platforms act as enablers of equity in the digital space. Historically, software development was restricted to those with formal programming skills, limiting participation from the non-technical staff and marginalized groups. LCNC platforms dismantle these barriers, allowing individuals from diverse backgrounds to contribute meaningfully to digital innovation. This inclusivity brings varied perspectives into problem-solving and strengthens the organizational resilience through collective intelligence (Clark, Scott, 2022).

As organizations pursue agility and inclusiveness, the convergence of LCNC and AI will accelerate this transformation. AI-augmented LCNC platforms will further reduce the technical thresholds, allowing users to automate tasks, build intelligent workflows, and refine applications with ease (Maes, Olivier, 2023). However, the success of this shift hinges on a robust governance, IT-business alignment, and strategic policies that ensure security, compliance, and scalability in a citizen-development environment (Clark, Scott, 2022).

The future of work lies in diverse, collaborative, and digitally empowered teams; where everyone, regardless of technical expertise, can contribute to innovation. Organizations that strategically adopt LCNC as a core digital enabler will be better positioned to lead in an inclusive and sustainable digital economy, where technology is a force for opportunity, creativity, and continuous transformation (Myles Suer, 2024).

References

Alamin, M. A. A., Uddin, G., Malakar, S., Afroz, S., Haider, T., & Iqbal, A. (2023). Developer discussion topics on the adoption and barriers of low code software development platforms. *Empirical Software Engineering*, *28*(1), 4. https://doi.org/10.1007/s10664-022-10244-0

Bernsteiner, R., Schlögl, S., Ploder, C., Dilger, T., & Brecher, F. (2022). Citizen vs. professional developers: differences and similarities of skills and training requirements for low code development platforms. In *ICERI2022 Proceedings* (pp. 4257–4264). IATED. https://doi.org/10.21125/iceri.2022.1036

Bhattacharyya, S. S., & Kumar, S. (2023). Study of deployment of "low code no code" applications toward improving digitization of supply chain management. *Journal of Science and Technology Policy Management*, *14*(2), 271–287. https://doi.org/10.1108/JSTPM-06-2021-0084

Bhavya Aggarwal. (2023, March 24). *Citizen Development: Why It's a Game-Changer in Innovation for SMBs* [Online post]. www.capterra.com/resources/what-is-citizen-development

Bies, L., Weber, M., Greff, T., & Werth, D. (2022). A mixed-methods study of low-code development platforms: Drivers of digital innovation in SMEs. In *2022 International Conference on Electrical, Computer, Communications and Mechatronics Engineering (ICECCME)*, pp. 1–6. https://doi.org/10.1109/ICECCME55909.2022.9987920

Binzer, B., & Winkler, T. J. (2022). Democratizing software development: A systematic multivocal literature review and research agenda on citizen development. In N. Carroll, A. Nguyen-Duc, X. Wang, & V. Stray (Eds.), *Software Business* (Vol. 463, pp. 244–259). Springer International Publishing. https://doi.org/10.1007/978-3-031-20706-8_17

Bock, A. C., & Frank, U. (2021a). In search of the essence of low-code: An exploratory study of seven development platforms. In *2021 ACM/IEEE International Conference on Model Driven Engineering Languages and Systems Companion (MODELS-C)*, pp. 57–66. https://doi.org/10.1109/MODELS-C53483.2021.00016

Bock, A. C., & Frank, U. (2021b). Low-code platform. *Business & Information Systems Engineering*, *63*(6), 733–740. https://doi.org/10.1007/s12599-021-00726-8

Brüggemann, L. (2023). *Securely extending and running low-code applications with C#* (Version 1). arXiv. https://doi.org/10.48550/ARXIV.2307.06340

Cabot, J. (2020). Positioning of the low-code movement within the field of model-driven engineering. In *Proceedings of the 23rd ACM/IEEE International Conference on Model Driven Engineering Languages and Systems: Companion Proceedings*, pp. 1–3. https://doi.org/10.1145/3417990.3420210

Clark, Scott. (2022, January 25). *The low-code and no-code revolution is driving innovation, growth and experimentation in the enterprise* [Online post]. www.reworked.co/digital-workplace/4-ways-low-code-and-no-code-drives-experimentation

Clay Richardson. (2016, January 15). *Vendor Landscape: The Fractured, Fertile Terrain Of Low-Code Application Platforms* [Online post]. www.forrester.com/report/Vendor-Landscape-The-Fractured-Fertile-Terrain-Of-LowCode-Application-Platforms/RES122549

Daniel, G., Cabot, J., Deruelle, L., & Derras, M. (2020). Xatkit: A multimodal low-code chatbot development framework. *IEEE Access*, *8*, 15332–15346. https://doi.org/10.1109/ACCESS.2020.2966919

Elshan, E., Dickhaut, E., & Ebel, P. A. (2023). *An Investigation of Why Low Code Platforms Provide Answers and New Challenges*. Hawaii International Conference on System Sciences. https://doi.org/10.24251/HICSS.2023.746

Elshan, E., Ebel, P., Söllner, M., & Leimeister, J. M. (2023). Leveraging low code development of smart personal assistants: An integrated design approach with the SPADE method. *Journal of Management Information Systems*, *40*(1), 96–129. https://doi.org/10.1080/07421222.2023.2172776

Gagik, M. (2023, May 31). *How No-Code Technology is Revolutionizing Accessibility for People with Disabilities*. www.moxly.io/blog/how-no-code-technology-is-revolutionizing-accessibility-for-people-with-disabilities

Goel, Vivek. (2022, August 17). *No-Code and Gen Z: The Productive and Future-Proof Match* [Online post]. https://readwrite.com/no-code-and-gen-z-the-productive-and-future-proof-match

Guest, G., & McLellan, E. (2003). Distinguishing the trees from the forest: Applying cluster analysis to thematic qualitative data. *Field Methods*, *15*(2), 186–201. https://doi.org/10.1177/1525822X03015002005

Guthardt, T., Kosiol, J., & Hohlfeld, O. (2024). Low-code vs. the developer: An empirical study on the developer experience and efficiency of a no-code platform. In *Proceedings of the ACM/IEEE 27th International Conference on Model Driven Engineering Languages and Systems*, pp. 856–865. https://doi.org/10.1145/3652620.3688332

Hoogsteen, D., & Borgman, H. (2022). *Empower the Workforce, Empower the Company? Citizen Development Adoption*. Hawaii International Conference on System Sciences. https://doi.org/10.24251/HICSS.2022.575

Ihirwe, F., Di Ruscio, D., Mazzini, S., Pierini, P., & Pierantonio, A. (2020). Low-code engineering for internet of things: A state of research. In *Proceedings of the 23rd ACM/IEEE International Conference on Model Driven Engineering Languages and Systems: Companion Proceedings*, pp. 1–8. https://doi.org/10.1145/3417990.3420208

Jacinto, A., Lourenço, M., & Ferreira, C. (2020). Test mocks for low-code applications built with OutSystems. In *Proceedings of the 23rd ACM/IEEE International Conference on Model Driven Engineering Languages and Systems: Companion Proceedings*, pp. 1–5. https://doi.org/10.1145/3417990.3420209

Jayatissa, K. A. D. U. (2023). Generation Z – A new lifeline: A systematic literature review. *Sri Lanka Journal of Social Sciences and Humanities*, *3*(2), 179–186. https://doi.org/10.4038/sljssh.v3i2.110

Jin, A., & Pan, Y. (2022). A study on citizen developer competency and development process in low-code/no-code development system. *The Korean Society of Culture and Convergence*, *44*(11), 119–131. https://doi.org/10.33645/cnc.2022.11.44.11.119

Johannes Hintsch. (2022, April 22). *Low-code Development Platform Usage* [Online post]. https://aisel.aisnet.org/acis2021/11

Kass, S., Strahringer, S., & Westner, M. (2022). Drivers and inhibitors of low code development platform adoption. In *2022 IEEE 24th Conference on Business Informatics (CBI)*, pp. 196–205. https://doi.org/10.1109/CBI54897.2022.00028

Kerv Digital. (2024, March 15). *Unlocking Accessibility with Low Code Solutions*. https://kerv.com/blog/kerv-digital/unlocking-accessibility-low-code-solutions/

Khorram, F., Mottu, J.-M., & Sunyé, G. (2020). Challenges & opportunities in low-code testing. In *Proceedings of the 23rd ACM/IEEE International Conference on Model Driven Engineering Languages and Systems: Companion Proceedings*, pp. 1–10. https://doi.org/10.1145/3417990.3420204

Kulkarni, M. (2021). Deciphering low-code/no-code hype – study of trends, overview of platforms, and rapid application development suitability. *International Journal of Scientific and Research Publications (IJSRP)*, *11*(7), 536–540. https://doi.org/10.29322/IJSRP.11.07.2021.p11570

Kurtzman, R. (2022, May 4). *Low-code and no-code make tech more inclusive*. https://dev.to/richkurtzman/low-code-and-no-code-make-tech-more-inclusive-27pe

Lebens, M., J Finnegan, R., C Sorsen, S., & Shah, J. (2021). Rise of the citizen developer. *Muma Business Review*, *5*, 101–111. https://doi.org/10.28945/4885

Luo, Y., Liang, P., Wang, C., Shahin, M., & Zhan, J. (2021). *Characteristics and challenges of low-code development: The practitioners' perspective*. https://doi.org/10.48550/ARXIV.2107.07482

Maes, Olivier. (2023, May 31). *What no-code can tell us about the future of AI in workplaces* [Online post]. https://builtin.com/software-engineering-perspectives/what-no-code-tells-us-about-future-ai-workplaces

Maiya, A. S. (2020). *ktrain: A low-code library for augmented machine learning* (Version 5). arXiv. https://doi.org/10.48550/ARXIV.2004.10703

Martinez, E., & Pfister, L. (2023). Benefits and limitations of using low-code development to support digitalization in the construction industry. *Automation in Construction*, *152*, 104909. https://doi.org/10.1016/j.autcon.2023.104909

Meegle Editor. (2025, February 17). *Multi-Language Support In No-Code Software*. www.meegle.com/en_us/topics/lowcode/multi-language-support-in-no-code-software

Moreira-Filho, J. T., Ranganath, D., Conway, M., Schmitt, C., Kleinstreuer, N., & Mansouri, K. (2024). Democratizing cheminformatics: Interpretable chemical grouping using an automated KNIME workflow. *Journal of Cheminformatics*, *16*(1), 101. https://doi.org/10.1186/s13321-024-00894-1

Muhammad, S., R. Prybutok, V., & Sinha, V. (2024). Citizen developers: The new accelerators for digital transformation. *Muma Business Review*, *8*, 173–180. https://doi.org/10.28945/5426

Myles Suer. (2024, December 16). *How are non-IT professionals driving enterprise agility?* [Online post]. www.vktr.com/ai-upskilling/citizen-development-the-future-of-enterprise-agility-in-ais-era/

Overeem, M., Jansen, S., & Mathijssen, M. (2021). API management maturity of low-code development platforms. In A. Augusto, A. Gill, S. Nurcan, I.

Reinhartz-Berger, R. Schmidt, & J. Zdravkovic (Eds.), *Enterprise, Business-Process and Information Systems Modeling* (Vol. 421, pp. 380–394). Springer International Publishing. https://doi.org/10.1007/978-3-030-79186-5_25

Paul Vincent. (2019, August 8). *Gartner Magic Quadrant for Enterprise Low-Code Application Platforms* [Online post]. www.gartner.com/en/documents/3956079

Popay, J., Roberts, H., Sowden, A., Petticrew, M., Arai, L., Rodgers, M., Britten, N., Roen, K., & Duffy, S. (2006). *Guidance on the conduct of narrative synthesis in systematic reviews: A product from the ESRC Methods Programme*. Lancaster University. https://doi.org/10.13140/2.1.1018.4643

Nimje, P. (2024). The rise of low-code/no-code development platforms. *International Journal of Advanced Research in Science, Communication and Technology (IJARSCT)*, *4*(3), 650–653. https://doi.org/10.48175/IJARSCT-18974

Rokis, K., & Kirikova, M. (2022). Challenges of low-code/no-code software development: A literature review. In Ē. Nazaruka, K. Sandkuhl, & U. Seigerroth (Eds.), *Perspectives in Business Informatics Research* (Vol. 462, pp. 3–17). Springer International Publishing. https://doi.org/10.1007/978-3-031-16947-2_1

Sahay, A., Indamutsa, A., Di Ruscio, D., & Pierantonio, A. (2020). Supporting the understanding and comparison of low-code development platforms. In *2020 46th Euromicro Conference on Software Engineering and Advanced Applications (SEAA)*, 171–178. https://doi.org/10.1109/SEAA51224.2020.00036

Sanchis, R., García-Perales, Ó., Fraile, F., & Poler, R. (2019). Low-code as enabler of digital transformation in manufacturing industry. *Applied Sciences*, *10*(1), 12. https://doi.org/10.3390/app10010012

Schroth, H. (2019). Are you ready for Gen Z in the workplace? *California Management Review*, *61*(3), 5–18. https://doi.org/10.1177/0008125619841006

Schwinger, W., Retschitzegger, W., Kapsammer, E., & Pröll, B. (2023). Getting started with low-code – A data-centric primer for oracle APEX. In *42nd International Conference on Organizational Science Development*, 1003–1016. https://doi.org/10.18690/um.fov.3.2023.74

Shridhar, S. (2021). Analysis of low code-no code development platforms in comparison with traditional development methodologies. *International Journal for Research in Applied Science and Engineering Technology*, *9*(12), 508–513. https://doi.org/10.22214/ijraset.2021.39328

Silva, J. X., Lopes, M., Avelino, G., & Santos, P. (2023). Low-code and No-code Technologies Adoption: A Gray Literature Review. In *Proceedings of the XIX Brazilian Symposium on Information Systems*, pp. 388–395. https://doi.org/10.1145/3592813.3592929

Sufi, F. (2023). Algorithms in low-code-no-code for research applications: A practical review. *Algorithms*, *16*(2), 108. https://doi.org/10.3390/a16020108

Tranfield, D., Denyer, D., & Smart, P. (2003). Towards a methodology for developing evidence-informed management knowledge by means of systematic review. *British Journal of Management*, *14*(3), 207–222. https://doi.org/10.1111/1467-8551.00375

Velásquez, A. P., Pérez-Salazar, C., Hernández-González, L. A., & Sánchez-García, Á. J. (2024). Systematic literature review of low-code and its future trends. In *2024 12th International Conference in Software Engineering Research and Innovation (CONISOFT)*, pp. 30–37. https://doi.org/10.1109/CONISOFT63288.2024.00015

Voelz, A., Muck, C., Amlashi, D. M., & Karagiannis, D. (2023). Citizen-centric design of consumable services for smart cities. *Digital Government: Research and Practice, 4*(3), 1–18. https://doi.org/10.1145/3597420

Wandhe, Dr. P. (2024). The new generation: Understanding millennials and Gen Z. *SSRN Electronic Journal*. https://doi.org/10.2139/ssrn.4716585

Waszkowski, R. (2019). Low-code platform for automating business processes in manufacturing. *IFAC-PapersOnLine, 52*(10), 376–381. https://doi.org/10.1016/j.ifacol.2019.10.060

Woo, M. (2020). The rise of no/low code software development—No experience needed? *Engineering, 6*(9), 960–961. https://doi.org/10.1016/j.eng.2020.07.007

Zhang, Y., Gitzendanner, M. A., Maxwell, D. S., Richardson, J. W., Smith, K. E., Stubbs, E. A., Stucky, B. J., Zhang, J., & Deumens, E. (2021). *Building an AI-ready RSE Workforce*. arXiv. https://doi.org/10.48550/ARXIV.2111.04916

Zohuri, B. (2024). Revolutionizing education: The dynamic synergy of personalized learning and artificial intelligence. *International Journal of Advanced Engineering and Management Research, 09*(01), 143–153. https://doi.org/10.51505/ijaemr.2024.9111

Zolotas, C., Chatzidimitriou, K. C., & Symeonidis, A. L. (2018). RESTsec: A low-code platform for generating secure by design enterprise services. *Enterprise Information Systems, 12*(8–9), 1007–1033. https://doi.org/10.1080/17517575.2018.1462403

14

Equitable Protection in Digital Spaces: Examining Cybersquatting in India Through a DEIB Lens

Janhavi A. Sakalkar and Ujwal Prabhakar Nandekar

14.1 Introduction

Branding is one of the most important aspects of any business, the basis for market awareness and consumers' trust. In the era of the internet, domain names become an important part of this process by offering a distinctive online presence for a company's products and services. Since every domain name is one of a kind, it is a valuable digital asset that can have a considerable impact on a brand's visibility and credibility. But with the growth of the e-commerce sector at a fast pace, a few people indulge in the illegal act of registering domain names that are very similar to existing business names or trademarks—a practice called cybersquatting. They are called cybersquatters. They usually aim to capitalize on the goodwill of genuine businesses for financial or personal benefits.

Although cybersquatting is a problem for every online business, it disproportionately affects smaller businesses, minority-owned enterprises, Indigenous peoples, and others from underrepresented or economically disadvantaged communities. Such communities are typically confronted by systemic obstacles to defending their online presence, such as scarce access to legal resources and information regarding domain dispute procedures. In India, the lack of specific legislation on cybersquatting only adds to these issues. Currently, such cases fall under the general purview of the Trademarks Act, 1999, which might not effectively deal with the subtle issues that crop up in cyberspace.

Additionally, the growing application of Artificial Intelligence (AI) in detecting and preventing cybersquatting poses its own challenges. Without deliberate efforts to make them fair and inclusive, AI technologies can inadvertently reproduce current social biases, potentially mislabelling culturally important domain names or ignoring abusive activity against marginalized

 DOI: 10.1201/9781003591078-18

communities. It is thus important to create AI solutions that are transparent, unbiased, and culturally sensitive.

This paper explores the intersection of cybersquatting, digital equity, and the role of AI in domain name dispute resolution. It aims to highlight the gaps in the current legal framework in India and proposes a more inclusive, AI-informed approach to protecting digital identities—especially for those who have historically been left out of the digital economy.

14.2 Literature Review

A few effective measures in order to control the practice of cybersquatting and resolve disputes arising due to it, i.e., online mediation and arbitration, administrative domain name challenge panels (Sangal, 1999). Further, WIPO mechanism is an effective way and a good start to solve the disputes related to cybersquatting. This approach of arbitration proceedings under WIPO has also been incorporated in the available literature (Zhao, 2000). In the researched literature, the study has linked both the concepts and has done a thorough analysis through case laws. The thorough delineation of domain names stimulated the understanding of the complex issues of cybersquatting and trademarks (Ebersohn, 2006).

Further, the other piece of literature deals with the importance of domain name as business identifiers and concise details with respect to WIPO Arbitration and Mediation decisions on domain names, UDRP, and has listed down the criteria for bringing an action (Mishra, 2013). Khanna and Shrivastava (2014) have shed light on the concept of ACPA Act, Lanham Act, and Trademark Dilution Act. The literature explains and throws light on India's Dispute Resolution Mechanism (INDRP), and the authors have suggested for the enactment of a new legislation and development of an independent body specifically dealing with cybersquatting. The researchers could grasp the nature and working of INDRP and comprehend the case laws mentioned in the article (Charan, 2015).

Vellakkat has expressed his view on how domain names are even more important than trademarks. The paper throws light on the development of Generic Top-Level Domains(gTLDs) leading to the rise in the threat of cybersquatting. It is been said in the paper that ICANN's Trade Mark Clearinghouse Mechanism is an effective way to resolve the domain name related disputes and trademark infringement caused due to that (Vellakat, 2016).

In the light of existing ICANN policy, the researcher has critically analysed the similarities and differences between both. The viewpoint of domain names used as trademarks in e-commerce is gained by the authors with the help of this article (Lukose, 2016). Jaybhave has majorly focuses on the concept of

Cyber Law and the IPR issues, i.e., copyright infringement in cyberspace and trademark law. The authors have dealt with latter issue by citing a number of case laws and analysing them in depth. The case laws in this article proved useful for the authors in its analysis and thus implement it in his research (Jaybhaye, 2016).

Tokas and Tyagi have recommended a few measures for the IT Act which apparently lacks in dealing with the cybercrimes related to IPR. It incorporates the issue of copyright and trademark in the digital medium. The authors at the end reiterated that there is a need for the IT Act to specifically include the provisions related to Trademark and Copyright Act in India (Rautdesai & Nandekar, 2017). It can be analysed that the researchers have a viewpoint of how IT Act could prove beneficial in combating cybersquatting, if amended (Tokas and Tyagi, 2020).

The abovementioned discussion of literature set forth the principles of domain name, cybersquatting and the resultant trademark infringement. Accordingly, the provisions for combating the same in India, USA, and other foreign countries have been articulated. However, there is a paucity of a consolidated research amalgamating the legal mechanisms for cybersquatting in India and its critical analysis.

14.3 Research Design

14.3.1 Research Objective

There is a need for research in this area as it would lead us to a better and in-depth understanding of the law and also recommend effective solutions in case if there are any lacunae in the existing laws and legislations.

The research objectives for this paper are:

- To analyze the laws existing in India with respect to cybersquatting and the trademark infringement caused due to that,
- To explore AI technologies that would help mitigate the problem of trademark infringement through cybersquatting,
- To scrutinize the IT Act, Trademark Law, INDRP and the existing dispute resolution mechanisms.

14.3.2 Research Gap

The research gap which the researchers try to fill in is:

- The lack of thorough analysis of the laws with respect to cybersquatting, domain squatting in India and the role of AI,

- A huge amount of available literature focuses on the legislations, provisions, and mechanisms relating to cybersquatting of the foreign land but there is paucity of in-depth research regarding the existing laws in India incorporating the trademark infringement.

14.3.3 Research Questions

The research questions for this paper are:

1. Whether existing laws/mechanisms in India are enough to counter the problem of cybersquatting and the infringement of trademark.
2. Whether the concept of Cybersquatting should be dealt under separate legislation.

14.3.4 Research Methodology

In order to get a better insight on the legal mechanisms of cybersquatting in India and thus analyse them, the authors have undertaken the doctrinal method of research. They have taken the help of online journals, articles, newspapers, etc.

14.4 Domain Names

14.4.1 What is a Domain Name?

As indicated by Merriam-Webster, a sequence of generally alphanumeric characters (for example, Merriam-Webster.com) that determines a gathering of online assets (starting at a specific organization or individual) and that structures part of the relating Internet addresses. (Merriam Webster Dictionary, 1828)

Domain names are a line of typographic characters used to depict the area of a particular location on the web. They are otherwise called Uniform Resource Locator, i.e., URL. Area names are utilized to distinguish IP locations and Webpages (Beal, 1996)

There exist different domain levels:

1. **TLD (Top-Level Domains):**
   TLD is the part after the dot. For example, in www.youtube.com, the TLD is .com.

2. **SLD (Second-Level Domains):**

   SLD is the word before the dot. Taking into consideration the earlier example, youtube would be the SLD.

   Every domain name essentially embodies a TLD and SLD.

3. **ccTLD (Country Code Top-Level Domains):**

   This type of domain name is associated with a particular country, for instance, the ccTLD is .in for India, .uk for the United Kingdom, etc.

4. **gTLD (Generic Top-Level Domains):**

   gTLD, unlike ccTLD, is not associated with any country. There are only two gTLDs left, viz, .net, and .org.

14.4.2 Significance of Domain Names

Domain names have great importance in today's era as the internet is progressively being used in the field of governance, education, and commerce (MEITY). In the case of *Lockheed Martin Corporation v Network Solutions Inc. [1999] 949 CD Cal,* the Court held that a domain name that comprises of a trademark name is a valuable business asset to its proprietor in that such a domain name makes it easier for the trademark owner's customers to find the trademark owner's Internet resources such as websites (Ebersohn, 2006). Therefore, it can be said that a company's presence on the Internet is corroborated by a domain name (Abel, 1999).

14.5 Conjugating Trademarks and Domain Names

Trademarks generally serve the purpose of products/business identifiers and create an image in the minds of the consumers with respect to particular goods. (Wadhera, 2009) Therefore, companies tend to use their trademarks or their businesses names as domain names because it is the general propensity of consumers to search for a company's website in a way which incorporates their trademark. For instance, if someone has to search for the website of Bata, he might enter www.bata.com on the browser with a presumption to come across the same (Anschell & Lucasm 2003). Several occurrences take place wherein third parties register domain names based on other company's trademarks in order to deceive the consumers and then profit by selling it to the original trademark owner (Zadna n.d.).

In the case of *Satyam Infoway Ltd vs Sifynet Solutions Pvt Ltd. AIR 2004 SC 3540,* the appellant sued the respondent for registering a similar domain name to theirs which in turn affected their business as well reputation. The Court in this matter emphasized on the importance of domain name as a business identifier in the ever-evolving commercial activity. The Court also decided that domain names and trademarks function differently. Trademarks can have multiple registrations in different countries and are governed by the indigenous laws available in the countries unlike, domain names that do not have any geographical constraints; therefore, exclusivity to domain names is required as a particular national law would not be competent to provide sufficient protection. (Singh & Associates, 2012)

14.6 Cybersquatting

14.6.1 What is Cybersquatting?

The anticybersquatting Consumer Protection Act (ACPA) enacted in the year 1999 aims to protect the rights of the trademark holders that are subjected to infringement due to the menace of cybersquatting and typo-squatting. *Section (2)(1)* of the Act defines cybersquatting.

In a nutshell, cybersquatting is a mendacious practice wherein a person registers for a domain name incorporating a trademark to which he has no legal rights. This is predominantly done with a view to gain ransom out of the trademark owner's goodwill by selling the domain name to them.

14.6.2 Categories of Cybersquatting

Cybersquatting is predominantly divided into four categories:

1. **Typo-squatting:**

   This is the most common form of cybersquatting and is also referred to as 'URL hijacking' or 'Fake URL'. (INFOSEC, 2017) The cyber squatters register domain names that are confusingly similar to someone's domain name. For instance, an extra 'a' could be added to the earlier existing domain name of www.bata.com which would make it www.bataa.com, this being extremely similar to the former one may deceive the consumers.

2. **Name Jacking:**

   Name Jacking is taken place when registration of a domain name incorporating a person's name is done. This is essentially done to lure the traffic by including a renowned person's name in it.

3. **Identity theft:**

   Registration of domain names is for a certain period of time after which if the owner does not renew the domain name. Cyber squatters may purchase the domain name. They get to know the information with the help of a software application. The intent behind doing this is to capture the traffic by using the duplicate domain name and linking it to other websites (INFOSEC, 2017).

4. **Reverse cybersquatting:**

   Reverse cybersquatting is accomplished when an owner of a company attempts to secure a domain name legally registered by a third party. This is primarily done by business companies who are in need of a particular domain name which is already registered by a third party (Domain Registration Services, 2011).

14.7 Statistics of Cybersquatting in India

According to the statistics of domain name disputes from the year 2010 to 2024 by WIPO, the lowest numbers of cases filed were 26 in the year 2012, and the highest has been 92 in the year 2022. Last year, 85 domain name disputes have been filed (WIPO). From the data below, it could be deduced that post-pandemic there has been a massive increase in the domain-name disputes, owing to the shift to the online platforms by most businesses and companies.

14.8 Legal Mechanisms for Cybersquatting in India

This part of the research paper attempts to set out the remedies that the trademark owners hold in case of cybersquatting against the cyber squatters. In countries like the USA, the ACPA Act is specific legislation dealing with the menace of cybersquatting. This allows the trademark owners to acquire appropriate countermeasures and hence protect their rights.

With regards to India, there is no exclusive legislation or provision to confront the peril of cybersquatting, albeit, the trademark owner has different recourse available under the Indian Legal System. If the rights of the trademark owner have been infringed, he has the subsequent correctives that could be undertaken to deal with the cyber squatter:

- *Cease and Desist Letters to the cybersquatter*
- *Arbitration proceedings under the ICANN or INDRP*
- *Litigation proceedings*

14.8.1 Cease and Desist Letters

When the trademark owners become cognizant of the fact that their rights with respect to trademarks are being infringed due to the practice of cybersquatting, the rightful owner can take immediate action by sending the cyber squatter a cease-and-desist letter. A cease-and-desist letter is a cautionary letter (Dev, 2020) which is sent to the alleged cyber squatter to serve it as a warning from abstaining to continue with the practice, noncompliance to which can prompt legal proceedings.

In 2015, Flipkart had sent a cease and desist letter to an Indian technology writer, Amit Bhawani alleging copyright infringement and cybersquatting (Saxena, 2015). The blogger owned a website with the URL amazonvsflipkart.com wherein he compared both the e-commerce giants based on a consumer satisfaction poll, the notice incorporated that the blogger used Flipkart's trademark in the domain name in order to benefit monetarily by diverting the traffic or by later ransoming the domain name back to Flipkart. Finally, it was revealed that the trademark infringement had been taken down, conforming to the legal notice (Saxena, 2015).

Cease and desist letter can be one of the most effective and expeditious ways to combat any sort of IP infringement if complied with. If juxtaposed with the legal proceedings, cease and desist letters prove to be less time-consuming and cost-intensive (Rana & Co. 2018).

14.8.2 Arbitration Proceedings

UDRP's course of action:

ICANN is a not-for-profit organization established in the year 1999 in the United States with a view to manage and administer the Domain Name System (DNS) (Internet Corporation for Assigned Names and Numbers, 2012). DNS aids people to access and locate the websites easily. Domain names are sold by registrars who charge a certain amount of fees, of which a part has to be paid to the ICANN.

UDRP formulated under the ICANN on 24th October, 1999 (Mishra, 2013) is a strategy to settle the disputes regarding the domain names. National or municipal laws concerning the domain names disputes and the issue of cybersquatting would not suffice. This is where the need for a stringent international regulation for cybersquatting entailed.

Under the UDRP, domain name disputes based on trademarks must be solved by the way of agreement, court action, or arbitration before the registrar cancels, suspends, or transfers the domain name (Internet Corporation for Assigned Names and Numbers, 2012). It is necessary for the complainant to prove elements in the administrative proceedings which are conducted by the ICANN accredited dispute resolution service providers. The current service providers include:

i. ACDR (Arab Centre for Domain Name Dispute Resolution)
ii. ADNCRC (Asian Domain Name Dispute Resolution Centre)
iii. CAC (Czech Arbitration Court)
iv. CIIDRC (Canadian International Internet Dispute Resolution Centre)
v. NAF (National Arbitration Forum)
vi. WIPO (World Intellectual Property Organization)

According to List of Approved Dispute Resolution Service Provider, WIPO, inter alia, is currently the principal domain name dispute resolution service provider. Each service provider follows the rules of UDRP coupled with their supplemental rules. The service providers have their set of panellists, from which one or three panellists are chosen to decide the matter. This process generally takes around 45 days and $1000 as fees has to be paid to the panellists (Khan et al., 2015).

UDRP accelerates the process of resolving domain name disputes, moreover, in a cost-effective manner. The remedies available under the UDRP are limited. Injunctions and damages are not given under UDRP (Arnot, 2014).

INDRP's Approach:

.in is India's country code top-level domain. NIXI, National Internet Exchange of India was formed under Section 25 of the Indian Companies Act, 1956 with a view to facilitate the internet services of the country. Under NIXI, the .in Registry was established to manage and maintain the .in ccTLD and ensuring its security and stability (Registry.in).

Since India does not subscribe to the UDRP, the IN registry developed the .IN Dispute Resolution Policy to specifically deal with the .in domain name disputes. (Rana & Co.) INDRP is aligned with the internationally accepted guidelines and the provisions under the Indian Information Technology Act, 2000. A complaint can be filed under INDRP on the grounds which are similar to that of the Rule 4(a).

Once the complaint is received, an arbitrator is appointed within 5 working days from the list of arbitrators to conduct the proceedings by the .IN Registry. According to INDRP Rules of Procedure, the Arbitrator is under the obligation to pass an award within 60 days and forward the same to the complainant, respondent and .IN registry (Registry.in). Under the INDRP, the complainant has to pay the entire fees (Registry.in). INDRP is an effective alternative to resolve the domain name disputes as the decisions are mandatory to be implemented, and it is relatively less time-consuming.

14.8.3 Litigation Proceedings

The third and significant recourse available to the aggrieved person is by filing a lawsuit in a civil court. There are comprehensive remedies under the common law against the squatter. Information Technology Act, 2000 deals with the offences of cybercrime but it does not incorporate any provision with respect to cybersquatting. Therefore, in case of infringement of domain names, an action can be taken on the ground of passing off or that there is an infringement of your trademark and intellectual property (Jain, 2016). Due to absence of a singular and stringent legislation concerning cybersquatting and domain name disputes, they are predominantly covered under Trademark law.

Under the Trade Marks Act, 1999, Section 28, 29, and 30 deal with the rights conferred by registration and infringement of trademarks and the limits of effect of registered trademarks respectively. With an eye towards obtaining relief, the aggrieved person in order to build a successful claim has to prove that the cyber squatter has used a similar mark to that of the owner which has led to create confusion among the persons at the receiving end.

Another action that could be taken by the claimant is on the grounds of passing off. The earliest and most rudimentary case law with respect to passing off is *Perry V Truefitt (1842) 6 Beav. 66.* This case articulated the principle of passing off and laid down a significant principle that *"A man is not to sell his own goods under the pretence that they are the goods of another man".* (McKenna, 2007). In simpler words, passing off is a form of unfair trading which causes misrepresentation with respect to the origin of goods and services. It is a practice where the infringer makes their consumers believe that their goods are connected to another business, when in reality they are not. This leads to deception and is considered to be a ground to sue for passing off.

The case of *Pandit Durga Dutt Sharma V Navaratna Pharmaceutical Laboratories AIR 1965 SC 980* signifies the distinction between trademark infringement and passing off. The Court in this case also sets out that for a successful claim for trademark infringement. It is essential to show that the trademark has been used by the Defendant which does not apply for passing off.

In *Reckitt & Colman Products Ltd. V Border Inc. 1 All E.R. 873.* case, the Court lays down three-part test for the claim of passing off, i.e., reputation, misrepresentation and damage. As long as the claimant does not prove the former part, a suit cannot be instituted. Finally, the claimant has to prove that he has suffered or is likely to suffer from damages caused due to the misrepresentation with respect to the origin of goods and services by the defendant.

14.9 Institutional and Judicial Approach

Comprehending the provisions and legal mechanisms pertaining to cybersquatting is preliminary, along with it, it is equally consequential to scrutinize the working of the institutions like WIPO under the UDRP, INDRP, and the courts in deciding the disputes relating to domain names and cybersquatting.

14.9.1 Cases decided by WIPO under UDRP

The very first cybersquatting case, i.e., *World Wrestling Federation case* in the world was decided by WIPO under UDRP on 14 January, 2000. The suit was filed by the World Wrestling Federation (WWF) based in the US against a resident of California who had registered the domain name 'www.worldwres tlingfederation.com'. Later, the respondent had also tried to sell it back to the WWF at an exorbitant price. This conduct could determine the bad intent behind the registration. Moreover, the registered domain name was extremely similar to complainant's trademark, and the respondent did not have legitimate right in the registration of the domain name. Therefore, WIPO ordered the respondent to transfer the domain name to the complainant.

In the case of *Bennett, Coleman and Company Limited, Worldwide Media Pvt. Ltd. v Hubert Louis Case no.: D2019-0221*, the complainants are quite renowned and they host number of events, symposiums, and beauty pageants. They filed a suit against the respondent for registering the domain name 'missindia.com'. It was proved that the domain name is closely similar to the trademark that the respondent had been using it for pay-per-click (PPC) advertising which generates money. Since the complainants' beauty pageants were known all over the world, the respondent had prior knowledge of its existence, it was implied that the respondent had registered the domain name and was using it in bad faith. Therefore, the panellists directed the respondent to transfer the domain name to the complainants.

The case of *Independent News Services Private Ltd. v Vijay Tayade Case no.: D2017-1464*, wherein, the complainant runs the television news channel 'India TV' filed a suit against the respondent as he registered the domain name 'indiatv10.com'. The Complainant has handful of trademarks which incorporate the name India TV which reiterated that the trademark is well-known and no rights are conferred upon any third-party for its use. The panel, thus, ordered that the disputed domain name should be transferred to the domain name.

14.9.2 Cases Decided under INDRP

In the case of *Eterno Infotech Private Ltd. v Zheng Wei*, the complainant is a company based in Bangalore and is the owner of the trademark 'Newshunt' since 2009 and is a coined term according to the complainant. Newshunt is a renowned software application with over more than 10 million downloads. The Respondent registered the domain name 'huntnews.in' to provide online news through the domain name. The domain name was confusingly similar to the registered trademark of the complainant, 'Newshunt', and is identical to the goods and services offered by both the parties. The Arbitrator, thus, ordered the respondent to transfer the domain name to the complainant and additionally pay Rs. 1 lakh to the complainant.

The case of *Google LLC v Titan Corporation* was decided based on the disputed domain name 'GOOGLEBANK.IN'. The proceeding was in accordance with the INDRP. The complainant is a highly recognized search engines and is used all over the world, resultantly, owns the trademark 'GOOGLE'. The respondent registered 'GOOGLEBANK.IN' in August 2018 which is identical to the complainant's trademark. Moreover, he had no rights with respect to that and had registered and used it in bad faith. Since the complainant was successful in establishing all the three elements that required under the policy, the Registry directed to transfer the domain name to the Complainant.

The respondent in the *CathayPacific Airways Limited v Hu Wei* registered the domain name 'cathaypacific.co.in' in light of existing CathayPacific trademark. The complainant has registered this trademark in over 35 countries, including India. This had also resulted in deception of the public and consumers who might link a connection between the complainant and respondent when there is none. On establishing the three requirements, the relief was granted.

14.9.3 Cases Decided by the Court

In the case of *Kesari Trust & Others v DLKesari Travels Private Ltd. 2016 SCC Online Bom 9483,* the plaintiff is a highly recognized travel agency based in Maharashtra and also owned the domain name 'kesari.in' which incorporates their mark Kesari. The defendant had recently commenced his travel business, by registering the domain name 'kesaritravels.in'. This had resulted in actual confusion of a customer who was deceived, as he thought that the latter agency was similar to the plaintiff.

The case of *Raymond Limited v Raymond Pharmaceutical Ltd. 2016 SCC Online Bom 5159.,* the plaintiff is a well-known Indian textile company, with the registered domain name Raymond.in. The defendant is a pharmaceutical company with the registered domain name 'raymondpharma.com'. But the order came as the adoption of the domain name by defendant was quite reasonable as it constituted as their corporate name and did not mean to take undue advantage of the plaintiff's reputation. Therefore, it was held on the basis of Section 29(4)(c) that this does not constitute as a case of cybersquatting.

14.10 AI Technologies

Besides the recourse through the legal system, among the most useful ways to tackle cybersquatting is embracing artificial intelligence (AI) technology. Machine learning algorithms based on AI can be utilized efficiently, particularly with the extensive adoption of AI in cybersecurity and internet brand protection. Such technologies are able to help companies identify cybersquatting attempts in real time and may be implemented by domain registrars to enhance domain registration processes, mark potentially infringing domain names, and determine deceptive tactics early. Machine learning techniques, specifically natural language processing (NLP), are able to assist in domain name classification, which is essential in tracking and detecting valid versus invalid domains (Garg et al., 2020).

Yet, AI technology deployment for cybersquatting detection risks perpetuating system biases unless appropriately considered with respect to diversity and inclusiveness. One such risk is the undue protection of well-known Western brands. Most AI systems are calibrated using trademark databases and domain conflict cases that significantly favor large multinational corporations from North America and Europe. As a result, these models may be more calibrated to recognize violations associated with internationally known brands such as "Apple" or "Google," but less so for threats targeting smaller Indian local businesses that might not be as well-represented in the training set (Chander & Krishnamurthy, 2021).

Yet another crucial bias exists in the linguistic dependency of AI systems. The majority of domain monitoring AI platforms are trained on English-language corpora, thereby discriminating against trademarks in India's multi-lingual environment. With 22 officially supported languages and countless more dialects, local businesses prefer to use domain names written in Hindi, Tamil, Bengali, or Marathi. NLP models that do not have strong multilingual features can miss phonetic or semantic matches in non-English domain names, thus diminishing the security afforded to Indian businesses conducting business in local languages (Joshi et al., 2020). For instance, a domain that closely resembles the Hindi name of a popular Indian brand but is spelled out in Latin script can go unnoticed because of shortcomings in language detection.

Moreover, contextual and cultural intelligence is frequently missing in AI models, particularly those built with Western-biased datasets. What could be thought of as "confusingly similar" in one cultural or linguistic context does not necessarily resonate well across geography. AI instruments could misidentify similarities in brand names because they lack cultural awareness, and so may miss culturally significant infringements. For example, in the case of symbolic references or usual idioms that are incorporated into Indian brand names, they might not be properly understood by AI programs not trained on culturally diverse data sets (Binns, 2018).

In order to counteract these biases, it is important to take a more inclusive stance regarding AI development for cybersquatting identification. This entails:

- Increasing training datasets to incorporate trademarks and domain dispute cases from developing nations, such as India.

- Improving NLP models with multilingual support that encompasses a wide variety of Indian languages.
- Adding culturally contextual training data to enable AI systems to learn local naming practices, linguistic patterns, and regional brand identifiers.
- Embracing transparent and accountable AI design processes that proactively tackle fairness and inclusivity in automated decision-making (Mehrabi et al., 2021).

Where AI presents substantial potential in combating cybersquatting, its effectiveness depends on the extent to which the technology is developed and implemented with equity. Unless conscious measures are taken to counter linguistic, cultural, and brand-based prejudices, AI-based systems can perpetuate global digital disparities by providing greater security to established Western brands against new local businesses in India and elsewhere in the Global South.

14.11 Cybersquatting, Trademark Enforcement, and Digital Equity

Cybersquatting is as much a matter of digital equity as it is a technological and legal concern. Securing and defending an online identity has become a critical requirement for engagement in digital economies, especially for small businesses, startups, and individual entrepreneurs. Existing legal and procedural frameworks for countering cybersquatting, however, do not adequately take into consideration structural inequalities and disproportionately harm marginalized or resource-poor communities.

14.11.1 Legal Barriers and Mechanisms for Small Businesses

Globally, the Uniform Domain-Name Dispute-Resolution Policy (UDRP), run by ICANN, and India's native forum under the Trade Marks Act, 1999, offer remedy against cybersquatting. Yet, these legal options are time-consuming, cumbersome, and expensive for small firms or individuals. It can cost from $1,300 to $4,000 USD in fees alone, without attorney representation, to file a UDRP complaint, for example. For small-scale enterprises or microenterprises in rural India, such costs can be too high, essentially pricing them out of access to the protection such mechanisms ought to offer (Kesan & Gallo, 2005).

In addition, the onus of proof in such proceedings—proving bad faith and confusing similarity—constitutes a heavy legal and evidentiary burden upon complainants, which better-capitalized corporations can more easily sustain. Small or local businesses do not necessarily have the legal experience, funds, or records needed to pursue an effective claim.

14.11.2 Unequal Access to Domain Name Registration and Literacy

Alongside conflict resolution, inequalities also emerge at the level of domain name registration. Identification, registration, and acquisition of relevant domain names involve a level of digital proficiency, access to technology, and knowledge of brand protection measures—assets more easily accessible to urban, technologically literate communities and established enterprises. In comparison, smaller businesses or those based in rural or underserved communities might not have knowledge of domain name strategy and are thus more susceptible to cybersquatting.

In addition, high-end domain names or exact brand matches are frequently purchased and resold at inflated prices by domain speculators, further distorting access to benefit more affluent individuals and organizations. This secondary market for domains values profit over equitable access and erodes digital inclusivity, especially for first-time entrepreneurs and grassroots innovators.

14.11.3 Cultural and Linguistic Marginalization

Cybersquatting enforcement also overlaps with linguistic and cultural equity. Given that legal and digital systems often are constructed considering English and Latin-script naming schemes, companies using regional Indian language or culturally imbedded brand identities might have difficulty establishing their rights within present systems. There is a danger of these businesses being doubly disadvantaged—first by poor linguistic representation in AI tools (as explored in Section 10), and second by law regimes that do not lend themselves to local naming conventions or informal economies.

14.11.4 Towards Inclusive and Fair Enforcement

For the creation of a more inclusive digital environment, reforms need to extend beyond narrowly legal and technological measures. Among key recommendations are:

- Tiered or subsidized fees for dispute resolution for small entrepreneurs and businesses based in low-income or rural backgrounds.
- Streamlined complaint procedures and multilingual assistance to minimize reliance on costly legal expertise.

- Mass awareness campaigns to establish digital literacy regarding domain name registration, risks of cybersquatting, and IP rights, especially among regional and underrepresented communities.
- Incentives for inclusive practices in domain registration, such as promotion of local language domain name systems and accessible registrar interfaces.

Confronting cybersquatting as an issue of digital equity involves the acknowledgment that present systems tend to mirror and entrench present-day socioeconomic hierarchies. A guarantee of equal access to protection of online identity is critical to a genuinely inclusive digital economy—where innovation and entrepreneurship can take root independent of geography, language, or financial means.

14.12 Cybersquatting, DEIB, and Domain Name Disputes in India

Cybersquatting—the practice of registering domain names identical or confusingly similar to well-known trademarks for profit from their goodwill—creates a major challenge for businesses and organizations, and especially those owned by marginalized groups. This is added to by the non-existence of specific legislation in India for the solution of cybersquatting, and hence the recourse to existing laws of trademark, which may fail to protect the interest of marginalized communities.

14.12.1 Effect on Indigenous and Cultural Organizations

Indigenous and cultural organizations tend to struggle in obtaining domain names that represent their heritage and identity. The lack of special legal safeguards exposes them to cybersquatting, where people register domain names belonging to these organizations to take advantage of their cultural value for financial benefits.

Case Study: Amul's Experience with Cybersquatting

Amul, India's largest dairy company, was the target of cybersquatting when scammers registered domain names like amuldistributor.com and amulboard.com. These domains were employed to set up phishing websites, which resulted in scams like spurious recruitment campaigns and demands for payment to become distributors. Amul was forced to publish public notices and seek legal recourse to clear the mess, underlining the difficulty in protecting even well-known brands' online identities.

14.12.2 Issues Affecting Small Underrepresented Business-owned Businesses

Small businesses, especially those underrepresented businesses, tend to have fewer resources at their disposal with which to observe and guard their domain names. Cybersquatters take advantage of this weakness by registering names resembling those of such businesses and agreeing to resell them at extortionate rates, thus causing business disruption and financial loss online.

Case Study: Arun Jaitley's Domain Name Dispute

Arun Jaitley, one of India's prominent politicians, approached registering the arunjaitley.com domain in 2011. Yet he learned the domain had previously been registered by a third party, who sought a significant fee for transfer of the domain name. Jaitley won a case against him at the Delhi High Court by stressing the fact that the domain name is as close as an individual trademark, and that defendant behaviour qualified as bad faith cybersquatting.

14.12.3 Domain Name Disputes Involving Regional Indian Languages

The proliferation of regional Indian language domain names has brought new challenges in cybersquatting. These domains tend to be symbolisms of local enterprises and cultural identities and have a strong appeal to be targeted by cybersquatters who aim to capitalize on their worth.

Case Study: Satyam Infoway Ltd. v. Sifynet Solutions Pvt. Ltd.

In this historical case, Satyam Infoway Ltd. complained that Sifynet Solutions Pvt. Ltd. had registered domain names like siffynet.com and siffynet.net, which were confusingly similar to Satyam's domain sifynet.com. The Supreme Court of India decided in favor of Satyam Infoway, holding that domain names are business identifiers and are equally protected as trademarks under the Trade Marks Act, 1999.

14.12.4 DEIB Considerations in Legal Decisions

Though Indian courts have dealt with cybersquatting via trademark law, very little evidence of direct DEIB consideration has been found impacting judicial decisions in domain name cases. The lack of a specific cybersquatting law leaves marginalized groups vulnerable to exploitation without specialized protections under the law.

Case Study: Tata Sons Ltd v. Monu Kasuri

Here, the defendant had booked domain names like tataindica.com, which were deceptively similar to Tata's trademark. The Delhi High Court held in favor of Tata Sons, laying stress on the protection of domain names as valuable corporate assets. The case did not touch upon the wider DEIB implications of cybersquatting, like its effects on small businesses or communities with fewer resources.

14.12.5 Suggestions for Improving DEIB in Cybersquatting Laws

To address the DEIB dimensions of cybersquatting and domain name disputes, the following suggestions are made:

Enact Specific Legislation: Pass legislation that explicitly deals with cybersquatting and sets up precise rules for resolving domain name conflicts, with a view to ensuring that marginalized groups are able to access legal recourse.

Provide Accessible Dispute Resolution Mechanisms: Develop low-cost and accessible systems of resolving disputes over domain names, like web-based arbitration services, to help small businesses and underrepresented communities defend their online identities.

Enhance Digital Literacy: Initiate programs to increase digital literacy among marginalized communities to enable them to comprehend and navigate the intricacies of domain name registration and protection.

Promote Cultural Sensitivity in Legal Rulings: Push for the integration of DEIB considerations into legal rulings on domain name disputes so that the cultural meaning of domain names is identified and preserved.

Support Community-Led Initiatives: Offer assistance to community-led organizations that help underrepresented groups acquire and safeguard domain names that represent their cultural identity and heritage.

By adopting these suggestions, India can build a more inclusive online space that safeguards the online identities of all communities so that cybersquatting does not disproportionately target underrepresented groups.

14.13 Analysis and Recommendations

It appears that the upset trademark owner now has various avenues of recourse against cybersquatters, ranging from cease and desist letters to arbitration processes such as UDRP and INDRP, and litigation pursuant to the Trade Marks Act, 1999. Yet, these remedies may or may not be effective and accessible, particularly from the perspective of **digital equity and community impact.

14.13.1 Cybersquatting and Marginalization of Indigenous and Cultural Organizations

Domain name conflicts do not impact all organizations alike. Indigenous enterprises, cultural communities, and civil society organizations in India do not have the institutional and economic resources needed to track, protect, or reclaim domain names associated with their identities, cultural expressions, or traditional knowledge. These groups may be outside the formal trademark registration system and lack the legal literacy necessary to file UDRP or INDRP cases.

For example, if a tribal artisan brand, a traditional healing ritual, or a regional cultural festival's domain name is cybersquatted and commercially exploited by a third party, there is limited recourse. Existing IP regimes are centred on formalized trademarks and do not account for the subtle forms of communal intellectual property prevalent in India's multicultural environment. Consequently, the digital presence and representation of these communities are susceptible to misappropriation and misrepresentation.

14.13.2 Insufficiency of Existing Legal Mechanisms

The current systems of dispute resolution under UDRP and INDRP are inclined to favor conventional, Western-oriented IP frameworks. Such frameworks might not acknowledge the informal or collective patterns of ownership prevalent in most Indian communities. Moreover, the procedural and economic costs of establishing "bad faith" or exclusive trademark rights constitute obstacles for marginalized groups to claim control over domain names associated with their identity or heritage.

In addition, neither the Trade Marks Act, 1999 nor the Information Technology Act, 2000 of the government of India incorporates provisions specifically protecting cultural expressions or traditional knowledge in the virtual space. This lacuna in legislation is a cause of the systemic exclusion of marginalized and indigenous communities from accessing the advantages of IP protection and digital representation.

14.13.3 Digital Representation and Inclusion

Domain names are more than virtual addresses—they are tools of identity, visibility, and agency online. For small businesses, local groups, and cultural organizations, having a domain name reflecting their brand or heritage is a key to exercising presence in India's growing digital economy. When these communities have their such domain names taken over by cybersquatters, it not only disrupts their capacity to communicate and trade online but also entrenches digital hierarchies.

The absence of fair access to mechanisms for protecting the domain is inextricably linked to more general concerns regarding **digital inclusion**. In the absence of equal chances to defend and advertise their identities in the digital sphere, historically excluded groups are relegated to the margins of India's digital revolution.

14.13.4 Recommendations

To make India's response to cybersquatting more robust and guarantee inclusive digital rights, which deals with Diversity, Equity, Inclusion, and Belonging (DEIB) in domain name dispute resolution and cybersquatting identification the following reforms are recommended:

- Protection of Cultural and Indigenous IP under Laws: Reform trademark and cyber laws to specifically acknowledge and protect indigenous, traditional, and cultural knowledge system domain names. This may include the inclusion of protections akin to those suggested under WIPO's Traditional Knowledge model.

- Inclusive Reforms to Domain Dispute Resolution (UDRP/URS): To bolster equity in domain name dispute resolution processes like the UDRP and URS, focused reform must centre on accessibility and inclusivity for underrepresented constituents. Implementing a sliding scale or subsidized fee structure can reduce economic barriers for small business, not-for-profits, and individuals from the Global South or Indigenous peoples. Enlarging multilingual availability and using plain language reports will demystify the process for users who have different legal and technical literacy. Legal aid and representation programs, established in collaboration with pro bono legal networks and nongovernmental organizations, can further equalize the playing field by providing necessary assistance to marginalized claimants. Guaranteeing diverse panellist rosters—indicative of gender, ethnicity, geography, and socioeconomic status—can overcome bias and promote more culturally sensitive decision-making. Lastly, making strong transparency controls and bias review processes, such as public release of dispute determinations broken out by demographics, will assist in detecting and addressing systemic disparities within the resolution process.
- Guidelines for Bias-Free AI Tools to Identify Cybersquatting: For AI tools for cybersquatting detection to function equitably and inclusively, they need to be designed with DEIB explicitly in mind. Bias auditing within training data is critical to avoid the disproportionate marking of domain names corresponding to Indigenous languages, regional trademarks, or culturally relevant expressions, which tend to get misclassified because they are underrepresented. The outputs of AI need to be explainable, presenting clear, interpretable grounds for flagging decisions so that the users understand, contest, and correct false positives—especially important for underserved communities with limited access to legal resources. Stakeholders from underrepresented groups should be included in the development and evaluation process to ensure that the tools represent diverse viewpoints and are culturally suitable. In addition, setting open access standards and clear APIs allows independent monitoring by researchers and civil society, fostering accountability and ongoing improvement in bias detection and mitigation.
- Education Initiatives for Digital Literacy and Domain Protection: In order to enhance digital literacy and enable various communities to protect their online presence, specific educational programs need to be made both accessible and culturally sensitive. Contextualized training programs presented in local languages and customized for specific groups—e.g., Indigenous peoples, immigrant business owners, and rural youth—can address key issues such as domain name

registration, renewal procedures, and the basics of intellectual property and cybersquatting threats. Cooperation with schools, NGOs, and community centres makes sure that such digital skills are integrated into prevailing education systems. Moreover, the creation of toolkits and "train-the-trainer" materials helps local leaders share knowledge effectively within their respective communities. Public awareness campaigns through mediums like social media, radio, and community newspapers can also further enhance the awareness of domain protection and digital rights. Lastly, underrepresented entrepreneur-focused mentorship networks and digital incubators can offer advice and support in order to obtain domain assets and establish long-term digital brands.

- Dispute Resolution with a Community Focus: Establish a low-cost, streamlined domain name dispute process for community groups, indigenous peoples, and small enterprises without formal trademark registration.
- Widen the IT Act's Scope Reform the Information Technology Act, 2000 to define cybersquatting as an act of cybercrime and provide provisions to take into consideration culturally symbolic domain names.
- Digital Literacy and IP Awareness Support: Introduce focused initiatives towards developing digital literacy, particularly in rural and tribal regions, such that communities learn how to register domain names and claim their rights.
- Set up a Cultural Domain Name Registry: Create a government-funded registry or guarded list of culturally important names, to bar their unauthorized registration by unrelated third parties, just as UNESCO protection schemes for cultural heritage.
- Inclusive Use of AI: Utilize AI in domain name surveillance in manners that are inclusive of Indian languages and culturally important words, so as to provide equitable protection across linguistic and ethnic communities (Mehrabi et al., 2021).

It is important to look forward for a just and inclusive framework of domain name resolution must look beyond commercial interests. It must also protect the virtual identities of all communities—particularly those who in the past were excluded from access to formal systems of IP protection. In the dynamic, multilingual environment of India, cybersquatting is not simply a commercial danger but a threat to representation in the digital space on fair terms. Legislative, administrative, and technology reforms need to target as a whole to ensure that everyone's voice—be it corporate, cultural, or communal—is guarded and brought forward in the cyber environment.

References

Abel, S. M. (1999). Trademark issues in cyberspace: The brave new frontier. *Michigan Telecommunications and Technology Law Review*, *5*(1), 91–129. https://repository.law.umich.edu/mttlr/vol5/iss1/4

Anschell, J., & Lucas, J. (2003). What's in a name: Dealing with cybersquatting. *Entertainment & Sports Law Journal*, *21*(3), 3–7.

Arnot, J. A. (2014). Navigating cybersquatting enforcement in the expanding internet. *Journal of Marshall Review of Intellectual Property Law*, *13*, 321–340.

Beal, V. (1996, October). *Domain name*. Webopedia. www.webopedia.com/TERM/D/domain_name.html

Binns, R. (2018). Fairness in machine learning: Lessons from political philosophy. In *Proceedings of the 2018 Conference on Fairness, Accountability and Transparency* (pp. 149–159). https://doi.org/10.1145/3287560.3287598

Chander, A., & Krishnamurthy, V. (2021). The myth of platform neutrality. *Georgetown Law Journal*, *109*(2), 445–497.

Charan, P. (2015). A survey of the prominent effects of cybersquatting in India. *International Journal of Information Security and Cybercrime*, *4*(1).

Dev, R. (2020). *Understanding cease and desist letter*. https://patentbusinesslawyer.com/understanding-cease-and-desist-letter/

Domain Registration Services. (2011, March 30). *What is reverse domain name hijacking?* www.domainregistration.com.au/news/reverse-domain-hijacking.php

Ebersohn, G. (2006). Cybersquatting, typosquatting and trade mark law (Part 1). *Journal of South African Law*, *2006*(3), 315.

Garg, A., Trivedi, N., Lu, J., Eirinaki, M., Yu, B., & Olumofin, F. (2020). An evaluation of machine learning methods for domain name classification. In *2020 IEEE International Conference on Big Data (Big Data)*, pp. 4577–4585. https://doi.org/10.1109/BigData50022.2020.9377787

Independent News Services Private Ltd. v. Vijay Tayade, Case No. D2017-1464. (2017). *WIPO Arbitration and Mediation Center*.

Internet Corporation for Assigned Names and Numbers. (2012). *ICANN annual report 2012*. www.icann.org/en/system/files/files/annual-report-2012-en.pdf

Jain, S. (2016). *Cybersquatting: Concept, types and legal regimes in India & USA*. https://ssrn.com/abstract=2786474

Jaybhaye, A. S. (2016). Cyber law and IPR issues: The Indian perspective. *Bharati Law Review*, *4*, 166–169.

Joshi, P., Kumar, S., & Mathur, P. (2020). Multilingual challenges in NLP for Indian languages. ACM Transactions on Asian and Low-Resource Language Information Processing, 19(6), 1–24.

Kesan, J. P., & Gallo, A. M. (2005). Domain name governance: The rise of the domain name marketplace and its effect on trademark law. *Michigan Telecommunications and Technology Law Review*, 11(2), 287–334.

Kesari Trust & Others v. DLKesari Travels Private Ltd., 2016 SCC OnLine Bom 9483.

Khan, Z. H., Charan, P., Ansar, M. A., & Khan, K. H. (2015). Cybersquatting and its effectual position in India. *International Journal of Scientific & Engineering Research*, *6*(2), 880–886.

Khanna, A., & Srivastava, S. (2014). Determining the 'domain' of trademark laws: Application in the interception of cyber squatters. *International Journal of Law and Policy Review, 1*(1), 63–76.

Lukose, L. (2016). Trademark infringement through cybersquatting: Law and policy: A study of UDRP and Indian system. *CNLU Law Journal*, *6*(3), 33–48.

McKenna, M. P. (2007). The normative foundations of trademark law. *Notre Dame Law Review, 82*(5), 1839–1913. https://scholarship.law.nd.edu/law_faculty_scholarship/226

Mehrabi, N., Morstatter, F., Saxena, N., Lerman, K., & Galstyan, A. (2021). A survey on bias and fairness in machine learning. ACM Computing Surveys, 54(6), 1–35. https://doi.org/10.1145/3457607

Mishra, P. (2013). *Cybersquatting and domain name disputes under trademark law* [Unpublished manuscript or institutional publication, if known].

Pandit Durga Dutt Sharma v. Navaratna Pharmaceutical Laboratories, AIR 1965 SC 980.

Perry v. Truefitt, (1842) 6 Beav. 66.

Rautdesai, R., & Nandekar, U. (2017). Online photographs in news: Copyright perspective. *Journal of Communication Media Watch, 8*(1), 133–142.

S.S. Rana & Co. Advocates. (2018). *Effects of sending cease and desist notices in cases of IP infringement*. www.mondaq.com/india/trademark/700068/effects-of-sending-cease-and-desist-notices-in-cases-of-ip-infringement

Sangal, P. S. (1999). Trademarks and domain names: Some recent developments. *Journal of the Indian Law Institute, 41*(1), 30–43.

Saxena, A. (2015, August 1). Blogger gets legal notice for using Flipkart logo. *The Economic Times*. https://retail.economictimes.indiatimes.com/news/e-commerce/e-tailing/blogger-gets-legal-notice-for-using-flipkart-logo/48752636

Singh & Associates. (2012). *Cyber squatting laws in India*. www.mondaq.com/india/trademark/208840/cyber-squatting-laws-in-india

Tokas, L., & Tyagi, A. (2020). Evolving IP issues and cyber laws. *Jus Dicere, 3*(1). https://indiankanoon.org/doc/1630167/

Vellakat, R. (2016). Trade mark clearinghouse: An anti-cybersquatting mechanism. *Practical Lawyer (IT)*, July, 88.

Wadhera, B. L. (2009). *Law relating to intellectual property*. Universal Law Publishing Company.

Webster's Dictionary (1828). *American Dictionary of the English Language*, from https://webstersdictionary1828.com/

Zhao, Y. (2000). A dispute resolution mechanism for cybersquatting. *Journal of World Intellectual Property, 3*, 1–15.

Part V

Technology and Marginalized Communities

15

Digital Inequality and Online Learning in Rural Sarawak

Nuurrianti Jalli, Ika Karlina Idris and Nala Edwin Widjaja

15.1 Introduction

The COVID-19 pandemic precipitated a paradigm shift in educational delivery. UNESCO (2022) reports that, in 2020, schools globally shuttered, impacting more than 1 billion learners across 150 countries. Subsequently, e-learning emerged as the predominant modality for educational continuity, endorsed by governments internationally. However, challenges with Internet connectivity impeded effective learning and teaching (Jalli, 2020). Online education, critics argue, privileges the few, excluding those in under-connected locales and socioeconomically marginalized homes (Jordan et al., 2021).

The rapid transition to online learning represents not merely a technological challenge but a critical equity, diversity, and inclusion (EDI) issue demanding urgent attention. When education becomes dependent on digital access, systemic inequalities transform learning platforms into gatekeeping mechanisms that disproportionately exclude those already marginalized by intersecting factors of geography, socioeconomic status, ethnicity, disability, and language (Van Dijk, 2020). This digital exclusion directly contradicts fundamental educational rights and perpetuates intergenerational cycles of disadvantage that undermine the social fabric of diverse communities.

Research has found that the pandemic exacerbated educational access disparities, primarily in communities already at a disadvantage (Milana et al., 2021). These communities—rural, impoverished, isolated, and less educated—suffer from preexisting inequalities (Van Dijk, 2020). For instance, Argentinian educators resorted to physical distribution of learning materials during school suspensions (Pini, 2020). Further exacerbating these disparities, students often lacked adult guidance in navigating online resources (Onyema et al., 2021). In certain areas, limited computer availability and subpar Internet services hindered connectivity (Khan et al., 2020). A systematic examination of the digital divide links educational impacts with various

DOI: 10.1201/9781003591078-20

factors, including socioeconomic status and infrastructural deficiencies (Badiozaman et al., 2022; Lythreatis et al., 2021).

In Malaysia, movement restrictions, such as lockdowns, curfews, and school closures, prompted a digital shift in education, eliciting varied public responses (Lin, Sim & Quah, 2021; Selvanathan et al., 2020). With physical classrooms shuttered and mobility severely limited, students were forced to rely entirely on digital platforms for continued learning (Azevedo et al., 2021). Concerns spanned Internet reliability, device access, digital literacy, pedagogical training, and the inundation of educational content across digital platforms (Johari, 2020). Sarawak, lagging in infrastructural development relative to other Malaysian states, faced pronounced challenges (Goh, 2021). This shift disproportionately affected Sarawak's marginalized and rural communities (Bong, 2020). Although intended to sustain education during movement restrictions, online learning inadvertently fostered systemic bias against those in connectivity-poor zones (Jalli, 2020). Post-online class implementation, social media highlighted the struggles of Sarawak's rural inhabitants in securing stable Internet, underscoring the financial strain of maintaining sufficient connectivity for educational purposes (Johari, 2020). These viral narratives spotlight online learning as an exclusionary, elite-centric educational model (Horn & Gifford, 2020).

This study investigates how the digitalization of education has impacted teachers and vulnerable communities in Sarawak, with fieldwork conducted in one of its polling districts. The research explores the extent of the digital divide experienced by these communities prior to the pandemic and examines whether the COVID-19 crisis exacerbated existing disparities. It also considers the specific challenges faced by teachers during the shift to online instruction, the difficulties students encountered as observed by educators, and community perspectives on what kinds of interventions are most needed. Ultimately, the study contributes to ongoing efforts to center equity and inclusion principles in education policy by offering grounded insights into how online learning systems can be more equitably designed to support teachers and students in rural and marginalized areas.

15.1.1 Digital Inequality

Digital inequality denotes the disparate access to and use of digital technologies across regions. Van Dijk and Hacker (2003) highlight that individuals in digitally deficient areas cannot reap the same benefits as those in digitally affluent regions. Van Dijk (2020) categorizes digital inequality into three domains: digital device and internet access, digital literacy, and societal and personal outcomes from digital engagement.

At its core, digital access entails the availability of technology and connectivity; advancements in infrastructure have facilitated faster internet, which is crucial for efficient online education. Nonetheless, geographical and developmental disparities lead to unequal access, with some relying on mobile internet, which is less suitable for educational needs due to slower speeds and instability (Cinnamon, 2020).

Digital literacy encompasses basic skills, like device usage and application navigation, and advanced competencies, including the strategic use of digital platforms for educational enhancement (Khan et al., 2019). Li et al. (2020) observed that during the pandemic, vulnerable urban communities depended on knowledgeable individuals to acquire digital skills. Concerning outcomes, while access and literacy improve, especially in developed nations, the use of digital technology for societal advancement remains uneven. Lower socioeconomic groups often engage with technology for entertainment rather than for life-enhancing purposes like employment or health services (Selwyn et al., 2005).

The 2020 Internet Governance Forum posited that post-pandemic existence will be inherently digital, necessitating a comprehensive digital transition in education. Educators are called to advance their digital pedagogy to align with the technology, learning theories, and appropriate digital tools for educational objectives (Howell & McMaster, 2022; Bećirović, 2023). The transformation extends beyond pedagogy to include knowledge management, systemic operations, assessments, and policy-making, all within a digital framework. The Organization for Economic Cooperation and Development (OECD) (2020) acknowledges that while sound educational policies exist, their implementation during the pandemic was often suboptimal, failing to meet educational demands effectively.

15.2 Digital Inequalities in Malaysia

In the wake of the COVID-19 pandemic, equitable access to information and communication technology (ICT) has become critically important. The Malaysian government, recognizing the necessity of digital inclusivity, has made strides in enhancing the affordability of devices and Internet services through initiatives like the Mandatory Standard on Access Pricing (MSAP) set by the Pakatan Harapan government in 2018, which limits the prices that service providers can charge users (Bernama, 2018). Despite these efforts leading to an Internet penetration rate exceeding 88% (Freedom House, 2022), this figure belies the true quality of connectivity experienced by users, particularly in rural areas.

Rural dwellers often report the necessity of traveling to urban centers for reliable Internet, with Sarawak being a notable example of such disparities (Johari, 2020). There have been numerous accounts of students and educators undertaking extensive treks to attain connectivity for educational purposes

(Banji, 2022). As of 2020, a disproportionate 75.6% of Internet users resided in urban centers, while only 24.4% were rural (MCMC, 2020), and around 20% of the nation still endured substandard Internet services (Bernama, 2020a).

The transition to online learning mandated by the Malaysian government in 2020 brought these issues into sharp relief, with social media amplifying the difficulties faced by rural students in engaging with online education exemplified by the viral video of a Sabah student climbing a tree for Internet access (Bernama, 2020b). In response, the government explored satellite technologies to extend Internet reach to rural and remote areas, yet these solutions are constrained by limited capacity, high costs, and susceptibility to weather (Government adopts VSAT technology, 2020).

In Sarawak, significant challenges in digital connectivity became increasingly evident during the COVID-19 pandemic (MCMC, 2020). Longhouse communities in Sarawak in this case, primarily inhabited by Indigenous groups such as the Iban, Bidayuh, and Orang Ulu, encountered significant barriers to accessing online education during the COVID-19 pandemic due to chronic limitations in Internet connectivity. These marginalized communities are located in remote and geographically challenging areas, often deep within forested interiors and accessible only by river or unpaved roads, which has historically hindered the development of digital infrastructure. Consequently, many longhouse residents either lack Internet access entirely or depend on unstable mobile data signals, often requiring students to climb hills or travel long distances simply to obtain a basic connection (New tower to overcome Internet access issue at Sarawak longhouse, 2022; UNESCO, 2021).

Longhouse communities in Sarawak have long faced critical challenges in accessing education, even prior to the implementation of online schooling during the COVID-19 pandemic. Their remote location makes daily travel to school both logistically difficult and financially burdensome (UNICEF Malaysia, 2019). As a consequence, many students from longhouse areas were required to stay in school hostels or undertake long and arduous journeys on foot or by boat, leading to irregular school attendance and elevated dropout rates, especially at the secondary level. These challenges were further exacerbated by inadequate educational infrastructure in rural areas, including limited availability of qualified teachers, insufficient learning materials, and a lack of access to specialized educational support services (Rickie & Alias, 2024).

Before the pandemic, the Malaysian government had limited integration of digital learning tools, especially in rural areas. While some urban and private schools had begun incorporating ICT in classrooms, most public schools relied on traditional teaching methods. National programs like the Smart School initiative, incorporation of the Frog Virtual Learning Environment in the classroom, and 1BestariNet aimed to digitize learning (Zainal & Zainuddin, 2020), but their impact was uneven and often constrained by infrastructure gaps, particularly in East Malaysia with Sabah and Sarawak located in this region (UNESCO, 2023).

In response to the COVID-19 pandemic, Malaysian government introduced several initiatives to support online learning, including the Digital Educational Learning Initiative Malaysia (DELIMa), the Teaching and Learning at Home (PdPR) framework, and collaborations with telecommunications providers to supply free data packages and devices for students (UNESCO, 2023). The rapid shift in the education system during the pandemic exacerbated the digital divide in Malaysia's remote and underdeveloped regions, which had already faced significant accessibility challenges before the health crisis. These existing limitations severely restricted students' ability to fully participate in the government's online learning programs. Although national efforts like the JENDELA initiative were launched to expand broadband coverage in rural areas, progress has been uneven particularly in Sarawak, leaving longhouse communities disproportionately disadvantaged in accessing equitable education throughout the crisis (UNESCO, 2023).

Academic inquiry into digital inequality has intensified, highlighting how it can worsen educational disparities for students in rural areas (Sulaiman & Halamy, 2021). These students face multiple challenges—from having to leave their homes to access the Internet during a global health crisis, to dealing with unstable connections and limited data availability. For low-income rural households, particularly those reliant on small-scale farming or informal work, the financial strain of online education is significant. The need to purchase multiple digital devices and maintain regular data usage places a heavy burden on families already struggling to meet basic daily needs.

This stark contrast in educational experiences casts doubt on the notion that online learning levels the playing field for urban and rural students alike. Rural students face a unique set of obstacles that risk leaving them behind in educational attainment. Moreover, educators in these areas must devise creative solutions to facilitate learning continuity, such as identifying Internet-accessible locations, distributing print materials, and personally seeking stable connections (Johari, 2020). Therefore, this analysis contends that in the Malaysian context, online learning acts as an exclusionary measure, effectively marginalizing those in rural areas and reinforcing systemic educational inequities.

15.3 Research Methodology

This study employed methodological triangulation by integrating an online survey with focus group discussions (FGDs), enhancing both the quality of data and the depth of analysis. Participants were educators from Layar, a state constituency in Sarawak that has been represented in the Sarawak State Legislative Assembly since 1968. The constituency comprises several polling districts—including Spak, Padeh, and Bebanggai—each reflecting varying levels of infrastructural and educational development.

Layar was strategically selected as the research site due to its demographic and geographic diversity. The area includes both urban and rural settings, encompassing a wide range of schooling environments. Within the constituency, there are regular day schools and boarding schools, as well as a mix of primary and secondary institutions. Students enrolled in these schools come from both urban centers and more remote rural villages, while the teachers serving in Layar also reside across this urban–rural spectrum. This spatial and socio-economic heterogeneity allows for a nuanced understanding of how connectivity and educational challenges manifest differently depending on geographic context.

The diversity of Layar offers a valuable comparative framework for analyzing disparities in digital access and educational experience. Because the constituency reflects the broader developmental and infrastructural challenges typical of many areas in Sarawak, the insights gathered here are potentially generalizable to other regions within the state and, to some extent, across Malaysia. This makes Layar a meaningful site for examining the intersections of digital inequality, geography, and educational access.

15.4 Online Survey (Quantitative)

A structured online survey was designed to capture broad trends among educators in Layar, particularly focusing on Internet connectivity, online teaching readiness, access to digital tools, and perceptions of policy support. Following initial consultations with Mr. Paul Langgang, Chair of the Layar Education Committee, the survey was deemed feasible given that most teachers had intermittent access to the Internet by traveling to towns such as Betong where connectivity was stronger. The survey instrument was pre-tested with a sample of 30 teachers representing both primary and secondary schools across different locations in the Layar constituency. These participants were purposively selected to reflect variation in geography, experience level, and subject expertise. The pilot test evaluated the clarity, internal consistency, and construct validity of the questionnaire. A Cronbach's alpha score of 0.83 was obtained, indicating good internal reliability and falling within the recommended range of 0.70 to 0.95 (Tavakol & Dennick, 2011). The finalized survey was hosted on Google Forms and distributed via WhatsApp, the most commonly used communication platform among teachers in the area. Distribution was coordinated with school administrators and local education stakeholders. The survey remained open from 3 September to 17 October 2020 and generated 359 valid responses, accounting for approximately 65.9%

of the total teaching population in Layar (N = 545). Data collected from the survey informed the development of targeted prompts for the qualitative phase.

15.5 Focus Group Discussions (Qualitative)

To gain deeper insight into the issues surfaced in the survey, seven FGDs were conducted between 28 September and 7 October 2020, involving 65 teachers from seven schools comprising four primary and three secondary institutions strategically selected based on geographic location and infrastructure variability. Participants were purposively sampled with the help of school heads to ensure diversity in teaching experience, gender, and subjects taught.

Each discussion lasted from 60 to 90 minutes and was moderated by the principal investigator using a semistructured focus group guide. Thematic areas of discussion included the following: (1) online teaching strategies and constraints; (2) Internet access and infrastructure; (3) support and communication from the Ministry of Education; (4) student participation and household support; and (5) recommendations for systemic improvement. Discussions were audio-recorded with participants' consent, transcribed verbatim, and analyzed using thematic analysis as outlined by Braun and Clarke (2006). As Kitzinger (1995) emphasizes, FGDs facilitate richer dialogue by allowing participants to interact, challenge, and build upon each other's perspectives, yielding a more dynamic and layered data corpus than individual interviews. This proved particularly effective in uncovering context-specific challenges and coping mechanisms related to the digital divide in rural Sarawak.

15.6 Triangulation and Use of Secondary Data

To ensure analytical rigor and contextual grounding, primary data from the survey and FGDs were triangulated with secondary sources, including national statistics from the Department of Statistics Malaysia, reports by the Malaysian Communications and Multimedia Commission (MCMC), and policy documents from the Ministry of Education. While national figures indicated that only 20% of Malaysians were without Internet access, data from Layar painted a more critical picture: more than 75% of surveyed educators reported that their current Internet service was insufficient to support online learning, and many were reliant on mobile data due to the lack of broadband infrastructure in longhouse areas. This triangulation not only contextualized local realities within national narratives but also highlighted the disconnect between top-down digital education policies and ground-level implementation challenges, reinforcing the need for localized interventions and infrastructural investment.

15.7 Findings

15.7.1 Survey Response Rate and Participant Profile

Between September 1 and October 17, 2020, an online survey was administered to teachers working in DUN 36, Layar, Sarawak, one of the rural state constituencies in Malaysian Borneo. Out of 545 teachers identified by the Layar Education Development Committee, 359 completed the survey, resulting in a response rate of 65.9%. The participating schools were all publicly funded and comprised both primary and secondary institutions serving predominantly rural and semi-rural populations. Respondents ranged in age from 18 to 65 years. The largest proportion were aged 25–34 years (35.1%), followed by those aged 35–44 years (31.2%), 45–54 years (23.7%), and 55–65 years (9.2%). A small number (0.8%) were 18–24 years old, likely interim teachers. Women made up 57.4% of the sample, while 42.6% were men. In terms of qualifications, 83.8% had a bachelor's degree, with smaller numbers reporting master's degrees (9.2%), professional teaching certificates (5.8%), or secondary school diplomas (1.1%). The majority of respondents had over five years of teaching experience, although the survey did not collect detailed data on their functional positions (e.g., head teacher and subject coordinator), which is acknowledged as a limitation.

15.7.2 Internet Access and Types of Connectivity

Most teachers (74.9%) indicated that they had some form of Internet access at home. However, access did not imply quality or reliability. The primary mode of Internet connectivity was via mobile phones, with 71.3% reporting that they relied primarily on cellular data. Only 28.7% reported using fixed broadband or other services. When allowed to select multiple responses, 94.2% indicated using cellular Internet, followed by 23.1% who used home broadband, 15.9% who used pocket Wi-Fi, and 3.1% who accessed satellite Internet. A few teachers (1.4%) reported relying on school Wi-Fi during lockdown, particularly those who lived near school compounds. The widespread reliance on mobile phones had significant pedagogical implications. Many parents owned older or low-spec smartphones, often with limited storage capacity and outdated operating systems. These devices were unable to support applications such as Google Classroom, Zoom, or even simple PDF viewers. In several cases, children shared a single mobile device among multiple siblings, delaying access to lessons or preventing synchronous participation altogether.

15.7.3 Barriers to Student Participation in Online Learning: Teachers' Observations during the COVID-19 Lockdown

Data from the online survey revealed that a significant majority of teachers—91.6% (n = 329) observed that their students were unable to participate in online learning due to a lack of Internet access at home. This quantitative finding was strongly corroborated by qualitative data from FGDs conducted across seven schools in the Layar constituency. Teachers consistently reported that once schools were closed and students returned to their family homes, often in remote longhouse communities any existing access to Internet services was lost.

At SK Nanga Spak, for instance, teachers estimated that more than 90% of their students, most of whom reside in longhouses without telecommunications infrastructure, had no Internet connectivity during the national lockdown. The closure of dormitories, which previously provided some students with limited but usable school-based Wi-Fi access, further exacerbated the problem. Without an alternative means of connection at home, students were effectively cut off from all forms of online instruction.

In addition to connectivity challenges, device unavailability emerged as another major barrier. A total of 87.5% of teachers (n = 314) reported that their students lacked the appropriate digital tools required for online learning. Many students did not own personal smartphones, tablets, or laptops. This problem was especially acute among families living in longhouses and rural settlements, where household incomes were limited and priorities were often directed toward basic needs rather than digital technologies.

At SK St. Mark, teachers described a situation in which nearly all students lacked individual access to suitable devices. In many cases, students relied on a parent's mobile phone, which was not only shared among several family members but also often incompatible with standard learning platforms due to outdated operating systems or limited storage. This rendered even basic tasks such as downloading learning materials or submitting assignments difficult or impossible. As one teacher put it during the focus group, "Even when families had smartphones, the devices were usually low-spec or full of apps, so students couldn't open Google Classroom or even PDF files."

These observations highlight the intersection of digital poverty and rural isolation, which made sustained participation in remote learning unattainable for the majority of students. Teachers noted that even students who were motivated to learn could not consistently engage due to infrastructural and socioeconomic barriers. Overall, the findings point to a structurally unequal educational environment in which students' ability to access education during the pandemic was determined not by interest or ability, but by geography, infrastructure, and income.

During the COVID-19 lockdown, many students and their families faced significant challenges when schools transitioned to online learning, as observed by teachers through a survey. The results revealed a staggering 83.8% indicated that their families had too few gadgets to allow all children to study simultaneously, forcing many to share devices. This issue was compounded by financial constraints, with 77.7% of families unable to afford unlimited Internet services, limiting their ability to maintain consistent online access. Moreover, 67.1% of parents lacked IT literacy, adding another layer of difficulty in supporting their children's learning. Even more concerning, 45.4% of students reported being unfamiliar with computer technologies, reflecting a deeper digital divide that exacerbated educational inequalities during the lockdown. These findings highlight the significant barriers faced by students and families, underscoring the need for targeted interventions to ensure equitable access to education in times of crisis.

15.7.4 Printed Materials as a Supplementary Strategy amid Widespread Connectivity Limitations

In response to the widespread lack of Internet access, teachers at several schools reported resorting to printed learning materials as an alternative means of instruction. These printed packets were delivered to students' homes, particularly to longhouses in remote areas, as a way to ensure some continuity in learning despite the absence of digital infrastructure. While this approach was logistically challenging, educators viewed it as a necessary stopgap measure to support students who were otherwise entirely disconnected from formal education during the lockdown period.

In addition to connectivity issues, the limited availability of digital devices posed a significant barrier. Although some households owned a smartphone or computer, these devices were typically shared among multiple children or family members. According to survey data, 83.8% of teachers (n = 301) observed that families with more than one school-aged child often struggled to facilitate simultaneous online learning, particularly in synchronous formats that required real-time engagement.

Furthermore, 78.9% of teachers (n = 282) noted that students were frequently dependent on a parent's mobile phone for accessing schoolwork. This arrangement was further constrained by parents' work schedules, limiting students' access to devices to evenings or off-hours. Financial constraints also played a major role. A large proportion of teachers—77.7% (n = 279)—reported that many families were unable to afford unlimited data plans or regular mobile credit top-ups. As a result, students' participation in online classes was sporadic or nonexistent.

Focus group discussions reinforced these findings. Several teachers recounted being contacted by parents who explained that their children could not join lessons due to insufficient credit on their prepaid mobile plans. Although the government introduced a policy providing 1 GB of free mobile data per day during the national lockdown, teachers widely agreed that this allocation was inadequate, particularly for students who had to attend multiple classes or download multimedia materials.

Teachers at SMK Datuk Patinggi Kedit shared that some families had to travel to the nearest town, despite strict lockdown measures—just to purchase prepaid credit. The problem was not only one of affordability but also of information gaps. Lim Hua Lip, the school's ICT coordinator (Guru Bestari), explained that many parents were unaware of cost-effective data plans available for educational use. He suggested that schools could play a more proactive role by compiling and disseminating information about affordable and reliable prepaid packages, especially for low-income households. His recommendation highlights a broader issue: that the success of online learning initiatives in rural areas depends not only on infrastructure but also on targeted community engagement and digital literacy support.

15.7.5 WhatsApp as the Primary Platform for Communication and Content Delivery

A significant challenge highlighted by teachers during the lockdown was the limited digital literacy among parents, which hindered their ability to support students in navigating online learning platforms. According to the survey, 67.1% of teachers (n = 241) observed that most parents lacked basic IT skills. Teachers from SK St. Mark, SK Nanga Ajau, and SK Nanga Spak emphasized that many parents were unfamiliar with even simple digital tasks such as logging into Google Classroom or downloading assignments. As one teacher from SK Nanga Ajau explained during an FGD, "Parents don't know how to help. Some don't even know how to open WhatsApp PDFs, let alone support their children on Google Classroom."

In response to these constraints, WhatsApp became the dominant platform for instructional communication. An overwhelming 97.8% of teachers (n = 351) reported using WhatsApp to share learning materials, send voice instructions, and maintain contact with students and their families. While 57.9% (n = 208) said they had used Google Classroom at least once, the majority preferred WhatsApp due to its lower data consumption and ease of use. As a teacher from SK St. Mark noted, "Google Classroom is too complicated. Students couldn't even log in, especially if they were using their parents' phones that were already logged into other accounts. WhatsApp was the only thing that worked."

Although the Malaysian Ministry of Education provided institutional Google accounts for both teachers and students, their usability was limited in practice. Students who attempted to access Google tools using shared devices frequently encountered barriers such as being locked out of their assigned accounts, inability to switch profiles, or prompts to verify information they could not provide. Teachers reported that many students simply gave up after multiple failed attempts. One teacher from SMK Ulu Layar stated, "We spent more time helping students figure out how to log in than teaching anything. In the end, we went back to WhatsApp."

These challenges were exacerbated by a lack of exposure to computer-based learning prior to the pandemic. Nearly half of the teachers surveyed (45.4%, $n = 163$) noted that their students, particularly those in primary schools, had never used a computer before. In many rural schools, computer labs were nonexistent or nonfunctional. At SK Nanga Ajau, for instance, the lab had been shut down for three years due to a damaged server. "Our students don't have laptops at home, and the only time they could learn to use a computer was in school but even that wasn't possible," shared one teacher.

For students living in longhouse communities, the digital divide was particularly stark. Lacking access to devices, stable power supply, and Internet infrastructure, most students could not participate in any form of online learning. These structural limitations severely undermined efforts to implement national-level e-learning programs in the region.

The situation was even more critical for students with special needs. At SK Nanga Spak, special education teachers reported that their students were completely excluded from online learning during the movement restrictions. "Our special needs students were left out. There was no platform or support for them. We couldn't do any interactive or adaptive learning," one teacher reflected. This highlights the urgent need for inclusive digital education strategies that address the unique needs of all learners, especially in marginalized rural settings.

15.8 Levels of Digital Inequality in Sarawak

The findings of this study reveal three interrelated forms of digital inequality in Layar, Sarawak, with the most acute challenges centering on digital access. Survey data indicated that five of the seven most frequently reported problems ranging from 77.7% to 91.6% of respondents were directly related to Internet connectivity and the ownership of digital devices. This reflects a severe access-related digital divide that hindered both teaching and learning during the COVID-19 lockdown period.

Prior to the pandemic, most teachers in Layar relied almost exclusively on face-to-face instruction and had minimal exposure to digital platforms. As a result, when movement restrictions were enforced and schools were forced to transition to remote learning, teachers turned to platforms they were already familiar with, primarily WhatsApp, as the main tool for student communication and instructional delivery. For students unable to access WhatsApp due to connectivity or device limitations, teachers took it upon themselves to print and physically deliver learning materials to longhouse communities. These efforts, while admirable, were constrained by limited Internet access and insufficient digital training, which significantly restricted the use of interactive learning content and pedagogical engagement.

To contextualize these findings, Figure 15.1 applies Van Dijk's (2020) framework of digital inequality to the rural Sarawak setting. Our study identifies three overlapping layers of digital divide: (1) access to devices and infrastructure, (2) digital skills, and (3) meaningful usage (in this case, the ability to access and benefit from interactive learning platforms and materials). While students in urban areas such as Kuala Lumpur were able to access resources through government-supported platforms like DELIMA and Google Workspace for Education (Sharon, 2020), students in Layar were unable to benefit from these initiatives due to poor connectivity and limited device ownership.

The first level of inequality device and Internet access goes beyond mere availability and includes device compatibility and the number of devices per household. In multi-child households, a single device shared among siblings severely constrained students' ability to participate in synchronous learning. Similarly, Internet access was not simply a matter of coverage but also of affordability and data availability. Many households could not afford unlimited Internet subscriptions or regular prepaid top-ups, resulting in inconsistent access that further disrupted learning continuity.

The second level, digital skill disparities, was observed at both the student and teacher levels. These disparities manifested in two forms: basic digital skills (e.g., operating mobile phones, logging into learning platforms) and more advanced competencies (e.g., evaluating Internet plans, designing interactive lessons, facilitating online engagement). A lack of training and exposure meant that even when devices were available, their use was often limited to one-way content sharing rather than interactive, student-centered learning.

The third and most complex layer of digital inequality relates to the meaningful use of digital tools, what Van Dijk terms the "third-level digital divide." This includes disparities in the capacity to access high-quality, interactive, and inclusive educational content. In high-income settings, such disparities are typically driven by differences in usage and digital fluency. However, in rural Sarawak, they are still rooted in infrastructural and economic barriers, highlighting Malaysia's uneven digital development despite its relatively high national Internet penetration rate.

This study also identified three particularly vulnerable groups in Layar's educational landscape: indigenous Iban households, digitally unskilled students, and students with special needs. The majority of the study's respondents came from Iban-majority schools. For many of these families, educational inequities stemmed not only from digital access issues but also

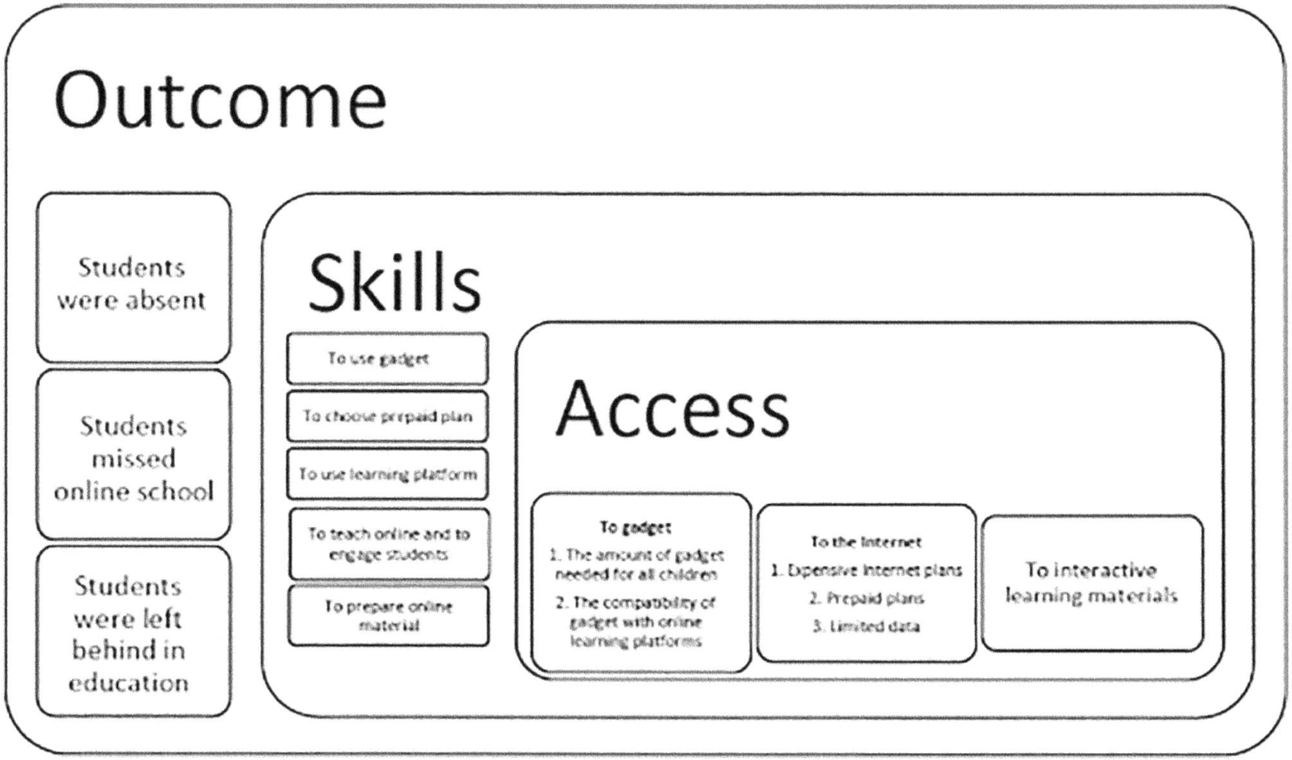

FIGURE 15.1
Level of digital inequalities in rural Sarawak. Diagram by the author.

from economic precarity. Most household incomes in Layar are derived from subsistence farming or informal labor, making it difficult for families to afford devices or sustain Internet subscriptions, especially in households with multiple school-going children.

The second vulnerable group comprised students with no prior exposure to digital learning. These students lacked the basic ICT literacy needed to navigate even the simplest learning platforms. Their parents, similarly unfamiliar with digital technologies, were unable to provide guidance or assistance. The abrupt shift to online learning during the pandemic thus deepened an existing educational divide, leaving these students largely disconnected from formal instruction.

The third group, students with special needs, were among the most affected during the pandemic. Teachers reported that no interactive or adapted materials were made available for these learners, particularly during the initial phases of the national lockdown. Without support mechanisms or inclusive digital tools, these students were entirely excluded from remote learning, effectively denied their right to education during a critical period.

Together, these findings underscore the layered nature of digital inequality in rural Sarawak. Addressing these disparities requires not only improving digital infrastructure but also enhancing digital literacy, tailoring instructional design to low-resource environments, and ensuring inclusive access for all learners, regardless of geography, ability, or income.

15.9 Recommendations for Strengthening Digital Access and Learning in Rural Sarawak

Teachers across all seven participating schools voiced an urgent need for substantial improvements in Internet connectivity and digital education infrastructure in rural Sarawak. Many emphasized that without reliable and stable Internet, neither teachers nor students could meaningfully engage in online learning. As one teacher from SMK Ulu Layar shared, "Schools in the cities were able to transition online, but we were completely left behind because we didn't have the tools or the connection."

The lack of reliable Internet access was compounded by the unavailability of compatible, high-spec digital devices. Teachers noted that while the government had previously distributed 1Malaysia laptops and Huawei tablets, these devices were of low quality, often outdated, and restricted by pre-installed limitations imposed by the Ministry of Education. Many teachers reported being unable to download or access essential applications. "The tablets were too low-spec, and even when we wanted to try new apps, the restrictions meant we couldn't use them," said one participant. Teachers called for the provision of durable, high-performance devices to students and teachers, along with the removal of unnecessary software restrictions that hinder pedagogical flexibility.

Another recurring recommendation was the creation of affordable, education-focused prepaid Internet plans, subsidized by the government for both students and teachers in low-connectivity regions. In tandem, teachers expressed frustration over the lack of functional computer labs in their schools. In communities where families cannot afford laptops or broadband, these school-based facilities would be students' only opportunity to build essential ICT skills. One ICT teacher from SK Nanga Ajau shared, "Some of my students have never touched a computer in their life. Everything they know, they have to learn here in school. But we don't have the equipment."

Beyond infrastructure, capacity-building emerged as a central concern. The majority of teachers (94%) reported that they never had received proper training in online teaching. The survey data showed that 48.5% of respondents believed that no one at their school had prior experience with online learning, while only 6% (n = 24) reported any extensive institutional experience. Teachers expressed difficulty in creating engaging online content, managing synchronous lessons, and maintaining communication with students across fragmented digital channels. They requested hands-on, face-to-face training with digital education specialists, focused on pedagogical strategies as well as technical tools. "We need more than just instructions. We need to learn how to make lessons interesting and keep students involved," said one participant.

In addition to professional development, 56.8% of surveyed teachers (n = 204) expressed the need for more structured guidance from the Ministry of Education on how to conduct online lessons effectively. Many reflected that during the initial national lockdown, both policymakers and educators were unprepared. As one teacher noted, "Everyone was caught off guard, but the problem was that the solutions we received weren't grounded in our realities." Participants stressed that national frameworks for digital learning must be informed by those implementing them, particularly educators in underserved areas.

This disconnect between policy and practice also extended to broader frustrations with Malaysia's Ministry of Communications and Multimedia. Teachers felt that rural schools and communities were being overlooked in infrastructure planning. Several called for site visits by decision-makers to gain firsthand insight into the conditions faced by teachers and students. "If the Ministry had come here, they would have seen we didn't even have phone signal in some classrooms," one teacher remarked.

Parental awareness and support also emerged as a critical challenge. Teachers reported receiving complaints from parents about the volume of learning materials shared via WhatsApp, the primary platform used to distribute assignments and maintain contact. Some parents even left WhatsApp groups or told their children to ignore schoolwork. Teachers from SJKC Chung Hua and other schools noted that many families did not understand that online learning was not optional, and often asked children to help with household chores or agricultural work during school hours. "One student told me he couldn't finish his assignment because he had to go tap rubber with his father," said a teacher from SK Nanga Spak.

To address this issue, teachers suggested that school- or district-level town hall meetings be organized to educate parents about the value of online learning and their role in supporting it. Survey responses echoed this recommendation: 70% of teachers (n = 244) said that parents need to stay in active communication with teachers; 64.6% (n = 232) recommended that parents set structured learning schedules for their children; 61.6% (n = 222) emphasized the importance of parents learning to use online platforms themselves; and 57.7% (n = 207) felt that creating designated home learning spaces would significantly improve student engagement.

15.10 Towards Inclusive, Community-Informed Digital Education Policy

Teachers' suggestions point to the need for a more holistic, community-centered approach to digital education policy. Feedback from the online survey and FGDs supports the development of a multi-level intervention framework, beginning with individual learners and extending to households, schools, communities, and government systems.

At the individual level, interventions should focus on improving digital literacy such as the ability to operate devices, access educational platforms, and engage in responsible online behavior. At the household level, efforts should target all family members, encouraging collaborative support for student learning. This includes learning to choose appropriate internet plans, developing shared learning routines, and setting up designated learning spaces within homes.

At the school and community levels, teachers recommended renewed investment in education infrastructure, updated computer labs, ongoing professional development, and revised assessment models that consider the unique needs of marginalized populations, including Indigenous and longhouse-based students. At the governmental level, teachers called for the distribution of compatible, durable devices, expanded broadband infrastructure, and the development of user-centered national education policies.

While the Malaysian government implemented several initiatives during the pandemic, including the daily 1 GB Internet subsidy and the distribution of free tablets, teachers felt these efforts were poorly designed and implemented. Consistent with observations from ECLAC-UNESCO (2020), top-down digital education policies often fail when they are not co-designed with the communities they aim to serve. In Sarawak, this disconnect resulted in policies that ignored the lived realities of rural educators and students.

To bridge this divide, future digital education frameworks must be grounded in local knowledge and co-created with teachers, parents, and students. Rural voices must be included not only as sources of anecdotal feedback but as central stakeholders in shaping policy, implementation, and evaluation. Without this participatory approach, digital interventions risk reinforcing existing inequalities rather than dismantling them.

15.11 Discussion: Theoretical and Practical Implications

15.11.1 Digital Skills and Media Literacy in an Unequal Digital Landscape

In today's digitally mediated world, Internet access and digital literacy are foundational to full participation in education, economic opportunity, and civic life. Ensuring that all citizens have reliable access to digital infrastructure, combined with meaningful media and information literacy, is increasingly recognized as essential to democratic equity. However, as this study reveals, structural inequalities in rural Sarawak and other underserved regions in Malaysia continue to exclude vulnerable populations from quality online education.

Although the Malaysian government has introduced digital access initiatives, these efforts have often failed to account for the ground realities in marginalized communities. The rollout of online learning strategies has largely followed a top-down approach, disproportionately benefitting urban populations with stable infrastructure, while neglecting the needs of Indigenous and rural communities. As evidenced by the experiences of teachers in Layar, such interventions risk becoming exclusionary rather than inclusive.

Applying Van Dijk's (2020) framework, this study extends the digital divide concept to include not only access to the Internet and devices, but also access to usable applications, learning platforms, and instructional content. In Layar, students and teachers were constrained by low-quality devices, restrictive software policies, and limited exposure to interactive educational platforms. This supports the findings of Khan et al. (2019), who argue that improving digital access must go hand-in-hand with efforts to enhance both basic and advanced digital competencies.

Learning loss among students in digitally excluded communities is an inevitable outcome under current policy structures. To mitigate this, we recommend a dual-intervention model: first, long-term digital literacy programs specifically tailored toward the realities of vulnerable groups and, second, incentives to promote participation among families and educators with limited digital exposure. Without these targeted efforts, national digital strategies will continue to reflect and reproduce existing inequalities. Additionally, this study finds that national assessment frameworks must evolve to reflect unequal learning conditions. In 2021, calls for adjustments to national examination standards went unheeded, with the Director-General of Education confirming that standards would remain unchanged ("National exams in Malaysia to go on as planned," 2021). Holding students in structurally disadvantaged communities to the same benchmarks as their urban peers, without accounting for unequal access to resources, exacerbates educational inequality.

The study findings also highlight the need for more context-aware interventions. Despite the availability of various digital platforms, teachers and students in Layar consistently relied on WhatsApp, citing its low data usage and familiarity. This suggests that national digital literacy campaigns should leverage platforms already embedded in community practices. For example, government initiatives could provide data subsidies or small monetary incentives to parents who complete online learning modules delivered through WhatsApp.

This study is not without limitations. Data were collected solely from teachers in Layar, Sarawak, during pandemic-related movement restrictions, without direct input from students. While this limits generalization of the study findings, the consistency of themes across schools suggests broader relevance to other rural Malaysian districts. Notably, data from this research have already been used by the Layar Education Development Committee to propose infrastructure improvements, digital device distributions, and targeted training for educators and parents (Jabu, personal communication, November 11, 2020; *Layar Education Development Committee donates Huawei*, 2022).

Future research should examine how digital exclusion affects other domains of public service, such as health, transportation, or employment, and evaluate what intervention models are most effective across sectors. Comparative studies across states or ASEAN member countries would also offer insights into regional disparities in digital governance and educational equity.

15.12 Conclusion: Addressing the Digital Divide through Inclusive Policy and Practice

This study concludes that the COVID-19 pandemic deepened existing digital inequalities in Malaysia, particularly between urban and rural populations.

In Layar, Sarawak, students and teachers were systematically excluded from meaningful participation in online education due to limited access to digital tools, infrastructure, and digital literacy training. These challenges were not isolated logistical issues—they were structural barriers embedded within Malaysia's digital and educational policy frameworks.

The transition to online learning during the first national lockdown in March 2020 disproportionately benefited those in well-connected urban areas, reinforcing a system that privileged the digitally equipped and excluded the rest. The experiences documented in this study highlight the need for multi-level interventions—across individuals, families, communities, and government—to address the digital divide in a meaningful and sustained way.

Equity-focused interventions must include community-centered digital literacy training, infrastructure upgrades, adaptive curriculum design, and revised education assessments. Federal and state governments should prioritize broadband expansion, provide durable and compatible devices, and develop policies that reflect the complexity of Malaysia's socioeconomic and geographic landscape. Failure to do so will have long-term consequences on academic outcomes and social mobility for students in rural communities.

Limited access to quality education restricts students' opportunities to perform well on national exams, enter higher education, and access stable, well-paying jobs. Without targeted interventions, these students are at risk of remaining in cycles of poverty, limited opportunity, and structural exclusion.

Despite these concerns, there are promising developments. This study's findings were used to advocate for improved infrastructure in Layar, including the installation of communication towers and allocation of digital literacy training funds. Devices have since been distributed to students and teachers, and local policymakers continue to push for equitable reforms based on the evidence collected.

Moving forward, Malaysia's education system must adopt a rights-based, inclusive approach to digital policy, one that centers the needs of its most marginalized populations. Access to digital tools, opportunities for skill development, and equitable educational outcomes must be treated as interconnected priorities. In short, bridging the digital divide is not simply a matter of technology—it is a matter of justice.

References

Azevedo, J. P., Hasan, A., Goldemberg, D., Iqbal, S. A., & Geven, K. (2021). Simulating the potential impacts of COVID-19 school closures on schooling and learning outcomes: A set of global estimates. *The World Bank Research Observer*, 36(1), 1–40.

Badiozaman, Adi., Fatimawati, Ida., & Segar, Augustus Raymond. (2022). Exploring online teaching competence in the context of the COVID 19 pandemic: Insights from Sarawak, Malaysia. *Journal of Further and Higher Education*, 46(6), 766–779.

Banji, Conny. (2021, February 17). Youth goes viral after trekking two hours up Sri Aman hill for an online interview. *The Borneo Post.* www.theborneopost.com/2022/02/17/youth-goes-viral-after-trekking-two-hours-up-sri-aman-hill-for-online-interview/

Bećirović, Senad. (2023). *Digital pedagogy: The use of digital technologies in contemporary education*. Springer Singapore.

Bernama. (2018, October 8). Cheaper broadband prices for consumers. *The Malaysian Reserve.* https://themalaysianreserve.com/2018/10/08/cheaper-broadband-prices-for-consumers/

Bernama. (2020a, August 3). Poor internet access in less than 20pc of Malaysia, Dewan Rakyat told. *Malay Mail.*www.malaymail.com/news/malaysia/2020/08/03/poor-internet-access-in-less-than-20pc-of-malaysia-dewan-rakyat-told/1890532

Bong, Karen. (2020, June 11). 50 percent of students in Sarawak unable to follow online learning. *Dayak Daily.* https://dayakdaily.com/50-per-cent-of-student-in-sarawak-unable-to-follow-online-learning/

Braun, Virginia., & Clarke, Victoria. (2006). Using thematic analysis in psychology. *Qualitative Research in Psychology*, 3(2), 77–101. ISSN 1478-0887.

Cinnamon, Jonathan. (2020). Data inequalities and why they matter for development. *Information Technology for Development*, 26(2), 214–233.

ECLAC-UNESCO. (2020, August 1). Education in the time of Covid report. *UNESCO.* https://repositorio.cepal.org/bitstream/handle/11362/45905/1/S2000509_en.pdf

Freedom House. (2022, January 27). Freedom on the Net (Malaysia). *Freedom House.* https://freedomhouse.org/country/malaysia/freedom-net/2021#footnote8_i5kb3t5

Goh, Pei Pei. (2021, September 27). People in Sabah, Sarawak to enjoy development similar to that in the Peninsula. *The Straits Times.* www.nst.com.my/news/nation/2021/09/731308/people-sabah-sarawak-enjoy-development-similar-peninsula

Government adopts VSAT technology to provide internet coverage in rural areas, says deputy communications minister. (2020, December 17). Malay Mail. www.malaymail.com/news/malaysia/2020/12/17/govt-adopts-vsat-technology-to-provide-internet-coverage-in-rural-areas-say/1932764

Horn, Christine., & M. Gifford, Sandra. (2020). ICT uptake and use and social connectedness in rural and remote communities: A study from Sarawak, Malaysia. *Information Technology for Development*, 1–26, 2021844

Howell, Jennifer., & McMaster, Natalie. (2022). *Teaching with technologies: Pedagogies for collaboration, communication, and creativity* (2nd ed.). Oxford University Press.

Jalli, Nuurrianti. (2020, March 17). Lack of internet access in Southeast Asia poses challenges for students to study online amid COVID-19 pandemic. *The Conversation.* https://theconversation.com/lack-of-internet-access-in-southeast-asia-poses-challenges-for-students-to-study-online-amid-covid-19-pandemic-133787

Johari, Zaheera. (2020, July 19). Grouses over poor internet access. *Borneo Post.* www.theborneopost.com/2020/07/19/grouses-over-poor-internet-access/

Jordan, Katy., Raluca, David., Phillips, Toby., & Pellini, Arnaldo. (2021). Education during the COVID-19: Crisis Opportunities and constraints of using EdTech in low-income countries. *Revista de Educación a Distancia (RED),* 21(65), 3750976.

Khan, M. Laeeq., & Idris, Ika Karlina. (2019). Recognise misinformation and verify before sharing: A reasoned action and information literacy perspective. *Behaviour & Information Technology,* 38(12), 1194–1212.

Khan, M. Laeeq., Welser, Howard T., Cisneros, Claudia., Manatong, Gaone., and Idris, Ika Karlina. (2020). Digital inequality in the Appalachian Ohio: Understanding how demographics, internet access, and skills can shape vital information use (VIU). *Telematics and Informatics,* 50, 101380.

Kitzinger, Jenny. (1995). Qualitative research: introducing focus groups. *BMJ,* 311(7000), 299–302.

Layar Education Development Committee donates Huawei tablets to 3 schools in Betong. (2022, October 1). DayakDaily. https://dayakdaily.com/layar-education-development-committee-donates-huawei-tablets-to-3-schools-in-betong/?fbclid=IwAR3LVH22RzJOdh7ityaOfk9boFFXZ1qewJKuPiwWyLXr7_euWeHtYO4eIz0

Li, Mingyong., An, Ziye., & Ren, Miaomiao. (2020). Student-centred webcast+ home-based learning model and investigation during the COVID-19 epidemic. *Inteligencia Artificial,* 23(66), 51–65. https://doi.org/10.4114/intartif.vol23iss66pp51-65

Lin, Sandra Sim Phek., Sim, Hannah., & Quah, Cheng Sim. (2021).Online learning: A post COVID-19 alternative pedagogy for university students. *Asian Journal of University Education,* 16(4), 137–151.

Lythreatis, Sophie., Singh, Sanjay Kumar., & El-Kassar, Abdul-Nasser. (2021). The digital divide: A review and future research agenda. *Technological Forecasting and Social Change,* 175, 121359.

MCMC. (2020, December 29). Internet users survey 2020. *Malaysian Communications and Multimedia Commission.* www.mcmc.gov.my/skmmgovmy/media/General/pdf/IUS-2020-Report.pdf

Milana, Marcella., Hodge, Steven., Holford, John., Waller, Richard., & Webb, Sue. (2021). A year of COVID-19 pandemic: Exposing the fragility of education and digital in/equalities. *International Journal of Lifelong Education,* 40(2), 111–114. https://doi.org/10.1080/02601370.2021.1912946

National exams in Malaysia to go on as planned despite calls for deferment. (2021, January 23). *The Straits Times.* www.straitstimes.com/asia/se-asia/national-exams-in-malaysia-to-go-on-as-planned-despite-calls-for-deferment

New tower to overcome internet access issue at Sarawak longhouse. (2022, February 17). *The Star.* www.thestar.com.my/news/nation/2022/02/17/new-tower-to-overcome-internet-access-issue-at-sarawak-longhouse?utm_source=chatgpt.com

OECD. (2020). *Lesson for education from Covid-19: A policy maker's handbook for more resilient system.* OECD.

Onyema, Edeh Michael., Nwafor, Chika., Obafemi, Faith Ayobamidele., Sen, Shuvro., Grace, Fyneface Atonye., Sharma, Aabha., & Alsayed, Alhuseen Omar. (2020). Impact of Coronavirus pandemic on education. *Journal of Education and Practice,* 11(3), 108–121. https://doi.org/10.7176/JEP/11-13-12

Pini, Monica. (2020). Digital inequality in education in Argentina: How the pandemic of 2020 increased existing tensions. In *12th ACM Conference on Web Science Companion*, pp. 37–40. ACM. https://doi.org/10.1145/3394332.340282

Rickie, G., & Alias, B. S. B. (2024). Students dropout in rural schools in Sarawak: Causes and proposed solutions. *International Journal of Academic Research in Progressive Education and Development, 13*(4), 3696–3712. https://doi.org/10.6007/IJARPED/v13-i4/24375

Selvanathan, Mahiswaran., Atikah, Nur., Hussin, Mohamed., & Azazi, Noor Alyani Nor. (2020). Students learning experiences during COVID-19: Work from home period in Malaysian higher learning institutions. *Teaching Public Administration,* 41(1),13–22. https://doi.org/10.1177/0144739420977900

Selwyn, Neil., Gorard, Stephen., & Furlong, John. (2005). Whose Internet is it anyway? Exploring adults'(non) use of the Internet in everyday life. *European Journal of Communication,* 20(1), 5–26. https://doi.org/0267323105049631

Sharon, Alita. (2020, June 19). Malaysia sets new digital learning ambitions. *Open Government Asia.* https://archive.opengovasia.com/2020/06/19/malaysia-sets-new-digital-learning-ambitions/

Sulaiman, Sharin, & Halamy, Suhaida. (2021). ICT education as a catalyst to bridge digital divide: The roles of UiTM Sarawak in rural areas. *International Journal of Advanced Research in Education and Society,* 3(2), 174–181.

Tavakol, Mohsen., & Dennick, Reg. (2011). Making sense of Cronbach's alpha. *International Journal of Medical Education,* 2, 53–55. https://doi.org/10.5116/ijme.4dfb.8dfd

UNESCO. (2021). Flexible learning pathways in Malaysian higher education. UNESCO. https://unesdoc.unesco.org/ark:/48223/pf0000378002

UNESCO. (2022, January 18). *UNESCO global education response*. UNESCO. https://en.unesco.org/covid19/educationresponse/globalcoalition

UNESCO. (2023). Technology in education: A case study on Malaysia. UNESCO. https://unesdoc.unesco.org/ark:/48223/pf0000387742

UNICEF (2019). Children without: A study of children in remote areas of Sabah and Sarawak. UNICEF. www.unicef.org/malaysia/media/621/file/Children%20Without.pdf

Van Dijk, J. (2020). *The digital divide.* Polity Press.

Van Dijk, Jan., & Hacker, Kenneth. (2003). The digital divide as a complex and dynamic phenomenon. *The Information Society,* 19(4), 315–326. https://doi.org/01972240390227895

Zainal, Azlin., & Zainuddin, Siti Zaidah. (2020). Technology adoption in Malaysian schools: An analysis of national ICT in education policy initiatives. *Digital Education Review,* 172–194. https://doi.org/10.1344/der.2020.37.172-194

16

E-Learning as a Pathway to Equity and Inclusion in Afghanistan

Siddiqullah Barikzai, Vijayakumar Bharathi S., and Arif Perdana

Introduction

Afghanistan's foray into e-learning exemplifies the transformative potential of digital education in post-conflict societies. In a nation grappling with significant development challenges, evidenced by its low ranking on the United Nations' human development index, adopting digital learning technologies represents more than just an educational shift. It embodies a complex interweaving of technological progress and societal rebuilding, offering insights into how innovation can be leveraged to overcome the educational hurdles endemic to conflict-affected regions (Sarwari et al., 2022).

The dawn of Afghanistan's e-learning era, coinciding with the fall of the Taliban regime in 2001, ushered in a new epoch of international collaboration in educational reconstruction. The Cisco Networking Academy Program at Kabul University in 2002 served as the harbinger of this digital awakening, laying the groundwork for future technological integration in education (Mikawa, 2006). This initial spark ignited a series of initiatives, including the Ministry of Communications and Information Technology's comprehensive digital learning program in 2003 and Kabul University's Next-Generation E-learning Program in 2005, each advancing the integration of digital competencies within the broader educational framework (Sokout & Usagawa, 2018).

Despite progress, Afghanistan's e-learning landscape faced significant hurdles, particularly in rural areas with poor information and communications technology (ICT) infrastructure (Wani & Mahdi, 2021). The Ministry of Higher Education's (MoHE's) 2015 policy aimed to address these issues, but implementation remained uneven due to security and resource constraints (Ministry of Higher Education Afghanistan, 2015). The COVID-19 pandemic unexpectedly catalyzed e-learning adoption, exposing vulnerabilities while showcasing the sector's resilience (Sarwari et al., 2022; Borazon et al., 2024). As Afghanistan navigates its post-conflict trajectory, e-learning emerges not

DOI: 10.1201/9781003591078-21

merely as an educational tool, but as a potential catalyst for broader socio-economic development.

Our chapter discusses the complex landscape of e-learning implementation in Afghanistan through the lens of a trifecta model: people, processes, and technology. It uncovers the complex interplay of these factors in shaping the digital learning ecosystem. When successfully navigated, this trifecta has the potential to transform higher education in Afghanistan, offering a beacon of hope for inclusivity and accessibility.

Overview of E-Learning Initiative in Afghanistan

Afghanistan, ranked 180th among 189 countries in terms of human development by the United Nations, has faced significant challenges owing to prolonged conflict and instability (Ministry of Higher Education Afghanistan, 2015; Sarwari et al., 2022). The higher education system in Afghanistan has been particularly impacted, with many institutions struggling to provide quality education amid political turmoil and security threats. However, since 2001, international efforts have been made to improve education through digital learning by leveraging technology to overcome some of the country's most pressing educational challenges.

In the aftermath of Taliban's fall in 2001, the establishment of a transitional government opened the door for international cooperation in rebuilding Afghanistan's education sector. One of the early successes of digital learning was the introduction of the Cisco Networking Academy Program at Kabul University in 2002. This program aims to enhance students' and faculty's ICT skills, providing a foundation for further digital learning initiatives (Mikawa, 2006). The success of the program at Kabul University has led to its expansion to other public universities across the country, highlighting the potential of digital learning to improve higher education in Afghanistan.

In 2003, the Ministry of Communications and Information Technology (MCIT) launched a digital learning program in collaboration with the Ministry of Education and MoHE. This initiative sought to integrate digital tools and resources into the education system, aiming to modernize the curriculum and teaching methods. However, the program faced significant obstacles, including limited access to ICT and poor computer skills of the target audience (Sokout & Usagawa, 2018). These challenges highlight the need for comprehensive strategies to build digital capacity in Afghan higher education institutions (HEIs).

Building on these early successes and challenges, Kabul University initiated the Afghanistan Next-Generation E-learning Program in 2005. This program was designed to advance computer and ICT skills among students and faculty, providing a more structured approach to digital learning (Sokout & Usagawa, 2018). The program emphasized the importance of integrating digital learning into a broader educational framework, rather than treating it as a stand-alone initiative. The MoHE supported these efforts by facilitating videoconference meetings for resource sharing among universities and fostering a culture of collaboration and innovation in digital learning.

Despite these efforts, the progress of digital learning in Afghanistan has been hampered by poor ICT infrastructure and limited Internet access, particularly in rural areas (Wani & Mahdi, 2021). The lack of reliable electricity and Internet connectivity has made it difficult for students and faculty to fully engage with digital learning platforms. The Central Asia and South Asia project, funded by the World Bank and regional states, was designed to address these infrastructure challenges by enhancing digital connectivity across the region. However, the project faced delays and funding setbacks due to changes in the government, slowing the pace of digital learning development in Afghanistan (Cabral, 2017).

Recognizing the need for a more strategic approach to digital learning, the MoHE formulated an e-learning policy and bylaws in 2015. This policy outlined a three-phase approach to enhance digital education in Afghan universities (Ministry of Higher Education Afghanistan, 2015). The first phase focused on assessing the existing ICT infrastructure in universities, identifying gaps, and prioritizing areas for improvement. The second phase aimed to integrate online and physical programs, allowing universities to offer blended learning opportunities that could reach a wider audience. The final phase involved developing fully online courses that enabled students to access higher education remotely.

Although this policy was a step in the right direction, its implementation has been uneven across the country. Many universities have struggled to meet the requirements of the first phase due to ongoing security concerns and limited financial resources. Moreover, the integration of online and physical programs in the second phase was hindered by the lack of trained faculty and some educators' reluctance to adopt new teaching methods. The development of fully online courses in the final phase has also been slow, with only a few universities managing to launch comprehensive online programs (Higher Education Development Program, 2019).

The COVID-19 pandemic, which hit Afghanistan in early 2020, has had a profound impact on the country's higher education system. With physical classrooms closed because of lockdowns, the MoHE introduced the Higher Education Learning Management System (HELMS) to facilitate remote learning (Alariqi et al., 2019; Asghari & Subriadi, 2021; Sarwari et al., 2022). The HELMS was designed to provide a centralized platform for universities to deliver online courses, conduct assessments, and manage student records. However, the sudden shift to online learning exposed the weaknesses of Afghanistan's digital learning infrastructure.

Many universities lack the necessary ICT infrastructure to support remote learning on a large scale. Students and faculty often struggle with unreliable internet connections, and many lack the devices needed to access online courses (Nasrat et al., 2020). To overcome these challenges, universities have begun using alternative platforms, such as Google Classroom and WhatsApp, to deliver course materials and communicate with students. While these platforms provided a temporary solution, they were not designed for the comprehensive delivery of higher education, leading to concerns regarding the quality of education during the pandemic.

The pandemic has highlighted the urgent need for robust infrastructure, ICT access, and continuous professional development to enhance digital learning in Afghanistan. Studies conducted during this period have identified several key challenges that must be addressed to build a resilient digital learning framework in the country. These challenges include inadequate ICT infrastructure, limited technology skills among students and faculty, poor Internet accessibility, resistance to change among educators, and financial constraints (Asghari & Subriadi, 2021; Nasrat et al., 2020; Oryakhail et al., 2021). Table 16.1 outlines the progression of E-Learning initiatives in Afghanistan over time.

The following section explains the trifecta of e-learning in Afghanistan (i.e., people, process, and technology). This trifecta explains the interdependence of each factor and collective importance for achieving successful e-learning implementation. It emphasizes that each component is essential, and when combined, they create a powerful synergy that can drive success.

E-Learning Challenges in Afghanistan

People Factors of E-Learning

The implementation of digital learning in Afghan universities is influenced by three critical factors: people (human), process (governance), and technology. Human factors highlight the importance of faculty members' and students' readiness for digital learning. While some faculty members, particularly those in computer science, exhibit high proficiency in educational technology, others, especially those from nontechnical disciplines, express a sense of inadequacy in their skills to develop standard online courses. This disparity underscores the need for comprehensive training programs to enhance digital teaching skills (Hu & Raman, 2024).

Our study found significant variation in faculty members' familiarity with learning technology and digital learning skills, primarily influenced by academic disciplines. Some faculty members, particularly those in computer science, demonstrated sufficient proficiency in educational technology, as

TABLE 16.1

Key Initiatives and Challenges in Advancing Digital Learning in Afghan Universities (2002–2020)

Year	Initiative	Description	Challenges/Outcomes
2002	Cisco Networking Academy Program	Introduced at Kabul University to enhance ICT skills among students and faculty. Later expanded to other public universities.	Provided a foundational ICT skills program; expansion highlighted potential for digital learning.
2003	MCIT Digital Learning Program	Launched by the MCIT in collaboration with education ministries. Aimed to integrate digital tools into education.	Faced challenges due to limited ICT access and poor computer skills among the target audience.
2005	Afghanistan Next-Generation E-learning Program	Initiated by Kabul University to advance computer and ICT skills among students and faculty.	Emphasized structured digital learning; supported by MoHE through videoconference meetings for resource sharing.
2015	MoHE E-learning Policy and Bylaw	Outlined a three-phase approach to enhancing digital education in Afghan universities.	Implementation was uneven; major challenges included limited ICT infrastructure, lack of trained faculty, and slow development of fully online courses.
2020	Introduction of HELMS	MoHE introduced HELMS during the COVID-19 pandemic to facilitate remote learning across Afghan universities.	The pandemic exposed weaknesses in digital infrastructure, including unreliable Internet and lack of access to devices. Alternative platforms like Google Classroom and WhatsApp were also used.
2020	Use of Alternative Platforms	Universities utilized platforms like Google Classroom and WhatsApp during the COVID-19 pandemic for remote learning.	These platforms provided temporary solutions but raised concerns about the quality and comprehensiveness of education.

evidenced by their ability to develop courses on multiple online Learning Management Systems (LMS). In contrast, others, especially those from non-technical disciplines, such as Islamic studies, expressed a sense of inadequacy in their skills to develop standard online courses, highlighting a gap in digital learning preparedness (Sarwari et al., 2022; Wani & Mahdi, 2021).

The shift to digital learning requires a significant change in pedagogical approaches (Lockee, 2021; Makda, 2025). Although faculty members are familiar with traditional teaching methods, the concept of online pedagogy remains relatively new and underexplored (Salas-Pilco et al., 2022). This gap highlights the need for targeted support and training in online teaching methodologies to develop high-quality online courses. Faculty members with a background in general education may understand traditional pedagogy and have basic computer skills but often lack experience in e-pedagogy and require additional support to create effective online courses.

Students face challenges, particularly in terms of their ICT literacy. There is a wide range of comfort levels with technology, with many students struggling because of economic constraints and limited access to necessary tools. The transition to digital learning demands a certain level of ICT proficiency that many students lack. Additionally, students accustomed to traditional learning styles often find it difficult to adapt to online environments, experience concentration issues, and feel disconnected from the interactive dynamics of physical classrooms.

Supporting staff is crucial in facilitating digital learning initiatives, as their technical skills are essential in assisting faculty with course development (Polly et al., 2021). However, there is a recognized need for further training and resource allocation to enhance the technical proficiency of these teams, ensuring that they can effectively support both faculty and students in the digital learning process. Staff who have received basic technical training are better equipped to assist the faculty in producing quality online content.

Attitudes toward digital learning among these stakeholders were also mixed. Administrators, faculty, and students recognize digital learning as a critical component of contemporary education; however, they face numerous challenges. These include infrastructural issues such as unstable electricity, inadequate Internet access, a lack of familiarity with learning technology, and the necessary ICT skills. These factors collectively contribute to varying attitudes toward digital learning, ranging from optimism regarding its potential to skepticism regarding its practical implementation. Table 16.2 provides an overview of the human factors influencing e-learning in Afghanistan.

Process Factors of E-Learning

The process factor in e-learning emphasizes the importance of user-friendly LMS and the quality of online course design. Experiences with the HELMS developed by the MoHE during the COVID-19 lockdown were mixed (Higher Education Development Program, 2019; Ministry of Higher Education Afghanistan, 2015). While some users found HELMS straightforward and easy to use, others encountered challenges, particularly with its high-speed Internet requirements and interface issues. Some administrators noted that HELMS, although developed urgently, was designed to be simple; however, it received varying feedback regarding its usability.

TABLE 16.2

Key People Factors Influencing E-Learning Implementation in Afghanistan

Aspect	Key Points
Faculty Readiness	• Faculty in technology-related fields demonstrated sufficient proficiency in online course development, while faculty from nontechnical disciplines struggled with the transition to online teaching, highlighting a need for more training in online pedagogy. • Need for comprehensive training programs to enhance digital teaching skills.
Pedagogical Shift	• Traditional teaching methods are well understood, but online pedagogy is new and less explored. • Faculty require support and training in online teaching methodologies.
Student ICT Literacy	• Varying levels of ICT skills among students, with economic constraints limiting access to necessary technology. • Some students struggle with adapting to digital learning, preferring traditional, physical learning materials.
Support Staff Role	• Technical skills of support staff are crucial for assisting faculty in digital course development. • Further training and resource allocation are needed to enhance technical proficiency of support staff.

Faculty members, in particular, struggled to efficiently organize course content and activities within the HELMS. As a result, many have turned to alternative platforms, such as Google Classroom, for a more reliable and user-friendly experience. These alternative platforms allow faculty to deliver course materials more effectively, as HELMS usability issues often impede student access. By contrast, several private universities developed their own LMSs before and during the pandemic, which were generally viewed more favorably. These platforms are characterized by better usability and more comprehensive features, making them more conducive to effective teaching and learning. Faculty members from these institutions noted that their systems, while initially facing challenges, had evolved to become user-friendly and well equipped to meet their needs.

The transition to online assessment has highlighted additional challenges in the shift to digital education (Turnbull et al., 2021; Otto et al., 2024). Faculty members have struggled to adapt traditional assessment methods to online platforms, revealing a significant need for training in digital assessment tools and strategies. One faculty member acknowledged that, while they are familiar with traditional assessment techniques, these methods often prove inadequate or ineffective in an online learning environment, underscoring the necessity for new approaches tailored to digital education.

Governance encompasses policy formulation, budget allocation, and capacity-building efforts. The MoHE laid the groundwork for the establishment of digital learning policies and bylaws in 2015. However, there is a growing consensus on the urgent need to revise these documents to better align faculty with Afghan universities' current educational realities and requirements. The gap between policy creation and its effective implementation is a significant hurdle. The lack of awareness and application of these policies, even among key stakeholders such as the MCIT, underscores the need for more inclusive policy-development processes.

There is a significant disparity between public and private universities in terms of budgetary allocations for digital learning. Public institutions face severe financial constraints that greatly hinder the development and maintenance of essential digital learning infrastructure. An administrator from MoHE acknowledged the lack of a dedicated budget for supporting and maintaining e-learning in public universities, emphasizing the need for the ministry to negotiate with relevant stakeholders to secure sufficient funding for advancing digital learning.

By contrast, private universities have greater autonomy in allocating funds for digital learning initiatives, which allows them to better support and maintain their e-learning systems. An administrator from a private university highlighted that their institution had successfully allocated a budget specifically for e-learning and system maintenance.

Capacity building has emerged as a critical issue with current efforts being insufficient and sporadic. Both faculty members and students across public and private universities require ongoing, detailed, and technically focused training programs to adopt digital learning methodologies effectively. An administrator from MoHE noted that while some workshops were conducted following the lockdown, overall efforts in capacity building have been lacking, particularly over the past three years. Table 16.3 presents a summary of the process-related factors affecting e-learning in Afghanistan.

Technological Factors of E-Learning

Technological factors in Afghanistan's e-learning landscape highlight the critical need for stable electricity, robust ICT infrastructure, and high-quality Internet access. The country faces significant challenges in these areas, particularly within public universities, where electricity supply is unreliable and computer labs are often inadequate. Despite generating over 600 megawatts from hydroelectric projects and importing additional power from neighboring countries, the electricity supply remains unstable, leading to frequent load shedding. This instability affects not only universities but also the homes of students and faculty, thereby impeding consistent access to digital learning platforms and resources. A faculty member noted that Afghanistan relies heavily on imported electricity, especially during peak usage seasons such as summer and winter, when neighboring countries prioritize their own needs before transferring the remaining electricity to Afghanistan. This

TABLE 16.3

Key Process Factors Impacting E-Learning Implementation in Afghan Universities

Aspect	Key Points
User-Friendliness of LMS	• Faculty often resorted to alternative platforms like Google Classroom for better reliability and user experience. • Private universities generally had more user-friendly and well-equipped LMS platforms.
Online Course Design	• Significant variation in instructional design quality across universities.
Online Assessments	• Faculty faced challenges adapting traditional assessment methods to online platforms. • There is a need for training in online assessment tools and strategies to improve the effectiveness of evaluations.
Policy and Budgetary Allocation	• Disparity between public and private universities in budget allocation for digital learning initiatives. • Public universities face severe constraints due to inadequate financial support, impeding digital infrastructure development. • Private universities have greater autonomy and allocate budgets for e-learning and system maintenance.
Capacity Building	• Insufficient and sporadic capacity-building efforts for both faculty and students. • Ongoing, detailed, and technically focused training programs are needed for effective adoption of digital learning methodologies.

dependency exacerbates the challenges of maintaining a stable and reliable power supply for educational purposes.

Computer laboratories, which are essential for providing hands-on experience with technology, are inadequate at most Afghan universities. The MoHE's initiative to upgrade computer labs by 2017 has seen some progress, yet the ratio of students to computers remains high, particularly in public universities. Private universities offer better access to technology-related majors. However, students from other disciplines often lack sufficient resources. Faculty members have also expressed dissatisfaction with the current status of computer laboratories, highlighting the need for more advanced and functional facilities (Haidari et al., 2021).

Internet accessibility, a crucial component of digital learning, is present in Afghan universities, but is often restricted to faculty and administrative offices. Students, particularly those not involved in computer science programs, frequently struggle with limited access to essential online resources. Even when Internet connectivity is available, its inconsistent quality further hampers digital learning experience. One administrator noted that while universities are connected to the Internet, access is primarily limited to administrative and faculty offices, leaving most students without reliable access to the Internet.

Despite these challenges, there are opportunities for improvement, such as the widespread use of smartphones by students and faculty. Smartphones,

TABLE 16.4

Key Technological Factors Affecting E-Learning Implementation in Afghan Universities

Aspect	Key Points
Electricity Supply	• Unstable electricity supply, leading to frequent load shedding, which impacts access to digital learning resources. • Afghanistan relies heavily on imported electricity, particularly during high-demand seasons like summer and winter.
ICT Infrastructure	• Inadequate computer laboratories, especially in public universities, with a high student-to-computer ratio. • Private universities offer better access to technology-related resources, but nontechnical majors often lack sufficient resources.
Internet Accessibility	• Internet access in universities is often limited to faculty and administrative offices, with inconsistent quality. • Students, especially those not in computer science programs, frequently lack access to essential Internet resources.
Opportunities for Improvement	• Widespread use of smartphones among students and faculty, which can facilitate access to educational resources. • Smartphones are used by students to store and access educational materials, providing a workaround for limited infrastructure.

which are affordable and multifunctional, have become valuable tools in the learning process, allowing students to store and access educational materials including notes, slides, and multimedia resources. This adaptability offers a potential workaround for the limitations of formal Internet access, helping bridge the digital divide in educational settings. Table 16.4 outlines the technology-related factors influencing e-learning in Afghanistan.

Figure 16.1 summarized the trifecta (i.e., people, process, and technology) as the insights shared by faculty members from Afghan universities on the critical factors needed for successful e-learning implementation in Afghanistan. It highlights the interconnected relationship between people, process, and technology, all of which must work in harmony for e-learning initiatives to thrive.

The people aspect encompasses faculty, students, support staff, and administrators. Faculty members emphasized the importance of their own readiness, particularly the need for enhanced digital literacy and pedagogical training to effectively transition to online teaching. They also highlighted the varying levels of ICT skills among students, indicating that both groups require more support and training to fully engage with digital education. The process covers key operational elements such as LMS implementation, course design, and assessment methods. Faculty expressed that without well-designed online courses and assessments, e-learning efforts would be less effective. Strong policies and governance structures are essential to ensure these processes are standardized and reliable. The technology component focuses on the infrastructure needed to support e-learning,

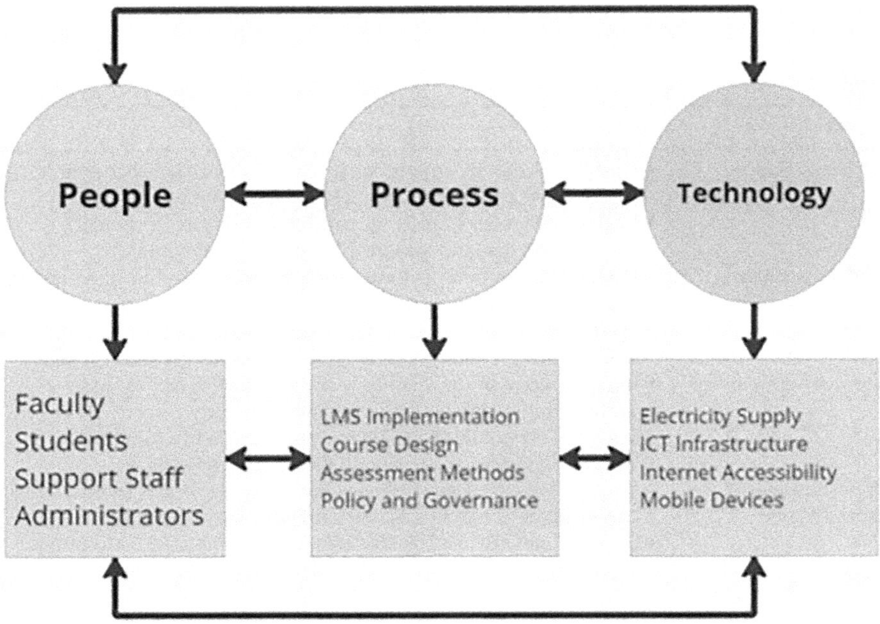

FIGURE 16.1
The trifecta of e-learning in Afghanistan.

including electricity, ICT resources, Internet access, and mobile devices. Faculty members underscored that without addressing these technological gaps, even the best people and processes would struggle to achieve success. Incorporating these factors, as identified by Afghan faculty, is essential for overcoming the unique challenges facing e-learning in Afghanistan.

Opportunities of E-Learning in Afghanistan

The advent of e-learning in Afghanistan presents a multitude of opportunities that extend beyond university education, offering a blueprint for broader educational access and national development. Despite formidable challenges, the interplay of people, process, and technology—the trifecta underpinning Afghanistan's e-learning ecosystem—demonstrates the potential for transformative change. By leveraging digital platforms, Afghanistan can expand educational reach, promote digital literacy, and equip students with essential modern workforce skills. This paradigm shift not only promises to enhance the quality of education but also contributes to economic growth, social development, and gender equality. The lessons learned from overcoming infrastructural, cultural, and policy hurdles in the university sector can inform and accelerate e-learning initiatives across all educational levels, paving the way for a more inclusive, resilient, and prosperous future.

Inclusive and Accessible Education

The COVID-19 pandemic has served as a catalyst for the adoption of e-learning in Afghan universities, simultaneously exposing infrastructure gaps and accelerating digital initiatives. This paradigm shift has transformed e-learning platforms into a vital alternative for Afghan girls and women who find themselves barred from secondary schools and universities.[1] In the face of stringent restrictions, virtual schools have emerged as beacons of hope, offering courses such as English and enabling female students to pursue their education from the relative safety of their homes.

Several notable initiatives have risen to meet this critical need. The Darakht-e Danesh,[2] Herat Online School,[3] and Daricha Schools,[4] all operated by non-governmental organizations (NGOs) outside Afghanistan, have witnessed a significant surge in enrollment[5]. These programs, conducted outside the formal education system and bridging geographical and political divides, exemplify the power of international collaboration in fostering educational continuity.

The Afghan diaspora has also played a pivotal role in this educational renaissance. The Omid Online School,[6] an example of diaspora-led innovation, provides a safe, virtual learning environment for 540 students from 7th to 12th grade. Offering seven regular subjects and three electives, it serves not only as an educational platform but also as a social hub, allowing girls to connect and nurture hope for their future despite the challenging circumstances.[7] These e-learning initiatives, born out of necessity and nurtured by global solidarity, embody a new educational paradigm that transcends traditional boundaries, empowering learners in challenging contexts while laying the groundwork for a more inclusive and resilient educational system in Afghanistan's future.

Digital learning empowers learners to take charge of their education through self-paced learning and active participation (Rathod & Kämppi, 2025). Customizable approaches cater to diverse needs and provide regular assessments and feedback for continuous progress. This transformative opportunity defies the imposed ban and empowers Afghan girls with their knowledge. Embracing digital learning in Afghanistan overcomes these barriers and offers a lifeline for knowledge and opportunities. The implementation of e-learning in Afghanistan has implications beyond its borders. The experiences and challenges faced by Afghan universities offer valuable lessons to other post-conflict and developing nations. The emphasis on inclusivity, overcoming infrastructure challenges, and adapting to cultural contexts can inform global efforts to enhance digital learning initiatives.

National Development and Economic Growth

Despite these challenges, e-learning presents a significant opportunity for Afghanistan to enhance the quality of higher education and to contribute to the country's economic and social development. By leveraging digital technologies, Afghan universities can expand access to education, promote digital literacy, and equip students with skills that are essential for the modern workforce. The potential of e-learning to bridge educational gaps and foster inclusive growth aligns with the broader goals of IT for development.

Our study suggests the potential of e-learning to contribute to Afghanistan's economic and social development. By providing access to quality education and skills training, e-learning can help to build human capital, foster innovation, and drive economic growth. Moreover, e-learning can contribute to gender equality and social progress by enabling more inclusive access to education, particularly for girls and women. As Afghanistan advances, e-learning has the potential to be a powerful tool for national development. Providing wider access to quality education can help build a skilled workforce capable of driving economic growth and social progress. It can also play a crucial role in promoting peace and stability by providing educational opportunities to marginalized groups and fostering a more inclusive society. The journey towards effective e-learning in Afghanistan is just beginning. Although challenges remain, the potential benefits are immense. With continued efforts, innovation, and collaboration, Afghanistan can harness the power of digital learning to transform its education system and build a brighter future for its citizens.

Strategic Collaboration and Continuous Improvement

To address the multifaceted challenges and harness the opportunities presented by e-learning in Afghanistan, a comprehensive strategy integrating digital, policy, and collaborative components is essential. The digital strategy should prioritize the development of inclusive, culturally sensitive learning platforms accessible on low-bandwidth Internet and mobile devices, ensuring widespread reach. This approach must emphasize digital literacy through comprehensive training programs, with a particular focus on promoting gender equality and female participation in digital learning. Content should be culturally relevant, respecting Afghanistan's diversity and available in multiple local languages (Farr, 2022).

The policy strategy should aim to cultivate a holistic digital learning ecosystem through collaboration among universities, government agencies, NGOs, and marginalized groups in decision-making processes. This approach involves raising awareness about the benefits of digital learning while addressing resistance to change. Strengthening infrastructure is crucial, including providing stable electricity, reliable Internet, and adequate computer labs. Policies and bylaws must be adapted to cater to the specific needs of educational institutions, with appropriate budget allocations.

In this context, organizations like Canadian Women for Women in Afghanistan are at the forefront of providing e-learning opportunities to Afghan girls[8]. They utilize technology to offer education to girls and women from their homes, circumventing the Taliban's restrictions on public education. The organization raises funds from Canadians, service clubs, and foundations to support this initiative. To extend this into a strategic collaboration, several approaches could be considered, including partnering with tech companies to improve Internet access and provide necessary devices, collaborating with other international NGOs to scale up the program, working with educational institutions to develop tailored curricula, engaging with diplomatic channels for recognition and protection of online education, and forming alliances with local Afghan organizations to ensure cultural appropriateness and on-the-ground support.

Our study highlights the need for a more nuanced understanding of the cultural and contextual factors influencing e-learning adoption in Afghanistan. While there is enthusiasm for digital learning among students and faculty members, resistance to change and preference for traditional teaching methods persist in some quarters. This underscores the importance of developing culturally sensitive e-learning strategies that respect local traditions while promoting innovation in education.

Furthermore, this chapter emphasizes the critical role of governance in the successful implementation of e-learning initiatives. There is a need for more comprehensive and consistently applied policies related to digital learning, as many participants reported a lack of awareness of existing e-learning policies. This suggests a gap between policy formulation and implementation, highlighting the need for more effective communication and enforcement of e-learning policies across all levels of higher education.

The path forward for e-learning in Afghanistan requires concerted efforts from all stakeholders. Universities must invest in developing their digital infrastructure and training their faculties and staff. The government must provide adequate funding and create supportive policies that encourage the adoption of e-learning. International organizations and NGOs can play a crucial role in providing technical expertise and financial support. Moreover, continuous research and evaluation of e-learning initiatives in Afghanistan are necessary to understand the long-term impact on educational outcomes, student engagement, and the overall quality of higher education, providing valuable insights for refining and improving e-learning strategies over time. Table 16.5 presents a synthesis of the primary opportunities for expanding e-learning initiatives in Afghanistan, distilling the key themes that emerged from our analysis.

Conclusion

E-learning presents a transformative opportunity for Afghanistan's higher education system, particularly in fostering diversity, equity, inclusion, and belonging. Despite the challenges of inadequate infrastructure, digital illiteracy, and resistance to change, the pandemic accelerated digital adoption, revealing both vulnerabilities and potential. The trifecta of people, processes, and technology underscores the interconnected nature of e-learning success. Faculty readiness, student digital literacy, and support staff training remain pivotal, requiring targeted investment and capacity-building efforts.

Strategic policy implementation and financial support are critical to bridging the gap between public and private institutions. Without stable electricity, reliable Internet, and functional ICT infrastructure, digital learning will remain fragmented. Yet, opportunities abound—smartphone adoption, international collaborations, and diaspora-led initiatives have created alternative learning pathways, particularly for marginalized groups, including women barred from traditional education.

For Afghanistan to fully harness e-learning's potential, universities, government agencies, and NGOs must work collectively to develop a holistic digital learning strategy. Investing in inclusive and culturally adaptive education models can drive long-term socio-economic progress. The future of Afghan education depends not only on technological advancements but also on the commitment to making learning accessible, equitable, and empowering for all.

TABLE 16.5

Key Themes for the Opportunities to Extend E-Learning in Afghanistan

Theme	Opportunity	Description
Inclusive and Accessible Education	Promoting Inclusive Education	• E-learning offers marginalized groups, especially girls, access to education, overcoming traditional limitations.
	Empowerment through Self-Paced Learning	• Digital learning allows learners to take control of their education, offering customizable, self-paced learning options.
	Addressing Gender Equality	• E-learning provides a platform to promote female participation and access to education, even amid restrictive environments.
	Creating Culturally Sensitive Platforms	• Development of inclusive digital platforms that are accessible on low-bandwidth Internet and mobile devices, ensuring broader reach.
National Development and Economic Growth	Economic and Social Development	• E-learning can contribute to building human capital, fostering innovation, and driving economic growth and social progress.
	Skilled Workforce Development	• Expanding access to education through e-learning can help build a skilled workforce essential for national development.
	Peace and Stability Promotion	• Providing educational opportunities to marginalized groups through e-learning can contribute to social inclusion and stability.
Strategic Collaboration and Continuous Improvement	Catalyst for Adoption	• The COVID-19 pandemic accelerated the adoption of e-learning, raising awareness of its benefits and challenges.
	Holistic Digital Strategy	• A comprehensive strategy involving digital literacy development, gender equality promotion, and culturally relevant content creation.
	Collaborative Policy Development	• Building a digital learning ecosystem through collaboration among universities, government agencies, NGOs, and marginalized groups.
	International Collaboration and Support	• Opportunities for international organizations and NGOs to provide technical expertise and financial support to enhance e-learning initiatives.
	Continuous Research and Evaluation	• Ongoing research to understand the long-term impact of e-learning, refine strategies, and improve educational outcomes.

Notes

1 How women and girls in Afghanistan can still access free education.
2 Darakht-e Danesh Academi offers asynchronous online courses in multiple languages (English, Dari, Pashto) for Afghan learners, including university-level, life skills, and professional development content. https://courses.darakhtdanesh.org/
3 Children on the Edge supports covert online schooling for over 800 Afghan women and girls, enabling access to education under repressive restrictions. www.childrenontheedge.org/heratschool.html
4 Daricha (Network of Community Schools for Girls in Afghanistan) organizes "home schools" and one-on-one tutoring to continue girls' education despite bans on formal schooling. https://darichaschool.com/
5 Afghanistan: Women locked out of schools, logging in online (www.youtube.com/watch?v=Xj88n36wsBE&t=46s)
6 Omid for Girls is a U.S.-based initiative pairing U.S. high school volunteers with Afghan girls to provide online lessons in mathematics and English, offering educational and moral support. www.omidforgirls.org/
7 Omid Online School—a diaspora-led initiative—offers girls in Afghanistan a secure virtual learning environment in the face of shutdowns and bans on female education. www.vidc.org/en/detail/omid-online-school-gives-hope-to-girls-in-afghanistan
8 Canadian organization provides online education to Afghan women and girls (www.youtube.com/watch?v=4_rfHS5M_eM&t=476s)

References

Alariqi, A. A., Najafi, M., Abdulrab, M., Murray, C., & Slimanzai, H. (2019). Factors affecting E-learning effectiveness in a higher learning institution in Afghanistan. *Proceedings of the 2019 11th International Conference on Education Technology and Computers*, 176–181. https://doi.org/10.1145/3369255.3372275

Asghari, M., & Subriadi, A. P. (2021). Virtual learning during Covid-19 pandemic in higher education of Afghanistan: Challenges and efforts in Kabul universities: A systematic literature review. *2021 International Conference on Electrical and Information Technology (IEIT)*, 233–238. https://doi.org/10.1109/IEIT53149.2021.9587381

Borazon, E. Q., Marques, S., & Saycon, D. R. (2024). E-learning adoption: A comparative analysis of public sentiments during COVID-19. *Information Technology for Development*, 1–29. https://doi.org/10.1080/02681102.2024.2423286

Cabral, J. M. (2017). *Environmental and Social Management Framework for Digital CASA Afghanistan Project* [Consultancy Services to Prepare Environmental and Social Management Framework (ESMF) and to Carry Out Relevant Capacity Building for Digital Casa Afghanistan Project].

Farr, G. (2022). Female education in Afghanistan after the return of the Taliban. *E-International Relations*. www.e-ir.info/2022/04/23/female-education-in-afghanistan-after-the-return-of-the-taliban/

Haidari, S. M., Safawi, S. S., & Yelken, T. Y. (2021). Investigating challenges facing Afghan university students during Covid-19 outbreak. *Shanlax International Journal of Education, 9*(4), 341–351. https://doi.org/10.34293/education.v9i4.4191

Higher Education Development Program. (2019). *Ministry of Higher Education (MoHE) Higher Education Development Program (HEDP) Operations and Monitoring Support Team (OMST) Bimonthly Progress Monitoring Report*. www.tandfonline.com/doi/full/10.1080/2331186X.2025.2457904#abstract

Hu, K., & Raman, A. (2024). Systematic literature review on the holistic integration of e-learning in universities: Policy, human, financial, and technical perspectives. *Contemporary Educational Technology, 16*(2), ep497. https://doi.org/10.30935/cedtech/14287

Lockee, B. B. (2021). Shifting digital, shifting context:(re) considering teacher professional development for online and blended learning in the COVID-19 era. *Educational Technology Research and Development, 69*(1), 17–20. https://doi.org/10.1007/s11423-020-09836-8

Makda, F. (2025). Digital education: Mapping the landscape of virtual teaching in higher education–a bibliometric review. *Education and Information Technologies, 30*(2), 2547–2575. https://doi.org/10.1007/s10639-024-12899-2

Mikawa, S. (2006). *Cisco-USAID-UNDP Networking Academy Alliance, Developing a sustainable Cisco Networking Academy Program in Afghanistan*. https://nsrc.org/regions/ASIA/AF/20060300-Cisco-USAID-UNDP.pdf

Ministry of Higher Education Afghanistan. (2015). *National Higher Education Strategic plan 2015–2020*.

Nasrat, N., Khamosh, A., & Lavangnananda, K. (2020). Challenges and hurdles to e-learning implementation during COVID-19 outbreak: A case of Shaikh Zayed University. *2020 International Conference on Informatics, Multimedia, Cyber and Information System (ICIMCIS)*, 242–246. https://doi.org/10.1109/ICIMCIS51567.2020.9354313

Oryakhail, M. S., Saay, S., & Nasery, H. (2021). Challenges in the implementation of E-learning in Afghanistan Higher Education. *2021 International Conference Advancement in Data Science, E-Learning and Information Systems (ICADEIS)*, 1–6. https://doi.org/10.1109/ICADEIS52521.2021.9702070

Otto, S., Bertel, L. B., Lyngdorf, N. E. R., Markman, A. O., Andersen, T., & Ryberg, T. (2024). Emerging digital practices supporting student-centered learning environments in higher education: A review of literature and lessons learned from the COVID-19 pandemic. *Education and Information Technologies, 29*(2), 1673–1696. https://doi.org/10.1007/s10639-023-11789-3

Polly, D., Martin, F., & Guilbaud, T. C. (2021). Examining barriers and desired supports to increase faculty members' use of digital technologies: Perspectives of faculty, staff and administrators. *Journal of Computing in Higher Education, 33*, 135–156. https://doi.org/10.1007/s12528-020-09259-7

Rathod, P., & Kämppi, P. (2025). Improving online and e-learning education through train-the-trainer model: A case study of European innovation project ECOLHE. *European Journal of Education, 60*(1), e12900. https://doi.org/10.1111/ejed.12900

Salas-Pilco, S. Z., Yang, Y., & Zhang, Z. (2022). Student engagement in online learning in Latin American higher education during the COVID-19 pandemic: A systematic review. *British Journal of Educational Technology*, *53*(3), 593–619. https://doi.org/10.1111/bjet.13190

Sarwari, K., Kakar, A. F., Golzar, J., & Miri, M. A. (2022). Distance learning during COVID-19 in Afghanistan: Challenges and opportunities. *E-Learning and Digital Media*, *19*(2), 144–162. https://doi.org/10.1177/20427530211044757

Sokout, H., & Usagawa, T. (2018). Analyzing the current situation of e-learning at Kabul Polytechnic University. *Proceedings of the 2nd International Conference on Education and Multimedia Technology (ICEMT '18)* (pp. 49–53). Association for Computing Machinery. https://doi.org/10.1145/3206129.3239428

Turnbull, D., Chugh, R., & Luck, J. (2021). Transitioning to E-Learning during the COVID-19 pandemic: How have higher education institutions responded to the challenge?. *Education and Information Technologies*, *26*(5), 6401–6419. https://doi.org/10.1007/s10639-021-10633-w

Wani, N. U. H., & Mahdi, M. I. (2021). Factors affecting e-learning adoption in Afghanistan: Empirical evidence from Technical and Vocational Education and Training Authority. *Kardan Journal of Economics and Manangement Sciences*, *4*(2), 1–22. https://doi.org/10.31841/KJEMS.2021.1

17

Bridging Divides: Technology as a Catalyst for Empowering Underrepresented Communities in India

Ananthanarayanan Venkateswaran and Shaji Joseph

17.1 Introduction

Technology is not just a tool. The idea behind using it is not just to be more productive or to replace human resources. When applied with the right focus and strategy, it has the ability to emerge as a transformative force that allows to bridge socio-economic disparities while fostering inclusivity. As we examine the undeniable and powerful role those digital advancements play in empowering underrepresented communities, particularly in India, we also explore ways to integrate global best practices. But, for a nation like India that has massive cultural, geopolitical and socio-economic diversity and disparity, there is a need for holistic approach to development. Hence, Amartya Sen's capabilities approach and the digital inclusion frameworks provide a good theoretical base to approach digital transformation in India. This chapter further explores the potential of technology focusing with an intent to expand freedoms, while enhancing well-being and at the same time also providing real opportunities for marginalised populations (S. Sharma et al., 2022). Through a comparative analysis of national and international models, this chapter identifies challenges, best practices, and policy interventions essential for driving inclusive technological development (Fisk et al., 2022). The idea is to enhance well-being while at the same time provide real opportunities for those in the marginalised populations (Rizvi & Nabi, 2021). With a central focus on India, the discussion integrates global perspectives while analysing initiatives such as the Digital India and Pradhan Mantri Gramin Digital Saksharta Abhiyan (PMGDISHA). At the same time, it works alongside international models, such as Sweden's gender-inclusive tech policies (Keshari, 2024) and the support for indigenous communities from countries such as New Zealand (Tripathi & Rajeev, 2023).

DOI: 10.1201/9781003591078-22

Despite a growing body of literature on digital infrastructure and e-governance, there remains a critical gap in analysing how digital technologies affect marginalised communities in India through a development lens. This chapter seeks to fill this gap by framing digital inclusion as a pathway to expand individual freedoms and capabilities, particularly for underrepresented groups. Using Amartya Sen's capabilities approach, this work goes beyond infrastructure metrics to assess how digital initiatives enhance agency, social inclusion, and well-being. It offers a comparative perspective grounded in Indian realities while drawing lessons from international best practices.

Some of the key challenges here revolve around affordability and infrastructure deficits and also discuss the systemic barriers (S. Khan, 2022; Tiwari, 2022). These, while being addressed by using practical strategies, also propose to include a holistic approach by enhancing the digital literacy. This will not only foster public–private partnerships but also help in creating a more localised content approach for messaging and communication. Special attention is given to intersectionality while also emphasising caste, gender, and income disparities. As we deal with specific sections focused on India, there are also targeted solutions for Dalits, for the indigenous populations, and for the rural women (Liu et al., 2024).

The chapter highlights the role of artificial intelligence (AI) and big data in not only optimising resource distribution but also working towards enhancing public welfare programmes. AI also helps in increasing the reach and efficacy of government schemes (Kuziemski & Misuraca, 2020). Some brilliant examples of global innovations include Kenya's mobile banking and Rwanda's drone deliveries (Millan et al., 2023). Kenya's credit cooperative banks make us of AI to make it more efficient and customer responsive. These serve as truly innovative inspirations for being able to adapt technology and, in a way, can serve as brilliant ideas and frameworks to be able to adapt them to India's unique socio-economic context. Nayak and Tiyadi (2024) studied how AI can become a means to bring in social inclusion, welfare distribution, better healthcare facilities predicting crime and reducing it, and overall to create a better decision-making by government bodies.

Corporate social responsibility (CSR) and impact investing are catalysts for inclusive technological growth. Some of the examples are Microsoft's AI for Good program and Salesforce's Trailblazer Community (Humphrey et al., 2020). These stand distinct as wonderful examples which empower skill development coupled with digital literacy and social enterprises. The use and integration of technologies such as blockchain and, at the same time, having a decentralised technology model, such as Estonia's e-residency program, are wonderful examples that demonstrate the potential for what a secure, transparent system can achieve. These showcase the ability to empower communities and at the same time also enhance governance. In rural contexts, technologies such as the solar-powered micro-grids and peer-to-peer energy trading clearly show how the integration of digital tools with sustainability can have a tremendous positive impact, not only on the nation, but also on the community as a whole (Khan et al., 2021). There are a number of good cases how companies in India extend their CSR in AI tools. TCS iON Digital Learning platform is aimed at providing personalised learning experiences to students and professionals especially in the rural areas. Wipro AI-based smart farming solutions help farmers to improve productivity and sustainability. HDFC bank has used AI-powered financial inclusion to provide micro-loans to underserved populations as part of their CSR activities. Mahindra & Mahindra's Rise for Good initiative focuses on creating sustainable rural livelihoods.

This chapter underscores the need for coordinated global and local policies which align with Sustainable Development Goal (SDG) and climate commitments. These global frameworks, for example, the UN's Digital Cooperation Roadmap and the EU's Green Deal, provide actionable insights. Grassroots innovations like Hasiru Dala and Trestle Labs are brilliant ways that not only exemplify how technology fosters circular economies but also showcase how these assistive solutions can positively impact vulnerable groups (Sambyal, 2023). Recently Tata Consultancy service (TCS) partnered with the World Economic Forum (WEF) to provide AI-powered insights into energy consumption patterns and carbon emissions. Microsoft India, through its AI for Earth initiative to monitor water resources, and ISRO's AI-driven satellite imagery help provide early warning to farmers on soil conditions, pest outbreaks, weather patterns, and irrigation needs. Another Indian start-up called CureMetrix has partnered with global health organisations to improve breast cancer detection using AI algorithms (Patra et al. 2024).

The chapter is structured as follows: it first outlines the theoretical foundations based on Sen's Capabilities Approach, followed by a discussion on the methodology and criteria for case selection. It then presents international examples of digital inclusion initiatives, organised thematically. This is followed by a critical assessment of India's digital inclusion efforts, corporate responsibility, and challenges faced. The chapter concludes with a discussion of key insights, policy implications, and recommendations to enhance the transformative potential of technology for inclusion.

17.2 Methodology and Case Selection

This chapter adopts a qualitative, exploratory approach to understand the dynamics of digital inclusion for underrepresented communities. The international and Indian case studies were selected based on their relevance to marginalised populations, the documented impact on digital empowerment, and their diversity in sociopolitical contexts. Countries such as Sweden, Finland, and Estonia represent technologically advanced welfare states with inclusive digital public services, while Kenya and Rwanda offer insights from emerging economies that have leapfrogged into mobile-based governance. Singapore and New Zealand were chosen for their strong digital literacy and indigenous inclusion frameworks.

The Indian case studies emphasise large-scale initiatives like Aadhaar, Common Service Centres (CSCs), and corporate programmes such as Microsoft's AI for Good. These were selected to reflect diversity in scale, implementation models, and stakeholder involvement (government, private sector, and non-governmental organisations [NGOs]).

Comparative analysis is based on thematic synthesis—examining how each initiative addresses access, capacity-building, and digital agency. This thematic lens enables a systematic understanding of strengths, limitations, and transferable lessons across different contexts.

Amartya Sen's capabilities approach serves as the core analytical lens for this chapter. The framework shifts the focus from economic utility or technological availability to human freedom and agency. According to Sen, development is the process of expanding the real freedoms people enjoy. In this context, digital inclusion is not merely about access to devices or connectivity—it is about enabling individuals to make meaningful choices, participate in society, and pursue goals they value.

Sen's concept of capabilities aligns strongly with digital empowerment: "functionings" such as accessing information, expressing opinions, or availing government benefits become possible when people have the capabilities supported by digital tools. However, these outcomes are contingent upon enabling conditions such as literacy, legal identity, and safety.

This theoretical framing helps assess whether digital initiatives in India and elsewhere expand real freedoms or merely increase superficial access. As Gigler (2015) also argue, digital development must be evaluated not just by reach but by its ability to enhance people's agency and well-being. This framework is thus used to critically assess how technology interventions affect marginalised communities across three pillars—access, capacity, and agency.

17.3 Digital Inclusion and Socio-economic Empowerment

Amartya Sen's capabilities approach integrated as a framework for this study helps to not only underscore the significance of expanding freedoms but also allows us the opportunities as a nation to lead a more valued life. In a country like India, technology cannot be approached merely as an answer to make things more accessible. The digital world needs to be able to translate with a clear intent to ensure that technology also assists in providing access while also ensuring higher and more secure skill development and social mobility. The integration of such a digital inclusion framework boosts this entire process further by emphasising affordability and at the same time accessibility, and usability (Nedungadi et al., 2018). These become critical pillars for equitable digital participation. Every state government in India has made it mandatory to have basic digital literacy in order to get a government job. The proliferation of smart phones to the remotest regions of India is another example of social inclusion through digital inclusion (Bhatia and Dawar, 2024).

17.3.1 The Digital Divide in India

Rapid technological advancements are not necessarily an indication of an equitable distribution. In fact, in spite of the massively booming advancements in terms of technology in India, the divide in terms of digital disparities seem to be widening more and more. There is no doubt that smartphones are cheaper, internet speeds have more than doubled, accessibility to internet data is easier and more affordable even for lower income communities. But, in spite of this, there are clear systemic barriers and digital literacy gaps. These gaps seem to be widening in terms of digital disparity. Some initiatives such as Digital India and PMGDISHA (Pradhan Mantri Gramin Digital Saksharta Abhiyan) are steps towards dividing this gap (Gahlot & Gahlot, 2020). These have made great progress while looking at various aspects with regards to systemic barriers such as affordability, infrastructure deficits, and digital literacy gaps, etc. But there still seems to be a pressing concern. The rural-urban divide, gender inequities, and caste-based discrimination have only contributed to further exacerbate the exclusion from digital opportunities. This is especially true in rural areas and for marginalised communities. It is also important to know that the age-old stratification method of Caste is also a factor in digital literacy in India (Rajam et al., 2021). Asrani (2021) observed that education, household demographics and income are the major determinants of ICT adoption. Education, age and gender plays as further aspects of digitisation in India. Similar challenges have been observed in Finland, where migrants often face structural difficulties in accessing digital public services due to low administrative literacy, underscoring the importance of tailored support in digital welfare systems (Safarov, 2023).

17.3.2 India-Specific Challenges and Solutions

For a nation like India, it is not only important, but extremely vital to address the needs of the underrepresented groups in India, which includes Dalits,

Adivasis and rural women. With the help of technology, we can understand the compounded challenges in accessing digital opportunities to address their needs. In this effort the government not only have to address the barrier but also answer some complex questions and even allow them to voice their issues and gain them access to essential services. This requires intersectional policy approaches that also take into consideration the various socio-economic, cultural, and gender-based inequities which they face (George, 2023). The Aadhaar initiative in India, which provides a biometric digital identity to over 1.3 billion people is a good start. The Aadhaar initiative has not only helped to empower and gain access to banking, subsidies, healthcare, and welfare schemes across groups but it has also contributed to an approach and a step towards decentralisation (Awasthi et al., 2024). Which is truly remarkable considering the size of a nation like India with its vast socio-economic disparities across various regions. Additionally, there are also programs like Digital Saksharta Abhiyan (DISHA) and Internet Saathi. They have contributed greatly in helping to improve the digital literacy among rural women. However, what is a pressing need today is that, we need to look at all of this in terms of empowerment, but with a clearly defined intersectional policy approach. One, that can also address caste, gender, and economic barriers simultaneously (Ghauri et al., 2022). A brilliant example of this is Brazil's Bolsa Família program. It allows for the integration of digital banking and mobile technology with an idea to be able to deliver financial aid to low-income families, particularly Afro-Brazilians and Indigenous groups (Pereira & Moroni, 2022). All these have to happen in a phased but with a holistic approach while addressing structural inequities. This will ensure equal access to digital opportunities across groups.

17.3.3 AI and Big Data for Social Welfare

The perfect use of technology is not about using it to create faster or more efficient and better digital tools alone. It is about ensuring that these technology tools can help us become more efficient and smarter in the process. We need to be able to use technology with a clear intent to add value to the society and in the process contribute to an equitable growth and development while ensuring a better quality of life (Sambasivan et al., 2021). With the rapid boost in Artificial Intelligence and Big Data, one can only wonder of the unlimited potential it has. For example, from our perspective, what we need to focus on is whether it can truly optimise aspects such as resource allocation while also helping to enhance public welfare programmes. We need to be able to use AI, big data, IoT, etc. to help us improve the effectiveness of government schemes. AI-driven predictive analytics has the power to ensure targeted delivery of social benefits, thus also helping us to improve a more strategic, structured and well planned outreach while improving the efficiency and even quality of delivery (View of the impact, 2024).

17.3.4 Corporate Responsibility and Impact Investing

Regulations and policies from government alone do not contribute to the success of CSR programmes. In-order to ensure the CSR reach the deserved groups there is a need for digital initiatives that are focused on marginalised communities. Further this has to be a connected effort of the government, non-governmental organisations and the citizen groups. There are some wonderful examples of brilliant corporate initiatives that have showcased the impact of contribution towards a stronger national digital literacy with a clear social goal in mind focused on equity. For example, Microsoft's AI for Good program and Salesforce's Trailblazer Community beautifully illustrate how businesses can contribute towards an equitable digital literacy and uniform skill development while ensuring social inclusion. By funding grassroots initiatives that integrate technology with social impact, the impact investing can be further driven towards a more sustainable digital transformation.

Corporate actors play a critical role in shaping digital inclusion, particularly through CSR programmes, public–private partnerships, and product design. In India, firms like Infosys Foundation and Wipro have invested in digital literacy programmes, while tech multinationals such as Google and Meta have launched training initiatives targeting women and youth. While these efforts have shown localised success, they often lack coordination and scalability. Moreover, private sector initiatives may prioritise brand positioning over long-term community empowerment.

The regulatory environment also influences corporate behaviour. For instance, the mandatory 2% CSR rule under the Indian Companies Act 2013 has increased funding for digital skill development, but its impact remains uneven across regions and sectors. Critics argue that without inclusive metrics and local participation, corporate programmes risk becoming top-down interventions.

To be truly impactful, corporate initiatives must align with participatory development principles, ensure data ethics, and be embedded in local socio-cultural contexts. Transparent impact assessments, open data collaborations, and co-creation with civil society could enhance outcomes.

17.4 Decentralised Energy and Rural Empowerment

For a nation to experience the true form of empowerment with regards to their underrepresented communities, it is vital to be growing across all sectors. Digital literacy alone cannot help this holistic development. A truly sustainable progress is the one that allows for a seamless technology integration with economic development, governance, and sustainability circular economy initiatives. For example, Indonesia's eFishery no doubt has leveraged IoT and

AI to help small-scale fish farmers. This program helped them optimise their processes in reducing waste improving yields (Zainudin et al., 2023). But this has also contributed to their financial inclusion programmes, coupled with the supply chain support, and sustainability efforts. Thereby, ensuring that farmers not only use digital tools but also gain economic benefits.

Similarly, in Mexico, the EncicloMedia programme is yet another brilliant example. In this, their public schools introduced interactive digital learning. Now if we look at it from a digital literacy perspective alone it is already a fantastic initiative. But to ensure it is long lasting and really contributing to their skill force development we need to understand and recognise that it has to incorporate other sectors. This programme's true impact came into light when it was combined with teacher training along with infrastructural upgrades (León-Duarte et al., 2024). This was further boosted with ensuring localised content development. This is what we call a holistic approach as it ensured every underrepresented student could meaningfully and effectively engage with this form of digital education. A good example of moving from macro top-down approach to micro decentralised bottom-up approach is a story of renewable energy project from Rajasthan narrated by the Barefoot College International. Here the onus of development was on the community members (Chakrabarty, 2023). They bring together political, economic, social and technological aspects together to help steer the development

17.5 Global Models of Digital Empowerment

The Digital Skills and Jobs Coalition, a brilliant initiative from the European Union, fosters women's involvement in technology, providing mentorship programmes, funding initiatives, and workplace policies that encourage gender diversity in the tech industry (Bauch, 2024). There are some brilliant and innovative national frameworks and policies that can be fantastic examples of integrating digital strategy policies that have been well embedded into the nation's system:

17.5.1 Digital Identity and Governance

1. **Aadhaar** (the Unique Identity Program of India)

   This probably is the most significant and most extensive activities conducted by the state to integrate every citizen digitally. This biometric based tool helps to document every data related to the individual. As almost all the services are linked to Aadhaar this provides a huge amount of data on India citizens. This can function as a major decision-making tool for Indian planners. Aadhaar is a 12-digit unique identification number assigned to every Indian citizen. It facilitates access to government services like subsidies, welfare programmes, and financial inclusion. It helps to identify the needy and provide targeted welfare schemes (Chaudhuri & König, 2017).

Despite its transformative potential, Aadhaar has also faced significant criticism. Civil society groups and legal scholars have raised concerns over data privacy, surveillance, and exclusion errors. Reports indicate that biometric failures have led to denial of entitlements such as pensions and rations, disproportionately affecting the elderly and disabled. The Supreme Court's 2018 judgement upheld the constitutionality of Aadhaar but mandated safeguards including restrictions on private sector use.

Moreover, the lack of robust grievance redressal mechanisms continues to undermine trust. Scholars such as Reetika Khera have argued that Aadhaar's techno-solutionism can exacerbate structural inequality if not accompanied by accountability and rights-based implementation. These concerns underscore the need for inclusive design, transparent governance, and community awareness to ensure Aadhaar empowers rather than alienates.

While government-led initiatives such as Aadhaar illustrate the scope and scale of public sector digital transformation, the private sector also plays an increasingly critical role in shaping the digital inclusion landscape.

2. **Estonia's e-Governance Model**

   Since 2003 Estonia has been gradually introducing a large-scale inclusive e-governance program. While introducing this they faced major challenges such as state readiness, local government readiness, transition and implementation, and analysis and assessment (Pappel et al., 2020). Today citizens can access services ranging from healthcare to business registration remotely. They use blockchain to authenticate these service transactions. They introduced a program called X-Road system to ensure networking and data sharing between government departments. This led to higher transparency and reducing bureaucratic inefficiency. This model highlights how India can enhance governance transparency through blockchain applications, particularly in the context of decentralised governance.

3. **Kenya's Mobile Banking Revolution**

   Kenya's M-Pesa is yet another innovative example. It showcases how financial inclusion can happen that can even embrace individuals without traditional bank access. It shows ways to empower and enable them to participate in the digital economy. This has been a revolutionising approach as this mobile banking innovation has truly become a blueprint for financial empowerment in emerging economies (Mbiti & Weil, 2015).

4. **Estonia's Blockchain-Based Governance**

   When we discuss e-governance, Estonia stands as a global leader. Its 100% digital public services in the form of its e-Residency program, e-tax, e-voting, etc., have showed the tremendous potential that digital can empower a nation with. Their integration of blockchain technology in governance, their digital identity management, and economic participation are truly remarkable. This has not only helped in reducing bureaucracy but also resulted in great efficiency (Semenzin et al., 2022). For example, their X-Road data exchange system is a key pillar in their entire digital society's framework and foundation. The focus on making their systems nationally secure, transparent, and decentralised is an inspiration for inclusive digital governance globally (Paide et al., 2018).

17.5.2 Digital Literacy and Capacity Building

1. **Singapore's Smart Nation Initiative**

   Singapore's Smart Nation Initiative is a masterclass in digital strategy focused on digital literacy, economic empowerment, and with that an equitable and sustainable future with overall skill development (Khanal et al., 2024). Their focus on AI, IoT, 5G, and fintech while ensuring digital inclusion is truly exceptional. The government is not only stressing on things like digital payments by promoting and incentivising cashless payments, digital ID systems (Singpass) and smart housing solutions but they are focusing on a lot more in terms of empowering societies and communities. They are heavily investing into AI-driven public services with real-time urban management systems, which are focusing on empowering transportation, security, and healthcare in a holistic way. Their emphasis on designing a policy and a national framework towards public–private collaboration, e-governance, and data-driven systems is truly remarkable and stands out as one of the most advanced digital strategies globally (Das & Kwek, 2024). This massive initiative aimed to connect the elderly, the underprivileged and marginalised to the mainstream through this platform. This was done through conducting workshops on digital technologies, providing free tools, and subsidised mobiles to the unconnected. By 2020 they were talking of a citizen-oriented smart city in Singapore (Chang & Das, 2020). Such strategic communication efforts involving digital engagement and public–private synergies echo practices highlighted by Lacarcel and Huete (2023), where digital platforms are purposefully employed to reach and include diverse populations.

2. **New Zealand's Indigenous Digital Inclusion**

   Now a brilliant and truly inclusive approach showcasing a nation's policy that caters to integrating indigenous knowledge is from the Government of New Zealand. They have prioritised digital literacy and economic empowerment for the Māori community. They have achieved this via localised content while ensuring culturally relevant tech solutions. The Māori Digital Strategy, which is a public–private partnership, stands as an amazing example showcasing supports for capacity-building efforts to seamlessly integrate indigenous knowledge systems into modern technology (Carnaby, 2008). Their policy is an example of how to prioritise, for example, in their case, the Māori data sovereignty, language preservation, and indigenous entrepreneurship, and it does so while promoting inclusion and all the while respecting Te Tiriti o Waitangi (Treaty of Waitangi) principles (Momo, 2022).

3. **Microsoft's AI for Good Initiative**

   This demonstrates how corporate technology platforms can contribute to inclusion, particularly through partnerships with governments and non-profits. In India, the company has supported accessibility tools for the visually impaired and AI models to predict dropout risks in education. While these programs offer significant potential, they also raise concerns related to algorithmic bias, lack of transparency in data governance, and dependence on proprietary technology. Scholars such as Eubanks (2018) argue that without checks, such initiatives may reinforce rather than reduce inequality. The effectiveness of AI for Good depends not just on technological innovation but on participatory design, inclusivity in training datasets, and open-source approaches. Hence, corporate digital responsibility must be understood as a multi-dimensional obligation, not a one-time CSR effort.

4. **Finland's Digital Literacy for Refugees**

   Finland has an open policy on refugees and want to provide all the support required to rehabilitate them. The Digital Inclusion of Immigrants program is aimed to train the refugees and low-income families in digital skills (Safarow 2023). Many of these refugees are victims of war and have physical handicaps. They observed that refugees, people with impairments and those who are underemployed for a long period have problems with digital technology. The immigrants also had cultural integration problems and the government launched an integrative Technology Design Model to bridge this gap (Hosseini, 2023).

17.5.3 Inclusive Public Service Delivery

1. **Sweden's Gender-Inclusive Tech Policies**

   Sweden here is a fantastic example to learn from. Its policies, "Digitaliseringsstrategi" (Digital Strategy) helps to ensure gender equity in digital literacy and STEM participation; these are truly remarkable. It beautifully brings together digital skills, infrastructure, cybersecurity and innovation into a converging well-founded national framework (Hallpers, 2019).

2. **Rwanda's Drone Deliveries for Public Welfare**

   Healthcare is a major concern for nations worldwide. Achieving equitable healthcare is a dream even for developed countries. Now, if a nation is able to integrate technology for optimising healthcare, then that is a case study that needs to be looked into with great attention. And that's exactly what the Rwanda's Zipline Drone Technology deserves (Gangwal, 2019). It has optimised healthcare delivery in remote regions. This policy has ensured timely access to essential medical supplies. At the same time, it has fostered the integration of AI-driven logistics into public health programmes (Bordenkircher & Egan, 2022), thereby demonstrating the true power and the right use of technology in addressing infrastructural challenges.

3. **Germany's Digital Strategy 2025**

   Germany's digital strategy is a perfect blend of Industry 4.0 as it brings together AI, digital infrastructure investment and gives a power boost to small-medium enterprises (SME) digitalisation while fostering a high-tech economy focused on a clearly defined roadmap for the future (Wittmann et al., 2020). The key here is to not only have clearly defined regulatory reforms but also boost the economy and nation by way of digital entrepreneurship in the process.

Similarly other developed nations such as Germany, Denmark, the Netherlands and France too have incorporated digital training and inclusion programmes. Germany's Platform Economy and Social Inclusion is aimed at integrating marginalised communities into the workforce. This is supported by corporate companies like Siemens to extend skill development programmes for the marginalised (Holzer, 2016). Denmark launched the Copenhagen AI Welfare State Model, which is used to help resource allocations in healthcare services based on the socio-economic data (Collington, 2021). Singapore's GovTech Open Data initiative allows small business and non-profit organisations to access anonymised government data for further innovation and development (Paud et al., 2022). The Netherlands uses digital technology to create a circular economy. Programmes such as Fariphone's e-waste reduction initiative and peer-to-peer energy sharing in Amsterdam are good examples of this digital transformation for sustainability (Dominish et al., 2018). France has pioneered cooperative digital platforms that promote financial inclusion among marginalised groups. La MedNum, a national cooperative, partners with local governments and businesses to provide affordable internet access and digital upskilling programmes for rural communities. This supports the public–private partnerships and governance section by demonstrating the power of community-driven digital initiatives.

Having examined both public and private sector efforts within India, along with comparative global insights, the following section summarises key takeaways and offers policy recommendations to enhance digital empowerment.

17.6 Policy and Governance Recommendations

17.6.1 Aligning Digital Policies with Global Climate and SDG Commitments

India has found it important to align its policies with international frameworks in order to ensure sustainable and inclusive digital expansion. The UN's Digital Cooperation Roadmap and the EU's Green Deal are examples of global initiatives to bring local development. This would be a great example of empowering a process in a seamless manner that will help to synergise in terms of a coordinated policy approach (Gritsenko, 2023). In the process, aligning digital policies with global initiatives will also add value in terms of bridging the digital divide and at the same time empowering people and the nation by promoting climate resilience and sustainable development. The UN Digital Cooperation Roadmap is aimed to break the monopoly of the large companies and countries on digital technologies. It aims to maximise the benefits and minimise the costs of digital transformation to ensure that everyone is included and the digital divide is removed. Clark et al. (2022) studied the concept of Just Digital Ethical Framework that has the potential to bring in sustainable development through digital inclusion.

17.6.2 Localised Content and Multilingual Digital Inclusion

India, the most populous country in the world, is also one of the most linguistically diverse nations. It has around 22 officially recognised languages under the Eighth Schedule of the Constitution, in addition to over 1,600 spoken languages and dialects. This linguistic diversity presents both challenges and opportunities, particularly in terms of digital adoption for marginalised communities. In other words, any form of support, access, or learning must be facilitated through strong access to content available in local languages. Bharatavani is an example of such a project, aimed at connecting dispersed communities across India (Choudhary et al., 2023). Many individuals, especially those in rural areas, still face significant barriers to accessing digital services, financial inclusion, and e-governance initiatives due to language barriers.

There are already many applications and tools that are focused on ensuring this gap is not widened and also with an attempt to bridge them. India, as a nation has seen successful AI-driven translation tools and many content initiatives that are localised for these reasons. For example, Jio's AI-powered multilingual voice assistant enables users to gain access to various information and services in multiple Indian languages. The idea here is to ensure that these digital tools become a lot more accessible to non-English speakers which is a big population' and in fact forms a majority percentage in a country like India. IBM's Spoken Web is another initiative to bridge this gap (Chengalur-Smith et al., 2020). Investing in regional language interfaces, speech-to-text tools, and localised e-learning platforms can further ensure inclusive digital participation. AI-driven translation tools and localised content creation are successfully launched in India. To make them scalable requires collaboration. Public–private partnerships undoubtedly play a crucial role in such initiatives. For example, ensuring that linguistic diversity is not a barrier to digital adoption in each of the projects launched till date, there can be a significant collaboration seen in the form of leveraging government initiatives and corporate innovation. That with community-driven efforts is what goes into making them become a widespread reality. In other words, India can build a brilliant ecosystem wherein digital inclusion is not just a possibility but a reality across the nation. It can do so with the help of timely and strategic partnerships and collaborations.

17.6.3 Strengthening Public–Private Partnerships

Technology is a tool for achieving sustainability. Many parts of the world however are not digitally connected or there is no infrastructure developed to connect everyone within the state. Governments along cannot reach the last mile to ensure digital connectivity. Many of the smaller nations are not financially and technologically equipped to ensure everyone is connected digitally. Nations like India also have the additional difficulties emerging from the large number of linguistic groups. Hence, it is observed that there is a need for public participation in improving the digital infrastructure of a nation. However, this is not possible without global support both in terms of technological know-how and financial support. NGOs play a crucial role in connecting the last mile as they are more flexible and have local influence. Thus, in order to successfully reach the last-mile digital connectivity, it is important to foster collaborations between government agencies, private enterprises through their CSR activities and community organisations. Some such initiatives are presented next.

i. The Google's Internet Saathi: In an article on the future of internet and sustainable development, European University Institute and Kulesza (2024) argue how Google's Internet Saathi provides digital literacy to rural women in order to help them access online services. This was their effort to empower the rural women. Here the purpose of the initiative is both to bring digital literacy to the grassroots and to achieve gender empowerment. Internet Saathi helps them access government schemes in their own language.

ii. e-District Services (Government of India): This is another example of how democratisation of digital technologies is used to bring development and essential services like certificates, pensions, and subsidies to the people in their own language. This initiative, started in Himachal Pradesh, makes use of *Lok Mitra Kendras* (Citizen Service Centres) to provide digital services to the people (Rajeshwar & Mahajan, 2020).

iii. Digital India Bhashini (Government of India): This is an AI-based initiative focused on developing digital platforms in local languages. This helps accessibility of online contents and digital services in various Indian languages. This helps create a national digital public platform to make available digital materials for free to the less privileged sections in the society (Gupta et al., 2023).

17.7 Various Digital Governance Initiatives in India to Create Digital Inclusion

The Government of India has introduced a series of tools and digital platforms to create inclusivity, empowerment and development. India has made significant strides in developing digital inclusion technologies to promote sustainable economic growth. These technologies have been designed to address social, economic, and environmental challenges, with a focus on accessibility, affordability, and environmental impact.

i. Digital Payment Systems: Another major milestone in the direction of digital transformation in India has been the introduction of the digital money. Today almost every Indian citizen irrespective of the class, caste, and whether urban or rural uses digital money for business transaction. The platforms such as *Unified Payments Interface (UPI)* and *Bharat Interface for Money (BHIM)* facilitate seamless money transfers, billpayments and other financial services. This has reduced reliance on physical banking infrastructure, and promotes financial inclusion. The widespread use of UPI has reduced barriers to accessing financial services, helping small businesses and individuals, especially in rural areas, participate in the digital economy (Kamble, 2022).

ii. e-Governance and Digital Services (e-District, e-Sign): Various states in India began digitising their registration departments as early as the year 2000. This digital shift has led to increased transparency and improved access to government services (Sharma & Sharma, 2023). It has also contributed significantly to reducing corruption. Furthermore, the introduction of the Goods and Services Tax (GST), a centralised taxation system, has facilitated the seamless movement of goods across states while promoting greater accountability and compliance among business organisations (Deshmukh et al., 2022).

iii. Smart Grids and Renewable Energy Solutions: Since early 2010 India has begun working on a concept called Smart Grid. However, post-Paris agreement this concept received much attention and the government established the National Smart Grid Mission in 2015. Post-2020 there has been acceleration of this process and function'to oversee the establishment of Smart Grid in different states.' It also aims to digitise power sector with the introduction of smart meter and providing EV charging stations connected to these grids. It will help in increasing the production of renewable energy, improving energy efficiency and reducing wastage (Khan et al., 2021).

iv. Digital Agriculture Platforms (eNAM, mKisan): Since 2000 there has been a lot of innovations taking place in agricultural technologies. At a national level the creation of eNAM (National Agricultural Market) facilitate a seamless trade between farmers and buyers across India. The launch of mKisan portal and mobile applications facilitated real-time weather updates, pest management solutions, and expert advice on crop management. Using technologies such as drones and remote sensing, IoT-based irrigation system and soil health monitoring, farmers are gradually able to move to precision farming. Platforms like eNAM and mKisan are designed to connect farmers with markets and provide real-time agricultural advisories and weather information. Under these schemes the government is also promoting climate-friendly agriculture through drought-resistant crops, agroforestry, etc. A lot of research is being carried out to help improve the crop yield and empower farmers (Tiwari 2022). Many private partners are also providing agricultural technologies to create a sustainable agriculture in India. ITC's eChoupal and Reliance's JioKrish are a few good examples.

v. Information and communications technology (ICT) in Education (Digital Infrastructure and Knowledge Sharing [DIKSHA] and Study Webs of Active-Learning for Young Aspiring Minds [SWAYAM]: Digital transformation is also revolutionising the education sector in India. To provide high-quality education to the less privileged and those who are not connected to metropolitan cities the government has launched a number of schemes. Platforms such as DIKSHA and SWAYAM provide high-quality learning materials and certifications to every one in the country. These platforms ensure access, quality and equity in education.

vi. Digital Health Platforms (eSanjeevani and Telemedicine): The Government of India launched the national digital health mission in 2020 with the aim to provide every Indian with a unique health ID that consolidates their health records digitally. In addition, the government has also launched Ayushman Bharat Digital Mission to provide a comprehensive digital health insurance to every Indian. eSanjeevani is another platform crated to help rural population to connect with doctors in the urban centre digitally. Private partnerships such as *Practo, 1mg, Docprime,* and *mfine* enable online consultations with doctors, prescription delivery, and diagnostics, making healthcare more accessible and affordable (Chakraborty et al., 2024).

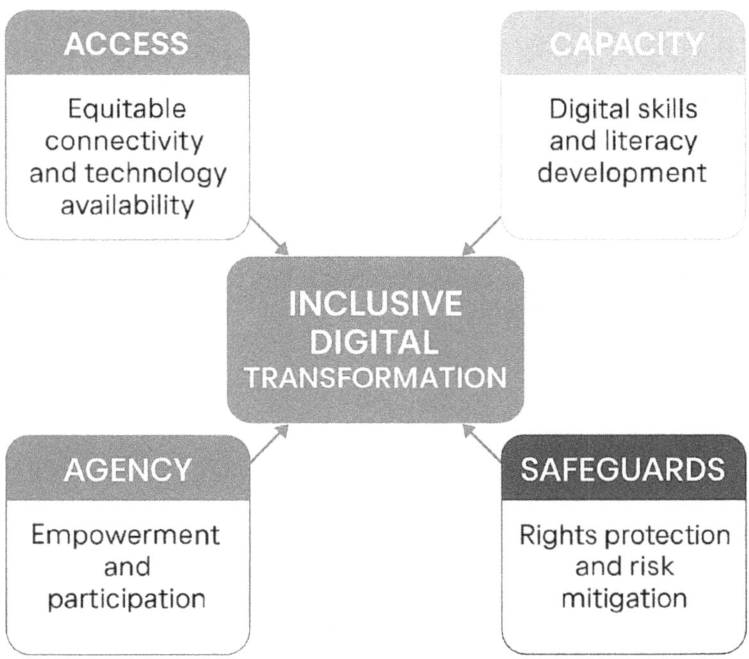

FIGURE 17.1
Visual framework for equitable digital empowerment.

Figure 17.1 provides a systems-based perspective on the key enablers of digital inclusion, including policy, infrastructure, social dynamics and capacity building. Its integrated design reflects the real-world complexity of empowering underrepresented communities and offers a practical foundation for both academic reflection and policy development aimed at advancing inclusive digital transformation.

17.8 Unintended Consequences and Ethical Risks

While digital transformation holds tremendous potential, it also presents significant ethical risks and unintended consequences, especially for underrepresented groups. Automated systems when poorly designed can reinforce existing inequalities through algorithmic discrimination. Examples include facial recognition technologies with higher error rates for dark-skinned individuals and gender biases in AI hiring tools. Data privacy is another major concern. In India, where a comprehensive data protection law has only recently been enacted, digital initiatives often outpace regulatory safeguards. Centralised identity systems like Aadhaar have raised fears of mass surveillance, especially when linked to financial and health records.

Further, the digital divide may be widened by rapid tech deployments that ignore contextual realities such as literacy, language, and infrastructure gaps. For instance, app-based welfare programmes often exclude non-smartphone users. The design of such tools can unintentionally privilege urban, English-speaking, tech-savvy populations. These risks call for inclusive technology design principles, human rights-based regulatory frameworks, and participatory governance models. Policymakers and practitioners must critically assess not only what technology can do but also whom it might leave behind.

17.9 Conclusion

In this chapter we have discussed a few of the initiatives taken by the Government of India towards digitising various services in India. This digitisation helps reduce the rural and urban divide. This also ensures that social and economic differences are reduced and everyone gets connected to a central system. Most of these initiatives are still evolving. In the field of eGovernance India has established some landmark achievements and functions as a benchmark for other nations to emulate. The digital payment portals have become more secure and widespread compared to many developed nations. However, in the area of health, agriculture and education there is a need for more investment and innovations. Integrating waste management and solar energy into India's digital transformation strategy can empower marginalised communities, create economic opportunities and advance sustainability goals. These insights align with India's SDG commitments, ensuring a more inclusive and climate-resilient future. By drawing insights from global best practices and tailoring them towards India's unique challenges, a multi-faceted approach integrating policy innovation, community participation and technological advancement can create a sustainable and inclusive digital future.

Technology holds immense potential to bridge socio-economic divides and empower underrepresented communities.. The alignment of digital initiatives with SDG and climate commitments will further ensure long-term equity and resilience in technological growth.

Based on the comparative and thematic analyses presented in this chapter, several policy recommendations emerge.

1. **Adopt Rights-Based Digital Identity Systems:** Ensure that identity platforms like Aadhaar are voluntary, privacy-protected, and designed with consent-based principles.
2. **Promote Inclusive-by-Design Digital Public Services:** Mandate multilingual, mobile-friendly, accessible interfaces with offline support mechanisms for last-mile users.
3. **Support Community-Led Digital Literacy Models:** Scale up NGO- and panchayat-driven digital education programmes with tailored content for women, rural youth, and marginalised caste groups.
4. **Establish Independent Oversight for Data Governance:** Operationalise an autonomous data protection authority to regulate consent, redress grievances and monitor algorithmic fairness.
5. **Foster Cross-Sectoral Collaboration:** Incentivise partnerships between government, academia, civil society and industry to co-create scalable, context-aware solutions for digital empowerment.

References

Asrani, C. (2021). Spanning the digital divide in India: Barriers to ICT adoption and usage. *Journal of Public Affairs, 22*(4). https://doi.org/10.1002/pa.2598

Awasthi, P., Ganapati, S., & Tai, K. T. (2024). Digital transformation in a large democracy: The case of India. *Asia Pacific Journal of Public Administration, 46*(4), 326–359. https://doi.org/10.1080/23276665.2024.2339874

Bhatia, S., & Dawar, G. (2024). The impact of financial inclusion on social and political empowerment: Mediating role of economic empowerment. *Journal of the Knowledge Economy, 15*(3), 13727–13744.

Bauch, P. (2024, May 28). European Union digital skills gap: Challenges and solutions in an evolving technological landscape. *SSRN*. https://doi.org/10.2139/ssrn.4859156

Bordenkircher, B. A., & Egan, D. (2022). Regulating UAS delivery: What can we learn from Rwanda? *Issues in Aviation Law and Policy, 22*(1), 155–179. https://las.depaul.edu/centers-and-institutes/chaddick-institute-for-metropolitan-development/research-and-publications/Pages/issues-aviation-law-policy.aspx

Carnaby, P. (2008). Creating a digital New Zealand: New Zealand's digital content strategy, opportunities and challenges for the education and research sectors. National Library of New Zealand. https://docs.lib.purdue.edu/cgi/viewcontent.cgi?article=1835&context=iatul

Chakraborty, A., Chawla, M., Pawar, B., Chakraborty, D., & Khanna, K. (2024). Attitude towards eHealth Services: Government initiatives in India. 1–7. 10.1109/ICRITO61523.2024.10522309

Chakrabarty, A. (2023). Feminizing decentralized renewable energy programs: A study of a community renewable energy project from India. *Journal of Asian Energy Studies, 7*, 107–120. https://doi.org/10.24112/jaes.070008

Chang, F., & Das, D. (2020). Smart Nation Singapore: Developing policies for a citizen-oriented smart city initiative. In Debolina Kundu, Remy Sietchiping, Michael Kinyanjui (Eds.), *Developing National Urban Policies* (pp. 425–440). Springer. https://doi.org/10.1007/978-981-15-3738-7_18

Chaudhuri, B., & König, L. (2017). The Aadhaar scheme: A cornerstone of a new citizenship regime in India? *Contemporary South Asia, 26*(2), 127–142. https://doi.org/10.1080/09584935.2017.1369934

Chengalur-Smith, I., Potnis, D., & Mishra, G. (2020). Developing voice-based information sharing services to bridge the information divide in marginalized communities: A study of farmers using IBM's spoken web in rural India. *International Journal of Information Management, 57*, 102283. https://doi.org/10.1016/j.ijinfomgt.2020.102283

Choudhary, N., Premkumar, L. R., Singh, C., Mondal, S., Priya, S., Sudarshan, B., Samy, P. P., & Mohan, S. (2023). Bharatavani project – Reviving linguistic diversity and cultural heritage in India: A case study. In *Proceedings of the 2nd International Workshop on Digital Language Archives (LangArc-2023), ACM/IEEE Joint Conference on Digital Libraries* (pp. 1–3). https://doi.org/10.12794/langarc2114300—

Clark, S., MacLachlan, M., Marshall, K., Morahan, N., Carroll, C., Hand, K., Boyle, N., & O'Sullivan, K. (2022). Including digital connection in the United Nations Sustainable Development Goals: A systems thinking approach for achieving the SDGs. *Sustainability, 14*(3), 1883. https://doi.org/10.3390/su14031883

Collington, R. (2021). Disrupting the welfare state? Digitalisation and the retrenchment of public sector capacity. *New Political Economy, 27*(2), 312–328. https://doi.org/10.1080/13563467.2021.1952559

Das, D., & Kwek, B. (2024). AI and data-driven urbanism: The Singapore experience. *Digital Geography and Society, 7*, 100104. https://doi.org/10.1016/j.diggeo.2024.100104

Deshmukh, A. K., Mohan, A., & Mohan, I. (2022). Goods and Services Tax (GST) implementation in India: A SAP–LAP–Twitter analytic perspective. *Global Journal of Flexible Systems Management, 23*(2), 165–183. https://doi.org/10.1007/s40171-021-00297-3

Dominish, E., Retamal, M., Sharpe, S., Lane, R., Rhamdhani, M., Corder, G., Giurco, D., & Florin, N. (2018). "Slowing" and "Narrowing" the flow of metals for consumer goods: Evaluating opportunities and barriers. *Sustainability, 10*(4), 1096. https://doi.org/10.3390/su10041096

Eubanks, V. (2018). *Automating inequality: How high-tech tools profile, police, and punish the poor*. St. Martin's Press.

European University Institute & Kulesza, J. (2024). Two sides of the same coin?: Future of the internet and sustainable development. European University Institute. https://data.europa.eu/doi/10.2870/4603450

Fisk, R. P., Gallan, A. S., Joubert, A. M., Beekhuyzen, J., Cheung, L., & Russell-Bennett, R. (2022). Healing the digital divide with digital inclusion: Enabling human capabilities. *Journal of Service Research, 26*(4), 542–559. https://doi.org/10.1177/10946705221140148 .

Gahlot, A., & Gahlot, S. (2020). Changing the state of literacy in the Digital Age in India. *EPiC Series in Education Science, 3*, 98–87. https://doi.org/10.29007/qbpr

Gangwal, A., Jain, A., & Mohanta, S. (2019). Blood delivery by drones: A case study on Zipline. *International Journal of Innovative Research in Science, Engineering and Technology, 8*(8), 8760–8765. Retrieved from www.ijirset.com/upload/2019/august/63_Blood.PDF

George, D. (2023). OneWeb: Revolutionizing digital connectivity in India. *Zenodo (CERN European Organization for Nuclear Research)*. https://doi.org/10.5281/zenodo.8264303

Ghauri, P., Fu, X., & Minayora, A. (2022). Digital technology-based entrepreneurial pursuit of the marginalised communities. *Journal of International Management, 28*(2), 100948. https://doi.org/10.1016/j.intman.2022.100948

Gigler, B. S. (2015). *Development as freedom in a digital age: Experiences from the rural poor in Bolivia*. World Bank Publications.

Gritsenko, D. (2023). Advancing UN digital cooperation: Lessons from environmental policy and governance. *World Development, 173*, 106392. https://doi.org/10.1016/j.worlddev.2023.106392

Gupta, S., Gupta, M., & Gupt, S. B. (2023). Analysis of AI-enhanced educational tools developed in India for linguistic minorities and disabled people. Retrieved from www.researchgate.net/publication/377115814_Analysis_of_AI-enhanced_educational_tools_developed_in_India_for_linguistic_minorities_and_disabled_people

Hallpers, A. (2019). "Allt förändras och förändringarna kommer att fortsätta": Om synen på digitalisering och det digitala imperativet wwwbiblioteksfor.cdn.triggerfish.cloud/uploads/2020/05/anna-hallpers.pdf

Holzer, H. J. (2016). *The role of skills and jobs in transforming communities* [Working paper]. Reinventing Our Communities: Transforming Our Economies, Federal Reserve Bank of Philadelphia Biennial Conference. https://penniur.upenn.edu/uploads/media/Holzer_PennIUR-Philly_Fed_working_paper_091416_(1).pdf

Hosseini, Z. (2023). *An integrative technology design model (TPCD) for cultural inclusion of immigrants in Finland*. Retrieved from www.researchgate.net/publication/373072206_An_Integrative_Technology_Design_Model_TPCD_for_Cultural_Inclusion_of_Immigrants_in_Finland

Humphrey, W., Laverie, D., & Muñoz, C. (2020). The use and value of badges: Leveraging salesforce trailhead badges for marketing technology education. *Journal of Marketing Education, 43*(1), 25–42. https://doi.org/10.1177/0273475320912319

Kamble, R. (2022). Impact of UPI technology to maintain sustainability during COVID-19 in Mumbai region. *International Journal of Creative Research Thoughts (IJCRT)*, 10(1). https://ijcrt.org/papers/IJCRTM020010.pdf

Keshari, N. (2024). Exploring the challenges to achieving gender diversity in Swedish IT firms: Perspectives of employers and employees – A qualitative study (Master's thesis, University of Gothenburg). GUPEA. https://gupea.ub.gu.se/bitstream/handle/2077/83145/Neha%20Keshari.pdf

Khan, R., Islam, N., Das, S. K., Muyeen, S. M., Moyeen, S. I., Ali, M. F., Tasneem, Z., Islam, M. R., Saha, D. K., Badal, M. F. R., Ahamed, H., & Techato, K. (2021). Energy Sustainability–Survey on technology and control of microgrid, smart grid and virtual power plant. *IEEE Access, 9*, 104663–104694. https://doi.org/10.1109/access.2021.3099941

Khan, S. (2022). Issues, challenges and opportunities in the digitalization of rural markets. *Human Systems Management, 42*(1), 73–87. https://doi.org/10.3233/hsm-220031

Khanal, S., Zhang, H., & Taeihagh, A. (2024). Building an AI ecosystem in a small nation: Lessons from Singapore's journey to the forefront of AI. *Humanities and Social Sciences Communications, 11*(1), 1–12. https://doi.org/10.1057/s41599-024-03289-7

Kuziemski, M., & Misuraca, G. (2020). AI governance in the public sector: Three tales from the frontiers of automated decision-making in democratic settings. *Telecommunications Policy, 44*(6), 101976. https://doi.org/10.1016/j.telpol.2020.101976

Lacarcel, F. J., & Huete, R. (2023). Digital communication strategies used by private companies, entrepreneurs, and public entities to attract long-stay tourists: a review. *International Entrepreneurship and Management Journal, 19*(2), 691–708. https://doi.org/10.1007/s11365-023-00843-8

León-Duarte, G. A., Castillo, M. M., Cázarez, C. R. C., & Rodriguez, L. a. O. (2024). Digital media competence in the Mexican Interactive generation. Have digital competence programs worked in Mexico? *Revista De Gestão Social E Ambiental, 18*(10), e09030. https://doi.org/10.24857/rgsa.v18n10-230

Liu, C., Saldanha, T., & Mithas, S. (2024). Can digital skills empower disadvantaged castes and women? Evidence from India. *Production and Operations Management, 34*(4), 760–776. https://doi.org/10.1177/10591478241248749

Mbiti, I., & Weil, D. N. (2015). Mobile banking: The impact of M-Pesa in Kenya. In S. Edwards, S. Johnson, & D. N. Weil (Eds.), *African successes, volume III: Modernization and development* (pp. 247–293). National Bureau of Economic Research.

Millan, E. N., Kamau, C. G., & Ibua, M. P. (2023). Effect of mobile banking technology on loan performance of deposit taking savings and credit cooperative organisations in Mombasa County, Kenya. *Universal Journal of Accounting and Finance, 11*(3), 53–62. https://doi.org/10.13189/ujaf.2023.110301

Momo, H. T. (2022). Building Indigenous knowledge: Exploring the pedagogy of Māori knowledge in the digital computing information technology tertiary sector of New Zealand. *Journal of Contemporary Issues in Education, 17*(2), 92–110. https://doi.org/10.20355/jcie29499

Nayak, M., & Tiyadi, J. (2024). Social Welfare and Artificial Intelligence's role: A comprehensive summary of the study. In *Bentham Science Publishers eBooks* (pp. 32–66). https://doi.org/10.2174/9789815256864124010004

Nedungadi, P. P., Menon, R., Gutjahr, G., Erickson, L., & Raman, R. (2018). Towards an inclusive digital literacy framework for digital India. *Education + Training*, *60*(6), 516–528. https://doi.org/10.1108/et-03-2018-0061

Paide, K., Pappel, I., Vainsalu, H., & Draheim, D. (2018). On the systematic exploitation of the Estonian data exchange layer X-Road for strengthening public-private partnerships. In *Proceedings of the 11th International Conference on Theory and Practice of Electronic Governance (pp. 86–92)*. Association for Computing Machinery. https://doi.org/10.1145/3209415.3209441

Pappel, I., Tsap, V., & Draheim, D. (2020). The e-LocGov model for introducing e-governance into local governments: An Estonian case study. *IEEE Transactions on Emerging Topics in Computing*, *9*(2), 597–611. https://doi.org/10.1109/tetc.2019.2910199

Patra, C. K., Mohammed, M. S., & Kandukuri, S. (2024, July). The strategic role of ISRO's polar ground station in space data acquisition and global collaboration. In *2024 IEEE Space, Aerospace and Defence Conference (SPACE)*. IEEE. https://doi.org/10.1109/SPACE63117.2024.10668299

Pereira Junior, A., & Moroni, J. (2022). Economic decision-making systems in critical times: The case of 'Bolsa Familia' in Brazil. *Cognitive Computation and Systems*, *4*(3), 304–315. https://doi.org/10.1049/ccs2.12056

Poudel, N. (2024). The Impact of Big Data-Driven Artificial Intelligence Systems on Public Service Delivery in Cloud-Oriented Government Infrastructures. *Journal of Artificial Intelligence and Machine Learning in Cloud Computing Systems*, *8*(11), 13–25. https://epochjournals.com/index.php/JAIMLCCS/article/view/2024-11-07/5

Puad, N. H. M., Suhaimi, M. A., & Hussin, H. (2022). Implementation of open government data in Asian countries: A review. *Journal of Information Systems and Digital Technologies*, *4*(1), 173–185. https://doi.org/10.31436/jisdt.v4i1.258

Rajam, V., Reddy, A. B., & Banerjee, S. (2021). Explaining caste-based digital divide in India. *Telematics and Informatics*, *65*, 101719. https://doi.org/10.1016/j.tele.2021.101719

Rajeshwar, K., & Mahajan, M. (2020). E-Governance: implementation of e-district application. In Janusz Kacprzyk (Ed.), *Lecture Notes in Networks and Systems* (pp. 691–699). https://doi.org/10.1007/978-981-15-8354-4_69

Rizvi, Y. S., & Nabi, A. (2021). Transformation of learning from real to virtual: an exploratory-descriptive analysis of issues and challenges. *Journal of Research in Innovative Teaching & Learning*, *14*(1), 5–17. https://doi.org/10.1108/jrit-10-2020-0052

Safarov, N. (2023). Administrative literacy in the digital welfare state: Migrants navigating access to public services in Finland. *Social Policy and Society*, *23*(4), 908–921. https://doi.org/10.1017/s1474746422000719

Sambasivan, N., Arnesen, E., Hutchinson, B., Doshi, T., & Prabhakaran, V. (2021). Re-imagining algorithmic fairness in India and beyond. In *Proceedings of the 2021 CHI Conference on Human Factors in Computing Systems* (pp. 1–14). Association for Computing Machinery. https://doi.org/10.1145/3442188.3445896

Sambyal, S. S. (2023). Social innovation for the circular economy: An example of informal waste recycling. In *Innovating for the Circular Economy* (1st ed., pp. 20). CRC Press. https://doi.org/10.1201/9781003201816

Semenzin, S., Rozas, D., & Hassan, S. (2022). Blockchain-based application at a governmental level: disruption or illusion? The case of Estonia. *Policy and Society*, *41*(3), 386–401. https://doi.org/10.1093/polsoc/puac014

Sharma, S. K., & Sharma, B. (2023). People perception towards e-Services in Hilly Area: A case study of e-districts in Himachal Pradesh. *Indian Journal of Public Administration*, *69*(3), 666–677. https://doi.org/10.1177/00195561231176982

Sharma, S., Kar, A. K., Gupta, M. P., Dwivedi, Y. K., & Janssen, M. (2022). Digital citizen empowerment: A systematic literature review of theories and development models. *Information Technology for Development*, *28*(4), 660–687. https://doi.org/10.1080/02681102.2022.2046533

Tiwari, S. P. (2022). Information and communication technology initiatives for knowledge sharing in agriculture. *arXiv (Cornell University)*. https://doi.org/10.48550/arxiv.2202.08649

Tripathi, S., & Rajeev, M. (2023). Gender-inclusive development through fintech: Studying gender-based digital financial inclusion in a cross-country setting. *Sustainability*, *15*(13), 10253. https://doi.org/10.3390/su151310253

Wittmann, F., Roth, F., Hufnagl, M., Lindner, R., Yorulmaz, M., Bratan, T., Arens, M., & Pfaff, M. (2020). First mission analysis report of the scientific support action to the German Hightech Strategy 2025 — Setting the stage: Positioning the missions in the socio-technical system. Fraunhofer Institute for Systems and Innovation Research ISI. https://doi.org/10.13140/RG.2.2.19153.04968

Zainudin, A., Habibullah, A., Arfiani, Y., & Mumpuni, S. D. (2023). digital transformation on aquaculture in Indonesia through eFishery. *IOP Conference Series Earth and Environmental Science*, *1147*(1), 012024. https://doi.org/10.1088/1755-1315/1147/1/012024

18

Technology, Trust, and Transformation: bKash's Role in Inclusive Finance and Women's Empowerment

Arif Perdana and Ridoan Karim

18.1 Introduction

Financial inclusion has emerged as a central objective for policymakers and business leaders seeking to foster economic growth and reduce poverty (Arner et al., 2020; Bharathi et al., 2023). In developing economies, the challenge of integrating underserved and unbanked populations into the formal financial system necessitates innovative solutions that leverage digital technology (Bharathi et al., 2023; Huda, Hossain et al., 2024; Huda, Rimthi et al., 2024). Bangladesh presents a compelling case in which digital financial services played a transformative role in extending financial services to millions of previously excluded citizens. At the heart of this transformation is bKash, the nation's leading mobile financial service provider, which has redefined the landscape of financial inclusion by utilizing technology to overcome traditional banking constraints (Aziz & Naima, 2021; Huda, Hossain, et al., 2024).

Our study addresses a critical gap in the literature on financial technology and development economics by examining how technological interventions such as bKash navigate the complex interplay between digital innovation, financial access, and socioeconomic empowerment. While existing research has documented the broad impact of financial inclusion, less attention has been paid to the specific mechanisms through which mobile financial services create sustainable ecosystems for unbanked populations. Through a conceptual analysis of bKash, we sought to answer three interconnected research questions.

1. How can mobile technology be adapted to diverse literacy levels and infrastructure limitations to enable inclusive financial access?

DOI: 10.1201/9781003591078-23

2. What service design elements are most critical for engaging traditionally unbanked populations?
3. How do improved financial services translate into meaningful socioeconomic change, particularly for women and low-income communities?

bKash emerged in a market with limited traditional banking infrastructure and widespread financial exclusion, especially in rural areas (Aziz & Naima, 2021). Recognizing this gap, bKash leveraged mobile technology to offer accessible financial services, setting the stage for socioeconomic progress in Bangladesh (Khatun et al., 2024). Instead of mimicking conventional banking, bKash redefined financial service delivery through a user-friendly mobile app focused on accessibility and affordability (Hasan, Lowe et al., 2020; Rahman et al., 2017). The company's service model centers on a simple yet robust mobile application that allows users to execute various financial transactions including money transfers, bill payments, and microloans (Aziz & Naima, 2021; Yesmin et al., 2019).

A key to its success is bKash's extensive agent network, which supports digital transactions and builds trust, especially in areas with low digital literacy (Yesmin et al., 2019; Hasan, Lowe et al., 2020). By empowering local entrepreneurs to serve as agents, bKash enhanced its reach and contributed to local economic development, reinforcing the broader goals of financial inclusion. The bKash case offers several insights into the broader discourse on digital financial inclusion.

First, the company's rapid growth demonstrates the viability of mobile financial services in markets traditionally underserved by conventional banking systems. With over 80 million verified users, bKash has succeeded in creating an ecosystem where digital financial services are not only an alternative, but also a preferred method of transactions.[1] This shift has profound implications for the formalization of economic activity in Bangladesh, as increased financial participation leads to more transparent and secure economic interactions. Second, bKash's experience underscores the importance of strategic partnerships in scaling digital financial services. By collaborating with banks, regulatory bodies, and technology partners, bKash has navigated a complex regulatory environment and ensured the security and reliability of its services (Islam et al., 2025). These collaborations are crucial in building user trust, which is a key factor in the adoption of digital financial services. The company's commitment to maintaining high-security standards and transparent operations has played an essential role in mitigating concerns about digital transactions, which can otherwise hinder the adoption of new technologies among risk-averse segments of the population. Furthermore, bKash's case study highlights the broader impact of financial inclusion on socioeconomic development. By providing access to digital financial services, bKash has contributed to economic empowerment, particularly among marginalized groups, such as women and rural populations (S. W. Ahmad & Wongsurawat, 2023; Islam et al., 2025). Access to credit, savings, and payment services has empowered marginalized groups to enhance financial resilience and economic participation while advancing broader goals of poverty reduction and development through technology-driven financial inclusion (Hasan, Lowe et al., 2020; Hasan, Shams et al., 2020; Rahman et al., 2017).

This chapter contributes to theory and practice by developing a conceptual framework for understanding how mobile financial services can be designed and implemented to maximize their social impact. Through an in-depth analysis of bKash's technological infrastructure, inclusion strategies, and socioeconomic outcomes, we derive insights that can guide similar initiatives in other developing economies facing the comparable challenges of financial exclusion.

The rest of the chapter is structured as follows: First, we explore the theoretical foundations that underpin digital financial inclusion, drawing on the Technology Acceptance Model, institutional theory, and the capability approach. Next, we describe the bKash story, its growth, strategic positioning, and impact on Bangladesh's financial landscape. We then analyze how its technological infrastructure and innovations have shaped accessibility and adoption. From there, we assess bKash's role in expanding financial inclusion and its broader socioeconomic effects, particularly on women's empowerment and poverty reduction. Finally, we distill key takeaways for other developing economies and conclude with reflections on future research and policy considerations.

18.2 Theoretical Framework

This study of bKash draws upon multiple theoretical perspectives to analyze how mobile financial services drive inclusion and socioeconomic transformation in developing economies. We integrate three complementary frameworks to examine the multifaceted dimensions of digital financial inclusion: the Technology Acceptance Model (TAM), institutional theory, and capability approach.

18.2.1 Technology Acceptance Model and Its Extensions

The TAM provides a foundation for understanding how users adopt financial technologies in resource-constrained environments (Davis et al., 1989). The TAM posits that perceived usefulness and ease of use determine attitudes toward the adoption of technology. However, for financial inclusion, standard TAM constructs require adaptation to account for the unique barriers faced by unbanked populations. Building on TAM, the Unified Theory of Acceptance and Use of Technology (UTAUT) incorporates additional factors relevant to mobile financial services: social influence, facilitating conditions, and trust (Venkatesh et al., 2003, 2016). For previously unbanked populations, these factors have a heightened significance. We extend this framework by incorporating elements specific to developing economies, including technological self-efficacy among low-literacy users, and the role of human intermediaries in technology adoption.

Chowdhury and Hussain (2022) found that perceived accessibility, security, and cost efficiency strongly influence FinTech adoption in Bangladesh, with perceived awareness acting as a moderator. Similarly, Hasan, Shams et al. (2020) emphasized the moderating role of income levels, where perceived usefulness has a stronger effect on adoption intention among lower-income consumers. The bKash case illustrates how perceived ease of use was achieved through simplified interfaces and agent-assisted transactions, while perceived usefulness was demonstrated through immediate benefits, such as secure remittance transfers (Rahman et al., 2020). Hasan, Lowe et al. (2020) further compared multiple adoption models and found that the Diffusion of Innovations model explained the highest variance in adoption intention, although the TAM and UTAUT remained influential. Their analysis of bKash users highlighted that perceived value positively influenced the adoption of bKash but negatively for Union Information and Service Centre (UISC), suggesting service-specific differences. These findings underscore the need for hybrid models that incorporate economic, social, and control factors in FinTech adoption research. The company's strategic emphasis on both technological and human touchpoints aligns with UTAUT's recognition that facilitating conditions critically influence adoption patterns (Rahman et al., 2020).

These technology acceptance insights provide the foundational lens through which we examine bKash's user-centered design strategies and adoption mechanisms. However, understanding individual-level technology acceptance alone is insufficient to explain how mobile financial services achieve widespread legitimacy and transform entire financial ecosystems. This necessitates a broader institutional perspective to complement the micro-level adoption dynamics.

18.2.2 Institutional Theory and Legitimacy

Institutional theory offers insights into how financial innovations gain legitimacy and transform established practices (Amenta & Ramsey, 2010; Dimaggio & Powell, 1983). For financial inclusion initiatives, legitimacy must be established across multiple regulatory, normative, and cultural-cognitive dimensions (Ehret & Olaniyan, 2023; Hsu et al., 2015). While prior research remains limited to investigating bKash from an institutional perspective, we argue that bKash success is critically influenced by institutional legitimacy.

Prior research, while not explicitly using institutional theory, aligns with these principles. bKash navigated this complex institutional landscape by securing regulatory approval, partnering with established institutions, and developing culturally appropriate service delivery models (Aziz & Naima, 2021; Huda, Hossain et al., 2024; Huda, Rimthi et al., 2024; Yesmin et al., 2019).

The institutional void perspective is particularly relevant, as mobile financial services such as bKash have emerged to fill gaps where traditional financial institutions have failed to serve specific populations. This perspective helps explain why bKash's agent-based model succeeded in addressing technological barriers and institutional gaps in the rural financial infrastructure (Aziz & Naima, 2021; Yesmin et al., 2019). We consider institutional theory to conceptually propose how bKash achieves the legitimate status necessary to overcome resistance to formal financial services among traditionally unbanked populations. The company's strategic partnerships with banks, mobile operators, and international organizations created an institutional foundation that enhanced trust and accelerated adoption.

The institutional legitimacy framework reveals how bKash's strategic positioning within Bangladesh's regulatory and social structures enabled its widespread acceptance. Yet, while technology adoption and institutional legitimacy explain the mechanisms of uptake, they do not fully capture the developmental outcomes and empowerment effects that mobile financial services generate for users. To address this gap, we turn to the capability approach to examine how bKash enhances human agency and expands opportunities for economic participation.

18.2.3 Capability Approach and Inclusive Development

Sen's capability approach provides a valuable lens for analyzing how financial inclusion contributes to human development and agency (Sen, 1993). This framework emphasizes that development should be evaluated in terms of the "capabilities" people have and their freedom to achieve the kinds of lives they value. Financial inclusion expands these capabilities by enhancing economic agencies, particularly marginalized groups. While research applying the capability approach and inclusive development remains limited, some studies have shown how bKash creates economic opportunities for marginalized communities in Bangladesh. Aziz and Naima (2021) argue that, while digital financial inclusion has improved access, its effectiveness is constrained by digital literacy, social networks, and infrastructure gaps. Hazra and Priyo (2021) further emphasize that mobile financial services (MFS) affordances, such as financial accessibility and self-sustainability, empower users by increasing financial autonomy, which is a core tenet of Sen's capability framework . Yesmin et al. (2019) note that bKash specifically targets the bottom of the economic pyramid by leveraging strategic partnerships and regulatory backing to enhance financial participation.

Huda, Rimthi et al. (2024) highlight that FinTech adoption, while progressing, remains uneven due to socioeconomic disparities. For women in Bangladesh, MFS represent more than transactional tools; they enable new forms of economic participation, previously constrained by social norms and limited mobility (S. W. Ahmad & Wongsurawat, 2023). The capability approach helps us analyze how bKash's services expand women's "capability sets" by providing secure savings, independent transaction abilities, and entrepreneurial opportunities. Collectively, these findings suggest that while bKash enhances financial inclusion, addressing structural inequalities such as education, gender gaps, and policy support is crucial for ensuring that digital finance translates into real improvements in well-being and economic agency.

Having established the capability expansion outcomes that mobile financial services can generate, we now synthesize these three theoretical lenses to develop a comprehensive analytical framework for examining bKash's transformative impact on Bangladesh's financial landscape.

These three theoretical perspectives–technology acceptance, institutional legitimacy, and capability expansion–converge in our bKash analysis. We propose an integrated model in which technology adoption (facilitated by perceived usefulness and ease of use) interacts with institutional legitimacy (established through strategic partnerships and regulatory alignment) to expand individual capabilities (manifested as an economic agency and inclusion). This theoretical triangulation provides a comprehensive framework for analyzing how mobile financial services contribute to socioeconomic transformation in developing economies.

18.3 Overview of bKash

bKash is Bangladesh's leading mobile financial service provider, operating under the regulatory oversight of Bangladesh Bank as a subsidiary of BRAC Bank. Founded in 2011 by Kamal and Iqbal Quadir in partnership with the BRAC Bank,[2] bKash was established to address the financial needs of the country's predominantly unbanked population (Islam et al., 2025; Yesmin et al., 2019). At its inception, the service focused on providing basic financial transactions, such as cash-in/cash-out and person-to-person transfers, offering a reliable way for urban workers to send money to their families in rural areas. Over time, bKash expanded its offerings, evolving into a comprehensive mobile wallet that supports salary disbursements, merchant payments, micro-savings, and microloans, while maintaining strict regulatory compliance to ensure financial safety and trust (Azim & Rahman, 2025). Figure 18.1 presents the bKash's key milestones and achievements.

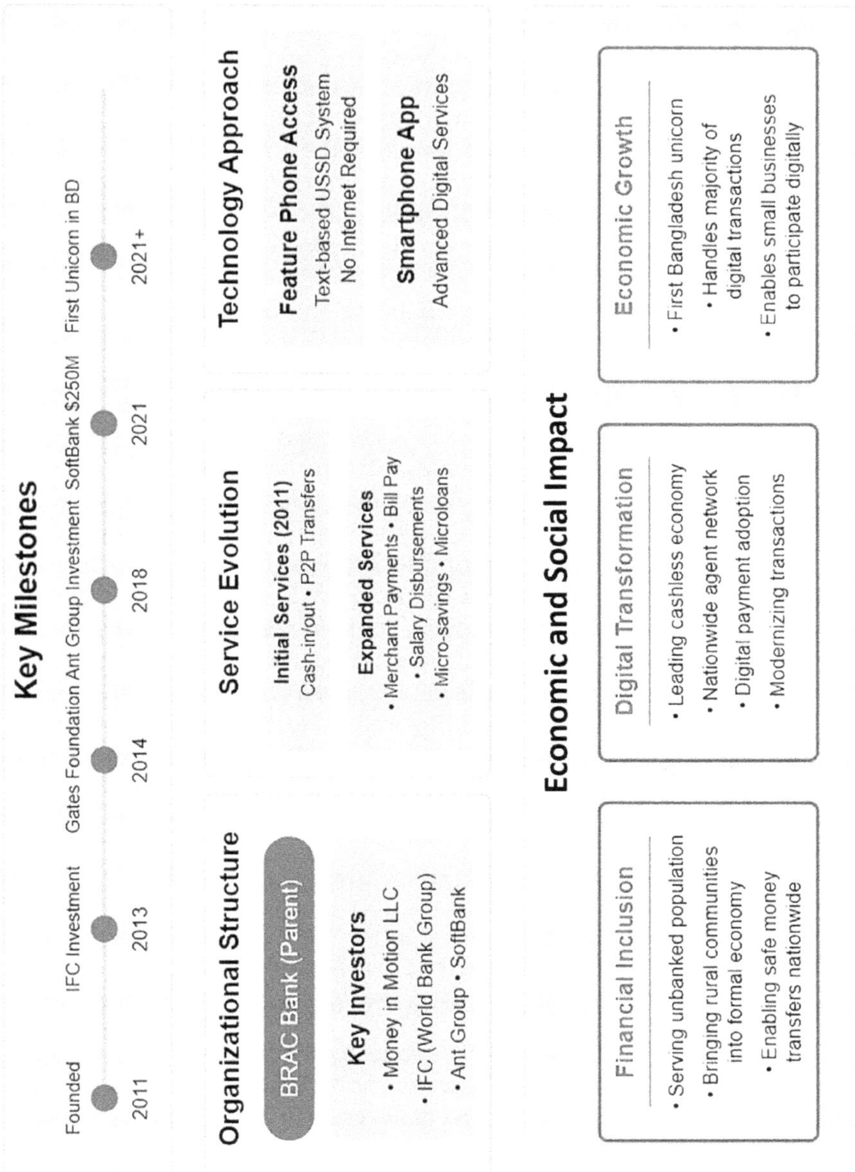

FIGURE 18.1
The bKash journey to financial transformation.

Strategic investments and partnerships with global financial and technology leaders have supported the company's rapid growth (Aziz & Naima, 2021; Yesmin et al., 2019). Initially launched as a joint venture between BRAC Bank and Money in Motion LLC, bKash soon attracted key stakeholders, such as the International Finance Corporation (IFC) of the World Bank Group in 2013 and the Bill & Melinda Gates Foundation in 2014 (International Finance Corporation, 2016). A significant milestone came in 2018 when Ant Financial, now Ant Group, an affiliate of Alibaba, invested in bKash, bringing in technical expertise to enhance its digital infrastructure[3] (Xiao, 2018). In 2021, SoftBank's Vision Fund invested $250 million, making bKash Bangladesh's first unicorn startup, valued at over $1 billion.[4] These partnerships injected capital and cutting-edge mobile payment technologies, enabling bKash to innovate and expand its services.

bKash has played a pivotal role in digitizing the Bangladeshi economy, building an extensive agent and merchant network that enabled millions of previously unbanked individuals to access financial services (Huda, Rimthi et al., 2024; International Finance Corporation, 2016, 2018; Islam et al., 2025).[5] The widespread adoption of bKash has accelerated the shift away from cash-based transactions, enabling seamless digital payments for everyday purchases, salary disbursements, and remittances (Hasan, Lowe, et al., 2020; Hasan, Shams, et al., 2020). bKash's ability to scale and serve diverse user groups was driven by combining digital technologies designed for feature phones and smartphones. One of the most important breakthroughs is the use of a simple text-based system that allows people to access financial services on their phones without requiring an internet connection (Nandhakumar, 2023). By entering a short code on their phones, even those with basic mobile devices can easily send money, pay bills, and relay their mobile balance.[6] This offline system is instrumental in onboarding millions of rural users and ensuring financial accessibility in regions with limited connectivity.

18.4 bKash Technological Infrastructure, Innovation, and Financial Inclusion: Expanding Access to Formal Banking

As smartphone usage expanded in Bangladesh, bKash launched a mobile app in 2018, offering a seamless and user-friendly digital experience in both Bangla and English. The app introduced features such as QR code payments, microloans, and fund transfers, becoming central to Bangladesh's digital economy. Through open APIs, bKash integrated with banks, FinTechs , and e-commerce platforms, allowing interoperability between mobile wallets and bank accounts. Many e-commerce and ride-sharing services now use bKash's payment gateway, embedding mobile money into daily financial activities. To ensure inclusivity, bKash adopted a dual-platform strategy, providing services both through its smartphone app and USSD technology for feature phone users without internet access. By dialing *247#, users can conduct transactions like sending money or paying bills using a simple text-based interface, particularly useful for low-literacy populations in remote areas where internet penetration is limited (Nandhakumar, 2023; Yesmin et al., 2019).

The app interface was designed for simplicity, using intuitive icons and a clean dashboard to reduce digital overwhelm, especially for first-time users. Common functions are prioritized, and the app supports screen readers and large text options for visually impaired users, reflecting bKash's commitment to digital accessibility (Rahman et al., 2017, 2020). Affordability is another core element of bKash's model. Users can open an account for free with only a national ID and photo, and there are no minimum balance requirements. Transaction fees remain low, making microtransactions feasible and appealing to low-income users who typically engage in small-value exchanges.

To expand financial access, bKash uses artificial intelligence to power credit scoring for nano-loans based on transaction data and mobile usage, bypassing the need for formal credit history and traditional collateral (Islam et al., 2025). These microloans have provided vital financial access to those excluded from traditional banking. AI also enhances user engagement through product recommendations and bolsters platform security with real-time fraud detection algorithms. Security is a top priority for bKash. The platform is built on a secure, encrypted Visa technology system and uses PIN protection and two-factor authentication. Fraud prevention is reinforced through real-time monitoring and public blacklisting of agents involved in misconduct (International Finance Corporation, 2016; Di Castri et al., 2015). Expanding its FinTech capabilities, bKash has adopted blockchain for remittances in collaboration with Malaysia's Mobile Money and Ripple, facilitating faster, cheaper, and more transparent cross-border money transfers (Hoque et al., 2024). It has also launched Bangla QR, an interoperable QR-based payment system aligned with Bangladesh Bank's vision for a cashless society (Uddin, 2023), and partners with companies like Huawei to improve rural digital connectivity (Aziz & Naima, 2021; Islam et al., 2025).

A vast nationwide agent network remains crucial to bKash's accessibility mission. These agents serve as on-the-ground facilitators, helping customers convert cash to digital money, open accounts, and learn how to use mobile financial services, effectively bridging the digital divide (Yesmin et al., 2019). This hybrid model, combining tech with human support, ensures even the most marginalized can access financial services. Education and outreach initiatives further support financial inclusion. Through community programs, NGO partnerships, and instructional campaigns, bKash enhances user awareness of financial literacy, security, and digital finance (International Finance Corporation, 2016, 2018). The impact of these strategies is evident: women, rural farmers, and low-income earners who were historically excluded from formal finance now actively use digital financial tools (S. W. Ahmad & Wongsurawat, 2023; Islam et al., 2025). By integrating low-tech solutions like Unstructured Supplementary Service Data (USSD) with high-tech innovations like AI and blockchain, bKash has developed a scalable, inclusive ecosystem that addresses real-world accessibility challenges. As Bangladesh advances toward a digital economy, bKash offers a model for other developing nations seeking inclusive FinTech solutions. Its emphasis on accessibility, innovation, and user-centered design proves that financial technology can be both transformative and equitable.

Nevertheless, financial inclusion has long been a challenge in Bangladesh, especially for rural and low-income populations with limited access to formal banking. The introduction of MFS has helped bridge this gap, with bKash emerging as a leading force in driving financial inclusion by offering secure, affordable, and accessible digital transactions. bKash's wide agent network across all districts has enabled people in remote areas to access financial services without relying on physical bank branches. A study shows 87.3% of farmers use digital financial platforms, with bKash being the most popular (Prodhan et al., 2024). This agent-based model, combined with a user-friendly mobile interface, allows users to deposit, withdraw, and transfer money efficiently. Holding 39.9% of the MFS market share, bKash outpaces competitors like Nagad and Rocket (Huda, Hossain et al., 2024). Despite recent financial losses, bKash continues to invest in technological upgrades to meet growing demand and expand financial access.

Beyond convenience, bKash has reshaped the banking landscape, offering alternatives to traditional branches. Around 88% of rural respondents now use mobile banking compared to fewer with conventional accounts (Khatun et al., 2024), highlighting bKash's role in bringing underserved groups into the formal financial system. bKash also introduced innovative services such as visa card payments and merchant voice alerts, further expanding its reach (Huda, Rimthi et al., 2024). By supporting both smartphone and basic phone users through USSD technology, bKash ensures accessibility for those with limited digital literacy (Nandhakumar, 2023; Yesmin et al., 2019). Low fees and flexible options have empowered entrepreneurs, housewives, and marginalized groups, contributing to broader economic inclusion. Offering 24/7 banking access, bKash removes time and location constraints common in traditional banking. By 2016, it had over 21.2 million users, representing 12.5% of the population, a figure that has since grown (Hasan, Lowe et al., 2020). According to Karmaker et al. (2025), bKash's seamless digital experience and strong merchant network enhance consumer satisfaction and foster digital financial habits. Its inclusive model, supported by agents across the country, ensures even the digitally unskilled are not left behind (Yesmin et al., 2019). These agents are critical for facilitating transactions, assisting users, and bridging the digital divide for those unfamiliar with mobile financial services. By integrating digital finance into daily life, bKash has created a more inclusive economy in which individuals from all backgrounds can participate.

bKash redefined financial inclusion in Bangladesh based on accessibility, affordability, and innovation. It has provided millions with a safe, reliable, and efficient way to manage their finances and reduce their dependency on cash transactions. This study's findings underscore bKash's role in transforming Bangladesh's financial landscape by making banking services available to those who need them the most. Continued investment in digital infrastructure and regulatory support is crucial in ensuring that mobile financial services remain sustainable and inclusive.

18.5 bKash, Women's Empowerment and Poverty Reduction: Socioeconomic Impacts

While financial access focuses on technical means of inclusion, bKash has generated profound socioeconomic impacts, particularly in women's empowerment and poverty reduction (S. W. Ahmad & Wongsurawat, 2023; International Finance Corporation, 2016, 2018; Islam et al., 2025). These outcomes represent the human dimensions of financial innovation, showing how technological solutions translate into meaningful social change.

A critical aspect of bKash's impact is women's empowerment, which has historically faced substantial barriers to banking access due to social and mobility constraints. By 2021, 43% of Bangladeshi women have a financial account, with mobile money playing a crucial role in closing the gender gap. Women's mobile money usage reached 20.3%, and rural women significantly contributed to this growth, benefiting from agent banking and digital financial services expansion (Alliance for Financial Inclusion, 2023). This suggests that mobile money reached women in villages who might never have access to a formal bank account. By giving women direct access to financial tools, bKash has increased its control over household finances, allowing them to receive stipends, remittances, and business payments without male intermediaries (Roy et al., 2024).

Mobile phone access plays a crucial role in empowering Bangladeshi women by enhancing their decision-making power, expanding their access to information, and fostering social connections. While its impact varies, even among housewives and women in male-headed households, mobile access remains a valuable tool for promoting financial and social empowerment (Manan & Farhana, 2023; Nandi & Duvander, 2025). The ability to save securely manage income and make independent purchases has shifted the dynamics of financial agencies in rural households. The Coronavirus disease

2019 (COVID-19) pandemic further underscores the importance of digital financial services for women (Alliance for Financial Inclusion, 2023). Women entrepreneurs leveraged bKash to sustain their businesses during lockdowns, receive payments via mobile transactions, and expand their online customer base.[7] This success story is emblematic of how digital finance can enable women to start and scale businesses without requiring a traditional banking infrastructure. Similarly, women-led micro-businesses, particularly in the cottage industry, have benefited from the ability to collect digital payments and ensure business continuity, even during economic disruptions.

Remittances, a crucial lifeline for many Bangladeshi households, have become more accessible and secure through bKash (Manan & Farhana, 2023). Women, often recipients of funds sent by migrant workers, now have greater control over financial decisions due to direct access to digital payments (Manan & Farhana, 2023). This shift has empowered rural women to allocate resources more effectively to household expenses, education, or small-scale investments. Despite these advancements, many women still require assistance in operating digital accounts and cultural norms limit full financial autonomy (Nandi & Duvander, 2025). Addressing these issues requires ongoing digital literacy efforts and targeted interventions to encourage greater female participation in mobile finance.

Beyond individual empowerment, bKash significantly reduced poverty by improving the efficiency of domestic remittances and financial transactions. Before mobile money, sending funds was slow, expensive, and risky (Manan & Farhana, 2023). Now, a garment worker in Dhaka can instantly transfer a portion of her wages to her village, which her family can access securely through a local agent. This system ensures that money reaches recipients on time, reduces reliance on informal lending, and prevents financial vulnerabilities during emergencies.

Prior studies have highlighted the correlation between mobile money usage and poverty alleviation (Djahini-Afawoubo et al., 2023; Senou & Houensou, 2024). Studies have shown that reliable and low-cost financial transactions enable families to manage financial shocks better, leading to improved long-term economic stability. In Kenya, mobile money users experienced fewer declines in consumption during economic crises, and similar trends were observed in Bangladesh (A. H. Ahmad et al., 2020; Bera et al., 2023). The ability to send and receive money effortlessly has made it easier for rural families to invest in health, education, and small enterprises, thus fostering economic growth.

The effectiveness of social safety nets was also improved by bKash. The government now disburses wages for programs like the Employment Generation Programme for the Poorest directly into beneficiaries' bKash accounts.[8] This method has streamlined payments for ultra-poor rural laborers, ensuring funds reach the intended recipients without leakages or delays. Other government-to-person payments, including education stipends and allowances for the elderly, are increasingly channeled through bKash. These digital transfers enhance the financial security of recipients and encourage greater adoption of financial services among previously unbanked populations.

The broader economic impact of bKash is also evident in job creation (Mahmud, 2024). The company's agent-based model has generated employment opportunities, particularly for microentrepreneurs who operate as bKash agents. These agents earn commissions by providing financial services to their communities, creating additional revenue streams, and fostering local economic development. In many cases, female agents have emerged that contribute to women's economic participation. Rahman et al. (2017) found that microentrepreneurs using bKash experienced a 20% increase in income, with 14.2% of respondents reporting financial gains after becoming bKash agents. This has created a ripple effect, with more individuals engaging in digital transactions and fostering economic growth.

Government policies have played a crucial role in enabling bKash expansion and, in turn, bKash has influenced financial inclusion strategies. Bangladesh Bank's progressive regulations allowed mobile financial services to scale rapidly, and during the COVID-19 crisis, the government incentivized garment factories to pay workers digitally through bKash (Khatun et al., 2021). These moves accelerated financial inclusion among women in the formal labor force, particularly in the garment sector, where millions of women received salaries in digital accounts for the first time. The impact of such policies is lasting, as digital wage payments continue to grow, strengthening women's financial literacy and inclusion. However, the dominance of bKash in the market raises new regulatory considerations, including ensuring fair competition and consumer protection. While the rise of competitors, such as Nagad, introduces diversity into the mobile financial sector, bKash remains the most trusted and widely used service. Figure 18.2 illustrates how the theoretical framework aligns with bKash's role in advancing financial inclusion, driving socioeconomic development, and empowering women. It offers a blueprint for understanding how mobile financial services can bridge gaps in underserved markets. This model may provide insights for policymakers and industry leaders looking to replicate bKash's success in other developing economies, highlighting key strategies that can be adapted to different contexts.

18.6 Lessons from bKash: Insights into Developing Countries

bKash's success in Bangladesh provides critical insights into how mobile financial services can drive financial inclusion and economic empowerment. By leveraging mobile technology, a robust agent network, and strategic partnerships, bKash redefined financial access in a country where traditional banking infrastructure struggled to reach the unbanked. Its model not only

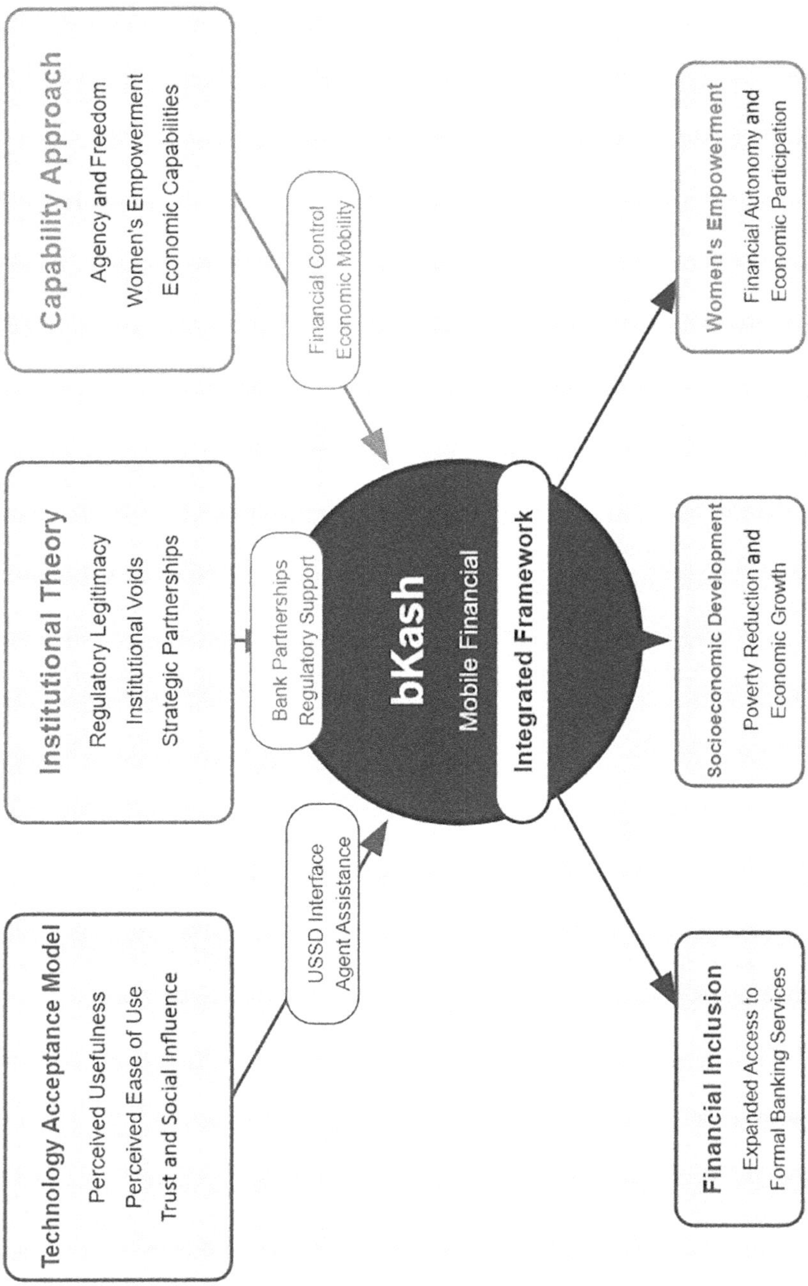

FIGURE 18.2
Theoretical framework mapping bKash's impact on financial inclusion, socioeconomic development, and women's empowerment.

highlights the power of digital finance but also underscores the importance of contextual factors, including regulatory support, telecom infrastructure, and user trust (Huda, Rimthi et al., 2024; Nandhakumar, 2023; Yesmin et al., 2019).

A key takeaway from bKash's growth is the strategic use of mobile technology to reach the underserved population. Traditional banks often face high costs in expanding to remote areas, but mobile penetration in many developing economies has outpaced the banking infrastructure. Using USSD technology, bKash enabled financial transactions even on basic feature phones, eliminating the need for Internet connectivity and ensuring access to marginalized communities (Nandhakumar, 2023). However, the replicability of this model depends on the local conditions. Bangladesh's dense population and relatively strong telecom infrastructure made nationwide agent network expansion feasible, whereas in countries with dispersed populations or unreliable mobile networks, implementing a similar approach could be more challenging.

The agent-based model was central to bKash's ability to build trust and expand its adoption. Agents serve as local financial intermediaries by providing cash-in and cash-out services, accounting registration, and transaction support (Aziz & Naima, 2021; Yesmin et al., 2019). The human touchpoint proved crucial in onboarding first-time users unfamiliar with digital finance, offering a level of guidance and reassurance that technology alone cannot provide. However, ensuring service quality across a vast agent network remains a challenge. Cases of unauthorized fees, fraud, and inconsistent customer support demonstrate the risks of decentralized agent management. In countries with weaker regulatory oversight, these challenges could be even more pronounced, making agent training and monitoring essential for sustaining user trust.

Affordability plays a major role in the widespread adoption of bKash. The removal of account maintenance fees and low transaction costs made digital finance accessible to low-income users, allowing them to engage in microtransactions without an excessive financial burden (Hasan, Shams et al., 2020; Rahman et al., 2017). This pricing model was designed to accommodate the economic realities of Bangladesh's working class, ensuring that even those earning daily wages can participate in digital finance. However, affordability must be balanced by financial sustainability. bKash operated at a loss for several years, relying on external investment to scale. Without venture capital funding, its pricing strategy might have been less inclusive, potentially limiting its impact. The tension between accessibility and profitability is a key challenge for FinTech providers in other markets where external funding may not be readily available.

Strategic partnerships play a crucial role in accelerating bKash growth. Collaborations with global institutions, such as the Ant Group, SoftBank, and the Bill & Melinda Gates Foundation, brought capital, technical expertise, and infrastructure improvements that strengthened bKash's capabilities

(International Finance Corporation, 2016, 2018; Xiao, 2018). These partnerships enabled the company to scale rapidly, enhance its cybersecurity, and introduce new financial products. However, the regulatory environment in each country determines the feasibility of such collaboration. Some nations impose restrictions on foreign FinTech investments, particularly from Chinese firms, while others lack the regulatory clarity needed to attract global investments. Policymakers seeking to replicate bKash's success must ensure a regulatory framework that fosters public–private collaboration while maintaining financial stability and data security.

The most significant contribution of bKash to financial inclusion has been its impact on women's empowerment (Alliance for Financial Inclusion, 2023; Roy et al., 2024). Historically, many women in Bangladesh have faced barriers to banking access owing to mobility constraints and social norms. Mobile money provides a solution, allowing them to receive payments, manage savings, and conduct transactions independently. By offering financial privacy and direct access to funds, bKash increased women's control over household finances, and enabled entrepreneurship. However, financial access by itself does not guarantee financial empowerment. Many women still rely on male family members for assistance with digital transactions, and low financial literacy remains a barrier to full participation. Addressing these challenges requires targeted financial education programs and the expansion of female-led agent networks to ensure that mobile finance truly serves as an enabler for gender inclusion.

Government support is another decisive factor in the success of the bKash. Bangladesh Bank's progressive policies encouraged MFS while ensuring consumer protection. Government-to-person (G2P) payments, such as digital wage disbursements and social benefits, further drive adoption by making digital transactions an integral part of daily life. In other markets, regulatory environments can enable or stifle FinTech growth. Some governments impose restrictive policies that slow innovation, whereas others lack sufficient oversight, leading to consumer protection concerns. Striking the right balance between regulation and market freedom is crucial to fostering financial inclusion.

Beyond individual transactions, bKash's success highlights the importance of integrating digital finance into broader economic ecosystems. The company's expansion into e-commerce, transportation, and utility payments created a seamless digital economy in which mobile money became more than a banking alternative (Karmaker et al., 2025; Khatun et al., 2021). This model suggests that financial inclusion efforts should not stop providing transaction services but should evolve into comprehensive financial ecosystems that include credit, insurance, and investment opportunities. However, many developing countries lack the digital infrastructure necessary for such an integration. Policymakers and private sector players must collaborate to incentivize digital transactions, develop interoperability standards, and create API-driven ecosystems that connect mobile money platforms with other financial services.

As mobile financial services expand, so do cybersecurity threats. bKash has encountered growing fraud and social engineering scams, largely due to users' limited digital literacy. While tools like AI-based fraud detection and biometrics offer protection, user education remains a critical gap. Enhancing financial literacy, voice-assisted transactions, and localized support can help mitigate these risks. bKash's near-monopoly enabled rapid growth but raised concerns about competition, pricing, and systemic risks. Encouraging interoperability and using regulatory sandboxes to test innovations can promote a healthier, more inclusive financial ecosystem.

Access barriers persist in remote areas due to weak network coverage and low smartphone penetration. Expanding digital infrastructure through public–private partnerships is essential to close this gap and support inclusive growth. Though bKash offers a strong example, its model is not universally applicable. Strategies must be tailored to each country's unique economic, cultural, and regulatory environment. In places with low digital literacy, hybrid models that integrate mobile and traditional banking may be more effective.

Table 18.1 outlines bKash's key success factors, current challenges, the lessons it offers, and the specific contextual conditions that shaped its growth in Bangladesh, providing a useful reference for adapting similar models in other developing economies..

Figure 18.3 illustrates how bKash can drive meaningful financial inclusion in developing economies based on Bangladesh's bKash success story. This figure also reflects on how we address our three research questions using bKash case. This three-pillar framework connects technological adaptation, service design, and socioeconomic impact, addressing the critical challenge of bringing financial services to previously excluded populations.

The first pillar demonstrates how technology must be adapted for diverse contexts. bKash's dual-platform approach combines USSD functionality for basic phones with smartphone applications, ensuring accessibility regardless of device ownership. Intuitive interfaces accommodate varying literacy levels, while advanced technologies like AI-driven credit scoring create opportunities previously unavailable through traditional banking.

The second pillar reveals that technology alone is insufficient, and human touchpoints remain essential. bKash's extensive agent network provides critical in-person support for first-time users unfamiliar with digital finance. The affordability model eliminates traditional banking barriers through zero minimum balances and low transaction fees, while ecosystem integration embeds financial services into daily activities.

The third pillar showcases the tangible socioeconomic changes that well-designed mobile financial services generate. For women, bKash provides

TABLE 18.1

Key Success Factors, Challenges, and Lessons from bKash in the Context of Bangladesh

Broad Category	Key Factor	Challenges	Lessons for Other Countries	Bangladesh-Specific Context
Technology and Infrastructure	Mobile technology	Network reliability, infrastructure gaps	Use existing mobile networks to bridge banking gaps, but adapt to local infrastructure conditions	High mobile penetration (95% by 2018), well-established telecom infrastructure
	Cybersecurity and digital literacy	Low digital literacy, fraud risks	Education campaigns and advanced security measures are essential for trust in digital financial services	Social engineering attacks increased as bKash adoption grew
Financial Model and Accessibility	Affordability	Balancing financial inclusion with profitability	Tiered pricing models can ensure sustainability while keeping services accessible	Strong investor backing allowed bKash to operate at a loss initially
	Remittances	Cross-border transaction costs and regulations	Collaboration with international FinTech firms can facilitate low-cost remittances	Large diaspora (7.5 million Bangladeshis abroad) created strong incentives for remittance innovation
Market and Business Model	Agent-based model	Service inconsistencies, fraud risks, regulatory oversight	Agent networks build trust but require strong oversight and consumer protection measures	High population density (1,265 people/km^2) made agent network easier to scale
	Market competition	Risk of overreliance on a single provider	Interoperability and competition ensure long-term market resilience and consumer protection	bKash controlled over 80% of the market, accelerating adoption but creating systemic risks
Strategic Partnerships and Policies	Strategic partnerships	Regulatory barriers, geopolitical concerns	Cross-sector partnerships drive innovation but must align with local political and economic conditions	Bangladesh attracted both Western and Chinese investment with minimal restrictions
	Government policies	Regulatory risk, financial stability concerns	Regulatory sandboxes and digital ID systems can create an enabling environment for mobile finance	Bangladesh Bank allowed flexible mobile financial service regulations
Social and Cultural Factors	Women's financial inclusion	Cultural resistance in some countries	Preexisting gender participation influences impact; tailored financial literacy programs are crucial	Microfinance (Grameen Bank) and garment industry had already normalized female financial participation
Technology and Infrastructure	Infrastructure gaps	Rural access issues, electricity shortages	Public–private partnerships can fund connectivity projects for financial inclusion	High urbanization and telecom coverage reduced these challenges compared to other countries

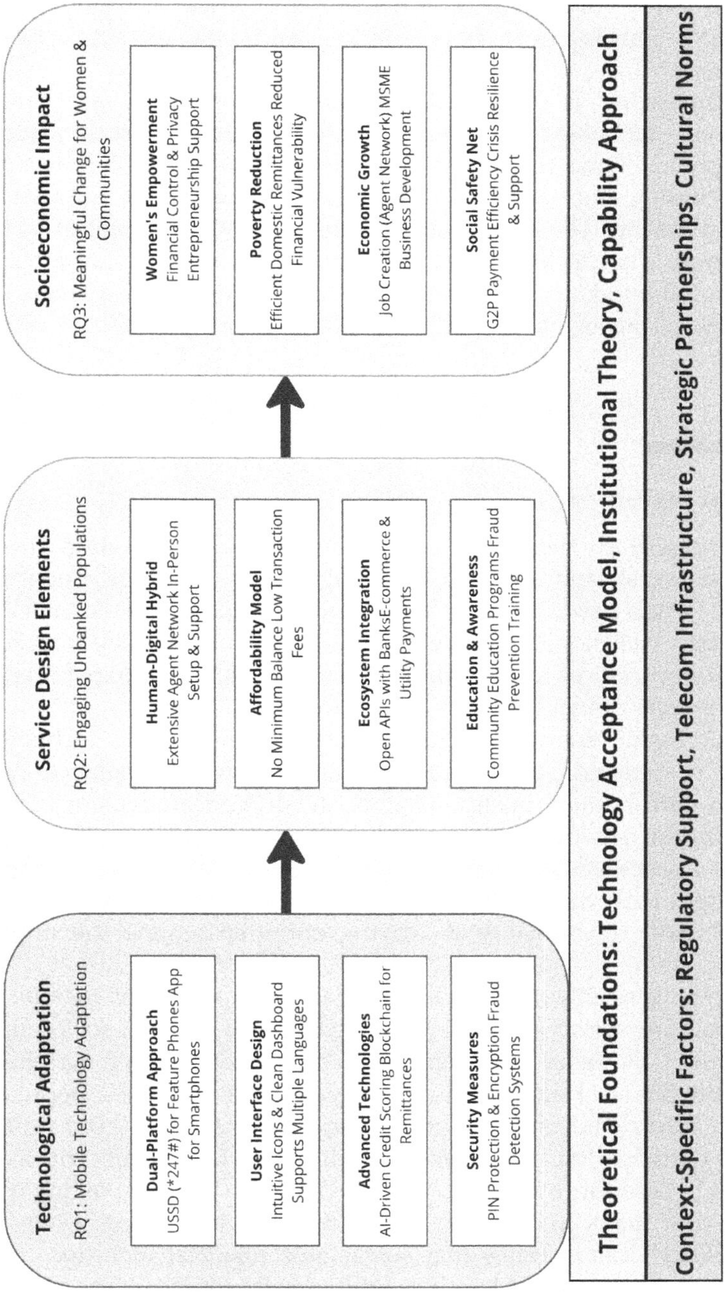

FIGURE 18.3
Lessons from bKash's three-pillar approach.

financial control, privacy, and entrepreneurial opportunities previously constrained by social norms. Efficient domestic remittances reduce financial vulnerability for low-income households, while the agent network itself creates employment opportunities and enables small business development.

This framework is anchored in three complementary theoretical perspectives – Technology Acceptance Model, institutional theory, and capability approach – and recognizes that success depends on context-specific factors including regulatory support, telecommunications infrastructure, and cultural norms. The bKash model demonstrates that financial inclusion requires more than technological solutions; it demands a comprehensive ecosystem that builds trust, addresses practical barriers, and delivers meaningful economic agency to previously excluded populations.

18.7 Conclusion

The bKash case study demonstrates how technological innovation can transform the financial landscapes in developing economies when adapted to local contexts and needs. bKash offers valuable insights into the intersection of technology, inclusion, and development through its journey from mobile money transfer services to a comprehensive financial ecosystem. Several key conclusions were drawn from this analysis.

First, successful financial inclusion requires more than technological solutions; it demands a sociotechnical approach that balances digital innovation with human touchpoints. bKash's hybrid model, combining an extensive agent network with digital platforms, creates a bridge between traditional cash-based societies and digital financial systems. This approach acknowledges that trust, accessibility, and user experience are as important as technological functionality in driving adoption among the unbanked population.

Second, the case illustrates that financial inclusion is not merely about access to banking services, but serves as a gateway to broader socioeconomic empowerment. Evidence from Bangladesh suggests that when marginalized groups gain financial agency, particularly women and rural populations, the impact extends beyond individual transactions to household resilience, economic participation, and poverty reduction. The significant increase in women's account ownership and economic decision-making power highlights how financial inclusion contributes to gender equality goals.

Third, bKash demonstrates that sustainable financial inclusion requires an ecosystem approach that involves multiple stakeholders. The company's partnerships with banks, telecom providers, regulatory bodies, and international organizations created the necessary infrastructure and regulatory environment for growth. This multi-stakeholder model suggests that financial inclusion initiatives should be conceptualized as collaborative endeavors rather than as isolated technological interventions.

From a theoretical perspective, the bKash case advances our understanding of how digital platforms can be designed to overcome both the physical and socioeconomic barriers to inclusion. It challenges conventional banking paradigms by showing that user-centric, mobile-first approaches can serve populations that traditional banking models have failed to reach more effectively. Several research directions have emerged from this case study. Further investigation is needed into the long-term socioeconomic impacts of mobile financial services, evolution of regulatory frameworks that balance innovation with consumer protection, and the role of digital financial literacy in sustaining inclusion. As digital financial services continue to evolve globally, the lessons learned from bKash provide a valuable blueprint for addressing the persistent challenges of financial exclusion in developing economies.

Notes

1 Leading mobile financial services provider in Bangladesh, founded in 2011, backed by BRAC Bank, IFC, Gates Foundation, Ant International, and SoftBank. www.bkash.com/en/about
2 Full-service commercial bank in Bangladesh offering retail, SME, corporate, and digital banking services. www.bracbank.com/en
3 Case study on bKash's role in financial inclusion through agent networks, regulatory compliance, and low-cost services. www.ifc.org/content/dam/ifc/doc/mgrt/bkash-final-low-res.pdf
4 SoftBank Vision Fund II invested ~$250M in bKash, raising its valuation to $2B. www.tbsnews.net/economy/softbank-investment-raise-bkashs-valuation-2bn-329299
5 Leading mobile financial services provider in Bangladesh, founded in 2011, backed by BRAC Bank, IFC, Gates Foundation, Ant International, and SoftBank. www.bkash.com/en/about
6 Allows money transfers to people without a bKash account. www.bkash.com/en/products-services/send-money-to-non-bkash-user
7 Highlights bKash's initiatives to promote women's participation in digital finance. https://businesspostbd.com/governance/bkashs-way-to-empower-women-2023-03-09
8 bKash used to distribute wages under Bangladesh's EGPP project. www.bkash.com/en/blog/bkash-will-disburse-wages-to-workers-under-govt-egpp-project

References

Ahmad, A. H., Green, C., & Jiang, F. (2020). Mobile money, financial inclusion and development: A review with reference to African experience. *Journal of Economic Surveys, 34*(4), 753–792. https://doi.org/10.1111/joes.12372

Ahmad, S. W., & Wongsurawat, W. (2023). Mobile financial services and household welfare in a developing economy: Boon and bane. *Journal of Science and Technology Policy Management, 14*(6), 1–20. https://doi.org/10.1108/JSTPM-03-2022-0046

Alliance for Financial Inclusion. (2023). *Women's Financial Inclusion, Digital Financial Services, and COVID-19 Policy Response: Case of Bangladesh*. Alliance for Financial Inclusion.

Amenta, E., & Ramsey, K. M. (2010). Institutional theory. In K. T. Leicht & J. C. Jenkins (Eds.), *Handbook of Politics* (pp. 15–39). Springer New York. https://doi.org/10.1007/978-0-387-68930-2_2

Arner, D. W., Buckley, R. P., Zetzsche, D. A., & Veidt, R. (2020). Sustainability, FinTech and financial inclusion. *European Business Organization Law Review, 21*(1), 7–35. https://doi.org/10.1007/s40804-020-00183-y

Azim, M. I., & Rahman, S. (2025). Digital financial inclusion: A lifeline for sustainable development goals—lessons from Bangladesh through crisis and beyond. In R. Arora & T. Sarker (Eds.), *Financing of Sustainable Development Goals (SDGs)* (pp. 193–216). Springer Nature Switzerland. https://doi.org/10.1007/978-3-031-80478-6_9

Aziz, A., & Naima, U. (2021). Rethinking digital financial inclusion: Evidence from Bangladesh. *Technology in Society, 64*, 101509. https://doi.org/10.1016/j.techsoc.2020.101509

Bera, S., Yao, Y., Palit, A., & Rahut, D. (2023). *Digital Transformation for Inclusive and Sustainable Development in Asia*. Asian Development Bank Institute.

Bharathi, S. V., Perdana, A., & Kulkarni, M. S. (2023). Exploring the synergy between financial technologies and financial inclusion: What we know and where we should be heading? *Pacific Asia Journal of the Association for Information Systems, 15*, 87–126. https://doi.org/10.17705/1pais.15104

Chowdhury, N. H., & Hussain, N. (2022). Using technology acceptance model for acceptance of FinTech in Bangladesh. *International Journal of Internet Technology and Secured Transactions, 12*(3), 250. https://doi.org/10.1504/IJITST.2022.122104

Davis, F. D., Bagozzi, R. P., & Warshaw, P. R. (1989). User acceptance of computer technology: A comparison of two theoretical models. *Management Science, 35*(8), 982–1003.

Di Castri, S., Grossman, J., & Sihin, R. (2015). Proportional risk-based AML/CFT regimes for mobile money. A framework for assessing risk factors and mitigation measures. Available at SSRN: https://ssrn.com/abstract=2928398

Dimaggio, P. J., & Powell, W. W. (1983). The iron cage revisited: institutional isomorphism and collective rationality in organizational fields. *American Sociological Review, 48*(2), 147–160.

Djahini-Afawoubo, D. M., Couchoro, M. K., & Atchi, F. K. (2023). Does mobile money contribute to reducing multidimensional poverty? *Technological Forecasting and Social Change, 187*, 122194. https://doi.org/10.1016/j.techfore.2022.122194

Ehret, M., & Olaniyan, R. (2023). Banking the unbanked. Constitutive rules and the institutionalization of mobile payment systems in Nigeria. *Journal of Business Research, 163*, 113845. https://doi.org/10.1016/j.jbusres.2023.113845

Hasan, M. R., Lowe, B., & Petrovici, D. (2020). Consumer adoption of pro-poor service innovations in subsistence marketplaces. *Journal of Business Research, 121*, 461–475. https://doi.org/10.1016/j.jbusres.2018.12.075

Hasan, M. R., Shams, S. M. R., Rahman, M., & Haque, S. E. (2020). Analysing pro-poor innovation acceptance by income segments. *Management Decision, 58*(8), 1663–1674. https://doi.org/10.1108/MD-09-2019-1301

Hazra, U., & Priyo, A. K. K. (2021). Mobile financial services in Bangladesh: Understanding the affordances. *The Electronic Journal of Information Systems in Developing Countries, 87*(3), e12166. https://doi.org/10.1002/isd2.12166

Hoque, M. M., Kummer, T.-F., & Yigitbasioglu, O. (2024). How can blockchain-based lending platforms support microcredit activities in developing countries? An empirical validation of its opportunities and challenges. *Technological Forecasting and Social Change, 203*, 123400. https://doi.org/10.1016/j.techfore.2024.123400

Hsu, C., Lin, Y.-T., & Wang, T. (2015). A legitimacy challenge of a cross-cultural interorganizational information system. *European Journal of Information Systems, 24*(3), 278–294. https://doi.org/10.1057/ejis.2014.33

Huda, S. S. M. S., Hossain, M. F., Rahman, S. M., Nazmul, S. B., & Hasan, R. (2024). An evaluation of FinTech in Bangladesh. *Journal of Information Technology Teaching Cases*, 20438869241236472. https://doi.org/10.1177/20438869241236472

Huda, S. S. M. S., Rimthi, R. R., Islam, T., & Mowla, S. M. (2024). Adoption of cashless economy in Bangladesh. *Journal of Information Technology Teaching Cases*, 20438869241279586. https://doi.org/10.1177/20438869241279586

International Finance Corporation. (2016). *Built for Change: Inclusive Business Solutions for the Base of the Pyramid*. International Finance Corporation.

International Finance Corporation. (2018). *Digitizing Merchants Payment in Bangladesh: Building the Business Case for Small Retailers*. International Finance Corporation.

Islam, Q., Brishty, S., & Islam, Q. (2025). *bKash: Revolutionizing Financial Inclusion and Sustainable Development in Bangladesh*. Sage Publications: SAGE Business Cases Originals. https://doi.org/10.4135/9781071959978

Karmaker, S., Oishi, Mst. E. F., Qasem, A., Sami, S. B. S., & Noor, J. (2025). Exploring influential factors of consumer purchase behavior on the adoption of digital payment apps in Bangladesh. *Computers in Human Behavior Reports, 17*, 100587. https://doi.org/10.1016/j.chbr.2025.100587

Khatun, M. N., Mitra, S., Sarker, M. N. I., Department of Agricultural Finance and Cooperatives, Bangabandhu Sheikh Mujibur Rahman Agricultural University, Gazipur-1706, Bangladesh, & School of Political Science and Public Administration, Neijiang Normal University, Sichuan, China. (2021). Mobile banking during COVID-19 pandemic in Bangladesh: A novel mechanism to change and accelerate people's financial access. *Green Finance, 3*(3), 253–267. https://doi.org/10.3934/GF.2021013

Khatun, M. N., Sarker, M. N. I., & Mitra, S. (2024). Adoption of mobile banking to promote financial inclusion among rural farming community: Drivers and satisfaction level perspective. *Journal of Agriculture and Food Research, 18*, 101448. https://doi.org/10.1016/j.jafr.2024.101448

Mahmud, J. (2024). Digital payments and economic growth: Analyzing the contribution of bKash to Bangladesh's GDP. *International Journal of Research and Innovation in Applied Science, IX*(II), 55–63. https://doi.org/10.51584/IJRIAS.2024.90207

Manan, K., & Farhana, K. M. (2023). Digital financial inclusion and remittances: An empirical study on Bangladeshi migrant households. *FinTech, 2*(4), 680–697. https://doi.org/10.3390/fintech2040038

Nandhakumar, J. (2023, September 6). How bKash became king: Three steps to balance purpose with profit. *Finance and Market WBS*.

Nandi, A. K., & Duvander, A.-Z. (2025). Mobile Phone Use and Women's Empowerment in Bangladesh: An Analysis of the Bangladesh Financial Inclusion Insights Survey 2017. *Social Sciences, 14*(3), 139. https://doi.org/10.3390/socsci14030139

Prodhan, Md. M. H., Ebn Jalal, M. J., Alam, H., Mostofa, Md. S., Khondker, B. H., & Khan, Md. A. (2024). State and potential of digital financial services among farmers in Bangladesh: An in-depth study. *Journal of Agriculture and Food Research, 16*, 101209. https://doi.org/10.1016/j.jafr.2024.101209

Rahman, S. A., Didarul Alam, M. M., & Taghizadeh, S. K. (2020). Do mobile financial services ensure the subjective well-being of micro-entrepreneurs? An investigation applying UTAUT2 model. *Information Technology for Development, 26*(2), 421–444. https://doi.org/10.1080/02681102.2019.1643278

Rahman, S. A., Taghizadeh, S. K., Ramayah, T., & Alam, M. M. D. (2017). Technology acceptance among micro-entrepreneurs in marginalized social strata: The case of social innovation in Bangladesh. *Technological Forecasting and Social Change, 118*, 236–245. https://doi.org/10.1016/j.techfore.2017.01.027

Roy, B. D., Ritu, S. A., Mrittika, A. P., & Noor, J. (2024). Bridging the gap: Exploring the factors influencing women's adoption of mobile financial services (MFS) in rural areas of Bangladesh. *Proceedings of the 7th ACM SIGCAS/SIGCHI Conference on Computing and Sustainable Societies*, 268–277. https://doi.org/10.1145/3674829.3675083

Sen, A. (1993). Capability and well-being. In M. Nussbaum & A. Sen (Eds.), *The Quality of Life* (pp. 30–53). Oxford University Press. https://doi.org/10.1093/0198287976.003.0003

Senou, M. M., & Houensou, D. A. (2024). From expanding financial services to tackling poverty in West African Economic and Monetary Union: The accelerating role of mobile money. *Journal of International Development, 36*(3), 1707–1737. https://doi.org/10.1002/jid.3881

Uddin, A. K. M. Z. (2023, January 17). Pilot kicks off for digital payment with QR code. *The Daily Star*. www.thedailystar.net/business/news/pilot-kicks-digital-payment-qr-code-3223756

Venkatesh, V., Morris, M., Davis, G., & Davis, F. (2003). User acceptance of information technology: Toward a unified view. *MIS Quarterly, 27*(3), 425–478.

Venkatesh, V., Thong, J. Y. L., & Xu, X. (2016). Unified theory of acceptance and use of technology: A synthesis and the road ahead. *Journal of the Association for Information Systems, 17*(5).

Xiao, L. (2018, April 27). Ant Financial to acquire stake in Bangladesh's bKash. *Caixin Global*. www.caixinglobal.com/2018-04-27/ant-financial-to-acquire-stake-in-bangladeshs-bkash-101240395.html

Yesmin, S., Paul, T. A., & Mohshin Uddin, Md. (2019). bKash: Revolutionizing mobile financial services in Bangladesh? In A. Sikdar & V. Pereira (Eds.), *Business and Management Practices in South Asia* (pp. 125–148). Springer Singapore. https://doi.org/10.1007/978-981-13-1399-8_6

19

Technology as an Equalizer in Kasikorn Bank's Inclusive Banking Strategy

Arif Perdana, Pearpilai Jutasompakorn, and Wei Kang

19.1 Introduction

In the evolving global finance landscape, the challenge of financial inclusion continues to outpace even the most sophisticated banking systems (Arner et al., 2020; Azim & Rahman, 2025). Despite rapid innovations, billions of people worldwide[1] remain underbanked or excluded entirely from formal financial services, a persistent gap that exacerbates socioeconomic disparities and hinders economic growth (Demirgüç-Kunt et al., 2022; Kamran & Uusitalo, 2024). Yet, amid this challenge, a growing number of institutions are beginning to view digital transformation not simply as an operational enhancement, but also as a strategic opportunity to redefine the scope of financial access. Traditionally, banks have functioned as gatekeepers of the financial system, offering deposit-taking, credit provision, and payment services primarily through physical branches. While effective in urban and formal sectors, this model has consistently fallen short in reaching informal and rural populations, due to high service costs, credit risk, and entrenched information asymmetries. Thailand's Kasikornbank (KBank) stands out as a prominent example. Through its bold embrace of digital technology, KBank illustrates how innovation can be leveraged not only for competitive advantage, but also as a powerful tool for expanding financial inclusion (Kasikornbank, 2023a).

KBank's transformation from the Thai Farmers Bank (founded in 1945) into a digital banking leader exemplifies how strategic deployment of technology can catalyze both institutional transformation and broader economic progress (Kasikornbank, 2023a; Paisarn & Intarawong, 2019; Wonglimpiyarat, 2005). Its strength lies not just in adopting digital tools, but in embedding them within a broader vision of financial democratization (Kasikornbank, 2025a). KBank's approach aligns commercial goals with social impact, using digital models that enhance financial inclusion while maintaining competitiveness (Kasikornbank, 2023a; Lu, 2024). By demonstrating that serving

 DOI: 10.1201/9781003591078-24

underbanked populations can be both socially meaningful and economically viable, KBank challenges the conventional view that inclusion compromises profitability (Lu, 2024).

KBank's digital strategy goes beyond traditional banking paradigms, recognizing that true financial inclusion requires more than just basic account access. Instead, the bank has built a comprehensive digital ecosystem designed to dismantle the structural barriers that have long excluded large segments of the Thai population from formal financial systems. Through its flagship mobile platform K-PLUS,[2] innovative social banking venture LINE BK,[3] blockchain-based services, and artificial intelligence (AI)-driven lending models, KBank has illustrated how technology can transform the economics of serving previously marginalized customer segments (IR News, 2017; Kasikornbank, 2025a). By embedding financial services into existing digital habits, particularly through LINE, Thailand's most widely used messaging app, KBank delivers accessible banking, credit, and payment services to rural, low-income, and underserved communities.

This success is particularly striking given Thailand's socioeconomic complexity. As a middle-income economy with significant rural populations and a substantial informal sector, Thailand epitomizes the challenges faced by many emerging markets in extending financial services beyond urban centers and formal employment (Lu, 2024). KBank's model highlights how strategic integration of digital platforms can effectively bridge geographical and economic divides.

A key example is KBank social banking platform, which enables users to open accounts, apply for loans, and manage finances directly through the LINE app, eliminating the need for physical branches, paperwork, or prior credit histories (Kasikornbank, 2023a). This streamlined onboarding process has significantly lowered access barriers and rapidly scaled user adoption. Crucially, this platform's alternative credit scoring methods have extended formal credit to first-time borrowers, directly addressing the persistent obstacle of limited credit history in financial inclusion efforts.

This integration of financial services into existing digital ecosystems represents a significant shift in financial inclusion strategy. Rather than expecting underserved populations to adapt to conventional banking models, KBank has brought banking to platforms where these customers already spend their digital lives (Lu, 2024; Potjanajaruwit, 2023). Beyond customer-facing innovations, KBank's digital transformation extends deep into operational infrastructure. For example, the adoption of blockchain technology in issuing Letters of Guarantee (LGs) has streamlined back-office processes, reducing friction and increasing access for small and medium enterprises. Similarly, the use of AI and machine learning in credit scoring, fraud detection, and personalized banking services illustrates how advanced analytics can enhance user experience while maintaining robust risk management—an essential balance when engaging with underserved and often risk-perceived customer segments (Bank Finance, 2025; The Digital Banker, 2023).

Equally vital to KBank's inclusive strategy is its commitment to financial literacy. Recognizing that access alone does not guarantee usage, KBank developed comprehensive educational initiatives delivered through digital channels. These programs specifically target marginalized communities, helping them develop knowledge and confidence in engaging with increasingly sophisticated financial services. This emphasis on capability building acknowledges that sustainable financial inclusion requires not only technological solutions but also concerted efforts to address knowledge gaps and build trust (Kantabutra & Aphiraks, 2016; Kasikornbank, 2023a, 2025a).

Further setting KBank apart is its integration of sustainability principles into its digital and financial inclusion agenda. The bank has leveraged its digital platforms to promote green financing, offering specialized products for renewable energy projects, energy-efficient appliances, and electric vehicles (Kantabutra & Aphiraks, 2016; Kasikornbank, 2023a, 2025a; Paisarn & Intarawong, 2019). This alignment of digital innovation, financial inclusion, and environmental responsibility exemplifies a forward-thinking approach to inclusive economic development.

KBank's experience offers timely lessons for financial institutions across emerging markets, as they navigate rapid technological change, evolving customer expectations, and persistent inclusion challenges (Murinde et al., 2022). Its journey invites a deeper reflection: How can banks leverage digital technologies to simultaneously advance inclusion objectives and strengthen their competitive positions? What strategic capabilities enable such dual-purpose innovation? KBank's case offers actionable insights for answering these critical questions.

This chapter makes several key contributions to the literature on digital banking and financial inclusion. First, it provides a comprehensive analysis of how traditional banks can successfully transform into digital-first institutions while maintaining financial inclusion commitments, offering a replicable model for emerging markets. Second, it exemplifies how alternative data sources and AI-driven credit scoring can expand formal credit access to previously excluded populations through embedded finance platforms like LINE BK. Third, it illustrates how digital transformation can simultaneously advance financial inclusion and sustainability goals through strategic technology deployment. Finally, the study challenges the conventional view that serving underbanked populations compromises profitability, providing evidence that digital inclusion can be both commercially viable and socially impactful.

The remainder of this chapter is organized as follows: First, we provide an overview of KBank's evolution from an agricultural lender to a digital banking leader, highlighting the key milestones in its transformation journey. Second, we examine the specific digital technologies that form the backbone of KBank's financial inclusion initiatives, including mobile banking platforms, blockchain applications, and AI-driven services. Third, we analyze how these technologies have catalyzed financial inclusion across diverse customer segments, with particular attention paid to innovative models such as LINE BK. Fourth, we explore the integration of sustainability principles into KBank's digital banking strategy, showing how technology enables both environmental and social impacts. Finally, we discuss the implications of KBank's approach to financial institutions that seek to leverage digital transformation for inclusive growth.

19.2 Overview of Kasikornbank

KBank has emerged as a dominant force in Thailand's financial landscape, evolving from its agrarian roots to a multifaceted banking institution that seamlessly integrates technology and sustainability (Liebena & Khiaonarong, 2009). Founded in 1945 as the Thai Farmers Bank (Lu, 2024), the institution was established with a singular vision: to support Thailand's agricultural sector by extending credit and financial services to farmers and rural communities. This vision aligned closely with the country's post-war economic priorities, during which agriculture served as the backbone of national growth. Early on, the bank focused on building a robust deposit base and extending credit to underserved segments (Kasikornbank, 2011). By 1962, it had already grown to become Thailand's ninth-largest commercial bank, with 36 branches nationwide. Its expansion strategy centered on branch proliferation, allowing it to deepen its reach among small businesses and agricultural clientele (Lu, 2024). This foundational commitment to financial inclusion laid the groundwork for its long-term trajectory, positioning it as a central player in Thailand's economic transformation.

As Thailand's economy modernized, KBank responded by adopting innovations that went beyond domestic banking, aspiring to integrate into global financial systems. In 1967, it was among the first Thai banks to expand internationally, opening branches in London (United Kingdom), Hamburg (Germany), and New York (United States, Lu, 2024). By the time the bank went public in 1976, listing on the Stock Exchange of Thailand, it had established itself as a formidable player with an extensive branch network and a growing portfolio of financial products. KBank showcased its innovative spirit by launching Thailand's first credit card in 1973, an early commitment to consumer finance that foreshadowed the country's shift toward a more consumption-driven economy (Liebena & Khiaonarong, 2009).

The 1980s and the 1990s marked a period of strategic financial innovations. KBank was ahead of its peers in raising capital through international markets, introducing Thailand's first floating-rate certificates of deposit in the London market in 1980. These efforts to modernize fundraising capabilities reflected their ability to navigate an increasingly complex financial landscape. However, the 1997 Asian financial crisis tested the resilience of Thailand's banking sector (Mahathanaseth & Tauer, 2014). KBank has responded by reinforcing its capital base and developing new financial instruments to sustain its operations. In 1998, it launched Stapled Limited Interest Preferred Stock as an innovative fundraising vehicle, ensuring liquidity and stability during a period of economic turmoil.[4]

In response to Thailand's rapid urbanization and economic diversification, the bank rebranded in 2003 as Kasikornbank Public Co. Ltd. (Kasikornbank, 2003). This shift in identity reflected a broader strategic transformation, transitioning from a rural-focused lender to a full-spectrum financial institution offering retail, small and medium enterprises (SME), and corporate banking, alongside digital and international services, aligning with the bank's growing emphasis on digital innovation, corporate finance, and international expansion. Under the leadership of Bantoon Lamsam and later Kattiya Indaravijaya, KBank adopted a "Customer-Centricity" philosophy, leveraging technology to enhance service delivery and operational efficiency (Kasikornbank, 2018a). This approach became particularly evident in the 2010s, as the bank accelerated its digital transformation, launching initiatives such as K-PLUS and LINE BK to expand access, improve user experience, and remain competitive in Thailand's evolving financial landscape.

KBank's technological leadership has been pivotal to its success. By integrating AI-driven services, blockchain platforms, and advanced analytics, it has redefined customer engagement and operational efficiency (Bank Finance, 2025; IBM, 2017; The Digital Banker, 2023). The foray into social banking exemplifies how banks leverage digital ecosystems to expand financial access (Banchongduang, 2025b; Hinchliffe, 2020). Launched in collaboration with LINE, the messaging app giant integrates banking services within a widely used social platform, allowing customers to perform transactions seamlessly. This approach has reached younger demographics and gig economy workers who may not have traditional banking relationships.

Parallel to its digital transformation, KBank has embraced a robust sustainability agenda. As part of its "Bank of Sustainability" vision, it has developed green finance programs that support businesses and individuals in transitioning toward a low-carbon economy (Kasikornbank, 2023a). The bank has structured lending frameworks that incentivise sustainable business practices, including preferential loan terms for companies that adopt renewable energy and environmentally friendly technologies. By aligning its financial products with environmental, social, and governance (ESG) principles, KBank positioned itself as a leader in responsible banking, setting a benchmark for financial institutions across the region. Figure 19.1 presents the historical timeline of the KBank.

Beyond environmental sustainability, KBank has exhibited firm commitment to diversity, equity, inclusion, and belonging (DEIB) (Kantabutra & Aphiraks, 2016; Paisarn & Intarawong, 2019). The bank has been recognized globally for its gender equality initiatives, creating leadership pathways for women, and fostering an inclusive workplace culture. This focus extends to its customer

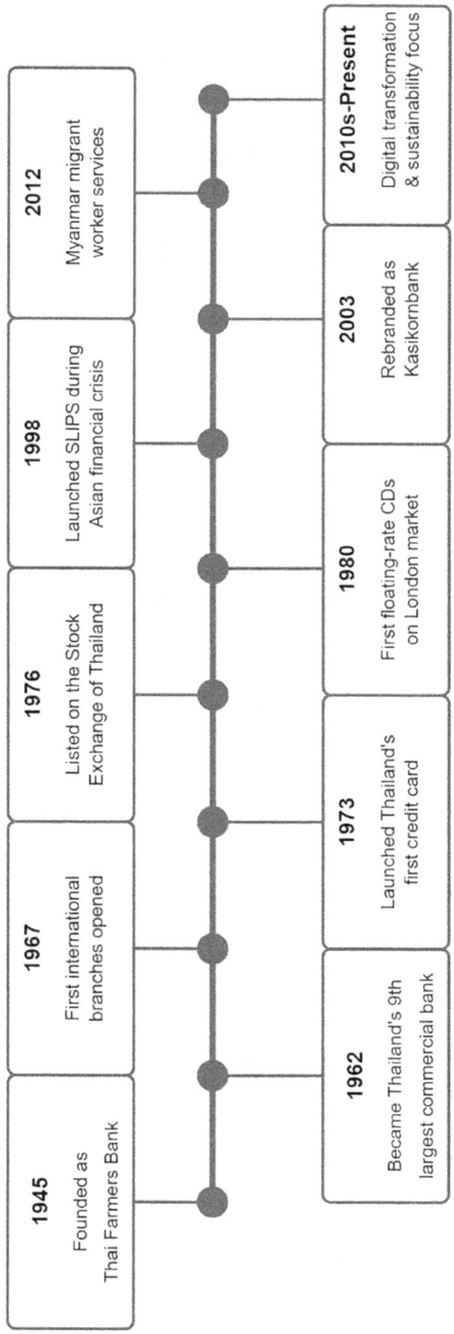

FIGURE 19.1
KBank's historical timeline.

base, where it designs financial products and services tailored to needs of the underserved communities. The introduction of specialized remittance services for Myanmar migrant workers in 2012, including ATM menus in the Burmese language, illustrates its proactive approach to inclusivity in banking (Nadi, 2012).

Regionally, KBank has expanded into key Southeast Asian markets, including Vietnam, Indonesia, and China. This cross-border growth is guided by deep market insights and regulatory acumen, allowing the bank to adapt its customer-centric model to diverse cultural and economic contexts. Through partnerships and digital banking solutions, KBank has successfully replicated its customer-centric model across borders, extending its financial access to millions beyond Thailand.

19.3 Methodology

This case study employs a qualitative research approach based on comprehensive secondary data analysis supplemented by contextual observations. The primary data sources include publicly available reports from Kasikornbank spanning from 2015 to 2025, including annual reports, sustainability reports, investor relations materials, and official bank publications that provide detailed insights into the bank's digital transformation journey and financial inclusion initiatives. These were complemented by extensive analysis of newspaper articles, industry magazines, and financial sector publications that documented KBank's strategic developments and market positioning over the research period. Additionally, the study benefits from the second author's direct observational insights as a Thai national with intimate knowledge of the local banking landscape, consumer behavior patterns, and regulatory environment, which provided crucial contextual understanding of KBank's innovations within Thailand's unique socioeconomic setting. This multi-source approach ensures comprehensive coverage of KBank's transformation while maintaining analytical rigor through triangulation of publicly available information with on-ground cultural and market insights, enabling a nuanced examination of how digital banking innovations translate into real-world financial inclusion outcomes.

19.4 Digital Technologies at Kasikornbank

KBank has positioned itself as a leader in digital transformation within the banking sector in Thailand (Lu, 2024). It signals a strategic commitment to integrate advanced technologies such as AI, blockchain, and platform-based fintech solutions. This leadership is evident in KBank's early launch of its mobile banking app, K PLUS, in 2010; the establishment of its technology arm, KASIKORN Business Technology Group (KBTG), in 2016; and the introduction of LINE BK, Thailand's first social banking platform, in 2020. For KBank, digital innovation is not a luxury but a necessity—central to competitiveness, financial inclusion, and operational efficiency. This commitment is operationalized through its technology subsidiary, KBTG, which leads the bank's research and development efforts in fintech and digital banking.[5]

AI plays a pivotal role in KBank's transformation agenda. KBTG has articulated an "AI-First" strategy, embedding AI across the bank's operational and customer-facing services (Bank Finance, 2025; The Digital Banker, 2023). This approach reflects a broader industrial trend in which AI is leveraged for natural language processing, machine learning-based risk assessment, and predictive analytics. KBank has made substantial investments in AI, exemplified by the launch of KXVC, a $100 million venture fund dedicated to AI, Web3, and deep-tech startups (Cordon, 2023). Through strategic partnerships with institutions such as AI Singapore and Google Research, the bank is actively developing AI models optimized for Southeast Asian languages to address the unique linguistic and cultural characteristics of the region's financial landscape (KBTG, 2024).

The practical application of AI spans multiple banking functions. Digital lending, for instance, has been enhanced through AI-based credit scoring mechanisms that incorporate alternative data sources (Banchongduang, 2025a). This is particularly evident in the bank's social banking platform, which facilitates responsible lending to customers with limited or no credit history (Banchongduang, 2025b). By leveraging behavioral data from users' LINE activity, mobile usage, and transaction patterns, LINE BK's AI models can assess creditworthiness beyond traditional financial records—enabling safe, small-ticket loans to the underbanked. By integrating AI-driven models, KBank has improved fraud detection, enhanced credit risk assessment, and delivered more personalized financial services. Internally, banks have deployed AI and machine learning to optimize decision-making processes, enhance operational efficiency, and streamline customer interactions, ensuring a seamless banking experience.

KBank has also been a pioneer in blockchain adoption, recognizing its potential to improve transaction security, transparency, and efficiency (IR News, 2017; Pathe, 2023; The Nation, 2024a). The bank was the first in Thailand to implement blockchain in its operations, collaborating with IBM in 2017 to develop a blockchain-based Letter of Guarantee platform using Hyperledger Fabric (IBM, 2017). The adoption of this platform significantly reduced the time required for issuing LGs, cutting processing times from days to within a single day and minimizing paperwork. Beyond internal applications, the bank played a leading role in establishing the Thai Banking Sector's Blockchain Community Initiative, which facilitated the use of distributed ledger technology for trade finance and verification services across multiple financial institutions.

Beyond trade finance, KBank has explored blockchain applications in sustainability and carbon trading. Banks are currently developing a blockchain-powered carbon credit trading platform that aims to enhance transparency and efficiency in green finance initiatives. This aligns with its broader sustainability agenda, which includes a commitment to mobilizing THB 200 billion in green financing by 2030 (Kasikornbank, 2023a). By leveraging blockchain technology in this manner, KBank not only enhances its financial services but also contributes to the broader sustainability goals of the financial industry.

In addition to AI and blockchain, KBank has embraced fintech partnerships and national payment infrastructure upgrades to extend its digital reach. It played a crucial role in Thailand's PromptPay QR payment system, facilitating cashless transactions and financial inclusion (Bangkok Post, 2024; Dharmaraj, 2024). It has since expanded its digital payment capabilities across borders, piloting QR payment linkages between Thailand and Laos and exploring further expansion to other regional markets, including India (Bank of Thailand, 2024). These initiatives are driven by the bank's vision of a digitally interconnected financial ecosystem that supports both local consumers and migrant workers with seamless cross-border transactions (Kasikornbank, 2024a).

KBank's digital banking app, K-PLUS, reflects the bank's long-term investment in digital banking (Banchongduang, 2025a). The platform has evolved into one of Thailand's most widely used mobile banking applications, contributing to banks' substantial market share in digital transactions. This success is underpinned by sustained investments in IT infrastructure, with the bank allocating billions of baht annually to ensure that its mobile, internet banking, and Application Programming Interface (API)-based services remain at the cutting edge of financial technology (Lu, 2024). By continuously upgrading these platforms, KBank ensures that its customers receive secure, efficient, and user-friendly digital banking services.

The bank's technology adoption strategy extends beyond traditional banking, embracing "beyond banking" fintech partnerships and investments. Through its venture arms, Beacon VC and KXVC, KBank strategically invested in fintech, AI, and blockchain startups across Southeast Asia (Kasikornbank, 2024b). These investments serve a dual purpose: generating financial returns, while also enabling the bank to integrate emerging technologies into its core services. A prime example of this approach is the partnership with LINE Corporation (Line, 2020), which led to the creation of LINE BK, a hybrid social media and digital banking platform (Hinchliffe, 2020). Additional partnerships with e-commerce and ride-hailing platforms have enabled the bank to offer embedded financial services, including in-app loans and digital payment tools.

A key enabler of KBank's open innovation is its embrace of open banking. By developing secure APIs, banks allow fintech partners to integrate into their financial systems, fostering an ecosystem in which financial services can be seamlessly embedded into third-party applications (Frei, 2023; Stefanelli & Manta, 2023). This approach has not only expanded KBank's digital footprint, but also enabled it to navigate market disruptions, such as those caused by the COVID-19 pandemic. The bank's ability to rapidly scale its digital services during a crisis highlights the robustness of its technology adoption strategy.

19.5 Digital Technology as a Catalyst for Financial Inclusion

In Thailand's rapidly evolving financial landscape, KBank has emerged as a pioneer leveraging digital technology to address one of the most persistent challenges of banking: financial inclusion (Chaisiripaibool et al., 2023; Potjanajaruwit, 2023). While traditional banking models have often struggled to serve underbanked populations profitably, KBank's digital transformation illustrates how technology can simultaneously advance social impact and business growth. The bank's journey offers valuable insights for financial institutions worldwide seeking to expand access while maintaining a competitive advantage in increasingly digital markets.

19.5.1 Redefining Access: Digital Innovation as a Tool for Inclusion

The Kasikorn Bank's approach to financial inclusion is not merely philanthropic; it represents a fundamental rethinking of how banking services can be delivered in the digital age. The bank has strategically positioned digital technology as the cornerstone of its inclusive banking strategy, moving beyond conventional branch-based models that historically have limited access to underserved communities (Lu, 2024; Potjanajaruwit, 2023).

At the heart of KBank's digital inclusion strategy is its open banking platform, K-PLUS (Kambosa, 2024; Kasikornbank, 2023c). Rather than viewing digital banking as simply a supplementary channel, KBank developed K-PLUS as an ecosystem connector, creating seamless linkages between financial services and the broader digital lifestyle of Thai consumers. This approach reflects a sophisticated understanding that financial inclusion is not just about access to banking products, but about integrating those services into everyday digital experiences.

The bank's focus on electronic channels, phone banking, and cash cards has led to significant gains, with digital users reaching 23.1 million by 2023 and steady monthly onboarding via social banking platform (Kasikornbank, 2011,

2018a, 2025a). This impressive acquisition rate reflects how digital channels can effectively scale inclusion efforts, while simultaneously supporting business growth objectives. By lowering operational costs through digital delivery, KBank made previously unprofitable customer segments commercially viable.

One of the key initiatives driving the KBank's inclusive approach is its commitment to financial inclusion through digital channels. The bank has embraced digital onboarding, allowing customers from various backgrounds, including those with limited access to traditional banking services, to open accounts and conduct transactions remotely. This not only removes the geographic and bureaucratic barriers often faced by marginalized groups but also provides a gateway for individuals historically excluded from the formal financial system. Digital transactions, facilitated by platforms such as the MAKE by KBank application, streamline financial services and provide greater accessibility to customers who may have been underserved by traditional banking methods (Kasikornbank, 2022b).

19.5.2 Breaking New Ground with Social Banking

Further advancing its inclusion agenda, KBank actively sought to integrate social chatbot technology to support customers with different levels of financial literacy. The KhunThong social chatbot serves as an interactive assistant, helping users navigate banking services in a way that is intuitive and accessible (Banking Frontiers, 2023). By incorporating natural language processing and multilingual capabilities, KBank ensures that customers from diverse linguistic and educational backgrounds can engage with their financial products. This technological intervention reflects a broader commitment to creating an inclusive financial ecosystem in which no customer is left behind due to language, literacy, or accessibility barriers.

One of KBank's most notable advancements in financial inclusion initiatives is social banking platform. Launched in partnership with LINE, the country's leading messaging app showcases the potential of embedded finance to expand financial access. By seamlessly integrating banking services into a widely used communication platform, KBank removed key obstacles for first-time banking customers. However, it is important to note that customers are still required to verify their identity either at a KBank branch, service point, or via K-PLUS using the same mobile device, potentially limiting access for individuals without proximity to a branch or existing digital banking setup. As such, while social banking platform enhances convenience and accessibility for many, its inclusivity may be limited for consumers without branch access or prior KBank engagement (Banchongduang, 2025b; Kasikornbank, 2023; Line, 2020; Line BK, 2023).

KBank social banking platform has shown significant potential in expanding access to banking services. However, the platform's most transformative influence is on its credit offerings. In its first year, the platform provided unsecured loans to many customers, with a notable portion gaining access to formal credit for the first time. This achievement was made possible through an innovative approach to credit assessments. With user consent, KBank leveraged LINE's rich data ecosystem, including mobile usage patterns and social network data, alongside traditional credit information to evaluate creditworthiness. An AI-driven backend system enables the rapid screening of applicants, allowing for near-instant loan approvals for individuals with limited or nonexistent formal credit histories but favorable alternative data signals.

However, the significance of this approach cannot be stated. By developing alternative credit scoring models, KBank effectively addressed one of the most persistent barriers to financial inclusion: the credit history paradox, where individuals cannot obtain credit without a history, yet cannot build a history without first obtaining credit. Via its social banking platform, KBank has created a pathway to formal credit that was previously unavailable for gig workers, informal-sector employees, and young consumers throughout Thailand.

19.5.3 Diversifying Inclusion through Alternative Lending Models

Beyond KBank social banking platform unsecured personal loans, KBank developed a diverse portfolio of alternative lending programs tailored toward specific underserved segments. The bank's "nano-finance" products exemplify this targeted approach. This nano-finance offers small, short-term unsecured loans to merchants and individuals with irregular income streams whom traditional banking models often exclude due to lack of credit history or collateral (Banchongduang, 2023).

One particularly innovative offering is a nanocredit line designed specifically for merchants using the LINE MAN delivery platform (Shin, 2025). The program provides essential working capital to street food vendors and small eateries, which typically cannot meet conventional lending requirements. By focusing on the specific needs of this segment, KBank has not only expanded its financial inclusion but also strengthened Thailand's vibrant street food economy.

Strategic partnerships have extended the KBank's inclusive lending reach. Collaborations with Srisawad Corp, a specialized microfinance and pawn loan company, have enabled LINE BK users to secure collateral microloans. Similarly, a partnership with Aurora, a major gold retailer, has facilitated gold-backed loans through the app (Line BK, 2023). These partnerships effectively blend KBank's digital infrastructure with the specialized expertise of niche lenders, creating more accessible financing options for those requiring immediate liquidity or small business capital.

In the traditional banking space, KBank has long supported SMEs through simplified account opening and streamlined credit evaluation processes for micro-SMEs and agricultural cooperatives (Lu, 2024; Potjanajaruwit, 2023).

The bank frequently collaborates with government programs to maximize the impact in this sector, recognizing that SME inclusion represents a critical dimension of broader financial inclusion efforts.

19.5.4 Expanding Access through Agent Banking and Digital Platforms

KBank's commitment to geographic inclusion is manifested in its innovative agent-banking model. The agent-banking model uses authorized local agents to deliver basic banking services in underserved areas, reducing costs and expanding access without physical bank branches. By enabling certain convenience stores and post offices to function as KBank service points in rural areas, the bank has dramatically reduced physical barriers to banking access. This approach allows individuals in remote villages to conduct basic financial transactions without undertaking costly and time-consuming travels to urban branches.

Cultural and linguistic inclusion also features prominently in KBank's strategy. The bank has deployed ATMs with Myanmar language options to serve the substantial migrant worker population in Thailand, and offers banking services in Thai, English, and Chinese to accommodate ethnic minorities and cross-border customers.[6] These seemingly small accommodations represent significant steps toward more inclusive financial services in diverse societies.

KBank's flagship digital platform, K-PLUS, plays a key role in promoting financial inclusion by simplifying access to banking services (Kambosa, 2024). By enabling many first-time users to onboard directly through the app, K-PLUS embodies the bank's vision of "banking everyone via mobile." This strategy supports Thailand's national financial inclusion goals. It also provides a sustainable model for growing the bank's customer base (Kasikornbank, 2023).

KBank's promotion of PromptPay QR code payment adoption has proven particularly impactful for micromerchants, such as market vendors (KBank News, 2024). By facilitating cashless payments via QR codes, KBank previously integrated cash-dependent businesses into the formal financial system with minimal setup costs or technical barriers. Thoughtfully implemented digital payment solutions such as these can benefit merchants, consumers, and the broader economy simultaneously.

19.5.5 Digital Inclusion in Action: Outcomes and Next Steps

Recognizing that access alone does not guarantee usage, KBank has developed comprehensive educational initiatives to support its digital inclusion efforts (Kasikornbank, 2015, 2023a). The bank regularly conducts campaigns to enhance customer digital finance literacy and maintains a network of financial education programs through its Learning Center and corporate social responsibility initiatives. These programs specifically target marginalized communities, helping them understand how to safely and effectively use banking services.[7]

The impact of social banking platform has been transformative. By focusing on alternative data for credit assessments, the platform has extended formal credit to many first-time borrowers, highlighting how digital technologies can scale financial inclusion. The flow of capital to underserved individuals, including gig workers and young consumers, showcases the commercial sustainability of this model. As KBank continues to refine its offerings, it underscores the potential for its social banking platform to address the financial needs of previously excluded populations, furthering the goal of a more inclusive financial system (Banchongduang, 2025b; Line BK, 2023).

As KBank continues to refine its digital inclusion strategy, several key lessons emerge for global financial institutions. First, embedding financial services into existing digital platforms that customers already use can dramatically accelerate adoption. Second, alternative data can effectively supplement traditional credit assessment models by providing formal credit to previously excluded populations. Third, partnerships that combine banking infrastructure with specialized expertise can create more accessible and relevant financial products for diverse customer segments.

KBank's experience suggests that financial inclusion through digital technology need not be viewed as a corporate social responsibility initiative separated from a core business strategy. Rather, when thoughtfully implemented, digital inclusion represents an opportunity to simultaneously expand market reach, drive customer acquisition, and fulfill the essential social purpose of banking. As financial inclusion continues to rise on the global policy agenda, KBank's approach offers a compelling blueprint for banks to remain relevant and impactful in an increasingly digital and inclusive financial future.

19.6 Kasikornbank's Digital Transformation: Advancing Sustainability in Finance

KBank has positioned itself at the forefront of sustainable finance by leveraging digital technology to integrate ESG principles into its core banking operations. As global financial institutions navigate evolving regulatory demands and growing customer expectations around sustainability, KBank has taken a proactive approach to embedding digital solutions into its ESG strategy. By utilizing blockchain, AI, digital payment infrastructure, and fintech partnerships, the bank redefines green finance, making sustainable investments accessible to both corporate clients and retail consumers.

19.6.1 Leveraging Digital Innovation for Green Finance

At the heart of KBank's strategy is its digital banking ecosystem, including platforms such as K-PLUS, K-PLUS SME, and K-payment gateways. These digital platforms not only streamline banking services but also enable sustainable financing by supporting green banking products and digital lending solutions (Kasikornbank, 2015, 2023a). By reducing reliance on physical banking infrastructure and paper-based transactions, banks minimize their operational carbon footprints while enhancing customer accessibility. These platforms also facilitate green financing initiatives, allowing individuals and businesses to access loans specifically designed for sustainable projects such as renewable energy installations and energy-efficient upgrades.

Beyond digital banking, KBank has adopted blockchain technology to improve transparency in sustainability-linked financing. The bank is developing a blockchain-based platform for carbon trading that aims to create a transparent and efficient marketplace for carbon credits. The platform supports Thailand's efforts to establish a structured carbon credit system, enabling businesses to trade emission reductions with greater accountability. By reducing transaction costs and ensuring the integrity of carbon credit transactions, KBank positions itself as a key player in advancing climate-finance solutions.

19.6.2 Sustainability, ESG Integration, and the Future of Banking

KBank's digital innovation extends beyond financial transactions to data-driven decision-making for ESG investments. Through AI and big data analytics, banks assess the environmental risks associated with their loan portfolios and provide sustainability-linked loans that incentivise businesses to achieve ESG targets. By embedding sustainability metrics into credit risk assessments, banks encourage corporate clients to adopt greener business practices while managing the financial risks associated with environmental regulations. This approach aligns with the bank's broader commitment to responsible banking, ensuring that financial decisions contribute to long-term sustainability goals (Kasikornbank, 2015, 2023a).

A landmark achievement in KBank's sustainability efforts is its leadership in issuing Thailand's first green bond, demonstrating its ability to mobilize capital for environmental and social projects. The bank's Sustainability Bond Framework, aligned with International Capital Market Association (ICMA) standards, ensures that funds are allocated to projects with measurable sustainability outcomes (Kasikornbank, 2018b). Digital platforms enable real-time tracking of these investments, offering stakeholders full transparency into their environmental and social impact.

In retail banking, KBank launched its digital-first green finance initiatives aimed at promoting sustainable consumption. The "Go Green Together" program offers Green Zero loans, which provide favorable financing terms for electric vehicle purchases, home solar panel installations, and energy-efficient appliances (Kasikornbank, 2022a). These loans include zero-interest introductory periods, which lower the financial barriers for consumers to transition to sustainable products. The bank's digital lending infrastructure ensures a seamless application process, allowing customers access to green financing with minimal friction. The initial allocation of THB 3 billion for Green Zero loans reflects KBank's commitment to driving consumer adoption of sustainable solutions, with the potential for expansion based on demand (Kasikornbank, 2023b). KBank also fosters sustainability across industries through digital marketplace solutions, connecting businesses with eco-friendly service providers. In sectors like education and travel, these platforms help companies adopt sustainable practices by facilitating financing for green initiatives.

Looking ahead, KBank plans to expand its green financing commitments by 2030, viewing sustainability not only as an ethical imperative but also as a strategic business opportunity. The bank has already channeled significant funding into renewable energy, sustainable agriculture, and energy efficiency, aligning with Thailand's national climate goals (Indonesia Business Post, 2024; Kasikornbank, 2023b).

Among its notable projects is a 21.5 MW floating solar farm, developed in partnership with Thailand's Export-Import Bank (EXIM Bank) (Kasikornbank, 2025b). Additionally, KBank collaborated with the Asian Development Bank to provide a THB 1.1 billion loan to solar energy developer Green Yellow Thailand, further advancing the region's renewable energy infrastructure (Kasikornbank, 2021).

19.6.3 Internal Sustainability and Industry Recognition

KBank leads by example, maintaining carbon neutrality since 2023 and committing to net-zero operations (Scopes 1 and 2) by 2030 (Bank Finance, 2024). The bank has invested in energy-efficient buildings, digital infrastructure, and green IT solutions, while also addressing Scope 3 emissions by integrating climate risk assessments into lending practices. Its alignment with global frameworks like the Task Force on Climate-related Financial Disclosures and the Partnership for Carbon Accounting Financials sets a benchmark for sustainable banking (Kasikornbank, 2023a, 2023b).

KBank's ESG leadership has earned it nine consecutive years on the Dow Jones Sustainability Indices (DJSI) (The Nation, 2024b), alongside recognition in the Bloomberg Gender-Equality Index—highlighting its commitment to social responsibility and governance excellence. These accolades validate KBank's nuanced approach to sustainability, proving that finance can be a powerful driver of environmental and social progress.

19.7 The Digital Transformation of Inclusion: Kasikornbank's DEIB Strategy

KBank has strategically positioned itself as a leader in integrating digital technology with its commitment to DEIB. As financial institutions increasingly recognize the role of digital transformation in promoting inclusivity, KBank has implemented a range of digital innovations aimed at reaching underserved populations, enhancing workplace equity, and ensuring that its services reflect the diverse needs of customers and employees.

19.7.1 Cybersecurity, Blockchain, and Workplace Equity

KBank's commitment to DEIB begins internally, with digital infrastructure designed to promote flexible work arrangements and equitable opportunities (Kantabutra & Aphiraks, 2016; Paisarn & Intarawong, 2019). By enabling remote and hybrid work models, the bank empowers women, caregivers, and employees with diverse needs to achieve better work–life balance—addressing systemic barriers to workforce participation.

Digital tools further support KBank's DEIB goals through data-driven HR analytics, which track metrics like gender representation, pay equity, and leadership diversity. AI-powered recruitment systems help mitigate unconscious bias, while performance management platforms ensure career advancement is merit-based. These efforts have earned KBank a place in the Bloomberg Gender-Equality Index for four consecutive years—making it the only Thai financial institution to achieve this recognition (Newswit, 2022).

The bank has prioritized the development of IT infrastructure that supports flexible work arrangements, ensuring that employees can participate fully in the workforce regardless of their personal circumstances. This is particularly relevant in promoting gender equity, as flexible work models empower women and caregivers by offering a greater work–life balance. Moreover, digital HR tools allow data-driven assessments of workforce diversity, helping leadership track progress in gender representation, pay equity, and leadership opportunities.

In addition to improving access and engagement, KBank has placed significant emphasis on the role of technology in creating a fairer and more secure banking environment. Cybersecurity and compliance measures ensure that all customers, regardless of their socioeconomic status, can safely engage with the bank's services. By implementing robust digital identity verification and fraud detection mechanisms, KBank protects vulnerable customers from financial exploitation and reinforces its commitment to equitable banking.

A particularly innovative aspect of KBank's digital strategy is its blockchain-based LGs service (IR News, 2017). Traditionally, the process of issuing LGs has been cumbersome, requiring significant paperwork and administrative effort. By transitioning to a blockchain-based system, KBank has enhanced its efficiency, transparency, and security in guaranteeing issuance. This not only reduces bureaucratic friction for businesses but also democratizes access to financial tools by making them more readily available to SMEs. By setting a target of issuing at least 35% of LGs through electronic channels, KBank demonstrates how digital transformation can facilitate economic participation for previously underrepresented businesses (Techsauce Team, 2017).

The application of blockchain extends beyond its operational efficiency. The decentralized nature of the blockchain ensures that financial transactions remain tamper-proof, fostering trust and security among all stakeholders. In regions where trust in financial institutions is still developing, this can be a game-changer in promoting financial inclusivity. Moreover, the transparency of blockchain-led systems aligns with KBank's broader efforts to create an equitable financial landscape by reducing the risks of fraud and corruption, which disproportionately affect marginalized communities (IBM, 2017; Kasikornbank, 2024a; The Nation, 2024a).

19.7.2 Sustainability, Socioeconomic Impact, and the Future of Inclusive Finance

KBank's digital transformation efforts extend beyond banking services to a broader socioeconomic impact. The bank's commitment to sustainability is closely intertwined with its DEIB initiatives, as it recognizes that financial inclusion and environmental sustainability are mutually reinforcing goals. By financing green projects and SMEs, the KBank contributes to economic equity, job creation, and long-term community development. These initiatives disproportionately benefit vulnerable communities, which often lack access to sustainable financial solutions. As shown in Figure 19.2, the interconnected technology pillars at KBank play a crucial role in fostering financial accessibility and socioeconomic progress.

KBank's ESG initiatives further demonstrate its commitment to equity. Through ESG-driven lending policies, the bank ensures that businesses it finances adhere to ethical labor practices and environmental responsibility. This approach helps safeguard workers' rights and promotes sustainable business practices that extend beyond immediate financial gains. In doing so, KBank not only upholds its corporate responsibility but also enhances economic resilience in the communities it serves.

Moreover, Kbank's digital financial literacy programs have played a crucial role in empowering the underserved population. By offering targeted educational resources on budgeting, credit management, and investment, KBank ensures that financial inclusion is not merely about access to banking services but also about equipping individuals with the tools to make informed financial decisions. This is particularly relevant for women, youth, and migrant workers, who often face structural barriers to financial literacy.

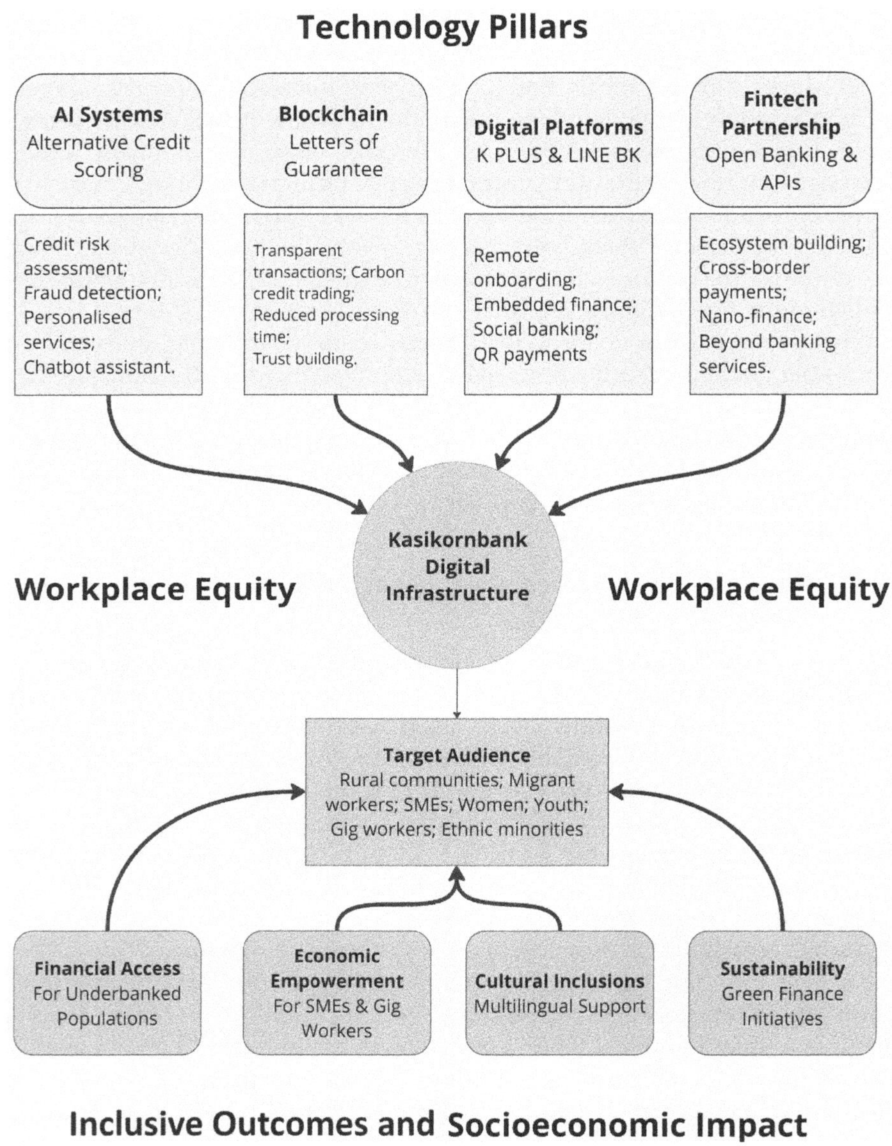

FIGURE 19.2
Overview of KBank technology pillars, inclusive outcomes and socioeconomic impacts.

19.8 National Policy Landscape: Toward Inclusive and Sustainable Banking in Thailand

Thailand has achieved a high level of basic financial access. A 2020 Bank of Thailand survey found that 99.7% of Thai households have access to formal financial services, with only 0.3% completely unserved and minimal gender disparity in access (Bank of Thailand, 2020).[8] However, deepening financial inclusion remains a critical challenge. The current access has not fully translated into widespread usage of diverse financial services. Substantial gaps persist in access to credit for low-income and informal segments such as self-employed microenterprises, agricultural workers, and those engaged in piecework. These groups made up 52% of total employment in 2021 (United Nations Capital Development Fund, 2024). A key policy priority is to broaden formal credit access for this large informal workforce.

Informal workers and micro-entrepreneurs often struggle to meet traditional banking requirements, including proof of income or collateral. As a result, many are pushed toward informal lenders, such as loan sharks, neighborhood investors, and retail installment schemes. These loans typically fall outside the regulatory oversight of the Bank of Thailand and the Ministry of Finance. They often carry high daily interest charges, frequently exceeding the legal ceiling on interest rates (Pinitjitsamut & Suwanprasert, 2022). This reliance on unregulated lending contributes to household overindebtedness and financial vulnerability.

To address this issue, national policy should prioritize the development of digital credit infrastructure that brings informal borrowers into the formal financial system. Regulators can support innovations in alternative credit scoring and data-sharing mechanisms that assess creditworthiness without requiring heavy collateral or conventional documentation. Thailand's regulatory sandbox for fintech has already enabled several such innovations. KBank social banking platform offers a compelling example. By using alternative data such as mobile usage patterns and social interactions for credit assessments, the platform has extended unsecured loans to gig workers, small-scale traders, and farmers who previously lacked access to formal credit (Banchongduang, 2025).

Scaling these models will require more banks, fintech firms, and upcoming virtual banks to adopt inclusive credit practices. Policy interventions could include support for public digital identity systems, streamlined electronic know-your-customer (e-KYC) processes, and credit bureaus that integrate data from mobile payments, utilities, or e-commerce activity. These reforms are aligned with ASEAN's Desired Outcomes, which emphasize a more inclusive and resilient financial sector that supports micro, small, and medium-sized enterprises (ASEAN, 2020). Even modest progress in transitioning informal businesses into formal finance can generate substantial gains in employment and gross domestic product growth.

Yet access alone is insufficient without financial literacy. Many low-income households in Thailand lack the knowledge required to make informed financial decisions, particularly regarding debt and credit management. To address this, the Ministry of Finance has promoted initiatives under its Financial Literacy Action Plan 2022–2027, which aims to enhance digital and financial literacy among vulnerable populations (ASEAN, 2020).

National authorities should therefore implement widespread and targeted financial education programs. These may include integrating personal finance modules into school curricula, offering community-based workshops on budgeting, savings, and responsible borrowing, and leveraging digital channels for outreach. KBank provides a useful model in this regard. It has implemented digital financial literacy initiatives that help first-time users navigate banking services safely and effectively, with a particular focus on marginalized communities.

Thailand's financial inclusion agenda must also contend with climate vulnerability. Ranked among the world's most climate-exposed nations, Thailand faces severe risks from flooding, rising sea levels, and erratic rainfall—threatening its agriculture-dependent workforce (Suthiwartnarueput, 2021). Advancing financial inclusion must therefore go hand in hand with promoting sustainable banking practices. Regulations can play a pivotal role in incentivizing financial institutions to align their lending and investment practices with ESG criteria. Thailand's central bank has encouraged such alignment in its strategic plans, and the Thai Bankers' Association issued Sustainable Banking Guidelines in 2019 to guide responsible lending (Thai Bankers' Association, 2019). Figure 19.3 outlines recommended actions for the Thai government to enhance financial inclusion and strengthen the sustainable finance ecosystem.

Progress is measurable through frameworks like the Sustainable Banking and Finance Network (SBFN), which benchmarks Thailand's advancements in ESG integration, climate risk management, and green financing. In 2023, SBFN benchmarked national progress across three pillars: ESG integration, climate- and Nature-related risk management, and financing sustainability (Sustainable Banking and Finance Network, 2024). These pillars are organized into six substages of advancement, ranging from commitment to mainstreaming behavioral change, and grouped into three overarching stages: preparation, implementation, and maturing.

Thailand demonstrated "Developing" status across all three pillars, with notable progress under ESG integration. It reached the "Advancing" substage, reflecting concrete actions in managing environmental and social risks in investment decisions and efforts to prevent greenwashing. This includes the 2020 issuance of the Sustainable Finance Framework by the Public Debt Management Office (Ministry of Finance, 2020).[9] In the second pillar, climate- and Nature-related risk management, Thailand remained at the Developing substage, having made strides in assessing long-term financial risks associated with climate and biodiversity loss. In the third pillar, financing sustainability, Thailand has taken steps to enable capital flows toward green and social objectives. This includes developing taxonomies, monitoring tools, and incentive mechanisms. One key milestone is the rollout of Thailand Taxonomy Phase 1 in July 2023, which focused on classifying sustainable activities in the energy and transport sectors. The government

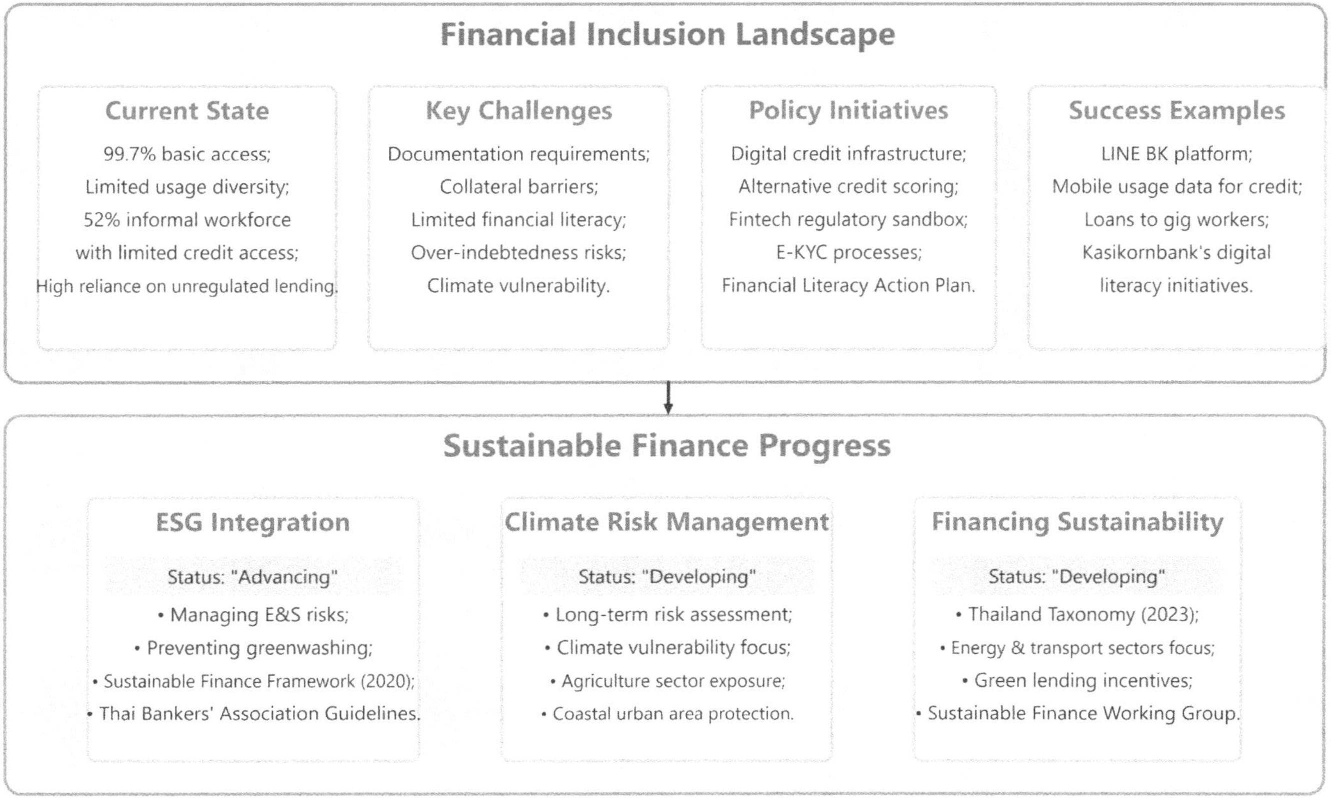

FIGURE 19.3
Key policy measures for improving Thailand's financial inclusion and sustainable finance landscape.

is now working to expand its scope to cover additional sectors and sustainability objectives (World Bank, 2024).

Complementing the taxonomy, the government could introduce targeted financial incentives to encourage green lending by banks. This is especially relevant since banks provide over 90% of private sector credit in Thailand (Suthiwartnarueput, 2021). Redirecting this credit toward renewable energy, sustainable agriculture, and climate-resilient infrastructure would not only support national development goals but also help financial institutions capture emerging market opportunities. Given that green loans can influence credit risk profiles and financial performance (Zhou et al., 2022), measures such as tax breaks or interest rate subsidies for green SMEs may serve as effective tools. This approach aligns with the priorities of Thailand's Sustainable Finance Working Group, which emphasizes robust incentives to mainstream green finance (UNEP, 2023).

19.9 Strategic Implications of KBank's Digital Transformation for Inclusive Growth

KBank presents a model of how digital transformation can be implemented not simply to improve operational performance, but to expand market reach by integrating underserved populations into the formal financial system. Its evolution from a traditional agricultural lender to a digital banking innovator shows the value of aligning digital initiatives with broader institutional strategy. This case provides a practical reference for financial institutions looking to position inclusion as a business driver, rather than a compliance obligation or philanthropic endeavor.

19.9.1 Embedding Technology within a Broader Inclusion Strategy

KBank's transformation underscores that digital tools, such as AI, blockchain, and mobile banking platforms, must be embedded into a long-term strategy that prioritizes customer access, data utility, and sustainable growth (Kasikornbank, 2023a; Lu, 2024). Tools alone are not sufficient; what matters is how they are integrated into delivery models that reach the right populations with the right services. KBank's deployment of AI-driven credit scoring for its social banking platform users, many of whom lack formal credit histories, illustrates how alternative data sources and consent-based behavioral analytics can unlock lending at scale (Banchongduang, 2025a, 2025b). This approach makes digital inclusion commercially sustainable, not just socially desirable. However, institutions seeking to replicate this model must design their AI systems carefully to avoid reinforcing bias or deepening exclusion (Bank Finance, 2025; Demirgüç-Kunt et al., 2022).

19.9.2 Using Platform Ecosystems to Extend Reach

KBank's decision to build LINE BK within Thailand's dominant messaging app reflects a broader principle: Institutions must meet customers in the environments they already use. This shift away from stand-alone platforms toward embedded finance allows banks to reduce acquisition costs, streamline onboarding, and minimize friction, particularly for populations unfamiliar with conventional financial services (Kasikornbank, 2023a; Potjanajaruwit, 2023). Financial institutions operating in similar contexts should evaluate existing digital platforms in their markets as potential partners or infrastructure layers. At the same time, customer data privacy and platform dependence must be managed carefully. KBank addressed this by investing in financial literacy campaigns and maintaining direct customer support within its own digital infrastructure (Kantabutra & Aphiraks, 2016; Kasikornbank, 2025a).

19.9.3 Aligning Financial Inclusion with Environmental Goals

Another defining feature of KBank's strategy is the alignment of its financial inclusion agenda with its sustainability commitments. Through products like the Green Zero Loan and blockchain-based carbon credit platforms, the bank has demonstrated that inclusion and environmental responsibility can be pursued together (Kasikornbank, 2023a; Paisarn & Intarawong, 2019). Institutions in other markets can take a similar approach by identifying green sectors with financing gaps—such as solar energy or electric transport—and creating digital channels to underwrite and distribute those products efficiently. Still, success requires more than innovative loan design. It demands impact measurement frameworks, third-party verification tools, and credible ESG reporting systems to prevent greenwashing and secure stakeholder trust (Arner et al., 2020; Murinde et al., 2022).

19.9.4 Principles for Scalling Digital Finance

KBank's experience highlights four actionable principles that financial institutions can adopt to scale inclusive digital finance. First, inclusion must be reframed as a strategic market opportunity rather than as a social obligation. Underserved populations represent viable customer segments with latent demand for financial services, if products are designed appropriately. Second, banks should leverage existing digital habits by embedding financial services into platforms already widely used by their target users. KBank's integration with the LINE app exemplifies how this approach lowers

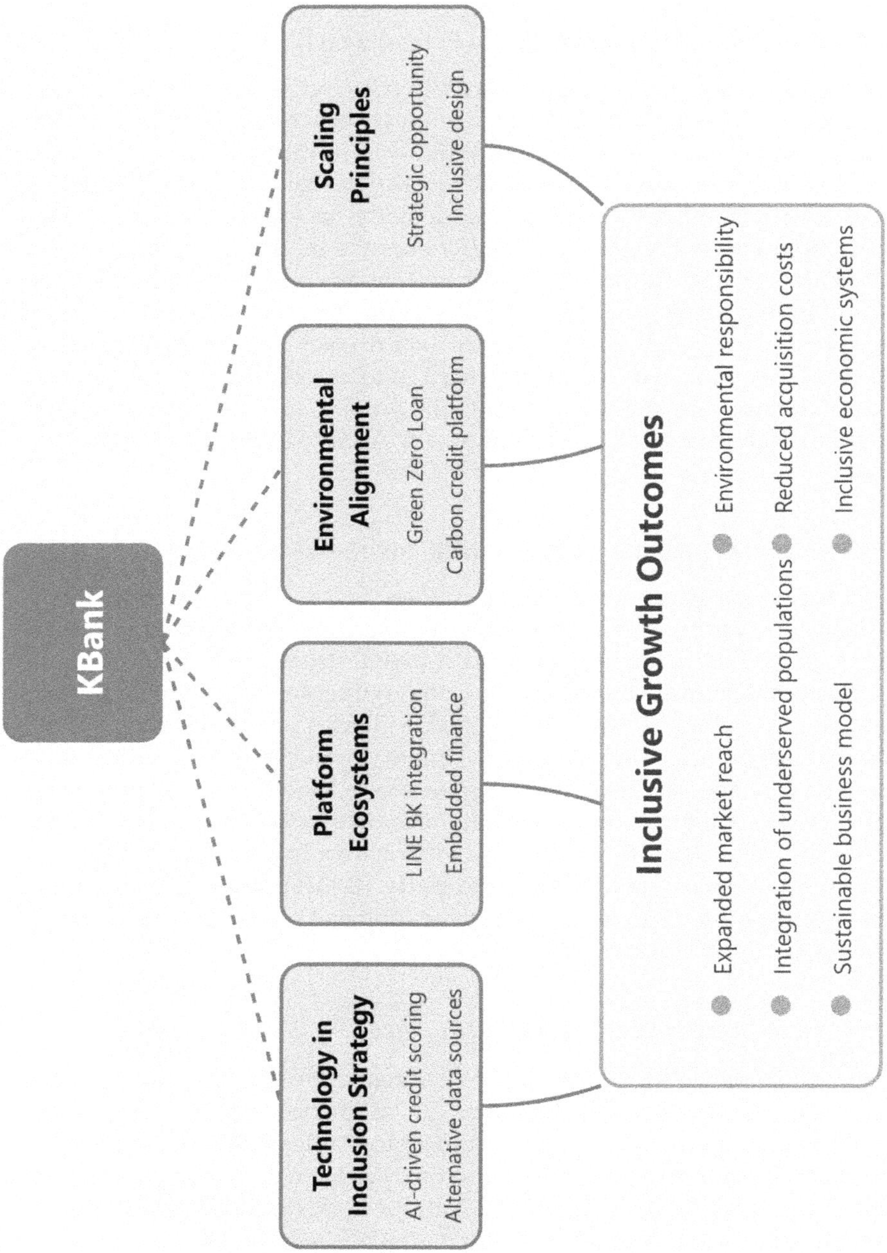

FIGURE 19.4
Lessons from KBank's digital strategy for advancing inclusive finance.

adoption barriers and increases engagement. Figure 19.4 presents the lessons from Kbank's digital strategy for advancing inclusive finance.

Third, institutions should adopt inclusive product design by incorporating alternative data sources and flexible underwriting criteria. This enables banks to assess creditworthiness even for customers lacking formal credit histories, expanding access without compromising risk management. Finally, financial inclusion efforts should be integrated with broader ESG objectives, aligning internal digital transformation initiatives with external societal and environmental impacts. This nuanced alignment not only strengthens business resilience but also enhances long-term stakeholder value.

These principles are particularly relevant for banks operating in emerging markets, where financial exclusion, informal employment, and environmental degradation often intersect. Institutions that successfully operationalize these strategies are better positioned to serve new customer bases while contributing to more inclusive and sustainable economic systems.

19.10 Conclusion

KBank's digital transformation journey offers insights into how financial institutions can leverage technology to simultaneously advance business objectives and social impact. By reimagining financial inclusion through a digital lens, KBank demonstrated that serving previously excluded populations can be commercially viable when powered by appropriate technologies. KBank's strategic integration of mobile platforms, social banking, blockchain applications, and AI-driven services has effectively addressed the structural barriers that have historically limited financial access.

Several key lessons have emerged for global financial institutions. First, embedding financial services within existing digital ecosystems that customers already use dramatically reduces friction and accelerates adoption. KBank's social banking platform exemplifies this approach, reaching millions of users by integrating banking into Thailand's dominant messaging applications. Second, alternative data can effectively supplement traditional credit assessment models when deployed responsibly, thus opening formal credit to previously excluded individuals. Third, back-office digitization enhances operational efficiency while simultaneously improving accessibility for SMEs, as evidenced by KBank's blockchain-based LG service.

Perhaps most significantly, KBank's experience illustrates that financial inclusion through digital technology need not be viewed as a corporate social responsibility initiative divorced from core business strategy. Rather, when thoughtfully implemented, digital inclusion represents an opportunity to simultaneously expand market reach, drive customer acquisition, and fulfill the essential social purpose of banking. By aligning digital capabilities with inclusive design principles, KBank created a sustainable model for unbanked banking.

As financial inclusion continues to rise on the global policy agenda, KBank's approach offers a compelling blueprint for banks seeking to remain competitive in an increasingly digital landscape, while maximizing their positive impact on society. The future of inclusive finance lies not in choosing between commercial success and social impact but in harnessing digital innovation to achieve both simultaneously.

Notes

1 Financial inclusion empowers individuals/businesses, drives economic growth, reduces poverty & supports social equality. Highlights the need for localized trust, transparent pricing, and tailored digital services. www.weforum.org/stories/2024/07/why-financial-inclusion-is-the-key-to-a-thriving-digital-economy/
2 Kasikornbank's mobile banking app providing full financial services, including payments, investments, and loans, widely adopted across Thailand for its security, reliability, and comprehensive features.
3 A social banking platform by LINE and KBank, offering account opening, loans, and transfers directly through the LINE app, targeting digital-native, underserved users.
4 Kasikornbank, founded 8 June 1945 with capital of 5 million baht and 21 employees; operates Corporate, SME, Retail businesses; early innovations among Thai banks. www.companieshistory.com/kasikornbank/
5 Tech-arm of Kasikornbank, established 2016, builds digital innovation, infrastructure and customer experience tools to support the bank's growth and digital transformation. www.kbtg.tech/
6 Examines Thailand's response to mixed migration from Myanmar post-coup; addresses human rights, protection, legal status of migrants. https://mekongmigration.org/?p=6983
7 Part of Kasikornbank's SR 2015, esp. pages 61-62: documents its social activities, community development, perhaps environmental or financial inclusion initiatives. www.kasikornbank.com/en/Social-Activities/Documents/SR2015/SR58_P61-62_EN.pdf
8 "Access" refers to households who used at least one financial service out of 11 key financial services: (1) deposits/savings, (2) loans (excluding credit cards), (3) money transfers, (4) payments, (5) credit cards, (6) life insurance, (7) nonlife insurance, (8) mutual funds, (9) government and central bank debt securities, (10) private securities, and (11) rotating savings groups.
9 Ministry of Finance (2020). Kingdom of Thailand Sustainable Financing Framework. Public Debt Management Office. Available at www.pdmo.go.th/pdmomedia/documents/2020/Jul/KOT%20Sustainable%20Financing%20Framework.pdf

References

Arner, D. W., Buckley, R. P., Zetzsche, D. A., & Veidt, R. (2020). Sustainability, FinTech and financial inclusion. *European Business Organization Law Review*, *21*(1), 7–35. https://doi.org/10.1007/s40804-020-00183-y

ASEAN. (2020). Measuring Progress 2020: financial inclusion in selected ASEAN countries. Association of Southeast Asian Nations. https://asean.org/book/measuring-progress-2020-financial-inclusion-in-selected-asean-countries/

Azim, M. I., & Rahman, S. (2025). Digital financial inclusion: A lifeline for sustainable development goals—Lessons from Bangladesh through crisis and beyond. In R. Arora & T. Sarker (Eds.), *Financing of Sustainable Development Goals (SDGs)* (pp. 193–216). Springer Nature Switzerland. https://doi.org/10.1007/978-3-031-80478-6_9

Banchongduang, S. (2023, August 3). KBank spins off investment business. *Bangkok Post*. www.bangkokpost.com/business/investment/2622513/kbank-spins-off-investment-business

Banchongduang, S. (2025a, January 8). KBank upgrades systems to fortify core infrastructure. *Bangkok Post*. www.bangkokpost.com/business/general/2935182/kbank-upgrades-systems-to-fortify-core-infrastructure

Banchongduang, S. (2025b, February 13). Line BK targets double-digit loan gain. *Bangkok Post*. www.bangkokpost.com/business/general/2960081/line-bk-targets-double-digit-loan-gain

Bangkok Post. (2024, July 26). Central Group rolls out QR code payments for tourists. *Bangkok Post*.

Bank Finance. (2024, December 17). Drive the green finance mission, create a Bank of Sustainability. *Money and Banking Online*. https://en.moneyandbanking.co.th/2024/145944/

Bank Finance. (2025, January 13). Powering AI transformation to drive AI-era banking. *Money and Banking Online*. https://moneyandbanking.co.th/en/2025/149906

Bank of Thailand. (2020). Financial access survey of Thai households 2020. www.bot.or.th/content/dam/bot/documents/en/research-and-publications/reports/financial-access-survey-of-thai-household/fin_access_survey_hh_full_report_2020_en.pdf

Bank of Thailand. (2024, April 3). *Joint Press Release Launch of the Cross-border QR Payment Linkage between Thailand and the Lao PDR*. www.bot.or.th/en/news-and-media/news/news-20240403.html

Banking Frontiers. (2023, November 22). Kasikornbank setting to become a regional digital bank of AEC+3. *Banking Frontiers*. https://bankingfrontiers.com/kasikornbank-setting-to-become-a-regional-digital-bank-of-aec3/

Chaisiripaibool, S., Kraiwanit, T., Duangsin, V., & Shaengchart, Y. (2023). The use of financial technology through banking agency in emerging economy. *Journal of Governance and Regulation*, *12*(4, special issue), 236–243. https://doi.org/10.22495/jgrv12i4siart3

Cordon, M. (2023, September 14). Kasikornbank launches $100m fund for fintech-focused AI, Web3 solutions. *Tech in Asia*. www.techinasia.com/kasikorn-bank-launches-100m-fund-fintechfocused-ai-web3-solutions

Demirgüç-Kunt, A., Klapper, L., Singer, D., & Ansar, S. (2022). *The Global Findex Database 2021: Financial Inclusion, Digital Payments, and Resilience in the Age of COVID-19*. World bank Group.

Dharmaraj, S. (2024, October 3). Thailand's accelerated journey to a cashless society. *OpenGov Asia*. https://opengovasia.com/2024/10/03/thailands-accelerated-journey-to-a-cashless-society/

Frei, C. (2023). Open banking: Opportunities and risks. In T. Walker, E. Nikbakht, & M. Kooli (Eds.), *The Fintech Disruption* (pp. 167–189). Springer International Publishing. https://doi.org/10.1007/978-3-031-23069-1_7

Hinchliffe, R. (2020, October 22). Line launches messenger-based banking platform in Thailand. *Fintech Futures*. www.fintechfutures.com/2020/10/line-launches-messenger-based-banking-platform-in-thailand/

IBM. (2017, August 8). KBank and IBM develop blockchain-based letter of guarantee service. *PR Newswire*. www.prnewswire.com/news-releases/kbank-and-ibm-develop-blockchain-based-letter-of-guarantee-service-300500502.html

Indonesia Business Post. (2024, October 18). *Kasikornbank targets THB200 billion in green financing by 2030*. https://indonesiabusinesspost.com/2951/Politics/kasikornbank-targets-thb200-billion-in-green-financing-by-2030

IR News. (2017). *KBank introduces world's first blockchain-based LG service targeting an increase in L/G issuance via electronic channel to 35 percent*. KASIKORNBANK PCL.

Kambosa, T. (2024, October 21). K Plus' new campaign via Grey Thailand highlights 'the moment of truth' on personal finance. *Marketech APAC*. https://marketech-apac.com/k-plus-new-campaign-via-grey-thailand-highlights-the-moment-of-truth-on-personal-finance/

Kamran, S., & Uusitalo, O. (2024). How informal financial service institutes facilitate the financial inclusion of low-income, unbanked consumers. *International Journal of Bank Marketing*, *42*(6), 1232–1263. https://doi.org/10.1108/IJBM-03-2023-0148

Kantabutra, S., & Aphiraks, T. T. (2016). Sustainable leadership and consequences at Thailand's Kasikornbank. *International Journal of Business Innovation and Research*, *11*(2), 253. https://doi.org/10.1504/IJBIR.2016.077989

Kasikornbank. (2003). *Kasikornbank Annual Report 2003*. http://asianbanks.net/HTML/Files/Thai/TFB%202003.pdf

Kasikornbank. (2011). *Kasikornbank Annual Report 2011*. www.kasikornbank.com/en/IR/FinanInfoReports/financialReports/kbank_en.pdf

Kasikornbank. (2015). *Bank of Sustainability*. Kasikornbank.

Kasikornbank. (2018a). *Investor Presentation as of 3Q18*. Kasikornbank. www.kasikornbank.com/en/IR/News/KBank_Investor_Presentation_3Q18.pdf

Kasikornbank. (2018b). *KASIKORNBANK Sustainability Bond Framework*. Kasikornbank. www.kasikornbank.com/en/sustainable-development/sustainability-bond/SustainableBondFramework/KBank%20Sustainability%20Bond%20SPO%20Update%20Final.pdf

Kasikornbank. (2021, December 16). *KBank with 2 partners in extending loan to Green Yellow (Thailand)*. Kasikornbank. www.kasikornbank.com/en/news/pages/syndication-loan-green-yellow.aspx

Kasikornbank. (2023a). *Bank of Sustainability: Annual Registration Statement and Annual Report 2023 (Form 56-1 One Report)*. Kasikornbank.

Kasikornbank. (2023b). *KBank's TCFD Report 2023: Task Force on Climate-related Financial Disclosures*. Kasikornbank. www.kasikornbank.com/SiteCollectionDocuments/sustainable-development/pdf/kbank-tcfd-report2023-th.pdf

Kasikornbank. (2025a). *Investor Presentation as of 4Q24.*

Kasikornbank. (2025b, February 26). *KBank, EXIM BANK jointly provide green loan for RE Energy to build a 21.49 MW floating solar power plant as part of its drive to create a sustainable society.* Kasikornbank. www.kasikornbank.com/en/news/pages/floating_solar.aspx

Kasikornbank. (2022a). *KBank unveil GO GREEN Together Project.* www.kasikornbank.com/en/news/pages/go-green-together.aspx

Kasikornbank. (2022b, August 17). *MAKE by KBank – the must-have money management app.* Kasikornbank. www.kasikornbank.com/en/news/pages/make-money-management.aspx

Kasikornbank. (2023c, March 21). *KBank digitisation drive adds more than two million new users to its K PLUS online banking app.* Kasikornbank. www.kasikornbank.com/en/news/pages/kplus.aspx

Kasikornbank. (2024a). *KBank partners with Orbix Technology and StraitsX to showcase cross-border blockchain payment innovation at Singapore FinTech Festival 2024.* Kasikornbank. www.kasikornbank.com/en/News/Pages/StraitsX.aspx

Kasikornbank. (2024b, July 15). *KX Venture Capital and AI Fund announce Strategic Partnership to Build AI Startups.* Kasikornbank. www.kasikornbank.com/en/news/pages/ai_fund.aspx

KBank News. (2024). *KBank launches Cross-Border QR Payment Service between Thailand and Lao PDR to accommodate Lao tourists paying via QR nationwide, aims for 30-percent growth of international QR payment services this year.* www.kasikornbank.com/en/news/pages/lao_qr.aspx

KBTG. (2024, September 27). KBTG announces strategic partnership with AI Singapore and Google Research to advance LLM development in Southeast Asia under Project SEALD. *KASIKORN Business-Technology Group (KBTG).* www.kbtg.tech/en/news/kbtg-announces-strategic-partnership-with-ai-singapore-and-google-research

Liebena, J., & Khiaonarong, T. (2009). *Banking on Innovation: Modernisation of Payment Systems.* Physica-Verlag HD. https://doi.org/10.1007/978-3-7908-2333-2

Line. (2020). *Introducing LINE BK, Thailand's First 'Social Banking' Platform.* Line. https://ffnews.com/newsarticle/introducing-line-bk-thailands-first-social-banking-platform/

Line BK. (2023, July 19). *LINE BK Reports Strong Growth in First Half of 2023 Company Sets Sights on Provincial Market Expansion and Insurance Broker Market Entry in Q3.* www.linebk.com/en/news/detail/line-bk-reports-strong-growth-in-first-half-of-2023-company-sets-sights-on-provincial-market-expansion-and-insurance-broker-market-entry-in-q3/

Lu, W. (2024). Ownership and business practice of the Thai banking sector after the Asian financial crisis: A case study of a family business. In W. Lu (Ed.), *Post-Asian Financial Crisis Reforms in Thailand* (pp. 117–145). Springer Nature Singapore. https://doi.org/10.1007/978-981-97-3771-0_6

Mahathanaseth, I., & Tauer, L. W. (2014). Performance of Thailand banks after the 1997 East Asian financial crisis. *Applied Economics, 46*(30), 3763–3776. https://doi.org/10.1080/00036846.2014.937036

Ministry of Finance (2020). Kingdom of Thailand Sustainable Financing Framework. Public Debt Management Office.

Murinde, V., Rizopoulos, E., & Zachariadis, M. (2022). The impact of the FinTech revolution on the future of banking: Opportunities and risks. *International Review of Financial Analysis*, *81*, 102103. https://doi.org/10.1016/j.irfa.2022.102103

Nadi, N. M. (2012, May 11). Thai, Burmese bank open remittance service. *Reliefweb*. https://reliefweb.int/report/myanmar/thai-burmese-bank-open-remittance-service

Newswit. (2022, January 27). *KBank chosen for the world-class Bloomberg Gender-Equality Index (GEI) for the fourth consecutive year, reflecting the Bank's commitment to equal opportunity promotion, inclusive culture and delivery of sustainable value*. Newswit. www.newswit.com/en/LUGn

Paisarn, P., & Intarawong, W. (2019). *Strategic leadership and employee engagement: The Antecedent of Performance of Kasikornbank Public Company Limited*. The International Academic Multidisciplines Research Conference.

Pathe, T. (2023, October 31). Kasikorn Bank snaps up 97% stake in cryptocurrency exchange Satang for $103m. *Fintech Futures*. www.fintechfutures.com/2023/10/kasikorn-bank-snaps-up-97-stake-in-cryptocurrency-exchange-satang-for-103m/

Pinitjitsamut, P., & Suwanprasert, W. (2022). *Informal Loans in Thailand: Stylized Facts and Empirical Analysis (No. 173)*. Puey Ungphakorn Institute for Economic Research.

Potjanajaruwit, P. (2023). Electronic financial services for environmental management entrepreneur in Thailand. In A. Beskopylny, M. Shamtsyan, & V. Artiukh (Eds.), *XV International Scientific Conference "INTERAGROMASH 2022"* (Vol. 575, pp. 2200–2205). Springer International Publishing. https://doi.org/10.1007/978-3-031-21219-2_247

Shin, J.-H. (2025, March 8). Line Man gains traction in Thailand. *The Investor*. www.theinvestor.co.kr/article/2085016

Stefanelli, V., & Manta, F. (2023). Digital financial services and open banking innovation: Are banks becoming 'invisible'? *Global Business Review*, 09721509231151491. https://doi.org/10.1177/09721509231151491

Sustainable Banking and Finance Network. (2024). *SBFN Global Progress Brief* – April 2024. www.sbfnetwork.org/global-progress-brief-2024/

Suthiwartnarueput, S. (2021). Creating a resilient future with sustainable banking. Bank for International Settlements. https://www.bis.org/speeches/sp120208.pdf

Techsauce Team. (2017, July 19). *KBank introduces world's first blockchain-based LG service Targeting an increase in L/G issuance via electronic channel to 35 percent*. Techsauce. https://techsauce.co/news/kbank-introduces-world%E2%80%99s-first-blockchain-based-letter-of-guarantee-service

Thai Bankers' Association. (2019). *Sustainable Banking Guidelines on Responsible Lending*. https://dicf.unepgrid.ch/thailand/sustainable-finance

The Digital Banker. (2023, September 22). Kasikornbank launches $100 million fund for Web3 and AI projects. *The Digital Banker*. https://thedigitalbanker.com/kasikornbank-launches-100-million-fund-for-web3-and-ai-projects/

The Nation. (2024a, Dedember). Blockchain payments to transform cross-border transactions. *The Nation*. www.nationthailand.com/pr-news/40044028

The Nation. (2024b, December 25). KBank maintains its position in globally renowned DJSI for the ninth consecutive year and is the first Thai bank to achieve this milestone. *The Nation*. www.nationthailand.com/business/corporate/40044480

UNEP. (2023). Sustainable Finance – Thailand. United Nations Environment Programme. https://dicf.unepgrid.ch/thailand/sustainable-finance

United Nations Capital Development Fund. (2024). 2023 ASEAN monitoring progress: Financial inclusion in selected ASEAN countries. www.uncdf.org/article/8770/2023-asean-monitoring-progress

Wonglimpiyarat, J. (2005). Banking technology, technological learning and competition: Comparative case studies in Thai banking. *Innovation*, 7(4), 402–415. https://doi.org/10.5172/impp.2005.7.4.402

World Bank. (2024). A Thai Recipe for Green Finance: What's Cooking in the World of Sustainable Finance? Available at: www.worldbank.org/en/news/feature/2024/08/01/a-thai-recipe-for-green-finance

Zhou, X. Y., Caldecott, B., Hoepner, A. G., & Wang, Y. (2022). Bank green lending and credit risk: an empirical analysis of China's Green Credit Policy. *Business Strategy and the Environment*, 31(4), 1623–1640.

20

Aligning Blockchain with Legal Constructs for Strategic Governance

Shruti Shree and Ujwal Prabhakar Nandekar

20.1 INTRODUCTION

The 21st century is defined by the rapid evolution of the knowledge economy, the ubiquitous presence of information, and unparalleled advancements in communication and transmission of technologies (Pandey & Sen, 2022). In this era of unprecedented connectivity, traditional information-sharing and product exchange paradigms have undergone profound transformations. Yet, amidst these advancements, fraud and opacity have affected many sectors, undermining trust and impeding progress. Blockchain technology emerges as a promising solution to address these critical issues. In recent years, incidents of fraud and lack of transparency have emphasized the urgent need for innovative governance mechanisms across various industries(al, n.d.). Traditional systems often struggle to provide the accountability and trust demanded by today's interconnected world. However, blockchain's decentralized and immutable nature presents a paradigm shift in governance structures, offering a transparent and secure framework for transactions and data management. Blockchain has emerged as a transformative force across various industries, offering high security, transparency, and efficiency (Zheng et al., 2018). Jurisdictions around the world are currently exploring different approaches to blockchain regulation. The European Parliament report of July 2018 recognized that blockchain technology is an opportunity for Europe to rethink its economic and societal models. However, legislatures and regulators are concerned about the legal questions raised by its use. The report suggests that it is necessary to develop clear legal standards to ensure that the technology and its applications in the digital environment respect fundamental rights and achieve legal certainty for all parties (Kopyto et al., 2020). Blockchain technology is increasingly being integrated into existing systems and processes in monetary transactions with cryptocurrencies, supply chain visibility, healthcare, and other myriad areas. Therefore, the successful use of a blockchain must be supported by the effective alignment

 DOI: 10.1201/9781003591078-25

of technology, legal constructs, and governance (Roth et al., 2023). Overall, aligning blockchain technology with legal compliance opens the doors for greater possibilities and transforms changes across industries (Javaid et al., 2022).

20.2 OVERVIEW OF BLOCKCHAIN

The term "blockchain" in the world of information technology has been derived from two words: "block" which means a digital information storage unit in a database and "chain" which is the collection of database sites where these blocks of information are kept (Ashurst & Tempesta, 2021). Blockchain is a decentralized digital ledger storing transactions on a connected chain of blocks. As each block becomes full, a new block is linked, forming a continuous chain. These blocks contain collections of transactions, effectively creating a chain that records the details of every transaction. The primary characteristic of blockchain is that once information is added to the chain, it cannot be altered, establishing a system that is both transparent and highly resistant to hacking attempts. To better understand blockchain, it can be linked to a Google Spreadsheet shared by multiple computers, where transactions are recorded. For a transaction to be included in the spreadsheet, all participants must acknowledge its legitimacy. This core principle of consensus forms the foundation of blockchain, ensuring a unique record and history of transactions. All users with a copy are immediately updated whenever a new block is appended. In contrast to traditional centralized systems, where a single entity holds all the data and is susceptible to hacking, blockchain technology distributes the ledger across a network of members. Consequently, no single point of failure enables the system to operate even if individual participants encounter issues. Each node in the network actively verifies and confirms transactions, upholding the integrity of the blockchain. By facilitating the development of a decentralized and trustless public ledger for cryptocurrencies and various other applications, blockchain has brought about a transformative revolution in data storage, security, and transparency. Its unparalleled levels of transparency and security have revolutionized operations in industries ranging from banking and cybersecurity to supply chain management and healthcare (Tyagi, 2023). Blockchain technology has fundamentally altered traditional data management paradigms, empowering users with greater control over their information while mitigating the risks associated with centralized systems. As blockchain continues to evolve and expand its reach, its impact on reshaping the data storage landscape and transparency across diverse sectors remains profound and far-reaching (Zheng et al., 2017). It will be crucial to navigate the complicated world of legal compliance as blockchain technology develops if it is to be successfully integrated and widely accepted.

20.3 EVOLUTION OF BLOCKCHAIN

Stuart Haber and W. Scott Stornetta's work represents a significant step in the history of blockchain technology and is often cited in dialogues about the origin and development of blockchain. Haber and Stornetta were two researchers looking for a way to time-stamp digital documents so that they could not be backdated or tampered with. In a paper they published in 1991, "How to Time-Stamp a Digital Document," they announced a cryptographically secure solution to the problem and introduced a method by which documents could be time-stamped and securely maintained, which they referred to as a "cryptographically secured chain of blocks." The introduction of this concept was monumental, and the term "blockchain" – the cryptographic concept that underpins digital cryptocurrencies – stemmed from their initial work. Haber and Stornetta's method used a chain of documents, each referencing its predecessor in time – very similar, in fact, to the structure of the Bitcoin blockchain. Each item in the list is bundled with data called "block," which is protected and bound using cryptographic principles, creating an effective chain. This idea formed the early basis for using this technology to secure digital documents (Hechler et al., 2020).

In January 2009, the first Bitcoin transaction took place, and Satoshi Nakamoto, the anonymous creator of Bitcoin, implemented the first blockchain for Bitcoin, known as the "genesis block." The genesis block is the initial block in a blockchain and is the only one that does not refer to the previous one because this block does not have a predecessor, known as "block zero." Nakamoto ingeniously designed Bitcoin so that money can be created and transferred without any central authority and with no risk of double spending. These concepts are not new. There have been many prior attempts at creating an online currency, such as E-gold and Reditum. However, the significant innovation behind Bitcoin was the creation of a decentralized network that could achieve consensus or agreement about the state of the database. Using the computational power of the decentralized nodes, combined with cryptography techniques, Nakamoto ensured that maintaining, verifying, and updating the blockchain was the "proof of work" required by each entity on the network (Panda, 2023).

Later, from 2014 onward, blockchain technology began exploring beyond currency, and one significant development came with the introduction of Ethereum, the second largest blockchain implementation after Bitcoin. Ethereum introduced its cryptocurrency called ether and allowed for the storage and execution of computer code on its blockchain, enabling the creation of smart contracts (Kshetri, 2021). Following the success of Ethereum, numerous other blockchains and cryptocurrency projects emerged, each with its own set of rules and applications. These included "altcoins" and entirely new blockchain-based systems like Ripple, which focused on real-time gross settlement, currency exchange, and remittance (*History of Blockchain*, n.d.). The versatility of blockchain technology led to its exploration in various sectors beyond finance, including supply chain management, healthcare, voting systems, and many more. In recent years, blockchain has seen increased adoption and interest from businesses and individuals. Moreover, blockchain continues to evolve and find new applications across various industries, promising to revolutionize how data is stored, verified, and transacted globally. To truly harness the potential of blockchain, it is important to ensure that its journey involves not only technological growth but also legal acumen and ethical responsibility.

20.4 SIGNIFICANCE OF BLOCKCHAIN

Blockchain technology has significantly revolutionized diverse sectors by providing decentralized, transparent, and immutable data records. Its significance lies in its ability to enhance trust, security, and efficiency in various applications, including finance, supply chain management, healthcare, voting systems, etc. By enabling peer-to-peer transactions without intermediaries, blockchain has immensely contributed to reducing costs and mitigating the risk of fraud and tampering. It has also helped reinforce the foundation for digital trust in an increasingly interconnected world. As governments, businesses, and individuals embrace blockchain, its potential to reshape legal constructs and regulatory frameworks becomes increasingly apparent, leading to a new digital innovation and collaboration era (Ashurst & Tempesta, 2021). With its decentralized nature, which means that transactions are verified by networks that are participants rather than any central authority like a bank or government, decentralization ensures that no single entity controls the network, reducing the risk of censorship or manipulation. With this, users have autonomy over their funds and can transact directly with others without needing intermediaries. The transparent nature of blockchain technology is a cornerstone of its significance, ensuring that all transactions are recorded and visible to all participants. Unlike traditional centralized systems where transactions are opaque and controlled by a single entity, this decentralized ledger is accessible to anyone on the network, which fosters trust among participants. For instance, in supply chain management, smart contracts can be utilized to automate and streamline processes such as tracking the origin and movement of goods. Each step of the supply chain can be recorded transparently, allowing all relevant parties to access real-time information about the exact status and the location of the products. This transparency enhances efficiency and reduces the risk of fraud and errors by providing a transparent and auditable record of transactions.

Blockchain technology plays a significant role in cost savings by eliminating transaction intermediaries, thereby reducing transaction costs. Traditional financial transactions often involve multiple intermediaries such as banks, clearinghouses, and payment processors, each adding their fees and delays to the process. By leveraging blockchain technology, these intermediaries can be bypassed, resulting in faster and more cost-effective transactions. A prime example of blockchain reducing transaction costs is RippleNet's blockchain solution. RippleNet is a global payment network built on blockchain technology to facilitate CRM border payments for financial institutions. Using Ripple's native digital asset, XRP, as a bridge currency, RippleNet enables direct and seamless transfers between different currencies, eliminating the need for multiple currency conversions and corresponding banking relationships. This streamlined process significantly reduces the time and costs associated with traditional cross-border payments, making it an attractive solution for financial institutions seeking to optimize payment processes.

Blockchains are transparent and auditable, facilitating regulatory compliance by providing a tamper-proof record of transactions and data. This transparency enables regulators and stakeholders to verify the integrity and accuracy of information, streamlining compliance processes and reducing the risk of fraud and misconduct. One example of blockchain facilitating regulatory compliance is TradeLens. TradeLens is a blockchain-based supply chain platform developed by IBM and Maersk designed to improve transparency and efficiency in global trade. TradeLens creates a transparent and secure documentation process for international trade transactions, ensuring compliance with international trade regulations and standards. All relevant parties, including shippers, carriers, ports, and customs authorities, have access to a shared ledger containing all information about the movement and status of goods. This transparent system enables tracking and verifying the flow of goods across borders, detecting discrepancies or anomalies, and enforcing regulatory requirements more effectively. It plays a crucial role across various sectors due to its distinctive features like decentralization, transparency, immutability, and security. With its potential to revolutionize industries through all sectors, widespread adoption of blockchain technology is vital to unlocking its full benefits. Law on the blockchain functions fundamentally differently from law in the physical world because there is no point in legal intervention. One of the best examples of how the law fills in the gaps in an incomplete contract and how it varies depending on the blockchain is found in business organization law; along with that, there is also a need for innovative approaches to address emerging opportunities and challenges.

Furthermore, blockchain's transparency and immutability serve as a vital mechanism to reduce systemic bias in technological systems. Every transaction recorded on the blockchain is permanent and verifiable, eliminating the possibility of unauthorized modifications or manipulation. This ensures accountability, particularly in sectors like finance, healthcare, and legal systems, where biased practices can disproportionately impact marginalized groups. Decentralized systems also help democratize access and governance by reducing the power asymmetries that exist in traditional centralized models. For example, in decentralized autonomous organizations, decision-making authority is distributed among network participants, not limited to a select few. This structure allows for wider representation, encouraging participation from diverse communities, and helps address inequities that stem from concentration of power. Thus, blockchain acts not only as a tool for operational transparency but also as a vehicle to challenge and mitigate institutionalized bias.

20.5 BLOCKCHAIN AND ITS DIVERSE USAGE IN INDIA

Blockchain has emerged as a transformative force in India, offering solutions to enhance transparency, security, and efficiency across diverse sectors. As India embraces blockchain technology, various state initiatives have been launched to explore and implement its applications.

- **Maharashtra:** The economic capital of India has adopted a "State Blockchain Policy" that aims to capitalize and streamline blockchain within the region. The state has already started working to implement blockchain solutions across various sectors with their "Four Pilot" projects that include health, transport, agriculture, and finance, showcasing the diverse applicability of blockchain technology. Recently Gokuldas Tejpal Hospital, located in Mumbai, has done corneal transplantation with the help of procedures based on blockchain technology, depicting its potential to enhance transparency and efficiency in medical processes. The transport sector, particularly the Regional Transport Office, has also introduced blockchain-based solutions to manage vehicle supply chains. This initiative helps to streamline operations and improve accountability within the transportation industry. Along with all these, the agriculture sector has benefited significantly from projects aimed at the state warehousing corporation focusing on developing a warehousing system, and this system aims to empower farmers by facilitating more accessible access to finance and enabling smoother exports of agricultural produce, mainly the pomegranate fruit (Radhakrishna& Roy, 2022).

- **Karnataka:** The state is actively developing blockchain technology, particularly in online property documentation. They have taken proactive steps by organizing a conclave in Bangalore to explore the prospects of blockchain technology within its borders. This gathering served as a platform for industry stakeholders, including government officials, technology enthusiasts, and representatives from various sectors, to exchange insights and perspectives on the potential applications of blockchain. At the inauguration of the conference in Bengaluru, Priyank Kharge, the minister of Information Technology of Karnataka, emphasized the importance of understanding blockchain technology thoroughly and invited input from startups and innovators across sectors. Karnataka aims to leverage blockchain's potential for innovation and efficiency, positioning itself as a leader in technology adoption and implementation (Pandey & Sen, 2022).
- **Telangana:** The state has been proactive in embracing blockchain technology. In 2019, the Telangana Academy for Skill and Knowledge, under the Department of Information Technology, Electronics and Communication, outlined a comprehensive vision for blockchain technology. This vision encompasses six key pillars: developing a talent pool, supporting infrastructure, promoting research and innovation, enabling collaboration, and building community and industry collaboration. Another significant initiative is the establishment of a "blockchain district" envisioned to be a hub for significant blockchain technology companies. This district will feature substantial means and state-of-the-art facilities to foster research, innovation, and industry collaboration. The aim is to position blockchain companies in Hyderabad on the global stage advantageously ("T to Develop a Framework to Boost Web3 & Blockchain," 2023).
- **Madhya Pradesh:** The state has emerged as a significant player in promoting blockchain technology, particularly agriculture. The Office of the Commissioner of Land Records and Settlement has used blockchain technology to manage land records. This move highlights the state's commitment to exploring innovative solutions to improve land records management's efficiency, transparency, and security. The state aims to modernize its land administration processes through blockchain technology and enhance trust and reliability in land-related transactions (Vayadande et al., 2022).
- **Jharkhand:** Jharkhand has made history by being the first state in India to implement blockchain technology for tracking seed distribution in collaboration with SettleMint India. This initiative aims to enhance transparency and authenticity in seed distribution under various agricultural schemes. By leveraging blockchain, Jharkhand seeks to ensure efficient management of distribution processes, eliminate middlemen, and provide quality seeds to farmers. This highlights the potential of

the blockchain to revolutionize agricultural supply chains, benefiting farmers and enhancing food security in India (Bureau, 2023).

- **Uttar Pradesh:** Uttar Pradesh, with its vast population, holds immense potential in terms of manpower. In a notable development, the state has partnered with India Smart Grid Forum, Power Ledger, and Abajyon Consulting to execute a pioneering project. This project, hosted by Uttar Pradesh Power Corporation, Madhyanchal Vidyut Vitran Nigam Limited, and Uttar Pradesh New and Renewable Energy Development Agency, involves a first-of-its-kind pilot project. It focuses on utilizing energy generated from solar rooftop systems installed on buildings in Lucknow. Moreover, Uttar Pradesh has taken a significant leap forward by launching India's and South Asia's first blockchain-enabled peer-to-peer trading of rooftop solar power on December 17, 2020. These initiatives signify Uttar Pradesh's commitment to leveraging innovative technologies like blockchain and renewable energy to drive sustainable development and energy efficiency in the state (*Uttar Pradesh Starts India's First Blockchain-Enabled Rooftop Solar Trading Platform – Mercom India*, n.d.).

20.6 LEGAL FRAMEWORK

Blockchain technology, till now, has immensely contributed to almost all the diverse sectors. However, due to rapid globalization and technological advancement, India has not adopted specific legislation for blockchain because awareness related to this technology is potentially lacking among most people, which creates different challenges for lawmakers. Currently, the National Informatics Centre, with the help of the Ministry of Electronics and Information Technology, is the sole agency responsible for implementing and coordinating the blockchain system in India. The Indian government regulates technology according to existing laws and regulations in the blockchain sector. Various laws, such as the Negotiable Instrument Act of 1881, the Securities Contracts (Regulation) Act of 1956, and the RBI Act of 1934, were mainly used to regulate blockchain. Later the Indian Copyright Act of 1957 and the IT Act of 2000 were also incorporated into the regulatory framework. In 2019, the Reserve Bank of India, in collaboration with digital banks and FinTech companies, proposed the concept of "Sandboxes" for blockchain regulation. Still, unfortunately, right now, it primarily focuses on financial transactions and payments with Non-Fungible Tokens and cryptocurrencies that are subject to taxation laws despite altogether banning them. Eventually, the budget of 2022 introduced certain amendments to the Income Tax Act of 1961, where the digital assets were incorporated under taxation laws. Now, these assets are outlined in the amendments to proposed tax rates and advance tax collection mechanism. Blockchain applications dealing with individuals' personal data must comply with the Personal Data Protection Bill 2019 provisions. This bill aims to regulate and provide specific guidelines and standards for government and private entities processing personal data, which helps ensure transparency and accountability in the data processing systems. It also provides clear and accessible information about the personnel data being used and processed within the blockchain. Smart contracts are crucial to blockchain technology and are governed by the Indian Contract Act of 1872, which provides the foundation for determining the enforceability of smart contracts within the country by meeting the same criteria as traditional contracts to be legally binding. Blockchain-related inventions, including algorithms and protocols, can be protected under intellectual property laws so that the owner can have exclusive rights to their creation and get maximum benefits from their innovation and investment. In addition, income derived from various blockchains, including cryptocurrency trading and many more, will fall under the purview of taxation regulations, such as the Income Tax Act of 1961, which has provisions for the applicable rates and mechanisms for compliance. Various regulations, including Combating the Financing of Terrorism and Anti-Money Laundering, are also crucial for blockchain-based business. These regulations come forward with robust Know Your Customer (KYC) procedures and suspicious transaction reports that are immediately sent to regulatory authorities to mitigate risk and ensure the security and integrity of blockchain technology. Indian initiatives for blockchain technology have been enormous in almost all the diverse sectors of the economy. Hence, it becomes the authorities' duty to adapt and enhance the current framework so that emerging challenges can be curbed effectively and a conducive environment can be built to use blockchain technology efficiently, leading to the country's overall development.

20.7 NEED OF BLOCKCHAIN GOVERNANCE

In the era of rapid technological advancement, blockchain technology continues to secure the highest position because of its various benefits, creating the need for effective blockchain governance. Blockchain governance refers to various processes, mechanisms, and structures that are put together to ensure the deployment, development, and operation of blockchain applications and networks. The need for blockchain governance arises because it is decentralized as it involves multiple participants in networking and decision-making processes; without proper governance, it can lead to conflicts, inefficiencies, and vulnerabilities. So, good governance helps to establish clear rules, standards, and protocols to govern the behavior of its decentralized participants, ensuring consensus and maintaining the integrity of the blockchain technology. Today, compliance is regarded as the DNA of all organizations, so blockchain governance plays a crucial role in addressing regulatory, legal, and compliance considerations linked with blockchains. Many international examples of blockchain governance highlight the diverse approaches taken to address the challenges and opportunities presented by blockchain technology.

- The United Arab Emirates has opted for the "Smart Dubai Initiative," making it the first city to be fully powered by blockchain. Its applicability is used in various sectors, from education and healthcare to environment sustainability and traffic management.
- The European Blockchain Partnership aims to develop a secure and trusted European blockchain infrastructure that helps to meet high standards of privacy, cyber security, and regulations in the applicability of policies.
- China has a system in which a unique global digital identity is assigned to its smart cities to improve connectivity and data sharing effectively in these cities. Along with this, they have also enabled blockchain notary services and are contributing immensely to their digital economy.
- Estonia has a "Keyless Signature Infrastructure," which is used by its government to prove the authenticity of its electronic records. It has also implemented an "X-Road," which is an open source of data exchange so that it can share information securely.
- Zug, located in Switzerland, is the first place in the world where Bitcoin payments are accepted for tax purposes. They have a successful voting system that functions with the help of blockchain technology and also created "Blockchain TaskForce" to implement the blockchain framework.
- Canada and Chile use Ethereum to bring transparency to the government's spending on various grants. They are also equally contributing blockchain benefits to the real estate sector.
- The UK and the USA use blockchain technology to ensure food standards, and the technology is equally used in the healthcare sectors to improve efficiency, security, and transparency.

The above examples clearly indicate the importance and urgency of having proper blockchain governance to ensure compliance and innovation that can help harness the potential of blockchain technology across various sectors for societal and economic benefits. In India, there has been considerable investment across various sectors by government bodies, private enterprises, and academic institutions actively engaged in research and development. The Ministry of Electronics and Information Technology has identified the potential of blockchain and its contribution to the research area with its application in governance. They have initiated projects by collaborating with institutes to look into the usage of blockchain in various sectors like property registration and cloud security assurance. They also encourage new inventions and their applicability to blockchain technology. Government agencies, including the National e-Governance Division and the National Informatics Centre, have established Centres of Excellence in blockchain technology to accelerate deployment and adoption in various government services. Academic institutes like IIT Kanpur and IIIT Hyderabad are involved in research on blockchain technology and its applications, focusing on the importance of governance in navigating the path of ethical considerations and standardizations. NITI Aayog is also working with Gujarat Narmada Valley Fertilizers & Chemicals Limited and has developed a unique blockchain system for fertilizers subsidy, which leads to tamper proof and a transparent system to move fertilizers across the value chain by reducing the time to activate subsidy. Overall, India can create a conducive environment for incorporating blockchain technology by having an effective governance system to help mitigate potential risks and challenges.

In addition to regulatory and structural needs, blockchain governance must also consider the challenge of algorithmic bias. Governance frameworks can be intentionally designed to identify and mitigate such bias by incorporating checks such as fairness audits, inclusive participation mechanisms, and transparent rule-making processes. For instance, blockchain projects like Algorand and Cardano emphasize inclusivity by distributing voting rights among diverse stakeholders, thereby preventing power from being concentrated in the hands of a few. Similarly, platforms like Gitcoin Grants use quadratic voting mechanisms that amplify the voices of underrepresented communities and reduce majority domination. By including diverse representation in governance processes, blockchain networks can build systems that reflect a wider range of experiences and needs, leading to more equitable technological outcomes. These inclusive strategies are crucial to ensuring that blockchain does not replicate or exacerbate existing societal biases.

20.8 EMPIRICAL ANALYSIS

20.8.1 Introduction

Blockchain technology has evolved since its emergence, providing security, transparency, and efficiency across various industries. It has the potential to completely revolutionize the older mechanisms that have brought various challenges in data management, accountability, and regulatory compliance. However, one must better understand current adoptions, benefits, challenges, and ethical considerations to utilize blockchain with its maximum benefit. In this empirical analysis, researchers have examined the intersection of blockchain technology and governance through various insights of people across industries by examining their perceptions toward blockchain, awareness, utilization, and visions for future applicability. Researchers have undertaken a non-doctrinal study to investigate how organizations in these sectors adopt blockchain technology, their challenges in regulatory compliance, and their strategies to enhance governance effectiveness. The findings below will provide policymakers, stakeholders, and organizations insights into aligning blockchain with legal frameworks.

Organization	Type of Industry
Bokaro Steel Plant (SAIL)	Steel Manufacturing
Tata Consultancy Services	Information Technology
PricewaterhouseCoopers	Professional Services
Indian Oil Corporation Limited	Oil and Gas
Infosys	Information Technology
Larsen & Toubro	Multinational Conglomerate
Aptech Limited	Education
Makarand M.Joshi & Company	Professional Services
National Agri-Food Biotechnology Institute	Agriculture
Procter & Gamble	Consumer goods
Bokaro General Hospital (SAIL)	Healthcare
Bank of Baroda	Banking
State Bank of India	Banking
Bharat Heavy Electricals Limited	Energy and Infrastructure
Oil and Natural Gas Corporation	Oil and Gas
Malabar Group	Retail
Cartus	Real Estate
Youtuber	Media

20.8.2 Classification of Respondents

Figures 20.1 and 20.2 below provide information about the respondents' age and gender to help understand any differences in opinions based on gender. The respondents were grouped into four age categories, ranging from 18 years as the youngest to 45 years and older as the oldest. Among the 18 respondents, 77.8% were male and 22.2% were female. Most of the responses came from the 25–34 years age group (61.1%), followed by the 45 years and above group (33.3%), while the smallest proportion came from the 18–24 years group (5.6%) (see Figure 20.1).

20.8.3 Awareness and Adoption of Blockchain Technology

Question 1: How aware are you of blockchain technology?
The findings reveal a diversity in the awareness levels: around 77.8% of the respondents are fully aware, 5.6% are moderately aware, 5.6% are somewhat

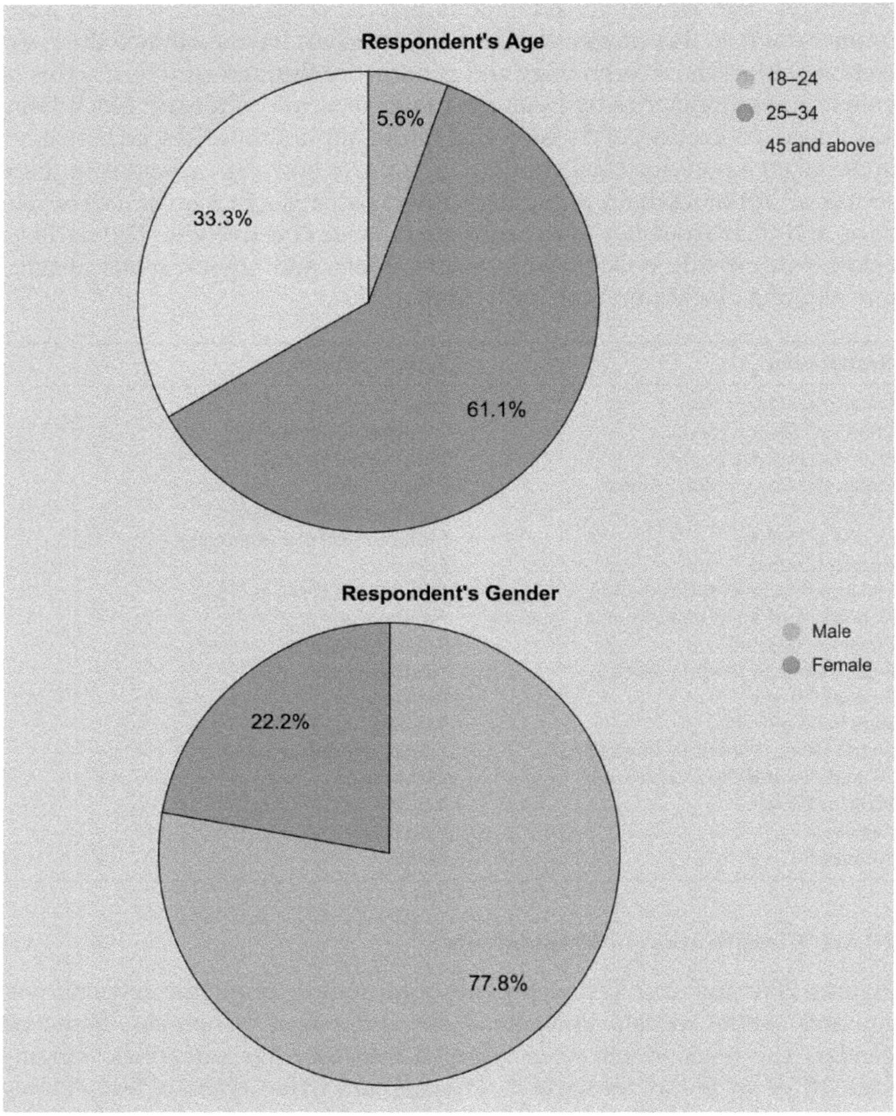

FIGURE 20.1
Respondent's age and gender.

aware, and 11.1% of respondents are unaware of blockchain technology (see Figure 20.2). Altogether, we have a heterogeneous nature of awareness levels. By addressing these gaps, we can promote awareness in different population segments so that blockchain technology could be widely adopted and its benefits can be availed in diverse sectors.

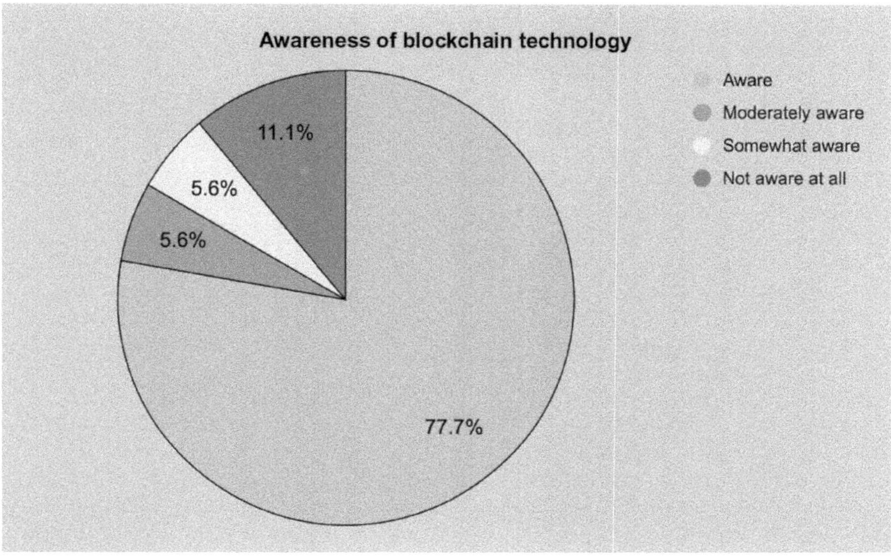

FIGURE 20.2
Awareness of blockchain technology.

Question 2: Have you ever used blockchain technology in your organization?
The findings reveal that only half of the respondents do know about blockchain, the rest 11.1% are still confused with the concept, and, lastly, 38.9% straightaway said that they do not have any knowledge, which creates a concern and alarms to familiarize individuals with blockchain's concepts and application to fill this gap and ensure that broader awareness is spread in terms of its potential benefits (see Figure 20.3).

20.8.4 Current Usage and Estimated Potential

Question 3: How is your organization currently utilizing blockchain technology?
The findings reveal a diversity of applications and approaches of blockchain for various organizations. Organizations have adopted blockchain technology for supply chain management, digital identity verification, and cross-border payments to enhance efficiency, transparency, and security in internal and external business processes. Specific organizations like PricewaterhouseCoopers have resources for research and development. They have a specialized lab that especially looks into exploring various potentialities of blockchain and its contribution to technological advancements. The Indian Oil Corporation (IOCL) has incorporated blockchain technology to

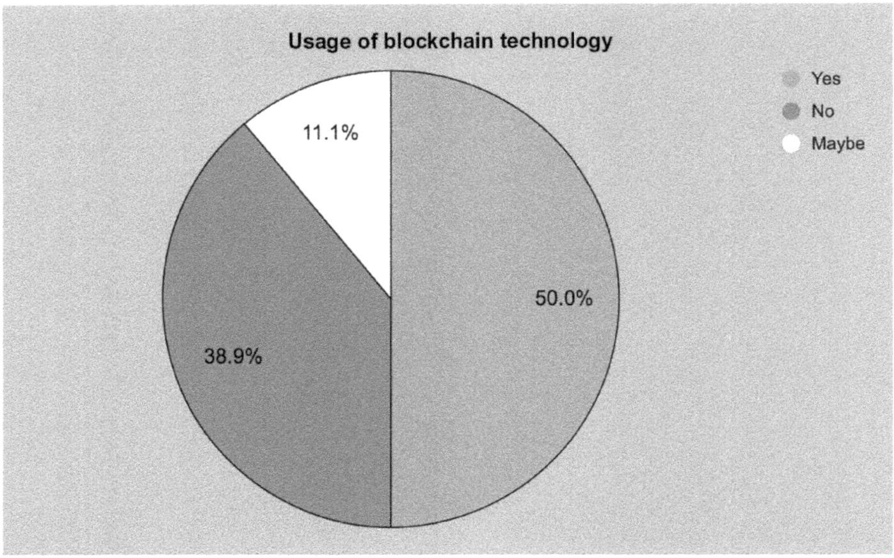

FIGURE 20.3
Usage of blockchain technology.

manage the distribution of their LPG. It also ensures accountability and traceability within its operations. Infosys focuses on unlocking business value through blockchain by simplifying its adoption integration with current technological advancements and pursuing a mission to achieve sustainability and innovation across industries. Financial institutions like the State Bank of India and Bank of Baroda have extensively used trade finance, invoice discounting, and e-KYC technology to enhance security. Energy sectors like oil and natural gas corporations also utilize Bitcoin mining technology to monetize gas flaring. Beyond the above-mentioned applications, some organizations, like the YouTube community, are still catching up as they use blockchain to maintain rationality and transparency in creating and editing processes. The wide-ranging applications and innovative initiatives led by blockchain highlight its potential to revolutionize governance within the legal framework as everyday blockchain technology evolves. Therefore, legal frameworks must adapt and evolve accordingly to realize blockchain's full potential.

Question 4: Which industries do you believe blockchain technology has the most potential for disruption or innovation?

The findings reveal that blockchain technology holds significant potential for disruption and innovation across diverse industries. Various sectors such as banking, health care, real estate, entertainment industry, steel industry, oil and gas, and energy sectors are all identified areas where blockchain has brought significant changes. These are some of the sectors that have reshaped

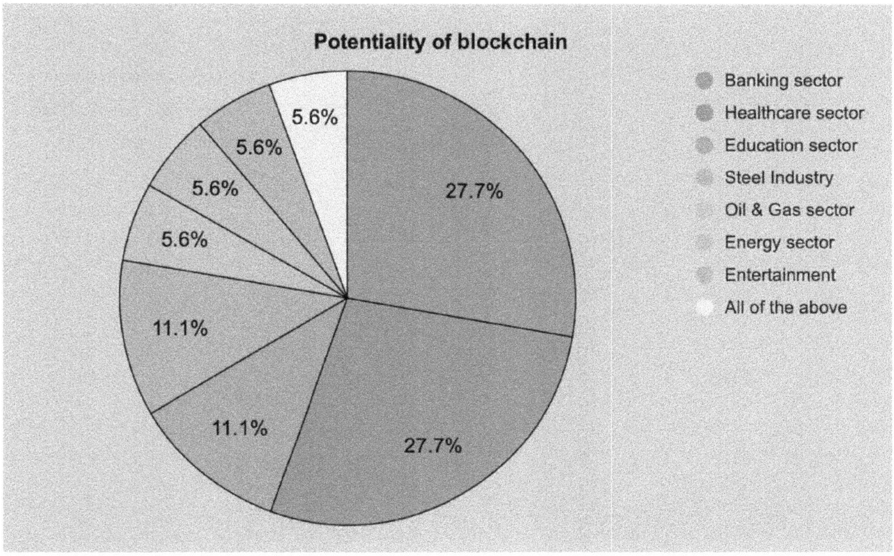

FIGURE 20.4
Potentiality of blockchain.

traditional practices and adopted blockchain technology to enhance efficiency and foster transparency and trust (see Figure 20.4).

20.8.5 Challenges and Barriers in Adoption

Question 5: What are the primary challenges or barriers to the widespread adoption of blockchain technology?
The primary challenges or barriers to the widespread adoption of blockchain technology include privacy and data protection concerns, regulatory uncertainty, complexity in its implementation, and, most importantly, the lack of awareness. Privacy and data protection concerns usually occur due to the immutable nature of blockchain, as the security it ensures often leads to breaches of existing privacy regulations and thus violates individuals' fundamental rights. Usually, blockchain requires particular technical expertise and various resources for its implementation, which often consumes time and money, so people tend to move away with this technology. Day by day, blockchain is evolving, and still, till now, no specific regulation has been brought that can secure the users and curb the conflicting regulations because of the various interpretations across jurisdictions, which lead to businesses deterring from investing in blockchain solutions. Lack of awareness about the benefits of blockchain technology creates hesitancy toward its adoption. The changes cannot happen just in the blink of an eye; they will require the combined efforts of policymakers, industrialists, and businessmen to work together to utilize the full potential of blockchain (see Figure 20.5).

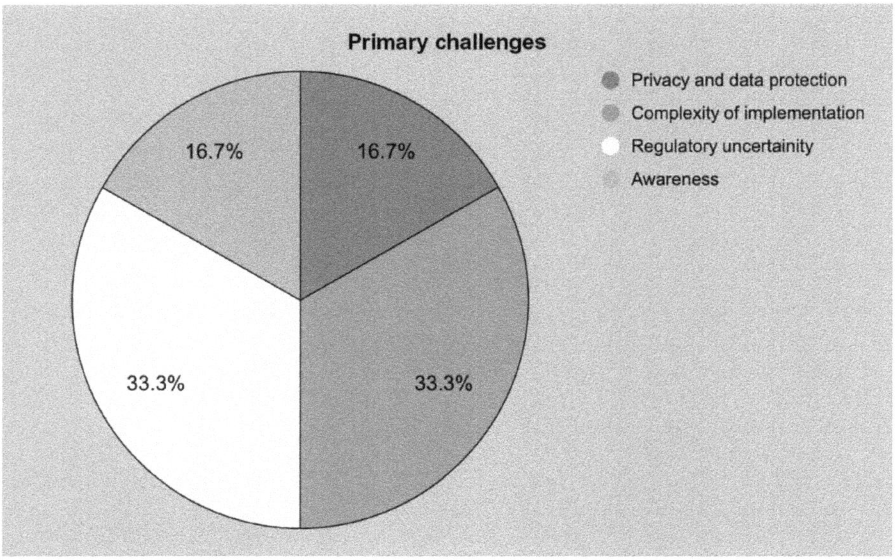

FIGURE 20.5
Primary challenges of blockchain adoption.

20.8.6 Future Governance and Ethical Considerations

Question 6: How do you envision the future of blockchain-based governance systems within the legal framework?
Blockchain-based governance within a legal framework holds immense potential to revolutionize the digital economy, bringing transparency, efficiency, and trust. These systems are essential for streamlining processes and decreasing inefficiencies. Reduction in fraud will enhance the stakeholders to build trust and thereby lead to sustainable growth and innovation. Therefore, a clear regulatory framework is essential to accommodate blockchain technology to bring legal certainty, and then, at large, its adoption can occur. Robust privacy regulations must be implemented to safeguard sensitive data and maintain the benefits of blockchain transparency. Successful blockchain implementation can only occur by overcoming the regulatory hurdles, considering privacy concerns, and adopting and fostering technological adoption through which organizations can pave the path for transparent, accountable, and efficient governance practices in the future (see Figure 20.6).

20.9 Conclusion and Suggestions

India's legal environment for blockchain technology is changing. Although there is still uncertainty around the regulation, the Indian government's

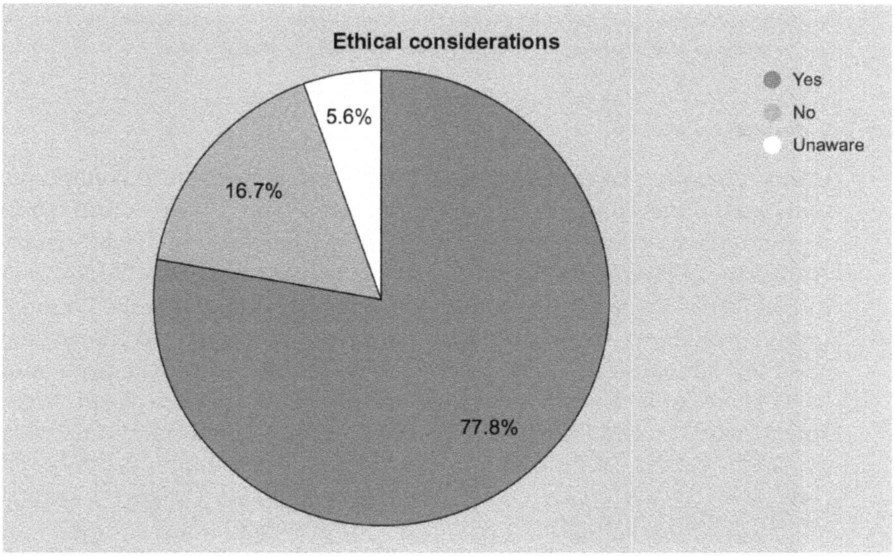

FIGURE 20.6
Ethical considerations of blockchain adoption.

interest in blockchain technology points to a promising future for the field. To navigate this ever-changing landscape, stakeholders in the blockchain field need to stay up to date on legal developments and ensure that current legislations are followed. Blockchain and its alignment with Indian legal governance have the potential to transform traditional processes and enhance the overall integrity and efficiency of the legal system. With its transparent and immutable records of legal proceedings, contracts, evidence, and judgments, blockchain technology has considerable potential to reduce the risk of fraud and manipulation, ensuring an individual's confidence in the judiciary and perpetuating impunity. Apart from that, blockchain-based smart contracts can bring greater efficiency and trust in legal transactions. We also see the future involvement of blockchain in keeping medical records and academic credentials, as it can be an ideal solution for storing sensitive information that can ensure accessibility and privacy protection for individuals. Cybersecurity is most important in safeguarding blockchain networks and data against cyberattacks, which can be achieved only by implementing robust encryption tools to secure access and regulate security audits to mitigate vulnerabilities to ensure the confidentiality and integrity of blockchain-based systems. Privacy and data protection regulations are necessary to balance transparency and people's right to privacy. Implementing privacy-enhancing technologies and establishing clear data protection guidelines will lead to trust and confidence in blockchain technology. Overall, blockchain technology in the future can perfectly revolutionize the management of intellectual property rights, land records, and government processes that can mitigate the risk of disputes, combat corruption, and promote fair compensation.

20.9.1 Suggestions

- **Comprehensive Legal Framework:** It is very important to collaborate with legal bodies and existing governments so that they can draft strict regulations specific to blockchain. The best example is the Monetary Authority of Singapore, which was established to oversee blockchain-related activities to ensure compliance with regulations in the country. Indian initiatives such as TCS's Quartz, which offers 20 blockchain solutions globally, are very good initiatives. Still, various aspects also need to be looked into, such as data protection, identity verification, smart contract execution, and dispute resolution. India should also consider various regulatory environments, including crypto-based solutions, so the legal framework accommodates diverse industry offerings while maintaining regulatory compliance.
- **Infrastructure development:** The collaboration between Bokaro Steel Plant and Telecommunications Consultants India Limited in utilizing 5G technology in mining operations highlights the need to implant robust infrastructure for blockchain technology's full potential, which includes high-speed internet connectivity, cybersecurity measures, and various other standards to facilitate seamless integration of blockchain across sectors. With the help of solid infrastructure, India can increase the efficiency of blockchain solutions, eventually leading to innovation and economic growth.
- **Ethical guidelines**: Ethical considerations and legal regulations are crucial for developing and implementing blockchain solutions. India should work with industrial organizations, academic institutions, and regulatory bodies to formulate ethical guidelines to promote transparency, accountability, and fairness in blockchain applications. These guidelines can help the stakeholders to take action and ensure that blockchain technologies are deployed responsibly and ethically.
- **Education and Training Programs:** To encourage the mass population to adopt blockchain technology, India must invest in education and training initiatives by conducting workshops and seminars for spreading awareness and building awareness among stakeholders, which includes policymakers, entrepreneurs, professionals, and the general public. Offering various courses and certified programs can help individuals equip with knowledge and skills to leverage blockchain effectively in their diverse sectors.
- **Continuous Monitoring and Evaluation:** There is a strict need to establish mechanisms for continuously monitoring and evaluating blockchain solutions, including regular assessments to check effectiveness,

relevance, and compliance with regulatory requirements. Staying vigilant on and responsive to the rapid technological advancements, we can, together as a whole, ensure that blockchain technology remains effective, relevant, and aligned with the needs of diverse sectors. By embracing a few measures, India can look forward to a future where blockchain technology could play a central role in the country's development and achieving economic growth, unlocking new opportunities for economic growth and overall societal development.

To fully realize the potential of blockchain technology, it is essential to adopt a stringent and adaptable legal framework or policies that can help integrate blockchain technology successfully. The framework should include the legal and regulatory aspects and consider the ethical conduct for its responsible implementation. Clear guidelines should be provided in data protection, identity verification, legal processes, and the execution of smart contracts so that clarity can be provided to stakeholders and a conducive atmosphere for innovation and adoption of blockchain solutions can be created through the integration of diverse perspectives and cooperation that are technically sound and legally compliant. This can be facilitated by knowledge sharing, resource pooling, and joint problem solving that will pace innovation and ensure blockchain technology can address all the challenges and needs in diverse sectors. Education and training programs are essential to build expertise in blockchain technology so that a workforce is fully prepared to explore the potentiality of blockchain. Launching awareness campaigns is necessary so that individuals can know the benefits of the technology and are not resistant to change in its adoption. Furthermore, strict monitoring and continuous evaluation should go hand in hand so that India can ensure that the technology remains effective, relevant, and responsive to the evolving trends and challenges of the diverse sectors. Therefore, it is the need of the hour to reshape blockchain technology and ensure that it gets aligned with legal governance to drive excellence and progress in the digital era.

REFERENCES

Ashurst, S., & Tempesta, S. (2021). *Blockchain Applied: Practical Technology and Use Cases of Enterprise Blockchain for the Real World*. Productivity Press. www.taylorfrancis.com/books/mono/10.4324/9781003132592/blockchain-applied-stephen-ashurst-stefano-tempesta

Bureau, D. (2023, July 4). Blockchain technology: A farm-to-plate traceability solution for seed value chain. *Krishak Jagat*. www.en.krishakjagat.org/global-agriculture/blockchain-technology-a-farm-to-plate-traceability-solution-for-seed-value-chain/

Hechler, E., Oberhofer, M., & Schaeck, T. (2020). *AI and Blockchain.* In Deploying AI in the Enterprise: IT Approaches for Design, DevOps, Governance, Change Management, Blockchain, and Quantum Computing (pp. 253–271). Berkeley, CA: Apress

ICAEW. (2018, November 30). History of blockchain. Retrieved [date you accessed] from www.icaew.com/technical/technology/blockchain-and-cryptoassets/blockchain-articles/what-is-blockchain/history

Javaid, M., Haleem, A., Singh, R. P., Suman, R., & Khan, S. (2022). *A Review of Blockchain Technology Applications for Financial Services. BenchCouncil Transactions on Benchmarks, Standards, and Evaluations.* www.sciencedirect.com/science/article/pii/S2772485922000606

Kopyto, M., Lechler, S., von der Gracht, H. A., & Hartmann, E. (2020). Potentials of blockchain technology in supply chain management: Long-term judgments of an international expert panel. *Technological Forecasting and Social Change*, 161, 120330.

Kshetri, N. (2021, April). *Blockchain technology for improving transparency and citizen's trust.* In Future of Information and Communication Conference (pp. 716–735). Cham: Springer International Publishing.

Panda, S. (2023). *Recent Blockchain Springer Book.* https://link.springer.com/book/10.1007/978-3-031-22835-3

Pandey, S., & Sen, C. (2022a). Blockchain technology in real-time governance: An Indian scenario. *Indian Journal of Public Administration, 68*, 397–413. https://journals.sagepub.com/doi/10.1177/00195561221105241

Radhakrishna, T & Roy., R. (2022, May 1). Maharashtra to come out with 'State Blockchain Policy' soon. ETGovernment (Economic Times). Retrieved from https://government.economictimes.indiatimes.com/news/technology/maharashtra-to-come-out-with-state-blockchain-policy-soon/74074086

Roth, J., Schär, F., & Schöpfer, A. (2020). The Tokenization of assets: using blockchains for equity crowdfunding. In Theories of change: Change leadership tools, models and applications for investing in sustainable development (pp. 329–350). Cham: Springer International Publishing.

T to develop a framework to boost Web3 & blockchain. (2023, July 23). *The Times of India.* https://timesofindia.indiatimes.com/city/hyderabad/t-to-develop-framework-to-boost-web3-blockchain/articleshow/102048749.cms

Tyagi, A. (2023). *Decentralized Everything: Practical Use of Blockchain Technology in Future Applications* (pp. 19–38). Academic Press.

Vayadande, K., Shaikh, R., Rothe, S., Patil, S., Baware, T., & Naik, S. (2022). Blockchain-based land record system. *ITM Web of Conferences*, 50, 01006. https://doi.org/10.1051/itmconf/20225001006

Zheng, Z., Xie, S., Dai, H.-N., Chen, X., & Wang, H. (2017, June 25). *An Overview of Blockchain Technology: Architecture, Consensus, and Future Trends.* https://ieeexplore.ieee.org/document/8029379

Zheng, Z., Xie, S., Dai, H.-N., Chen, X., & Wang, H. (2018). Blockchain challenges and opportunities: A survey. *International Journal of Web and Grid Services, 14*, 352. www.inderscienceonline.com/doi/abs/10.1504/IJWGS.2018.095647

Part VI

Embedding DEIB in Digital Foundations

21

The Safety Algorithm: How Safetipin Translates Women's Experiences into Urban Policy

Arif Perdana, Vijayakumar Bharathi S., Eka Permanasari, and Kanchan Patil

21.1 Introduction

At the heart of Delhi on the evening of 16 December 2012, a tragic incident shocked the nation and sparked global outrage (BBC, 2020; Bhandari, 2024). The brutal gang rape and subsequent death of a young woman on a moving bus catalysed unprecedented public discourse on women's safety in urban India (Kohli, 2024). This watershed moment demanded not only outrage but also actionable change. Amid growing concerns over urban security, a critical gap became evident in conventional approaches: an absence of preventive, data-driven, and community-centred strategies that reflect how women experience safety. Traditional methods (such as police patrols, CCTV installation, and post-incident investigations) mainly respond after incidents occur, rather than preventing them. It overlooks the power of real-time insights and localised data to drive meaningful changes (Polonyi, 2021; Viswanath, 2016).

India has advanced women's education, employment, and legal rights, yet fear of violence and harassment in public spaces restricts women's freedom and social participation. Women's safety intersects with gender inequality, patriarchal norms, inadequate infrastructure, and policy implementation gaps. Beyond preventing violence, empowering women's rightful community and economic participation requires understanding their urban interactions as co-creators of safe spaces, not merely users. This necessitates recognising lived realities shaping women's navigation decisions and safety perceptions. Urban spaces embody power dynamics creating different experiences for various users, demanding comprehensive approaches that address structural inequalities rather than surface-level interventions (Xu

DOI: 10.1201/9781003591078-27

et al., 2025). For women across India's rapidly growing cities, navigating public areas involves complex mental calculations regarding routes, timing, transportation options, and contingency plans, which are largely invisible to traditional urban planners (Jagori, 2009; Mandal, 2020; Polonyi, 2021). The resulting restriction of mobility represents not merely an inconvenience but also a fundamental barrier to economic participation, social engagement, and civic access.

Safetipin transforms traditional Women's Safety Audits into a scalable digital platform, integrating technology, community participation, and institutional partnerships to enhance urban safety for women. Using mobile apps like My Safetipin, Safetipin Nite, and Safetipin Site, it collects real-time feedback, images, and safety data. The platform conducts city-wide audits, collaborates with partners like Uber for dashcam footage, and employs manual analysis with machine learning to generate location-based safety scores using parameters like lighting and walkability. This data informs urban stakeholder interventions, modernising traditional safety assessment methodologies for broader implementation. (Jagori, 2009; Mandal, 2020; Viswanath, 2016). By converting subjective safety perceptions into quantifiable data points, Safetipin created a language through which women's experiences could be translated into policy actions (Polonyi, 2021; Sil et al., 2023).

What distinguishes Safetipin from conventional urban safety initiatives is its fundamental reconceptualisation of safety as measurable, preventive, and deeply connected to spatial design (German et al., 2023; Manazir et al., 2019). Rather than focusing exclusively on post-incident responses or law enforcement, the platform builds a multidimensional understanding of safety using nine carefully selected parameters: lighting, openness, visibility, crowd density, security presence, walkway quality, transport access, gender usage, and subjective feeling (Dubey et al., 2024a; Sil et al., 2023). This approach recognises that safety is produced through both physical infrastructure and social dynamics, a breakthrough in urban planning that has traditionally treated these elements in isolation (Gupta et al., 2022).

Safetipin's technological architecture represents a sophisticated blend of mobile applications, geographic information systems (GIS), cloud computing, and artificial intelligence (AI) that collectively enable unprecedented community participation in urban governance (Dubey et al., 2024a; Sil et al., 2023). By creating a three-tiered system (i.e., My Safetipin for individual users, Safetipin Nite for large-scale data collection, and Safetipin Site for professional audits), the platform balances accessibility with analytical rigor (Dubey et al., 2024a; Dubey et al., 2025; Manazir et al., 2019). The resulting datasets provide information that city officials, researchers, and community advocates have long lacked empirical evidence of safety disparities that can guide targeted interventions.

The platform's impact extends across multiple dimensions. At the infrastructure level, Safetipin's mapping has directly informed the installation of thousands of streetlights, improved pedestrian pathways, and optimised public transit access points across Delhi, Mumbai, Bengaluru, and beyond (Uteng, 2021). At the institutional level, it has transformed how municipal authorities approach safety planning, creating accountability mechanisms that make women's concerns visible within formal governance systems (Dubey et al., 2024a; Dubey et al., 2025; Prabhakar et al., 2024). Perhaps most profoundly, at the community level, Safetipin empowered ordinary citizens, particularly women, to become active participants in shaping their urban environments, rather than passive recipients of planning decisions (German et al., 2023; Polonyi, 2021; Uteng, 2021).

Safetipin's journey is, however, not without its challenges. The platform confronts a digital divide, which potentially excludes the most vulnerable population from participation. It grapples with fluctuating user engagement, which threatens data continuity (Dubey et al., 2024a; Prabhakar et al., 2024; Puthige et al., 2021). It must navigate the implementation gap between the identified problems and the actual interventions. Critically, it faces the limitation that physical infrastructure improvements alone cannot address the sociocultural factors underlying gender-based violence.

As cities worldwide confront intensifying urbanisation alongside growing demands for inclusive development, Safetipin offers vital insights into how digital innovation can advance broader diversity, equity, inclusion, and belonging (DEIB) objectives. The platform demonstrates that women's safety is not a niche concern but a fundamental indicator of urban functionality, and that addressing it creates environments that better serve all residents, including seniors, children, persons with disabilities, and other marginalised groups. This case study examines an essential question at the nexus of technology, gender equity, and urban governance: *How can digital platforms transform subjective experiences of the socially excluded into actionable data that reshapes physical environments and institutional practices to create more inclusive cities?*

The remainder of this chapter is structured as follows: First, we explore Safetipin's technological architecture, examining how mobile applications, crowdsourcing, GIS mapping, and analytics create a comprehensive digital ecosystem for safety assessment. Second, we analysed Safetipin's implementation across major Indian cities, identifying key successes, challenges, and variations in local adoption. Third, we evaluated the platform's impact on women's safety and broader DEIB promotion, considering both quantitative infrastructure improvements and qualitative shifts in community empowerment. Finally, we assess strategic challenges and future directions, offering recommendations for enhancing Safetipin's effectiveness, as it scales globally while addressing limitations in access, engagement, and implementation.

21.2 Overview of Safetipin

Safetipin represents a compelling intersection between grassroots advocacy and digital innovation. It reshapes urban safety through participatory data collection. Rooted in the concept of the Women's Safety Audit, a methodology pioneered by feminist groups such as Jagori in India[1] and METRAC in Canada,[2] Safetipin translates community-driven safety assessments into actionable urban planning insights (Jagori, 2009; Mandal, 2020; Viswanath, 2016). Women's Safety Audit methodology combines subjective perception with objective indicators that allows users to evaluate the safety of public spaces. At the core of Safetipin's methodology is a Safety Audit, a structured survey designed to assess safety perceptions and conditions in public spaces (Manazir et al., 2019; McIlroy, 2023; Polonyi, 2021). The audit considers nine key parameters: lighting, openness, visibility, population density, security presence, walk-path quality, access to public transport, gender distribution of space usage, and an overall subjective sense of safety (Polonyi, 2021; Prabhakar et al., 2024; Viswanath, 2016). Each data point is geotagged and timestamped, allowing for granular spatial analysis of urban safety (German et al., 2023; Uteng et al., 2019). By integrating objective infrastructural factors and subjective perceptions, Safetipin constructs a multidimensional understanding of how safety is experienced across different locations. For instance, a well-lit street bustling with pedestrians and visible security measures would be safe, whereas an isolated, poorly lit street would be unsafe. This approach ensures that the analysis reflects not only physical conditions but also the lived experiences of diverse urban populations.

The initiative took shape when a team of urban safety researchers led by Dr. Kalpana Viswanath recognised a fundamental weakness in conventional security measures: their reactive nature and failure to incorporate preventive, community-driven strategies. Existing frameworks largely overlook how safety is experienced in daily life, relying instead on enforcement-led interventions rather than proactive, data-informed approaches that empower local communities to shape safer environments (Viswanath, 2016). By digitising the Women's Safety Audit into a mobile app, Safetipin built a scalable model that enabled cities to incorporate gender-sensitive data into infrastructure development and policy design (Polonyi, 2021; Viswanath, 2016). It refers to data collected, analysed, and presented considering gender differences and inequalities. It goes beyond simply disaggregating data by sex; it captures the diverse experiences, needs, and outcomes of individuals based on their gender identities and roles within society. Gender-sensitive data is crucial for identifying disparities, informing inclusive policies, and promoting equity in health, education, employment, and access to technology. It helps ensure that interventions and decisions do not unintentionally reinforce gender biases or discrimination.

Safetipin's foundation rests on understanding how urban environments affect women, girls, and marginalised genders' experiences, mobility, and access, converting these into tangible urban improvements. The name "Safetipin" embodies both technological and symbolic meaning. This represents digital map markers showing safety scores and referencing everyday tools Indian women use as makeshift weapons against harassment in crowded spaces.[3] Since inception, the organisation has evolved beyond startup origins, establishing partnerships with city governments, non-governmental organisations (NGOs), and global institutions including UN Women and the World Bank, expanding its transformative impact on urban safety infrastructure and policy development[4] (Safetipin, 2024a; World Bank Group, 2020). This trajectory demonstrates its transition from a localised initiative to a globally recognised force in urban safety planning.

Community participation was integral to the Safetipin model. Local residents, particularly women, contribute by conducting safety audits using mobile applications (Dubey et al., 2024a; Puthige et al., 2021; Uteng et al., 2019). This participatory approach democratises urban data collection, ensuring that the insights originate from those most affected by public space vulnerabilities. In addition, Safetipin deploys trained auditors in collaboration with municipal authorities and urban planners to systematically assess critical areas. The app design facilitates real-time data capture, making it an effective tool for monitoring urban safety trends over time (German et al., 2023).

The impact of Safetipin extends beyond data collection, as it actively informs policy interventions and urban planning decisions (Uteng & Turner, 2019). City authorities use Safetipin's insights to guide investment in street lighting, pedestrian pathways, and public transport accessibility. The organisation's collaboration with global agencies has positioned its data-driven approach as the best practice in urban safety governance. Safetipin's My Safetipin and Safetipin Nite apps collect data on nine safety characteristics, including "gender usage" which measures women's and children's presence as indicators of inclusivity. The 2022 She RISES framework provides structured measures for evaluating cities' responses to gendered safety experiences. Through perception surveys and safety audits, Safetipin captures women's subjective safety assessments, informing urban planning and real-time evaluations. The platform collaborates with grassroots organisations like Pravah and Mahila Jan Adhikar Samiti to ensure community engagement with women and youth. By embedding gender-sensitive safety considerations into city planning, Safetipin ensures that infrastructure developments align with the needs of all urban residents, particularly those with vulnerable demographics (Jagori, 2009; Uteng, 2021; Uteng & Turner, 2019).

Safetipin's model also highlights the potential for technology-driven social innovation. The integration of geospatial data, mobile technology, and participatory auditing creates an agile system that is capable of addressing urban safety challenges at scale (German et al., 2023; Manazir et al., 2019). Traditional crime mapping in India reactively uses police records and accident reports to identify hotspots after incidents occur, focusing on recording rather than preventing crimes. This retroactive approach lacks real-time accuracy and ignores unreported incidents, particularly gender-based harassment that women hesitate to reporting publicly. Safetipin offers proactive safety mapping through crowdsourced, geotagged data from users, especially women and youth, evaluating perceived safety across lighting, walkability, visibility, presence, and gender usage factors. This enables real-time monitoring and identifies dangerous areas before incidents occur. Unlike institutional reporting-dependent crime maps, Safetipin transforms subjective experiences into actionable data through individual contributions. Its adaptable, scalable model works effectively in megacities like Delhi and Mumbai, plus smaller towns lacking reliable crime data, shifting safety paradigms from reactive to preventive urban interventions.

21.3 Digital Technology Used by Safetipin

Urban safety perceptions and realities significantly influence mobility patterns, particularly for women. While urban planners and policymakers acknowledge these concerns, systematically capturing and translating lived experiences into actionable insights remains a persistent challenge. Safetipin, a technology-driven platform, addresses this gap by redefining how cities assess, quantify, and enhance safety through digital infrastructure. By integrating mobile applications, crowdsourced data, GIS mapping, and advanced analytics, Safetipin enables a data-driven approach to the inherently subjective domain of urban safety, offering policymakers and stakeholders a more systematic framework for intervention.

21.3.1 Mobile Technology as the Foundation

Safetipin's technological architecture begins with a suite of purpose-built mobile applications that serve distinct, but complementary functions. The flagship app My Safetipin puts the power of safety assessment directly in citizens' hands through an intuitive interface that allows users to rate locations on nine parameters (Viswanath & Basu, 2015). Beyond simple data collection, the app delivers immediate value to users with features such as safety-optimised routing between locations, real-time alerts when entering higher-risk areas, and a "Track Me" function that enables virtual accompaniment through trusted contacts (Domde et al., 2017). The platform's data collection capabilities extend far beyond individual user input through Safetipin Nite, a specialised application that transforms ordinary vehicles into mobile data collection units (Dubey et al., 2024b). By mounting smartphones on car dashboards, the app captures geotagged photographs at regular intervals, allowing for rapid, systematic auditing of entire street networks. This represents a fundamental innovation: the conversion of everyday vehicles into urban sensing platforms that can efficiently cover vast areas.

For structured professional assessments, Safetipin deploys Safetipin Site, designed for tablets and web interfaces (Dubey et al., 2024a; McIlwaine & Ansari, 2024). This application enables trained auditors to conduct comprehensive surveys of specific infrastructure points, such as bus stops, parks, or marketplaces, capturing detailed parameters from lighting quality to the presence of security personnel. Three mobile phone applications—My Safetipin; Safetipin Nite and Safetipin Site—ensure comprehensive data collection across different urban contexts and stakeholder needs. The My Safetipin app democratises safety assessment by engaging ordinary citizens, Safetipin Nite enables efficient large-scale data gathering, and Safetipin Site facilitates professional and structured evaluations of critical infrastructure. Together, these applications create an integrated ecosystem that balances subjective user experiences with objective measurements, producing a multidimensional understanding of urban safety that neither citizens nor professionals can capture.

21.3.2 Digital Participation at Scale

What distinguishes Safetipin from conventional urban surveys is its fundamental embrace of crowdsourcing as both a methodology and a philosophy (Dubey et al., 2024a; Puthige et al., 2021; Viswanath & Basu, 2015). The platform goes beyond data collection, empowering citizens to become active participants in the urban governance process. Thousands of users across cities, such as Delhi, Mumbai, and Chennai, have contributed audits, creating a living repository of safety perceptions that evolve in real time (Bansal et al., 2022; Datta, 2022). This approach serves a dual purpose: it gathers granular insights from daily experiences that would be invisible to conventional urban surveys while simultaneously raising awareness and building agency among participants. A college student auditing her daily commute, for instance, not only contributes valuable data but also gains a deeper awareness of urban safety factors that shape her own decision-making.

Safetipin amplified this participatory dimension through strategic integration with social media and municipal campaigns. By making its data accessible through platforms such as the India Urban Data Exchange (IUDX), it extends the principle of crowdsourcing beyond collection to utilisation, enabling researchers, civic technologists, and ordinary citizens to analyse and build upon accumulated knowledge.[5] The platform strategically partners with local NGOs to expand its reach and to enhance community engagement. In Mumbai, Safetipin collaborated with Akshara, a women's rights organisation, to collect data and advocate for safer public spaces (Shah et al., 2017).

Similarly, Chennai's implementation involved cooperation with Prajnya, a local NGO that mobilised volunteers to conduct safety audits (Safetipin, 2024b). These partnerships not only increase data collection capacity but also ensure that safety improvements reflect the specific needs of those most affected by urban insecurity. This represents a sophisticated application of citizen science principles: communities are not merely sources of data, but co-producers of knowledge that directly affect their living environment. Digital infrastructure thus facilitates not only measurement but also mobilisation, a critical factor in sustaining urban reforms beyond initial interventions.

21.3.3 Geographic Information System as the Analytical Engine

At Safetipin's core lies a robust GIS that transforms thousands of discrete data points into comprehensible spatial narratives (German et al., 2023; Le, 2022). Each safety audit is stored with precise latitude-longitude coordinates and visualised on interactive maps, converting complex data patterns into instantly recognisable visual signals through colour-coded pins and heat maps (Hawken et al., 2020). This spatial approach is more than visualisation, and it enables analytical insights that would be impossible using tabular data alone. In Kolkata, for instance, Safetipin's mapping revealed striking correlations between infrastructure quality and women's presence in public spaces (Safetipin, 2023b). By overlaying "gender usage" patterns with factors such as lighting and security, the platform identified wards where women were virtually absent after dark, corresponding directly to poor infrastructure ratings.

The GIS framework integrates seamlessly with existing municipal systems, providing standardised data formats such as Shapefiles or Excel sheets that authorities can incorporate into their urban planning databases. In Gwalior, Safetipin's safety data were integrated into the city's "One City One App" system, making safety insights accessible to both the public and city planners (Safetipin, 2021). This interoperability ensures that safety considerations become embedded in broader urban development processes rather than remaining isolated in specialised systems. GIS functionality allows Safetipin to generate targeted, actionable outputs for specific stakeholders. Transit authorities receive maps of poorly lit corridors around stations, municipal corporations visualise dark spots requiring immediate intervention, and police departments obtain spatial analyses of high-risk zones requiring enhanced patrols.

In Delhi, this approach identified thousands of dark spots that the authorities subsequently addressed with additional lighting (Viswanath & Basu, 2015). More importantly, spatial intelligence creates a common visual language between citizens and authorities. When municipal officials see red clusters indicating safety hazards directly overlaid on familiar city maps, the abstract concept of "women's safety concerns" becomes concrete and specific (Dhawale et al., 2023). As one observer noted, the quantitative data and visual mapping "act like a foot inside the door" to initiate discussions with officials who might otherwise overlook sex-specific urban experiences (Dhawale et al., 2023).

21.3.4 Analytics and Artificial Intelligence

With hundreds of thousands of audit points collected across multiple cities, Safetipin operates firmly in the realm of big data analytics (Hawken et al., 2020). The platform aggregates diverse inputs, such as numeric safety ratings, textual comments, and thousands of street photographs and applies analytical techniques to extract meaningful patterns (German et al., 2023; Safetipin, 2021, 2023b; Viswanath & Basu, 2015). These analytics operate on multiple scales. At the macro level, Safetipin computes citywide safety scores that enable comparative analysis across urban centres and longitudinal tracking of improvements (Safetipin, 2015). At the micro level, the platform can isolate specific parameters such as lighting or visibility to identify precise intervention points.

Data has been gathered using the My Safetipin and Safetipin Nite apps in more than 80 cities worldwide as of 2023–2024 annual report, including those in India, Asia, Africa, and Latin America.[6] In four Rajasthani cities—Jaipur, Udaipur, Ajmer, and Jodhpur, the Cities for Youth initiative alone produced over 35,200 geotagged data points, carried out 4,800+ safety assessments, and completed 1,380+ user perception surveys. In 2023, a citywide safety mapping project in Delhi generated over 200,000 photos for processing, identified important safety indicators spanning 3,054 bus stops and 90 metro stations, and covered 2,338 km of streets with 17,927 audit sites. As data volumes have grown exponentially across multiple cities, Safetipin has increasingly incorporated AI and machine learning to enhance its analytical capabilities. Image recognition algorithms help classify photographs captured through Safetipin Nite, automatically detecting streetlights, pedestrian activity, and infrastructure conditions ((Dubey, et al., 2024a; Dubey et al., 2025; Manazir et al., 2019). This AI-powered approach reduces manual review efforts while increasing the platform's ability to efficiently process massive datasets. The platform also explores predictive analytics to forecast emerging safety risks. By correlating historical audit data with crime statistics and infrastructure records, Safetipin can identify potential safety issues before they manifest themselves as security incidents. For example, patterns of deteriorating lighting in a district might correlate with increased vulnerability, allowing authorities to take preemptive action before the safety conditions worsen significantly.

As data volumes have grown, Safetipin has increasingly incorporated AI, particularly for processing vast image libraries captured through the Safetipin Nite. The platform maintains a "certified team for the review and codification" of photos, suggesting a semi-automated approach to identifying elements such as broken streetlights, poor sidewalks, or empty streets in nighttime images. Computer vision algorithms are likely to supplement human reviews to handle the scale of visual data being processed (Le, 2022; Topham et al., 2023). The analytics infrastructure also supports impact assessment by enabling before-and-after comparisons following the interventions. Delhi's significant reduction in dark spots between 2015 and 2018, for example, was precisely quantifiable because the platform could systematically compare safety parameters across time periods.[7] Drawing from numeric safety scores, geo-tagged photographs, and user-generated textual insights, the system combines crowdsourced intelligence with AI-driven processing and predictive analytics. The methodology, as tabulated below, illustrates how Safetipin enables data collection, processing, and presentation to inform actionable urban safety and inclusion decisions (see Table 21.1).

21.3.5 Cloud Computing

Underpinning Safetipin's technology stack is a robust cloud computing architecture that enables seamless data flow, storage, and distribution (Dubey, 2024). This cloud-first approach allows the platform to scale across cities without requiring local infrastructure investments; auditors in Delhi can simultaneously contribute to the same system in real time. Cloud storage facilitates Safetipin's open data initiatives, making audit scores available through standardised application programming interfaces. This interoperability has proven crucial for integration with government systems. In cities like Chennai, municipal corporations have incorporated Safetipin's data layers directly into their existing GIS platforms for planning purposes.

The cloud architecture significantly enhances Safetipin's commitment to open-data principles. By hosting safety data on shared platforms, such as the IUDX, the platform encourages wider utilisation beyond its immediate partners. Government agencies, academic researchers, urban planners, and social enterprises can access these data to inform their own initiatives, creating a multiplier effect that extends Safetipin's impact beyond its direct interventions.[8] Cloud-based deployment also streamlines integration with emerging smart-city initiatives. Urban management platforms and command centres can incorporate Safetipin's data streams into their dashboards, ensuring that safety intelligence is embedded in broader urban governance frameworks. This alignment with smart city infrastructure positions Safetipin as both a standalone safety solution and a critical enabler of data-driven urban development (Bansal et al., 2022; Datta, 2020; Hawken et al., 2020). Cloud architecture also enables collaborative projects across organisational boundaries. International partners such as UN Habitat and the World Bank can access dashboards displaying data from multiple project cities simultaneously, facilitating cross-city learning and comparative analysis that would be impossible with localised systems (World Bank Group, 2020).

TABLE 21.1

Data Management in Mysafetipin app for Informed Decision-Making

Method	Description	Purpose	Decision-Making Support
Crowdsourcing via MySafetipin App	Citizens contribute safety audits, geo-tagged photos, and qualitative feedback directly through the app.	Captures public perception and real-time situational feedback.	Empowers individuals and communities to map safety, while supporting civic participation in decision-making processes. Enables hyperlocal insights for planners.
Project-Specific Audits via Safetipin Site App	Trained personnel conduct structured assessments tailored to infrastructure or stakeholder requirements.	Standardised and repeatable data collection across project sites.	Informs city authorities and urban planners about area-specific interventions using structured, comparative datasets.
City-Wide Visual Mapping via Safetipin Nite App	Smartphone-mounted vehicles capture nighttime street imagery, which is then semi-automatically processed.	Generate comprehensive nighttime safety datasets at scale.	Enhances planning at macro and micro levels—identifies lighting gaps, isolated areas, and infrastructure deficits. Supports longitudinal tracking.
AI & Machine Learning-Based Image Processing	Computer vision algorithms classify street imagery to detect lighting, walk paths, visibility, and crowd density.	Reduces manual review; scales processing of massive image datasets.	Speeds up risk detection and identifies precise intervention points like broken lighting or poor sidewalks. Enables predictive maintenance planning.
Integration with External GIS and Crime Data	Datasets are layered with local authority information (e.g., infrastructure, police zones, crime data).	Creates a multidimensional understanding of urban safety.	Facilitates evidence-based policymaking and prioritisation of safety upgrades. Supports preemptive interventions using risk forecasting.
Data Visualisation in Maps & CSV Formats	Data is accessible through dashboards, downloadable tables, and geo-maps.	Enables public transparency and stakeholder accountability.	Supports monitoring, evaluation, and "before-after" comparisons to assess intervention outcomes. Aids budget allocation and policy reporting.

21.3.6 The Technology-Governance Interface

Safetipin's most significant achievement may be how its digital infrastructure interfaces with the governance processes. The platform actively integrates itself as a conduit between citizen experiences and government action, ensuring that lived realities inform policy and urban interventions

(Dubey, et al., 2024b). Formal agreements with municipal bodies in cities such as Delhi, where the Department of Women and Child Development commissioned citywide safety mapping, ensure that data flows directly to decision-makers.[9] This technology–governance interface extends to multiple stakeholders: law enforcement uses data to optimise patrol routes, urban planners incorporate safety parameters into design guidelines, and transit authorities address vulnerabilities around transportation nodes.

The platform demonstrated remarkable versatility in engaging with different governance structures. In Delhi, the Municipal Corporation and Police Department both leveraged Safetipin's insights to make coordinated interventions. The former addressed infrastructure deficiencies by installing additional street lights at over 7,000 locations, while the latter optimised patrol routes to cover identified high-risk zones. In Gurgaon, the Municipal Corporation used Safetipin's findings to upgrade street lighting at more than 800 locations, directly improving the conditions in previously neglected areas (Dhankar, 2024). This collaborative approach creates accountability mechanisms that are often absent in traditional urban safety initiatives. When safety data are transparently shared between citizens, civil society organisations, and government authorities, it becomes more difficult to ignore the identified problems. Safetipin has effectively created a data-driven framework that makes women's safety concerns visible, measurable, and actionable within formal governance systems (Dhawale et al., 2023). Figure 21.1 presents an overview of Safetipin core technology infrastructure and external system integration.

By serving as this digital intermediary between lived experience and policy response, Safetipin accomplished something remarkable: inserting women's safety concerns into mainstream urban agendas through the universal language of data. This platform demonstrates how thoughtfully designed digital infrastructure can bridge subjective experiences and objective interventions, ultimately creating more inclusive cities that work better for everyone.

21.4 Safetipin across India

Urban safety, particularly for women, remains a critical issue in India's rapidly growing cities. Safetipin, a technology-driven initiative, has emerged as a key player in addressing this challenge by providing data-driven insights that can guide urban safety interventions. Through comprehensive safety audits, the platform influenced city planning, infrastructure improvements, and policy changes. This case study examines Safetipin's implementation and impact in major Indian cities, highlighting the key successes, challenges, and lessons learned. Figure 21.2 shows an overview of Safetipin's implementation across several cities in India.

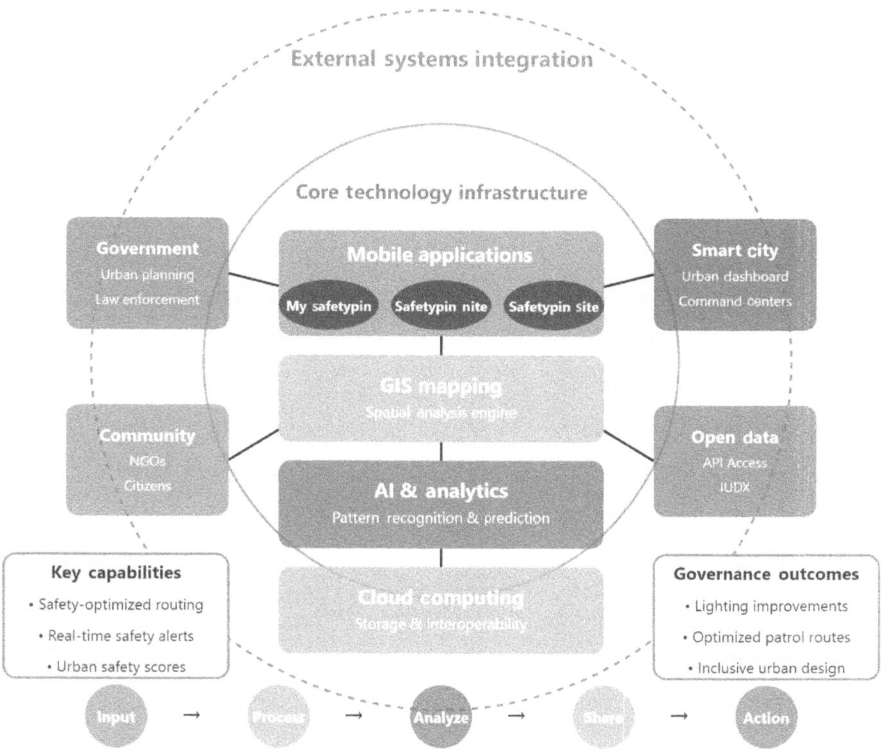

FIGURE 21.1
Safetipin technological infrastructure.

21.4.1 Delhi: A Model for Scalable Urban Safety

As a pilot city, Delhi was Safetipin's first major implementation and remains the most comprehensive case study. Beginning in late 2013, Safetipin conducted safety audits across upscale neighbourhoods, low-income areas, and transit hubs. Partnering with the local NGO Jagori, volunteers conducted nighttime manual audits, while the Safetipin Nite app collected photographic data through vehicles equipped with mobile devices (Jagori, 2009).

By 2014, Safetipin had established itself as a trusted data partner for the Delhi government, conducting safety audits that helped to identify and address lighting issues throughout the city. Their data assisted the Delhi Police in reformulating patrol routes to improve safety. From 2016 to 2023, there was a dramatic reduction in dark spots across Delhi from 7,438 in 2016 to 2,780 in 2019, and further down to just 727 in 2023, representing over 90% reduction in seven years. The Delhi government proactively responded to these findings by launching the "Mukhya Mantri Street Light Yojana" (Chief Minister's Street Lights Scheme) with dedicated annual budget allocations

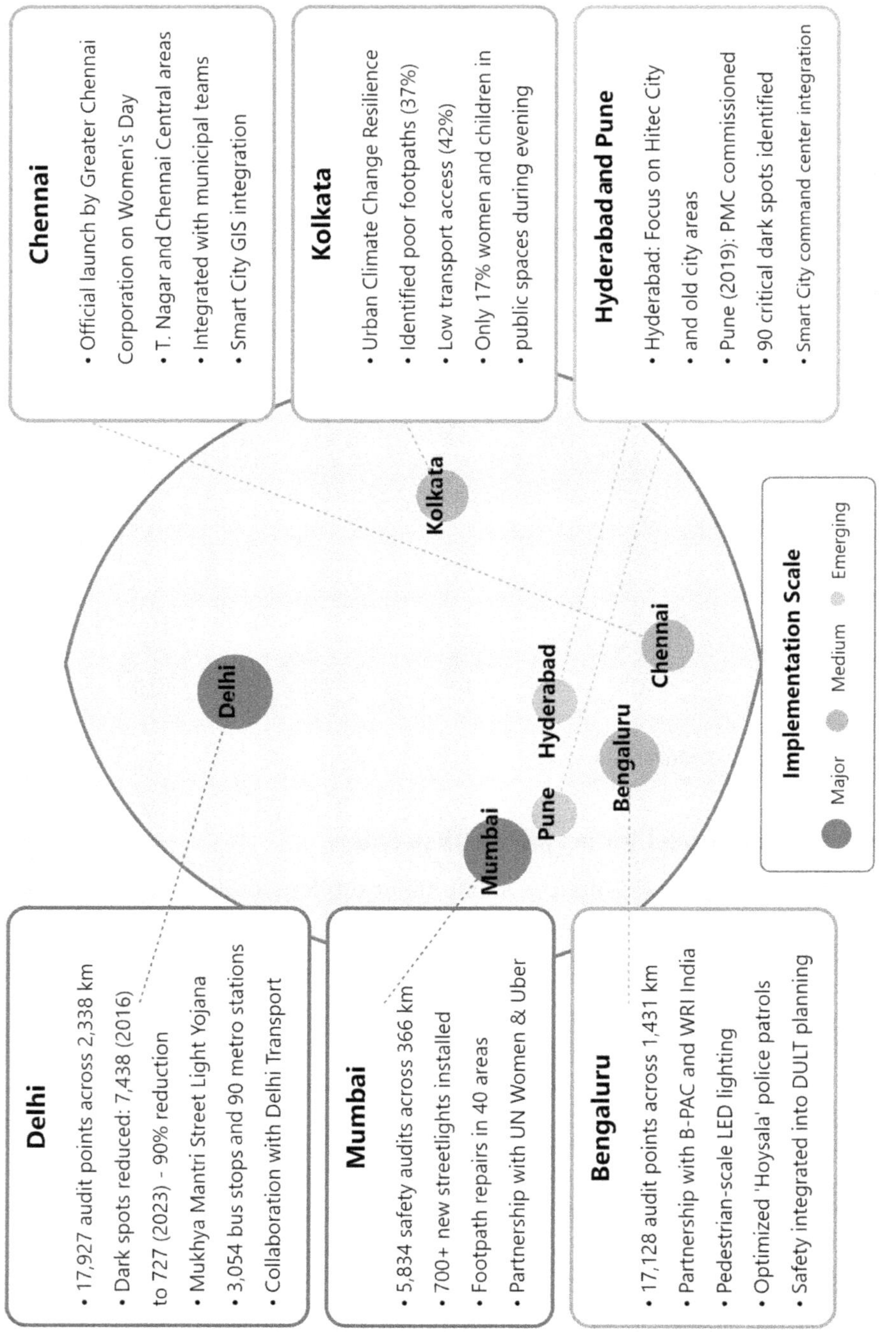

FIGURE 21.2
Overview of Safetipin implementation across several cities in India.

for lighting improvements. The 2023 comprehensive audit covered 2,338 km of streets with 17,927 audit points, including 3,054 bus stops and 90 metro stations, generating over 200,000 images analysed across eight safety parameters (Safetipin, 2015, 2024a).

Although significant progress has been made in improving street lighting infrastructure, Safetipin's work has expanded to address broader transportation safety issues. Their collaboration with the Delhi Transport Corporation focuses on increasing bus ridership and improving women's employment in the transport sector, including specific studies at Nehru Place and Mehrauli bus terminals in 2023. These comprehensive efforts demonstrate how data-driven approaches can systematically improve the urban safety infrastructure over time.

21.4.2 Mumbai: Infrastructure Gains and Public Accountability

Mumbai's engagement with Safetipin began in 2015–2016, with support from UN Women. Partnering with the Akshara Centre and Uber, the project focused on public transit routes, commercial districts, and informal settlements (Safetipin, 2017b). By 2017, data from 5,834 safety audits across 366 km of city roads were compiled into a comprehensive Safety Score Map that provided granular insights into intra-city variations. The key findings highlighted poor lighting, inadequate pedestrian infrastructure, and low natural surveillance in several areas. These findings prompted the Brihanmumbai Municipal Corporation to install new streetlights at over 700 identified dark spots and repair footpaths in 40 high-priority areas. The Mumbai Police increased night patrols and stationed female constables at key transit hubs (Safetipin, 2017b). However, its implementation was uneven. While improvements in high-footfall areas such as Marine Drive and major train stations were swift, marginalised areas such as Mankhurd and Dharavi saw slower progress due to administrative coordination challenges. Nevertheless, Safetipin's ability to mobilise public interest and media pressure created an ongoing accountability mechanism, compelling municipal authorities to respond more effectively.

21.4.3 Bengaluru: Aligning Safety with Smart City Goals

Bengaluru integrated Safetipin into its Smart City and urban transport initiatives in 2017, with support from the Bangalore Political Action Committee (B-PAC) and UK Aid (Safetipin, 2017a). In 2017, safety audits conducted by Safetipin, in collaboration with WRI India and B-PAC mapped 1,431 km of road length and generated 17,128 audit points across Bengaluru. The audits identified key infrastructure gaps, including broken or missing footpaths, inconsistent street lighting, and poorly illuminated transit hub. These findings have contributed to urban planning improvements by emphasising pedestrian-scale lighting and enhanced footpath infrastructure (Safetipin, 2017a).

Following these assessments, the Bangalore Metro Rail Corporation integrated safety considerations into metro station designs and the surrounding public spaces. Efforts have been directed toward installing pedestrian-scale LED lighting along major transit corridors and improving walkability near key employment hubs such as Electronics City and Whitefield. Additionally, Bangalore Police leveraged Safetipin's data to optimise their "Hoysala" patrol placements, ensuring improved safety coverage in high-risk areas. Despite these advancements, sustaining engagement with Safetipin's safety audits remains a challenge. While the initial assessments provided valuable data, infrequent public participation limited regular updates to the safety scores. Furthermore, rapid infrastructure expansion and metro construction projects have introduced evolving safety hazards, necessitating dynamic, real-time updates that are yet to be systematically implemented. The institutionalisation of safety reviews within the Directorate of Urban Land Transport, however, reflects a long-term commitment to integrate gender-sensitive urban planning and prioritise public safety in city development.

21.4.4 Chennai: Institutional Adoption and Community Engagement

Chennai's adoption of Safetipin in 2023 marks a city-led approach to women's safety. The Greater Chennai Corporation officially launched the My Safetipin app on International Women's Day, integrating safety audits into municipal operations (The Times of India, 2024). Initial assessments in commercial hubs, such as T. Nagar, and transit points, such as Chennai Central Station, revealed a mixed picture: affluent areas rated highly, while older districts and transit zones scored lower. A notable early success was the integration of the app with the civic maintenance teams. Residents can now report nonfunctional streetlights directly through the app, expediting repairs. Additionally, the Chennai Smart City initiative has begun overlaying Safetipin safety maps onto existing city GIS frameworks to holistically address infrastructural gaps. Maintaining public engagement remains a key challenge. While the app's launch generated enthusiasm, sustaining long-term participation required consistent outreach and incentives. Moreover, expanding audits beyond the city core to suburban areas remains an important next step in ensuring equitable safety improvements across metropolitan regions.

21.4.5 Kolkata: Integrating Safety with Non-Motorised Transport Planning

Kolkata engaged with Safetipin as a part of a study that focused on social vulnerability and accessibility in public spaces (Safetipin, 2023b). This Safetipin's study, funded by the Urban Climate Change Resilience Trust Fund, aimed to assess safety and walkability, particularly for women, children, the elderly, and persons with disabilities. Audits conducted across major pedestrian corridors, heritage areas, and residential zones revealed significant concerns including poor footpath quality (37%), lack of adequate transport access (42%), and low visibility (51%) in many areas. A key finding was the under-representation of women and children in public spaces during the evening (6–8 p.m.), accounting for only 17% of the observed foot traffic. This reinforces concerns about gendered mobility constraints, particularly in areas with limited lighting and visibility. To address these challenges, Safetipin's recommendations informed interventions, such as street lighting improvements, enhanced pedestrian pathways, and increased public transport accessibility (Safetipin, 2023b).

As part of the Comprehensive Mobility Plan 2025, authorities have focused on improving the lighting conditions and enhancing public surveillance in strategic areas. The New Town Kolkata Development Authority piloted "safe walking corridors" featuring continuous lighting, designated seating areas, and emergency helpline access, aiming to create a more pedestrian-friendly environment . However, implementation challenges remain. Kolkata's dense urban fabric and heritage preservation constraints limit large-scale infrastructure changes, making gradual improvement a more feasible approach. While donor-supported projects have catalysed change, long-term sustainability depends on sustained institutional commitment beyond the scope of time-bound funding (Safetipin, 2023b).

21.4.6 Hyderabad and Pune: Emerging Engagements

Hyderabad's Safetipin engagement has been relatively limited, but is growing. Early audits focused on HITEC City and old city areas, identifying disparities between planned business districts and informal settlements (Safetipin, 2024c). Although the city has not fully institutionalised Safetipin's methodology, independent audits have influenced infrastructure improvements, including expanded street lighting and Closed-Circuit Television (CCTV) installations. Future efforts could benefit from a structured, citywide, and Safetipin implementation.[10] Pune's engagement began in 2019, when the Pune Municipal Corporation commissioned citywide safety audits. The findings identified 90 critical dark spots, prompting lighting improvements and integration of safety metrics into the city's Smart City command centre. Although Pune's response has been proactive, addressing safety concerns in rapidly urbanising peripheral areas remains a challenge.

21.4.7 Future Areas of Improvements

Future developments indicate Safetipin's capacity for expanded influence across digital innovation, gender inclusion, and urban safety domains. Institutional integration of the She RISES framework represents a primary objective, facilitating data-driven, gender-responsive planning mechanisms within municipal governance structures across additional Indian cities. Youth engagement through the Cities for Youth model remains central to organisational strategy, particularly enabling young women to leverage technological tools and advocacy networks for urban development initiatives. The My Safetipin application will undergo continued enhancement, incorporating improved usability interfaces, real-time responsiveness capabilities, and hyperlocal safety functionalities. Platform adaptation for peri-urban and rural contexts with limited internet infrastructure constitutes another development priority. Institutional capacity building involves integrating safety audit protocols within municipal frameworks and incorporating safety datasets into existing urban planning platforms.

Public transportation infrastructure revision emphasises inclusive design principles, addressing specific requirements of female commuters and youth demographics. The organisation will explore emerging challenges including online gender-based violence and digital safety concerns. International expansion involves promoting cross-border collaboration and knowledge exchange, advancing feminist urban development principles that support inclusive, secure, and equitable urban environments globally.

21.5 Insights from Safetipin Users

Our analysis examines 98 Google Play Store and 25 iOS user reviews of the My Safetipin app spanning 2019–2024, systematically investigating user experiences to identify areas where the application successfully advances its safety objectives and where improvements are needed. The My Safetipin app generates safety scores through user audits of nine parameters: lighting, openness, visibility, people, security, walk path, public transport, gender usage, and feeling, which collectively assess perceived safety in physical environments.

Six primary themes emerged from user review analysis, corresponding closely with the app's nine safety audit parameters: safety and social impact, technical functionality, usability, data quality and privacy, community participation, and user support. The safety and social impact theme correlates with parameters including lighting, visibility, security, gender usage, and feeling, as users evaluate how these elements influence their empowerment and security perceptions in public spaces. Technical functionality and usability align with walk path and public transport parameters, reflecting users' experiences recording safety concerns and navigating urban environments.

Data quality and privacy concerns relate to crowdsourced data reliability across all parameters, particularly subjective measures like feeling and people, alongside personal data security considerations. Community participation operates through the auditing process itself, where users contribute observations regarding gender usage, openness, and people parameters, transforming individual experiences into collective urban intelligence. User support effectiveness influences feedback mechanisms and app responsiveness across all parameters. These themes demonstrate how My Safetipin operationalises subjective safety experiences into structured, actionable urban planning data.

21.5.1 Safety and Social Impact

The app's core proposition, to enhance safety for women and marginalised groups, resonates with users. Many describe My Safetipin as a "must-have" tool, particularly for navigating cities like Delhi. It is praised for features such as neighbourhood safety scoring, safe route suggestions, and its "find support" directory connecting users to local services such as police stations and crisis centres. Users from varied backgrounds, e.g., students living away from home, concerned parents, and everyday commuters, highlight the app's importance in helping them make informed decisions. This segment of the feedback shows a deep emotional connection with the app's mission. One user summarised the sentiment succinctly: "It helps me track which areas of my city are safe for women." Yet the praise is often accompanied by a sobering reflection, like the need for such an app reveals the persistence of unsafe public spaces and the lack of institutional guarantees around women's mobility. Some users express unease that personal safety now relies on private technological tools. One comment captures this discomfort: "Ah, the fact that women now need an app to feel a bit safe." The app's social utility is recognised, but it is also clear that it exists within a wider societal failure to ensure safety. In this sense, the app fills a critical gap, but its use is also a symptom of broader structural shortcomings.

21.5.2 Technical Functionality

Despite the conceptual strength of My Safetipin, persistent technical issues threaten its viability. A large proportion of negative feedback centres on fundamental problems, that is, frequent app crashes, login failures, one-time password (OTP) issues, and session timeouts. These are not minor usability concerns; they are critical failures that prevent users from even accessing the platform. Several reviews describe scenarios where users successfully install the app and register, only to be locked out by failed OTP delivery or repeated error messages such as "wrong password" despite correct inputs. Others report being stuck in a loop, such as being shown the frequently asked questions (FAQ) screen repeatedly without any navigation options. These issues do not merely frustrate users; they erode trust. In the context of a safety application, technical instability has a disproportionate impact. If users cannot rely on the app to function during times of need, its value proposition collapses. Comments such as "worst app" and "bogus" may appear emotionally charged, but they reflect the high expectations users place on safety-oriented technology. When those expectations are not met, the fallout is severe.

21.5.3 Usability and User Experience

On the surface, the app features a design that appears user-friendly to some. A subset of reviews describes the app as intuitive and straightforward, with specific praise directed at the Global Positioning System tracking and real-time location sharing functionality. These features are particularly valued by users who need to keep family members informed of their whereabouts. However, a more dominant pattern in the feedback reveals significant gaps in usability. Navigation is not intuitive for many users, and the absence of an effective onboarding process leaves some unsure about how to use key functions like contributing to a safety audit or reporting a concern. The interface sometimes fails to respond or loops back to the home screen or FAQ section, offering no clear path forward. Language accessibility also surfaces as a concern. One review suggests that support for local languages, such as Tamil, would broaden the app's utility. Others mention that the guidance and labels in the interface are too general, leading to confusion over what constitutes a useful contribution. The overall pattern is clear: the app is well-intentioned and offers valuable features, but usability inconsistencies limit adoption, especially among first-time users and those less familiar with mobile apps.

21.5.4 Data Quality, Privacy, and Trust

In an app that depends heavily on crowdsourced data, accuracy and transparency are paramount. Unfortunately, this is an area where user trust appears to be declining. Multiple users raise concerns over the reliability of safety scores and the completeness of the data. One comment specifically questions, "Why is the safety score of the area always changing?" These concerns point to either a lack of clarity in how data is collected and updated or actual inconsistency in the underlying algorithms. Even more concerning are privacy-related complaints. A few users note that deactivating an account does not necessarily remove their data from the app's servers. Phrases like "they can't entirely delete your account" suggest that the app has yet to establish clear data governance protocols or communicate them effectively to users. Trust, once lost, is hard to regain, especially for a platform centred on personal safety. Transparency about how user data is used, stored, and shared is not just a compliance issue; it is a functional requirement for legitimacy in this domain.

21.5.5 Community, Support, and Communication

A core premise of My Safetipin is that users themselves can contribute to improving the safety of public spaces by conducting audits and reporting concerns. In theory, this is a powerful model—decentralised, participatory, and scalable. Some users acknowledge this strength, noting that the app's effectiveness will increase as more people contribute. Comments like "the more the number of people using this app, the bigger impact it will create" reflect this belief in collective action. However, the implementation appears to lack guidance. Reviews indicate that users are unsure how to add a safety audit or rate an area. This is a missed opportunity. Crowdsourcing can only function when contributions are intuitive, low-effort, and clearly explained. Improving clarity around how users can engage, and perhaps adding gamification or incentives, could unlock significant value. Until then, the app's full potential remains unrealised. Figure 21.3 and Table 21.2 provide an overview of the themes and sample of positive and negative feedback.

21.6 Safetipin Impact on Women's Safety and DEIB Promotion

In cities across the globe, women navigate urban spaces differently than men, often taking longer routes, avoiding certain areas after dark, or limiting their mobility entirely owing to safety concerns (Fisher & Naidoo, 2016; Shucksmith & Brown, 2016). Spatial inequality extends beyond personal inconvenience, constituting a structural barrier to economic participation and civic engagement. Safetipin, a social enterprise, is reshaping how cities address safety disparities by integrating innovative data collection methodologies that align with broader DEIB objectives. Departing from conventional urban planning frameworks that assume safety to be gender-neutral, Safetipin has developed a system that systematically captures women's lived experiences in public spaces. By quantifying key environmental factors such as lighting, visibility, and crowd density, the platform generates actionable insights that bridge the gap between subjective perceptions of unsafety and data-driven municipal interventions (Dhawale et al., 2023; Jagori, 2009; Polonyi, 2021).

21.6.1 Translating Data into Urban Transformation

Safetipin's approach has led to tangible infrastructure enhancements in various cities, with Delhi as a prime example of data-driven policy reform. A thorough audit conducted in 2013–2014 revealed thousands of unlit areas

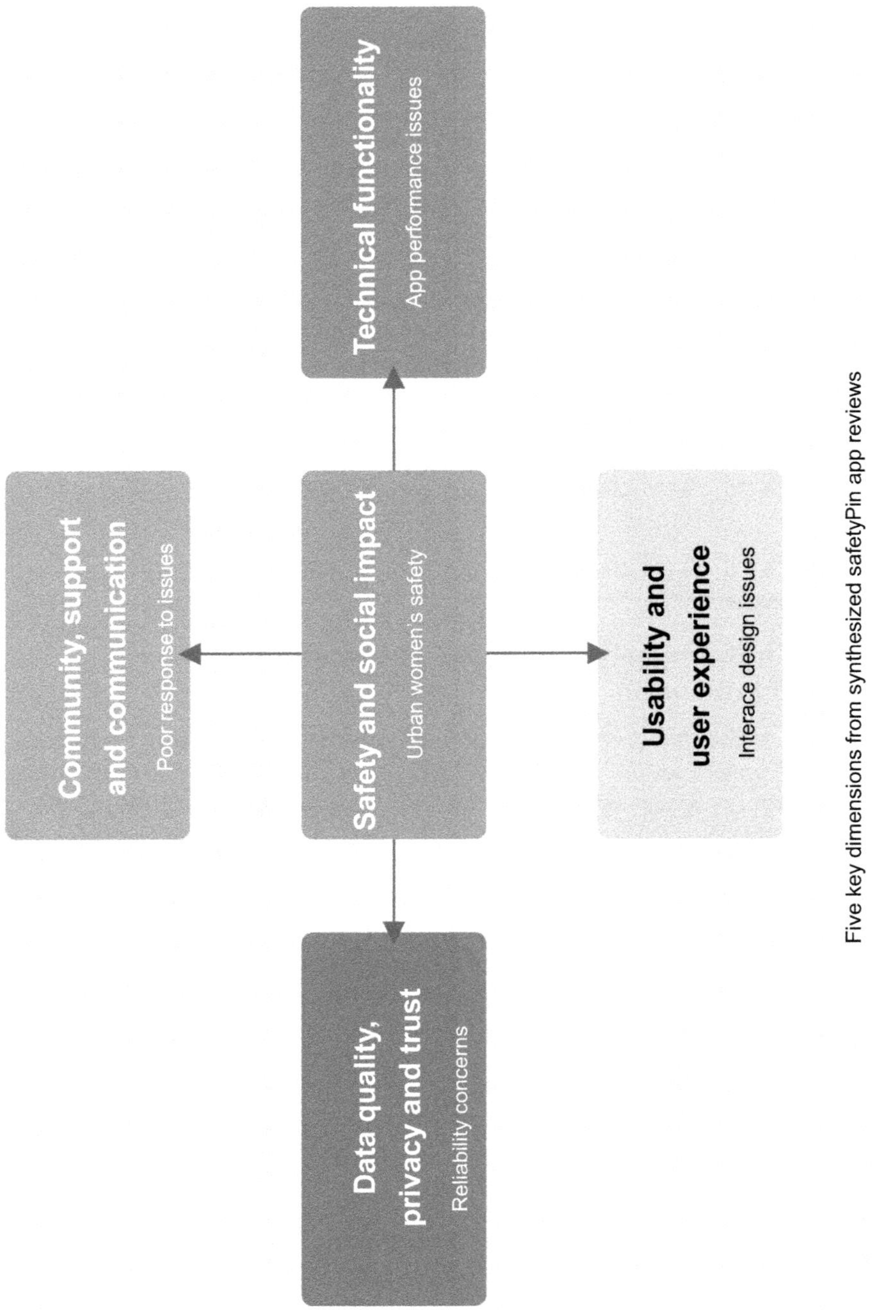

FIGURE 21.3
What users are saying about the My Safetipin App.

TABLE 21.2

Safetipin Users' Sentiment Summary Table

Theme	Sample Positive Feedback	Sample Negative Feedback
Safety and Social Impact	Valuable for women's safety, good for awareness, socially relevant	Frustration over societal need for such apps, inefficient routes, needs more user data
Technical Functionality	Rarely mentioned	Crashes, login failures, OTP issues, poor stability, erodes trust
Usability & Interface	User-friendly for some, good tracking features	Confusing UX, poor navigation, lack of onboarding, accessibility issues (e.g., language)
Data Quality, Privacy & Trust	Supports route planning and awareness	Inaccurate data, privacy concerns, lack of transparency, trust issues
Community, Support, and Communication	Encourages crowdsourcing, promotes awareness	Poor instructions for contributing, low engagement; No response to issues, lack of guidance, poor support system

across the city, prompting local authorities to initiate "Roshan Dilli" (Light Up Delhi).[11] Within three years, this effort successfully brought lighting to a significant portion of the dark spots. Beyond simply installing streetlights, the initiative also introduced routine maintenance procedures and strategically positioned police patrols in isolated or unsafe areas.

This pattern of data-informed intervention was repeated across contexts. The Delhi Transport Corporation leveraged Safetipin's "Safety & Accessibility assessment" of bus terminals to redesign pedestrian access routes and lighting systems (Safetipin 2023a). Cities such as Mumbai and Kolkata have begun formalising street vending in isolated zones, a strategy straight from Safetipin's playbook that simultaneously increases natural surveillance and supports local economies (Safetipin, 2017b, 2023b). The granular nature of Safetipin's data also enabled hyperlocal intervention. In Delhi's low-income Madanpur Khadar neighbourhood, young women used the platform to audit their streets through the "Aana-Jaana" (Coming and Going) project (Datta & Thomas, 2022). Their findings secure new streetlights and paved walkways, dramatically improving residents' nighttime mobility. Similarly, a Residents' Welfare Association in South Delhi's CR Park leveraged Safetipin's digital audit tool to identify and rectify broken infrastructure from missing street signs to overgrown shrubs that compromised visibility (Safetipin, 2019).

What makes these changes significant is their measurable impact on women's behaviour. Areas previously rated "Poor" on Safetipin's safety index improved to "Average" or "Good" following targeted interventions. Internal assessments documented corresponding increases in women's use of public spaces after the dark, particularly in zones with enhanced lighting, improved footpaths, and greater human presence. The virtuous cycle is clear: better data lead to more effective action, which enables greater freedom of movement for women.

21.6.2 From Gender-Responsive Design to Universal Inclusion

While Safetipin frames its mission as women's safety, its approach delivers broader societal benefits that advance comprehensive DEIB objectives (Hawken et al., 2020; Shah et al., 2017; Viswanath & Basu, 2015). The platform operates based on a fundamental insight: a city designed for its most vulnerable users improves the conditions for everyone. Better lighting, accessible walkways, and activated public spaces benefit seniors, children, people with disabilities, and individuals from marginalised communities. The data often reveal stark disparities between well-serviced affluent areas and neglected low-income neighbourhoods. In a study across Bhopal, Gwalior, and Jodhapur, Safetipin found that over 90% of women felt unsafe in significant portions of these cities, which coincided with inadequate basic amenities and infrastructure (Safetipin, 2024c). By highlighting these inequities, Safetipin advocates for more balanced urban development, where every district receives comparable attention, regardless of its socioeconomic profile.

Perhaps most telling is Safetipin's "Gender Usage" parameter, which quantifies the presence of women and children in public spaces (Safetipin, 2018). This metric serves as a direct indicator of inclusion; areas with zero female presence (especially after dark periods) represent clear zones of exclusion. The Safetipin audit in Kolkata revealed that women and children were present in only 17% of the city's streets during evening hours, with the remaining 83% having little to no female presence. These data highlight the need for targeted intervention to improve safety and accessibility. In response, authorities introduced measures, such as increased police presence in key areas and awareness programs, to encourage more inclusive public spaces (Safetipin, 2023b).

The participatory nature of Safetipin's methodology further advanced inclusion by inviting diverse stakeholders to conduct safety audits. This collaborative approach creates dialogue between groups that rarely interact; college students, homemakers, and police cadets might work together to assess neighbourhood safety. Such engagement validates women's experiences while educating men and officials about spatial inequities through concrete data rather than anecdotes. The platform's influence has been increasingly extended to formal policy frameworks. India's Smart Cities guidelines now incorporate safety audits and gender-disaggregated data as recommended indicators of inclusive development. The institutionalisation of Safetipin's approach suggests a meaningful shift in how urban planning conceptualises and prioritises safety.

When examined through an intersectional lens, Safetipin's interventions delivered multiple benefits. Improved street lighting helps LGBTQIA+ individuals who face harassment, better sidewalk design enables independent navigation for persons with disabilities and increased "eyes on the street" through commercial activities can enhance safety for religious or ethnic minorities in otherwise isolating environments. Ultimately, Safetipin demonstrates that urban safety is not merely about crime prevention, but also about creating environments where everyone feels they belong. Its data-driven methodology transforms abstract discussions on inclusion into concrete and measurable changes in the built environment. The result is a powerful model for gender-responsive urban planning that advances equity while creating more functional and vibrant public spaces for all city dwellers.

As cities worldwide face challenges of inclusion and belonging, Safetipin offers a replicable approach that recognises women's safety not as a niche concern, but as a fundamental indicator of urban health. By quantifying the previously unmeasured factors that shape women's mobility, the platform has created a powerful framework for building cities where everyone, regardless of gender, ability, or background, can move freely and confidently.

21.7 Navigating the Complexities of Urban Safety Innovation

At the intersection of technology and social change, Safetipin has emerged as a pioneering data-driven approach for transforming urban safety. The platform converts subjective safety experiences into actionable insights, empowering individuals at the grassroots level, while driving meaningful infrastructure improvements. Despite its impressive achievements in redefining how cities approach safety planning, Safetipin is now confronted with critical challenges that constrain its transformative potential.

21.7.1 The Power of Digital Empowerment

Safetipin's most significant achievement lies in the transformation of passive urban dwellers into active agents of change. Women in communities report feeling "heard" when their safety audit data translate into tangible improvements. The platform shifts community advocacy from subjective complaints to evidence-based recommendations, a particularly powerful shift for marginalised communities, whose concerns are frequently dismissed in traditional planning processes. Digital empowerment creates solidarity networks that extend beyond technological interfaces. When community members contribute multiple audits in a single area, they develop an awareness of shared concerns and often unite to address them collectively. In cities like Bangalore and Delhi, these digital connections have materialised into real-world safety committees and neighbourhood vigilance groups, with the data providing not only evidence for authorities but also rallying points for communities to self-organise.

This empowerment model is, however, constrained by digital divide. The app-based approach inevitably favours smartphones, reliable data connectivity, and technological literacy. The most vulnerable women, including domestic workers in urban slums and elderly residents unfamiliar with digital interfaces, often remain excluded from direct participation. While Safetipin has attempted to bridge this gap through partnerships with NGOs which represent these communities in data collection, truly inclusive participation remains elusive, leaving certain areas and populations at risk of underrepresenting their safety concerns (Manazir et al., 2019)

21.7.2 Confronting Implementation Challenges

Perhaps most critically, identifying safety issues presents an opportunity for timely intervention. When cities effectively address dark spots documented through data collection, they can overcome bureaucratic delays, budget constraints, and competing priorities to enhance women's safety in public spaces. This implementation gap reveals a fundamental truth: Technology alone cannot overcome governance challenges, and political will remains essential. This inconsistency in governmental response creates a demotivating feedback loop: When citizens see their data contributions lead to no visible changes, continued participation diminishes, particularly in communities that have historically experienced neglect from authorities (Uteng, 2021).

The platform's adoption by key stakeholders such as transport authorities and law enforcement remains inconsistent. Ambiguity in transport policies and the absence of clear gender inclusion guidelines complicate Safetipin's institutionalisation within urban mobility frameworks. Law enforcement agencies often adopt a reluctant approach to addressing rarely reported sexual harassment incidents, undermining user trust in reporting mechanisms. Inefficient systems and inadequate protective laws for women further weaken the platform's ability to translate safety audits into actionable policies (Sil et al., 2023). Accountability mechanisms can help close this implementation gap. Public dashboards tracking the status of reported issues or regular scorecard meetings with city officials can increase transparency and create pressure for action. While some cities such as Delhi have implemented follow-up audits to measure progress, making this practice standard across all participating locations would significantly enhance accountability (German et al., 2023).

21.7.3 Beyond Infrastructure: Addressing Social Dimensions

Safetipin's focus on environmental design represents both its strengths and limitations. While enhancing lighting and infrastructure contributes to safer physical environments, these interventions must be complemented by efforts to address the deeper cultural factors underlying gender-based violence.

The platform effectively tackles the opportunity for crime through environmental modifications but cannot directly address the underlying social motivations for such behaviour. The app's "feeling" parameter attempts to capture subjective dimensions of safety, but it cannot fully encompass complex fear drivers like social harassment patterns. A well-lit street might score highly on physical parameters while still being avoided by women because of frequent harassment in which information remains uncaptured unless explicitly commented upon. The platform's inability to systematically document behavioural elements of safety, including verbal harassment trends and targeted intimidation in otherwise well-designed spaces, represents a significant gap in its analytical framework (Puthige et al., 2021)

By labelling spaces as either "safe" or "unsafe," the platform may inadvertently shift the burden of safety onto women rather than addressing systemic vulnerabilities in urban planning. This approach also enables increased surveillance while overlooking intersectional issues, such as socio-economic disparities, disability, and ethnicity, potentially reinforcing existing inequalities through algorithmic bias (Gupta et al., 2022; Prabhakar et al., 2024).

21.7.4 Sustaining Engagement and Participation

Initial enthusiasm rarely translates to sustained participation. Many users download the app after workshops or awareness campaigns but discontinue regular audits unless they see immediate benefits. This engagement drop-off has pushed Safetipin away from its original vision as a purely crowdsourced platform towards greater reliance on structured data collection through dedicated volunteers and partners, a shift that makes the model less "bottom-up" than initially conceived. The solution may lie in a deeper community integration. Embedding Safetipin within existing community institutions, such as resident associations, women's collectives, or school safety clubs, could create sustainable data pipelines while fostering local ownership. If community groups conduct quarterly Safetipin audits as a civic responsibility, data flow would become more consistent while reinforcing citizen-driven safety improvements (S. Dubey et al., 2025). The digital divide in emerging markets exacerbates these challenges. Low percentages of female mobile internet users, combined with technical glitches, inaccurate location detection, and a lack of user tutorials, reduce engagement with the platform. Interface challenges make it difficult to report safety concerns effectively, and the inconsistent performance of the app across urban and rural settings further limits its reach (Manazir et al., 2019).

21.7.5 Strategic Path Forward

Several strategic enhancements deserve consideration for safety to maximise its impact. Deeper integration of AI could enable predictive analysis, identifying areas likely to become unsafe based on urban development patterns, while using natural language processing to extract themes from qualitative comments not captured in numerical ratings. Enhanced inclusivity in design represents another critical frontier. Multilingual interfaces supporting regional languages, simplified audit protocols for users with limited literacy, and specialised parameters capturing accessibility concerns would significantly broaden their participation. Rather than treating wheelchair accessibility as a subcategory of walkability, dedicated metrics can ensure that safety planning accounts for diverse mobility challenges.

Expanding beyond pedestrian safety to comprehensively address the entire urban mobility experience, including public transportation, last-mile connectivity, and daytime harassment in crowded spaces, will create a more holistic safety framework. By systematically evaluating waiting areas, vehicle interiors, and transfer points, Safetipin can address safety throughout the mobility chain (McIlroy, 2023). Formalising partnerships with national urban planning bodies could embed Safetipin's methodology into standard governance practices, while an annual City Safety Index might incentivise improvements through constructive competition. When integrated with existing urban development frameworks, such as Smart Cities initiatives, safety data collection becomes institutionalised rather than exceptional, ensuring that gender-responsive design becomes a fundamental consideration in urban planning.

As Safetipin aims to expand its global footprint and strengthen its position within the Global Safe Cities network, the focus must remain not only on geographic expansion but also on the deepening impact within each location. The most sustainable model will create an iterative loop of improvement, re-evaluation, and sustained commitment from both communities and governments, transforming cities not through one-time interventions but through continuous data-informed evolution towards safer urban spaces for all (Datta, 2022; Uteng et al., 2019).

Adapting Safetipin's data-driven model to urban planning offers significant potential, as its framework can be operationalised in multiple ways to enhance gender-inclusive governance. The model can be translated into public transportation policy, participatory governance via application, and legislative framework reinforcement. It requires integrating its participatory, data-driven approach into policy frameworks and infrastructure design, supported by global best practices and academic insights. For instance, Mexico City's 2008 *Viajemos Seguras* program offers a critical case study: designed to combat gender-based violence in public transport, it introduced women-only Metrobus carriages, pink buses under the Athena program, and supports for reporting harassment (Infante-Vargas & Boyer, 2022). However, enforcement of gender-segregated spaces sparked tensions, with male passengers sometimes forcibly removed by police or women riders, revealing the complexities of implementing exclusionary safety measures in mixed-use systems (McIlwaine et al., 2024). This underscores the need for nuanced, culturally adaptive strategies such as Safetipin's focus on infrastructure improvements rather than segregation to avoid social friction.

Meanwhile, through this participatory governance via digital technology, community engagement and gender perspectives can be significantly enhanced through hybrid models (Listerborn, 2016). As demonstrated by initiatives like Chennai's My Safetipin app, it enables residents to report infrastructure issues in real time, triggering prompt municipal repairs. Similarly, Jakarta's smart city ecosystem employs platforms such as JAKI app for reporting troubles connected to geotagging and fast response units. The JAKI app also integrates public service access, from transportation schedules to health facility locations, empowering citizens to navigate urban life efficiently. These apps exemplify the transformative potential of smart technologies when rooted in transparency, connectivity, and participatory governance (Zhu & Alamsyah, 2022). Technology can also facilitate gender participation in urban governance. For instance, the *Msheireb Downtown project* in Qatar integrates smart city technology such as surveillance, lighting, waste management, climate-responsive design, and emergency system to create a safe and inclusive public space (Grichting Solder & Alfaraidy, 2024). The project also employs digital monitoring systems to track sustainability metrics and enhance women's sense of safety, encouraging women participation in public space.

Further, adapting the Safetipin model can also influence legislative frameworks reinforcement. For instance, Chile's *Ley de Acoso Callejero* (Street Harassment Law) institutionalises gender-sensitive safety audits, embedding accountability into urban policy and ensuring marginalised voices shape public space design.[12] Together, these cases underscore the necessity of balancing participatory data collection, inclusive design principles, and ethical governance to scale tools like Safetipin into universal instruments for equitable urban development. Both technological innovation and sociocultural responsiveness bridge digital divides while fostering resilient, citizen-centric environments. As much as the strategic path ahead, Safetipin should mitigate ethical risks. For instance, Safetipin could anonymise location data at the point of collection, ensuring that audits of dark spots or harassment zones do not inadvertently expose individual identities. Further, Safetipin could also adopt several safeguards, particularly in contexts where authoritarian regimes might misuse surveillance tools.

21.8 Conclusion

Safetipin represents a groundbreaking convergence of technology, social innovation, and urban governance, and has fundamentally redefined how cities approach safety planning. By transforming the subjective experiences of women navigating urban spaces into quantifiable data points, the platform bridges the critical gap between community perceptions and municipal action. Its success across diverse Indian cities demonstrates that gender-responsive design is not peripheral, but essential to creating functional urban environments for all residents. The platform's journey illuminates both the transformative potential and the inherent limitations of digital solutions to complex social challenges. While Safetipin has catalysed tangible infrastructure improvements and institutional changes, it continues to navigate tensions between technological capability and social reality, in which the digital divide excludes vulnerable populations, engagement fluctuations that threaten data continuity, and implementation gaps that undermine trust in the process.

Looking forward, Safetipin's evolution will depend on addressing these core challenges through the deeper integration of AI for predictive analysis, enhanced inclusivity in design for diverse user groups, comprehensive mapping of entire mobility chains rather than isolated points, and formalised partnerships with urban planning bodies to institutionalise gender-responsive practices. As cities worldwide face intensifying urbanisation alongside growing demand for equity, Safetipin offers a replicable model for how technology can make invisible concerns visible, ensuring that urban spaces serve all citizens equally. The platform's most profound insight may be its demonstration that safety is not merely about security but also about belonging; when cities are designed with their most vulnerable users in mind, they become more accessible, vibrant, and inclusive for everyone.

Notes

1 Indian feminist organization focused on informing, inspiring, and empowering women via research, advocacy, capacity building, safety in public spaces, creative strategies. www.jagori.org/
2 Metrac (also known as Metropolitan Action Committee on Violence Against Women & Children) works on advocacy, research, legal support, and awareness to reduce violence against women and children. (No exact summary found in result set.). https://metrac.org/
3 Social impact organisation using technology and data (apps, audits) to create safer, inclusive, equitable urban spaces, especially for women. https://safetipin.com/about-our-company/
4 "Take Five – the idea is to make safety…" — Campaign/initiative highlighting collective responsibility, community engagement for urban safety of women. (Specific date: 2019) https://asiapacific.unwomen.org/en/news-and-events/stories/2019/03/take-five-the-idea-is-to-make-safety
5 Data for Change — Using collected safety data to inform education, planning, and policy for urban safety. https://safetipin.com/data-for-change/
6 Details Safetipin's work during 2023-24: progress, projects, impact in enhancing urban safety, inclusiveness, especially for women and youth. https://safetipin.com/wp-content/uploads/2024/09/Annual-Report-I-2023-24.pdf.pdf

7 The Safetipin Impact on Delhi — A study/report on how Safetipin interventions have affected safety / public space usage in Delhi. https://safetipin.com/the-safetipin-impact-on-delhi/
8 IUDX (Indian Urban Data Exchange) data platform for urban planning, enabling exchange of city-related data for decision-making. https://iudx.org.in/
9 Case study analysing safety audits, mapping, and interventions in Delhi through Safetipin. https://safetipin.com/case-study-delhi/
10 Safety Audits in Pune 2019 — Documenting safety audits in Pune, India (2019), mapping elements like lighting, walkability, infrastructure affecting women's safety. https://safetipin.com/report/safety-audits-in-pune-2019/
11 Making Delhi Safer for Women – Partnership with NDTV and Uber — Collaborative project to raise awareness and implement safety-related infrastructure / services for women's mobility in Delhi. https://safetipin.com/making-delhi-safer-for-women-a-partnership-with-ndtv-and-uber/
12 Colectivo Rosa Roja / Ley de Acoso Callejero que cambio — In Spanish-speaking contexts; about laws against street harassment ("ley de acoso callejero") that changed, possibly due to activism / policy change by Colectivo Rosa Roja. www.cosecharoja.org/ley-de-acoso-callejero-que-cambio/

References

Bansal, T., Roychowdhury, P., Rawat, P., Choubey, A. N., & Hoda, Md. N. (2022). Gender and smart city: Canvassing (in)security in Delhi. *GeoJournal*, *87*(3), 2307–2325. https://doi.org/10.1007/s10708-020-10369-z

BBC. (2020, March 20). Nirbhaya case: Four Indian men executed for 2012 Delhi bus rape and murder. *BBC*. www.bbc.co.uk/news/world-asia-india-51969961

Bhandari, H. (2024, December 16). Delhi 2012 gang-rape: A decaying witness to a crime that left India shocked. *Hindustan Times*. www.hindustantimes.com/cities/delhi-news/delhi-2012-gang-rape-a-decaying-witness-to-a-crime-that-left-india-shocked-101734285441637.html

Datta, A. (2020). The "Smart Safe City": Gendered time, speed, and violence in the margins of India's urban age. *Annals of the American Association of Geographers*, *110*(5), 1318–1334. https://doi.org/10.1080/24694452.2019.1687279

Datta, A. (2022). 'Thick time': Experiments with feminist urban futures in community podcasts. *Geoforum*, *134*, 108–117. https://doi.org/10.1016/j.geoforum.2022.06.007

Datta, A., & Thomas, A. (2022). Curating #AanaJaana [#ComingGoing]: Gendered authorship in the 'contact zone' of Delhi's digital and urban margins. *Cultural Geographies*, *29*(2), 233–252. https://doi.org/10.1177/1474474021993415

Dhankar, L. (2024, August 27). Street lights cry for attention in Gurugram. *Hindustan Times*. http://hindustantimes.com/cities/gurugram-news/street-lights-cry-for-attention-in-gurugram-101724697217748.html

Dhawale, K. R., Jha, S. S., Gube, M. S., & Guduri, S. M. (2023). Empowering women's safety: Strategies, challenges, and implications. In S. Ponnusamy, V. Bora, P. M. Daigavane, & S. S. Wazalwar (Eds.), *Advances in Computational Intelligence and Robotics* (pp. 139–159). IGI Global. https://doi.org/10.4018/979-8-3693-2679-4.ch009

Domde, A., Dhole, A., Rekhate, P., & Goel, M. (2017). SecureU emergency system using GSM and Android application. *International Journal for Research in Applied Science & Engineering Technology*, *5*(2), 11–18.

Dubey, P., Birha, P., & Bambodkar, R. V. (2024). Emergency response mobile apps. In P. Dubey, G. S. Chhabra, B. T. Hung, & U. Ghugar (Eds.), *Developing AI, IoT and Cloud Computing-based Tools and Applications for Women's Safety* (1st ed., pp. 71–86). Chapman and Hall/CRC. https://doi.org/10.1201/9781003538172-6

Dubey, P., Chhabra, G. S., Hung, B. T., & Ghugar, U. (2024a). *Developing AI, IoT and Cloud Computing-Based Tools and Applications for Women's Safety* (1st ed). CRC Press LLC.

Dubey, P., Tamhankar, A., & Mallick, B. (2024b). Successful Implementations: Case studies. In P. Dubey, G. S. Chhabra, B. T. Hung, & U. Ghugar (Eds.), *Developing AI, IoT and Cloud Computing-based Tools and Applications for Women's Safety* (1st ed., pp. 236–245). Chapman and Hall/CRC. https://doi.org/10.1201/9781003538172-15

Dubey, S., Bailey, A., & Lee, J. (2025). Women's perceived safety in public places and public transport: A narrative review of contributing factors and measurement methods. *Cities*, *156*, 105534. https://doi.org/10.1016/j.cities.2024.105534

Fisher, B., & Naidoo, R. (2016). The geography of gender inequality. *PLOS One*, *11*(3), e0145778. https://doi.org/10.1371/journal.pone.0145778

German, S., Metternicht, G., Laffan, S., & Hawken, S. (2023). Intelligent spatial technologies for gender inclusive urban environments in today's smart cities. In P. Droege (Ed.), *Intelligent Environments* (pp. 285–322). Elsevier. https://doi.org/10.1016/B978-0-12-820247-0.00012-6

Grichting Solder, A., & Alfaraidy, M. (2024). Women, sustainable development and heritage regeneration in Qatar and Bahrain. *ArchNet-IJAR*, *18*(3), 481–500. https://doi.org/10.1108/ARCH-09-2023-0263

Gupta, S., Janicki, S., Casula, P., & Parvin, N. (2022). Rethinking safe mobility: The case of Safetipin in India. *International Conference on Information & Communication Technologies and Development 2022*, 1–6. https://doi.org/10.1145/3572334.3572392

Hawken, S., Leao, S. Z., Gudes, O., Izadpanahi, P., Viswanath, K., & Pettit, C. (2020). Safer cities for women: Global and local innovations with Open Data and Civic Technology. In S. Hawken, H. Han, & C. Pettit (Eds.), *Open Cities | Open Data* (pp. 85–105). Springer Nature Singapore. https://doi.org/10.1007/978-981-13-6605-5_4

Infante-Vargas, D., & Boyer, K. (2022). Gender-based violence against women users of public transport in Saltillo, Coahuila, Mexico. *Journal of Gender Studies*, *31*(2), 216–230. https://doi.org/10.1080/09589236.2021.1915753

Jagori. (2009). *Understanding Women's Safety: Towards a Gender Inclusive City*. Jagori. www.endvawnow.org/uploads/browser/files/understanding_womens_safety.pdf

Kohli, S. (2024, August 19). "Why Should We Fear to Go Out?": A march for women's safety—On roads, at workplace. *The Times of India*. https://timesofindia.indiatimes.com/city/gurgaon/why-should-we-fear-to-go-out-a-march-for-womens-safety-on-roads-at-workplace/articleshow/112616335.cms

Le, T. (2022). Crowdsourcing women's experiences of space: Empowerment, (in)visibility, and exclusions – A critical reading of Safetipin map. *Platform: Journal of Media and Communication*, *9*(1), 43–55. https://doi.org/10.46580/p62073

Listerborn, C. (2016). Feminist struggle over urban safety and the politics of space. *The European Journal of Women's Studies, 23*(3), 251–264. https://doi.org/10.1177/1350506815616409

Manazir, S. H., Govind, M., & R, R. (2019). My Safetipin mobile phone application: Case study of e-participation platform for women safety in India. *Journal of Scientometric Research, 8*(1), 47–53. https://doi.org/10.5530/jscires.8.1.7

Mandal, R. (2020). *Guidelines for an Index on Gender Friendly Cities*. Safetipin. https://asiafoundation.org/wp-content/uploads/2024/08/Guidelines-for-an-Index-on-Gender-Friendly-Cities-Report_India.pdf

McIlroy, R. C. (2023). Mobility as a service and gender: A review with a view. *Travel Behaviour and Society, 32*, 100596. https://doi.org/10.1016/j.tbs.2023.100596

McIlwaine, C., & Ansari, M. R. (2024). Gender-based violence in an urban world. In L. Peake, A. Datta, & G. Adeniyi-Ogunyankin (Eds.), *Handbook on Gender and Cities* (pp. 366–375). Edward Elgar.

Polonyi, T. (2021, April 14). *CityChanger Kalpana Viswanath: Technology for safety – How an App Is Giving Women a Sense of Security*. CityChangers.org. CityChanger Kalpana Viswanath: Technology for Safety – How an App is giving women a sense of security

Prabhakar, P., Pati, P. B., & Parida, S. (2024). Navigating legal and ethical dimensions in AI, IoT, and Cloud Solutions for women's safety. In P. Dubey, G. S. Chhabra, B. T. Hung, & U. Ghugar, *Developing AI, IoT and Cloud Computing-based Tools and Applications for Women's Safety* (1st ed., pp. 155–191). Chapman and Hall/CRC. https://doi.org/10.1201/9781003538172-11

Puthige, I., Bansal, K., Bindra, C., Kapur, M., Singh, D., Kumar Mishra, V., Aggarwal, A., Lee, J., Kang, B.-G., Nam, Y., & R. Mostafa, R. (2021). Safest route detection via Danger index calculation and K-means clustering. *Computers, Materials & Continua, 69*(2), 2761–2777. https://doi.org/10.32604/cmc.2021.018128

Safetipin. (2015). *How Safe is Your City? Sadety Audit Report of 8 Cities*. Safetipin. https://safetipin.com/wp-content/uploads/2020/01/Safety-Audit-Report-of-8-Cities_Safetipin_2015.pdf

Safetipin. (2017a). *Bengaluru: A Safety Analysis Report*. https://safetipin.com/wp-content/uploads/2020/01/Bengaluru-A-Safety-Analysis-Report_2017.pdf

Safetipin. (2017b). *Safetipin Mumbai*. Safetipin. https://safetipin.com/wp-content/uploads/2020/01/mumbai-safetipin-2017.pdf#:~:text=This%20report%20has%20been%20prepared,from%20Akshara%20organization%20using%20My

Safetipin. (2018). *Delhi: A Safety Assessment*. Safetipin. https://safetipin.com/wp-content/uploads/2016/01/delhi_a_safety_assessment_2016.pdf

Safetipin. (2019). *Safetipin Newsletter August 2019*. Safetipin. https://safetipin.com/wp-content/uploads/2020/02/Safetipin-Newsletter_August19.pdf

Safetipin. (2021). *Women's Safety Audit of Tondiarpet: Final Report*. The World Bank. https://safetipin.com/wp-content/uploads/2021/12/womens-safety-audit-of-tondiarpet-safetipin-2021.pdf.

Safetipin. (2023a). *Safetipin News Letter April 2023*. The Delhi Transport Corporation leveraged Safetipin's "Safety & Accessibility assessment"

Safetipin. (2023b). *Social Vulnerability Audit Report of Kolkata*. https://safetipin.com/wp-content/uploads/2021/04/social-vulnerability-audit-report-in-kolkata-safetipin-2021.pdf

Safetipin. (2024a). *Safetipin Annual Report 2023-2024*. https://safetipin.com/wp-content/uploads/2024/09/Annual-Report-I-2023-24.pdf.pdf

Safetipin. (2024b). *Safetipin Newsletter March 2024*. https://safetipin.com/wp-content/uploads/2024/03/March-2024-Newsletter.pdf

Safetipin. (2024c). *Women and Mobility: A Case Study of Bhopal, Gwalior & Jodhapur*. Safetipin. https://asiafoundation.org/wp-content/uploads/2024/08/Women-and-Mobility_India.pdf

Shah, S., Viswanath, K., Vyas, S., & Gadepalli, S. (2017). *Women and Transport in Indian Cities* [Policy Brief]. ITDP and Safetipin.

Shucksmith, M., & Brown, D. L. (2016). *Routledge international handbook of rural studies*. Routledge.

Sil, A., Chowdhury, S., & Thoreau, R. (2023). Moving towards an inclusive public transport system for women in the South and Southeast Asian region. *Transport Reviews*, *43*(6), 1144–1164. https://doi.org/10.1080/01441647.2023.2200983

The Times of India. (2024, March 9). Safe Areas for Women: App Shows Them. *The Times of India*. https://timesofindia.indiatimes.com/city/chennai/my-safetipin-app-identify-safer-areas-and-routes-for-women-in-chennai/articleshow/108339213.cms

Topham, S., Boscolo, P., & Mulquin, M. (Eds.). (2023). *Personal Data-Smart Cities: How Cities can Utilise Their Citizen's Personal Data to Help Them Become Climate Neutral*. Taylor & Francis.

Uteng, T. P. (2021). Gender gaps in urban mobility and transport planning. In *Advances in Transport Policy and Planning* (Vol. 8, pp. 33–69). Elsevier. https://doi.org/10.1016/bs.atpp.2021.07.004

Uteng, T. P., Singh, Y. J., & Lam, T. (2019). Safety and daily mobilities of urban women—Methodolgies to confront the policy of "invisibility." In *Measuring Transport Equity* (pp. 187–202). Elsevier. https://doi.org/10.1016/B978-0-12-814818-1.00012-3

Uteng, T. P., & Turner, J. (2019). Addressing the Linkages between Gender and Transport in Low- and Middle-Income Countries. *Sustainability*, *11*(17), 4555. https://doi.org/10.3390/su11174555

Viswanath, K. (2016, September 16). *Using Data to Improve Women's Safety in Cities, Transport*. Asian Development Bank. https://blogs.adb.org/blog/using-data-improve-womens-safety-cities-transport

Viswanath, K., & Basu, A. (2015). SafetiPin: An innovative mobile app to collect data on women's safety in Indian cities. *Gender & Development*, *23*(1), 45–60. https://doi.org/10.1080/13552074.2015.1013669

World Bank Group. (2020). *Safety Mapping for Women's Mobility*.

Xu, F., Wang, Q., Moro, E., Chen, L., Salazar Miranda, A., González, M. C., Tizzoni, M., Song, C., Ratti, C., Bettencourt, L., Li, Y., & Evans, J. (2025). Using human mobility data to quantify experienced urban inequalities. *Nature Human Behaviour*, 1–11. https://doi.org/10.1038/s41562-024-02079-0

Zhu, Y.-Q., & Alamsyah, N. (2022). Citizen empowerment and satisfaction with smart city app: Findings from Jakarta. *Technological Forecasting & Social Change*, *174*, 121304. https://doi.org/10.1016/j.techfore.2021.121304

Index

For Product Safety Concerns and Information please contact our EU representative GPSR@taylorandfrancis.com
Taylor & Francis Verlag GmbH, Kaufingerstraße 24, 80331 München, Germany

www.ingramcontent.com/pod-product-compliance
Ingram Content Group UK Ltd.
Pitfield, Milton Keynes, MK11 3LW, UK
UKHW020025200926
475702UK00014B/2065

* 9 7 8 1 0 3 2 9 6 8 8 4 1 *